W9-CZU-713

AMERICAN NATIONAL GOVERNMENT IN ACTION

AMERICAN NATIONAL

DICKENSO

GOVERNMENT IN ACTION

Edited by

KARL M. SCHMIDT

Maxwell Graduate School of Citizenship

and Public Affairs

Syracuse University

UBLISHING COMPANY, INC. BELMONT, CALIFORNIA

American National Government in Action edited by Karl M. Schmidt

L.C. Cat. Card No.: 65–25016
Printed in the United States of America

FOR MARY

PREFACE

Modern American government is an instrument of such complexity that it frequently defies even the most expert analysis. Yet, in our democratic system, we have dedicated ourselves to the Jeffersonian proposition that the common man, when well informed, can govern himself better than can any set of masters or any elite corps of leaders. This proposition has become so ingrained that we seldom stop to reappraise the John Adams philosophy that government should be entrusted to the more politically capable citizens.

Any assessment of the practice of government in America must of necessity start with this basic political controversy. To what extent and how well does the common man understand and participate in his *government in action?* Any response based on objective appraisal seems somewhat less than encouraging. As some of the authors included in this volume point out, the modern American often seems ill informed on the major issues of the world, to say nothing of that world's physical characteristics and geography. Worse still, he sometimes seems little aware of his own ignorance, if not apathetic toward attempts at alleviating his lack of knowledge. Still more discouraging, before the common man can begin to move past the mere acquisition of factual knowledge toward an increased depth of understanding, he must "unlearn" much of what he already "knows"—or thinks he knows.

The task is a formidable one. The fundamental question remains unanswered. Can Americans come to a better understanding of their government, despite its complexity?

American National Government in Action stems from my long-standing belief that an affirmative answer to this question is both possible and necessary. It also reflects my increasing conviction that many of the most valuable aids to an improved understanding—many of the finest insights and most perceptive writings of recent years—have been all too evanescent because of their publication in periodicals and newspapers, which, by their very nature, are ill adapted to continued reference.

Fortunately, an opportunity for me to test these beliefs with adult community leaders was provided a few years ago by a grant from the Fund for Adult Education to University College of Syracuse University and the Carrie Chapman Catt Memorial Fund, affiliated with the League of Women Voters. This grant allowed me to conduct a systematic study of recent periodical literature and to test selected articles on groups of mature, well-informed adults. Two conclusions emerged from this initial study, and from further trials with my undergraduate students at the Maxwell Graduate School of Citizenship and Public Affairs: (1) that this approach, employing current journalistic sources, is sound; (2) that the articles made the greatest impact on their readers when the original authors were allowed their full say, untrimmed by any editorial shearing. This book reflects both findings.

The readings that have been included represent a wide spectrum of political thinking, a broad range of governmental experience and outlook. Nonetheless, I freely admit that certain prejudices, including the view that government is one of mankind's most useful servants, may be rather transparently reflected in my choices. Furthermore, I have selected the articles on the assumption that the environment and the operation of American government require greater understanding than does its structure. These articles, from Senators and Supreme Court Justices, from administrators, journalists, and college professors, have been selected because they provide new and valuable insights into American democracy and into the conduct of our government in action.

In the introductions to the chapters, I have attempted to summarize some of the prevalent American belief systems and to suggest (a) criteria by which some of the governmental institutions may be judged, and (b) goals by which the effectiveness of public policy may be measured. In addition, I have tried to identify some of the most pressing problems, with an occasional hint as to possible alternatives. The final acceptance of such criteria and goals, the ultimate analysis of the problems and solutions, must, however, of necessity rest with the reader and his 195,000,000 fellow Americans, who make up our government in action.

I am deeply indebted to the Fund for Adult Education for the generous grant that permitted initiation of the work. For their support and encouragement in the early phases of the project, I owe thanks to Harlan Cleveland, Dean of the Maxwell School at the time, and to Alexander Charters, former Dean of University College. I am also grateful to Dean Clifford Winters of University College for his continuing assistance. But, above all, my greatest debt is to my students and to the participants in the Government in Action program, who have been so thoughtful and generous in their suggestions. To my colleagues Alfred Cope and Stephen Koff, who have shared the teaching burdens of the Government in Action course in my absences, I am grateful for sound advice and constructive criticism.

Finally, to the many authors whose skilled words and experienced judgments provide the sole justification for this volume's existence, as well as to the publishers who have so generously made possible the reproduction of those words and judgments, I express my sincere appreciation. For selection of the works included, and for provision of the introductory passages, I accept full responsibility.

K.M.S.

CONTENTS

AMERICAN NATIONAL GOVERNMENT IN ACTION

1 THE DEMOCRATIC IDEAL

Before inquiring into the institutions and processes that shape our government in action, it seems appropriate first to examine briefly the democratic ideal—that vague, ill-defined, but nonetheless real set of goals that has governed the thinking of most Americans throughout their history. Although they may possess a varied and sometimes less than accurate understanding of the theory and manner in which their government operates, Americans tend to concur in defining those goals for which it *should* operate. Thus, even extremely heterogeneous groups agree that, if their ideal of democracy is to be fulfilled in practice, conclusive answers are needed to some half-dozen basic questions.

First, most Americans want to know: "Is the individual the end for which the government has come into being?" Without necessarily ever having heard of the *social compact*—that government is a contract entered into with the consent of the governed—they instinctively suspect those nations where it appears that the individual exists to serve the state and that rule has been imposed against the will of the ruled.

Second, they ask: "Is there equality of opportunity?" Granting that individual differences in ability distinguish people just as much as long and short noses, black, brown, blond, and red hair, their concern is whether the individual may have an equal opportunity to make use of his God-given talents, however abundant or sparse they may be

Third, they raise the question "Is there freedom of choice?" Although few Americans would argue for any absolute freedom—recognizing that, in the words of the familiar saying, "One's freedom to swing his fist stops where the other fellow's nose begins"—fewer still seem willing to accept more than minimal limitations on their basic independence.

Fourth, most are concerned with inquiring: "Is there majority rule?" The more sophisticated, concerned with the nationwide hysteria of the McCarthy era and mass displays in such communities as Little Rock, Arkansas, and Oxford, Mississippi, add significantly: "In addition to majority rule, are minority rights secure—protected not only in theory but also in practice?" Furthermore, these citizens want to know whether that protected minority accepts the majority decisions—at least until the minority may, by constitutional processes, achieve majority status.

Fifth is the closely related question "Can political differences be peacefully resolved?" Not only on the international level, where the prospect of a hydrogen holocaust may be all too vivid, but on the local scene, where the necessity of day-to-day living with sometimes unpleasant neighbors is all too real, the majority of Americans view *accommodation* as essential. They instinctively recognize that the alternatives to coexistence and compromise are but two in number—subjugation or submission. Most Americans automatically reject the latter; and only a few, once they have fully examined the implications, yearn for the former.

Their sixth question deals with their fellow citizens: "Are the people interested and informed, and do they participate in public affairs?" Most Americans agree that in a democracy, the level of government cannot long be sustained at a level above that of the participants. In this respect, Americans look upon themselves and their fellows as both an end and a means to an end. They concede, sometimes reluctantly, that the days are forever vanished when democracy could be absolute ("pure," in the sense of everyone's direct participation), that a representative system has emerged of necessity, and that it is up to the people to select wise and capable leaders. Thus, they are led to inquire: "Are these leaders democratically responsible? Are they willing to guide and inform their followers while remaining responsive to the informed judgments of the rank and file?"

These questions reflect some aspects of the American consensus on the democratic ideal and pinpoint some of the goals and criteria by which governmental performance may be judged. We may keep these questions in mind as we proceed, chapter by chapter, to a more detailed examination of the way American government works in practice. Thus we begin the inquiry into our government in action.

WHAT IS DEMOCRACY?
Walter Lippmann

Walter Lippmann, newspaper columnist and former editor of the *New York World,* is one of America's most distinguished political commentators. He is the author of many books, including *Public Opinion, A Preface to Politics, The Good Society,* and *The Public Philosophy.*

THE UNATTAINABLE IDEAL

A false ideal of democracy can lead only to disillusionment and to meddlesome tyranny. If democracy cannot direct affairs, then a philosophy which expects it to direct them will encourage the people to attempt the impossible. . . .

The private citizen today has come to feel rather like a deaf spectator in the back row, who ought to keep his mind on the mystery off there, but cannot quite manage to keep awake. He knows he is somehow affected by what is going on. Rules and regulations continually, taxes annually and wars occasionally, remind him that he is being swept along by great drifts of circumstance.

Yet these public affairs are . . . for the most part invisible. They are managed, if they are managed at all, at distant centers, from behind the scenes, by unnamed powers. As a private person he does not know for certain what is going on, or who is doing it, or where he is being carried. No newspaper reports his environment so that he can grasp it; no school has taught him how to imagine it; his ideals, often, do not fit with it; listening to speeches, uttering opinions and voting do not, he finds, enable him to govern it. He lives in a world which he cannot see, does not understand and is unable to direct. . . .

There is then nothing particularly new in the disenchantment which the private citizen expresses by not voting at all, by voting only for the head of the ticket, by staying away from the primaries, by not reading speeches and documents, by the whole list of sins of omission for which he is denounced. I shall not denounce him further. My sympathies are with him, for I believe that he has been saddled with an impossible task and that he is asked to practice an unattainable ideal. I find it so myself for, although public business is my main interest and I give most of my time to watching it, I cannot find time to do what is expected of me in the theory of democracy; that is, to know what is going on and to have an opinion worth expressing on every question which confronts a self-governing community. And I have not happened to meet anybody, from a President of the United States to a professor of political science, who came anywhere near to embodying the accepted ideal of the sovereign and omnipotent citizen. . . .

The actual governing is made up of a multitude of arrangements on specific questions by particular individuals. These rarely become visible to the private citizen. Government, in the long intervals between elections, is carried on by politicians, officeholders and influential men who make settlements with other politicians, officeholders, and influential men. The mass of people see these settlements, judge them, and affect them only now and then. They are altogether too numerous, too complicated, too obscure in their effects to become the subject of any continuing exercise of public opinion.

Nor in any exact and literal sense are those who conduct the daily business of government accountable after the fact to the great mass of the voters. They are accountable only, except in spectacular cases, to the other politicians, officeholders and influential men directly interested in the particular act. Modern society is not visible to anybody, nor intelligible continuously and as a whole. One section is visible to another section, one series of acts is intelligible to this group and another to that.

Even this degree of responsible understanding is attainable only by the development of fact-finding agencies of great scope and complexity. These agencies give only a remote and incidental assistance to the general public. Their findings are too intricate for the casual reader. They are also almost always too uninteresting. Indeed the popular boredom and contempt for the expert and for statistical measurement are such that the organization of intelligence to administer modern affairs would probably be entirely neglected were it not that departments of government, corporations, trade unions and trade associations are being compelled by their own internal necessities of administration, and by compulsion of other corporate groups, to record their own acts, measure them, publish them and stand accountable for them. . . .

It may be objected at once that an election which turns one set of men out of office and installs another is an expression of public opinion which is neither secondary nor indirect. But what in fact is an election? We call it an expression of the popular will. But is it? We go into a polling booth and mark a cross on a piece of paper for one or two, or perhaps three for four names. Have we expressed our thoughts on the public policy of the United States? Presumably we have a number of thoughts on this and that with many buts and ifs and ors. Surely the cross on a piece of paper does not express them. It would take us hours to express our thoughts, and calling a vote the expression of our mind is an empty fiction.

A vote is a promise of support. It is a way of saying: I am lined up with these men, on this side. I enlist with them. I will follow. . . . The public does not select the candidate, write the platform, outline the policy, any more than it builds the automobile or acts the play. It aligns itself for or against somebody who has offered himself, has made a promise, has produced a play, is selling an automobile. The action of a group as a group is the mobilization of the force it possesses. . . .

I do not wish to labor the argument any further than may be necessary to establish the theory that what the public does is not to express its opinions but to align itself for or against a proposal. If that theory is accepted, we must abandon the notion that democratic government can be the direct expression of the will of the people. We must abandon the notion that the people govern. Instead we must adopt the theory that, by their occasional mobilizations as a majority, people support or oppose the individuals who actually govern. We must say that the popular will does not direct continuously but that it intervenes occasionally. . . .

The attempt has been made to ascribe some intrinsic moral and intellectual virtue to majority rule. It was said often in the 19th Century that there was a deep wisdom in majorities which was the voice of God. Sometimes this flattery was a sincere mysticism, sometimes it was the self-deception which always accompanies the idealization of power. In substance it was nothing but a transfer to the new sovereign of the divine attributes of kings. Yet the inherent absurdity of making virtue and wisdom dependent on 51 percent of any collection of men has always been apparent. The practical realization that the claim was absurd has resulted in a whole code of civil rights to protect minorities and in all sorts of elaborate methods of subsidizing the arts and sciences and other human interests so they might be independent of the operation of majority rule.

The justification of majority rule in politics is not to be found in its ethical superiority. It is to be found in the sheer necessity of finding a place in civilized society for the force which resides in the weight of numbers. I have called voting an act of enlistment, an alignment for or against, a mobilization. These are military metaphors, and rightly so, I think, for an election based on the principle of majority rule is historically and practically a sublimated and denatured civil war, a paper mobilization without physical violence.

Constitutional democrats, in the intervals when they were not idealizing the majority, have acknowledged that a ballot was a civilized substitute for a bullet.

"The French Revolution," says Bernard Shaw, "overthrew one set of rulers and substituted another with different interests and different views. That is what a general election enables the people to do in England every seven years if they choose." . . . Hans Delbruck puts the matter simply when he says that the principle of majority rule is "a purely practical principle. If one wants to avoid a civil war, one lets those rule who in any case would obtain the upper hand if there should be a struggle; and they are the superior numbers." . . .

To suport the Ins when things are going well; to support the Outs when they seem to be going badly, this, in spite of all that has been said about tweedledum and tweedledee, is the essence of popular government. Even the most intelligent large public of which we have any experience must determine finally who shall wield the organized power of the state, its army and its police, by a choice between the Ins and Outs. A community where there is no choice does not have popular government. It is subject to some form of dictatorship or it is ruled by the intrigues of the politicians in the lobbies.

Although it is the custom of partisans to speak as if there were radical differences between the Ins and the Outs, it could be demonstrated, I believe, that in stable and mature societies the differences are necessarily not profound. If they were profound, the defeated minority would be constantly on the verge of rebellion. An election would be catastrophic, whereas the assumption in every election is that the victors will do nothing to make life intolerable to the vanquished and that the vanquished will endure with good humor policies which they do not approve.

In the United States, Great Britain, Canada, Australia and in certain of the Continental countries an election rarely means even a fraction of what the campaigners said it would mean. It means some new faces and perhaps a slightly different general tendency in the management of affairs. The Ins may have had a bias toward collectivism; the Outs will lean toward individualism. The Ins may have been suspicious and non-cooperative in foreign affairs; the Outs will perhaps be more trusting or entertain another set of suspicions. The Ins may have favored certain manufacturing interests; the Outs may favor agricultural interests. But even these differing tendencies are very small as compared with the immense area of agreement, established habit and unavoidable necessity. In fact, one might say that a nation is politically stable when nothing of radical consequence is determined by its elections. . . .

The test of whether the Ins are handling affairs effectively is the presence or absence of disturbing problems. . . . It is my opinion that for the most part the general public cannot back each reformer on each issue. It must choose between the Ins and the Outs on the basis of a cumulative judgment as to whether the problems are being solved or aggravated. The particular reformers must look for their support normally to the ruling insiders.

EDUCATION FOR DEMOCRACY

Education has furnished the thesis of the last chapter of every optimistic book on democracy written for one hundred and fifty years. Even Robert

Michels, stern and unbending antisentimentalist that he is, says in his "final considerations" that "it is the great task of social education to raise the intellectual level of the masses, so that they may be enabled, within the limits of what is possible, to counteract the oligarchical tendencies" of all collective action. . . .

The usual appeal to education as the remedy for the incompetence of democracy is barren. It is, in effect, a proposal that school teachers shall by some magic of their own fit men to have had a free hand in writing the specifications. The reformers do not ask what men can be taught. They say they should be taught whatever may be necessary to fit them to govern the modern world.

The usual appeal to education can bring only disappointment. For the problems of the modern world appear and change faster than any set of teachers can grasp them, much faster than they can convey their substance to a population of children. If the schools attempt to teach children how to solve the problems of the day, they are bound always to be in arrears. The most they can conceivably attempt is the teaching of a pattern of thought and feeling which will enable the citizen to approach a new problem in some useful fashion. But that pattern cannot be invented by the pedagogue. It is the political theorist's business to trace out that pattern. In that task he must not assume that the mass has political genius, but that men, even if they had genius, would give only a little time and attention to public affairs. . . .

At the root of the effort to educate a people for self-government there has, I believe, always been the assumption that the voter should aim to approximate as nearly as he can the knowledge and the point of view of the responsible man. He did not, of course, in the mass, ever approximate it very nearly. But he was supposed to. It was believed that if only he could be taught more facts, if only he would take more interest, if only he would read more and better newspapers, if only he would listen to more lectures and read more reports, he would gradually be trained to direct public affairs. The whole assumption is false. It rests upon a false conception of public opinion and a false conception of the way the public acts. No sound scheme of civic education can come of it. No progress can be made toward this unattainable ideal.

This democratic conception is false because it fails to note the radical difference between the experience of the insider and the outsider; it is fundamentally askew because it asks the outsider to deal as successfully with the substance of a question as the insider. He cannot do it. No scheme of education can equip him in advance for all the problems of mankind; no device of publicity, no machinery of enlightenment, can endow him during a crisis with the antecedent detailed and technical knowledge which is required for executive action. . . .

The fundamental difference which matters is that between insiders and outsiders. Their relations to a problem are radically different. Only the insider can make decisions, not because he is inherently a better man but because he is so placed that he can understand and can act. The outsider is necessarily ignorant, usually irrelevant and often meddlesome, because he is trying to navigate the ship from dry land. That is why excellent automobile manufacturers, literary critics and scientists often talk such nonsense about politics. Their congenital excellence, if it exists, reveals itself only in their own activity. The aristocratic theorists work from the fallacy of supposing that a sufficiently excellent square peg will also fit a round role. In short, like the democratic theorists, they miss the essence of the matter, which is, that competence exists only in relation to function; that men are not good, but good for something; that men cannot be educated, but only educated for something. . . .

Democracy, therefore, has never developed an education for the public. It has merely given it a smattering of the kind of knowledge which the responsible man requires. It has, in fact, aimed not at making good citizens but at making a mass of amateur executives. It has not taught the child how to act as a member of the public. It has merely given him a hasty, incomplete taste of what he might have to know if he meddled in everything. The result is a bewildered public and a mass of insufficiently trained officials. The responsible men have obtained their training not from the courses in "civics" but in the law schools and law offices and in business. The public at large which includes everybody outside the field of his own responsible knowledge, has had no coherent political training of any kind. Our civic education does not even begin to tell the voter how he can reduce the maze of public affairs to some intelligible form. . . .

Education for citizenship, for membership in the public, ought, therefore to be distinct from education for public office. Citizenship involves a radically different relation to affairs, requires different intellectual habits and different methods of action. The force of public opinion is partisan, spasmodic, simple-minded and external. It needs for its direction . . . a new intellectual method which shall provide it with its own usable canons of judgment. . . .

THE ROLE OF THE PUBLIC

If this is the nature of public action, what ideal can be formulated which shall conform to it?

We are bound, I think, to express the ideal in its lowest terms, to state it not as an ideal which might conceivably be realized by exceptional groups now and then or in some distant future but as an ideal which normally might be taught and attained. In estimating the burden which a public can carry, a sound political theory must insist upon the largest factor of safety. It must understate the possibilities of public action. . . .

We cannot, then, think of public opinion as a conserving or creating force directing society to clearly conceived ends, making deliberately toward socialism or away from it, toward nationalism, an empire, a league of nations or any other doctrinal goal. . . .

The work of the world goes on continually without conscious direction from public opinion. At certain junctures problems arise. It is only with the crises of some of these problems that public opinion is concerned. And its object in dealing with a crisis is to help allay that crisis.

I think this conclusion is inescapable. For though we may prefer to believe that the aim of popular action should be to do justice or promote the true, the beautiful and the good, the belief will not maintain itself in the face of plain experience. The public does not know in most crises what specifically is the truth or the justice of the case, and men are not agreed on what is beautiful and good. Nor does the public rouse itself normally at the existence of evil. It is aroused at evil made manifest by the interruption of a habitual process of life. And finally, a problem ceases to occupy attention not when justice, as we happen to define it, has been done but when a workable adjustment that overcomes the crisis has been made. . . .

Thus we strip public opinion of any implied duty to deal with the substance of a problem, to make technical decisions, to attempt justice or impose a moral precept. And instead we say that the ideal of public opinion is to align men during the crisis of a problem in such a way as to favor the action of those individuals who may be able to compose a crisis. The power to discern those individuals is the end of the effort to educate public opinion. The aim of research designed to facilitate public action is the discovery of clear signs by which these individuals may be discerned.

The signs are relevant when they reveal by coarse, simple and objective tests which side in a controversy upholds a workable social rule, or which is attacking an unworkable rule, or which proposes a promising new rule. By following such signs the public might know where to align itself. In such an alignment it does not, let us remember, pass judgment on the intrinsic merits. It merely places its force at the disposal of the side which, according to objective signs, seems to be standing for human adjustments according to a clear rule of behavior and against the side which appears to stand for settlement in accordance with its own unaccountable will.

Public opinion, in this theory, is a reserve of force brought into action during a crisis in public affairs. Though it is itself an irrational force, under favorable institutions, through leadership and decent training the power of public opinion might be placed at the disposal of those who stood for workable law as against brute assertion. In this theory, public opinion does not make the law. But by canceling lawless power it may establish the condition under which law can be made. It does not reason, investigate, invent, persuade, bargain or settle. But, by holding the aggressive party in check, it may liberate intelligence. Public opinion in its highest ideal will defend those who are prepared to act on their reason against the interrupting force of those who merely assert their will. . . .

These in roughest outline are some of the conclusions, as they appear to me, of the attempt to bring the theory of democracy into somewhat truer alignment with the nature of public opinion. I have conceived public opinion to be, not the voice of God, nor the voice of society, but the voice of the interested spectators of action. I have, therefore, supposed that the opinions of the spectators must be essentially different from those of the actors, and that the kind of action they were capable of taking was essentially different too. It has seemed to me that the public had a function and must have methods of its own in controversies, qualitatively different from those of the executive men; that it was a dangerous confusion to believe that private purposes were a mere emanation of some common purpose. . . .

It is a theory which puts its trust chiefly in the individuals directly concerned. They initiate, they administer, they settle. It would subject them to the least possible interference from ignorant and meddlesome outsiders, for in this theory the public intervenes only when there is a crisis of maladjustment, and then not to deal with the substance of the problem but to neutralize the arbitrary force which prevents adjustment. It is a theory which economizes the attention of men as members of the public, and asks them to do as little as possible in matters where they can do nothing very well. It confines the effort of men, when they are a public, to a part they might fulfill, to a part which corresponds to their own greatest interest in any social disturbance; that is, to an intervention which may help to allay the disturbance, and thus allow them to return to their own affairs.

For it is the pursuit of their special affairs that they are most interested in. It is by the private labors of individuals that life is enhanced. I set no great store on what can be done by public opinion and the action of masses.

I have no legislative program to offer, no new institutions to propose. There are, I believe, immense confusions in the current theory of democracy which frustrate and pervert its action. I have attacked certain of the confusions with no conviction except that a false philosophy tends to stereotype thought against the lessons of experience. I do not know what the lessons will be when we have learned to think of public opinion as it is, and not as the fictitious power we have assumed it to be. It is enough if with Bentham we know that "the perplexity of ambiguous discourse . . . distracts and eludes the apprehension, stimulates and inflames the passions."

WHERE THE AMERICAN TRADITION LIVES
Bruce Catton

Bruce Catton received the Pulitzer Prize for History in 1954 for his work *A Silence at Appomattox*. A leading historian of the American Civil War, he is also the author of such books as *War Lords of Washington* and *Glory Road*.

A real national tradition is something that we live by rather than something that we talk about. We seldom try to define it: We feel that we don't have to, tradition—we simply respond to it. We respond to it instinctively, because it is so deeply a part of our lives that it has us in its possession.
because if it is a real, living, moving force—and it is, if it is a genuine national

From *Saturday Review,* July 6, 1957. Reprinted by permission.

The greatest of all American traditions is the simple tradition of freedom. From our earliest days as a people this tradition has provided us with a faith to live by. It has shaped what Americans have done and what they have dreamed. If any one word tells what America really is, it is that one word, Freedom.

This is a word that is eternally growing broader. If any single thing gives us reason to have confidence in this infinite future of the American people it is the fact that this most basic of our traditions is capable of infinite expansion. It does not limit us. On the contrary, it forever invites us to grow—to see beyond the horizon, to look ahead to a fairer and a brighter day, to develop and to strengthen the noble concept of brotherhood by which we live.

I think we can say now that this national tradition is as strong and as healthy as it ever was. Today, as always in the past, its best and strongest defense lies in the reactions which individual Americans make when they find the tradition under attack. The tradition may be a national thing, but it resides finally in the hearts of individual men and women. These men and women do not always bother to work out elaborate rationalizations of their sets of defense. They simply respond instinctively to specific cases. When they encounter a situation which denies the tradition of freedom, an inner force which they do not need to define impels them to go out and do something about it. They move, without thought of what the cost to themselves may be, to put themselves in between the oppressor and the oppressed. They strengthen freedom simply by going ahead and living it.

We find them, quite literally, everywhere. A state legislator in Florida discovers that his stand for school integration makes him a minority of one in his legislature; no matter, he goes on as he had started and attainment of the brotherhood of man comes one step nearer as a result. A Catholic priest in Indiana finds immigrant farm laborers suffering medieval exploitation and injustice; he refuses to walk on the other side of the road but stops to demand that the exploitation and injustice be remedied—and, after months of unremitting effort, finally sees his demand made good; and fifty or sixty human beings move out of peonage into the sunlight of American life. A handful of Protestant ministers risk their careers to stand against bigotry and intolerance in their own Tennessee town—and, after a long struggle see the area in which bigotry and intolerance can operate perceptibly narrowed. A young Oklahoma schoolteacher loses his job in order to make his lone protest against racial discrimination—and, telling why he had done so, gives a noble and eloquent explanation of the spirit that moves Americans who love freedom: "In a thing like this you don't stop to think. You just do what you feel you have to do."

You don't have to stop to think: You just do what you feel you have to do. From the earliest days, the presence of that spirit in the breasts of American men and women has been our most profound national asset. It is where this tradition really lives. Not all the petty malignant forces of reaction—the men who think the people need a guardian and a keeper to guide their way into a blighting conformity; the men who dread freedom unless it be limited to those who think and talk as they themselves do; the men who believe that there should be classes and grades in American citizenship, and dread anything that tends to remove the barriers that set men apart from men—not all of them together, operating in a time of confusion and danger, can summon a simple, instinctive reaction that rises in the breast of the ordinary American when he sees American freedom being cut down.

We seem to have begun, in this country, with a demand for freedom of religious belief—in Plymouth colony and Providence plantation, in William Penn's settlement of Pennsylvania and in the charter for the first colonization of Maryland.

We moved on to see that freedom must also mean freedom from foreign oppression, and fought the American Revolution.

Then we came to see that there must also be freedom from domestic tyranny, and we put together the Constitution of the United States.

We came, as well, to see that freedom has to be unlimited—that it has to apply all across the board, to men of all colors, all races, and all conditions—and we struggled through a terrible Civil War in order to make such an extension of freedom possible.

All of these are not separate freedoms so much as they are varying forms of an undivided whole. For one of the things we have learned in this country is that freedom has to be indivisible. Anything that limits any part of it, for anyone, is a menace to all of us, a threat to the tradition by which we live.

American freedom today is under attack—very often by people who insist that they are trying to defend it. In a short-range view conditions are extremely ominous. Yet I think if we look at our present situation long-range we can see that we have little reason to be afraid. We get waves of reaction in this country, periodically, in times of extreme national stress, and the great national tradition comes under attack—seems, indeed, to be in a fair way to be overwhelmed entirely. But the waves always pass—with however much incidental injustice and oppression for certain individual victims—because the instinct of the American mind and heart which the tradition is based on is, finally, irrepressible.

In the early days of the Republic we had, for instance, the Alien and Sedition Acts. Europe was torn by a great war and by an unpredictable revolutionary movement. America's position seemed insecure; external pressures were becoming all but intolerable, and men hardly knew which way to turn to find national security. Out of this came these almost unbelievably repressive laws. Freedom of the press and freedom of speech were effectively outlawed. It was made a crime to criticize acts of the national administration. Editors who spoke out against these laws were imprisoned. Thomas Jefferson's mail was opened, in the hope that some paragraph or sentence could be found on which he could be arrested. A man who tried to get signatures to a petition to Congress urging repeal of these laws was arrested and sentenced to jail. Lawyers who defended victims of this oppression were denounced by judges as traitors. To all appearances American freedom had been done to death.

All of this lasted two years or more. Then came a change. Jefferson himself, against whom so much of this attack had been directed, became President. The laws expired. The freedom that had been assailed so malevolently was restored —stronger than ever for the very virulence of the onslaught that had been made upon it. Today the men who inspired and supported the Alien and Sedition Laws are remembered only because they have come to symbolize the stupidity and the viciousness of those who tried, briefly and unsuccessfully, to turn backward the mainstream of American life.

Similar things have happened at other times. During the early part of the Civil War a brigadier general in the Union army was called before a Congressional committee and questioned because of suspicion that he had been having traitorous dealings with the Confederates—his real offense being that by following the instructions of his superior, and returning fugitive slaves to their Maryland owners, he had given offense to the powerful and suspicious abolitionists who were rising to dominance in Congress. He was accused of nothing whatever; indeed, he never quite realized that he was even under suspicion; but he was finally removed from command and sent off to prison by a War Department which dared not oppose a powerful Congressional committee, and his career was ruined. He was released, finally—not exactly cleared, because nobody had ever formally accused him of anything, so there was no charge from which he could be cleared—but at least released. And the episode comes down in history as a melancholy illustration of the way in which fear and hysteria, operating together, can lead even a committee of Congress to narrow the area of American freedom and justice.

I have cited two cases out of the past. There are many more that could be cited, some of them, indeed, matters of tolerably recent memory. But the thing to bear in mind is that these spasms to which we are now and then subjected are always of temporary effect. We do come out of them; their authors pass on and are forgotten, surviving only as melancholy footnotes in history; and our great tradition, down the years, grows broader and stronger despite these temporary setbacks.

We are today emerging from the latest of these spasms of terror. We have seen some highly discouraging things in recent years. We have seen an atmosphere in which the mere fact that a man was accused of something was taken as proof of his guilt. We have been reminded of Mark Twain's comment on the reign of terror that prevailed in late medieval times under the Doges of Venice, when a committee on public safety received anonymous accusations against the loyalty of citizens; as Mark Twain remarked, if the committee could find no proof to support an accusation, it usually found the accused guilty on the ground this simply showed how deep and devious and inscrutable the man's villainy really was. We have witnessed an era in which it was widely taken as a crime for an accused person to invoke the Bill of Rights itself in his own defense —as if the provisions of the Bill of Rights were not meant to operate in precisely a time like the present. We have seen times in which no one in authority seemed willing to place the slightest amount of trust in the innate loyalty, good faith, and intelligence of the American people; times which led former Senator Harry

Cain to burst out with the cry: "A whole clique of spies could hardly do as much damage to us as could our failure as a government to have confidence in the people."

We have seen all of this, and we can still see too much of it if we look around carefully. Yet the crest of the wave is passing. It is passing because the American people are responding once more to that deepest and most profound of all of their instincts—the instinct to defend the tradition of freedom when it comes under attack. It is passing because the courts of America have stood firmly in defense of individuals and their liberties. It is passing because many groups and individuals have stood up for the rights of their fellow Americans.

Scientists have made a contribution by their efforts to promote rational discussion of the dangers of too much secrecy about their work. The Congressional committee headed by Representative Moss has thrown much light on the secretive practices of some government agencies. The press, through its reports on the Moss Committee's work and through the efforts of individual newspapermen, has helped to break through some of the official barriers to the free flow of information. The American people are gradually getting the materials for a more factual understanding of Communism in the United States and the world. The events in Hungary have clearly demonstrated the essential falsity of Communist claims to a concern for civil liberties—and have contributed to the decline of the Communists here and in other free countries.

When I say that the crest of the wave is passing I don't mean that no threats to liberty exist. Arbitrary censorship both by private and governmental groups has continued to affect a wide area of American life. Government restrictions on the flow of information are still excessive in some agencies. Much confusion remains in the administration of security measures; some unfair procedures have become institutionalized. The pressures of conformity are still strong in many places. Yet I feel confident that the American tradition will flourish in the future as it has in the past. That tradition, to repeat, is something that lives inside of us. It is not a set of laws; and freedom itself is not simply the absence of restraint. Rather, it is an abiding inner faith that cannot be limited by doubt or by confusion or by fear. It is something built into the American soul, and in the long run it is unconquerable.

The secret of the American tradition is freedom—freedom unabridged and unadulterated, freedom that applies to everybody in the land at all times and places, freedom for those with whom we disagree as well as for those with whom we do agree.

And the secret of freedom, in turn, is—just courage. The kind of courage, welling up instinctively in the breasts of individual citizens, which over and over again leads to the kind of actions that are commemorated in the experiences I have been writing about; the kind of courage which led the poet to cry:

> Yet, freedom, yet, thy banner,
> torn but flying,
> Stream like the thundercloud
> *against* the wind—

Freedom rests on courage; and courage, in its turn, rests on faith—on faith in ourselves and faith in our fellows, on faith that the thing which we believe in and which we live by is immortal and everlasting, a fundamental truth of the universe with which we move on toward the future. It is on this faith that our confidence finally rests. For out of this faith come those noble statements which show why this American tradition is in the end invulnerable; statements like that one of the Oklahoma schoolmaster—

"In a thing like this you don't stop to think. You just do what you feel you have to do."

On that spirit, and in that spirit we can go ahead to broaden the great American tradition.

IS DEMOCRACY POSSIBLE?
Robert M. Hutchins

Robert M. Hutchins is President of the Fund for the Republic. A former President of the University of Chicago, he has devoted a lifetime to strengthening the fibers of democracy. He is the author of *Freedom, Education and the Fund: Some Observations on American Education.*

The faith in which I was brought up was as simple and confident as the environment. Democracy was the answer to everything, including the ills of democracy. These ills would be cured by more democracy. The ideal toward which we were moving was the civilization of the dialogue where everybody talked with everybody else about everything; where nobody tried to get his way by force or fraud, where everybody was content to abide by the decision of the majority as long as the dialogue could continue. Democracy meant self-government, and self-government meant primarily participation by the individual, at least through the selection of his representatives, in decisions affecting his life and happiness. Since decisions affecting the citizen's life and happiness were taken not merely by his government, but also by many other institutions, corporations, trade unions, and political parties, for example, the thing to do was to democratize them, as well as the government.

In this view the great crime is to try to prevent other people from speaking up, or to say that there are certain things you won't talk about, or certain people you won't talk to, either at home or abroad. In this view education and communication are of prime importance, because if you can't hear what the

From *Saturday Review,* February 21, 1959. Reprinted by permission.

others are saying, or can't understand it, or if they can't hear or understand you, there can't be any dialogue, and democracy becomes meaningless.

The democratic faith is faith in man, faith in every man, faith that man, if he is well enough educated and well enough informed, can solve the problems raised by his own aggregation.

One advantage of this faith is that it is practically shockproof. Industrialization can sweep the world; nationalism and technology can threaten the extinction of the human race; and population can break out all over. Man can take off from this planet as his ancestors took off from the primordial ooze and try to make other planets from which to shoot. Education can be made trivial beyond belief. The media of communication can be turned into media of entertainment. The dialogue can almost stop because people have nothing to say, or, if they have something to say, no place to say it. And still it is possible to believe that if democracy and the dialogue can continue, if they can be expanded, if they can be improved, freedom, justice, equality, and peace will ultimately be achieved.

Some shocks I have received lately have bothered me a little. The first came when during the excitement of last year I was recommending my democratic panacea as a remedy for the ills of the labor unions to the people on the trade union project of the Fund for the Republic. They informed me that the idea of government by the people had little application to labor unions and that in any event democratic forms in unions were no safeguard against antisocial behavior on their part. In fact, they said, some of the unions in which democratic forms were most conspicuous were the most antisocial.

The second shock came when at the conclusion of my usual tirade against the wild irrationality of our foreign policy I explained to the people on the common defense project of the Fund for the Republic that we should subject that policy to democratic control. My colleagues pointed out to me that in addition to being impossible this was unconstitutional, and had always been regarded as such, and that whatever I might think of the policies followed by the President and the Secretary of State, and however much I might dislike being blown up or suffocated as a result of these policies, the Founding Fathers intended that I should be in precisely this position. At any event, they said, there was no way, particularly in view of the enormous technical problems of modern warfare and international relations, in which the citizens could actually participate in the decisions upon which their lives depended.

The third shock came when I was proposing my usual remedy to the people on the project on political parties, which deals with the political process in a free society. Participation was my watchword. Get out the vote. Or, as the Advertising Council has it, "Vote as You Please, but Please Vote." My associates indicated to me that getting people out to vote when they did not know what they were voting for was not helpful, and might be harmful, to the objects I had in view. Under modern conditions, they said, it might be that responsible political participation and decision by the citizens would prove to be impossible, anyway.

Somewhat shaken, I went to the conference on the Island of Rhodes on Representative Government and Public Liberties in the New States. The basic problem of the conference turned out to be whether government by the people is possible, or even desirable, in the modern world. The sense of relief with which members from the new states welcomed military dictatorships in their countries and with which the Frenchmen present welcomed de Gaulle was a measure of the current disenchantment with democracy. These men saw no way of adjusting democratic institutions to contemporary realities. What they hope for is a period of order in which the most acute problems, like Algeria in France and corruption in Siam, may be solved; after which they may, or may not, try government by the people again.

Eminent European philosophers and political scientists present reassured the members from the new states, three of whose governments turned into military dictatorships while the conference was in session, by telling them that democracy was an illusion in both old and new states, for different reasons. The new states could not expect government by the people because they lacked education, communication, organization, and law. In the old states it had been out of date since the Peloponnesian War, and even then it was not what we mean by democracy now. Pericles, a leader of the Left, struck thousands of voters from the rolls because they could not prove that both their parents were native-born Athenians. Greek democracy was based on a uniformity of ideas and practices appropriate to an extended family group. The kind of government by the people that may be said to have worked in Athens and in the New England town meeting could not possibly work in a large, heterogeneous, industrial, bureaucratic society. The most we could hope for was order, efficiency, and the maintenance of civil liberties, those rights historically carved out against governmental interference with private life. Alexander Pope, whose celebrated lines had always seemed to me as false as they were celebrated, was justified at last:

> For forms of government let fools
> contest
> Whate'er is best administered is best.

I came away from Rhodes with the foreboding that we might be at the beginning of something new in the last 100 years—a worldwide antidemocratic trend that had little or nothing to do with the intimidations or seductions of the Kremlin. (It was significant that in eight days of discussion no member from any new state said a word about Communism or Russia.) This antidemocratic trend would reverse the aspirations of all men of good will—at least since 1848—for government by the people. It would have alarming connotations for the United States in the realm of foreign policy. It should force us to re-examine the assumption and slogans by which we have lived in the light of the actual operation of our institutions in the new industrialized, polarized, bureaucratic world.

If you ask how my democratic faith is doing

> Whither is fled the visionary gleam,
> Where is it now, the glory and the dream?

I reply that it is still here. Perhaps the gleam is not quite as bright as it used to be, and somewhat more visionary, but it is still here. Yet, even at my age, I cannot long sustain a position to which my reason will not assent. The shocks I have received are recent; and I cannot claim that I have absorbed them or that I know how to repel others in the future. Perhaps what I can do is to communicate the sense of crisis that I feel and to ask others to join in thinking for a moment how that faith can be defended.

The faith rests on the propositions that man is a political animal; that participation in political decisions is necessary to his fulfillment and happiness; that all men can and must be sufficiently educated and informed to take part in making these decisions; that protection against arbitrary power, though indispensable, is insufficient to make either free individuals or a free society, and that such a society must make positive provisions for its development into a community learning together. For this is what political participation, government by consent, and the civilization of the dialogue all add up to.

If we are to become a community learning together, as I insist we can, the first thing we have to do is to make up our minds that we want to learn. We have lived on a note of triumphant philistinism. Here is a characteristically triumphant proclamation made by Carl D. Becker, perhaps the most celebrated American historian of his day, in 1931. He said, "Our supreme object is to measure and master the world, rather than to understand it. . . . Viewed scientifically, it appears as something to be accepted, something to be manipulated and mastered, something to adjust ourselves to with the least possible stress. So long as we can make efficient use of things, we feel no irresistible need to understand them. No doubt it is for this reason chiefly that the modern mind can be so wonderfully at ease in a mysterious universe."

At ease, indeed! Anybody who feels at ease in the world today is a fool. And anybody who would say now that he was content to master and manipulate the environment without bothering to understand how it worked or what to do with it would show first that he did not know what science was, for science is nothing but organized understanding, and second that he had no grasp of the kind of problems we now confront. The great overwhelming problems of our country are how to make democracy a reality, how to survive in the nuclear age, and what to do with ourselves if we do survive. None of these problems is technological, though technology has helped to create all of them, and none of them will yield to the kind of measurement, manipulation, or mastery that Professor Becker had in mind. We may, in fact, reverse his statement of 1931 and come nearer the truth of 1959. Then it would go like this: no doubt it is because we have felt no irresistible need to understand the world that the modern mind can be so wonderfully ill at ease in a mysterious universe.

The next question is, how are we going to learn? History will have trouble with American education in the twentieth century. It will see a people who say they are dedicated to education and who are the richest in the world indifferent to education and unwilling to pay for it. It will see an educational system that delivers less education per dollar than any I can think of, saying that all it needs is more money. The people and the educators are united only in this: They both want education without pain, either intellectual or financial. History will find it hard to explain how a nation that is one, a nation in which the political subdivisions have almost no relation to social or economic life and very little to political life, can entrust its future to these subdivisions by relegating education to them. History will smile sardonically at the spectacle of this great country getting interested, slightly and temporarily, in education only because of the technical achievements of Russia, and then being able to act as a nation only by assimilating education to the Cold War and calling an education bill a defense act.

We might as well make up our minds to it. If our hopes of democracy are to be realized, every citizen of this country is going to have to be educated to the limit of his capacity. And I don't mean trained, amused, exercised, accommodated, or adjusted. I mean that his intellectual power must be developed. A good way to start finding the money that is needed for education would be to kick out of it the subjects, the activities, and the people that make not a contribution to the development of intellectual power. Such an operation would produce just sums. I suggest that two things might be done with this money and with any more that may be needed: first, we should double teachers' salaries, not because all the teachers we have deserve twice as much as they are getting, but because we want to attract the ablest people into the profession; and second, we should establish a national system of scholarships that makes it possible for every citizen of this country to be educated to the limit of his mental capacity, regardless of the financial capacity of his parents.

If life is learning, and I think it is, and if our object is to become a community learning together, education ought to continue throughout life. Here is the great educational opportunity and obligation of the next generation. The education of adults is not only indispensable to the continuation, expansion, and improvement of the dialogue, but it is also an answer to the question of what we are going to do with ourselves if we survive. As automation advances, as new sources of energy are applied in industry, as the hours of labor decline, we have the chance to become truly human by using our new and disturbing leisure to develop our highest human powers to the utmost. Here we can build on the experience of such organizations as the Great Books Foundation, which has succored tens of thousands of refugees from television.

This brings me to the media of mass communications. If our hopes of democracy are to be realized, the media must supply full and accurate information on which the people can base their judgment on public affairs, and they must offer a forum for the discussion of those affairs. I doubt if there are six cities of any size in the United States in which the newspapers come anywhere near meeting these requirements. As for radio and television, with a few distinguished exceptions now and then, they make no attempt to meet them. A dozen years ago the Commission on the Freedom of the Press recommended the establishment of a continuing independent agency, privately financed, to appraise and report periodically on the performance of the media. Everything that has happened since, and especially the use of the most marvelous electronic methods of communication for the communication of the most insignificant material, makes the adoption of this recommendation more urgent every day. If we were well educated and well informed could we make ourselves felt in the realm of political action?

In the Republic as I have described it every act of assent on the part of the governed is a product of learning. Could we learn by doing in politics? Or would the archaic structure of our government and the vast bureaucratic machine that goes creaking on, following the right procedure instead of seeking the right result, prevent us from using our newly won education and information as active, deciding, responsible citizens?

Today the dialogue is impeded by obsolescent practices and institutions from the long ballot to the presidential primary, from the electoral college to the organization of cities, counties, and states. In too frequent elections unknown persons by the hundreds running for insignificant offices, and improper questions, like the dozens submitted at every California election, are presented to the electorate. This is not democracy, but the perversion of it. The political anatomy is full of vermiform appendices, many of them, like Arkansas, inflamed.

Some of these obsolescent practices stop the dialogue in its tracks, like the failure of the FCC and Congress to develop any concept of the public interest, convenience, and necessity. Some of them distort the dialogue by throwing false weights into it, as the electoral college gives a false weight to the large state and the laws on campaign expenditures give money an overwhelmingly false weight in elections. One thing is certain: if our hopes of democracy are to be realized, the next generation is in for a job of institutional remodeling the like of which has not been seen since the Founding Fathers.

Well, suppose we got this remodeling done. Could we then turn ourselves into active, responsible, participating citizens? Wouldn't the bureaucracy, though better, and administering better laws, still have us by the throat? The answer depends partly on our capacity for political invention, which in 1787 was quite large, and partly on what participation means. If we can be equipped for the dialogue and then invent the means by which the bureaucracy can hear it and be made responsive to it, we shall have come a long way from where we are now in relation for example, to the State Department and the Atomic Energy Commission. Then political participation would mean not only what it too often means exclusively now, the ballot, but also participation in the dialogue about the ends and means of the political society. We would be a community learning together, and the bureaucracy would be learning, too.

The notion that the sole concern of a free society is the limitation of governmental authority and that government is best which governs least is certainly archaic. Our object today is not to weaken government in competition with other centers of power, but rather to strengthen it as the agency charged with the responsibility for the common good. That government is best which governs best. Mr. Hoover could see no constitutional way of coping with depression, as Buchanan before him could see no constitutional way of coping with secession. We started out to show in 1932 that our institutions were sufficiently flexible to care for the welfare of all the people. The demonstration was never made. We have got instead the pressure-group state, which cares for the welfare of those who are well enough organized to put on the pressure.

The genealogy of this development is strange. When I was a boy, we knew what stood between us and freedom, justice and equality: It was special privilege. Get rid of special privilege, we said, and the common good will be achieved. In our time pacification has been attained not by getting rid of special privilege, but by extending it, by extending it to those well enough organized to threaten the special privileges under attack.

Is the tariff hurting the farmers? Retain the tariff and subsidize the farmers. Are administered prices hurting labor? Let's have administered wages, too. Is industry demoralized by expense accounts and tax dodges? Let's have featherbedding in labor, too. Is something done by some group antisocial? Let's all of us—all of us who can put on the pressure—be antisocial, too. And if a Federal agency is established to regulate us, never fear, we have the pressure that will shortly make the agency the servant and mouthpiece of the interests it was intended to control. And as we laughingly count our gains at the expense of the public, we can reverently repeat the solemn incantation that helped to make them possible; that government is best which governs best.

The Constitution must protect the citizen against the government. The government must protect him against the pressure groups. The government must protect him against society and the rapacity of organizations in it by seeing to it that these organizations pursue purposes and programs consonant with the common good.

The stresses and strains in our society are obscured for us partly by our preoccupation with Russia, which plays a curious double role in our lives as the devil in our world and as the standard by which we measure our progress. If we weren't getting ahead of Russia, or falling behind her, how could we tell where we were?

Our real problems are also concealed from us by our current remarkable prosperity, which results, in part, from the production of arms that we do not expect to use and in part from our new way of getting rich, which is to buy things from one another that we do not want at prices we cannot pay on terms we cannot meet because of advertising we do not believe.

But beneath these superficial manifestations, fantasies of fear on the one hand and wealth on the other, are moving those great, fundamental, historic forces which will put our institutions and our democratic faith to the test. This is the basic fact of our life as people.

I have never subscribed to the proposition once debated in the Oxford Union, that in the opinion of this House Columbus went too far. Nor can I bring myself to refer to man as he is now referred to in military technology, as a "biomechanical link." If Columbus had not gone so far, man might never have had the chance to become anything more than a biomechanical link. It is still our responsibility, now more than ever, to see to it that government of the people, by the people and for the people does not perish from the earth.

2 POLITICS, POWER, AND PUBLIC PARTICIPATION

Before we can adequately assess the role of politics in the power structure and the decision-making process of democratic government, we must examine the belief systems that determine the attitudes of many Americans toward their political parties.

Underlying most Americans' attitudes is a fundamental contempt for politics; a widespread belief that its practitioners are inevitably corrupt and dishonest. The word *politician* is more often used by them as an epithet than as the name of a profession. Reflecting another basic misunderstanding is the all-too-common statement "Both parties are just the same." On the local level, this misconception frequently takes form in the time-worn saying "There is no Republican, there is no Democratic way to pave a street"; at the polling place, it may be reflected in the conclusion "I'm going to vote for the best man, since the parties are both bad." The individual thus expressing himself often holds an ill-disguised contempt for those who admit to straight-ticket voting. He feels that he is an "independent" and hence possessed of more objective judgment—that he has risen above the level of the political party. To others, the party appears a necessary—or, in some instances, an *unnecessary*—evil. Reinforcing this viewpoint has been the frequency with which political figures blame the other party for all the evil that befalls the nation and claim for their own the credit for all the good. Understandably the public often rejects both sides of the argument and concludes that the parties have no relationship whatsoever to the implementation of public policy—except, perhaps, a negative one. This conclusion has been reflected in the frequent drives to "take politics out of government," to institute nonpartisan elections, and to separate the nomination of candidates from the party process.

Another set of complaints, concerns the lack of honesty and the organized graft, fraud, and corruption that are thought by some to be the inevitable concomitants of party operation. These complaints note the regular recurrence of bosses, machines and dictatorial organizations, though frequently without any serious attempt to identify the causal link—a link that would be absent were the parties more democratic.

Still another widely held belief is that political parties are nasty compromisers. *Compromise* is a loaded word on the American scene. For an older generation, it raises visions of Chamberlain, Munich, and umbrellas; for a younger generation, the fear of "giving in to the Communists." Consequently, this view of the party as compromiser is a negative one, suggesting that the party is lacking in principle and concerned only with getting its candidates into office.

Finally, there is the reaction of untold others, who take the ultimate retreat from political responsibility, asking, "What difference does my vote make? After all, I'm only one among millions. Why should I bother?"

In order to establish some firmer ground for our consideration of the readings in this chapter, it seems essential to define as accurately and clearly as possible some of the terms commonly employed by political scientists in the realm of partisan politics. For instance what is a *political party?* Three elements are essential: (a) a *group,* or numbers; (b) some degree of *organization;* and (c) a *common purpose*—certainly the purpose of taking control and accepting responsibility for the conduct of the government. In this definition, the third characteristic distinguishes a political party from a private-interest group. A pressure group may seek to elect candidates and to influence official policy, but it does so without accepting public responsibility.

We frequently hear talk of *principles, issues,* and *policies.* In the partisan context, a *principle* may be defined as a long-held fundamental belief concerning the over-all conduct of government. Thus, one might contend that the Republican Party is a party that holds to a belief in property rights and personal rights, and that the Democratic Party is a party that adheres to a belief in personal rights and property rights. The distinction would lie in the emphasis, or in the order of priority assigned by each. An *issue,* on the other hand, is a specific difference, stemming from a concrete problem that has arisen —a problem for which each party provides a different answer. For example, public housing for low-income groups might constitute a concrete issue, with the Democrats urging a federally subsidized program and the Republicans supporting a state-financed one, or a completely private one. Finally, *policies* are the programs developed by the parties, in line with their fundamental principles, to meet the issues of the day. One example might be a Democratic (or Republican) program to meet the farm problem by providing income supports (or marketing assistance) for small farmers.

Some of these observations may suggest a basic similarity between the two great American political parties. But are the parties as identical as is commonly believed? A certain amount of light may be shed on this question by an examination of the characteristics of the American two-party system. A brief historical survey will serve to focus their many similarities and some of their differences. Both parties accept the Constitution, with its concepts of limited government and popular sovereignty. In this sense, both parties are republican and both are democratic. Neither party strives to overturn the government by extralegal means. Both parties are broad and somewhat lacking in precision. They unquestionably overlap. Nevertheless, year in and year out, there has been a discernible difference in their respective philosophies. This difference has been measurably reflected in their consistently varying approaches to such matters as public housing, farm policy, fiscal policy, aid to education, taxation, social security, unemployment compensation, and—through many an earlier day—the tariff.

Yet often the lines have seemed blurred, particularly since party discipline has seldom proved strong enough to array the partisan troops in orderly, opposed lines. Moreover, there has been a notable looseness attached to party membership; for the most part, the individual voter has remained free to come and go at will. Despite this fluidity, however, there has been a persistence of party adherence, loyalty, and devotion on the part of a substantial majority—indeed, some studies suggest that as many as three out of four partisans never deviate from their paternally inherited political affiliation.

Throughout our nation's life, the alignment of opposing party interests has remained basically the same. Thus, the direct descendants of the early Federalists became Whigs and, later, Republicans. The Jeffersonian Republicans and Republican-Democrats continue in a straight line of succession through the Jacksonian Democrats to become the modern Democratic Party. The Federalist-Republican succession has reflected an ongoing community of interest among the relatively well-to-do and affluent of the society—the businessman and the industrialist, later joined by the farm owner and the craft unionist. The Jeffersonian-Democratic succession has evidenced a general orientation toward the "common man"—at least in the dominant, New Deal wing of the party. The Civil War produced a major shift in the previous homogeneity, preventing the erstwhile Whigs of the reconstructed South from rejoining their Northern colleagues under the Republican banner, and driving them instead into the ranks of a Democratic Party that ever since has been uneasy with their presence.

Finally, a careful evaluation of congressional voting patterns demonstrates the existence of a substantial difference in the "center of gravity" between the two major parties. This legislative record shows that the preponderant voting strength of the more liberal Democratic Party is identifiably to the left of center, that of the more conservative Republicans well to the right.

With some of these background factors in mind, we are now in a position to raise some of the questions that the articles in this chapter discuss. First, what functions are served by the political parties in our governmental system? Numerous observers have suggested that our Constitution—with its separation of powers, its checks and balances, and its varied attempts to insure individual freedom—has set up an essentially unworkable mechanism. They point to the requirement of an electoral-college majority to elect a president, the single-member-district method of congressional election, and the federal system itself; and conclude that these technicalities have created a governing system admirably suited to the slower tempo of the eighteenth century but inadequate to the demands for action of the twentieth. Only the parties, they claim, have provided a bridgework for surmounting these structural barriers. By their nominating devices, the parties provide a limited number of candidates among whom to choose. By their selection, emphasis, and discussion, they stimulate an awareness and knowledge of the issues upon which to base our decisions. Once the election verdict has been rendered, they organize a government to effectuate the mandate, and an opposition to criticize and suggest alternatives.

Second, what are the problems and deficiencies of existing party organization, operation, and behavior? Analysis suggests that many problems arise from a lack of party responsibility—a lack created partly by the imprecision of ideological alignment and partly by the absence of effective discipline in each party. Other problems result from a want of citizen participation in policy making, organizational work, and financial support. Thus, by default, party control often gravitates to the bosses and "fat cats"—the people with time, money, and interest. Finally, it is suggested that the failure of the two parties to centralize in pace with the increasing federalization of our formal government has left political power highly diffuse—in the hands of some three thousand county chairmen for each party.

What are some of the more promising proposals for improving the political parties? Party realignment, with all the liberals in one party and the all conservatives in the other, as has often been suggested? Increased "responsibility," as proposed in the 1950 report of the American Political Science Association? Better integration, greater resistance to pressures, greater internal cohesion? Or does the only solution lie in increased public participation; and, if so, how is that participation to be achieved? There is no dearth of answers to these questions. Perhaps some of the divergent views presented in this chapter may shed light on them—as well as provide an answer to that most important question: "Does party make a difference in our government in action?"

THE VOTER AND THE PARTY
Joseph C. Harsch

Joseph C. Harsch, news correspondent, commentator, and foreign-affairs columnist, has been with the *Christian Science Monitor* since 1952. He is the author of *Patterns of Conquest* and *The Curtain Isn't Iron.*

The relationship of the individual voter to the American political party is undergoing a transition.

We have witnessed a growth of the "independent" class of voters.

The party label tends increasingly to be worn in the open by those engaged in active work, less frequently by the mere voter, the customer in the American system as it is operating in mid-twentieth century.

This is not necessarily a good or a desirable thing.

Those who take pride in being "independent" miss out in the selection process for candidates and thus fail to participate in efforts to raise the level of candidate quality. Their seclusion in an ivory tower above party can contribute to concentration of party control in the hands of an oligarchy or machine. And sometimes machines get together and form what becomes a political monopoly in fact, although it may still retain the outward form of the two-party system.

Also when independence becomes apathy such machines are allowed to

From *The Role of Political Parties U.S.A.* (pamphlet), 1955. Reprinted by permission of the League of Women Voters Education Fund.

continue, thus depriving all voters of a bona fide choice on election day. A monopoly machine may govern well or poorly, but it governs arbitrarily, and it is free from the useful restraint of the competitive system.

Add that the *active* party worker tends to be a livelier and more experienced voter.

However, in actual practice two sets of reasons impel a minority of American voters into active party work and leave the majority in a state of "independence."

One group goes into party work to obtain a political career, to get a job, to seek advancement for a special interest. These are the most influential reasons and account for the work of the most active party workers.

Others go in to preserve the two-party system, or to raise the quality of the preferred party.

In both parties there are patriotic men and women who seek to promote the public welfare and to carry out their citizen responsibility through active party work.

For better or worse, the majority of American voters have become shoppers from one party store to the other, and back again. The flow of their inclination between the parties has become the principal stimulus to good deeds and proper behavior by the parties.

The American party itself is a business corporation, not an ideological vehicle. Its accepted task is not to further the special interest of some single group in the population, but to arrive by theory and practice at the given formula which at any given time will best serve the general welfare of the whole community. It is the trial-and-error method, if you like, but this is safer for us than a party governed by a rigid dogma which attempts to govern by some ideological book of rules. The Soviet Union has tried that and it is fairly clear by now, even to some orthodox communists, that the ideas of Karl Marx evolved in mid-nineteenth-century Europe are not ideally suited to all the needs of today. As *Harper's* magazine brightly pointed out, Karl Marx was a city boy and didn't know anything about farming. The attempt of the Russians to solve their farm problems out of Marx became the most open and dangerous failure of the communist system. Government out of a book doesn't work. The man who wrote the book, no matter how wise, couldn't foresee everything. Pragmatism is the only safe way of meeting the problems of tomorrow.

The average American has long since come to express his group interest not in his political party, but in his trade association, labor union, church or chamber of commerce. Each such organization has group interests which it promotes, but by indirect rather than direct, political action. These organizations have learned by long experience that they do better for themselves by the indirect method.

If, for example, business men formed a political party and sought to win the White House they would probably fail. Then, because they had alienated themselves from the winning coalition they could expect little consideration from the winner. But if they remain independent of party they can make the best case they have to both parties. If business men did succeed as business men in winning an election the country would be divided on sharp economic lines. The country would be split vertically instead of horizontally, and we would have a condition which at the very least would not resemble our present and reasonably workable system. Such divisions lead to civil war.

As it is in our country, the great issues between groups of citizens are fought to a decision inside the two parties, rather than in open political action between the parties. True, there was a tendency during the New Deal period for the parties to begin to divide by social and economic groups. Labor moved significantly although never totally into the Democratic party, and business and the professions moved towards the Republican party. We came uncomfortably close in those days to dividing by economic class. The bitterness and intensity of the period was a reminder of how dangerous such a division could become.

When World War II ended and the two parties had time to reconsider their attitudes on domestic matters it was quickly evident that they preferred to avoid plunging back into the New Deal strife. Harry Truman made immediate gestures towards a reconciliation of Democrats with business and industry, suffered a relapse during the 1948 campaign, but promptly thereafter sent his Secretary of Commerce, Charles Sawyer, on an extended new mission among the "heathen." Republicans, on their part, developed a vocal new-dealish wing which went about the land urging what their more orthodox brethren called "me-too-ism." Henry Cabot Lodge, Jr., and Phillip Willkie broke into the "slick" magazines with arguments for the new Republican "modernism" and a crop of post-war young Republican Governors, like Driscoll in New Jersey, stole the reforming lead from local Democratic machines.

This trend of the two parties towards the center became pronounced with the Republican election of Dwight D. Eisenhower in 1952 followed by the Democratic capture of Congress two years later. Mr. Eisenhower achieved more harmony with a Democratic Congress than most Presidents had been able to enjoy with Congresses of their own party persuasion. The Eisenhower-Democratic coalition government of 1954–55 produced the nearest thing to political harmony in Washington since the nostalgic days of "normalcy" under Calvin Coolidge.

So changed was the relationship of the parties in 1955 from what it had been in the New Deal period that Republican party strategists had to consider what they would do if the Democrats were suddenly to swing right by nominating a deeply conservative candidate. If such a thing were to happen Republicans could find themselves outflanked on the right with a possibly profitable opportunity for a leftward move of their own. To persons mentally conditioned by the New Deal battles it seems incredible that such a shift of relative positions could ever happen. Yet it is a fact that over the span of American political history since 1860 the Republicans have been the radical or left wing party about as much of the time as they have been the conservative or right wing party.

There is nothing inherent in the political system which prevents such a thing from happening again, for there is no firm and abiding commitment by either party to right or to left. There is a ceaseless search for opportunities to profit from the mistakes of the other, and such opportunities can occur on either right or left.

In this situation the average American seeks the furtherance of his personal economic or social ends by working through his economic group organization. A farmer has the Grange or the Farm Bureau or the Farmers' Union. If he is a big industrialist, the National Association of Manufacturers is looking out for his interests. If he is a businessman he will probably be a member of the U.S. Chamber of Commerce. Every labor union has its architectural palace in Washington from which it projects the strongest influence it can upon Congress and the White House. The latest of these almost literally casts its shadow on the White House from just across Lafayette Park, and just around the corner from the classic marble facade of the U.S. Chamber of Commerce.

The group and class interests of the individual American are well tended, nourished and nurtured by these vast, wealthy and powerful institutions which are ever vigilant in presenting their views to Presidents, legislators and the respective National Committees of the two parties. In fact, the staffs of the two committees reflect in their composition the kaleidoscope of group or "lobby" interests in Washington.

Come Presidential election year, each party produces a campaign "platform" which reflects its best judgment at the time of the most expedient, and vote winning, blend of the views of the "pressure" organizations. The tendency, of course, is for the platforms to express a substantial degree of similarity whenever they deal with promises for the future. They manage to conceal this largely by devoting long passages to ingenious and zestful accounts of each other's real or imagined misdeeds of the past.

But the substantial, and usually transparent, element of genial fraud in all of this does not detract from the fact that year by year, through this process, the voter directs and controls the evolution of the two major parties in a direction which serves his political needs. True, he does this less by being impressed by campaign promises than by his ability to reject the party in power. It is frequently, and truthfully, said that the voter seldom votes "for," he votes "against." After twenty years of Democrats in Washington, he voted "against" another tour of duty for Democrats. He wanted to try something else for a change.

But by rejecting a party in power the voter induces both the loser and the winner to revise its policies and plans in order to avoid the condition which brought the governing party down. There is a constant, gradual assimilation of new ideas and new approaches. The voter checks or encourages the new trend by selecting the party which, in any given year, is ahead or behind on the particular issue.

The plain voter reaches his moment of greatest influence through the simple process of putting his ballot in a box on election day. At other times, he influences the direction of a party more by outside activity than by participating in the renewal of the faith at party gatherings.

Active party membership and a system of party dues are characteristic of continental European parties, which are more nearly like the American trade associations and labor unions, and lay church societies. The American voter is a customer, not a communicant. His vote provides the acid test of the validity of a party's policies and performances. His tastes determine the style and horsepower of next year's model in politics, precisely as in the automobile industry.

But, to do this we must have a choice between two parties.

THE PARTIES AND RESPONSIBLE POWER
Stephen K. Bailey

Stephen K. Bailey is Dean of the Maxwell School of Citizenship and Public Affairs. Formerly a Professor of Political Science, he has had an active political career, including a term as Mayor of Middletown, Connecticut. He is the author of *Roosevelt and His New Deal, Congress Makes a Law,* and several American government textbooks.

The American government today suffers from three weaknesses:

1. Its difficulty in developing a flow of imaginative, informed, consistent, and power-related responses to pressing national and world issues.
2. Its difficulty in generating sustained political power.
3. Its difficulty in making policy truly accountable to a national popular majority.

These are serious defects, not only because they interfere with wise and coherent governing in these dangerous days, but because they undermine the faith of the citizen in the reality or even the possibility of responsible representative government.

The temptation to blame all this on the President, the 22nd Amendment, the split election of 1956, or the present Democratic majorities in Congress is easy—and perhaps partly justified. But the defects are not new. Occasionally, in the past, they have been masked by brilliant presidential leadership in times of crisis or by the virtuosity of congressional leaders in times of presidential ineptitude. But the underlying defects have not disappeared. Nor, in spite of the hopes of a few recent writers, are they going to be overcome by countervailing pressure groups or by the expertness, decency, and continuity in office of civilian and military career officials, important as these factors are in the conduct of free and effective government.

V. O. Key sounds not a hopeful but an ominous note when he writes:

From *The Condition of Our National Political Parties* (Fund for the Republic, 1959). Reprinted by permission of the author.

> Representative bodies, the institutional embodiment of democratic ideology, have by the compelling force of events lost both power and prestige. Their role in the initiation of public policy has been diminished by losses to pressure groups and administrative agencies; their authority to decide many issues has, of necessity, been delegated to the administrative services. They have been driven towards a role of futile and uninformed criticism, at its worst motivated either by partisan or picayune considerations.

Even if we assume that the work of modern government is so technical and complex that enormous discretion must be lodged in the hands of experts, their capacity to act steadily in the public interest depends upon the effectiveness of the very institutions whose influence is threatened by the expert mind. This dilemma will continue until we recognize that our representative institutions invite disuse and denigration because their structure is inadequate to perform the functions required of them. It is increasingly obvious that there are innovative, integrative, and perhaps sacrificial tasks ahead for which our government is not institutionally equipped.

IS LEADERSHIP THE BASIC ISSUE?

To say that we need a new kind of political leadership may be true, but it begs the question. Where and how does political leadership arise in the United States? How can the process of selection be improved? How can leadership be sustained? How can first-class political executives be found to run our great public departments? Why is their present tenure so ephemeral? By what means can presidential and congressional purposes be brought into working relationship? And why cannot leadership be held more fully accountable to the desires of popular majorities?

All these questions are related to the structural handicaps under which the American government now operates. At first glance, the problem seems to be constitutional—and in part it is. But the only two structural faults of the Constitution which really get in the way of responsible power in the national government are the 22nd Amendment, which limits the President to two terms, and the provisions for staggered elections. The only two constitutional reforms that this paper will suggest are the repeal of the 22nd Amendment and changes in the term of Member of the House from two to four years and of United States Senators from six to eight years (half the Senate coming up every four years at the same time as the presidential elections). The real problem is *political.* If our *political* institutions can be modernized by certain changes in statutory law and in political party rules, the old problems associated with separation of powers, checks and balances, and federalism would, it seems probable, largely disappear.

The root of the weakness is that while the two national parties for years have genuinely competed for the Presidency they have not made a similar effort in the election of United States Senators and Members of the House of Representatives. Nor have they been of sufficient help to the President and the

Congress in providing candidates of high quality for the grand patronage of departmental and agency direction. So long as we lack strong national parties operating as catalysts in the Congress, the executive branch, and the national government as a whole, and between the national government and state and local governments, power will continue to be dangerously diffused or, perhaps what is worse, will whip-saw between diffusion and presidential dictatorship.

THE NATURAL PARTY DISTINCTIONS

Contrary to the view of many writers, the parties do not need to be strongly ideological or even strongly programmatic—that is, beholden to comprehensive and distinct sets of policies—in order to accomplish the kind of re-alignment of the party system that would stabilize the national power and help to make it responsible. There are vast areas of overlap in the rather vague programmatic shadows that our two great parties cast over the nation—and this is as it should be if consensus is to continue in the making of public policy and in the administration of foreign policy.

But the centers of gravity of the two parties are quite distinct. The Democratic party basically is a party of innovation, with a "pro-government" bias. The Republican party is an essentially "consolidating" party with a limited-government bias. The distinction has become blurred in the last two generations, largely because of the extreme economic and social conservatism of one-party areas in the South—a conservatism which has been reflected in the Congress through its seniority rules and some other carefully contrived rules and myths. But now, the peculiar condition which has smudged party images for so long is on its way out. The economic base of the solid South has shifted monumentally in the past fifteen years: one-party areas across the land are on the wane; the northern migration of the Negro is having vast political consequences.

Political reform does not include making the parties any more ideological than they are now. It does include making them competitive across the nation, allowing them to appeal to the natural ideological divisions within the population and within us as individuals. The stumbling block in this task is that neither party has a sufficiently unified structure to enable it to dramatize its program around its ideology: neither has the power, even if it had the right structure, to carry out the program; neither has sufficiently clear and unambiguous lines of political accountability running to the voters.

THE RESULTS OF PARTY DIFFUSION

The structural limitations of the parties have grave consequences. First, they virtually insure a government by fits-and-starts. Some historians claim that the United States was wise in having rejected the League of Nations; but few would claim that the *process* by which the League was rejected was a rational way of arriving at a major foreign policy decision. In more recent times presidential requests for an adequate United States Information Agency budget have been listened to one year and ignored the next by the House Appropriations Committee. As a result, cultural officers abroad have had to spend much of their time hiring and firing—inflating and deflating programs like an accordion. This has made us look ridiculous as a nation, and has also made it extremely difficult for a coherent information program to develop as a vital element in our foreign policy. The same has been true of foreign economic aid.

Spasms in domestic policy have been equally obvious and equally unsettling. The executive department and the Congress have been unable to agree on any coordinated methods of applying the kind of devices needed to stabilize the economy and promote the goals of the Employment Act of 1946. Similar fits and starts have been noticeable in defense policy, atomic energy policy, welfare policy, and conservation policy. They have been quite as apparent when the Presidency and both Houses of Congress have been in one party as when the control of the government has been divided.

The second consequence of the structural limitations of the parties has been the lack of rationality and consistency in the substance of much public policy. In Paul Appleby's phrase, in this day and age someone or something has to "make a mesh of things." In a world in which, for example, the indiscriminate dumping of rice on the world market in order to erase a temporary glut in Louisiana could cost the friendship of Burma, there are huge dangers in having unlinked centers of power making their own policy for the nation. And yet, parochial groups in the Congress (often in league with sections of the executive branch and with outside pressure groups) still carry an inordinate amount of power.

The third consequence of the absence of coherent party machinery truly responsive to popular majorities is that congressional compromise tends to fall with considerable regularity on the side of minority rather than majority interests. Committee chairmen from "safe" and often sparsely populated, one-party states and districts; the minority-weighted bipartisan rules committee; and the myths, rules, and influence structure which enable congressional leaders to ignore demands for greater majority representation in policy decisions—all these combine to inflate the power of minority interests at the expense of the national popular majority. The pages of the *Congressional Record* or the *Congressional Quarterly Almanac* in any year since the war offer substantiating evidence. The bills and policies introduced or supported by Senators and Congressmen from the areas of greatest popular concentration in America have almost without exception been substantially watered down according to the predilections and petitions of powerful minority interests in and out of the Congress.

This is government by tollgate. It leads directly to consequence four; the increasing danger of public cynicism and apathy toward the Congress, partly because its power is too diffused, too subtle to comprehend; partly because when the power is clearly identifiable it seems to work more consistently for minorities than for the majority.

The last and by no means the least important consequence stemming from the absence of unified party structure is that desperately needed criticism of both domestic and foreign policy is dissipated and discouraged. There is no effective vehicle for responsible opposition criticism of programs; there is no machinery for anticipating the implications of social changes and their effects on policy. With the help of a huge and in part brilliant staff, members of Congress may fill the air and the *Congressional Record* with daring solutions to our dilemmas. But without some sort of party sanction, these ideas are worth little more than an inch or two in *The New York Times*.

In sum, the absence of effective party machinery in each House, and in the government generally, means that policy is fragmentally developed by an infinitely intricate system of barter and legerdemain.

Some defenders of America's traditional disorder have discounted the dangers to policy-making of these intermittencies and irresponsibilities. They argue that our survival suggests that presidential leadership and a congressional desire to cooperate during periods of crisis can save us in the future as they have in the past; that the thermidor between crises allows the divergences in our society to have their day without being subject to the tyranny of a transient numerical majority; and that the accepted American tradition of government by extraordinary or "concurrent" majority has not stopped innovation or social criticism, it has only slowed change, and in the process has insured a healthy unity behind public policy.

In relation to the past, these may be strong arguments. But are they addressed to a world of big bureaucracies, sustained cold wars, and chronic international periods between crises? As long as the frontier was open and the spirit of laissez faire encouraged political parties to be barriers against government action, anarchy in program and uncontrolled shifts in power within the national government were of little consequence. For many years the parties were anti-governmental vehicles, so to speak, minimizing public policy and fencing off large sections of the population and of the domain for private exploitation and private dreams. But we are now in a very different world. As E. E. Schattschneider has pointed out:

> The revolution in communications, the dissolution of nationality blocs, the impact of the labor movement, urbanization, the revolution in public policy, the expansion of the practising electorate in recent years, and the new world position of the United States are only a few of the influences likely to give impetus to political reorganization in the present generation. It is obvious that the purposes of political organization are not what they once were. There was a time when it might have been said that the purpose of the party system, or large parts of it, was obstruction. In an era of perpetual crisis, political organization is reasonably certain to reflect the anxieties that now dominate all public life.

THE PROPHETS

For three quarters of a century America has heard warnings from a variety of distinguished political prophets about its governmental weaknesses. Whether their solution has been constitutional revision or political revision, they have

Woodrow Wilson, Henry Jones Ford, and A. Lawrence Lowell, and continuing through William MacDonald, William Y. Elliott, E. E. Schattschneider, Henry Hazlitt, Thomas K. Finletter, James M. Burns, and Paul T. David, criticism has been directed at a single issue; the difficulties of achieving sustained and responsible political power adequate to contemporary necessities.

All seem to accept one proposition: Such power can be achieved though a greater synthesis is impossible without broad constitutional revisions along the lines of the British parliamentary system, including provision for the executive dissolution of the legislature in case of loggerheads and provisions for concurrent terms for President and Congress. Others believe that the catalytic effect of a reformed party system, together with certain changes in congressional organization and procedure, will make drastic constitutional reform as unnecessary as they believe it to be impossible.
all argued about the limitations of our governing instruments. Starting with

Two statements—one from Woodrow Wilson and one from Thomas K. Finletter—sum up seventy-five years of prophetic writing on this subject. In the 1880's, Wilson wrote:

> The Constitution is not honored by blind worship. The more open-eyed we become as a nation, to its defects, and the prompter we grow in applying with the unhesitating courage of conviction all thoroughly-tested or well-considered expedients necessary to make self-government among us a straight-forward thing of simple method, single, unstinted power, and clear responsibility, the nearer will we approach to the sound sense and practical genius of the great and honorable statesmen of 1787.

Two generations later, Thomas Finletter wrote:

> The question thus is whether means, that is the procedures of our government, are adequate in relation to its objectives, or its ends. The usual pattern has been long periods of negative government interlarded with short periods of strong action . . . The irregular flow of power endangers representative government in the United States . . . You cannot have a government capable of handling the most difficult problems that peace-time democracy has ever faced with the two main parts of it at each other's throats . . . A government of fits and starts is no longer good enough for our purposes.

In 1950, a Committee on Political Parties of the American Political Science Association brought out a report which was in the direct line of this earlier prophetic writing. Called "Towards a More Responsible Two-Party System," the APSA report discounted the possibility of drastic constitutional change, but put forward a series of suggestions for political reform designed to create a party system capable of enabling the national government to cope effectively and responsibly with the great national and international issues of the twentieth century.

Nearly a decade has elapsed since the publication of the Committee's report.

Nothing has happened in that time to suggest that the basic issues raised have dwindled in significance. The report itself has been subject to academic debate. Some of its recommendations have been misunderstood or misinterpreted by its critics: other recommendations and assumptions have been justly criticized.

What is increasingly apparent is that the authors of the report were closer than its critics to the spirit and necessities of the age. And inexorable forces, only dimly observable when the report was being written, are now clearly at work preparing the soil for a crop of politics far different from what we have known in the past century.

It is time for a stringent look at the national politics we have had, the kind of national politics we want, and the reasons for believing that our traditional party system, like a vast glacier may now have reached the edge of the sea.

WANT TO BE ELECTED?

Martin Abramson

Martin Abramson is a magazine writer who has contributed many articles dealing with social and civic problems to leading national publications. He also writes for the United Features Syndicate and contributes to the *London Express*. He is a former New York newspaperman and a one-time writer of "We the People," a TV show. Together with his wife, Mr. Abramson has helped manage and publicize the campaigns of a number of "good government" candidates.

One evening about two years ago a tall, dark-haired, community-minded young mother named Marie Santagata got a telephone call from a group of home owners who called themselves the Efficiency party of Westbury, Long Island. Would Marie care to run for trustee of the village of Westbury? Marie ordinarily commands an impressive arsenal of words but this time she reacted like the shy maiden of the melodramas who gets an unexpected proposal and can't think of anything to say—except, of course, "This is so sudden."

Once the element of surprise wore off and Marie regained her usual self-possession, she decided she'd indeed like to run. The political sages of Westbury greeted this decision with a loud and meaningful yawn. The village had been under the control of one political group for eons and, as a candidate of a "rump" party, Mrs. Santagata was at a decided disadvantage.

Besides, she was a woman, and no female representative had ever been elected to legislative office in Westbury. Like most of the suburban communities in the New York metropolitan area, Westbury had always considered females un-

From *New York Herald Tribune Magazine, Today's Living,* July 2, 1961. Reprinted by permission.

desirable (or ineligible) for public stewardship. Therefore, this woman's race was classed as nothing more than spirited exercise.

To the astonishment of almost everyone in town—including, probably, the Efficiency party itself—Marie not only won her election but rolled up a margin large enough to cause the surprised *Westbury Times* to headline the event with two giant words—"Oh Marie!" To prove this was no fluke, Marie ran for re-election with fellow Efficiency candidate Tom Johnson and amassed another large plurality. Her male compatriots on the village board were so impressed that they broke another precedent and gave the woman trustee the extra chore of serving as commissioner of police and public safety—probably the only such post in the country held by a female.

Until recently the mere act of running under the Republican emblem in villages that have the elephant-donkey political setup, or being chosen as candidate of the "old settlers" group in other communities, was all that was necessary to get elected to local office. But the floods that have washed new populations into Suburbia and that have created the headaches of helter-skelter growth and high taxes have also done violence to established political mores. More and more fresh faces are replacing in office the familiar personalities who used to get elected by force of habit.

"After the scandals investigations of recent years here, people became a lot more mature politically," says James E. Jarvis, chairman of the Fusion Economy party of Huntington, Long Island. "We're getting more discerning people to the polls in suburban communities these days, and they aren't interested so much in party as they are in individuals who, they feel, can give them the best government at the lowest cost per tax dollar."

"We tell the members of our organization that they have to go out and prove their value to the community before they can be considered for nomination to office," says John R. Dunne, president of the Republican Recruits of Nassau County, New York. "Just being a party worker isn't, in my opinion, enough to warrant a nomination anymore—let alone an election."

"The day of the cut-and-dried local election is past," says Mrs. Helene Rosenberg, vice chairman of the town of Eastchester Democratic Committee in Westchester County, New York. "We've elected Democrats in some staunchly Republican villages when we were able to show that they could provide better government than the incumbents."

Could *you* get elected to local public office? On the basis of conversations with local officials, political leaders, civic leaders and the League of Women Voters in Westchester, Long Island, New Jersey and Connecticut, we're ready to say that you can—provided you have or can develop certain personality traits and are willing to follow a specific program of action. "We desperately need new blood in many of our local offices," says a League of Women Voters official in Bergen County, New Jersey. "And the blood should be not only new but also capable." . . .

The attributes are these:

1. An outgoing manner.

2. An affinity for liking and getting along with people.

3. A forceful voice that carries and a habit of expressing decisive opinions. "Voters don't want a shilly-shallier in office; they want someone who represents leadership," a Westport, Connecticut, selectman points out.

4. An ability to listen patiently to others and give their remarks thoughtful appraisal.

5. Plenty of free time and an understanding spouse who doesn't mind your spending that time on public business.

"My wife *does* mind the time but I've appeased her by turning over to her my stipend as mayor the minute I get it," says Sidney Haber, commuter-mayor of Cedarhurst, Long Island.

"My wife objects too but my job doesn't pay anything, so I've just cultivated the habit of not listening to her," says Joseph Dalfonso, mayor of Mamaroneck, New York. "I guess I'm an exception," he adds.

6. A full pocketbook, or friends with full pocketbooks, or a talent for coaxing strangers with full pocketbooks to contribute to your campaign cause. "Inflation has come to local politics," says Eli Wager, former president of the Hempstead, Long Island, town civic council. "Today it costs thousands of dollars to run for the school board or even, in many cases, for sanitary commissioner. I know of a candidate who ran uncontested for the school board and yet spent $2,500 to advertise himself. He was afraid of a write-in opposition."

7. A thick skin. Traditionally, village, school and local district elections have been considered Alphonse-and-Gaston affairs but the winds of change have made that too an obsolete concept. "It now takes more courage to run for a local office, in which you get very little for your public efforts, than for a well paid state or federal office," a Fairfield County, Connecticut, civic leader says.

"The local officeholder is the only remaining public official who'll sooner or later meet his critics face to face in the town hall," maintains Marie Santagata.

"The mud that's thrown in a local election is the hardest to take because it comes from your own people, not from outsiders," says Frank Bear, a veteran of Long Island school board service.

"A local election here is about as mild as a battle between a cobra and a mongoose," says a League of Women Voters worker in Stamford, Connecticut.

"It takes a particular brand of courage to run for office in a small town," says Matthew Feldman, mayor of Teaneck, New Jersey. "The pressures exerted on local officials are considerable. New York City residents write or wire their complaints to the mayor but suburbanites simply pick up the telephone. They rightfully feel that the officials should be responsive to their needs, so we hear on the phone about sewers backing up, about stray dogs, about a skunk having been run over, about unplowed streets. Nevertheless, one Bergen County, New Jersey, mayor, who'd announced his decision not to run again because of hundreds of calls he received in the wake of a February snowstorm, changed his mind and was re-elected in May." . . .

A former school board trustee in suburban New Jersey, who describes himself as a Republican, an Episcopalian and a fifth-generation American, heard himself called a "damned Red," an atheist and a "damned foreigner" when he advocated a hike in school expenditures during a bitterly fought school election. "I never ran for office again after that experience and you can bet your life I never will," he says.

"When election time gets close, there'll be whispers that you drink heavily, chase redheads, are in trouble with the Internal Revenue Service, or intend to use public office for your personal gain," says Jerry Kremer, assistant corporation counsel of Long Beach, Long Island, and an official of the Long Beach Young Democratic Club. "How do you fight these things? You don't spend your time going around denying the whispers, that's sure. Instead, you brush them off and paint a positive picture of yourself so that people will forget the rumors."

This is your course of action:

Become a member, become active, become a leader of local organizations. "It's important to work in charity groups, in service organizations such as Kiwanis and Rotary, and in educational groups," says John Dunne. "But the most important field of activity for anyone interested in public life is the civic association. These associations get involved directly in problems of zoning, taxes, recreation, public improvement projects and the like, and experience in these areas is the right preparation."

See that your activities are publicized in the local press by sending out news releases. "It's important that *all* the people in the community, not just the members of your civic or charity group, get to know your name and what you're doing," says Eastchester's Mrs. Rosenberg.

Become affiliated with a church or synagogue as a worshipper and a worker. "People feel that their officials should be identified with an organized religious group," says Mayor Haber.

Once you've become established as a civic personality, a local political organization may tap you as good candidate material. If it doesn't, you'll have to become active in the organization to earn your nomination. If you're out of sympathy with the party or parties dominant in your community, form your own. In most areas only three people are required to form a political party legally.

"We formed the Independent party in Norwalk several years ago because we felt that neither the Democrats nor the Republicans were doing a job," says Peter Leavitt, a Norwalk, Connecticut, community leader. "That was the time of the teachers' strike—when our whole educational system was in danger. I'd been outspoken in public meetings about the failure of our local government to deal properly with education, to correct an inequitable tax system and to do a lot of things they should have been doing. So, when we started our own party, I was asked to run for councilman. I didn't think I had a chance; I ran as a token candidate—merely to present our case to the public. But we were able to convince the people that the status quo simply had to be changed and I ended up being elected and then re-elected several times." . . .

Put color into your campaign. "If you can get volunteer help from somebody in publicity or advertising to dramatize your activities, it will help you considerably," says Julian Kane, an official of the Levittown, Long Island, Property Owners Association. "Too many of the brochures that are sent out in local campaigns are as dry as dust. Political literature that has an artistic presentation will get read instead of being dropped into the garbage. Anything that stimulates public interest and also gets across an important point can be used to advance a good cause. A restaging of the Boston Tea Party by candidates in Nassau County, who were protesting inequitable representation, got a lot of attention and something similar was done in Westchester. In Suffolk County, New York, candidates who were demanding a cleanup of corrupt government made their point by having housewives parade in front of town hall with brooms."

Present a specific program. "Too many outs who want to get in base their whole campaign on the argument that the ins are no good and should be out," a White Plains, New York, Republican leader notes. "People in local communities don't fall for that. They want specifics; they want to be told just what the outs can do that the ins haven't done."

"The candidate we backed for supervisor—Bob Flynn—had plenty to say about the boss-ridden political machine he was fighting; but, more important, he had a program of action that the voters liked," says Huntington's James Jarvis. "Flynn said he was going to cut political padding and waste out of the government, adopt the first code of ethics for a township government in New York State, cut taxes, set up a new recreation program and institute planning studies to deal with the impact on the township of the sudden population growth. As supervisor he's done what he promised, which is the best way I know of for a man to get re-elected."

It should be noted here that the things you should not do when running for public office are as important to your political hopes as the things you should do. Suburban politicos of all stripes agree, for example, that you should not dwell on the problems of the Congo, Castro's Cuba, or unemployment in West Virginia's depressed areas when campaigning for local office.

"We had one candidate who was wonderfully eloquent when it came to discussing foreign affairs, but he acted as if he felt that garbage disposal and building codes were much too mundane for him; so when the election results came in he was trounced," a Rockland County, New York, political leader recalls.

It's important, too, when you're working in civic organizations with an eye toward a political future, that you don't give your civic associates the idea that you're exploiting them for personal gain.

"There's nothing wrong with having political ambition. But if you don't do your civic and charity work sincerely and you adopt the cynical approach—'This is all right for today but, thank God, I'll be done with it tomorrow'—the people you expect to have working for you later will instead mark you as a bad apple," says Dr. Jacob Fried of Woodmere, Long Island, professor of political science at the New School for Social Research.

Westbury's Marie Santagata recommends, surprisingly, that you *don't* ring doorbells. "It may be all right for the party workers, but not for the candidate himself," she says. "When I rang my first doorbell, the door opened and the cry of a young child, awakened from his nap by my ring, greeted me. When I rang my next bell, the door opened and out ran a dog with its mistress in hot pursuit. Having lost two votes, I decided to stop ringing and start meeting people instead at prearranged coffee parties, small house meetings, neighborhood socials and the like—and also by asking for invitations to speak or debate before any and every local organization that would have me."

One final warning: If you finally win election to local office, don't expect caviar and cream. Garden City's Mayor William J. Maslanka devotes every night and most weekends to his village duties. In order to attend special luncheons or consult with county officials who work during the day, he'll sometimes leave his office in Manhattan (where he works as a production executive), take a midday train to Garden City, do whatever he has to do there, rush back to Manhattan, stay late at the office to catch up, take a late train home, bolt his supper, and then hurry to a night meeting.

Maslanka used to enjoy family outings with his wife and four children on weekends but since he became a mayor his outings, picnics and fishing dates with the youngsters have fallen by the wayside. Also public offices in local communities carry salaries ranging from zero to about $2,750 a year; Maslanka is in the zero category and pays all his own expenses.

Then why should anybody want such a job?

"Primarily because it gives you a chance to perform a public service on behalf of all your neighbors and friends," says Maslanka. "If you don't care about public service, you shouldn't get involved in local politics.

"Of course," he adds, "there's the factor of ego, too. When somebody comes up to me and says, 'Good morning, Mr. Mayor,' it makes me feel very good, very proud. After all, I'm only human."

3 DECISION MAKING IN A DEMOCRACY—THE VOTERS

Although the debate over party realignment goes on, and the inquiry into the possibility of "more responsible" parties continues along the lines suggested in the preceding chapter, certain political questions may be answered only by examining the behavior of the voters, the participating members of the democracy themselves. Therefore, we must ask two significant questions about the voters. First, what factors determine the voting patterns and behavior of the individual in the polling place? Second, since much evidence suggests that party affiliation is one of these determining factors, what factors determine party affiliation?

With respect to the latter question, studies indicate that people seem to be swayed far less by party principles and party issues than by environmental factors and institutional surroundings, such as family influence, traditional geographical patterns, national origins, religious affiliation, economic status, social environment, friends, education, and, perhaps to a lesser extent, age. In short, party preferences are seldom based on purely intellectual or cold-bloodedly rational lines.

In the area of voting behavior, regular or traditional party adherence seems to be the primary determinant for an overwhelming majority of voters. For such citizens, voting is much more an affair of the heart (an emotional reaction) than of the head (a rational decision based on the issues). A second major factor affecting electoral decisions seems to be an economic one—the pocketbook. Indeed, if the pocketbook has been hurt enough, the voter's reaction may overcome his underlying traditional motive. When the voter's decision is more or less reasoned, or based on issues, negative influences usually rate high, as reflected in the broad tendency of people to "vote against"—to voice their discontent with programs that have failed, rather than to rally in support of proposed alternatives.

Do party platforms serve as guides to issues-oriented voting? The widespread disregard for party platforms among the voters suggests that the public views them—not without some perspicacity—more as devices for getting elected than as guidelines to prospective action. In the absence of more systematic surveys and data, we can conclude only that voting behavior seems little affected by the issues so laboriously spelled out in formal party programs.

If issues do not determine the voting, is it "the man"? What about the candidates? What moves people to vote *for* one candidate, or *against* another? Is it some aspect, revealed or hidden, of personality? Is it press coverage—favorable or unfavorable treatment at reportorial hands? Or is it "image"—that carefully contrived but seemingly spontaneous build-up of a candidate's reputation? Is it physical appearance, the capacity to project a photogenic or videogenic impression? Is it speaking ability or appearance of sincerity? Or is it some factor half-hidden in inheritance or history—ethnic or racial ties, religious affiliation, or marital status? Limited inquiry suggests that all these items may be far more important than the basic intelligence of a candidate, his stand on the issues, or the record he has made in public life. Once again, we are faced with a lack of sufficient studies in depth, of final evidence on which to base our conclusion. Nonetheless, even a brief inquiry into some of these factors may help us to understand better the decision-making processes of the voters who shape our government in action.

THE HEAD, THE HEART, OR THE POCKETBOOK?
Louis Bean

Louis Bean, a career civil servant and statistician in the Department of Agriculture, is the author of *How to Predict Elections*. He was also the only major prognosticator to forecast the victory of Harry S. Truman in 1948. In 1952, however, he predicted that Adlai Stevenson would win the election.

Why do people vote as they do? This is as complex a question as any in the whole field of politics. There is no single answer nor is there a simple classification of the thousand and one reasons influencing voters. If you want to visualize the extremes within which the answers may lie, think first of the traditional solid Republican or the solid Democrat who votes as he does because his father and grandfather voted that way. Then think of the kind-hearted Republican lady, ready to vote for Dewey in 1948 but so affected by the public opinion polls showing Dewey far in the lead that she voted for Truman, not wanting at all to elect him but unwilling to see the President so crushingly defeated.

Apparently people vote as they do for reasons that may go back as far as grandfather's genes or no farther back than the emotional response to the breakfast headlines just before going to the polls.

People vote as they do for reasons related to every facet of human behavior. Education, occupation, income status, sex, age, race, nationality, religion, even regional differences are some of the standard items of classification against which the political scientist tests the issues of an election. Issues, in turn, may be grouped "anatomically" as pertaining to:

(1) The head, applying to voters who try to reason things out, to evaluate issues and candidates, and also to those who vote on the basis of their prejudices, acquired or hereditary.

(2) The heart, for those voters who respond emotionally.

(3) The pocketbook, whether full, empty or squeezed.

If you scan the political fever chart of the United States over the last 100 years you are forced to two broad conclusions: One, that there is a general tendency for people to vote along traditional lines which hold election results within certain percentage bounds; the other, that the greatest variations in voting behavior, the greatest shifts from one party to the other, are associated with pocketbook issues.

The general magnitude of traditional voting is suggested by the fact that each party, judging from past experience, can expect to receive a minimum of about 35 to 40 percent of the votes cast. The Democratic bloc of traditional voters is centered in the Southern states. The Republican bloc is more widely distributed throughout the Northern states, particularly in the rural areas. This means that there is usually an in-between group, the so-called independent group of 20 to 30 percent of the voters, which in reality determines the outcome of the national elections.

But even this independent group is not entirely uninfluenced by tradition; it is not, perhaps, as independent as is supposed. Public opinion tests have shown that most of the independent voters voting Republican come from Republican backgrounds whereas those independents voting for Democratic candidates for the most part come from Democratic backgrounds.

Just as we cannot draw a firm line between Democrats and independents and between independents and Republicans so we are unable to draw exact lines between head, heart and pocketbook reasons for voter behavior. Voters are human beings and human beings are mechanisms in which intellect and emotion operate in complex relationship, a relationship further complicated when you attach a pocketbook to that mechanism. The pocketbook issues which I find creating the greatest amount of variation in political behavior should therefore not be taken as entirely unrelated to the head and heart reactions; nor should the head and heart issues that I point out be taken as entirely unrelated to the pocketbook reactions.

The 100-year record of political tides from 1854 to 1954 is clear on this point. Unemployment, financial crisis and collapse, industrial and agricultural depressions—these, in combination, have been the basic reasons for major shifts in control of the Federal Government.

The Republicans were thrown out by the Democrats with the aid of the great depression set off by the financial and industrial collapse of 1873. Twenty years later the Democrats, in turn, were ousted by the Republicans with the aid of the financial and industrial collapse of 1893. The Democrats were returned to control in Congress in 1910 and in the White House as well in 1912, aided by a delayed reaction to the sharp but brief industrial depression of 1907–08 and the economic reform movements that culminated in the election of Woodrow Wilson.

The depression of 1914 whittled down Wilson's support in Congress and the post-war deflation of 1920 and the onset of the 1920–21 depression completed the downturn in the Democratic political tide with the Democratic defeat in 1920. Then in 1929 came the peak of the greatest boom ever erected during any previous Republican era, or Democratic for that matter, to be followed by the greatest collapse and worst industrial and agricultural depression this country had ever experienced.

Empty dinner pails, envelopes with little take-home pay, abundant farm products sold dirt cheap, empty brokerage houses in the financial and commodity markets and idle money in the lending houses have marked every one of our abrupt, conclusive political upheavals and justify the conclusion that the pocketbook issues have been prime factors in voting alternately for Democratic or Republican control of the Federal Government.

But doesn't recent experience go contrary to this generalization? Didn't the Republicans take over in 1946 and again in 1952 when this country was enjoying economic prosperity? Every rule must have its exceptions or there would be no place in the dictionary for the word "uncertainty."

It is true that in 1946, as in several other mid-term election years, the party in power lost control of the legislature but the 1946 episode was not devoid of the pocketbook issue. In fact it may have been dominated by it.

There was much dissatisfaction in 1946 with the way the Democrats were helping the country to shift from war to peacetime activity and much confusion in matters of foreign as well as domestic policy, but the Republican campaign took full advantage of the sharp rise in prices that squeezed the pocketbooks of consumers. The Republican gains were in the urban centers, not among the farmers who benefited by the high prices.

The 1952 exception to this pocketbook rule must be credited to the power of hero worship. Without Eisenhower's extraordinary popularity among Democrats as well as among Republicans, the Republicans, in my estimation, could not have capitalized so effectively as they did on the various issues that filled the air in 1952, particularly the issues of Korea and corruption and communism in Government, or the catchy line "it's time for a change." But the pocketbook issue was there nevertheless, even if less dominant, in the form of the desire of businessmen to have businessmen run the Government, and the universal desire to lower taxes, to lower living costs and to "take Government out of business."

The heart and the head issues are, of course, present in all elections but, unlike the pocketbook issues that sweep one party out and the other in, these tend to set up conflicting tendencies among voters. Given a general depression, which means a nationwide depression all groups, all regions are affected. Bankers, industrialists, farmers, workers, professors, ministers, men, women, Catholics, Protestants, Jews, Easterners, Southerners, Northerners, Westerners, all were, in 1932, for example, swept by a common economic disaster into the Roosevelt-Democratic tide. The usual reasons for voting Republican gave way under the impact of the need for economic security. Under more nearly normal business conditions voters respond to head and heart issues and it is here that the differences among voters create counteracting cross-currents that tend to give stability to election results.

Scanning the national elections for issues of the head and heart I find several outstanding cases. I bypass the silver and other economic or pocketbook elections of the Eighteen Nineties and early Nineteen Hundreds and come to the election of 1916. On the eve of our entry into World War I, the re-election of

Woodrow Wilson in 1916 was a close affair, made so by the fact that the international issues of that campaign did not sway voters uniformly. The nationality factor, whether you classify this under head or heart, was perhaps the most important feature in the voting behavior of 1916.

Wilson received relatively more support in the Eastern and Far Western states, where voters are more positively interested in issues of an international character, less support in the Midwestern states, the so-called isolationist states, where there were and are many voters of German origin or with other German ties. The nationality issue also cost Roosevelt some support in certain Italian-American communities because of his "stab in the back" remark in referring to Mussolini's declaration of war on France and Great Britain in 1940.

Religion is another strong heart or emotional reason. For the most part, religion is of only local significance, though there have been occasions when national elections were clearly shaped by cleavages along religious lines. The Al Smith election campaign is the prize example. Many Southern Protestant voters turned against him because of his Catholic religion and put a sharp dent in the otherwise solid Democratic record of the Southern states. Just the opposite reaction showed up in the Northern and other states where Catholics constitute large segments of the voting population. Those two opposite responses tended to offset each other.

We skip the Democratic defeat in 1920, having already indicated that it was a pocketbook defeat, though I must recognize that most political scientists attribute it to the League of Nations issue—chiefly a head and heart issue—and move to the 1940 campaign.

The 1940 Roosevelt election was a close parallel to the 1916 Wilson election. In this campaign, too, the nationality cleavage showed up. Roosevelt's strength increased in the internationally minded Eastern and Pacific states but sagged decidedly in the Middle states where Willkie gained substantially among the German-American communities and the isolationist groups.

Another recent instance where voting behavior touches religious affiliation is the 1950 mid-term election. The McCarthy efforts against Senator Tydings in Maryland were more consistently effective in predominantly Catholic communities and the same observation may be made regarding the 1950 Senatorial results in such states as Pennsylvania, Illinois, Utah and California. Politicians of both parties consider this factor as important in 1952 also. Republicans hope and Democrats fear that it may play some part again in this year's results.

For a combination of all kinds of issues, head, heart and pocketbook, the 1952 election is our best example. Voters' fears were played upon by means of the Communists-in-Government issue. Voters' emotions were played upon by the publication of shocking war pictures in some of the most widely read national magazines. Voters' hatreds were played upon in Southern states and focused against Truman, therefore against Stevenson. Voters' intelligence was influenced by the logical sounding argument that twenty years of one party is too long, that in a two-party country the Republicans should be given a chance at control and responsibility.

Voters in general were approached by Republicans through mass-media advertising devices that have proved effective in selling commodities to consumers. Above all, the young, the old, the educated, the uneducated, the rich, the poor were all influenced by idol worship, by the power of the well-known name of the general who had led the troops to victory in the greatest of all wars.

In this brief review, what more can be said for the standard classifications of voter behavior? Can we put them into categories of education, occupation, income, status, sex, age, race, region, religion and nationality and expect to find them behaving according to a common pattern in any election? Obviously not, although there may be greater stability in some categories than in others.

You can expect the South to be dominantly Democratic just as you can expect Maine, Vermont, Nebraska and the Dakotas to go Republican. You can expect women to vote about as men do. You can expect farmers, outside the South, to be predominantly Republican while the majority of workers will be found on the side of the party in power. Businessmen for the most part still think that there is more profit to be gained under a Republican than under a Democratic Administration.

Religious and nationality groupings will be predominantly in one political column or the other depending on the election and its dominant issues. Age groups, especially the voters in the younger brackets, do not stay put. Youth in 1932 favored the New Deal. Youth in 1952, not having lived through the experience of the Nineteen Thirties, was inclined to hero worship and in recognition of that fact the Republicans have proposed lowering the voter age level.

Local issues may not be as significant generally as people think. A survey conducted by Elmo Wilson's International Research Associates in eleven states, from Massachusetts to California and from Minnesota to New Mexico, on issues and other problems in this election indicates, among other interesting things, that the results are more likely to be determined by voters' opinions of the attitude of the two parties in matters of human welfare and enterprise.

While the 1954 campaign was tailored to the localities in recognition of the importance of local issues and personalities, the survey, in September, revealed the astonishing fact that about 80 per cent of those questioned could name neither their Democratic nor Republican Congressional candidates and nearly 75 per cent were unable even to name their Senatorial candidates. Such popular figures as Gillette in Iowa, Humphrey in Minnesota and Anderson in New Mexico are exceptions.

The survey also showed that, among the reasons for their preferences, party affiliation counts most heavily. About 80 per cent of the Democrats chose on a party and personality basis, whereas among Republicans party and personality reasons add up to about 85 per cent. Recommendations of a candidate by family or friends are relatively minor factors both among Republicans and Democrats.

The real difference shows up in two other sets of reasons given: among Democrats the fact that the party of the candidate favors "underdog" groups has an importance of 15 per cent, but only 2 per cent among Republican voters.

On the other hand, among Republican voters association with Eisenhower rates about 6 per cent, the need for a Republican Congress to support Eisenhower 4 per cent. This is a total for the Republican Eisenhower factor of 10 per cent in contrast with Democratic concern with issues affecting "underdog" groups of 15 per cent.

This leads me to the conclusion that the 1954 election is essentially a pocketbook election, even though a strong effort has been made through emotional appeal to convert a mid-term election favoring the Democrats into the equivalent of a Presidential, Eisenhower election. There is some unemployment, concentrated chiefly in the northeastern quarter of the country, where many of the marginal seats are located. There is farmer dissatisfaction with lowered farm income. The basic underlying fact is that more people consider the Democratic party the party of the "underdog" groups and the Republican party the party of business groups. This essentially pocketbook cleavage constitutes a basic reason for people voting as they have—and as they will.

IS IT THE MAN OR IS IT THE ISSUE?

Henry Steele Commager

Henry Steele Commager is one of America's most distinguished historians and the author of many studies, including *The American Mind* and *Living Ideas in America.* After many years on the faculty of Columbia University, he now is Professor of American History at Amherst.

The framers of our Constitution gave more, and more elaborate, consideration to the executive office than to any other feature of our Federal Government. Yet we look in vain through all the prolonged debates in the Convention, and through the eleven Federalist papers on the executive, for any suggestion that there is any relation between the election of a President and political principles or issues.

The framers were not political innocents; they were hardheaded realists. But they hoped, nevertheless, to create a Chief Executive who would be above party and above faction, who would decide on issues impartially and dispassionately. They thought that they had contrived an ingenious method of selection of the executive which would guarantee such impartiality, and would guarantee a lofty eminence as well.

As long as Washington was willing to serve as Chief Executive, these expectations were not disappointed. But no sooner was Washington out of the reckoning than the whole machinery so carefully provided by the framers fell apart. Parties came in to take over the job of selecting a candidate; electors—who were supposed to exercise independent judgment—came to be morally committed to the party choice. Presidential nominees were selected first by caucuses, then by popular conventions, and the careful arrangements of the framers were frustrated.

Thus for well over a century now our Presidential elections have been characterized by what Winston Churchill calls two grand climacterics: first the choice of candidates of the major parties, second the choice between them. From beginning to end it is the candidates who dominate the political scene —or who fail to do so at their peril. Does this mean that Americans are more interested in candidates than in issues, and that their votes are given to men rather than to parties or principles? Superficially it does, but only superficially.

After all, it is relevant to note that the choice of candidates itself is dictated, in large part, by the outcome of intraparty contests over issues. Thus the selection of Alton B. Parker instead of Bryan, in 1904, was a public confession that the conservative Democracy was back in the saddle. Eight years later, the victory of Woodrow Wilson, over the party war-horse, Champ Clark, was proclamation of the triumph of the progressive wing of the party. To take an example fresher in our minds, the nomination of General Eisenhower was not a personal tribute only, but a verdict on the struggle between internationalism and isolationism inside the Republican party.

The issues that candidates choose to talk about, the manner in which they discuss them, the attitudes they reveal, consciously or unconsciously, the interests they come to represent—all these are important in the elections themselves—and may be decisive. Thus it may be argued that the ability of McKinley—or of Mark Hanna—to dramatize the issue of "sound money" was largely responsible for Republican victory in 1896; thus the position, or the supposed position, of the two opposing candidates of 1916 on the question of war or peace proved decisive in a very close election.

Parties may not have firm principles but they do sometimes have firm reputations. The vague feeling that the Democratic party is liberal and the Republican party conservative, that the Democratic party represents the interests of the forgotten man and the Republican of the man who could never be forgotten —these feelings are none the less effective for their vagueness or even for their error.

And there is usually a long psychological lag before opinion catches up with reality. It took half a century for the Democratic party to overcome the onus of slavery and the Civil War; only now is the Republican party recovering from the embarrassment of the Depression.

But before we discuss further the question whether Americans vote for men or for issues, we must face the fact that we still do not know why people vote or fail to vote, and we do not know why they vote as they do.

It is indeed a bit embarrassing how little we actually know about voting or non-voting. Although every party in power during a major depression has been swept out or repudiated at subsequent elections, we do not really know the effect of economic conditions on voting. Even prosperity is no automatic guarantee of victory; thus, 1884, 1912, and even 1920 fell in periods of general prosperity, but in each case the election went against the party in office. Although war is supposed to be unpopular, no party or Administration has been thrown out during a war. The political pendulum swings so erratically that it is next to impossible to draw a reliable pattern.

What, after all, influences or controls voting? Is it party loyalty, hereditary or acquired? Is it habit? Is it geography? Is it class or group interest? Is it argument and propaganda? It is doubtless some or all of these considerations with various people at various times. Surely something explains our voting patterns. If Vermont or Westchester County invariably vote Republican and South Carolina or Jersey City invariably vote Democratic, we may be allowed to suspect that something besides rational arguments are operating. If four-fifths of the newspapers of this country support the Republican ticket, year after year, through thick and thin, we may wonder whether it is always because the Republican candidates have an intellectual appeal not vouchsafed the Democrats or whether the Republican platform is invariably more logical and more eloquent.

It is doubtless true that long before the nominations and campaigns a substantial proportion of all voters have committed themselves to one party or another as certainly as they have to one church or another, and are no more likely to be weaned from party than from church allegiance. It is equally true that these fixed voting habits seem to run in certain patterns which persist from election to election, and that it is possible to predict these patterns with considerable accuracy.

Thus, regardless of candidates, it has been true for some time that big cities tend to vote Democratic and small towns Republican; that skilled and semi-skilled workers vote Democratic and professional men and women Republican; that Negroes tend to vote Democratic and that voters under 25 are more likely to be found in the Democratic than in the Republican ranks.

Nor is this tendency to vote along lines of real or supposed economic or social interests confined—as some campaign orators would have us believe—to the ranks of labor and of farmers, who are somehow unpatriotic for consulting their interests in voting. After all there is little doubt about the way Westchester and Nassau Counties are going to go in any election; the medical profession is probably more of a unit in voting than, let us say, the railroad unions, and John Hersey's statistics on the class of '36 suggests that there is more uniformity of voting in graduates of Yale than in graduates of any Midwestern secretarial school.

Yet granted all this, it still cannot be said that any major group, except perhaps in the Deep South, is committed in advance to party or to candidate. There is not, in the United States, such a thing as a labor vote, a farm vote, a Negro vote, a Protestant or a Catholic or a Jewish vote, an Irish or a Polish vote, a teacher vote—or be it noted—a civil servant vote, or a Social Security vote.

While it is no doubt true that the groups indicated by these terms *tend* to vote in one way rather than another, the groupings are overlapping and blurred and unreliable. Any careful study of, for example, the farm vote would have to analyze it county by county and almost farm by farm, and would quickly discover that politically there was no such thing as the "farmer" but that there were instead Connecticut Valley tobacco farmers and Maine potato farmers and Georgia cotton farmers and Minnesota wheat farmers and Long Island truck farmers and California fruit farmers.

Furthermore, the various factors that condition party allegiance and voting are important but they are not decisive. They are not decisive for two reasons: first, because they cannot be counted on with certainty—witness the vast swings of the popular vote from 1916 to 1920 and from 1928 to 1932 for example. And second, because in so large and diversified a nation as ours most of these special interests cancel out. What these two qualifications mean is that within each group, class, section, or interest there is always a substantial number of independent votes, and that these along with the traditionally independent vote can be decisive.

What then decides the large floating vote? What decides the marginal independent vote within each supposedly committed group—Texas Democrats, for example, or Iowa corn farmers or New York Negroes—and the broad floating vote that is never wholly committed? What determines—parties or principles, men or issues, or a combination of them all?

Now the first thing that strikes the observer who looks objectively at the American political scene is that the American voter is rarely confronted with real issues—with issues that take on the dignity of principles. And the second thing that must impress him is that only very rarely do parties actually divide on issues or on principles; that even when—as this year, for instance—there are genuine issues, they are not such as to divide the major parties ideologically.

A third consideration at once qualifies these two. It is that Americans commonly think that they are confronted with great questions of principle and that the division between the parties is profound.

This elementary fact that the division between parties is more notorious than real pains most of our European friends, and astonishes a good many Americans who ought, by now, to have got over their astonishment. It is, however, not only an elementary but a wholesome fact. For it is the essential character of our major parties that they are the great common denominators of the American people, embracing within their hospitable folds men and women of all classes, faiths, interests and sentiments. And it is the historical function of parties, in normal times at least, to be all things to all men. It is this, indeed, which enables our two-party system to function at all.

History furnishes us innumerable examples of this party parallelism, as does, for that matter, the contemporary scene. Thus outraged Federalists insisted, correctly enough, that Jefferson had out-Federalized them, and, in revenge, they themselves adopted a good many former Republican principles. Thus, a century later, cartoonists displayed T. R. stealing the clothes of Bryan, off swimming in the Democratic pond. And thus in our own day Governor Stevenson can observe, somewhat wistfully, that he would be glad to stand on the Fair Deal platform if only General Eisenhower would move over and make a little room.

There are, of course, important exceptions to all this. Once in a while—fortunately not too often—the country is called upon for decisions on real issues. There was a real issue in 1892—an issue of Bank versus Government and of nationalism versus states' rights. In 1856 the people were confronted with very real issues in Kansas and the Fugitive Slave Law—issues so real that they destroyed the Whigs and largely destroyed the new American or Know Nothing Party. By 1860, people and parties were divided on the tragically real issue of the maintenance of the Union.

Then in 1896 Americans appeared to be confronted with real issues, and on these the parties divided: free silver or the gold standard. In 1912, too, there was a division, at least between the right and left wings of the Republican party—and again in 1916, although the division of that year was canceled by the swift events in the next few months.

It is worth noting that on most of these occasions parties broke into fragments—in 1856, 1860, 1896, and 1912. For just as our parties manage to hold together their varied and often conflicting elements by the calculated avoidance of vital issues, so the necessity of embracing such issues tends to divide and to destroy them.

In recent years we have witnessed a division on issues and on personalities as well—in 1932 and in 1936. If we look to party platforms, or to what candidates and parties are actually prepared to do rather than merely to say, it is difficult to find any genuine division after 1936.

To those who remember clearly the heat and excitement and acrimoniousness of the three campaigns of the Forties, this statement may arouse astonishment. But we have only to compare the party platforms of these years, or to recall the practical proposals of the candidates—as distinguished from their rhetoric—to realize that the statement is essentially true. We have only to ask ourselves what important features of the New Deal the opposition would have repealed or modified if it had won office, or what essentials of foreign policy it would have reversed.

But while it is probably true that parties are not really divided on principle, and that there are but few genuine issues in a normal campaign, it is equally true that a great many people, including the candidates themselves, persuade themselves that there are genuine issues and that parties are divided on matters of principle.

The human mind—and not least the American—yearns for simplification, loves the dramatic, and prefers its issues painted in black and white. Our political oratory, our campaign literature, often our very conversation, falls into stereotypes of issues and principles. . . . How much more dignified, after all, and how much more heroic to contend for great principles than merely for office! How dramatic to stand at Armageddon and battle for the Lord!

And what of the candidates? So Americans normally vote, then, for men? Again no generalization is possible. This much can be said: the vast majority of Americans know more about the candidates than about the issues; a powerful candidate can rise superior to party and ignore issues; candidates are most effective when they appear as symbols for some great principle, and it is only in third or minor parties (and not always there) that principles pretty consistently overshadow the personality and character of the candidate.

History, again, affords abundant illustration for those rather broad observations. Jefferson all but created his party and as long as he cared to, he dominated it. Jackson, one feels, could have run on any ticket and won—Jackson who in the beginning did not rightly know what his political convictions really were. Clay was as much Mr. Whig as Senator Taft is Mr. Republican, but the former dominated his party as no twentieth century politician has dominated the Republican party, commanding the allegiance of his followers for almost forty years. Bryan, too—perhaps the most neglected major figure in our political history—captured not only the Democratic party but the hearts and imaginations of his devoted following; alone among political candidates he survived three sharp defeats and remained a figure to reckon with.

The first Roosevelt dominated the whole political scene, not by virtue of his principles but by force of personality, by energy, vigor and excitement. Franklin Roosevelt overshadowed his party as had Jefferson and Jackson and —as with these predecessors—passed his power on to a successor.

Some of these men, so powerful, so dazzling, in their own right, were significant, too, as symbols. Thus Jackson came to be a symbol of democracy and Lincoln of the Union. Clay came to be a symbol of compromise. Bryan, too, and F.D.R. were not only spokesmen but symbols of great popular movements, of revolt and reform. General Grant had no known political convictions, but when Robert Ingersoll declaimed,

> When asked what state he hails from
> Our sole reply shall be
> That he comes from Appomattox
> And its famous apple tree,

Grant was irresistible. McKinley—not a strong character—was a persuasive symbol of prosperity and respectability, as Coolidge came later to seem a symbol of frugality and security.

When we come to symbols, we are in the realm of the intangible. No one who studies the American political past or observes the contemporary scene can doubt that the intangibles are important and may be decisive.

One final observation is, perhaps, relevant. At least, three of our Presidents who clearly stood for principles failed to win either contemporary popularity or historical acclaim for their courage. John Quincy Adams was very much a man of principle, of such firm principles, indeed, as all but disqualified him for the rough and tumble of American politics. After an unhappy Presidency he was defeated by a man who had yet to learn what he believed about public questions. James K. Polk was another man of principle—a man who boldly announced a program and carried it through, item by item: Oregon, Texas, bank reform, tariff reform. He, too, was allowed to retire after a single term. Andrew Johnson was most certainly a man of principle, a man who endured every indignity that a reckless Congress could heap upon him rather than surrender. Probably a fourth name should be added to this brief list—that of Herbert Hoover. Few will deny that he was a man of principle, as candidate, as President and as party mentor.

What emerges from all this? We do not know what men vote for, but we may conclude that they rarely vote for a candidate alone, or for issues alone. To be successful a candidate must have more than charm and eloquence and magnetism, important as these are. He must have more than principles and popular issues, important as these are. He must persuade the voters that he understands the vital issues, that he has a practical program, that his program is based not alone on immediate needs but on eternal verities, and that he can carry through the program and vindicate the principles.

THE CHANGING U. S. ELECTORATE
Samuel Lubell

Samuel Lubell is a political analyst who has spent a career in newspaper reporting and free-lance writing. He is a columnist for the United Features Syndicate and the author of *The Future of American Politics, Revolt of the Moderates, and White and Black: Test of a Nation.*

To many Republicans, 1964 seems hardly worthwhile. Often during recent months I have been told, "This isn't a Republican year" or "What difference does it make whom we nominate?" This sense of depression has been only deepened by the fact that the bitterly fought series of primaries in New Hampshire, Oregon, and California produced three different winners. To their distress, the Republicans must go into their convention this month with the sharp policy disagreements among themselves painfully exposed and a leading candidate for the nomination who is more popular with the delegates than with the Republican voters.

This sense of Republican futility about 1964 is unjustified for two reasons. First, an election is never settled until it is over. No one can predict the turn of events over the next months, and President Johnson's recent remark ("I hope that they feel in November as they do in April") was a pertinent one. Second, the feeling of helplessness overlooked the true significance of the election. Every Presidential election has an importance beyond mere victory or defeat. Each election is inescapably a step in the growth of both political parties—in the emergence from the past into the future or both parties and the nation.

In these terms, 1964 is a crucial year for the Republicans. Its import arises less from the remote chance of a stunning upset in November than from changes taking place in the electorate itself. The challenge to the Republicans is to recognize and adapt to these changes, some of which are working to their long-term advantage and against the Democrats.

These changes can be summed up by saying that both parties are in the process of being restructured. The South, long a one-party citadel, is in transition toward having two competing parties. Simultaneously, through the whole nation all sorts of nonpolitical changes are making the country more homogeneous. But this breakdown of traditional barriers does not mean that the American electorate is now huddled together in one great mass of unanimity. Far from it. The steady drift toward a managed economy ("mismanaged" if you don't like what is going on) is rearranging our politics into new divisions and patterns, largely reflecting group—rather than individualistic—economic interest. The political test of the future revolves around the skill with which both parties adjust to these nationalizing forces.

To continue as the majority party, the Democrats must keep their followers happy and committed. But keeping the party glued together is becoming more and more difficult, and only President Johnson's personal popularity makes it look easy this year. The danger to the Democrats—and the opportunity for the Republicans—can be discerned in the three great running conflicts of our era: economic policy, race, and foreign affairs.

On economic issues many voters find themselves torn and divided. Our affluent electorate is marked by a basic conservatism, in the sense that the citizens want to preserve what they believe has helped them in their economic climb. They identify approvingly with some government actions—like social security and minimum-wage laws. But they also are impatient with government spending when carried too far, with inflation that cuts into their purchasing power, with taxes that take money they would like to spend on other needs and wants. When a Democratic Administration proposes, as has Johnson's, to expand welfare programs, some Democrats will applaud—but many would prefer a cut in federal spending.

The racial issue also threatens wholesale defections from the Democrats in the years ahead, not just in the South but in the North as well. The heavy vote for Governor George Wallace of Alabama in the Maryland, Wisconsin, and Indiana primaries shows the increasing political explosiveness of racial feeling outside the Deep South. Some of this "white blacklash" is strongly anti-Negro, but more of it reflects divided emotions—a recognition that Negroes deserve equal treatment wars in the minds of most voters with the tensions stirred by Negro pressures to gain these rights.

In foreign policy many voters are subject to a conflict of hopes and fears, which poses distinct problems for both parties. The electorate wants to see war avoided and is willing to go along with efforts to negotiate better relations with Russia. But at the same time people are wary of strengthening Russia and, even more so, Communist China. Asked on what basis we should trade with Russia, most voters say, "Sell them food or consumer goods but not machinery that will help them in war." The public generally doubts that the Russians can be trusted to keep any agreement they sign. The Democrats seem committed to seek a basis for relaxing tensions with the Russians. Most voters are going along with this effort—with fingers crossed. Relaxation of international tensions will have political value for the Democrats only so long as it seems to work.

The Democratic party's travail, postponed though it appears to be by Johnson's wide appeal, should give Republicans hope for the future growth of their party. A minority party draws unto itself, whether it wants them or not, the voters who dislike the policies of the majority. But the Republican opportunity in the years ahead is far wider than merely harvesting disaffected Democrats. The Republicans have a chance to transform themselves into a truly national party, breaking down the old one-party South and encompassing a wide range of viewpoints of different interest groups.

My surveys indicate that this opportunity has not been fully exploited by the Republican leaders. The shaping of the G.O.P. into an effective national party will have to be done mainly in the areas of the conflicts over economic policy, race, and foreign affairs. But before discussing these in detail it may be helpful to examine the changing social patterns reflected in today's electorate.

A HARVEST OF SOCIAL CLIMBERS

As I see it, the orbit of political conflict that binds both parties has been shaped by a historic migration. For seventy years after the Civil War the Republicans were in the majority. But immigrants were pouring into the country from Europe during this period, filling the tenements of the great urban slums. Joining them were the native American migrants—people leaving the land and seeking opportunity in city factories. With the depression and the New Deal, these slum dwellers, their children, and grandchildren swung over into the Democratic party. The old Republican role as the majority party in the nation was taken over by the Democrats, who have held it ever since.

Even after these onetime minorities came together as the new majority, they did not stop migrating. They continued marching and climbing toward middle-class blessedness, first inside the cities and then into the suburbs. This migration, as important in its latter-day way as that which pushed back the nation's frontiers, could be scoffed at as social climbing of a sort. But social climbing is the great Americanizing institution, the necessary process by which the country has assimilated its different elements.

As the migration of these urban masses proceeded, their economic and political interests changed. In 1936, the year of the greatest Roosevelt sweep, hardly a Democrat paid taxes. Today these Democratic families are affluent or in debt, or both—and strongly tax-conscious. Their gains of recent years have set up a conflict with old underdog attitudes. They still tend to distrust Republicans, whom they thought of as the "haves" in the bad old days when they were "have-nots," but this new middle class no longer buys, sight unseen, all the New Deal slogans. Their values have changed with their net worth. The change was helped along by the Eisenhower years. Two terms of a Republican President without a depression virtually erased the memory link that had tied the Republican party to Hoover and the great depression in the minds of many Democrats.

The memories and interests of these prospering Democrats no longer entirely jibe. They really are voters in transition. Some, if they advance far enough in their economic climb (or if they identify with management), may make a deliberate decision to go over to the Republicans. Most of these in-transition voters, however, just stay in the middle, voting Democratic if their political habits are undisturbed, but ready to shift politically if troubled sufficiently. In 1952 anger over the stalemate in Korea brought a landslide break from old loyalties. One can point to a long roster of Democratic governors who were defeated in recent years largely because of a revolt against the taxes that had been levied to pay for the services demanded by their citizens.

The existence of these restless Democrats has shaped the dominant G.O.P. strategy in the North, a strategy calling for the blurring of party differences. Nelson Rockefeller in New York and William Scranton in Pennsylvania are only two examples of Republicans who have won with this strategy. During these gubernatorial campaigns I interviewed a cross section of the electorate. Repeatedly, Democratic voters who said they intended to vote Republican would explain that they did not feel this meant any change in basic party loyalty. A Democrat did not have to renounce his party and become a Republican for all time to vote for Rockefeller or Scranton.

Some Republican politicians in the North have insisted on sharpening rather than blurring the sense of party difference. This has brought some disastrous Republican defeats, as happened in 1958 when Senator John Bricker was toppled in Ohio and Senator William Knowland in California. Both men were beaten largely because of the bitter resentments kicked up by efforts to push through "right-to-work" laws in those states.

The great right-to-work fiasco of 1958 reflected a misunderstanding of voter attitudes toward labor unions. In my interviews with union members over the years I have found that they draw a distinction in their own minds between the union, which they will fight to preserve, and their leaders, whom they often dislike or disagree with. Frequently union members will protest against what their union proposes—as, for example, with union demands that many members feel may intensify inflation. When a political issue involving unions is presented as a "reform"—a step in a new direction—it will gain the support of many union members. But if the issue is posed as it was in 1958—as an effort to destroy the union—the membership solidifies in opposition. I remember a bakery driver's wife in Carrollton, Ohio, saying: "Sure, our union leaders are crooks. But we need our union and we'll keep it, crooks and all." So deep were the emotions stirred that even workers who had been lifelong Republicans broke and voted Democratic in 1958.

In most northern states, one must remember, there are sizable numbers of voters who are Republican primarily because of inherited family tradition rather than any sense of current economic interest. When the lines of economic conflict tend to be drawn more sharply, as happened during the recession of 1958 and in the farm-belt reaction to Ezra Benson's economic ideas, some of these Republicans-by-tradition are likely to break with their traditional loyalties.

In the South the pattern is almost exactly the reverse. There the Republicans need to sharpen economic issues to free lukewarm Democrats of party tradition. The south's political insurgency is primarily economic in motivation and traces back to the region's awakening to the rewards and excitement of industrial progress. To win over the new middle-class elements in the South, the Republicans need to sharpen their differences on economic issues with the Democrats.

This divergence between the northern and southern political strategies could prove as embarrassing to the Republicans as a similar conflict has proved to the Democrats in the past. In their search for maneuverability, the Republicans may need to develop the equivalent of the "border states" Democrats, who have served as "brokers" to bridge Democratic extremes, both economic and racial. Both Alben Barkley and Harry S. Truman kept open the lines of communication between the anti-Negro South and the big-city machines, to which the Negro vote was important. For the Republicans, Minority Leader Everett Dirksen appears to be filling such a role on the civil-rights bill, partly because of his position in the Senate but also because Illinois is a state with a large Negro vote. Probably the chief need for Republican "brokers" lies in the economic area.

THE BIG SPENDING MACHINE

Today it is the economy that does most to shape the basic party allegiance of the average voter throughout the nation. Not too many years ago, high-income southern precincts were almost as Democratic as low-income precincts. The historic significance of Dwight D. Eisenhower's victories was that they extended into the South this pattern of economic voting. In the last three presidential elections in every southern city the precincts at comparable income levels have shown much the same Republican vote as in the North. The higher up on the economic scale the more Republican the precinct has been. This economic voting pattern now seems so strongly rooted in the South that I don't believe it can be entirely wiped out by Lyndon Johnson's "local boy" appeal or by a continuance of Johnson's success in pleasing many members of upper-income groups, North and South. The relative showing of the Republicans in the South this year will constitute one measure of the G.O.P.'s progress toward becoming a national party.

In a context broader than the South, the key factor determining how people feel about economic issues has become their relation to the big spending machine that is now the federal government. Over the years one of my standard questions has been, "What is the biggest difference between the two parties?" In pre-Eisenhower days the answers nearly always ran: "The Republicans will bring another depression," or "The Republicans are the party of business, while the Democrats are for the workingman" (or "little people," or "middle class," depending on how the person interviewed saw himself).

But today most voters respond to the question with comments on spending, taxes, and inflation. Opposition to increased government spending may be more vocal among Republicans than Democrats, but it exists among all groups. A strange kind of balance prevails on this issue. Most people want to keep spending up to a level that will assure prosperity (though they may be confused on cause and effect), but will oppose spending that increases taxes or prices. Both the Kennedy and Johnson administrations seem to have tailored their economic programs to this public sentiment. Income taxes have been cut; and some effort has been directed toward keeping a lid on price increases, even while new welfare programs have been instituted to benefit specific voting segments.

Opposition to spending, however, does not signify universal disillusionment with government programs. The citizenry has come to prize the economic stabilizers instituted by the New Deal, and each economic group tends to want to hold onto the program that subsidizes it, even while grumbling against spending generally. Continuing these programs does not seem radical or even liberal to many voters, but conservative.

This attitude showed up as early as 1948. Many voters I talked with that year told me they voted for Harry Truman because they considered Thomas E. Dewey "too risky" a candidate. Overconfident of victory, Dewey failed to spell out what parts of the New Deal he proposed to keep and what he would scrap or change. Today I continue to find that to many voters "conservatism" means holding on to much of the legislation begun by the New Deal, retaining the gains they have made in recent years.

It was this personalized definition of "conservative" that hurt Senator Goldwater so badly in the New Hampshire primary. Nothing cut into his support there more than his statement that the social-security system should be made voluntary. Those who favor a voluntary system argue that young people should be free to do anything they want to do with their savings. But this appeal is countered by a double argument raised by many Republicans. One was that without forced savings of this sort, most people would do no savings at all, and the welfare burden would be even heavier than it is now. The other was that loss of the social-security system after all these years would penalize the prudent more than the imprudent.

In Dover, New Hampshire, I recall one old couple's telling me, "If we didn't have social security, we'd have to sell our home and go on relief." Republicans who voiced conservative views by almost any standard were appalled by Senator Goldwater's suggestion. Men and women who said staunchly, "We don't want any more of this welfare state" would still come to the defense of the social-security system. "We've lived with this for twenty-five years," said one storekeeper in Pittsfield. "You can't just drop it."

In contrast, Senator Goldwater's ideas are much more attractive in areas of rapid economic growth, such as southern California and parts of the Southwest. There people find it easier to make money, to start a new enterprise, to sell a piece of property at a profit, to strike it rich by tapping the population rise. These entrepreneurs are ambitious, active types. They really do not want to turn the clock back, but are seeking to hold a larger share in the returns from their activities. This desire encourages them to a more militant resistance to government policies which skim off so large a part of the profits that can be earned in this region.

These contrasting examples from New Hampshire and California point the need for Republican leaders to view primary campaigns not as "disruptive" but as a means of arriving at a unifying definition of what the party is to stand for. As a result of New Hampshire, I am sure the Goldwater forces learned to respect the electoral sentiment that attaches a high value to preserving the social-security system. From the voting in southern California anti-Goldwater forces should learn that these self-styled "conservatives" cannot be dismissed as merely "crackpots" or "backward looking."

A GAIN ON RACE

The second of the great policy conflicts in our present society—over race—poses perhaps the most pressing political danger to the Democrats, not only in the South but in the North and West as well. In such a situation some Republican strategists seem to be tempted to adopt a hands-off policy calculated to let the white South do as it pleases racially. To yield to this temptation would be unwise politically because the nation is looking for political leadership on the racial issue. Indeed, the chief defect of the Democratic party's recent record is its failure to unify the nation on policy questions arising from relations between the races. Deadlocked on race, the Democrats have bought time—and wasted the time that was bought, spreading the cancer of racial strife ever wider. The ultimate challenge before the Republicans is whether they can succeed where the Democrats failed in achieving a unifying national policy toward race problems.

Unification cannot be achieved on the basis of so-called "states' rights." That approach has already been tried and proved utterly inadequate. The inescapable fact is that civil rights has long been a national issue, requiring national policy. My own study of this tangled problem suggests that the course of unification lies in a quickening of the pace of desegregation, even while pursuing a gradualistic, moderate course. The emphasis must be on action. "Gradualism," if it is to be effective, cannot be used as a cloak for doing nothing. On this issue, in short, the Republicans should stand for real progress through moderate action, not for inaction under the guise of "states' rights."

The Republican need is to think beyond the temptations of the next election and aim at the failure of the Democrats as a unifying force. If insurgencies develop because of the enforcement of integration decrees or other racial tensions, the political reaction will need to champion a course of racial progress that avoids extremism on either flank, moving desegregation forward at a unifying pace. The ground that makes unification possible is where the Republicans should take their stand.

The last of the three great political conflicts in our society is over foreign policy. At this writing, my voter interviews show no single foreign-policy issue that is so tied to people's emotions as to endanger Lyndon Johnson's election. Vietnam seems far away to the average voter, despite the years of our involvement there. Republican campaign orators may hope to fan a Korea-type resentment over this struggle, but so far voters remain more uneasy and puzzled than emotionally aroused about Vietnam.

Cuba sparks more emotional interest. Republicans and Democrats alike nurse anger over a Communist base "only ninety miles off our shores." But President Kennedy's firm stand on Soviet missiles in Cuba in 1962 erased much of the political stain of the Bay of Pigs fiasco, while Johnson has been in office too short a time to absorb any blame for anything about Cuba. Most voters, when asked about Cuba, say, "We should have gone in earlier, but now it's too late." A new threat or provocation from Castro's Cuba might spur new demand for U.S. action. But, at this stage, Cuba is no political burden on Johnson. Voters feel that he didn't make our foreign-policy bed; he's just sleeping there. Every honeymoon ends, however, and Johnson—or at least the Democratic party—will in time be called to account for his stewardship of our foreign policy.

In this, as in other arenas, the Republican party will attract those who disagree with the majority party's policy. Because Roosevelt was President when the U.S. started lend-lease prior to entering World War II, those who disagreed with his actions—the so-called isolationists—automatically moved into the Republican party. Memories of Roosevelt's foreign policy have remained a basic divider between Republicans and Democrats ever since. Although Eisenhower was internationalist in his outlook, and was "imaged" as such by his speech writers, his greatest voter gains in 1952 came among Democrats with an isolationist tradition. The more international-minded Democrats stuck with Adlai Stevenson. Ike won the people who were disillusioned by Democratic foreign policy—many saw Korea as an extension of Roosevelt's policy—and who felt they wanted a change in it.

Too many politicians act as if in each new election people were voting for the first time. Actually, all elections begin as a projection of the past. Because of its past appeal the Republican party will continue to be a haven for those who are distrustful of the U.S. course abroad. This remains true even though the internationalist aspect of that policy was left relatively untouched in the Eisenhower Administration. Recently, for example, I conducted a survey on

Red China. Republicans were more opposed to admitting Peking to the United Nations than Democrats (though a majority of Democrats also opposed its admittance). Even more interesting were the responses to the question "Which is the bigger threat to the U.S., Russia or Red China?" Democrats tended to pick China while Republicans tended to see Russia as the bigger threat and to be less hopeful of the prospects of attaining a genuine relaxation of tensions between the U.S. and the Soviet Union.

One major difficulty the Republicans face is how to campaign for a stiffer foreign policy without seeming to be warlike. In California more adverse criticism was voiced against Senator Goldwater on this point than on any other aspect of his views. Goldwater's proposal to send the Marines in to turn on the water at Guantanamo Bay was recalled by many voters with the comment, "He'd rush us into war." Justly or unfairly, they concluded: "He doesn't talk like a President. He shoots off his mouth without thinking."

In an age of nuclear weapons and missiles, belligerent political partisans—whether Republican or Democratic—defeat their own purposes when they pound the table. The need of the nation is for an opposition party that can point out the risks and weaknesses in Administration policy without sounding as if it were issuing a call for war. The American voter will respect differences of opinion on foreign-policy issues when supported by reasonable arguments. It is worth noting that Senator Goldwater lost no public support by his vote against the nuclear-test-ban treaty. Many voters were as doubtful of its wisdom as he was, even when they resolved their doubts by being ready to take a chance on the treaty. A number of voters told me: "I can see how anybody could be suspicious of that test ban."

WHAT IS POVERTY?

Not just on foreign policy but on all the great issues of our time there is a pressing need for genuine cause-and-effect study of the problems facing the nation. On the Democratic side too much energy is devoted to keeping in line the party faithful and too often there is a tendency to deal with problems in quick headlines and New Deal imagery. The Republicans, on the other hand, in their efforts to chip away Democratic support, tend to react too often in terms of quick opposition to whatever Democratic leaders propose. In place of quick appeals and quick opposition, the nation needs to get down to fundamentals on many questions.

The opportunity to do so is perhaps greater for the Republicans, since Democratic thinking has hardened almost into dogma. There is scarcely a problem for which the Democratic strategists do not trot out the same solution—spend more money. The tax cut was presented as a way of ensuring "full employment" by priming more spending, with little real attention given to the many varied causes of unemployment.

Last year I did an exhaustive survey of unemployed workers to determine why we had so high a jobless rate in a booming economy. I concluded that the unemployment figures on which both Democrats and Republicans rely are no longer an accurate measure of our economic performance. Largely because of labor unions and corporate economic strength, we have turned most of our economy into a protected fortress. The worker with enough seniority to be within the fortress gets the high wages and fine fringe benefits of our modern society. Those who are outside the fortress bear the brunt of the unemployment.

The same people get thrown out of work repeatedly because they are low in seniority. With any downturn in the economy, they are the first to go. If inflation pushes up labor costs, those without seniority are most vulnerable when efforts to cut costs are made. I have interviewed young people of thirty and thirty-five who have never held a steady job in their lives. They have been laid off time and time again. Many live mainly for the time when they will finally build up enough seniority to be assured of working steadily. Waiting for seniority has become part of the pattern of industrial living. Often the wives of those without seniority must go to work to supplement the family income.

This unemployment survey emphasized the need for examining the different kinds of unemployment on a cause-and-effect basis. Neither party has yet given the unemployment problem the kind of study that is needed.

The "war on poverty" is another example of a headline in search of analysis. The statistics being used of the people who are supposed to be living in poverty are not good figures at all. Some professor-politicians set up arbitrary statistical dividers and say, "This is poverty." Their proposed solution is not soundly based because it is not derived from a diagnosis of poverty, of the many different causes of "poverty," of why particular people are poor. One should also question whether poverty is what the government says it is. I remember interviewing one Iowa couple who had moved from fertile Story County to southern Iowa, where the land is poor and eroded. When I asked why they had left good land for poor, the wife replied, "Up in Story County people had dollar signs for eyes; all they thought about was money." This couple was willing to accept a lower standard of material comforts in order to escape competitive pressures. Is that true "poverty?" I told this couple, "Some people in government think that you should not be farming such poor land, that you ought to be retrained for other work." The husband replied stiffly, "I don't want to be retrained. We're doing all right."

What is called "poverty" involves more situations than can be dealt with under one statistical headline. Instead of having just a label, we need more digging to determine the numerous kinds and causes of poverty. Then our corrective efforts should be addressed to those causes.

WHO CAN DO BETTER?

To sum up, I believe the nation needs a change in the terms of party competition. Ordinarily, the majority party is in the better position to set the terms of party competition, with the minority party left to wait for sizable segments of the majority to fall out among themselves. But the trend toward a managed economy, the spreading racial strife, the dangers of both nuclear and submarine war require a party competition that will be more sensitively attuned to the emerging problems of the future rather than the lingering quarrels of the past.

This is why, as a nonpartisan student of politics, I feel the interests of the whole country will be advanced by a strengthening of the Republican party so it can be an effective national party. The nation's interests would be advanced even further if either party were to change the terms of party competition by framing policy proposals that go to the heart of the difficulties we face in economic affairs, foreign relations, and the racial conflict.

This, it seems to me, is the real challenge to the Republican party in 1964. My interviews with voters in every part of the country show this need to move the party competition closer to realistic solution of national problems. It is a challenge that the G.O.P. may find easier to pick up, if only because the Democrats, with their deadlocked majority, may not be capable of much more than a holding action for some years ahead. American history suggests that political power ultimately goes to the party of unification in the nation. The Democrats, despite a masterful blurring of differences by Lyndon Johnson, seem to have lost this unifying power, at least temporarily. One way of looking at 1964—and beyond—is to ask: can the Republicans transform themselves into the party of national unification?

4 PUBLIC OPINION AND NEWS MANAGEMENT

The importance of public opinion in a democracy can scarcely be overstressed. As the famed pollster George Gallup has pointed out, "What we don't know *can* hurt us." The need for an enlightened people has been recognized throughout American history by virtually every leader identified with the advancement of democratic principles. From Thomas Jefferson through Abraham Lincoln and Woodrow Wilson down to Dwight D. Eisenhower, John F. Kennedy, and Lyndon B. Johnson, all have agreed on the significance of participation by an informed public—if enlightened decisions are to be reached, errors are to be corrected, and wise leadership is to be selected.

Analysis of public opinion suggests the existence of a threefold relationship between government and its citizens in a democracy. First, there is the problem of determining what public opinion is; second, there is the task of reflecting that opinion; and third, there is the creation of opinion, a task of leadership even in a democracy.

In its First Amendment, the American Constitution undertakes to guarantee that there shall be a broad and unrestricted realm for the development of public opinion—with freedom of speech, freedom of the press, and freedom of assembly. Most state constitutions repeat these guarantees. But how do these protections emerge in actual practice?

The attempt to determine public opinion leads first to the question "What public?"—for, indeed, there seem to be many. Apparently, a crisscross network exists, in which one segment of the public may believe one thing and another segment the opposite. But frequently there is no precise way of determining the outlook of a mathematical majority. Furthermore, opinions may be held with varying degrees of intensity, with virtual indifference at one extreme and strong, emotionally held points of view at the other. Then, too, many degrees of knowledge and understanding may underlie the opinion—in short, the basis of opinion may be rational and enlightened or just the reverse. Moreover, public opinion may be latent rather than crystallized and clearly formulated; it may be more a subconscious feeling than a well-defined credo.

The measurement of public opinion—still far from an exact science—has come a long way from that day in 1936 when the *Literary Digest* so confidently predicted, on the basis of a sample drawn from its own subscription list and the telephone directory, a triumph for Landon over Roosevelt. Even today, as the more recent experience of 1948 suggests, polls are not yet completely accurate barometers. Nonetheless, they have their place—together with the more subjective personal-interview surveys (of the Samuel Lubell type), press samplings of editorial comment, and letters from constituents—in estimating the public pulse.

But how should opinion, even if susceptible to increasingly precise measurement, be reflected in public policy? This remains one of the most perplexing questions facing the public servant, whether he is a ward politician or chief executive, an administrator or legislator, or any combination thereof. Phrased perhaps oversimply, is it the duty of the representative in a democracy to follow, as accurately as polling techniques will permit and as slavishly as individual conscience will allow, the voice of the people? Or does he have an obligation to pursue a stronger and more forthright position than the statesman in the possibly apocryphal story, who admits, "There go my people. I must follow them for I am their leader"?

Certainly, if he chooses a more independent course, today's leader has many powerful weapons at his disposal. For public opinion, it is well recognized, is amenable to many types of manipulation—covert as well as open, subliminal as well as visible; for better or worse, it may be created or destroyed, used or abused.

The institutions that shape public opinion may be divided into two distinct categories—the *unconscious* and the *conscious* movers. In the first group is the over-all pattern of cultural heritage and of social institutions: home, school, and church, and the personal environment, including friends and family, associates, neighbors, and co-workers. In the second are the activities of advertisers and editorialists, press agents and pamphleteers, panacea peddlers and politicians, news reporters and news "managers."

It is the latter group that has been the subject of most the recent public concern. In the light of this group's reputed ability to mold public thinking, such attention is well merited. But perhaps in the long run the subconscious influences—the more basic and less publicized—are the more important, in that they are responsible for the very definition of the society—the society whose underlying attitudes shape our government in action.

WHAT WE DON'T KNOW *CAN* HURT US
George Gallup

George Gallup, America's best-known pollster, founded the American Institute of Public Opinion. He is the author of *The Pulse of Democracy, Guide to Public Opinion Polls,* and other publications.

The most disturbing fact about the present American scene is the ignorance on the part of a large segment of our population regarding issues vital to their very existence. Like the poor, the ignorant are always with us. Normally, lack of information on the part of some of the voters has little effect upon national policy. But when this same lack of knowledge is widespread, the consequences can be dangerous.

Today for the first time I must confess that I am concerned lest lack of information lead the American people to decisions which they will regret. When the public is reasonably well informed on any issue, it generally comes to the right conclusion. Today, however, poll takers daily bring to light misconceptions and ignorance which I think should be corrected. I have listed five of the most important of these "areas of ignorance" which affect the thinking of large segments of the population.

The first area of ignorance concerns foreign affairs.

What is the state of knowledge regarding some of the problems of combating Communist aggression which face us in the Orient and Europe? To get some idea of how well informed the voters of this country are we devised a very simple set of questions which our interviewers put to a cross-section of the adult population in a . . . survey.

These are the questions which we asked of this cross-section: (1) Will you tell me where Manchuria is? (2) Will you tell me where Formosa is? (3) Will you tell me what is meant when people refer to the 38th Parallel? (4) Will you tell me what is meant by the term "Atlantic Pact?" (5) Will you tell me who Chiang Kai-shek is? (6) Will you tell me who Marshal Tito is?

Certainly there is no question here that should stump any citizen. Yet only 12 percent of all adults we questioned could answer all six correctly. A higher percentage—19—could not answer a single one. The amazing thing is that virtually all of these people read a newspaper and listen to their radio daily. . . .

When the Iranian situation was boiling to a crisis, only four Americans in ten knew where Iran was, and only three in ten knew what the trouble in Iran was all about.

Keystone of our European foreign policy is the Marshall plan. Yet after the plan had been in effect for more than two years, one-third of the American voting population either knew nothing at all about the Marshall plan or had mistaken ideas concerning it.

Ignorance of domestic affairs is likewise alarming.

It was shocking to learn . . . that 34 per cent of the American people could not correctly identify Dean Acheson [when he had been] Secretary of State . . . for two years. One third didn't know who Senator Joseph McCarthy is either.

Six out of every ten [didn't] know what the Reconstruction Finance Corporation (R.F.C.) is, despite all the publicity over questionable R.F.C. loans. Fewer than one-third of the adult population has followed any of the discussions about the Brannan plan. In one survey the public was asked to state approximately how much the Federal debt is. The average guess was $150 billion short of the mark.

It is little wonder that the Herbert Hoover Commission reports on reorganizing the executive branch of the Government to save money and increase efficiency are largely Greek to the great majority of Americans. Only about four voters in every ten (44 per cent) have ever heard of the Hoover Reports, and only 24 per cent know what they recommend.

Another misconception has to do with the destructiveness of the atom bomb.

Some six years ago the world witnessed the collapse of Japan shortly after we had dropped atom bombs on two of her cities. I am not competent to say just what part these bombs played in the surrender of Japan.

However, it is easy to see how this success in the war against Japan could give many persons the fantastic idea that all we have to do to bring Red China and Red Russia to their knees is "drop an atom bomb" on their cities.

Further questioning of these same individuals reveals the extent of their misinformation about the bomb. They do not seem to realize that its effectiveness is a matter of a few miles. In their minds, just a few A-bombs are capable of destroying virtually a whole nation.

I am not an authority on the A-bomb. But I do believe it is a threat to this country to permit so many persons to have an exaggerated idea of its destructive power.

The fourth major area of ignorance is the inability of many Americans to envisage the awesome effect of another world war on our present civilization.

Polls show that only a fraction of the population has any conception of the staggering cost of war in money alone, to say nothing of blood. Only 13 per cent of Americans polled were able to make even a rough guess as to the amount—approximately $57 billion—being spent on defense in 1951–52.

Moreover, most Americans really cannot conceive of our not winning any war we undertake. The delusion is that we can fight World War III, get home quickly, and live happily ever after. Consequently, many voters tell our poll interviewers: "War with Russia is inevitable. So let's get it over with, so we can stop worrying."

The only proper rejoinder to this is that death, too, is inevitable; so let's all go out and jump in the river and have done with this waiting and worrying.

The confidence in our ability to win a war is encouraging evidence of our national morale and patriotism. But it fails to take into account that even the victor in the next war is likely to suffer more than the losers of past wars.

Europeans, whose lives are more directly affected than ours ever were even at the height of World War II, do not share the sanguine belief that everything would return to normal if the Soviets were defeated in World War III.

Lastly, few Americans seem to understand or take much interest in the possible alternatives to a shooting war.

Our polls show that 77 percent have never even heard of the Point Four program and only 5 per cent understand what it is trying to accomplish.

A surprisingly large number—more than half—don't know what the "Voice of America" is or what it does.

Our national lack of appreciation of the importance of ideological warfare is particularly disturbing in view of the fact that we are going to have to live in the same world with the Communists for a good long time to come. We not only have to outsmart the Communists in the struggle for men's minds, we have to understand what's going on in the minds of men all over the world, rather than expect them to think as we do. As a nation, we're still largely ignorant of the impact of ideas on other nations. Witness the sudden dismay of many Americans at starving India's acceptance of Russian grain.

Only our failure to see what is going on in the world and to face up to the realities of the struggle we are engaged in keeps us from doing the things which we need to do to win the war of ideas.

Who is to blame for our ignorance about current world problems?

First, I think, the chief blame lies with the people themselves.

We have become so bent on entertainment that anything which doesn't fit easily and unconsciously into this groove tends to be ignored. The old-fashioned idea that everyone should "keep abreast of the times" apparently has lost much of its early appeal. Either this must be true or that admonition has become corrupted to mean keeping abreast of winning football teams or the latest bulletins on Hollywood marital affairs.

Next, let's look at our educational system. It is my conviction that educators have succeeded admirably in making learning dull and lifeless in this era of universal education. The conception that the ultimate goal of education is to inspire students to carry on the process of learning throughout their lives, to give them an unquenchable thirst for knowledge, seems to be lost in the struggle to equip students to capitalize on what they have been taught in the classroom.

What about the role of the newspaper in this situation? The historical function of the newspaper has been to keep the public informed about issues of the day. It is, in a very real sense, "the schoolmaster of the people." But have the newspapers of the country lost a sense of mission in this respect? Have they begun to worry too much about having the most popular comic strips and the most complete sports pages and too little about keeping their readers interested in, and informed about, the important problems of the day?

I recently conducted a small survey among working newspaper men actively engaged in processing the daily flow of reporting—copy desk chiefs—asking them to rate on a scale of 100 the quality of the job being done today by daily newspapers in treating news of world events and issues in such a way as to interest the maximum number of newspaper readers.

Interestingly, the copy desk chiefs rated this aspect of today's journalism *lower* than any other practice. They gave it a score of only 36. In other words, their combined judgment is that the press today is doing a pretty poor job in presenting national and foreign news to readers. Or put in a more encouraging way, there is tremendous room for improvement in this department.

An important part of the job of a public opinion polltaker, as I see it, is to keep uncovering and reporting the more serious "areas of ignorance." What people know has an important bearing upon what they think. And what they think almost invariably influences the course of action taken by government.

That is why it is so vital today to see that decisions which the government makes aren't influenced by lack of information on the part of voters. Our very lives are at stake.

Perhaps we should revise the old statement, "What you don't know won't hurt you," to read: "What you don't know may destroy you."

GOVERNMENT BY PUBLICITY

Douglass Cater

Douglass Cater, Special Assistant to President Lyndon B. Johnson, was formerly Washington Editor of *The Reporter* magazine. He is the author of *The Fourth Branch of Government,* and *Power in Washington.*

More than in any other capital in the world or any other city in the United States, there is prestige and privilege belonging to the lowly reporter in Washington. Even those who have graduated to the higher callings of columnist or bureau chief still take a modest pride in identifying themselves by the lesser title. Within the press corps, faint derision attaches to one who prefers anything more pretentious.

The Washington correspondent clings to the image of the reporter as the supreme individual in the age of the organization man. His prestige symbols encourage him in this notion. The Pulitzer Prizes, the Heywood Broun and Raymond Clapper Awards handed out each year, all go to the individual who has beaten the system and gotten the "scoop." Even the hoary myth of the swashbuckling, free-wheeling, heavy-drinking reporter who pursues news with a hunch and a hangover dies hard. It is desperately nourished in the literature of the profession and in the tall tales swapped around the Press Club bar.

The reality is a bit different. The Washington correspondent's business, like most big businesses, has become specialized, compartmentalized, channelized, even routinized to a degree that would shock his predecessor of a few decades ago.

The backbone of the business and, to a certain extent, its central nervous system are the giant wire services with a labor force large enough to monitor every major news outlet in the capital and to maintain a steady outgoing flow of words. The wire-service employee scarcely conforms to old-fashioned notions of the reporter who each twenty-four hours dictates a first draft of history. He is rather the bucket boy for a never-ceasing stream of news that may be scooped up at any hour of day or night and poured into print by the far-flung distributors.

There are the Washington bureaus of the big-city dailies and the chain papers—highly varied operations ranging from the twenty-three man princely state maintained by the *New York Times* to the one- and two-man outposts of the Denver *Post* and the Providence *Journal.* These reporters are the most direct spiritual heirs of the ancient tradition of the Washington correspondent. They range widely in their purpose. For some it is an unending search for scandal and expose. Some consider their function to be the more leisurely digestion of the raw meat of the headlines. Another sizable contingent of the Washington press corps is composed of the "localizers" of the news. They bear daily testimony to the fact that the United States has become a world power whose interests are still heavily provincial. These reporters view Washington through the eyes of Dubuque, or Kalamazoo, or Nashville.

Other reporters view the Washington scene from other perspectives. Reporters for the news weeklies—artisans on a different type of assembly line from the wire services—dig out the primary components necessary to give a factual shape and color to the week's events. Other components—style, polish, "meaning"—are added further along the assembly line, in the skyscraper workshops of New York. Reporters for radio and television scan the horizon with restless radarscopes in search of news in shapes than can be heard and seen. And syndicated columnists, the most independent of the news merchants, batter the barricades for their "inside news" purveyed three times or more weekly and ranging in content from foreign policy to freight rates.

The reporter is the recorder of government, but he is also a participant. He operates in a system in which power is divided. He as much as anyone—and more than a great many—helps to shape the course of government. He is the indispensable broker and middleman among the subgovernments of Washington. He can choose from among the myriad events that seethe beneath the surface of government which to describe, which to ignore. He can illumine policy and notably assist in giving it sharpness and clarity; just as easily, he can prematurely expose policy and, as with undeveloped film cause its destruction. At his worst, operating with arbitrary and faulty standards, he can be an agent of disorder and confusion. At his best, he can exert a creative influence on Washington politics.

In no other major capital does the reporter have quite this political role. Patrick O'Donovan, correspondent for the London *Observer,* has commented: "Most strangers are astonished by the power of the American and, more particularly, the Washington press. It fulfills an almost constitutional function. And it works with a seriousness and responsibility which—even though it may lack the luxuries of style—cannot be matched in Britain today."

During the latter years of the Truman administration, the widely publicized Congressional challenge to Presidential leadership aroused deep concern among those anxious about America's role in the free-world alliance. Yet, viewed with the hind-sight of a very few years, it appears a curious sort of challenge. It is doubtful whether a single prerogative of the Presidency was actually diminished. What had in fact happened was simply that *the focus of public attention shifted from the White House to the committee rooms of Congress.* Prior to 1950, the major events of government that attracted public attention included the Truman Doctrine, the Marshall Plan, Point Four, the Berlin airlift, and the North Atlantic Treaty Organization with its accompanying Military Defense Assistance Program—all Executive-inspired and carried out with the "advice and consent" of Congress. From 1950 to 1953, in any newsman's book the major Washington stories would include the Tydings investigation of the McCarthy charges, the MacArthur dismissal inquiry, the McCarran hearings, and McCarthy's continuing warfare against the State Department. Congress, not the President, became the principal source of news, explanation, and opinion.

The investigations themselves were singularly barren of conclusions. Despite all the furor, they did not result in drastic legislative reforms or even in substantial defeats to the administration's foreign-policy program. Yet it would be idle to claim that this shift in public attention had not affected the workings of the American government. It served to diminish the usefulness of a great many of the President's chief lieutenants and to elevate into positions of commanding importance hitherto obscure members of Congress. It enabled one comparatively junior senator lacking the conventional trappings of seniority and prestige to sustain for a considerable time a threat to the President's control over the Executive branch. It created serious doubts at home and abroad whether the President did in truth stand at the helm of government during a critical time in world affairs. This era, in brief, illustrates the degree to which the reporting of events can itself be a major political event.

Publicity is a force that has become uniquely essential to the American system of government, in which "public opinion" is called on daily to arbitrate between two competing branches of government that are supposedly separate and co-ordinate to what Woodrow Wilson called the "literary theory" of our Constitution.

In recent years, U.S. government has, in fact, experienced a curious turnabout in the exercise of powers from what was envisaged in Constitutional doctrine. The President, aided by a growing staff of experts, has become the prime formulator of legislative programs and the chief budget maker. Congress, on the other hand, with the proliferation of its investigative committees, ever attempts to serve as board of review and veto over the ordinary administration of the Executive departments. Each, in testing the undefined limits of these new claimed prerogatives, must resort unceasingly to public explanation to sustain the logic of its claims.

Within the Executive branch itself, grown large and infinitely compartmentalized, the publicity competition often takes on the character of a life-and-death struggle. Inside the Pentagon, where a sizable chunk of the Federal budget is divided up, the highest classifications of military secrecy often go out the window in the rivalry among the three services. When an Army colonel was court-martialed in 1957 for leaking to the press information about the Army missile Jupiter, Dr. Wernher von Braun, head of the Army Missile Program, testified in his defense: "Jupiter involves several million dollars of the taxpayers' money. One hundred per cent security would mean no information for the public, no money for the Army, no Jupiter. . . . The Army has got to play the same game as the Air Force and the Navy."

The Reporter in Washington has witnessed on numerous occasions how the journalistic mask of a public figure can take possession of the man himself. More than witnessed—he has often played an active role in the transformation. A leading correspondent who prefers to remain anonymous has provided a revealing illustration of this creative function of journalism in a letter to a friend: "I have had one very important experience in this town. I knew Arthur Vandenberg when I thought he was the most pompous and prejudiced man in the United States Senate. I saw him change partly by the processes of mellowing old age, but mainly by accident and particularly as a result of public reaction to his famous speech of January 10, 1945. I happen to know that that speech, or rather the main parts of it, were largely accidental. I can say to you privately that I was, myself, quite by chance responsible for that change in the speech. But my point is that what changed Vandenberg was not the speech itself, but the press of public reaction to the speech, and from then on, as you know, he played an important role in winning bipartisan support for the concept of collective security."

What the writer failed to add was that the "public reaction" was in large part stimulated by the tremendous fanfare that leading newspapers gave to Vandenberg's speech—a build-up that took the senator quite by surprise, as he confessed in his private papers, published posthumously. It was not the first time—nor will it be the last—that the Washington journalist has hailed the policy declaration that he himself had a hand in ghosting.

This tendency for the development of news to influence reactively the development of events is a force that cannot be precisely charted. The interaction can be a result of pure chance. It can, as modern practitioners of the art of public relations appreciate, be made the object of manipulation. It can even be a product of conscious co-operation, or lack of it, between the politician and the press.

News standards go to the very core of policy formulation by high officials. At a gathering of newsmen to pay honor to him for his famous plan, General George C. Marshall described the publicity problems of putting the plan across. And Paul G. Hoffman, at the same gathering, paid glowing tribute to certain members of the Washington press corps. "We would have never gotten the dollars," said Hoffman, "if it hadn't been for the support of the reporters of the Overseas Writers' Club." The tribute was duly and modestly accepted by those present.

Yet there is a basic conflict of interest between the government and the press that creates continuing unrest in Washington. On Dean Acheson's last day in office as Secretary of State, he was paid a visit by James Reston, Washington correspondent for the *New York Times*. The purpose of Reston's call was to ask quite bluntly why the Secretary and he had not enjoyed better working relations. Underlying his question was the unhappy conviction that Acheson, who brought unusually high talents to the office, had been unwittingly caught in the riptides of publicity. His effectiveness had been gradually eroded by failures of communication.

Secretary Acheson answered with equal bluntness that better relations would have been impossible, since there was a basic conflict of purpose between the two of them. A Secretary of State, Acheson said, had to germinate new policies and to nurse them along until they have reached the stage of development when they can withstand the battering assaults of the political arena. The reporter's primary purpose, on the other hand, is to get news for his paper, no matter what the effect on policy.

Reston stoutly denies that the conflict can be defined in quite these terms. He admits that it is the duty of the reporter to get at the news while it is still news. In government today, when so many policy decisions are made in the closed precincts of the Executive departments, the press would be abdicating its function if it were to sit by until these decisions are formally announced. But Reston argues that Secretary Acheson failed to understand and make use of the creative power of the press to muster public support for sound policy and, alternatively, to gauge the full extent of public reaction to unsound or unrealistic policy.

This dialogue between the Secretary and the reporter—both able and earnest men, both anxious that democratic government also be effective government—reveals a dilemma of government and the press. It is more recognizable in the American system than in those parliamentary democracies where the press does not play nearly so intimate a role.

The American fourth estate today operates as a *de facto* quasi official fourth branch of government, its institutions no less important because they have been developed informally and, indeed, haphazardly. Twelve hundred or so members of the Washington press corps, bearing no authority other than accreditation by a newspaper, wire service, or network, are part of the privileged officialdom in the nation's capital. The power they exercise is continuing and substantive.

Yet the interaction of the government and the press needs to be examined to discover how much or how little it contributes to a continuing disorder in American democracy when government fails to explain itself clearly and candidly to the citizens. It is equally a failure when the press fails to communicate intelligibly the news of government or when that news becomes an instrument in the hands of self-seeking interests.

"THANK YOU, MR. PRESIDENT"

No monarch in history has had a retinue like that which gathers about the American President and calls itself the White House press corps. The reporters hang about his antechamber with the self-assurance of privileged courtiers at some federal court, keeping under constant surveillance and interrogation those who pass in and out—governors, cabinet members, senators, ambassadors. They dog the President's every step and turn his most casual conversation into a mass meeting. Their special plane takes off after the one carrying the President and alights just in advance of it. Thus even the contingency of a fatal crackup has been calculated so as not to interrupt the flow of prompt and plentiful publicity about our President.

Just to the right of the entrance to the White House's west wing where the President has his office, a special room has been set aside for the press, its typewriters, its telephones, its poker table. There the twenty to thirty White House "regulars"—reporters whose sole assignment is to cover this tiny beat—spend much of their day. Directly across the entrance hall, the Press Secretary has offices connected by private corridor to the President's own office. Two and three times daily the Press Secretary meets with the regulars and any other reporters who may wander in. And throughout the day the reporters are in constant touch with the Press Secretary and his assistants, checking leads, listening for tips, or simply killing time.

But the chief event of the week is when the reporters, one hundred and fifty to two hundred strong, file into the ornate little room in the old State Department Building once used for signing treaties. They pack themselves into row on row of tightly spaced steel folding chairs and overflow onto the rococo balcony up near the ceiling. Along the back of the room a solid bank of floodlights and cameras adds to the congestion. In the heat of Washington summer it is almost unbearable. At the appointed hour the doors are closed against the laggards, and the nation's leading citizen hurries in from a side entrance to meet the press. His assistants march in behind him to listen, but seldom to intercede. There may be a few prepared words, and then, with a barely perceptible Presidential nod, it begins. Reporters rise and vie for recognition. For the next half hour, the President's gaze scans the assemblage and the President's nod designates who shall be his interrogators. His choice is generally a random one and as a consequence the interchange of question and answer is apt to be quite haphazard. The ceremony is not very solemn, but the underlying solemnity of the occasion can never be entirely forgotten. For a time the President of the United States stands alone, unshielded by the layers of officialdom that lie between him and thc Amcrican public.

The conference may follow a smooth and gentle course. Or it may explode with unabashed savagery, the reporters probing relentlessly into a touchy subject and the President lashing back angrily at question and questioner. Then, at a signal from the press itself, it is all over. The grand finale is a scene of frenzy. Turning their backs on the still standing President, reporters from the wire services and networks who occupy the frontmost seats charge down the center aisle in a pushing, shoving race to reach telephone booths just outside the door.

Foreign visitors to the President's press conference depart from this undisciplined ritual with a feeling of awe, consternation, or outright disgust. But they rarely fail to be impressed by its importance as a central act in the high drama of American government.

Why such mutual fascination between the President and the press? What prompts the editor and publisher to devote so much money and space to the Presidential press conference? And what, in turn, causes the President to put up with the incessant inroads on his privacy? The answer lies in the very nature of modern American government. Proper relations with the press are as essential to its orderly functioning as the power to levy taxes and pass laws.

The Press Beats the Measure

Any President who may lightly consider abolishing the press conference, as Eisenhower reportedly did during the hectic months before his inauguration, must come to recognize its value as a device for keeping public attention focused on himself as the single most important person in the United States and, for that matter, the free world. By having the floodlights thus fixed, the President can give his words and gestures subtle gradations of meaning, and avoid the stark black-and-white they would acquire in a formal announcement. He can, if he chooses, address words of intercession or exhortation to Congress that would not be altogether effective for him to speak in his weekly conferences with Congressional leaders of his party. He can, with a casual word at his press conference, break an administrative log jam in the vast Federal Bureaucracy spread out beneath him. Finally, he can speak to the foreign governments, for which his slightest nuance may have considerable meaning.

All this the press conference can do for the President. Yet the blunt fact remains that to a large extent, its ritual has been shaped by the specialized needs of the press rather than by his needs. While the President and his aides must give considerable thought to anticipating the questions that will be directed to him, he can never be altogether certain that one will not come hurtling his way to catch him completely unawares. The press, not he, regulates the pattern, the flow, and to some extent the mood of the conference. The press even controls, within limits, its duration. It is the prerogative of the senior wire-service man to call out "Thank you, Mr. President" in order to terminate it. There have been times when the conference was terminated well ahead of the usual half hour because, in the judgment of the senior wire-service man, there was news enough.

During his press conference, the President is exposed. He knows his moment of truth as clearly as any matador. Of course he can refuse, he can evade, or he can angrily rebuff an impetuous questioner. But he must do it before curious eyes. Frequently what he does not say may prove just as newsworthy as what he does say. He must endure the stupid question and maintain his composure. He must be prepared to leap from a penetrating query about a most delicate policy matter to one about the appointment to a district judgeship, and then leap back again without growing rattled. His questioner may serve him false or misleading information on which to comment. He may suddenly find himself confronted with a diplomatic question from a foreign correspondent who is really an agent of his government.

Almost as irritating to the President are the questions never asked for which he has prepared an answer. After one of Eisenhower's conferences, a White House aide listed for me six major questions involving events, policies, and programs that had gone unasked at that week's conference, despite their prominence in the news. One time Eisenhower commented wryly as the reporters trooped out of the conference room, "No one gives me an opportunity to talk about defense."

Misadventures

The Presidential press conference can result in startling fiascoes. The most celebrated, which occurred in November 1950, resulted in news stories all over the world that President Truman was considering use of the atom bomb in Korea. It brought Prime Minister Attlee flying to America for consultation, and indirectly hastened the death of the President's Press Secretary, Charles G. Ross. John Hersey has provided a masterful account of this ill-fated conference. Having been present in the White House at the time to gather research material for a *New Yorker* profile of Truman, Hersey was able to describe in detail the development of what was a major failure in communication.

The Chinese Communists had just entered the Korean War and the situation was admittedly grave. Several days before the conference, a number of top United States policy planners had worked to prepare a statement which the President dutifully read at the beginning of his press conference. At no time, according to Hersey, had there been any mention of using the atom bomb. But Truman's prepared statement, expressing general determination to remain steadfast in the face of the new peril, was not particularly newsworthy and the reporters probed for "hard" news. They got it when, in response to a question, the President affirmed that the use of the atom bomb was "always under consideration." The headlines that resulted dropped the "always" and played heavily upon the "under consideration."

Hersey's analysis, which tends to place all the blame on the reporters, could be criticized as the work of someone who was not accustomed to the routine of the press conference. The reporters could legitimately argue that there was no way for them to know what had gone on in the minds of those who had planned the President's statement. They could only assume, in the light of the President's vague intimations, that he deliberately intended to raise the specter of the atom bomb at that critical time. By their recurrent questions—there had been five or six—they had sought to alert him to the significance of his utterances. A final definite warning had been sounded by Anthony Leviero of the *New York Times* when he asked if the President's remarks could be quoted directly. The President refused but made no effort to clarify his remarks until after the conference, when the first wire-service bulletins had already begun to spread the alarming story.

But regardless of any specific finding of guilt, Hersey's documentary was in fact a damning indictment of the slipshodness of the press conference as an institution for conveying vital information. It gave meaning to the judgment of Charles A. Beard, who declared "no President should be encouraged or forced to speak offhand on any grave question of national policy." On the press's side, it illustrated the unspeakable folly of measuring the President's utterances with the same yardstick of "newsworthiness" as that used on a minor news event. It bordered on complete irresponsibility to take his words and edit them for the sensational headline and the startling lead paragraph, which was the way Mr. Truman's atom-bomb remarks were handled. All the qualifying details were left out of the early bulletins. The President's statement was given shape by the inexorable pattern of "the news."

Whereas Mr. Truman was the backwoods Baptist laying down a personal testament of God and Mammon to the congregated reporters, President Eisenhower has preferred to be the high priest, whose utterances contain less fire, more theology. Matured in the practice of conducting military briefings for the politicians, he is a master at the art of saying little while talking a great deal.

President Eisenhower has had his rough moments with the press. One such occasion was in late 1953, when reporters took him to task for Attorney General Brownell's speech accusing ex-President Truman of knowingly promoting a Communist spy in his government. From abroad Harold Callender of the *New York Times* cabled an account of the astounded European reaction: "Few would believe that the reporters would dare address the President with the challenging questions asked or that their editors published the questions and answers."

Once, in response to persistent queries about the McCarthy forays against his administration, Eisenhower stalked angrily from the conference room. On a number of occasions, he has flushed deep red when prodded about a sensitive subject and rejected the questioner abruptly. But in the main he has achieved a gentleness in his conferences that contrasts strangely with the flamboyant Truman ones. Questions involving high policy matters are asked with the broadest kind of hook, on which the president can hang any answer he likes. There are dark suspicions that the partisan preferences of newspaper publishers have caused this. Certainly a more direct cause has been the fact that these are the kinds of questions the President will answer.

Eisenhower's use of the press conference has not furthered it as an instrument of lucid communication. His penchant for the vague generality as well as his willingness to comment volubly on almost any subject has tended to debase the currency value of his words. After one notable conference, a reporter observed that if the President's remarks that morning were to be taken as policy, it could be assumed (1) that he was in conflict with his own administration on the right and duty of public officials to state opinions on Supreme Court decisions; (2) that United States commanders in the field might or might not have authority to use atomic weapons in defense of their commands—he was not sure; (3) and that the United States might or might not wait to be attacked in a major war. There have been a number of times when the reporter would have devoutly preferred a terse "no comment" to the President's rambling soliloquy in which they could find neither sense nor syntax no matter how they searched.

For both the two latest Presidents, the press conference has been in a deeper sense a failure. For Truman it produced an impression of Presidential arrogance and obstinacy that worsened his working relations with Congress. Eisenhower, on the other hand, has conveyed through it an impression of irresolution. He has maintained the image of the President who reigns, but there has been a blurring in the eyes of the world of the image of the President who rules, of the leader who stands for specific issues and against specific issues, who likes certain people and, yes, detests certain people.

It can be argued that in both Truman's and Eisenhower's cases the failure of the press conference has been merely symptomatic of more fundamental failures of leadership. Most observers, however, would concede that it has tended to aggravate their problems. It has compounded the difficulty of leadership for the President in an era when he grapples with issues incapable of easy or quick solutions.

The President's press conferences have not contributed the way they should to the formation of a truly enlightened public opinion. As Zechariah Chafee has noted, "They tempt a President to blurt out anything that boils up in his emotions and do his thinking out loud in public." There are times when the thoughtful onlooker is dumbfounded by the offhand manner in which unmatured convictions on critically grave issues are voiced by the nation's chief executive. The difficulties provoked by this practice are not lessened now that the President's every word becomes a part of historic record.

The Interpellative Branch

Quite a few people have critically examined the shortcomings of the President's press conference. By and large they fall into two groups: the abolitionists and the reformers. The abolitionists claim that the conference is one of the worst abuses in a capital where publicity has become a policy in itself, rather than a product of policy. But a telling riposte to the abolitionists was voiced by one veteran Washington correspondent: "O.K., cut out the President's press conferences—better cut out the Secretary of State's and the other cabinet officers' while you're at it. Then let the administration's enemies on the Hill dominate the headlines." His answer reveals the extent to which the need for publicity must be a dominating concern among those responsible for Executive leadership in America.

Those who would reform the President's press conference have suggested such changes as more systematic preparatory briefing; active participation by the President's advisers, especially when they sense something going wrong; a brief post-conference session conducted by the Press Secretary to clear up possible misunderstandings; and a delayed release time on publication of conference news. Most practicing newspapermen are strongly opposed to a return to the requirement of submitting written questions in advance—a practice that evokes memories of the stuffy days of Harding and Hoover. Instead, many support James Reston when he suggests that to certain difficult questions the President might promise to provide studied answers in writing, later in the week. With a newspaperman's shrewdness, he points out that this practice would lighten the burden imposed on understaffed Washington news bureaus, which can hardly do justice in a single day to the great variety of questions and answers presently evoked at the press conference. The President would thus reap the benefit of providing "more front page copy on more days of the week."

It is noteworthy that all of these reforms would in effect give formal recognition to the Fourth Estate as the interpellative branch of the American government. It would, however, be less a Constitutional revolution than the admission that such a revolution has already taken place, and that the time has come to set our new house in order.

MAKING NEWS ON THE HILL

The member of Congress is uniquely both a creator and creature of publicity. By the very nature of his job, with its relative insecurity of tenure, he is concerned with the processes by which the public attention is attracted. He lives in a state of intimacy with the newspaperman that outsiders mistake for pure cronyism. He employs his highest-paid assistant to diagnose and fill the prescriptive needs of the press.

The individual publicity drive of any particular congressman may seem a minor and even ludicrous phenomenon. But collectively, reinforced by the publicity-making mechanisms of Congressional committees, it gives a distinct Congressional bias to the news, and creates certain advantages for the Legislative branch of government in its continuing power struggle with the Executive. It contributes at times to a Constitutional imbalance that seems to be a recurrent disorder of American government.

The press is omnipresent on the Hill. Room for its ever-expanding needs has been carved out of every strange nook and cranny of the ancient Capitol. Just over the presiding officer's desk in each House hovers the press gallery, its occupants constantly monitoring the proceedings and frequently outnumbering the legislators present on the floor below. For the wire services there are special muted telephones within the chamber itself, ready for the instant communique about a critical Congressional action. Behind swinging doors, off the gallery, the press has its quarters for work and relaxation. Teletypes stand ready to relay copy to the central offices of the wire services. The walls are lined with typewriters and telephone booths. Great leather couches offer all-night accommodation should the legislative session drag on. In nearby studios the reporters for radio and television can originate their broadcasts.

Favor for Favor

The reporter's access to individual legislators is frequent and intimate. Near each chamber there are private rooms to which members of Congress are summoned, in a never-ending file, for communion with the press. They come, obediently and willingly. During a lively session, the President's Room just off the Senate Lobby is continuously crowded with little clusters of solons and scribes, two by two, exchanging earnest confidences. Special doormen stand ready at the request of reporters to call still others away from the debate. At times this little anteroom contains more senators than the Senate Chamber. The creation of the public image of the debate is more engrossing to most of them than the actual debate itself.

Across the Capitol, a similar drama is being enacted in the House of Representatives. There, even the members' lobby is open to the prowling correspondent. The senior reporters assigned to the Hill share an intimacy with Congressional leaders far beyond that possessed by lesser members of Congress. At least once daily the wire-service representatives are invited in for sessions with the Speaker of the House and the Senate majority leader. On countless occasions the reporter may attend informal convocations at which down-to-earth matters of politics are explored. He may find himself a direct witness to, even a participant in, the drafting of laws.

At times the raw competition by congressmen to serve the press takes on bizarre proportions. The following account appeared in a "Footnote to the News" column of the *Washington Post and Times Herald:*

> A freshman Senator outslicked his veteran colleagues to pick off his easiest publicity plum available last week. He was Clifford P. Case (R.-N.J.) whose reaction comment to the President's decision (to veto the natural-gas bill) was the first to hit the Senate press gallery. His prize was a prominent play in the afternoon newspapers.
>
> Behind his speed was the quick thinking and faster legs of Sam Zagoria, Case's administrative assistant and former *Washington Post and Times Herald* reporter.
>
> Zagoria had run off several copies of the Senator's "isn't-it-grand" statement early Wednesday morning. He then parked himself by the Associated Press teletype in the Senate lobby. When the flash came through, he hightailed it back to the press gallery, one floor above, where eager reporters were waiting to write reaction accounts. Zagoria beat a runner for Senator William A. Purtell (R.-Conn.) by one minute flat.

For the reporter, it is more than easy access that makes Congress a primary news source. The business of Congress is the stuff of which good news reporting is made. Congress is a continuing scene of drama, conflict, and intrigue. Its battles can be described in terms of colorful personalities rather than amorphous and complicated issues that may confound the copy desk and confuse the reader. It is therefore perhaps inevitable that there should be this "Congressional bias" to the news. But some of the results need to be examined.

Powerful pressures dissuade the reporter from being as zealous a prober of Congress as he is of the Executive departments. His obtaining of news "exclusives" depends upon the preservation of a chummy relationship with members of Congress. A great amount of news is dispensed to him as a favor, and must be regarded as such. Furthermore, retaliation for unfavorable publicity can be swift and vengeful. It is by no means unusual for a member, enraged by something appearing in print, to take to the floor in a violent attack against the offending reporter. And such is the clublike atmosphere of the two houses that no member is likely to come to the reporter's defense.

Thus, on April 10, 1950, Senator Harry Cain rose on the Senate floor to answer an assertion by *Time* magazine that he was among the Senate's "expendables." For the better part of the afternoon he centered an attack on *Time's* Congressional correspondent. "If ever I sat with a human being who was smug, arrogant, self-centered, vain and frustrated . . . This ulcer-burdened young American who could neither vote nor fight . . . The agent *Time* magazine has today was a 4-F in war . . . (He) has undoubtedly encouraged other men to die, but he has never . . . watched them die." Not one senator raised a protest against this stream of abuse.

There are countless instances when Congressmen demand special privileges which go unpublicized but which would provoke a furor if made by an administration official. Members of the press often apply a deliberate censorship to a legislator's unwise public utterances. One neophyte reporter who unwittingly quoted a rash remark revealing bigotry on the part of a leading congressman was afterward chastised by his press colleagues for this indiscretion.

Women correspondents covering Capitol Hill circulate among themselves a list of those members of Congress with whom it is unsafe to be alone. One or two solons have been known to be outrageous sex reprobates. But no word of their misdemeanors ever reaches the reading public. Senators have been seen to stagger drunkenly onto the Senate floor and deliver unintelligible harangues without creating a ripple in the press.

Amid the publicity drives of Congress, the investigating committee exerts the most powerful thrust. It is geared to the production of headlines on a daily and even twice-daily basis. It is able to create the news story that lingers week after week on the front pages to form an indelible impression on the public mind. No institution of the Executive branch is capable of such sustained and well-manipulated publicity.

The most notable committee investigations are seldom in point of fact "investigations" once the public hearings commence. They are planned deliberately to move from a preconceived idea to a predetermined conclusion. The skill and resourcefulness of the chairman and a sizable staff are pitted against any effort to alter its destined course. Whatever investigating takes place is done well in advance. The hearing is the final act in the drama. Its intent, by the staging of a spectacle, is to attract public attention, to alarm or to allay, to enlighten or sometimes to obscure.

How to Run a Hearing

In 1943, the counsel of a House committee investigating the Federal Communications Commission distributed a confidential memorandum to committee members that fell into the hands of outsiders. It had been prepared for the committee by a reporter for International News Service, whose talents later carried him high in the employ of the Republican National Committee. Its seven points remain a classic disquisition on the publicity requirements for an investigation:

1. Decide what you want the newspapers to hit hardest and then shape each hearing so that the main point becomes the vortex of the testimony. Once that vortex is reached, adjourn.
2. In handling press releases, first put a release date on them, reading something like this: 'For release at 10:00 a.m., EST July 6,' etc. If you do this, you can give releases out as much as 24 hours in advance, thus enabling reporters to study them and write better stories.
3. Limit the number of people authorized to speak for the committee, to give out press releases or to provide the press with information to the fewest number possible. It plugs leaks and helps preserve the concentration of purpose.
4. Do not permit distractions to occur, such as extraneous fusses with would-be witnesses, which might provide news that would bury the testimony which you want featured.
5. Do not space hearings more than 24 or 48 hours apart when on a controversial subject. This gives the opposition too much opportunity to make all kinds of countercharges and replies by issuing statements to the newspapers.
6. Don't ever be afraid to recess a hearing even for five minutes so that you keep the proceedings completely in control so far as creating news is concerned.
7. And this is most important: don't let the hearings or the evidence ever descend to the plane of a personal fight between the Committee Chairman and the head of the agency being investigated. The high plane of a duly-authorized Committee of the House of Representatives examining the operations of an Agency of the Executive Branch for constructive purposes should be maintained at all costs.

The allusion in point 5 to "the opposition" simply means those who are being investigated. It is a rare investigation, and certainly a poorly publicized one which has not passed judgment on the "opposition" long before the hearings commence.

The Uses of Laughter

The proliferation of publicity-inspired investigations has taken us in the direction of what might be called "government by concurrent publicity." Decisions tend to be taken not in an orderly, procedural way but on the basis of what is instantly explainable to the public through the mass media.

The investigated, too, have turned to publicity as a weapon. Last year, there was a fantastic case study when the House Special Subcommittee on Legislative Oversight began to probe the affairs of the New England tycoon Bernard Goldfine and particularly his dealings with the Assistant to the President, Sherman Adams. Goldfine, accompanied by a retinue of lawyers and publicity agents, set up headquarters in a Washington hotel, staged press and television conferences day and night, timed releases to compete with committee-inspired headlines, and pursued a calculated public-relations policy to make himself appear, as one aide put it, "a simple, innocent, underdog type being persecuted by a powerful congressional committee."

Philip Deane of the London *Observer* cabled home a graphic account of his visit to the Goldfine publicity headquarters:

> We were shushed into silence while the television news was switched on. One of the well-known commentators was speaking of the latest developments in the Goldfine case. When mentioning Goldfine himself, the television star lost control and an Homeric laugh spread across his distinguished face. . . .
>
> "Great! Great!" said Mr. Jack Lotto, Public Relations Counselor to the Goldfine interests. "That's what we want; we want people to laugh."
>
> "Please!" said a European journalist. "Did you say you wanted people to laugh at your employer?" . . .
>
> "It's like this," explained a fellow journalist. "When McCarthy attacked Senator Millard Tydings, of Maryland, Tydings tried to defend himself with dignity and failed miserably. His Public Relations firm made a fascinating study of this and decided that the only way to fight an attack by Congressional investigation is to raise more noise than your opponent, make the whole thing into a farce."
>
> "People don't think of you as a villain when they are laughing at you," said Williamson thoughtfully.
>
> "Doesn't Goldfine mind being made a clown?" asked the European.
>
> "You're thinking in terms of your own country. People here are different," said the American journalist. "Actually, there's a good deal of sympathy for Goldfine. He has done less than most business men do. He gives vicuna coats. Others give mistresses to married men. Have you seen salesmen entertaining buyers at Las Vegas?"
>
> This is sad because Goldfine is cute and he is not such a bad example of the great American dream—poor immigrant boy makes good. Lotto here is applying the conclusions of the Tydings case, defending the Goldfine integrity by destroying the Goldfine dignity while incidentally, the whole United States Administration goes down gloriously in a cloud of fudge.

The net effect of this and similar publicity brouhahas has been to divert the public's attention from the underlying ills in government that need legislative attention. Amid the aimless airing of charges, the quest reduces itself to a confused chase after individual villains rather than a purposeful inquiry to get at the root causes and to devise lasting solutions.

A NEW KIND OF DEMAGOGUE

The American politician has always been something of a dramatist in search of an audience, more flamboyant, a greater individualist than his European counterpart. Recently, however, there has begun to emerge in the halls of Congress a new type of politician conditioned to the age of mass media and more keenly aware of the uses of publicity. He is not apt to be a member of what William S. White calls the "Inner Club," where emphasis is still put on seniority and skill in negotiation. He need not be in the forefront among those who uphold the ancient traditions of eloquence in Congressional debate. Nor need he be assiduous in preparing legislation and attending to the thousand and one chores of pushing it through to enactment. Rather he is a man versed in the subtleties of appealing beyond Congress directly to the mass audience. He knows the formula of the news release, the timing, the spoon-feeding necessities of the publicity campaign. He assesses with canny shrewdness the areas of enterprise that will best lend themselves to a sustained publicity build-up. He is a master at shadow play, creating the illusion of magnificent drama from a reality that may be quite mundane. Usually he lacks direct influence among his colleagues, but he acquires a special standing commensurate with his reflected power as a "nationally known" figure.

To a greater or lesser degree, every politician who makes his way in Congress today must have something of this new sense. But it is possible to isolate advanced specimens of this *genus politicus* for which publicity has been a more durable stock in trade than seniority or legislative prestige. Among these, one would have to include Richard Nixon, Republican, who was catapulted to national prominence and power—from newly elected congressman to Vice-President—in the brief span of six years without having his name tied to a single notable achievement except the exposure of Alger Hiss.

Also to be included high on this list of the new politician is Senator Estes Kefauver, Democrat, who has been regularly rejected by his more powerful colleagues from membership in the Inner Club but stands as the symbol of senator for countless Americans. A quiet-spoken, not particularly eloquent man, he scarcely fits the picture of the new-type politician. But as reporters who have worked closely with him can testify, he shows an uncanny knack for lifting an idea or an issue out of the slough of neglect and placing it squarely on page 1. On one occasion during the Dixon-Yates controversy, Kefauver exposed with resounding headline clatter the name of a Budget Bureau official who was reputedly guilty of attempting to sabotage the Tennessee Valley Authority. It turned out that the same man had been named months earlier by Senator Lister Hill, a more traditional politician without the flair for publicity. No one had noticed.

McCarthy and the Press

The career of Senator Joseph McCarthy is, of course, by now a classic case. Whereas the traditional demagogue could be measured by how skillfully he sized up and played on fears and prejudices existing in a region or within a social group, McCarthy's skill lay primarily in his capacity to "stage" a single issue so as to dominate the channels of communication and to distract a national audience. Huey Long or Tom Heflin knew how to sway the crowd, stirring its emotions, playing on its vanities. McCarthy was never terribly good before a large crowd. But he knew how to rule the headlines.

In February 1950, brandishing stage-prop documents that he never let anyone examine, McCarthy showed his talents for the first time. As Richard Rovere has pointed out, *Senator charges communist influence in state department* might have produced a two-inch story on page 15 of the local newspaper. *Over two hundred with communist ties* would have done slightly better. But *205 card carrying communists* was something else. It was as if the press yearned for the really big lie.

Responsible newspapers tried hard to live up to the American Society of Newspaper Editors' ethical rule entitled "Fair Play"; "A newspaper should not publish unofficial charges affecting reputation or moral character without opportunity given to the accused to be heard." But in practice it worked like this: Late one afternoon Senator McCarthy might name a person, more likely a series of them. All through the evening the accused's telephone kept ringing. He was told briefly the nature of the charge made against him—let us say, "top Soviet agent"—and asked for a brief reply. McCarthy's charge was controversial and unexpected—a news count of two. The denial was controversial and completely expected—a news count of one. Both were equally lacking in proof. Nobody, after all, carries the credentials on his person to prove that he is not the "top Soviet agent."

By such means, McCarthy held the headlines. Day after day, several times a day, in time for the morning, afternoon, the seven o'clock, and late evening editions, he served up the scabrous material that he was attempting to make the national folklore. He knew the ingredients for the "lead," the "overnight," and the "sidebar." He could evoke the most publicity bounce from the ounce. Not one of the succession of department and agency heads who came up against him was able to find an effective defense. Neither of the two Presidents who had to reckon with him ever discovered a truly satisfactory counter-publicity weapon. He threw great governmental establishments like the State Department and the Army into confusion and provoked precipitate decisions on policy and personnel resulting in untold damage.

Unlike certain senior members of Congress, McCarthy lacked the capacity to insert a crippling rider into legislation or to tamper with an appropriations bill in committee as a way of blackmailing the Executive. He never had the physical means, as his apologists frequently point out, to intimidate or to punish those who aroused his ire. There was no violence, in the ordinary sense of that word, during the reign of McCarthyism. All McCarthy could do was to carry his vendettas into the public headlines. That was enough. It produced unparalleled fear and pusillanimity in Washington.

Few of the reporters who regularly covered McCarthy believed him. Most came to despise and fear him as a cynical liar who was willing to wreak untold havoc to satisfy his own power drive. But though they feared him, it was not intimidation that caused the press to serve as the instrument for McCarthy's rise. Rather it was the inherent vulnerabilities—the frozen patterns of the press—which McCarthy discovered and played upon with unerring skill. "Straight" news, the absolute commandment of most mass journalism, had become a strait jacket to crush the initiative and the independence of the reporter.

McCarthyism was an unparalleled demonstration of the Congressional publicity system gone wild, feeding on the body politic like a cancerous growth. It demonstrated that public opinion when incessantly nagged by the instantaneous communications of the mass media and prodded by the pollsters is not capable of rendering sure verdicts on matters of great complexity. It showed that the publicity-generating power of Congress can be a dangerous force when it is not subject to check and review by higher bodies in or out of Congress.

McCarthyism sought to provide a vocabulary for our fears that had no relevance to the world we actually live in. Responsible men, talking to each other in this synthetic language, for a time lost contact with reality. McCarthyism's greatest threat was not to individual liberty or even to the orderly conduct of government. It corrupted the power to communicate which is indispensable to men living in a civilized society.

As a group, the reporters have made Washington the most thoroughly covered and most heavily reported capital in the world. Well over a hundred thousand words daily, the volume of a good-sized novel, pour out over wire, radio, and television. In periods of peak stress, the sheer productive capacity of this industry defies the imagination.

Ever since the arrival of the New Deal, the press corps has forsaken its old simple ways just as government has. The old-fashioned general-assignment reporter in Washington, who nibbles at news wherever he can find it, still survives but in reduced circumstances. In his place, Washington reporting has discovered new methods of organization, new ways of packaging news in response to the newly felt needs and the newly developed media of communication.

Reporting has moved to keep up with the changing times. Yet it would be preposterous to argue that the press has met the enormous challenge confronting it. For the dimension of the challenge goes beyond the requirements of speed, specialization, and clever new ways of packaging news. It is, rather, to be measured by how well our system of government, which is dependent on publicity to ensure its orderly functioning, is actually being reported. Viewing the problem in these terms, the reporter in Washington has cause for sober and troubled reflection.

The McCarthy era came as a deeply unsettling experience to many Washington correspondents. The demagogue has been defined as the undetected liar. Yet all the elaborate reporting mechanisms of the press seemed unable to detect McCarthy's lies and to communicate the basic fact that he *was* lying. As McCarthyism mushroomed in the nation's capital, the public dialogue grew strangely distorted. Serious reporters understood that the press was adding to the distortion rather than helping bring things into focus.

HOW STRAIGHT IS STRAIGHT NEWS?

"The job of the straight reporter," a wire-service editor once defined for me, "is to take the place of the spectator who is unable to be present. Like the spectator, he does not delve into motives or other side issues except as they become a part of the public record." Unfortunately, the spectator is a casual witness, usually bewildered by any unexpected event. The reporter who limits himself to this role often becomes an unwitting agent of confusion. The trouble with "straight" reporting is that it attempts to deny the creative role the reporter in fact plays in government. It is myth that even the most passionately objective reporter can be truly "straight" in translating the multiple events he covers into the staccato of the teletype. He must constantly make decisions—for good or bad.

Even the purely technical aspects of news production raise their own problems so far as objectivity is concerned. Let us examine the candid account of a typical working day described for me by an able wire-service reporter whose beat has been Capitol Hill:

> A central fact of life for the wire-service reporter in Washington is that there are a great many more afternoon than morning papers in the United States. This creates a problem because the early afternoon paper on the East Coast goes to press between 10 and 10:30 A.M.—before the "news development" of the day. It means the wire-service reporter must engage in the basically phony operation of writing the "overnight"—a story composed the previous evening but giving the impression when it appears the next afternoon that it covers that day's events.
>
> Let's take as an example the day the Austrian treaty came up in the Senate. The evening before, I prepared a story of which three-quarters was mere "background" concerning the treaty. In the progressive developments that followed, this part of the story remained untouched. But I had to have a "lead" on my overnight, so I called on Senator Walter George, chairman of the Foreign Relations Committee, and tried out an "angle" on him. Would there be any U.S. military aid for the Austrian army? George said, "No money. Only long-term credits." That became my lead. I had fulfilled the necessary function of having a story that seemed to be part of the next day's news.
>
> Next day, when the treaty came up for debate in the Senate, it was my job to get some "top" on this story. Senator Sparkman led off for the supporters of the treaty. He had in his speech a couple of newsy items though nothing worthy of filing as a "bulletin." So I dictated a new lead and picked up the main body of the story from my overnight. I threw away the George lead because it was a phony one.
>
> After Sparkman came Senator Jenner. He was vitriolic against the treaty. It was close to 2:30, which meant the deadline for the late afternoon papers. Was he worth a lead? I thought "No" because he represented such a minute minority in the Senate. But that was where a matter of judgment entered.
>
> Suddenly, Jenner made a nasty crack about Eisenhower which was certainly newsier than anything Sparkman had said. How should I handle it? In deciding problems like this, I always have to consider what the other wire-service reporters covering the same story may be doing. I decided not to lead with Jenner, but instead to move his section of the story into the office as an insert. (All my decisions are reviewable in the office, where the editors may make a decision based on factors I know nothing about.) But the Jenner paragraph moved as an insert, which meant that there was a slug on the A-wire: "Insert—"Austrian Treaty paragraph after 'It was said . . .' "
>
> A little after 3:30 P.M. the treaty was adopted. That automatically con-

> stituted a bulletin to be sent out immediately on the A-wire even though Senate passage had been accepted by everybody as a foregone conclusion. So I wrote a third lead for that particular story and then it was time to write a completely new story for next day's A.M. papers.
>
> But my job had not finished. The treaty-adoption bulletin had gone out too late to get into most of the East Coast afternoon papers except for the big-city ones like the Philadelphia *Evening Bulletin,* which has seven editions. I had to find a new angle for an overnight to be carried next day by those P.M.S which failed to conclude the treaty story.
>
> They don't want to carry simply a day-old account of the debate. They want a "top" to the news. So, to put it quite bluntly, I went and got Senator Thye to say that Jenner by his actions was weakening the President's authority. Actually, the Thye charge was more lively news than the passage of the Austrian treaty itself. It revealed conflict among the Senate Republicans. But the story had developed out of my need for a new peg for the news. It was not spontaneous on Thye's part. I had called seven other senators before I could get someone to make a statement on Jenner. There is a fair criticism, I recognize, to be made of this practice. These senators didn't call me; I called them. I, in a sense, generated the news. The reporter's imagination brought the senator's thinking to bear on alternatives that he might not have thought of by himself.
>
> This can be a very pervasive practice. One wire-service reporter hounded Senator George daily on the foreign-trade question until he finally got George to make the suggestion that Japan should trade with Red China as an alternative to dumping its textiles on the American market. Then the reporter went straight-way to Senator Knowland to get him to knock down the suggestion. It made a good story, and it also stimulated a minor policy debate that might not have got started otherwise. The "overnight" is the greatest single field for exploratory reporting for the wire services. It is what might be called "milking the news."

The point of this description is to indicate just how complex the business of reporting really is. The phantasmagoria of "straight" news can itself produce a departure from true "objectivity." Within the routines that govern the straight reporter, there is abundant room for bias to enter. Unless he makes reasonable choices, difficult and long-drawn-out issues become progressively more distorted. He finds himself granting the forces of confusion greater access to the loudspeaker system of the press than the forces of clarity. McCarthy proved how pliant such "objectivity" can be in the hands of the skilled manipulator.

GOVERNMENT BY LEAK

By conservative estimate, ninety per cent of the conflicts arising between government and the press in Washington lie in that shadowy no man's land of news that is ahead of the public event. This quest for what is variously called "background reporting," the "news behind the news," and "inside dope" engages the highest talent of the less restricted Washington correspondents. It is frequently a source of bafflement to the public official. Senator Robert Taft used to complain bitterly that reporters in Washington were so busy trying to find out what was going to happen that they didn't provide a decent account of what had already happened.

In Washington it is always embarrassing when the lid blows off a background story that was meant to be strictly "not for attribution." Like the small-town gambler who gets word from the police department that the heat is on, the reporter knows that for some time there are going to be slim pickings in that particular vicinity. For the government official, it is no less embarrassing. Not only have policies got caught and perhaps irredeemably mangled in the machinery of publicity; the official himself has been exposed in a practice that officialdom can never admit goes on. In all the formal literature on the functioning of the American government, there is not one word on what has been variously called the "leak" or "cloaked news."

For the average citizen, who can be expected to bring only so much sophistication to the business of reading his newspaper, the problem is also serious. Unattributed news can be a highly confusing matter. Take, for example, what happened during the spring of 1955 when there was one of those recurrent crises over the islands in the Formosa Strait. On Saturday, March 26, the reader found a three-column thirty-six-point headline in the upper right-hand corner on page 1 in the *New York Times:* "U.S. Expects Chinese Reds to Attack Isles in April; Weighs All Out Defense." Three days later, the reader found another headline in the same position, same type: "Eisenhower Sees No War Now over Chinese Isles."

If the reader studied the two stories closely, he noted one similarity. Neither had a single word to indicate who had presumed to speak in the first instance for the United States or in the second for President Eisenhower. The reader was obliged to take the word of the reporters—in these two instances highly reliable men—that these contradictory stories had some basis in fact. Actually, the source of the first story was Chief of Naval Operations Robert B. Carney, speaking to a select group of reporters at a background dinner. The second was none other than the White House Press Secretary, James Hagerty, who attended a hastily called second background conference in order to repudiate the stories arising out of the first.

The newspaper reader is obliged to accept a sizable quantity of news in this fashion. He has been given lengthy and varying descriptions of the timing, the extent, and the conditions of potential war—frequently without being told who was making these life-and-death judgments. A newspaperman once catalogued five basic contradictions in "authoritative" reports about American policy in the Far East during a single crisis. It was truly a period of the background story gone wild. But it was by no means a unique period. Cloaked news has become an institution in the conduct of modern government in Washington, part of the regular intercourse between government and the press. During periods of high tension when more formal channels of communication—such as the President's and the Secretary of State's press conferences—are cut off, it often becomes the major means by which important news is transmitted. As one reporter described a critical period, "At a time when any word out of Washington was considered of international significance, what had developed, it appeared, was government by leak."

Compulsory Plagiarism

The ritual of the formal leak is fairly uniform. On a specified evening, a dozen or so correspondents gather in one of the private dining rooms in the Metropolitan Club or in a nearby downtown hotel. They are joined by the guest of honor, usually a high government official. It is not always clear who has initiated the meeting. Usually, the official has graciously "responded" to a standing invitation to meet with the reporters. He may or may not wish to admit that he has something to disclose. Drinks are served and all sit down to dinner. Until the meal is completed, the conversation follows an aimless pattern. No one likes to appear eager. Then chairs are pushed back, the presiding correspondent raps on his glass, reminds his colleagues of the rules, and the session begins.

Usually the official makes no formal remarks. He exposes himself to questions from the correspondents. If he knows his business, he can always manage to steer things in the direction he wishes to move. Frequently he does not openly admit that he is outlining a new government program or a drastic new approach to policy. He is merely "talking over" with the reporters some of the problems that confront him. He relies on them to have sense enough to grasp his meaning without having it spelled out for them. This studied casualness, at times, can breed misunderstanding and produce woeful consequences. The session sometimes goes on till quite late. Afterward, the chairman reminds everyone of the rules and each goes his separate way.

As background briefings grew more frequent, the rules of the game also began to multiply and become more complex. Partly because the matters discussed at the conferences were not so delicate as during wartime, partly because the newsmen chafed at information given purely for self-edification, there was an inevitable trend toward relaxing the strictures against publication. Now, conferences may range from "deep" background to a variety of lighter hues, depending on the secretiveness of the informant. In the main, the so-called Lindley Rule, first developed by Ernest K. Lindley of *Newsweek,* governs the proceedings. It requires what has been called compulsory plagiarism. The journalist may use what he has learned, but strictly on his own authority. Sometimes there are variations permitting him to quote "informed circles" or "a high government spokesman."

Usually there is at least one day's moratorium on the news coming out of such background briefings. If the news is especially hot, it may be arranged that nothing will be printed until the informant gets out of town so that he can establish a convenient alibi. But nothing is hard and fast about the arrangements. Misunderstandings are frequent, increasing in direct ratio to the importance of the news.

The postwar uses of the background session have been varied. It has been a means of alerting the press to the gravity of a situation being overlooked in the news. Dean Acheson, while still Under Secretary of State, once called in a small group of reporters and gave them the "background" on current Soviet demands against the Turks. It helped focus world attention on a situation that might have grown much worse.

The background conference is also used to play down the gravity of a situation. A dubious instance occurred when George Kennan, then chairman of the Policy Planning Board of the State Department, arranged a briefing at the time of President Truman's announcement of Russia's first atomic explosion. Contrary to the facts, Kennan assured reporters that the timing of the Soviet feat did not come as a surprise to American policy planners. He was deliberately trying to minimize the news value of the story in an effort to avert a strong public reaction.

Most frequently, the leak is symptomatic of rivalry in the higher echelons of government itself. Harold E. Stassen, once Special Assistant to the President on the disarmament question, would hold a background conference to discuss his thoughts on modifying U.S. proposals for arms controls. Promptly, Secretary of State Dulles would hold his own background conference to "clarify" the news coming out of the Stassen conference. Both conferences resulted in "news" about American policy. Unfortunately, the sum total of "news" on this crucial subject was and continues to be highly confusing.

The leak is traditionally used as a method of promoting a new program before it is formally unveiled before Congress. In Great Britain, where the cabinet has an obligation to report initially to the House of Commons, such use of the press to launch legislative programs would be unthinkable. In Washington it is habitual. Prior to the announcement of the so-called Eisenhower doctrine for the Middle East, Mr. Dulles engaged in three days of systematic leakage to reporters of the details of the new policy. By the third day, when Congressional leaders were themselves briefed on the proposal, a news dispatch in the *New York Times* noted that they ". . . were cautious in their reaction . . . but the Administration's plan had been so widely publicized before the leaders reached the White House that . . . they can do little more than adopt the new policy as presented."

The Cloak of Semi-Anonymity

The often sorely pressed Washington official sees numerous advantages in this system. It gives him a semi-anonymous voice in the cavernous echo chambers of the nation's capital. By keeping members of the press informed the official can engage in preventive action against the thousand and one stories that crop up from nowhere and do damage to sound policy. In addition, it permits greater flexibility in taking policy initiatives. Without risking either his own . . . or his department's reputation, he has an opportunity to take the measure of public and—more immediately important—Congressional opinion. If it is hostile, he can always fall back on what has been called "the technique of denying the truth without actually lying."

This latter technique works as follows: Secretary Dulles, in 1953 held a background conference in which he revealed to reporters that he had been doing some tentative thinking about a Korean boundary settlement along the line of the narrow waist of the peninsula. The news stories that emerged provoked criticism on Capitol Hill, particularly from Senator Knowland. Forthwith, the White House issued a denial, drafted by none other than Dulles himself, which stated that "the Administration has never reached any conclusion that a permanent division of Korea is desirable or feasible or consistent with the decisions of the United Nations." The pertinent words of course were "conclusion" and "permanent." The White House statement was not, in fact, what it seemed—a clear repudiation of what Mr. Dulles had told the reporters and what they had written, perforce on their own authority.

Despite its ambiguities, cloaked news has at times played a creative part during the malleable period of policy formation. Historian Bruce Catton has concluded that "our particular form of government wouldn't work without it." The critics—and there are a lonely few among the newsmen who stubbornly refuse to attend any news conference that is not on the record—make a number of arguments. They decry the informality that curses the whole practice. Mixing business and pleasure at the background dinner, with usually a goodly number of drinks thrown in, serves to befuddle the newsmen as well as the official. The reporter usually does not take notes while the official is present. (This might cramp the official's style.) There is a painful reconstruction afterward of what exactly was said. No one ever seems to be quite sure what the rules are. Moreover, because the reporter cannot quote a source, he finds it almost impossible to convey in his story the subtle gradations of meaning that good reporting requires. The background briefing provides a field day for those who prefer to present the news in stark, dramatic terms.

Agent or Tool?

Inevitably, the case against cloaked news gets down to fundamental concepts of reporting. What is the reporter's responsibility? Is he an intelligence agent for his paper and, ultimately, for the American public? Or is he to be made a tool of the government's counterintelligence operations? Arthur Schlesinger, Jr., once put the problem this way: "Washington newspapermen today hardly know whether to believe the Secretary of State, because they do not know if he is speaking to them as reporters or seeking to use them as instruments of psychological warfare. . . . What is the responsibility of a newspaperman when he discovers that some rumored development of policy is really only a psychological warfare trick? Should he print the truth at the risk of wrecking the plans of the Secretary of State? Or should he suppress the truth, betray himself, and deceive the American people?"

In this, as in much that concerns reporting in Washington, the absolutist position has little relevance to the reporter's workaday world. He cannot narrowly demarcate his sphere of operations. He is caught and intimately involved in the ceaseless battle of intelligence versus counterintelligence in Washington.

He can remove himself from the battlefield only at the risk of negating his role as a reporter.

A more fruitful inquiry may be directed into the conditions that should be imposed on cloaked news as a technique of communication. On the government's part, there needs to be a clearer recognition of the limits to which this practice can go. No matter how compelling the exigencies, the press in a free society should not be turned into the government's propaganda instrument. A fine line has to be drawn between the diplomatic and the deceitful. Secretary Dulles went over that line when, during the Quemoy-Matsu crisis of August, 1958, he issued a public statement of official policy, then immediately afterward made more sweeping pronouncements to reporters on a not-for-attribution basis. He was transferring an unfair burden to the reporter.

The main responsibility in guarding against the misuse of counterintelligence, however, lies not with the government but with the press. Just as government must take initiative in safeguarding its essential secrets, so the reporter must in the first instance decide what is proper and what is improper practice in the handling of the leak.

There are grounds for thoughtful review in this field. In his eagerness to get at the inside news, even the good reporter frequently loses the keen discrimination as shows in his more open reporting. As William S. White has written:

> Often reporters handle a leaked story with a solemn uncriticalness. The documents, or whatever, are ceremoniously produced for the public which at times must scratch its head in perplexity as to what the devil they are all about. The motivation for the leak usually is not mentioned, although that may be the most significant part of the story.

The reporter himself is often guilty of deceit in the business of cloaking the news. He refers vaguely to "informed circles," implying a plurality of opinion when in fact he may be quoting the views of one person. He also plays up leaks with an importance they would not deserve if their sources were made known.

There is no reason why the rules for cloaked news cannot be made to fit more adequately the needs of honest reporting. For example, when anything of a highly controversial nature comes forth at a background session, the moratorium should be extended long enough to enable the reporter to check other sources. Few instances occur when anonymity needs be carried to the point that the reporter must deliberately confuse his reader about what is being related. The reporter's first obligation is to present a clear and balanced story.

No matter what improvements are made, however, this war of intelligence and counterintelligence is likely to remain one of the perplexing phenomena of the Washington scene. Though limits may be imposed on its excesses, there is no possibility of ever declaring a permanent truce. The conditions that give rise to it are basic to the American system of government and the free condition of American society. For the reporter, few hard and fast rules can be laid down to serve him as a permanent code of conduct. Instead, he must be governed in his daily work by his best judgments. It is one more measure of the creative role he has to play in the political life of Washington.

"MANAGED" NEWS

When James Reston appeared before the Moss Committee investigating "Availability of Information from Federal Departments and Agencies," he voiced an uneasiness felt by many:

> Most of my colleagues have been talking primarily about the suppression of news. I would like to direct the committee, if I may, to an equally important aspect of this problem which I think is the growing tendency to manage the news. Let me see if I can illustrate what I mean:
>
> I think there was a conscious effort to give the news at the Geneva Conference (in 1955) an optimistic flavor. I think there was a conscious effort there, decided upon even perhaps ahead of time, for spokesmen to emphasize all the optimistic facts coming out of that conference and to minimize all of the quarrels at that conference. . . .
>
> After the Geneva Conference a decision was taken in the government that perhaps this was having a bad effect, that the people in the western countries were letting down their guard, and therefore a decision was made, primarily upon the appeal of Chancellor Adenauer of Germany, that the government should strike another note. So that after the Geneva smiling, the new word went out that it might be a good idea now to frown a little bit, so the President made a speech at Philadelphia, taking quite a different light about the Geneva Conference. That is what I mean by managing the news. And I would urge your committee to look into that a bit, because, while it is bad to suppress a bit of information, it would seem to me to be even worse if all of the news-making powers of the Federal government were to blanket the newspaper situation with the theme which perhaps they did not believe was quite true, but might be an instrument of their thought.

Ethics in Action

From time to time the reporter in Washington becomes uneasily aware of a developing technique among the politicians for giving shape and direction to the news. In 1953, for example, there were telltale signs to indicate that Attorney General Herbert Brownell's attack on former President Truman for "knowingly" promoting "a Communist spy," i.e., Harry Dexter White, was part of a carefully planned operation calculated to garner maximum publicity. Shortly before Brownell made the attack, the Republican National Committee had ordered fifty thousand reprints of a Senate Internal Security Committee report on "Interlocking Subversion" in which White's name was prominently mentioned. The timing of the attack itself was most delicate. Brownell made it in a speech before the Chicago Executives Club at approximately 12:30 P.M. Chicago time (1:30 in Washington). Advance texts of two other speeches he gave that day had been distributed to the press the preceding afternoon, but this one, ironically entitled "Ethics in Government," was held up until an hour before Brownell spoke. As a result there was no chance for reporters to alert Truman until the story began to move on the press wires and out over radio and television. When frantic calls reached him in Missouri, Mr. Truman had to answer fast if he wanted to get his statement into the afternoon papers along with Brownell's charges. Inevitably, he reacted too quickly. He said that he did not remember any FBI memorandum on White and that he had gotten rid of him when he found that White was "wrong." By four o'clock that afternoon (Washington time), Press Secretary Hagerty had called in reporters and made public the text of a Truman letter in 1947 accepting Harry Dexter White's "resignation" and praising him for his services. Hagerty did not bother to explain how a six-year-old letter had been dug out of the files so quickly—in plenty of time for the evening papers and newscasts.

The G.O.P. publicity director gave this reporter an account of what went on at the Republican National Committee that same afternoon: "We put four men on the telephone to alert members of Congress. Three placed simultaneous calls to Velde, Jenner, and McCarthy." Those three gentlemen, of course, were chairmen of the investigating committees and could be counted on to pick up the publicity ball and carry it for an indefinite period. A secret FBI memorandum on White and others was leaked to reporter Richard Wilson of the Cowles publications. Wilson reported its contents in a series of stories. (For this piece of enterprise, Wilson was later awarded a Pulitzer Prize.)

Despite the careful publicity planning, the White affair took a strange turnabout when Senator McCarthy demanded and got free time on a nation-wide radio and television hookup to answer a televised reply Truman had made to Brownell. Instead of answering Truman, however, McCarthy launched a biting attack on the Eisenhower administration for not being sufficiently tough on Communists. The whole episode with its farcical climax was a distasteful case study in the misuse of publicity.

The Washington correspondent does not always know how to handle the "managed" news event, which he is expected to report while pretending to be blind to the props and staging devices. Too often, he tamely falls in with the purpose of the publicists. For a prolonged period, administration spokesmen were able to carry on a fantastic game of juggling the numbers of "security risk" dismissals in such a way as to create the impression that a wholesale cleanup of "subversives" in the government was taking place. Diligent reporters compiled documentary proof that the mounting totals furnished to them included a loose accumulation of resignations and dismissals on grounds other than security. But it was a complicated story, and most reporters were content to play it just the way the government spokesmen wished.

Manipulated news can also be used as an instrument against an administration. In 1954, Democratic National Chairman Stephen Mitchell suddenly accused Eisenhower's friend Bobby Jones of having conspired with the President on the golf course to destroy the Tennessee Valley Authority. Jones was supposedly an agent for a private power combine, Dixon-Yates, seeking to invade TVA. The particular charge was utterly without foundation. Yet because it was so sensational it succeeded in returning the Dixon-Yates story to the front pages and, as a direct consequence, revived interest in a lagging Congressional investigation. Once again an unsubstantiated attack served to trigger the publicity mechanisms and yield calculated results. The press was used as a vehicle for the transmission of managed news. A complex and important issue was reduced to an absurdity.

Mr. Hagerty at Work

A more subtle case study in the management of news is provided by the recent career of James Hagerty, who, in the opinion of an admiring critic, *Time* magazine, has been "by every standard the best—and most powerful—White House press secretary in U.S. history . . . Day in, day out, year in, year out, between Presidential speeches and press conferences, during Eisenhower's vacations and Eisenhower illnesses, Hagerty is the authentic voice of the White House and, to an extent rarely recognized, of the whole Administration."

With Washington reporters, and especially the group who are assigned on a continuous basis to the White House, Hagerty has proved thoroughly skilled and obliging in meeting the vexing demands of their business. He knows particularly well their nagging need to produce a steady flow of news. Twice a day and sometimes more he holds informal press conferences in a diligent effort to meet this need.

Hagerty has shown shrewd and farsighted judgment on occasion. When the President was stricken with his heart attack in 1955, passing along the word "Tell Jim to take over," the Press Secretary instituted a publicity operation remarkably candid in view of the grave situation. On the other hand, Hagerty is capable of rather subtle judgments in this business of public relations. Less than a year later, when Eisenhower was again hospitalized for the ileitis operation, the Press Secretary was not nearly so obliging to the press. "A Presidential heart attack is the property of the people," he explained afterward. "But we did not consider the ileitis something that endangered the President's life."

All these qualities may be considered virtues in the public-relations business. But an underlying suspicion that has disturbed a number of correspondents in Washington has been that Hagerty has carried these virtues too far. He has made of public relations an end in itself rather than a means to an end.

This was most apparent during the prolonged periods when the President has been ill or on vacations. As *Time* has since reported:

> Hagerty struggled valiantly and, to a point, successfully, in stressing work over play. He took with him on trips briefcases full of executive orders, appointments, etc. and parceled them out daily to make news under the Augusta or Gettysburg dateline. He encouraged feature stories on the Army Signal Corps' elaborate setup to keep Ike in close touch with Washington. He produced Cabinet members in wholesale lots (Does Hagerty

> really call for Cabinet members? Says he: "Maybe sometimes I do"). He did anything and everything, in short, to keep the subjects of golf and fishing far down in the daily stories about the President.

Hagerty has not been above hocus-pocus. Once, during an Eisenhower illness, he handed a visiting cabinet member a statement to read to reporters about how well the President was looking. The man had not yet been in to see the President.

The trouble is that Hagerty has so arranged the lights and shadows that he has distorted the public image of the President and, more importantly, of the Presidency itself. For prolonged periods, he has attracted public attention away from compelling problems of leadership with a succession of makeshift and inconsequential diversions. His skill has been so great that the editors of at least one major United States newspaper felt obliged to cut down the number of frontpage stories coming out of the White House because they judged they were causing a false public impression of the President's activities.

The Hagerty-type operation, despite its technical proficiency, cannot substitute for having a responsible source of explanation at the highest level of government. In his management of news, Hagerty has in fact discouraged such explanation. He has rebuffed the reporter's attempts to approach other White House sources for briefings on important questions. The office of the President has become a no man's land for the reporter seeking guidance on major policies in flux.

THE NEWS AND THE TRUTH

When, on rare occasions, he takes time to review his many mandates, the reporter in Washington is apt to be overwhelmed. His preparation of the news cannot help but be conditioned by the audiences for whom he writes. Amid competitive, ofttimes contradictory pressures he must somehow achieve equilibrium. And he must do it, usually in a hurry, while the waiting presses set the one unyielding pressure.

There is the audience composed of his sources, the various protagonists in the Washington arena, who read his copy with great care and sensitivity. The correspondent who intends to survive must be ever mindful of them. Even the most powerful reporter learns to ration his enemies. Too open an approach to the news can mean too many closed doors.

There is the audience of his bosses. Their cupidity and their influence have been berated and at times overrated. It varies, of course, from boss to boss. But a more continuous and compelling pressure upon the Washington correspondent comes from basic economic trends in the communications industry. News is big business. News is a commodity that must be purveyed to an ever-expanding audience by increasingly monopolistic distributors.

There is the audience of his readers—a frenetic group who, he is told, spend eighteen and a half minutes a day reading five columns of news, of which only one-eighth is international. The reader, it has been said, is the median man, destined, like Orphan Annie, never to grow an inch. To hold his attention, the reporter feels a gnawing compulsion to devise ever more resourceful ways of perfecting the "leads" and "angles" of his stories.

When he is in a philosophical frame of mind, the Washington reporter asks himself whether news was ever meant to serve as the vehicle for communicating the "Truth" about government. Many years ago, Walter Lippmann, while still a comparative newcomer to journalism, examined the proposition and reached a pessimistic conclusion. "If we assume . . . that news and truth are two words for the same thing, we shall, I believe, arrive nowhere," he wrote. The function of news, Lippmann pointed out, is "to signalize an event," whereas the function of truth is "to bring to light the hidden facts, to set them into relation with each other, and make a picture of reality on which men can act." Lippmann ridiculed the notion that the press, by acting upon everybody for a few minutes each twenty-four hours, "can create a mystical force called Public Opinion that will take up the slack in public institutions."

Yet this is precisely the job that the Washington correspondent has been called upon to attempt. As the business of government has become more complicated, responsible reporters have felt a driving urge to expose the "hidden facts," to relate them, and to furnish a realistic picture of what is happening. It is a job that has to be done if the American system of government is to function properly.

The reporter knows that he has done his job well at times. On occasion, he has stimulated public controversy when even members of the opposition party have maintained a discreet silence. He has broken up petty conspiracies among politicians too long vested with arbitrary power. He has exposed the corruption that desire for power and, conversely, the careless use of power breeds. On the positive side, he has served as middleman and broker for important new ideas and policies. He, as much as anyone, has helped to keep Washington in healthy ferment.

Still, it comes as a shock to realize just how precarious is the base from which the responsible reporters in Washington operate. The constituency to which they communicate about the state of the nation is pitifully small compared, say, to the constituency of the television comedian or the comic-strip artist. Outside of Washington they are not big guys. Most are aware that they are allowed to operate not because of economic benefits they bring in but because their bosses believe that their work is in the public interest. They are aware, too, that concepts of the public interest can change radically.

Finally, the reporter in Washington has had to consider the subject matter with which he deals daily. He has watched politics—the stuff of his trade—explode like the now familiar mushroom cloud, engulfing economics, military strategy, and at last the worlds of nuclear and space science. He suspects darkly that somewhere along the way the essentials of a reporter's knowledge moved into a new order of magnitude. He looks back nostalgically to the time when the subjects government dealt with did not seem so alien or formidable to the gifted amateur.

This fantastic role the reporters play in Washington must be in large part self-directed. Yet they lack even a set of guiding principles commonly imposed within the press corps to satisfy the ethical exigencies. "Shyster lawyers can be disbarred, quack doctors can have their licenses revoked, and unworthy ministers can be unfrocked, but the newspaper profession had no method of dealing with black sheep," wrote a disgruntled critic about an earlier period in Washington. The profession has no such method even today.

But the good reporters are linked by a sense of the importance of what they are doing that compensates for all the low pay, long working hours, high tensions, and unending dilemmas of the business. "Above all reporting offers the sense of being "engagé" in the political process of one's own time," the brothers Alsop have remarked. It is only the very bad and unsuccessful reporter in Washington who does not share this sense.

WHO DECIDES WHAT'S FIT TO PRINT?
T. S. Mathews

T. S. Mathews, presently an editor of the Sunday *New York Times,* joined the staff of the *New Republic* in 1925 and then moved to *Time* Magazine in 1929, where he was managing editor and editor from 1943 to 1953. He is the author of *The Sugar Pill.*

The main business of the press, supposedly, is news, as the main business of banks is money. It may surprise the public to discover how incurious many bankers are about the real nature of money, and how unclear they are about it. In just the same way, and perhaps to a greater extent, many journalists are incurious about the real nature of news and just as unclear about it. This particular question has been begged for so long that it now seems either self-evident or insoluble. Ask a journalist "What is news?" and you'll get one of a number of answers, ranging from "It's what interests *me*" (meaning "the paper I work on") to "how should I know?" (meaning "I just work here").

Perhaps the neatest as well as the most generally accepted definition of news is "what happened yesterday." I remember once totting up the front-page news stories (the news of the day considered most important) in a good provincial newspaper, in America. Of the eleven stories on the page, seven had not happened at all—in the sense of man biting dog, or even of dog biting man. Some of the speculations about the future—and there were many—might have come true, but so far they were just speculations. If news is

From *Saturday Review,* January 24, 1959.

what happened yesterday, the newspapers print an awful lot of phony news. But we have seen how the practical definition of news varies from paper to paper. Journalists never have been very keen on defining news theoretically, except in a parlorgame spirit. Someone whose faith in the news was simple, like C. P. Scott, the famed editor of the *Manchester Guardian,* took news for granted; news was the sacred facts. An equally inexact but more inclusive description might be, "News is what the press produces." It isn't only physics that's getting more complicated: we now know the facts, like the atom, can be split.

I mustn't push the analogy with banks too far, but there is one striking similarity between banks and the press. Both, to a great extent, manufacture their product, though they are not popularly supposed to. By far the greatest part of the world's "money" is issued by banks in the form of credit. Most of the world's "news" is manufactured by the press itself: Interviews with important men; reports on grave situations; press conferences; press investigation; political surveys; "informed speculation," etc., etc. Most "hard news" falls into the press's lap like the meteorites or manna from heaven: murder and suicide, rape, war, pestilence, famine, catastrophes of all kinds. This bad news is the best news to the press—it's not only exciting to read but it comes ready-made. Mongers of sensational news, like *The London Daily Mirror,* admitting that the supply of this sort of news is unsteady, meet the daily demand for sensation in two ways; by dressing up small news to look big, and by ballyhooing daily features. There is no essential difference between the inevitable screaming front-page headline of the *Mirror* and the "running story" from a wire service of a diplomatic conference. Both are manufactured news. They are said to have happened big; actually, they either didn't happen at all, or they only happened a little.

Some of the more exacting followers of C. P. Scott still insist that their paper deals in sacredly regarded facts. That is probably true in spots, although they conveniently overlook the other spots in the paper that are profanely opinionated rather than sacredly factual. A large part of the press has, in effect, abandoned the pretense of dealing exclusively with facts, or the pretense that their source is invariably as pure as the Pierian spring. A great many newspapers, for example, make no bones about printing gossip. They still, officially at least, exclude rumor (except from the gossip columns, or unless it can be attributed to a "hitherto unimpeachable source," when it rises from "rumor" to "speculation" or "inside information").

The only journalists who are consistently successful in keeping rumor and gossip out of the news are the Communists. The Communists' press, an avowed instrument of government, is dedicated to the proposition that facts equal propaganda equals truth. The facts are chosen, the propaganda ordered, and the truth announced. It's much simpler than with us. And the Russians have a great contempt for the confusions of the Western press, which all stem from this inadmissible search for news. "News" in Russia is issued as a valuable, State-controlled ration.

When Ilya Ehrenburg, one of the dark stars of Communist journalism, visited the United States a few years ago, he was much bothered by reporters who pried into what he considered irrelevant personal questions—the one that moved him to most sardonic mirth was whether a suit he was having made at a New York tailor was to have trousers with buttons or a zipper. There, he said triumphantly, you have a picture of the Western press, which concerns itself with gossip; buttons or zipper, that is all they care to know about. In the doctrinaire Communist view, our free press makes too little distinction between public news (which is the press's only business) and private news (which is none of its business). Moreover, say the Communists, nobody but they know what news is fit to publish, or what news really is.

One defense to this is apt to be: "The truth shall make you free"—by which we mean that if everybody talks continuously at the top of his lungs, somebody from time to time will probably say something true, somebody else may hear it, and it may have some good effect, by and large. Nevertheless, we have an uneasy suspicion that there should be some distinction between public and private news, and that the press doesn't make the distinction clear—no doubt because of the general confusion about what news really is. Public or private, the news must affect our individual lives, it must be translatable into our personal terms, before we will pay attention to it. Even the news in Russian papers can be so translated, I should imagine. Everything *Pravda* or *Izvestia* publishes means some action or threat of action by the Government; the trick is to see: "How is that going to affect *me?*" We read the newspapers that way in time of war, when all governments are gray. In peace-time, public news for most of us is just something to quack about, and it rolls off our backs; the news that really concerns us comes by word of mouth or by mail. The opening door, the doctor's verdict, the expected letter, the telegram that says "death" or "life"; this is the kind of news that comes home to us. Perhaps it is the only real news there is.

Nevertheless, we feel that there should be bigger news than this, and the press continually assures us that indeed there is. The press keeps on telling it, in big headlines; big good news and big bad news. The big good news is mainly manufactured, not so much because the press is sanguine by nature as that it is committed to the encouraging notion of progress. The big bad news is what has actually happened. When our candidate is elected or the war ends, we may call the news both big and good; but what will it be called by the people who voted for the other man, or who lost the war? No, real good news, in the public sense, is either incredible or beyond our understanding. And yet we crave it, its absence seems wrong, we want it to be. The press, which is as human as the rest of us, shares this craving and gropes for big news—however incredible or beyond our understanding. When the *New York Times* printed the text of Einstein's theory, it was in this mystical and groping spirit. The hope was that Einstein had found a large piece of truth—even if nobody, or almost nobody, could understand it; and in that hope the *Times*' editor was willing to bow his uncomprehending head, and take the whole congregation of the *Times* to their knees with him.

In less than two generations science has become untranslatable, and its speculations about the world come to us more and more faintly, like the dwindling shouts of a search-party that have disappeared into an enormous maze. The news they succeed in sending back to us (with the press as messenger) often seems contradictory of earlier bulletins; the gist of it comes across as a progressive disillusionment with accepted facts and an immense widening and deepening of the unknowable. But this is depressing and therefore unacceptable to our optimistic habit of mind—as if, with all our advantages, we were just catching up with Socrates, and as it were from behind! So the press continues to hail scientific "discoveries" (the substitution of a new theory for an abandoned one) as if they were real news, big news and good news. And the public, official view of science's search for knowledge is one of untiring hope and faith. In private, however, there is skepticism and doubt, and not just among illiterate peasants either.

The only big news, private and public, that human beings are really concerned about is news of life and death. There has been no new news on either subject for some time—nearly 2,000 years, in fact. The Resurrection was tremendous good news, if true; the best news ever reported. But though it has been told wherever Christian missionaries have gone and a large proportion of the earth's population must have heard it, it is still widely disbelieved or believed only in a poetic or mystical sense, as "an honorable thought" or an incomprehensible symbol. Even those Christians who believe that the Resurrection was an event that actually happened and a demonstration that individual human beings are literally immortal would nowadays hesitate to apply it without qualification to their own personal lives and deaths. As for agnostics and unbelievers, they have accepted and spread the persistent rumor that the news of the Resurrection was exaggerated or false.

The press is only a reflection of the world it reports, and like the world it reports, is quite unable to recognize or accept really good news—a saint for the ages, a hero both immediate and lasting, a revelation of permanent truth; it can only exaggerate or minimize, ignore, misreport, or doubt, just like the rest of us. Big bad news it can't miss; big good news it never sees—though it pretends a lot of little good news is big, and manufactures all the big good news it can. What keeps the press going is mainly snippets; some news, much gossip, loads of rumors—not to speak of all the features, extras, special acts and entertaining etceteras.

The biggest piece of clap-trap about the press is that it deals almost exclusively, or even mainly, with news.

And the next-biggest piece of clap-trap is that the press has enormous power. This delusion is persistent and widespread. It is taken for granted by the public-at-large, who are apt to be impressed by anything that is said three times; it is continually advertised by the press itself; and it is cherished by press lords, some of whom, at least, should know better. The Hutchins Commission of the Freedom of the Press, which represented a more-than-usually-intelligent public-at-large in the United States, not only took the power of the press at the Press's own valuation, but thought it very alarming:

> We have the impression that the American people do not realize what has happened to them. They are not aware that the communications revolution has occurred. They do not appreciate the tremendous power which the new instruments and the new organization of the press place in the hands of a few men.

In what way is the press supposed to be so powerful? The general notion is that the press can form, control or at least strongly influence public opinion. Can it really do any of these things? Hugh Cudlipp, editorial director of *The London Daily Mirror,* and a man who should know something about the effect of newspapers on public opinion, doesn't share this general notion about their power. He thinks newspapers can echo and stimulate a wave of popular feeling, but that's all. "A newspaper may successfully accelerate but never reverse the popular attitude that common-sense has commended to the public." In short, it can jump aboard the bandwagon, once the bandwagon's under way, and exhort others to jump aboard too; but it can't start the bandwagon rolling, or change its direction after it's started.

Like other habit-forming pills, the press can stimulate or depress, but it cannot cure. It can fan fear and hatred of another nation (when the fear and hatred are there, waiting to be fanned) but it cannot make peace. As more and more people have painful reason to know, the press has a nasty kind of power—the same kind of power a bully has, of hurting somebody smaller and weaker than himself. An individual's only defense against the press is the law of libel, but considerable harm and much pain can be caused without going as far as to commit an actionable libel. Journalists themselves generally have a horror of being interviewed, "written up" or even noticed by the press—they know too well from their own experience how inept and cruel a distortion the result is likely to be. Nine times out of ten, as they know, ineptness is to blame rather than conscious cruelty; but there is always that tenth case. And a blundering friendly fist. The press is often like a clumsy giant who gives you a pat on the back and knocks the wind out of you, if he doesn't cause internal injuries. I remember once coming upon an elderly professor of my university who had just been "written up" by the paper I worked on. When he saw me, tears came into his eyes, and he said, "What have I done to them? What have I done to deserve this?" He was deeply wounded by the article, and regarded it as an extremely unkind caricature. Knowing that it had been written by one of his former students who liked and admired the professor, I tried to reassure him that it was at least kindly meant; I don't think I succeeded.

The press has a negative power—to titillate, alarm, enrage, amuse, humiliate, annoy, even to drive a person out of his community or his job. But of the positive power to which it pretends, and of which the press lords dream—to make and break governments, to swing an election, to stop a war or start a revolution—there is no tangible evidence. Its vaunted might is a gigantic spoof. Professor David Mitrany, speaking in 1932 on "The Press and International Relations," put the case with delicate irony: "There is no need to spend time in an attempt to show how great is the influence of the press. It is greater in certain fields than in others. It is greater, one could say, in any field in which the knowledge and interest of the man in the street is lesser. For in that case the reading public is apt to think that the press speaks with the voice of authority; while the authorities are apt to assume that the press is speaking the voice of the people . . ."

Everyone has heard of the "power of the press"; no one has seen it. The greatest believers in this exaggerated "power" and the loudest promoters of it are, naturally, the press lords themselves. One of the most deluded of these, not even excepting Northcliffe or Beaverbrook, was Robert McCormick, Publisher of the *Chicago Tribune* (still emblazoned with his modest motto: "The world's greatest newspaper"). McCormick, and of course his paper, were always in bitter opposition to the Roosevelt Democrats, as well as to the liberal element in his own Republican Party. A story used to be told about the *Tribune*—no doubt apocryphal but in essence true—that one of the janitors in the Tribune building always bet against any political candidate the paper supported, and gave odds to boot; and that he found this sideline so profitable that he was able to buy two sizable blocks of flats.

The people in Chicago who bought the *Tribune* didn't buy it to find out how to cast their votes: they bought it in spite of its advice and its bias, because on the whole they liked its personality and found it entertaining. Does this seem to argue a too shrewd, calm and sensible attitude on the part of the ordinary newspaper reader? The press is generally appreciated by the public for what it is rather than for what it pretends to be. They don't feel it as a power in their lives, but as a working-day prerequisite.

5 GOVERNMENT UNDER PRESSURE

In recent years, Americans have become increasingly aware of the existence of pressure groups in their society. They have heard tales of the not quite reputable operations by which Big Business, Big Labor, Big Agriculture, and others seek to influence the legislative process. They have read about the subterranean workings of wily lobbyists and the assorted blandishments with which legislators are reputedly plied. All these tales are a part of the popular folklore; and yet the real world of pressure politics, where the administrator is often a more important target than the lawmaker, and where the lobbyist openly provides invaluable services for the harried official, is not well understood. Indeed, the simple identification of pressure groups inevitably omits one of the very largest—the military-industrial complex spotlighted by President Eisenhower in his farewell message of January 1961. Other top interest groups frequently go unrecognized—the many foreign governments, large and small, that seek to reinforce their American favor, and the federal government itself, its administrators often linked to formally organized clients in a binding community of interest.

It is not easy to determine the magnitude of pressure operations. The best "hard" figures available date back more than a decade, to the days before court decisions revealed the loopholes, which lobbyists have since taken advantage of, in the Lobbyist Registration Act of 1946. In 1950, we learned that some two thousand registered lobbyists spent an annual $10,000,000 to influence the work of the Congress alone. Congressman Frank Buchanan of Pennsylvania, who had conducted one of the most searching inquiries into the subject, used the analogy of the iceberg to estimate the total expenditure at some six or seven times the visible portion. Today, lobbying—even when defined in a limited sense, as direct attempts at legislative influence—is probably a $100,000,000-a-year business. Direct congressional lobbying, however, represents only a portion of the total outlay in a nation where the creation of "image" and the building of "grass-roots" attitudes annually involve the expenditure of corporate and organizational millions in so-called "institutional advertising."

The techniques of lobbying are as varied as their practitioners, and attempt to influence not only the legislator and administrator but even the courts—particularly those on the state and local level—as well as influential citizens and community leaders, the molders of local opinion. Although illicit methods of influence, such as bribery and corruption, are still occasionally uncovered, they have generally given way to more honorable and more effective techniques. The lobbyist today may do research for the administrator, draft bills for the legislator, or direct community-improvement projects to create a favorable climate of opinion.

Pressure groups provide a valuable reflection of economic and social interests in a pluralistic society whose formal representation is geographically based. Consequently, pressure activity has at least two dimensions: (a) it provides certain desirable services; and (b) it creates certain significant problems. A series of questions may suggest some of the difficulties involved. Since not all pressure groups are balanced by "countervailing power," one may well ask: "Who speaks for the consumer, the nonveteran, the atheist, the agnostic, or for the nonunion worker?" "To what extent do the interest-group leaders reflect the views of the rank and file?" "Are American Legionnaires as reactionary as some of their Commanders' views would indicate?" "Is there dissenting opinion within the monolithic facade of the American Medical Association?" "How many businessmen share the progressive economic ideas of their colleagues in the Committee for Economic Development?"

These are some of the queries, perhaps unanswerable, that we should keep in mind as we examine the workings of the special interests in and on the American society. And yet, as we explore the problems, and the reforms suggested by some, we should bear in mind the wise guarantee of the First Amendment—the right to petition for a redress of grievances. For it seems not only inevitable but, indeed, a necessity that there be pressure—democratic pressure—if our government in action is to serve the needs of all its people.

HOW PRESSURE GROUPS OPERATE

Henry A. Turner

Henry A. Turner is Associate Professor of Political Science at the University of California, Berkeley. His articles have been published in a number of professional journals, and he is the editor of *Politics in the United States.*

Pressure groups have participated actively in politics from the establishment of the first governments in America and must, therefore, be considered as an intrinsic element of our political system.

The manner in which pressure groups operate in the United States today is determined basically by the political environment: the federal form of government; separation of powers; electoral system; political parties; technological development; and the economic, social, ethnic, and religious composition of the population. Individual interest groups generally function in

From *The Annals of the American Academy of Political and Social Science,* September 1958. Reprinted by permission.

a pragmatic and opportunistic fashion, using any method or technique which they believe will serve their purpose effectively. Undoubtedly dictating most pressure group activity is the criterion: what action will produce the maximum desired result with the minimum expenditure of time and resources. The techniques and tactics which any particular group employs will be determined largely by such factors as size and geographic distribution of the membership, cohesion of membership, financial resources, prestige position of the organization, quality of leadership and staff, and relations with the political parties and other organized groups.

Where are pressures applied? Depending on the aims and characteristics of the individual organization, an interest group may attempt to influence its own membership; other pressure groups; the electoral process; the legislative, executive, and judicial branches of the government; and public opinion.

INFLUENCING THE MEMBERSHIP

One characteristic of virtually every large organization is the tendency for a few individuals to gain effective control of the group. In some associations the officers may enjoy near permanent tenure, and in others they may be selected from a relatively small elite. These officers and the paid bureaucracy in many instances literally run the organization. Hence, from the standpoint of origination of policy, they become the organization.

In some organized groups, a considerable portion of the time and energy of the staff may be expanded to influence the members of the group and potential members. Most associations wish to retain and enlarge their membership—if for no other reason—in order to increase the political strength of the group. In group meetings, publications, and direct communications, to the membership, efforts are also directed toward producing greater group cohesion, to "educating" the membership to accept and support the policies of the organization, and to inducing the members to engage in desired political activity. Types of activity urged on group members include: registering and voting; working in political campaigns and making financial contributions; and communicating via personal conversations, letters, telegrams, and telephone calls to public officials and those who control the media of mass communication.

CO-OPERATION BETWEEN GROUPS

In a sense, pressure groups lobby other pressure groups. Organized interest groups seek the active support of their allies or potential allies, the endorsement of groups less directly interested, and the neutralization of their opponents. Such co-operation may be achieved by one group merely activating another, by promising future assistance, or by making concessions or compromises. In some cases co-operating groups develop only informal working arrangements, but there are instances in which organizations have signed formal agreements to pool their political efforts in working for a program. Examples may also be cited of groups co-operating through interlocking directorates.

In 1950, a Congressional committee investigating lobbying found that interest groups co-operate not only "within so obvious a functional area as an industry," but also on an ideological basis, for "there is a growing joint effort in lobbying by groups whose unity is philosophical rather than functional in character." The Committee added, "The general theme of combination rather than conflict grows bolder and more insistent every year."

A particular type of pressure organization, the catalytic pressure group, has been developed to promote joint action by interest groups. Catalytic groups usually consist of representatives of several pressure organizations, but an established pressure group may itself serve as a catalytic organization. Some catalytic groups have been established on an *ad hoc* basis for the purpose of stimulating and coordinating the activities of several organizations to secure the adoption of a specific policy; and once the policy has been effected, the catalytic group has been disbanded. An example of such a group is the Citizens Committee to Repeal Chinese Exclusion. Other catalytic groups such as the National Tax Equality Association have been established on a permanent basis.

PRESSURE ON THE ELECTORAL PROCESS

By definition, pressure groups are nonpartisan organizations which attempt to influence some phase of public policy. They do not, themselves, draft party platforms or nominate candidates for public office. Pressure associations do, however, appear before the resolutions committees of the political parties to urge the endorsement of their programs as planks in the parties' platforms. They often attempt to secure the endorsement of both major parties and thus remove their program from the area of partisan controversy. Many groups are also active in the nomination and election of party members to political offices.

Most interest groups which are active in election campaigns will support a candidate of either party if his general outlook is similar to that of the group. Thus organized labor has followed the policy, first prescribed by Samuel Gompers, of "rewarding friends and punishing enemies" by support or opposition in campaigns and at the polls. Apparently, however, some labor, business, farm, professional, and other organizations have found most of their "friends" in one party and most of their "enemies" in the other, for they have tended to align themselves with one or the other of the two major parties.

The most common method of aiding in a campaign is through financial contribution. Labor unions and corporations are prohibited by law from making "a contribution or expenditure in connection with any election" at which a member of Congress or the President and Vice-President are selected; but they have devised means for evading the spirit, if not the letter, of the law.

Testimony before the Senate subcommittee investigating the 1956 election campaign revealed that both labor unions and corporations pay salaries to officers and employees working full time for a party or candidate, publish political arguments in their house organs, and purchase television and radio time and newspaper space to present political views. In addition, the subcommittee was informed that corporations make political contributions by permitting party officials or candidates to use offices and equipment without charge and pay bonuses and permit expense accounts to be padded with the understanding that political contributions will be made from the bonuses and padded accounts.

Influencing Legislators

A century ago pressure groups concentrated most of their efforts on promoting and opposing legislative proposals. During recent decades, their activities have been expanded into other areas; yet even today, the methods employed to influence legislative decisions are the most obvious actions of pressure groups.

The major organized interests maintain permanent staffs of professional lobbyists, research personnel, press agents, and secretaries in Washington throughout the year and have similar but smaller staffs in most state capitols during legislative sessions. Associations which have only an incidental interest in legislative proposals customarily do not have a full-time lobby staff, but may employ a lobbyist to represent them on occasions when legislative issues of interest to their members arise.

Some interest groups have "stables" of legislators who will work closely with them either because they owe their election largely to those groups or because they are themselves members of those groups. Pressure organizations with like-minded spokesmen in the legislature, or "inside lobbyists," naturally have an advantage over other groups.

Available information indicates that pressure associations originate a large percentage of the bills introduced in Congress and the state legislatures. Many organizations have their staff members read all bills introduced to determine which they wish to support, which to oppose, and which to attempt to have amended. As would be expected, lobbyists customarily watch the bills which they have sponsored to help expedite their movement through the various stages of the legislative process to enactment.

Committee hearings on bills provide the various organizations with opportunities to present their information and arguments and also to show how strongly the members of the group favor or oppose a given proposal. Officers of the association, their lobbyists, or lay members will testify before committees, often with charts and graphs to show statistical data. Sizable delegations may be organized to attend committee hearings. At crucial times—such as when a committee is considering a bill or when the measure is being debated by one of the houses of the legislature—pressure associations often have their members write, telegraph, or call their legislators. Some groups attempt to flood the legislators with messages, while others concentrate on having communications sent by the principal supporters of each legislator and other key persons in each district.

Basically, lobbying consists of communicating with the legislators. Organized groups utilize every available opportunity to inform legislators of their wishes; to provide them with facts, information, and arguments; and to impress upon them the ability of the organization to reward or punish the legislator by giving or withholding support at the polls, campaign contributions, or gifts and items of value to the legislator. In spite of the pressures brought upon them, most legislators agree that private groups perform a valuable function in presenting information regarding a multitude of bills—many of them of a highly technical nature—introduced in each legislative session.

Any survey of pressure group operations would be incomplete that omitted reference to the social lobby and the use of unethical or illegal methods. There is widespread agreement that both types of practices still exist, but that they are of much less importance than in the days of the "old lobby." It should also be noted that these methods are undoubtedly employed as much today to influence administrators as legislators. Although the social lobby, minor favors, and practices of a distinctly corrupt nature may influence some public officials, their total impact on the political process is probably not great today.

Pressure on the Executive Branch

One of the most noteworthy changes in pressure-group activity during this century is the increased effort to influence the executive branch of the government. Pressures are applied on executive and administrative personnel who are in the position to render decisions or take action of interest to organized groups. As in earlier years, after a bill has been passed by the legislature, interest groups may inundate the Chief Executive with statements, letters, telegrams, and memorials; and they may appeal to him personally to veto or sign the measure. Well aware of the importance of the Chief Executive's recommendations regarding legislative policies and budgetary matters, organized interests urge the President or governors to incorporate or omit specific proposals from their legislative programs and to increase or decrease budgetary requests for particular administrative departments or agencies.

The vast expansion of governmental regulation of economic life and the tendency of the legislatures to grant administrative officials broad discretionary powers have caused pressure associations to evince more interest than in the past in the selection of administrative personnel. Moreover, it is apparent to most groups that administrators may forcibly execute a statute or virtually nullify it. For these reasons it is not uncommon for groups to seek the appointment of their members or of individuals friendly to their group to administrative posts of particular interest to them. Pressure organizations with friends in top administrative positions have found that they have advantages not available to other groups in securing permits, licenses, contracts, subsidies, favorable adjustments of tax problems and antitrust suits, and various other types of privileges and favors.

Administrative agencies which have been granted quasi-legislative powers find that representatives of interest groups commonly appear before them to oppose or support rules and regulations. On the national level, the Administrative Procedure Act requires most administrative agencies to hold public hearings on proposed rules and permits interested individuals to request the issuance, repeal, or amendment of rules. Pressure associations have availed themselves of these rights and lobby the administrators in much the same fashion as they lobby Congress or the state legislatures.

Interest groups may importune the legislature to amend the statutes under which an agency operates and to increase or decrease its appropriation in order to expand or curtail its operations. In some instances, organized interests have been able to get legislators to investigate administrative agencies in an effort to punish administrators for uncooperative or unfriendly action. It is incorrect, however, to assume that the relationship between private associations and governmental agencies is typically one of antagonism. On the contrary, it is not uncommon to find pressure organizations, legislators, and administrative agencies working together harmoniously for their mutual benefit.

Pressure Groups and the Judiciary

Although pressure organizations expend considerably less energy and time attempting to influence the judicial branch of the government than either the executive or legislative branch, reference should be included of their efforts to influence the courts. Whether judges are elected or appointed, organized interests often participate in their selection.

Occasionally groups seek to advance the cause of their members by initiating litigation to test the constitutionality of legislation or the action of public officials. For a number of years the National Association for the Advancement of Colored People has relied on litigation as a principal means for upholding Negro rights. Some organizations also file briefs as friends of the court to support other groups involved in litigation, or they have articles prepared for publication in law reviews with the expectation that they will be used as briefs or may be read by judges and possibly influence their decisions.

Pressure Groups and Public Opinion

The continual increase in the efforts of interest groups to win support for their organizations and programs by using the mass media of communication to influence public attitudes is perhaps the most significant recent development in pressure-group activity. Among factors contributing to this development are the increasing awareness on the part of interest-group leaders that public opinion is an entity which must be considered; the development and refinement of new propaganda techniques and devices; and the revolutionary changes in communication media which make it possible for literally millions of Americans to be reached daily via television, radio, the motion pictures, newspapers, and periodicals.

The rise of the public-relations counsel has occurred concomitantly with the growth of pressure groups and the extraordinary development of the communication media. To advise their highest officials on public relations and to direct propaganda programs many business organizations, labor unions, farm groups, professional associations, government agencies, and other organizations now employ public-relations counsels—some on a full-time basis in the top-echelon-planning and strategy group; others only occasionally to direct specific campaigns.

PROPAGANDA

Although the term propaganda is not new, there is general agreement that propaganda as employed today is a "new thing." The distinctive feature of modern propaganda is that it is disseminated principally through the media of mass communications by pressure groups who employ public-relations experts to develop their propaganda themes and techniques.

Pressure groups use propaganda both as a tactical means of accomplishing specific short-term goals and as a part of their long-range political strategy. From a tactical standpoint, a well-organized public-relations campaign may have either of two results. It may give the impression that there is such broad public support for a proposal that the campaign itself will result in the effectuation of the desired policy. Or, the campaign may activate the citizenry to the extent that they will demand through letters, telegrams, and other means that the officials make the decision wished by the organized group. In either event, the basic aim is to make the program of the group appear synonymous with the general welfare.

The strategic or long-term goal of a public-relations campaign tends to be ideological. Groups employing propaganda for strategic purposes often have as their aim selling the public a particular philosophy of government. In effect, they wish to condition the attitudes of the people so that a state of public opinion will be created in which the public will almost automatically respond with favor toward programs desired by the group and reject programs opposed by the group. The National Association of Manufacturers has referred to their strategic concept of public relations as the "bank account theory." In one of their publications they explain: "It necessitates making regular and frequent deposits in the Bank of Public Good-Will so that valid checks can be drawn on this account when it is desirable. . . ."

Virtually all major interest groups attempt to influence public attitudes, but business organizations tend to exert more effort and to enjoy more success than most. Business groups usually have the financial resources with which to employ public-relations personnel and to purchase advertising space and time; they often have the added advantage of being able to compute these expenditures as normal operating expenses for taxation purposes. The fact that American culture is basically a business culture and that such traditional American values as low taxes and limited government are among the propaganda themes of organized business has undoubtedly contributed to the success of their campaigns.

As V. O. Key has noted, an organization's public-relations program may increase the prestige of the group and its leaders. Indeed, an organization may elevate itself in the esteem of the public by using proper publicity in a manner not dissimilar to that by which movie stars, athletes, and presidential contenders are made national celebrities. Definite political advantages accrue to the group with status: their views are heard with more respect and given greater weight than those of lower prestige groups, and their members may be appointed to important advisory committees or influential governmental positions.

Propaganda Campaigns

Pressure organizations usually direct their propaganda campaigns at specific target groups. For example, Richard Gable notes that the public-relations programs of the National Association of Manufacturers—which he describes as "the most intensive, comprehensive, and expensive means by which it attempts to influence the formation of public policy"—are directed toward particular groups of individuals. He states:

> The NAM's public relations and propaganda programs can be classified according to the audience as external, indirect, and internal. The audience of the external appeal is the general public. The indirect approach covers educators, churchmen, women's club leaders, agricultural leaders, and similar community leaders who in turn mold specific publics. Internal programs are directed at state and local associations affiliated through the National Industrial Council as well as the NAM membership. Their purpose is to induce and assist members and affiliates to conduct community public relations programs using manuals and materials supplied by the Association.

Nationwide propaganda campaigns directed by public-relations experts often are organized and executed with the care for detailed planning and proper timing characteristic of highly successful military campaigns. One notable example was the American Medical Association campaign, directed by the Whitaker and Baxter firm, Campaigns, Inc., against the Truman national health insurance program. The total cost of the three-and-a-half year campaign was $4,678,000, of which approximately $775,000 was spent for propaganda skills. In this campaign, as in most others of this scope, virtually every conceivable communication medium was utilized. Physicians and laymen were enlisted to deliver to various clubs speeches prepared by the Whitaker and Baxter staff. In 1949 aone, 54,233,915 leaflets, pamphlets, booklets, and other pieces of literature were distributed. Radio, television, newspaper, and periodical advertising was purchased. Physicians placed literature in their waiting rooms, discussed the issue while treating their patients, wrote letters to patients, and placed enclosures in bills mailed to patients. One physician even dropped 50,000 leaflets from his airplane on a community.

Of the various methods of disseminating propaganda, the distribution of press releases, clipsheets, and prepared editorials apparently is one of the more effective. If used, such material gives the impression of straight reporting or editorials conceived and written by the staff of the local press. Through its public-relations department, the National Association of Home Builders has supplied its local associations with such items.

Pressure organizations in their efforts to influence public attitudes have not overlooked the educational system. The National Association of Manufacturers and other groups have prepared and distributed to the public schools posters, booklets, books, radio skits, film strips, and other "teaching aids." In 1957 the NAM announced that it distributed "at least two million booklets" free to the schools every year. The gas and electric public utilities during the 1920's surveyed textbooks and suggested changes in the presentation of materials regarding public utilities. Approximately three decades later an official of the National Association of Real Estate Boards told a Congressional committee that his organization had stimulated the writing of textbooks that were used "in 127 colleges and universities in teaching . . . the economics of real estate."

Institutional Advertising

Institutional advertising, which may be defined as the use of paid space or time in the communication media to promote or oppose ideas, has been used extensively to shape public sentiment since the early part of World War II. In 1954 the editors of the *Saturday Review* wrote: "one of the extraordinary things about American business is that it feels a responsibility to communicate with the American people about the ideas and philosophy that animate business and govern its multiple relations with society." And the Senatorial committee investigating the 1956 election reported finding "numerous instances of institutional advertising, either clearly political in nature or with definite political implications." Thus another recently developed activity of pressure groups is their use of institutional advertising to establish a climate of opinion which will promote their political objectives.

COMMITTEES, FOUNDATIONS, COUNCILS, AND INSTITUTES

The dynamic nature of interest-group activity may perhaps be seen most vividly by noting a new type of pressure organization, the oldest of which was established slightly over two decades ago. These organizations have as their primary purpose the publication and dissemination of leaflets, pamphlets, and books which present a particular viewpoint on current political and economic problems. Some of the more active of these groups are: The Committee for Constitutional Government, the Foundation for Economic Education, the National Economic Council, the Constitution and Free Enterprise Foundation, and the Public Affairs Institute. Of these five groups, the first four have been financed primarily by donations from large corporations and wealthy individuals, the Public Affairs Institute, on the other hand, has been supported in part by contributions from labor unions. All of these organizations receive some income from the sale of their publications.

The Committee on Lobbying Activities noted that to these organizations "the dissemination of literature is both the reason for the group's existence and a primary means by which it exists." Much of the success of these organizations in raising funds may be due to the fact that they have succeeded in getting the United States Treasury Department to classify them as educational foundations with contributions to them deductible for income-tax purposes. A Senatorial committee recently commented that "such foundations may be used as a device to avoid controls upon political expenditures and to provide tax benefits for political contributors."

The efforts of organized interests to propagandize the public have caused some concern regarding the future of the American democratic system. The very fact, however, that pressure groups believe it necessary to make extraordinary expenditures of time and resources to shape public attitudes may be evidence of the fundamental strength of American democracy; although interest groups can on occasion manage public sentiment, they are aware that they court defeat if they flout it.

American democracy is based on the premise that the people if provided sufficient information can be trusted to make correct decisions. The general public is not well informed regarding pressure groups. The basic problem, then in controlling pressure-group activity is how to give the people more adequate information about organized interests, their methods of operation, and their aims for "an informed and vigilant public is the only lasting guarantee that pressure groups will operate in an open and aboveboard manner."

THE FOREIGN LEGION OF U.S. PUBLIC RELATIONS
Douglass Cater and Walter Pincus

Walter Pincus, Washington correspondent for *News Focus,* has been the recipient of several awards for distinguished journalism.

Douglass Cater, formerly Washington editor of *The Reporter,* has served since 1964 as Special Assistant to President Lyndon B. Johnson.

The article presented below gained for its authors the Page One Award of the American Newspaper Guild, New York.

On January 30, 1959, the president of the Mutual Broadcasting System, Alexander L. Guterma, accompanied by the chairman of Mutual's board of directors, Hal Roach, Jr., and several other associates, flew to Ciudad Trujillo, Capital of the Dominican Republic. There he entered into an unusual agreement with representatives of dictator Rafael Trujillo. For a consideration of $750,000, paid in advance, Guterma agreed that for an eighteen-month period Mutual would broadcast a "monthly minimum of 425 minutes of news and commentary regarding the Dominican Republic." Trujillo's government would serve as its own news agency, supplying Mutual with items of news interest "by telegrams, air-mail dispatches, or telephonic beeper calls." Guterma also gave the Dominicans power of censorship by guaranteeing not to broadcast news inconsistent with their country's best interests, "in your sole and exclusive judgment."

Subsequently, a series of legal actions proceeded out of this deal—a hearing under the Bankruptcy Act involving Mutual, a civil action filed by the Dominicans to get their money back, and a Justice Department case against Guterma for failing to register as a foreign agent. From these proceedings, a fairly detailed account of what happened can be pieced together.

The origins of the agreement Guterma made in Ciudad Trujillo may be traced back to several earlier encounters between Saul S. Nevins, an attorney seeking capital for Guterma, and Porfirio Rubirosa, the celebrated international bridegroom who at the time was serving as Dominican ambassador to Cuba. During one meeting, Rubirosa complained about the unfavorable press coverage his government was getting in the United States. Nevins had earlier shown how Mutual could do something about it. Nevins had phoned in a story from Ciudad Trujillo about anti-Batista sentiment in the Dominican Republic that subsequently was broadcast twice from Washington, with Nevins identified as Mutual correspondent in the Dominican Republic. Mutual's Washington news director testified later that the practice of taking such information was not unusual. "We get a good deal of our news from people (who are not) newsmen. These can be fire chiefs, senators, congressmen."

Evidently the idea that such news coverage could be a salable commodity did not take long to develop. When Guterma's group met with Otto Vega, special assistant to Generalissimo Trujillo, they came right to the point. "They said they were in a position to secure . . . in the United States an outlet for our news," Vega testified later. Guterma produced a map of the Mutual Network and pointed out the number of stations that would be involved.

BROKER RUBIROSA

Guterma also provided another quick demonstration of the product he was prepared to sell. According to Vega's testimony: "He said, 'Give me an idea, some piece of news you would like to broadcast.' I said that I did not have anything. He said, 'Well, since we have Mr. Rubirosa here and Mr. Roach here, why not say Mr. Rubirosa is going to make a picture for Hal Roach in the Dominican Republic and they are negotiating that.' " The very next day, returning to New York in Guterma's private plane, the group heard Walter Winchell recite their make-believe news item over the Mutual Network.

During that same flight, Guterma showed Nevins a draft copy of the specific terms he was prepared to offer the Dominicans. The lawyer later professed amazement at their boldness. It amounted to nearly fifteen minutes daily to be "carried by the entire network . . . in a normal course of our broadcasting day." There was only one restriction: "We will not carry any news extolling the Communist cause but agree that the primary purpose is to exemplify the stability and tranquillity of the Dominican Republic and its unequivocal position and stand against Communism."

Nevins was fearful that the contract might run afoul of the law requiring agents of foreign governments to register with the Justice Department. To get around this requirement, he arranged to draw up papers creating for Guterma a new corporation, Radio News Service, which could claim exemption from the act on the grounds that it was a bona fide news-gathering agency.

The terms were acceptable to both sides, and on February 5, the negotiators having returned to Ciudad Trujillo, Vega brought to Guterma's suite at the El Embajador Hotel a cloth sack containing the $750,000, mostly in thousand-dollar bills. Not all of it, however, went to Guterma. Later, in trying to account for it, he claimed that he had been obliged to pay "brokerage fees" of $50,000 to Rubirosa, $25,000 to Vega (Vega denied receiving it), $37,500 to Nevins, and $57,500 to his other associates.

What remained was evidently insufficient to meet Guterma's pressing financial needs. In mid-February, 1959, he lost control of F. L. Jacobs, the holding company in which he combined his various enterprises, and was forced to resign as president of Mutual. Not long afterward, he was indicted for stock fraud in connection with his F. L. Jacobs dealings and he is now serving a five-year prison term. When that is completed an additional eight- to twenty-four-month sentence awaits him for failing to register as a Dominican agent.

How seriously did Guterma ever intend to live up to the terms of this agreement with Trujillo? The Dominican government, in filing suit for the return of its money, now claims that the contract was "not performed, was incapable of performance and was entered into by claimant on the basis of mistake in law and fact."

Because Guterma pleaded *nolo contendere* to the illegal-agent charges filed by the Justice Department, there was only fragmentary evidence of the extent to which Guterma managed to turn Mutual into a propaganda outlet of the Dominicans. Robert Hurleigh testified that as Mutual vice-president, he once received a call at his Washington office from Guterma in Ciudad Trujillo. He "said he had a congressman there who had . . . made a speech before the Legislature, or whatever the name is, and he thought this would be a good broadcast, so we took the Congressman in on a beeper . . ." Tapes of the visiting congressman, Gardner Withrow (R., Wisconsin), were used on newscasts during the day. On another occasion Hurleigh sent Guterma a note calling his attention to a "Capitol Cloakroom" interview with Senator Allen Ellender (D., Louisiana) on the Caribbean situation. Guterma promptly forwarded tapes of the two network broadcasts to Vega as proof the contract was being fulfilled.

Apparently Hurleigh, who succeeded Guterma as president of Mutual was unaware at the time of what lay beneath this sudden interest in the Dominicans. The first he learned of it, according to his testimony, was in May, 1959, when he and a Mutual reporter visited Ciudad Trujillo on a press junket arranged by the Dominicans. Hurleigh was shocked when Vega made inquiries about the contract. To stave off further involvement in this embarrassing affair, the Dominican government was paid $12,500, and it returned the eleven hundred shares of Mutual stock that Guterma had turned over to Vega as "good faith" collateral.

In becoming a publicity agent for a foreign government, Guterma was going into a business that has been expanding rapidly in this country during the last few years. Several hundred agents of foreign governments are duly registered at the Justice Department (as Guterma was not), and the number is constantly increasing. Many of these foreign agents are simply promoting tourism, while others are lawyers carrying on the various legal and lobbying activities in Washington that are considered necessary to backstop diplomatic missions. As the files at Justice indicate, a good many—comparative newcomers but more numerous all the time—are professional public-relations experts engaged in the business of influencing American opinion.

In the main, of course, this expansion of P.R. in the United States on behalf of foreign governments is no more surprising or sinister than the growth of the domestic variety as an adjunct to private or public business. They are, in fact, parallel efforts to meet the same basic need. The systematic cultivation of public opinion is frequently more fruitful than more direct attempts to influence government officials. But the ways of communicating with the public are intricate indeed. As Harold Oram, Inc., put it in a memorandum soliciting the P.R. account of the government of Ghana: "The services of a professional public relations firm are . . . becoming more of a necessity than ever before. The vast and complex network of media outlets, both mass and specialized, require, for effective utilization, long years of experience and understanding . . ."

UNLABELED COMMERCIALS

In seeking this "effective utilization" of the "media outlets," not every P.R. agent of a foreign government has done its work as openly and candidly as the Oram firm. A great temptation for many of them lies in the fact that the press and the other media have proved to be peculiarly vulnerable to the infiltration of blatant propaganda.

For example, in 1954 the government of Guatemala, then headed by Carlos Castillo Armas, hired John A. Clements Associates at a fee of $8,000 a month to engage in a public-relations campaign on its behalf. This job, according to the Justice Department registration, was to be handled by Clements and Patrick McMahon, who were at the same time serving as editor and Washington editor, respectively, of the *American Mercury*. As a further coincidence, that magazine published a number of articles on Guatemala during the period, three of them of a political nature. While on the Guatemala payroll, McMahon also acted as consultant to the House committee which investigated Communism in Guatemala and, according to his statement to the Justice Department, "prepared (its) report and helped edit the hearings . . ."

Or take the special case of the Nationalist Chinese government, which has long displayed an anxious regard for its public image in this country:

Item: Early in 1959, the North American Newspaper Alliance carried a series of stories written from Formosa by Don Frifield. The reader was not informed that NANA's correspondent was also employed by Hamilton Wright, the U.S. public-relations firm handling the Nationalist China account. Frifield has received $19,700 during the past two years for "editorial services."

Item: In June, 1958, during one of the periodic crises over the offshore islands of Quemoy and Matsu, there was shown at Radio City Music Hall in New York a documentary film entitled "Fortress Formosa," which had been "produced" by Twentieth Century-Fox. It was subsequently distributed to movie theaters all over the country. In the screen billings, a credit line indicated that it had been "Arranged by Hamilton Wright," but the viewer had no way of knowing that Hamilton Wright serves as Nationalist China's registered agent. The film, in Technicolor and CinemaScope, had actually been shot by the P.R. firm's camera crews and then turned over without cost to Twentieth Century-Fox.

Item: Last October 14, the morning after the third "Great Debate," in which the presidential candidates tangled over Quemoy and Matsu, NBC's "Today" carried on its news roundup a report of Chiang Kai-shek's angry rejection of Kennedy's position on those islands. While the television viewer heard Chiang quoted as voicing firm determination to resist the surrender of the islands, he watched a film clip depicting Nationalist Chinese troops and tanks parading in full battle array. This film was another production of Hamilton Wright supplied gratis to the NBC film library and used without credit.

Item: Since 1957, the *Saturday Evening Post* has carried a series of signed editorials by Geraldine Fitch in which she has defended Chiang's policies and criticized others for their lack of sympathy with those policies. The *Post* has identified Mrs. Fitch as an author who "spent many years in China and now lives in Formosa." But it has made no mention of the fact that she is also employed in Taipei as "consultant editor" of the Government Information Office, Republic of China.

Item: In a catalogue of free programs offered to independent television stations, Radiant Films of 358 West 44th Street, New York, includes a half-hour documentary, "Miracle in Free China" (". . . where Madame and Generalissimo Chiang Kai-shek and their ten million followers are marking time for the return to the mainland!") and "Face of Free China" ("How American defense in the Pacific is tied into the general defense of the free world through the U.S. Alliance with the Republic of China"). The only hint of who produced and paid for this entertainment is the cryptic mention that it was "Filmed by the world-renowned Hamilton Wright Organization." Neither Hamilton Wright nor Radiant Films, which is not registered as a foreign agent, has supplied the Justice Department with information about the distribution of these films, which were paid for by the government of Nationalist China.

Item: On a number of occasions in recent years, the *New York Times* has published letters to the editor, supporting the Chinese Nationalist stands, from Harold Riegelman, a New York attorney who has been both the city's acting postmaster and the Republican candidate for mayor. Though Mr. Riegelman is registered as a foreign agent of Nationalist China, he has not felt an obligation to label his communications under the Foreign Agents Registration Act. Neither the *Times's* editors nor its readers could be expected to know from his letters of Mr. Riegelman's connections with the Nationalist Chinese.

PRIVATE VS. PUBLIC P.R.

Foreign governments have provided Americans with information about themselves for a good many years. The British, starting with a modest library shortly after the First World War, have expanded the British Information Services in the United States into an efficient operation that now spends $1 million a year, with publishing and film facilities in New York and a B.I.S. representative stationed in Washington's National Press Building, where he is an accessible companion and counselor to the capital's reporters. Thirty-five other countries have established more or less similar information facilities, and have reported expenditures in 1959 totaling nearly $7 million. We do the same thing on a large scale in our U.S. Information Service missions around the world.

But the use of private P.R. firms in the United States on behalf of foreign governments dates largely from the end of the Second World War. Sometimes it was a matter of special necessity. The Roy Bernard Company of New York, which works for West Germany, took the account when its government was not entitled to send an official information mission to this country. A number of firms quickly moved into what was fast becoming a highly profitable field of enterprise. In addition to Nationalist China, Hamilton Wright's clients include Italy and Mexico. Hill & Knowlton, Inc., handles Japan; Harold L. Oram, Inc., has South Vietnam; Curtis J. Hoxter, Inc., works for Austria, Guatemala, and Brazil; Max Rogel, Inc., which formerly had the South Korean account, also takes care of Nicaragua.

During the past two or three years there has been a scramble among American P.R. firms to sign up the emerging African nations. When Vice-President Nixon visited Africa in 1957, one enterprising P.R. man got himself included in the entourage and tried to sell his services along the way.

The size of a foreign government's P.R. operation in the United States is by no means related to the country's size or relative power. The Dominican Republic, for example, has spent during the past five years more than $2,500,000 for assorted P.R. projects here. In 1946, the Dominicans hired Harry Klemfuss of New York to set up a Dominican Republic Information Center at $1,500 monthly. In 1952, a Miami *Herald* columnist, Jack Kofoed, was paid $2,300 monthly, which included $800 for expenses, to prepare a book on Trujillo and to write magazine and newspaper stories about the Dominican Republic. ("General Trujillo isn't as well known to the American people as he could be," ran one of several Kofoed columns that year dealing with the Dominicans. "Even his enemies can't deny that Trujillo has, single handed, lifted his country from the lowest state it could reach to the place it occupies now.") In 1957, A. Tyler Hull, a maker of documentary films, was paid $35,000 to prepare a thirty-minute color film and a twenty-six-minute black-and-white film for television, guaranteeing in his contract "a minimum of 300 television broadcasts in the United States to an estimated audience of more than 15 million viewers within a period of twenty-four months."

During that same year, Trujillo hired Sydney Baron, Inc., to combat adverse publicity arising from the mysterious disappearance in New York City of Dr. Jesús de Galindez, an outspoken opponent of the Dominican dictatorship. Baron listed receipts for 1957 and 1958 amounting to $562,-855, of which more than $200,000 went to the well-known attorney Morris Ernst, who was retained "to undertake an investigation of the so-called Galindez affair in so far as it touches upon implications and accusations against . . . the government of the Dominican Republic and persons holding high office in that government." In 1959, even as Guterma was making his deal with the Dominicans, By-Line Newsreel Productions was hired to produce a fifteen-minute sound movie each month for the purpose of "making increasingly known the progress achieved in the Dominican Republic." The agreement specified that these newsreels, which cost $3,000 apiece, would be shown in nine hundred movie houses throughout the United States.

As any reporter can testify, much of foreign P.R. performs a useful service in keeping the press informed about facts they need to know. Taken as a whole, it is no more mysterious or unscrupulous than P.R. work done for domestic clients. It varies, of course, from firm to firm and client to client, since in this unlicensed and unlimited profession the practitioners are pretty much able to devise their own rules and ethics as they go along. But in one respect the work done for a foreign government does differ from that performed in behalf of, say, an American manufacturer. For one thing, the American public's familiarity with the domestic client's product is apt to exert some check on the activities of those who promote it. But such restraints do not apply so rigorously to a foreign client, particularly if it happens to be the government of a country not visited by many American tourists, congressmen, and journalists who may snoop around a little during their travels.

Obviously in our days, nearly all nations are engaged in some sort of direct or indirect public-relations activities abroad. The United States, it is hoped, operates constantly and efficiently in this field. But the activities and the policies of a large country are always the object of scrutiny and debate. The same does not apply to small countries, or rather to their governments—all too often when the very survival of those governments depends to a large extent on the assistance they receive from us. The facts we need to know are often concealed, or get to us too late. All of a sudden there may be a blow-up in a country with which we have been deeply involved. When that happens, it not only upsets the best-laid plans of the P.R. men but greatly harms America's prestige.

'HOW MUCH WOULD IT COST?'

A foreign government's assumptions about how to handle press relations in the United States are heavily conditioned by the way it treats the press back home. Generalissimo Trujillo had no reason to doubt that he could buy the services of a radio network. When General Batista was still boss in Cuba in 1958, he approached a New York P.R. firm with a query about how much it would cost to get favorable stories in the *New York Times* (Batista felt sure that Herbert Matthews of the *Times* was in the pay of Castro).

False expectations, it must be added, have sometimes been encouraged by overzealous P.R. firms. On file at the Justice Department is a copy of a prospectus prepared by Max Rogel, Inc., soliciting the Nicaraguan account. It makes this claim: "We now have a comprehensive news service that makes it possible to flash a story or a photograph to every major daily newspaper in the United States. This story will come across the wire into the offices of these newspapers. It will be treated as a news story and will be received as such. . . . This is an operation that is very similar to the workings of the two major news services in the United States. It is, in actuality, a service extended to us by one of these two news services on an exclusive basis." What the prospectus apparently referred to was the PR Newswire in New York, which transmits releases around the city and which, of course, has no official connection with either AP or UPI.

A similar impression of accessibility to the heartbeat of the news system was contained in the Rogel proposal to the Korean government that the first step in its operations would be "to secure a newspaper person who could act as our leg man or stringer in Seoul. . . . This individual will be someone who is known in Seoul and approved by your government. He will be attached to one of the wire services." In a recent interview, Rogel's executive vice-president, Clyde Matthews, has stated that his firm never obtained such a wire-service stringer in Korea. But he pointed out that it is not out of keeping with P.R. practice. In Nicaragua, according to the firm's filings with the Justice Department, payments were made to one Leonardo Lacayo, who also serves as a UPI stringer in Managua as well as editor of the pro-government newspaper *Novedades*. Matthews estimates that half of the news stories that come out of Nicaragua are in one way or another the products of the firm's initiative.

SWEETNESS AND LIGHT

Naturally those who are in the business of creating favorable impressions about their clients are not apt to underestimate their own accomplishments. Many of the reputed feats of the P.R. men prove after investigation to be pretty trivial stuff, a conspicuous waste of a foreign government's money.

But it would be a mistake to think that P.R.'s foreign legion is ineffective. Perhaps the most dramatic example of what it can accomplish occurred in 1955, when the Cubans were faced with the imminent threat that their quota of sugar exports to the United States would be slashed in order to favor domestic producers. Forty-nine senators had gone on record for revising the Sugar Act ahead of its scheduled expiration at the end of 1956. In desperation, the Cuban sugar industry hired Samuel E. Stavisky, a Washington newspaperman turned public-relations counsel.

Stavisky, who has described what ensued in a document entitled "The Sweetest Story Ever Sold," launched a campaign that was responsible in large measure for thwarting Congressional action in 1955 and led the next year to a new and highly favorable quota for Cuban sugar that lasted until Castro upset everything. Stavisky estimates that "Effective public relations helped the Cuban sugar industry gain an extra million tons of sugar quota in the American market." It was, according to Stavisky, a P.R. job with a $100 million payoff for his client.

The operation was directed more at the press than at the politicians. Stavisky reasoned that he had a good but complex story to get across on a subject about which most reporters were notably ignorant. Liked and respected by his former colleagues, he gathered small groups of them for lunch at Washington's Colony Restaurant and discussed the political ramifications of sugar with an old newsman's sense for the interesting "story angle." With the help of a liberal expense account, he "encouraged" reporters to visit Cuba. Some were provided with travel subsidies when they couldn't make it on their own. One correspondent even charged off his gambling losses.

More important, Stavisky soon worked out a news angle that made the fate of Cuban sugar important local news all over the United States. Using an IBM punch-card breakdown of shipping invoices, he traced the origin of the more than $400 million in U.S. exports to Cuba the previous year by state, city, Congressional district, product, industry, and company. Soon a steady flow of stories began to appear in local papers around the country about the importance of the Cuban market to Texas oil, California beans, Arkansas rice, and Ohio lard. In the western tier of the North Central States, whose congressmen were generally hostile to sugar imports, it was discovered that 708 manufacturers had sold Cuba more than $22 million in 1953. This was considered news throughout that region.

A newsman's intimate connections on Capitol Hill served Stavisky in good stead. In early 1955, Stavisky relates, when Vice-President Nixon visited Cuba during a Caribbean tour he was briefed with a Stavisky memo and the Havana reporters were loaded with Stavisky-inspired questions for Nixon.

Publicity counterattacks against the domestic sugar interests were also part of the Stavisky operation. When Senator Ellender took two "experts" representing those interests into a closed Senate committee session, the fact was soon published in a Drew Pearson column that proclaimed, "Ellender Works for Sugar Lobby."

Stavisky measured his impact on newspapers in column-inches. His scrapbook is crammed with clippings from newspapers all over the country, many bearing a word-for-word identity with his press releases. Frequently they have omitted any mention of their origin.

WHO PICKS UP THE TAB?

In assessing the abuses that crop up, those involved in public relations often pass the blame to the press. One veteran P.R. man for a Central American client estimates that his firm "places" between a hundred and two hundred stories a week in the newspapers, often used verbatim and sometimes with a prominent reporter's by-line added. He finds that it is getting easier all the time to do the newsman's job for him. "From my point of view as a P.R. man, this is good," he remarks, "but from journalism's point of view it is not good. The number of reporters with time to dig beyond the surface facts seems to be getting smaller and smaller. We fill a vacuum in the flow of news."

He ascribes this condition in part to the economics of U.S. news coverage. Despite the hordes of reporters who congregate in Washington or accompany the President on his good-will missions, the ranks of American journalists covering the rest of the world are remarkably thin. By his estimate, nine-tenths of our news from the smaller foreign countries is handled by stringers who piece out their income with other jobs. The Associated Press claims that it services eighty countries, maintaining regular correspondents in more than fifty of them. In many places, at least until events reach a crisis point, news coverage is very much a hit-or-miss proposition.

In Cuba, for example, it turned out after the Castro revolution that the AP stringer at the Presidential Palace had been on Batista's payroll. The Dominican Republic long controlled stringers working for U.S. publications by its control over all domestic papers.

To get coverage for the countries they represent, both great and small, P.R. agencies frequently provide travel subsidies for the press. But many feel that the practice has been increasingly getting out of hand and has dubious benefits. Curtis Hoxter says he receives as many as ten calls a week from reporters looking for junkets. Among a dozen or so P.R. firms we interviewed, none had failed to get requests for travel subsidy or other gifts, ranging from a case of liquor on up, as incentives to do a "good" story.

Among reporters, whose income averages far less than that of their P.R. counterparts, there are no generally agreed-upon ethics about these practices. Free-lancers particularly, having no guarantee that their articles will be bought, accept it as part of the game. The Society of Magazine Writers does not include in its Code of Ethics and Good Practices anything on the subject of accepting or labeling such financial assistance. James Doyle, who wrote a story for North American Newspaper Alliance after a week's trip to Nicaragua last August, paid for by the P.R. firm of Max Rogel, argues: "You are not deceiving editors. They know somebody pays your way. But no good reporter is going to be seduced by room, board, or an airplane ride." Doyle claims that for "marginal" stories like Nicaragua, its government must pay the freight or nobody will go. "After all, who gives a damn about Nicaragua?"

Neither Doyle nor John McBride, Latin-American columnist for the New York *Mirror,* who also went on the Nicaraguan junket, believes it would be appropriate to state who paid for such trips in published copy. "When you do something like that," McBride says, "it takes away from your writing no matter what you say. It would hurt if readers knew the paper wouldn't send you down but the Nicaraguan government would."

Economics plays an even bigger role in the newsreel business. Placing films seems to be a nearly sure-shot proposition for the knowledgeable P.R. man. The firm of Hamilton Wright, for example, has some of the finest camera crews and equipment in the business. One of its typical contracts, drawn up with the government of Chile, provides that newsreels with commentary will be prepared and delivered free of charge to Fox Movietone, MGM Newsreel, Paramount, Warner Pathé, and Universal International: "This organization guarantees that five or more of the above newsreels shall be accepted and shown by at least one of the above-mentioned companies throughout its entire chain of theaters in the United States." Much the same guarantee has been made to Nationalist China.

According to Hamilton Wright, Jr., such a guarantee is "based on past experience." The normal procedure in placing a newsreel for a client is to prepare seven hundred feet on a subject and supply an informational sheet that will permit the editors to edit it for themselves. Last spring for example, the firm offered footage on the Formosan elections that Fox Movietone used in its regular newsreels.

The documentary "Fortress Formosa" was turned over to Twentieth Century-Fox with a grant of full ownership rights for a five-year period. But Wright minimizes the propaganda value of these efforts. "For theatrical distribution, they must be subtle," he declared. "They cannot have much political content."

He was seconded on this point by John Kuhne, a veteran documentary producer for Twentieth Century-Fox, who claims that he turns down most film submissions even though they are free. The ones he accepts, like "Fortress Formosa," are picked solely for their entertainment value. He rejects the suggestion that the source of such films might be clearly labeled: "It would look like a direct propaganda bit." He points out that Twentieth Century-Fox does not label the Defense Department films that are supplied regularly to all major distributors.

Jerome Kahn, assistant news editor of Twentieth Century-Fox, has said he will incorporate P.R. film in his newsreels only when it contains a legitimate news story. There have been times, he claims, when Hamilton Wright has had the only footage of areas Chiang bars to regular photographers. He doesn't object to having a P.R. outfit handle the Dominican Republic because this is the only way to get films. The newsreel company simply can't afford to send its own crew.

Among P.R. firms, there is general agreement that the theater newsreel is in a declining state and pretty well forced to live on handouts. Even those who do this handing out sometimes feel the pinch. An executive at Harold Oram, Inc., which handles the account of South Vietnam for an annual fee of a mere $38,000, has said, "You never see a film on Vietnam in your theaters because we don't have the money to make it."

Television networks generally keep a sharp eye out for attempts at infiltration by P.R. operators. "They try to use us," said Piers Anderton of NBC News, who handles the Huntley-Brinkley newscasts, "but we use them." He will accept footage but not the accompanying scripts. In reference to the film clip of Chiang's forces that was shown on "Today" right after the Nixon-Kennedy debate over Quemoy, Bill Fitzgerald, news director for the program, points out that it was only a brief sequence and that it had been stored for some time in the NBC film library. He does not feel that the network was under any obligation to identify those who originally provided the film. "They are satisfied with the exposure. There is no prerequisite to mention their name." What about responsibility to the public? "I don't think the public is too interested in knowing," Fitzgerald said.

By far the most fertile field for the planting of P.R. film has been in direct submission to independent television stations. It has, in fact, become such an active market that there are now a number of middlemen who specialize in distributing free films being offered for television use. These distributors are paid for each showing, not by the station but by the supplier of the film.

One of the biggest of these distributors, Sterling Movies U.S.A., Inc., puts out quarterly a fat catalogue of offerings that have been prepared to fill half- and quarter-hour time slots in a TV station's schedule. The catalogue usually makes no mention of who has paid for the production of these films. It is obvious that many are veiled advertisements for tourist resorts or industrial sponsors. In its foreign listings, the Spring 1960 catalogue listed eight films on Algeria ("The background story on this critical area in world affairs. . . . Enlightening information on the movement toward nationalism"), four on the Sahara, two on Morocco, three on Tunisia, one of Turkey, and six on South Africa "Points up similarities between U.S. and South African history"). On investigation, it turned out that several of the Algerian films had actually been paid for by the French government, which then hired New York producers to edit them, dub in English voices, and pay for the distribution. Essentially the same procedure is known to have been followed by South Africa and governments of several of the other countries involved.

"Public advocacy" by a foreign country's diplomats, argues the Ghana memorandum prepared by Harold L. Oram, Inc., is generally regarded as "improper interference in the internal affairs of the United States" and "a highly ineffective method to convert or persuade the American public . . ." Therefore, the memorandum goes on, "One of the cardinal rules of effective public relations, particularly in the political sphere, is to remove the source of the ideas (in this case the Government of Ghana or its representatives) as far as possible from the advocates (whether they be private individuals, organizations or media)."

THE DIM SPOTLIGHT

Oram may be right. But one trouble with his argument is that it does not entirely square with the terms of the Foreign Agents Registration Act of 1938, amended in 1942, which specify that a public-relations agent employed by a foreign government is required, after registering with the Justice Department, to make full disclosure of activities and expenditures and to label all communications intended to influence "any section of the public . . . with reference to the political or public interests, policies, or relations of a government of a foreign country . . ." The act grew out of Congressional concern over Nazi propaganda agents in this country. "Resting on the fundamental Constitutional principle," according to an interpretation by Justice Hugo Black, "that our people adequately informed may be trusted to distinguish between the true and the false, the bill is intended to label information of foreign origin so the hearers and readers may not be deceived by the belief that the information comes from a disinterested source." The chairman of the House Judiciary Committee, Representative Emanuel Celler, who helped draft the law, counted on fighting fire with fire by using "the spotlight of pitiless publicity" to expose foreign propaganda.

But the law has had a hard time keeping up with expanding P.R. activities in the postwar period. Nathan B. Lenvin, chief of the Justice Department's registration section, is quite confident "that the vast majority who come within the purview of the statute have registered." Over its twenty-two-year history, there have been twenty-three prosecutions for failure to do so and twenty-one convictions.

But the spotlight in which Congress placed its trust has certainly been less than pitiless. Few people come to look at the files in Lenvin's outer office, and few of the documents give the kind of details that Congress ordered. Many of the reports filed there make only the barest statement about expenditure or activities in behalf of foreign clients. Some P.R. agents who submitted fuller details in former years have dropped the practice. (One, who admits that his reports are not very lengthy, says frankly that he has no intention of telling his competitors what he is doing.)

The act's most neglected provision has been the requirement to label the source of political information. Time and again in our investigations we came across what appeared to be clear violations. But the Justice Department has never brought a test case in this area. No one is certain, for example, how precisely a distributor or a television station is supposed to identify films prepared by foreign agents. The Federal Communications Commission has also failed to explore this field despite its regulation that "a station disclose to its audience exactly who is paying for or furnishing the broadcast material . . . (on) political matters or controversial issues of public importance."

The FCC's own precedents governing domestic P.R. would seem to be pertinent. In 1958, the commission censured Westinghouse Broadcasting for failing to label film used on a news program that had been provided free of charge by the National Association of Manufacturers. Such a practice, the FCC held, required "the highest degree of diligence on the part of the licensee . . . in ascertaining . . . the actual source . . . and identifying this source plainly to the viewing audience."

Perhaps the law is too cumbersome to cope with the way some news finds its path to the public nowadays; foreign agent to producer to distributor to middlemen to media representative. Frequently, it is a difficult matter to determine the origin of something that finally appears in print or on the screen. And it could quickly become a rather absurd pursuit if the Justice Department were to try to monitor all the stages of this very broad enterprise. Too much that passes for high-powered P.R. work is too picayune to matter.

In the long run, the responsibility for keeping the communications channels open and working properly must be borne primarily by those engaged in the business of communication. It is up to those who control the spotlight of publicity to see that it is bright enough and properly focused. The press and other media surely ought not to pass along cheap propaganda simply because they haven't the time or the cash to check stories for themselves. Ultimately, it is not just a matter of economics but even more one of ethics.

There are no cut-and-dried rules to be laid down in this game. A reporter or a broadcaster would be a fool to chuck pertinent information in the wastebasket simply because it came to him from a P.R. source. Foreign P.R., as practiced by reputable private firms as well as official government information agencies, has done a great deal to break down the barriers of isolation and lack of interest that once kept our public opinion aloof and ill informed.

But the press must apply its criteria of selection very carefully in an area of communication that vitally affects our understanding of what is going on in the rest of the world—and of what we are asked to do about it.

A SENATOR LOOKS AT THE LOBBIES
Eugene J. McCarthy

Eugene J. McCarthy has served as Democratic Senator from Minnesota since 1959. He is the author of *Frontiers of American Democracy.*

The word "lobbying" has a derogatory ring. This is not surprising for good or bad lobbying occurs in the processes of democracy at the point of rough transition where interests conflict and judicial processes fall short. Lobbying is a test—sometimes a raw test—of the judgment and integrity of political officeholders, both elected and appointed.

Who are the lobbyists? What do they do in order to affect the course of government? How effective are they? Is lobbying a threat to democracy? Do government officials need more protection from lobbyists? What can or should be done about lobbying? It is important that these questions be asked and that an attempt be made to answer them.

This has been a most active year for lobbyists in Washington. They were drawn especially by the tax bill, the Trade Expansion Act, the medical insurance program and by the Sugar Act.

The activities of lobbyists on the Sugar Act, which involves foreign countries, have moved the Senate Foreign Relations Committee to make a special study of lobbying—or, as the committee described it, of "non-diplomatic activities of representatives of foreign governments or their agents in promoting the interests of those governments." Investigation or inquiry into the operation of lobbyists in other fields has been suggested by some members of Congress.

By statute, the lobbyist today is any person who solicits money or anything of value to be used principally to secure or influence the passage or defeat of any legislation by the Congress of the United States.

Lobbying has a long history. The word "lobby" appeared first in the English language about the middle of the sixteenth century. It was derived from the medieval Latin word *lobium,* a monastic walk or cloister.

Three hundred years later the word was in politics. It was used both to identify a hall or corridor in the British House of Commons and as a collective noun applied to all those who frequented these lobbies. It covered those who sought to influence men in office as well as newspaper men and others looking for news and gossip.

Today the word "lobbyist" is used both in its narrow legal sense and, more broadly, as a description of all attempts to influence not only the legislators, but also any agency or officer of government. Registered lobbyists in

Washington number approximately 1,100, but the number of persons and agencies involved in efforts to influence the Government is much greater.

Some lobbyists represent big interests and well organized groups. The Chamber of Commerce and the National Association of Manufacturers have registered lobbyists along with the A.F.L.-C.I.O.; so do the American Petroleum Institute, the Association of American Railroads, and nearly all major industrial and financial interests. The so-called "little people" and the unorganized or less organized also have lobbyists. For example, the American Committee for Flags of Necessity, the Hualapai Reservation, and the Arthritis and Rheumatism Foundation are among those groups or organizations represented by lobbyists.

Some lobbyists are well paid; some get little more than expense money. Some operate directly on government officials, others primarily by indirection through appeals to constituents or voters. Some are professional, others amateur. Some lobbyists represent only one position or program, while others are available as free lancers on an issue-by-issue or client-by-client basis.

Some lobbyists are quite open—they seek their own gain, the protection of an economic advantage, or the elimination or reduction of advantages held by their competitors. These cry more often for equity than they do for justice. Others speak for the arts, for morality, for aid to the sick and for the oppressed among the family of man.

What do lobbyists do in order to affect government decisions?

The methods used by the lobbyists are almost as varied as their causes. Some appeal on a purely personal basis, as friend to friend. Some undoubtedly use monetary or material appeals, but there is little evidence of direct pay-off in lobbying activities affecting the Congress. In some fourteen years of membership in the Congress, I know of no case in which a member was moved to support or to oppose a position in response to any kind of direct financial or material reward. The indirect influence of campaign contributions is more difficult to assess but it is, I believe, more important.

The most common method of lobbying is that of simply appearing before a committee of Congress or speaking to individual members in an attempt to bring them to understand one's position or to influence them to support that position.

How effective are the lobbyists?

Some are wholly ineffective but take credit for what happens without, in fact, having in any way influenced events.

Among the regular lobbies, the postal employes' organizations are usually very active and, whenever postal pay legislation is before Congress, they are listed at or near the top in terms of total expenditures. In order to raise wages or to change working conditions significantly, the spokesmen for the postal workers of the country must influence either the Congress or the Administration—or both—for Government employe unions are not recognized and dealt with in the same way as other labor unions are by private employers. There is little doubt that the existence of this Washington lobby has influenced the Congress and successive Administrations to raise salaries and to improve working conditions not only for postal employes, but for all Government workers.

The major farm organizations in the country maintain regular lobbies in Washington. The American Farm Bureau Federation and the National Farmers Union usually take opposite sides on farm legislation. The apparent success of the two organizations parallels closely the success of the two major political parties. The Farmers Union position is favored when the Democrats are in power, and the Farm Bureau position when the Republicans are in power.

One of the most interesting and continuing lobbying efforts of recent years has been that in support of a bill which is known as H.R. 10. This bill proposes to change existing income tax laws to allow members of professions and other self-employed persons a limited income tax credit on money invested in private pension or retirement programs. Starting almost from scratch, the supporters of this legislation have secured the approval of the House of Representatives and of the Senate Finance Committee. Victory in this case—if it comes—must be credited in great measure to the efforts of a lobby registered as the American Thrift Assembly, a kind of holding company or organizing lobby, which was supported in testimony by the U. S. Chamber of Commerce, the National Association of Manufacturers, the Farm Bureau, the American Medical Association and others.

In this session of Congress, lobbies have been most active in four major areas: taxes, trade and tariffs, medical aid for the aged and extension of the Sugar Act. Undoubtedly the lobbyists did have or will have some effect on action in each of these areas.

Any significant change in tax laws attracts the attention of those who may be affected. The changes being considered this year were significant and controversial and the lobbying effort extensive.

THE BIG ONES

As reported, according to law, to the Clerk of the House of Representatives and the Secretary of the Senate, the ten biggest-spending lobbies in Washington in 1961 were:

American Medical Association	$163,405
A.F.L.-C.I.O.	139,919
American Farm Bureau Federation	111,364
American Legion	103,566
U.S. Savings and Loan League	101,801
National Committee for Insurance Taxation	90,058
National Farmers Union	88,273
National Housing Conference	88,141
American Trucking Associations, Inc.	84,986
International Brotherhood of Teamsters	81,918

Industries likely to be affected by trade and tariff policies are always well represented in Washington. Whenever an issue even remotely bearing upon trade is brought up for consideration, the representatives of these industries seek permission to testify. The hearings on the President's new tariff and trade program have attracted them in great numbers. Members of the House Ways and Means Committee and the Senate Finance Committee, which ordinarily hold trade and tariff hearings, are generally familiar with the testimony of these witnesses. They have been described as somewhat like professional soldiers who regularly go to battle, seldom win wars and suffer few casualties.

One of the most active Washington lobbies this year, and through the years, is that of the American Medical Association—better known in Washington for what it is against than for what it is for. The spokesmen for the A.M.A. have effectively opposed the inclusion of doctors in the Social Security retirement program. They were strongly opposed to amending the Social Security Law to provide for the payment of Social Security pensions to people who are permanently or totally disabled after they pass the age of 50. And in the present session of Congress, the A.M.A. lobby led the opposition to the establishment of a medical insurance program for the aged as a part of the Social Security program. Action in this Congressional session has been a real test of the power of the A.M.A. lobby.

Lobbying activities with reference to the Sugar Act revision this year involved lobbyists in greater numbers than ever in the past, and the lobbying activities were more intensive. At least twenty-two lobbyists testified before Congressional committees in behalf of the countries they represented. The list of lobbyists included former members of both the Eisenhower and Truman Administrations, Washington lawyers, and public relations men. Their agreements with their principals varied from flat fees to contingency agreements, depending upon the action taken by Congress.

The massive lobbying activity this year arose from the fact that the Administration recommended that the Cuban sugar quota of some three million tons, withdrawn from Cuba because of Castro, be purchased in the world market at something like 2.8 cents a pound rather than on a quota basis from designated countries at traditional premium prices. At the premium price the supplying country would receive approximately $54 a ton more than it would receive at world prices. The Administration's counterproposal was an open, almost demanding invitation to every sugar-producing country interested in getting a share of the premium market to seek representation. Most of them did.

We now come to the basic question: Is lobbying a threat to democracy?

The effects of lobbying can be good or bad, helpful or harmful to democracy, depending upon two things: the purposes or objectives of the lobbying effort, and the methods or devices by which the lobby seeks to accomplish its objectives.

There are some who take the extreme view that lobbies are by their very nature power blocs and therefore inconsistent with democratic government;

that since lobbies represent special or limited interests, their objectives are of necessity not directed to the general welfare and, therefore, they should be abolished.

There are some who see nothing wrong with lobbies except when they represent economic interests.

There are some who hold that the dangers in lobbying arise from secrecy and behind-the-scenes operations and from the amount of money that may be spent by lobbyists.

There are regular demands that more publicity be given to lobbying activities, that lobbying be more closely regulated, and that the amount of money which can be spent by a lobbyist or lobbying groups be limited and fully reported.

Positively, the activity of lobbyists is often very helpful. Lobbyists can help maintain a balance between Congress and the Executive Branch of the Government. The Executive Branch has a prepared case, usually sustained by expert witnesses. The Congress can offer in opposition the knowledge and experience of its own members and that of the Committee staff or Congressional assistants. Often this is an unfair contest. The expert testimony of lobbyists or witnesses from outside may help to bring the contest closer to balance.

Congress, of course, does not depend entirely upon lobbyists for its information. It is the usual practice to call upon governmental experts and also on independent experts drawn from groups directly affected by the legislation under consideration or from related fields and from the academic profession.

For example, in special hearings on unemployment in 1959, invitations to testify were sent to these organizations: the National Association of Manufacturers, the U. S. Chamber of Commerce, the National Coal Policy Conference, the A.F.L.-C.I.O., the United Mine Workers, the National Small Businessmen's Association, the Railway Labor Executives Association and others. Representatives of the U. S. Departments of Labor, Commerce, and Defense were called. Leading labor economists were asked to submit papers, to testify, and to meet with the members of the committee. Hearings were also held in the field. These hearings were open to the testimony of anyone who wished to speak on the subject.

Apart from laws and regulations, there are some built-in protections against the power and influence of lobbyists. One safeguard is that usually there are organized lobbies on both sides of controversial issues: protectionists on the one hand versus free-traders on the other; the A.F.L.-C.I.O. opposed by the National Association of Manufacturers; growers' associations against those seeking to improve working conditions of migratory farm workers; anti-vivisectionists against those who favor medical experimentation with animals.

Sometimes the opposition is not direct but involves competition for a larger share of a quota or a subsidy, or for greater participation in advantageous tax concessions.

Political party positions and programs, too, tend to eliminate large areas of political action from the influence of lobbyists. The political campaign in the United States is a rather severe testing. Most of the important national issues are raised during political campaigns, and most men who are elected to office have made firm commitments on most issues.

The President of the United States is called to account and judged by the people every four years; members of the United States Senate must run for re-election every six years, members of the House of Representatives every two years.

The activities of members of Congress are watched closely by colleagues, particularly by those of the opposite party. They are watched by newspaper men whose reputations in many cases are based upon their ability to ferret out and report any action and conduct unbecoming Government officials.

In addition, of course, everyone who holds office must assume that there are at least two or three people—perhaps in his own party and certainly in the opposition party—who are quite willing to replace him and consequently are likely to give more than ordinary attention to his conduct in public office.

What can or should be done about lobbying?

Members of Congress cannot be fully protected from lobbyists by regulation. They cannot be expected to keep a check list of registered lobbyists or demand proof of registration or defense of non-registration before responding to a request for conversation or for a conference. Yet, members of Congress and other Government officials can be given some protection by law.

The present lobbying registration act should be fully enforced, and financial reporting should be checked carefully. Fees contingent on successful lobbying should be outlawed. Care should be taken to remove from direct legislative determination those questions which should be settled by other branches of government: by the President, by special commissions, by departments and agencies of government or by international agreement.

Much of the agitation over the Sugar Act could have been prevented if the Administration, acting directly or possibly in cooperation with the Organization of American States or the signatories to the International Sugar Agreement had determined the way in which the Cuban sugar quota was to be allocated. There would have been some Congressional protest, since in a broad way Congress has determined sugar allocations since the Sugar Act was passed in 1934. But the protest would have been limited and the compromises so minor that extensive lobbying activities, brought on when the whole question of re-allocation was left open by the Administration, would have been discouraged.

Better salaries for Government officials and sounder methods of financing campaigns would also lessen the likelihood of undue financial influence on public officials by lobbyists and others.

There is always the risk that public officials may be unduly subject to outside influence. But it is hard to imagine a meeting of a national legislature today that could or should be insulated from public pressure or demand. The practice of some primitive tribes, in which the wise men or elders withdrew from society periodically to consider laws and practices, is not likely to be revived.

The whole concept that lobbying opposes the majority, that it seeks to manipulate and subvert the majority will and the public interest, is unrealistic. Lobbyists seldom manufacture a problem. They call attention to an existing problem and try to guide the course of events. Action in Washington sometimes supports the judgment of J. B. S. Hardman, the philosopher and intellectual mentor of industrial trade unionism in America: "Majorities never rule, they merely give credentials to contending minorities."

Although lobbying does not usually involve a physical assembly—such as the 1932 veterans bonus march on Washington or current picketing of the White House—it does involve organization, a bringing together of citizens seeking a common objective. Thus, the act of lobbying is basically an exercise of the right to petition the Government—a right set forth in the Constitution. Lobbying also involves, in a way, the exercise of the right of assembly.

In a democratic society there must be a point at which influences, both good and bad, are brought to bear upon government. The point at which these influences meet finally is in the elected and appointed officials of the country. They are supposed to be men skilled and experienced in politics and possessing the character to withstand improper pressures and improper demands.

Until a clear case can be made against the lobbyist, his voice should be heard in Washington. But his voice must be identified and, insofar as possible, restricted to that influence which is justified by the facts and the conclusions to be drawn from those facts.

6 THE CONGRESS AT WORK

What are the attitudes of most Americans toward their national legislative body?

For the most part, popular attitudes reflect the negative, hostile treatment of the Congress by the press, which has tended to emphasize the errors, shortcomings, and wrongdoings and to ignore the positive accomplishments. Many Americans view their congressmen and senators as little more than "party hacks," "errand boys on missions of trivia," or compromisers who are all too willing to jettison principles for the sake of political expediency. They often think of their representatives as wasters—wasters of time, in such fruitless activities as filibustering, or as wasters of money on "junkets" that are invariably reported as heading for Hawaii in the winter or Alaska in the summer. In another vein, no less hostile, the public has viewed its representatives, through the eyes of the press, as lacking in leadership, deficient in initiative, unrepresentative of the popular will (whatever that may be), mere rubber stamps for presidential legislation, and far too responsive to pressure groups.

In order to make a fair appraisal of the Congress, however, we must establish more definite criteria than these popular impressions afford. Several questions are pertinent. For example: Is the Congress truly representative? Is it responsible? Is it democratic? Does it operate in the public interest? That is, does it understand that "what's good for General Motors" may *not* necessarily be good for the United States? Is it constructively critical?

These questions suggest a conclusion that has become increasingly apparent to observers of the Washington scene—namely, that we expect far more of Congress than mere legislating. Thus, it is necessary to clarify the functions of Congress before we may pass judgment on the way Congress performs.

Two of its four leading functions have involved substantial changes since the Constitution was written; the other two have evolved more nearly as planned. First, in enacting legislation, Congress now has a *screening* rather than an originating role; it regularly reviews, but it seldom creates major public policy.

Second, the function of *popular representation* has also undergone a subtle mutation: congressmen today, in a very real sense, *must* be the errand boys for the American public, since some public body must provide popular checks on an administration grown so necessarily large. How else may bureaucracy be kept responsive to the desires of the people that it serves?

A third valuable function of Congress is *compromise*. Despite its negative aspects, compromise is a vital part of the democratic process; for its alternatives, suppression or surrender, are generally unacceptable to thoughtful persons everywhere.

Finally, the Congress has the major task of *informing and educating* the American public. Not only is it charged with reflecting public opinion; it must lead and create that opinion, as well as discover what public opinion is.

With these functions in mind, what elements are essential to an understanding of our Senate and our House of Representatives? First is the changing nature of the American representative system. Contrary to the expectations of the Founding Fathers, the Senate has emerged as the voice of the nation—despite its states'-rights intonations and its occasional southern accents. On the other hand, the House, created as the popular spokesman, has emerged as a more provincial body, far more subject than the Senate to the importunings of local pressures.

The second essential element, the lack of strong party leadership, reflects the shortcomings of our national political organizations. While the nation has been centralizing its federal system for more than 175 years, the political parties have remained much as they were a century and a half ago—county-oriented groups far more interested in getting their henchmen elected to local offices than in the subtleties of national policies. Lacking in discipline and more concerned with candidates than with issues, the parties have frequently been irresponsible in their behavior, and since the Civil War they have been guilty of mislabeling—with Northern liberals retained for nearly a century in a predominantly conservative G.O.P., and with Whig-type Southern conservatives still to be found among progressive Democratic ranks.

The third element is personality—the personality of the House Speaker, the personality of the Senate Majority Leader, and the personalities of the key committee chairmen. Here one encounters the seniority system, with its negative impact on party legislative programs. One finds the House Rules Committee—that "traffic cop of legislation," which, for the Democratic Party at least, has proved more of a road block than a traffic regulator, seldom signaling a green light without exacting an undue toll of concessions. There are other committees: the standing committees, with virtual life-or-death powers over proposed legislation; and the conference committees, those "third houses" of the Congress with powers to mold the final shapes of laws. These are some of the elements at work in the nation's Capitol—elements which, despite extensive press coverage, are too little understood by the public as it views the legislative branch of our government in action.

PORTRAIT OF A "TYPICAL" CONGRESSMAN
David S. Broder

David S. Broder, a political reporter for the *Washington Star,* regularly observes congressmen at work on and off Capitol Hill.

If Congress is, as its critics say, a sickly institution, then those who run for Congress presumably have no objections to catching some sort of Capitol fever. About 900 of our fellow citizens are seeking the 435 House and 39 Senate seats available this November—a record number. And for what? For the honor of serving in a body whose reputation with its critics has rarely been lower?

In order to know what lures these men and women to Congressional service—why an institution that has been pronounced a failure by its critics should exert such magnetism across the land—we must understand the nature of the office itself.

What is a Congressman, really? Is he legislator or errand boy, an ambassador from his state or district or an officer of the national Government? By what standards should he be judged? The chances are these questions will be raised in few of the current campaigns. And yet one cannot shake the suspicion that they are overdue for discussion.

The burden of this article is that the Congressman is a most misunderstood creature. He is not one man, as the critics would have it, but three. He is a legislator for the nation; he is a mediator between his district and the central Government; and he is a teacher of his people. His performance in his three roles varies. In the first, he is adequate; in the second, excellent, and in the third, deficient.

But before pulling him apart this way, let us see him whole, as he is in life.

The typical Congressman is an unbashful, churchgoing fellow of 52, a veteran and a college graduate. He has made his living as a lawyer or businessman and has learned something of the management of human affairs. He also has behind him some years in public office—as a prosecutor perhaps, or as a mayor or a state assemblyman. He is, in all likelihood, a man of above-average sensitivity, stamina, ambition and acumen.

This bears importantly on the Congressman's performance in his first role, as a national legislator. The critics of Congress sometimes talk as though ignorance, indifference and inertia are so inbred in Senators and Representatives that they are literally incapable of writing good legislation.

The contrary seems closer to the truth. Most Congressmen are far ahead of their constituencies, both in sensing national problems as they arise and in understanding the strengths and weaknesses of proposed solutions. It is not just accident that the average Congressman is better informed than almost any of his voters. He has to be, for in the Washington arena knowledge is power, whether the struggle concerns the tax code, the merits of rival weapons systems or the mechanisms of the farm program.

Because he is a decision maker, the Congressman is the beneficiary of a constant flow of information and instruction from committee staff members, from his colleagues, from the Administration and from representatives of interest groups. Even the dullest Senator or Representative cannot fail to learn something from this process and most of them learn a great deal more than a little.

Is the problem, then, that the mechanism of Congress will not enable its members to put their knowledge to work? Lately, it has become fashionable to suggest that this is the answer. The seniority system must be abolished, it is said. Committees must be curbed, or perhaps strengthened. Debate must be curtailed, or perhaps extended. The leadership must be broadened, or made more responsive, or something.

The pertinent point about these criticisms is not that they are irrelevant but that they are not new. The conflict-of-interest problem, so much discussed recently, was not unfamiliar to Daniel Webster. The struggle between the party leadership in each house and the committee chairmen is routine, not novel. Congress operates now very much as it has throughout its history.

What has changed is the amount of time, energy and brains Congressmen can devote to the tasks of devising legislation and overcoming the built-in obstacles to its enactment. The main reason, I suggest, that Congress does not legislate better is simply that most Congressmen can no longer afford to regard legislation as the most important part of their jobs.

Indeed, many of them find it very difficult to sandwich legislative work into the busy schedule of what they describe—correctly—as their more important functions. These functions relate to their second role, as mediators between their districts and the central Government, and we will examine in a moment why the burdens they carry in this area have increased so in recent years.

But first it is important to understand that the conflict between the Congressman as national legislator and the Congressman as agent for his district is not just a theoretical struggle.

The practical problem the Congressman faces is well described by Representative Clem Miller, a California Democrat, in his revealing little book about the realities of Congressional life, just published under the title, "Member of the House."

In one of the letters comprising the volume, he explains to his friends at home that most of the vital decisions on the floor of the House are made on teller votes, with the opponents and supporters of the bill or amendment passing up the aisle between counters to indicate their stand. Mr. Miller reports, accurately, that "at least 150 members can be counted on to be absent from any teller vote."

"What is it that happens to these members of Congress?" he asks. "Presumably they were elected for this very task above all others: to be in the chamber, to vote.

"The fact is that this objective is blurred with time and circumstance. . . . What is of overriding significance gives way to what is immediate. The competing interests, the endless details of Congressional routine, take hold.

"Members are called to the floor . . . as the afternoon's debate begins . . . Most stay for a while listening and chatting. Then, inevitably, the drift begins. Pages hurry up and down the aisles with sheaves of messages . . .

"Gradually . . . (the Congressman) is caught up in the inescapable workaday world of Congress. Almost without volition, he finds himself back in his office, trying to keep up with the mail, interviewing and being interviewed by streams of callers. Now he is too far away to get back to the floor for a teller vote.

"Once away from the chamber, he is far away. The urgency, the insistence, is gone. A million words of testimony, the results of a thousand patient meetings may be going down the drain. But it is another world from the Congressional office."

The conflict between these two worlds has another dimension, because it is also a conflict between pleasure and duty. Most Congressmen find the pleasures of their work lie mainly in the legislative world, in the personal relationships between competitors and cohorts in the Insiders' World of Washington Influentials, a world where strength and shrewdness, wit and will are savored as much as wealth in Dallas.

But pleasurable as his life in the Insiders' World may be for the Congressman, his job security and his political future depend chiefly on how well he serves the residents of the Outsiders' World—the people of his state or district. Cultivating his relationship with them must be given first priority, no matter what his personal tastes dictate and no matter what the critics of Congress may think.

The plain fact is that a man's legislative work is commonly a matter of indifference—if not outright suspicion—for his constituents. What can hurt politically is the charge that he has failed to look after his district. Neglect of correspondence, of constituent services or of vital local needs lies behind the defeat of a vast majority of those few in Congress who fall of re-election.

No wonder, then, that the first move of distinguished chairman of the Senate Foreign Relations Committee, Senator J. W. Fulbright, made in preparation for his current campaign in Arkansas was to turn over leadership of his committee for the year to the next-senior Democrat, Senator John Sparkman of Alabama (whose term does not expire until 1967). Rice, cotton and flood control projects are safer concerns for a man seeking re-election than U.N. bonds or foreign aid.

There is no sense mourning the fact that the Congressman's constituent-service role is interfering ever increasingly with his work as a legislator. It is the inevitable result of the changes that have taken place in our society and Government in the past 175 years.

The Founding Fathers knew the conflict would exist, but they misjudged the dimensions of the problem. In Federalist Paper No. 56, Madison recognized that the Congressman "ought to be acquainted with the interests and circumstances of his constituents." But in a simple society under a government of limited powers, this requirement, he believed, could easily be met.

"This principle," he argued, "can extend no farther than to those circumstances and interests to which the authority and care of the Representative relate. An ignorance of a variety of minute and particular objects, which do not lie within the compass of legislation, is consistent with every attribute necessary to a due performance of the legislative trust."

The increase in our population, the growing complexity of our economy and the proliferation of government functions have made it far more burdensome than Madison ever dreamed for the Congressman to define and defend "the interests and circumstances of his constituents"—to serve as a mediator between them and their Government. This function is consistently undervalued by critics of Congress, particularly those who are Washington-based, who fail to comprehend the gulf between the constituencies and the capital.

To the average citizen preoccupied with his own affairs, the central Government is a remote colossus, incomprehensible, almost unapproachable, but not safely ignored. His link—his sole link—with it is his Congressman.

The Congressman must protect his district and its people from the mischance and mischief that almost inevitably accompany bureaucracy's rather rigid way of doing its work. He *must* do it, for his people have no one else to look to. Because the work is essential and unavoidable, most Congressmen have become very proficient at the task. And that is the main reason why, in recent elections, less than one incumbent in ten seeking re-election has been denied another term.

But the Congressman's position as the middleman between his district and the central Government imposes another duty on him—one which he meets less adequately. I refer now to his third major role—not as legislator, not as a broker, but as a teacher, an educator and a shaper of opinion back home.

To some it will seem strange to charge the Congressman with this responsibility. It has become customary to say that the President has the job of telling the people where the country stands and what it needs to do. He does. President Kennedy has been criticized for failing to do this sufficiently, and so were his predecessors. The inescapable fact is that all our Presidents for the last quarter-century have been preoccupied with foreign affairs. Most of their speeches have sought public understanding of our responsibilities in that area.

Domestic affairs have been left largely to Congress. If domestic needs are unmet—as many believe—the blame must rest on the Congressmen for failing to bring their people to an understanding of the programs required.

How can Congress do this job? One of the most effective devices is the public hearing. Look, for example, at the way in which the 1959–60 revision of the labor law came about. A Senate committee held a series of hearings that gave the public dramatic evidence of the extent of criminal infiltration into labor unions. Another committee drafted remedial legislation. The topic was discussed in the districts by virtually every member of Congress. Only in the final stages of the debate did the President join the dialogue, and then his intervention was a marginal influence. It was a Congressional project.

"The job of a Congressman," Representative Miller says in his book, "in major degree is communicating—making our political world understandable."

Congressmen communicate through their newsletters and radio and television reports to their districts; through the frequent speeches they make to civic and political groups at home; and through their innumerable conversations with individual constituents.

But how well do they communicate? Too often, I am afraid, the same Congressman who will tell a bureaucrat bluntly and honestly how a proposed policy would affect his constituents will equivocate and hesitate before giving his constituents the blunt truth about what can and cannot be done in the national interest.

Nothing is more important to our democracy than the kind of information our Congressmen spread. The operations of the representative system enable the vast majority of these men to stay in office as long as they wish. Do they use their time preparing their constituents to cope with the world as it is, or do they conceal the world from them? That is the crucial question about this year's election, as about every Congressional election.

Will the Midwestern conservative who is certain to be back for another term give his constituents the old line about balancing the budget first and then cutting taxes? Or will he help them try to understand that our present tax structure is keeping us from balancing the budget and achieving a lot of other economic goals as well?

Will the Eastern liberal from a safely gerrymandered district go back to his voters with the same shopworn promise about passing a massive aid-to-education bill? Or will he tell them what he knows to be true: that those sincerely interested in helping education must define the goals and limit the scope of the program much more strictly than they have in the past in order to meet the legitimate objections of those who, for a variety of reasons, fear the impact of massive Federal aid?

Too frequently in Washington one hears a Congressman say, "I understand the need for this, but my people back home don't, so I won't vote for it." That may be acceptable as an excuse on that particular day, but it ought to oblige that Congressman to spend a good many days helping his people grasp the situation as well as he does.

By way of summary, then, our scorecard on Congress looks something like this:

As the agent for his constituents in protecting their interests in Washington, the average Congressman does an excellent job. The role is a vital one from his district's point of view and, if the critics of Congress want to be fair, they should give him high marks for the quality of his performance in this field.

As a national legislator, the Congressman is at least adequate. Men will disagree on how many desirable bills are left unpassed, on how many bad ones become law, and on what provisions any particular measure should contain. But it seems fair to say that most of the bills Congress does approve are well-designed for their purpose, are drawn with some attention to the technical, legal and political niceties of the problem and generally emerge in a more satisfactory form than they began.

As a teacher of his people, the average Congressman leaves much to be desired. The gap between the reality of the situation the nation faces and the public's understanding of it seems to be growing, not shrinking. This trend must be reversed if our Government is going to remain both representative and effective.

By now it must be obvious why so many men and women this fall are seeking to gain or retain membership in Congress.

The power and the pleasures of a Congressman's job are unique in the structure of American public offices. He is a key member of the small world of Washington Influentials, sharing in the secrets and the satisfactions that attend the management of the world's most powerful nation.

He is also the protector of his people in their dealings with the central Government and, frequently, the dispensing angel through whom that Government lavishes its gifts upon the land. He is able, in other words, to perform a great many services of great importance for people who are of personal concern to him.

Finally, he is, or can be if he wishes, a great source of wisdom to his people—an influence upon their thinking and upon their lives.

Because he is all of these things, he is also a very busy man—so busy, often, that he cannot do any of these jobs as well as he would like.

The second-commonest remark on Capitol Hill is, "I don't know why I put up with this rat race." But the commonest is, "I don't know anything I would rather be doing."

THE SENATE ESTABLISHMENT
James McCartney

James McCartney is in the Washington Bureau of the *Chicago Daily News.*

Early this month, Senator Joseph Clark, the studious, liberal Democrat from Pennsylvania, astonished his fellow Senators by opening a speech with these words: "Mr. President, I desire to address the Senate on the subject of the Senate Establishment and how it operates." For, of course, the one subject that by unspoken rule is taboo in this most exclusive club in the world is the power structure of the club itself, or the impugning, no matter how indirectly, of the motivations of any of its members.

Senator Clark's remarkable speech deserves the closest attention of all those who tend to confuse the *forms* and the *substance* of democratic gov-

From *The Nation,* March 15, 1963. Reprinted by permission.

ernment. In sum, Clark charged that the Senate as a whole was a virtual prisoner of about twelve of its members—eight Democrats and four Republicans—who, by virtue of seniority and their alliances with essentially conservative interests, can direct legislation by rigging committees and by the control they can exert over the destinies of individual Senators. These dozen men constitute, in Senator Clark's phrase, the "Senate Establishment"—and its power became dramatically evident even as the Senator was attacking it.

A few days earlier, it had become apparent that the Establishment had seen fit to deprive a raft of liberal Senators of important committee assignments to which they were clearly entitled. Yet so great was the victims' fear of further punishment that not one of them had dared to complain publicly. Nor, with two exceptions, was this silence broken when Clark made his speech: only William Proxmire (D., Wis.) and Paul Douglas (D., Ill.) had the temerity to agree openly with their colleague from Pennsylvania.

Clark elaborated his thesis for three days, off and on. At no time did he attempt to list completely the members of the Establishment by name and rank. But some of his research aides, together with aides of other liberal Senators, have pieced together a reasonable version of the membership and made a number of illuminating points concerning this *ex-officio* "in-group."

For example, they say that Senate Majority Leader Mike Mansfield, theoretically the most powerful figure in the Senate, may not be a member, although he is often a spokesman for it. On the other hand, the Minority Leader, Everett Dirksen of Illinois, is definitely a member, even though he has only half as many Republicans to "lead" as Mansfield has Democrats. Moreover, two men who are not even Senators and who are almost unknown outside of Washington, are considered by some observers to be members: Robert Baker, secretary to the Democratic majority, and Mark Trice, who holds the comparable job for the Republicans.

Mr. Clark's description of the Senate Establishment at work began with a general summary of its significance and *modus operandi:*

> The Senate Establishment is almost the antithesis of democracy. It is not selected by any democratic process. It appears to be quite unresponsive to the caucuses of the two parties, be they Republican or Democratic.
>
> It is what might be called a self-perpetuating oligarchy with mild, but only mild, overtones of plutocracy. The way it operates is something like this:
>
> There are a number of states, most of them Democratic, but one or two of them Republican, which inevitably and always return to the U.S. Senate members of one party, and under a custom which has grown up over the years of following the rule of seniority in making committee assignments, and in connection with the distribution of other perquisites of Senate tenure, the result has been that those who have been here longest have become chairmen of committees.
>
> As such, they have exercised virtual control over the distribution of

> favors, includings committee assignments and other perquisites of office in the Senate and largely . . . determine who shall be selected to posts of leadership in this body.

The point is hardly new that conservatives, most of them Southerners with seniority, dominate the Senate, but Clark brought the mathematics of their power up to date. Of the Senate's hundred members, 67 today are Democrats and 33 are Republicans. Of the Democrats, 23 are from the South (the 11 states of the old confederacy plus Oklahoma and Arkansas). The hardcore Southerners, in other words, make up 34 per cent of the Democratic bloc. But on the vital Appropriations Committee, for example, they hold 50 per cent of the Democratic seats; on the Armed Services Committee, 42 per cent; of the important Foreign Relations Committee, 42 per cent; on the Democratic Steering Committee (which selects other committee members), 47 per cent.

In this session of Congress especially, no body is more important than the Senate Finance Committee, which will handle President Kennedy's top-priority legislative items—his tax-cut program as well as medicare. Thus a battle has been waged over the committee's composition, and the winners are now more than clear: the Southerners wind up with 6 out of the 11 Democratic members for a representation of 55 per cent.

Senator Clark had sought to get the committee enlarged in order to give the President's programs a better chance. The justification for his attempt was mathematical. There have been 11 Democrats and 6 Republicans on the committee and, according to Clark's theory, the Democrats—outnumbering the Republicans in the Senate by 2 to 1—should be entitled to at least a 2 to 1 ratio on the committee. He proposed that the ratio be 12 to 6 or 14 to 7, or any one of several other combinations which would have reflected the party balance of the Senate as a whole. But it was not to be. The Establishment was able not only to maintain the present inequitable ratio, but to deliver another blow at the liberals by appointing to the committee Senator Dirksen to replace the late Senator Robert Kerr (D., Okla.), oil man and frequent spokesman for business interests.

Senator Mansfield supported Clark's proposal. But by his own admission on the Senate floor, the Majority Leader could line up only 40 to 42 votes in favor. The point was that neither the Republicans nor the Southerners would "buy" the proposal, and Mansfield must have help from one group or the other or he gets nowhere, clearly exposing the deficiencies of the official and formal Democratic leadership's position.

Clark emphasized that a key instrument of the Establishment is the Democratic Steering Committee. In a careful analysis, he showed that 9 of its 15 members are Southerners and conservatives and only 6 might be called liberals, in spite of the fact that Democratic liberals actually outnumber conservatives in the Senate. Stated the Senator:

> I suggest in all candor that the Steering Committee does not fairly represent either the geography or the ideology of the Democratic members of

the Senate. . . . Whom does the Steering Committee of the Democratic Party represent? It represents the Democratic side of the Establishment.

And how does the Steering Committee wield its power? Clark produced an analysis of committee appointments in an effort to indicate possible motivations, although he refrained from drawing conclusions. His analysis suggested a relationship between votes by nonfreshman Senators on the filibuster issue and the degree to which the Democratic Senators received their requested committee assignments from the Steering Committee. Six of eight Senators who voted with the South on the issue got their first choice of committee; only one who voted against the South got his first choice—and that was the Majority Leader, who traditionally can go to any committee he wants.

The role of the Republicans in the Establishment should not be overlooked.

> The senior ranking members of the minority party are a part of the Establishment (said Clark) and they, in conference—usually informal, always friendly—with their colleagues on the other side of the aisle pretty well decide who is going to do what to whom. That is what is happening in the Senate today.

Who are the actual members of the Establishment? There is a considerable amount of friendly disagreement among Senate liberals on just how powerful a number of individuals are, but there is wide agreement on the key figures. The following list of eight Democrats and four Republicans is based largely on the judgment of Clark and his aides.

The most powerful figure of all is Senator Richard Russell (D., Ga.). Among the Democrats, the number two man is probably Senator Lister Hill, of Alabama. Other Democratic members are Senators George Smathers of Florida, the close personal friend of President Kennedy; Carl Hayden of Arizona, John McClellan of Arkansas, Allen Ellender of Louisiana, John Stennis of Mississippi, and, perhaps, Harry Byrd of Virginia (although his influence has declined with his advancing years).

Heading the GOP membership is Dirksen, whom Clark terms "the champion of the Republican Establishment." The other Republicans are Bourke Hickenlooper of Iowa, Norris Cotton of New Hampshire and, perhaps, Carl Curtis of Nebraska.

The significance of all this, as far as Clark is concerned, is what the Establishment has been doing to President Kennedy's programs. A large majority of Congressmen supported the Democratic platform adopted at the Los Angeles Convention in 1960—the platform on which President Kennedy won office. Then Clark added:

> We now stand at the beginning of the third session of what might be called a Kennedy Congress, but actually it is not a Kennedy Congress. . . . The principal reason . . . so far as the Senate is concerned, is, in my opinion, that we are operating under archaic, obsolete rules, customs, manners, procedures and traditions—and because the operation under those obsolete

> and archaic setups is controlled by this oligarchical Senate Establishment, a major part of the members of which, by and large, are opposed to the program of the President. . . .
>
> The two-thirds majority of the Democratic Senators who are Kennedy men, and therefore liberals, and therefore want to get the country moving again, and therefore believe in the inevitability of change, are represented sparsely, if at all, in the Senate Establishment.

Senator Paul Douglas noted:

> The Democratic Party wins its Presidential elections by the votes of the great industrial states. It wins those elections on platforms which are believed in by the voters and which pledge to carry out legislative programs which will be in the interest of the great masses of the American people; namely, the wage earners, the small farmers, the white-collar workers, the small businessmen, the housewives and the consumers.
>
> That is how we win our Presidential elections. Then the Congress convenes, and we are not able to pass any considerable portion of the program upon which we have gone to the country.
>
> We find that the machinery of the Senate, and I think largely of the House, is in the hands of those who fundamentally do not believe in the program by which the Presidential election was won and for which the great mass of voters in the country cast their ballots.

One may well ask: Why did Clark, after seven years of relative silence on the subject, decide that 1963 was the time to start talking publicly about the Establishment? The answer offers some encouragement to liberals, if not for this year, then for the future. For Clark's underlying motivation was the belief that the time is coming when the Establishment can be overthrown.

Clark's message to the liberals, in other words, is one of hope, in spite of many disappointments and disillusionments—some of them with the Kennedy Administration itself—in recent years. His theory is that the voters, beginning especially in the off-year Congressional elections of 1958, clearly expressed themselves as supporting an essentially liberal approach to legislation. Conservatives, however, by controlling Senate machinery, have seen to it that the wishes of the voters haven't been turned into legislation. Now, Clark believes, the conservative Establishment that runs the Senate is on the ropes, or at least close to it. The Establishment has already lost control of some committees and, inevitably, in the years to come, will lose control of more as the number of liberally inclined votes grows.

Watching the Senate in operation now, one hardly gets the impression that the liberals are about ready to take over. Liberals like Clark, Douglas, Proxmire, Albert Gore of Tennessee, Estes Kefauver of Tennessee, Wayne Morse of Oregon and Phil Hart of Michigan are clearly not members of the Establishment. Douglas, for example, in spite of the fact that there is a Democrat in the White House, clearly has less influence in the Senate than his fellow Senator from Illinois, Dirksen—even though Dirksen represents the party out of power. The White House recognized this all but formally last year when, over Douglas' strong objections, it gave a friend of Dirksen's an Illinois federal judgeship.

The fact is that some of the pragmatic operators on the White House staff —who have a tendency to value pure political muscle over principle—privately joke about some of the fruitless efforts of the liberals in Congress.

The White House group, for example, had a vast respect for the late Senator Kerr, a thoroughgoing pragmatist. And the White House tends to admire the work of such as the secretary to the majority, Robert Baker, a friend of Lyndon Johnson's. Asked why the White House seemed to like to deal with Baker more than with some of the Senate liberals, one Presidential aide put it bluntly: "He can count." The statement meant that Baker respected votes in the Senate—respected practical possibilities. The liberals, in the view of the White House, often waste their time tilting at windmills.

The underlying question posed by Senator Clark, then, is one that the White House itself might ponder. Clark is saying that the liberals actually have political muscle at the polls—where it counts in Presidential elections. They just haven't been able to defeat the powers of the Establishment in the Senate to put that muscle to work.

> We are playing (as Clark put it) with a stacked deck. The deck is stacked against the President of the United States and I want to shuffle that deck so that in the end the President of the United States will have his fair share of trumps and we can play the game with an honest deck of cards.

TO MOVE CONGRESS OUT OF ITS RUTS
Hubert H. Humphrey

Hubert H. Humphrey, Vice President of the United States, was formerly Democratic Senator from Minnesota. In addition to his role as majority whip, he served on four committees, including one on reorganization of government.

Sixteen years ago, the United States held a monopoly of atomic weapons. Jet aircraft were barely operational. The Space Age could be found only in science fiction magazines. Television was an eight-inch infant in electronics laboratories. The nation's elementary schools had classrooms to spare. The cold war could be seen on the horizon only by a handful of political wise men. Europe was near economic collapse, Africa was still a continent of colonies and Chiang Kai-shek still ruled the Chinese mainland. Cuba, to

From *The New York Times Magazine,* April 7, 1963.

most Americans, was a plush and pleasant vacation spot. And Fidel Castro was a teenager.

It was 16 years ago when the United States Congress last turned to the tedious task of self-criticism and produced a major legislative reform. Since the Legislative Reorganization Act of 1946, Congress has changed little. The structure is the same. The committee lineups are almost identical. The traditions are preserved. And the basic attitudes of Congress toward its own prerogatives and centers of power are still tuned to 1946 or the more distant past.

But the needs of the nation and the demands of Congress have multiplied. Since 1946 the nation's population has increased 33 per cent, its government has grown to include many more services and duties, its problems are infinitely more complex, and its involvement in world affairs is no longer fractional and irregular but rather total and constant.

The essential problem of Congress today is simply that there is more to do but only the same number of men to do it. The members of Congress have to find enough time to fulfill their thousands of obligations and to develop a Congressional system in which they can use their time most effectively.

The most pressing day-to-day demands for the time of Senators and Congressmen are not directly linked to legislative tasks. They come from constituents. And the constituency of a member of Congress is not limited to his home state or district. He gives priority attention to the people "back home," but as a United States Senator or Representative, his constituency is the whole nation.

The image of a member of Congress engaged in debate of issues or in study and reflection on the problems of the nation and freedom is accurate for only a fraction of his time. At any point in his workday, the Congressman is more likely to be talking about a housing development with municipal officials, or phoning an executive agency for an answer to a constituent complaint, or dictating a letter to a citizen who wants some information for his son's term paper for a school civics class.

Speedy air travel, the low cost of telegrams or long-distance telephone calls and campaigns to encourage citizens to "write your Congressman" have turned most Congressional offices into operations resembling a complex of train station, post office, airline terminal and communications center. My own experience may or may not be typical, but it is significant of the increased personal workload for members of Congress.

In 1949, I moved into an office of four rooms. My staff and I had the use of two telephone lines. An average of 50 letters a day were received. Thirty telephone calls a day were considered heavy. A personal visit to the office by a constituent on any day was a special event.

In 1962, my office had doubled to eight rooms. Now, 12 telephone lines funnel an average of 500 calls into the office each day, and I keep two private lines just to be sure I will be able to get through the crowded switchboard to reach my staff. One hundred and twenty personal visitors—not counting large groups of students or tourists—come into the office each day, about half of them constituents from my home state.

How does the member of Congress handle this workload? He has a staff to help, and he and his assistants work long hours at a fast pace. Any citizen who doubts that he is getting "an honest day of work" for the salary he pays his Congressman need only walk by the Senate or House office buildings late at night or on weekends. Most of the lights are burning through the evening hours, and many still shine after midnight on any night of the week.

Congressmen do not complain about the demands on their time for service to constituents. They perform that service because it is their job, because it is vital for their political survival, and because they know that the individual citizens with a need, complaint or idea cannot even hope to dent the surface of big government unless he works through his elected representative.

But members of Congress do complain often that they have little time to perform their duties as legislators. This is perhaps the central, general problem and defect of Congress today: the inability of Congressmen to find the time to inform themselves of the issues they face, to give their best talents to committee assignments, and to legislate responsibility.

The day is long gone when a member of Congress could be satisfied with mastery over two or three limited, precise subjects and follow a policy of voting the party line on other issues. Today, the Senator or Congressman is expected to be thoroughly informed on hundreds of different subjects and issues—from agricultural economics in Minnesota to the administration of foreign aid in Bolivia, from federal housing needs in New York to Soviet strategy in the Middle East, from a flood control project in California to the merits of a "man on the moon" spaceship project.

The complexities and variety of issues which members of Congress must master will continue to increase in an age of nuclear power, scientific advances, fast-changing social patterns and international involvement and leadership by the United States.

The pattern is already evident: At the time of the last Legislative Reorganization Act, the 79th Congress (1945 and 1946) initiated 12,656 bills or resolutions. The 87th Congress (1961 and 1962) initiated 20,316 bills or resolutions—a 60 per cent increase in the Congressional workload.

Most of these measures were relatively routine, but each took some time from Congress in general and individual members in particular.

There has been a comparable increase in the flow of major, controversial and thus time-consuming legislative proposals. Traditionally, the average Congressional session has seriously considered and attempted to hammer out one major new program or reform in a single year. The second session of the 87th Congress last year made a serious effort on many major legislative programs, including the trade bill, tax reform, Social Security financing of health insurance, authorization to purchase United Nations Bonds and the Communications Satellite Act.

A realistic accounting by the White House concluded that the 87th Congress approved, and the President signed into law, 73 major legislative proposals. The 83rd Congress, representing the first two years of the Eisenhower Administration, approved 29 major legislative proposals. The 87th Congress of 1961 and 1962 approved a total of more than 1,000 public bills. The 83rd Congress of 1953 and 1954 approved about half that number.

These figures are not mentioned to play a sort of partisan numbers game, but rather to emphasize the increased legislative workload of Congress and its members.

The result of that heavy workload, in 1962, was one of the longest peacetime sessions of Congress in history. Congress met continually from early January to mid-October. In the final months, a few old-timers on Capitol Hill grew frustrated enough to look back fondly on the year 1923, when Warren Harding was President and the Congress convened in March just long enough to recess until December.

But even nine or ten-month Congressional sessions do not solve the problem of the individual Senator or Congressman who must find the time to inform himself about the legislative issues he faces.

Most members of Congress are dedicated and conscientious legislators and public servants, aware of the power they hold over the dollars and destiny of the American people and so many others throughout the world. If they are given extra time—or rather freed from unnecessarily time-consuming duties—they will spend most of it tackling the huge task of informing themselves.

Several steps can be taken to give them that extra time. These are not the final answers to the time problem of members of Congress, but they would help.

First, more joint meetings of Congressional committees. A legislative question involving disarmament and arms control, for example, normally requires consideration by the Foreign Relations and Armed Services Committees of the Senate and the House and the Joint Committee on Atomic Energy. Joint meetings would save the time of members serving on more than one of these committees.

Second, more standing joint committees including members of both the House and the Senate. Such committees would save time, particularly toward the end of each Congressional session, by paving the way to speedier conference agreements between the Senate and the House on controversial issues.

Third, more efficient scheduling of the work days of Congress. Certain days could be scheduled specifically for floor debate and action by the full House or Senate. Other days could be restricted exclusively for hearings and action by the Congressional committees.

In the early months of the session, the full House or Senate would meet only a few days each week. As committees completed their action in the later months of the session, the Senate and House would meet more often.

This pattern would save time for members, and end the absurd necessity of members literally running from committee room to Senate or House chamber when issues in which they are involved are up for action at different places at the same time.

Fourth, modification of the "Morning Hour" in the Senate, in which members read miscellaneous speeches of marginal or undated importance and insert various articles into the Congressional Record. Instead, members would be permitted to send their "morning hour" speeches and articles to the clerk for insertion in the Record, without taking their own time and the time of other Senators to read them word-for-word.

Fifth, a requirement in the Senate that members restrict their remarks to the issue formally listed as the business of the Senate. In a debate over agricultural programs, for example, a Senator would not be able to spend an hour discussing a totally unrelated subject. This "Rule of Germaneness" now applies only to debate in the House of Representatives.

Sixth, a summer recess of Congress of at least three weeks. This would take time away from legislative duties, but ultimately, I am convinced, would save time. The immediate value would be the opportunity for members of Congress to spend some time with families and constituents in a period (June or July) when schools are closed and citizens are not tied at home because of weather.

The indirect value would be the change of pace and rest such a recess would give to each member. He would return for the final busy weeks of the session refreshed for more efficient performance of his legislative duties. Congressmen are human beings; they get tired and their nerves can become frayed from long months of pressure and hard work. A summer recess would probably reduce the inevitable tensions and bickering so common in the final weeks of Congressional sessions.

Seventh, modification and adoption of the British "Question Period," in which Administration leaders would report on and answer questions of general importance before the full Senate and House. This would save time, help to keep members of Congress better informed on Administration programs and policy and sustain the necessary frequent contact between the Executive and Legislative branches of government.

This final suggestion—and some of the others—would have a valuable side-effect; it would save the time of high Administration leaders who have their own crucial problems of too many duties for too few hours.

It is not unusual for the Secretary of State and the Secretary of Defense and other Cabinet officers to give basically the same testimony and answer basically the same questions for several different congressional committees. The Secretary of State, for example, might be called early in the session to outline the foreign aid program—including military aid—to the Senate Committee on Foreign Relations. He will then repeat the same testimony to the Senate Armed Services Committee, and again to the House Armed Services Committee.

The result, I believe, is an excessive demand on the time of these officials. Secretary of State Dean Rusk made 54 personal appearances before Congressional committees during the 87th Congress—29 in 1961 and 25 in 1962. Secretary of Defense Robert McNamara spent a total of 203 hours before Congressional Committees during the 87th Congress—88.75 in 1961 and 114.23 in 1962.

Standing Joint Committees, more joint meetings of committees and a "Question Period" for the full House or Senate would save the time of Congressmen and these high officials—and serve to inform all members of Congress more thoroughly.

Another Congressional defect which tends to waste time—and to cause confusion and occasional conflict between members—rests with the lineup of Senate and House Committees. New problems and programs created by a world transformed by nuclear power and the space age are being handled by a Congressional committee system which has changed little in 50 years.

There were two weeks of confusion following introduction of my bill in 1961 to establish a United States Arms Control and Disarmament Agency. This measure was first assigned to the Foreign Relations Committee, then switched to the Government Operations Committee, then back to the Foreign Relations Committee. At one point, it almost went to the Armed Services Committee. (The bill finally remained with Foreign Relations, was approved and signed into law.)

The Communications Satellite Act bounced from committee to committee before it was finally processed and sent to the floor last year. At one time or another, this bill involved the Interstate and Foreign Commerce Committee, the Foreign Relations Committee, the Government Operations Committee, the Space and Astronautics Committee and, of course, the Appropriations Committee.

Is a more up-to-date committee lineup, responsive to modern problems and modern opportunities, needed? I believe it is, and that a thorough review of the present committee and sub-committee lineups and jurisdictions is necessary.

That review would be one of the prime responsibilities of a "Joint Committee on the Organization of Congress," which would be established by a resolution sponsored by Senator Joseph S. Clark (D., Pa.) and 31 other Senators representing both parties. A companion measure in the House agrees that this committee of seven Senators and seven Representatives should conduct a complete review—the first since 1946—of Congress and produce recommendations for its improvement.

I expect this "Joint Committee on the Organization of Congress" to be established. Its work will be one of the most significant efforts of the 88th Congress. And its task will be difficult, because there is little popular interest or direct political advantage in the tedious effort for procedural reform within Congress.

But the American people want good government, and sense that the legislative branch has not been performing its functions with the order and effectiveness the nation deserves. The waning weeks of the 87th Congress included fights over such petty issues as what room the Appropriations Conference Committee should meet in, and long delays over minor details of legislation.

Displays of bickering and pettiness tend to obscure the real record of achievement written by recent Congresses and to diminish the respect and confidence of the people in their own representative government. Perhaps the greatest need in Congress today is not so much for studies, procedural changes and committee modernization. It may rather be a more thoroughly responsive attitude by members of Congress, who need to realize that the rules and traditions of Capitol Hill are not sacred, and that the national interest and public service are more important than individual or committee powers and prerogatives.

7 THE PRESIDENCY

The American presidency has been called the most powerful democratically filled office on earth. But just what is the presidency? In a timeworn yet descriptive phrase, it is an empty vessel waiting to be filled—filled to the brim by strong presidents or in much shorter measure by the less willing or less able. Constitutionally, the incumbent is free to fill the job much as he wishes; although he will discover maximum limits to his power, he is unlikely to find minimal requirements for his performance.

There is no training, either formal or informal, that can begin to match the twentieth-century demands of the job. Forged by various craftsmen with varying designs for over 175 years, the presidency has emerged as an alloy of four main elements—executive leadership, legislative leadership, party leadership, and popular leadership.

Executive leadership incorporates two significant aspects. A president is both chief executive and chief administrator. He is charged with law enforcement—a straightforward task which, nonetheless, may vary from the overstrict application of a McCarran-Walter immigration law under a Truman to the virtual cessation of enforcement of a Volstead Act (Prohibition) under a Hoover. The president alone possesses the responsibility for administrative leadership, including decision making, policy determination, and departmental coordination. Although he may delegate a portion of this task to his subordinates, he finds, in the motto that adorned the desk of Harry S. Truman, that "The Buck Stops Here." He possesses a full power of appointment and removal of subordinates, subject only to those limits imposed by the workings of "senatorial courtesy" [1] and the Humphrey decision.[2] He is commander-in-chief, possessed of significant powers at home, as witnessed in the Little Rock incident of Eisenhower's time, the Pullman strike of Cleveland's day, and the Whiskey Rebellion put down by Washington; and abroad, as displayed by such strong presidents as the two Roosevelts and by only slightly less powerful incumbents, including Polk and Truman.

The total power of the White House in foreign affairs is clearly superior to that of the Congress, despite constitutional limits. For example, the president may bypass the treaty-ratification requirement with an executive agree-

[1] According to the workings of "senatorial courtesy," the Senate of the United States will refuse to confirm the president's appointment of an individual to a federal post, such as judge or marshal, within a state, if the appointee is "personally distasteful" to the senior senator, of the president's own party, from that state.

[2] In the case of Federal Trade Commissioner Humphrey (*Rathbun v. U.S.*), the Supreme Court ruled that the presidential removal power was constitutionally limited, in the instance of those independent commissions to which the Congress has delegated "quasi-legislative" powers, by those conditions, such as removal only "for cause," set by the Congress itself.

ment, and he may grant recognition or withdraw diplomatic representation—thus establishing or severing our international relations—without any action on the part of the House or Senate. He alone receives communications from foreign nations, passing them on to the Congress or the public at his discretion. (A notable instance is McKinley's failure to inform the public that he had received a virtual surrender by cable the night before he asked Congress for a declaration of war against Spain.) He may make all kinds of commitments, open or secret, which the nation must then fulfill. Franklin D. Roosevelt summed up these tremendous executive powers in a single sentence, penned to Winston Churchill November 9, 1941: "I do not have the power to declare war, I may only *make* war."

The president is clearly the nation's legislative leader, primarily because the parochial nature of our national legislature does not provide or promote leadership in public policy. Unlike the state or local representative, the president (with administrative experts to advise him, and with the public support he can command through television, radio, and the press) is in a strong position to initiate policy, to prevent conflicting policy through the use of the veto, and to exercise financial leadership through the executive budget.

In addition, the president is the leader of his party—he has the high-level contacts, the power of patronage, and the prestige of his office, if he is inclined to use these weapons to enforce his party command. If he fails to take the helm, his party can only drift.

At home and abroad, the president is considered the leader of the free world. Domestically, he is the representative of all the people—a father image and royal head combined. Overseas he is the symbol of American prestige. Representing the power of democracy and freedom, he is a tower of strength, or a crumbling pillar, as viewed by the people of the world.

For all the respect the president commands, however, he is not possessed of power without limit. The resident of the house that Harry Truman called "the great white jail" at 1600 Pennsylvania Avenue finds certain bounds beyond which he cannot move with impunity. There is the sheer magnitude of the job—an overwhelming task for some, because of the multiple skills required. There is the inertia of bureaucracy, the separate empires, the status quo within the departments—departments that exist presumably to carry out the president's will but that so often delight in frustrating it. There are the special interests with their constant importuning, their many friends in high places. There is the public itself, whose ultimate support must be retained—the public with its sometimes fickle responses to actions consequential and minute alike. The ability to keep these conflicting interests satisfied is essential to a favorable "public image." A president ignores them only at the risk of rejection at the polls.

A further problem is the political opposition a president encounters—frequently more bitter from within his own party than from without. He must be ever wary of the "nine old men"—the Supreme Court, with its power of judicial review. In recent years, the president has come to know the force of the congressional inquiry—whether designed for self-seeking, witch-hunting, or more constructive purposes. And finally, the president, like any lesser man, is frequently the captive of events—events not only in the United States but throughout the world. Over these he may have little control, but they may make him a hero or a goat (perhaps both) in short order.

These, then, are some of the aspects of the presidency that we shall keep in mind as we analyze the decision-making process that revolves around our chief executive, and as we review the changes the American presidency has undergone throughout our history. For the president in the twentieth century is clearly the focal point of our national government in action.

THE U.S. PRESIDENCY

Gerald W. Johnson

Gerald W. Johnson is one of America's most respected political journalists and historians. A former editor of the *Baltimore Sun,* he is the author of *American Heroes and Hero Worship, The Lunatic Fringe,* and *A History for Peter.*

The Presidency of the United States has come down from George Washington to Dwight D. Eisenhower in a succession uninterrupted for nearly 175 years by any exterior force save that of human mortality. The contingency of death was foreseen, and the succession provided by law. Even when there was no clear election by the people, as in 1800 and 1824 when no candidate received an electoral majority, and in 1876 when the apparent majority was challenged, those crises were successfully met by legal devices without resort to force.

This gives the Presidency an appearance of great stability. It is probable that the typical American, if questioned, would confidently assert that no political office in the world is more solidly established, or has been less affected by the sweeping changes that have transformed almost everything else since the establishment of the republic. But the appearance is deceptive. The real characteristic of the office has been and is now a malleability that amounts almost to fluidity. Under no two men has the Presidency been exactly the same, and even its constitutional significance has altered until it is, in important respects, the opposite of what it was in Washington's time.

The impact of personality upon the office has been too conspicuous to

From *Saturday Evening Post,* June 11, 1960. Reprinted by permission.

pass unnoticed by the most superficial observer; but the changes forced by events are more important, although subtler and hard to perceive except in historical perspective. Everyone knows that the Presidency changed radically when Abraham Lincoln succeeded James Buchanan, and the facile explanation that Lincoln was a war President is inadequate. The country was at peace when Theodore Roosevelt succeeded William McKinley, yet the change in the Presidency in 1901 was, if anything, more spectacular than the change in 1861. Far more important than the effects of individual temperament, although less readily observed, are such changes as that between the time when Jefferson established the rule that the President receives, but makes no social calls, and the time when Eisenhower set out on his 1959 odyssey across the world.

Temperament has nothing to do with these changes. All men know that as far as his personal desires were concerned, the last thing Mr. Eisenhower wished was to undertake that physically and mentally arduous journey; he went because he deemed it his duty, not his pleasure, to go. It was the same motive that impelled President Washington to make his even more taxing trips through the country. The difference is that the first President could halt at the national boundary, while the thirty-fourth must cover the world. But nobody planned it so; it is the effect of the trend of events, not of human volition.

Washington did not expect this kind of development. The "Farewell Address" is full of foreboding, but the changes he foresaw and dreaded were to be effected by ambition, not by necessity. "In the most solemn manner" he warned us "against the baneful effects of the Spirit of Party . . . a fire not to be quenched; it demands a uniform vigilance to prevent its bursting into a flame, lest, instead of warming, it should consume." The Spirit of Party, he thought, must in the end "incline the minds of men to see security and repose in the absolute power of an individual; and sooner or later the chief of some prevailing faction, more able or more fortunate than his competitors, turns this disposition to the purposes of his own elevation, on the ruins of Public Liberty."

A dismal prospect indeed, but severely logical in view of the information available to Washington. The power of the presidential office has increased, not steadily, but by fits and starts, speeded up by strong Presidents, slowed down by weak ones, but never reversing its general trend; until today it vastly exceeds anything dreamed of at the beginning of the nineteenth century.

Yet the calamitous results foretold in the "Farewell Address" have not yet come upon us. They may be impending, for it would be fatuous to deny that the Presidency contains the seeds of dictatorship; but they are not here yet, and an inquiry into why the seeds have not sprouted, flourished and borne their deadly fruit ought to be suggestive, at least, of means by which we may hope to keep them latent indefinitely.

Washington's anxiety was based upon the assumption that any additional powers accruing to the Presidency must of necessity be subtracted from those of one or both of the other branches of government. It was his belief that the "system of checks and balances" in the Constitution had separated the powers of government and distributed them all; he and his contemporaries accepted the theory that the powers of Government consist of the legislative, the executive and the judicial, and that once these were lodged in different and independent hands, government would be completely organized. The problem thenceforth would be to keep any one from encroaching on the authority of the others.

What the men of 1787 did not suspect—and is, indeed, but imperfectly realized by our own generation—is that there is a fourth power of government difficult to define legally and not disposed of by the Constitution, yet as important in a democracy as the executive, legislative or judicial. This is the power of the initiative, which we commonly term leadership. The history of the Presidency is a story of the slow accretion of this power in the hands of the man in the White House.

To understand why this factor was overlooked by statesmen as far-sighted as those who dominated the Constitutional Convention, one must remember that they were theorists, guided by reason, not by experience. The only form of government under which any of them had lived was monarchial; parliamentary government was indeed taking shape in England, but it was not yet clearly defined, and parliament was far from being a representative democracy, such as our Constitution envisaged. Thus the Americans had no pattern to follow; for the direct, not representative, democracies of ancient times were horrible examples rather than models, since all of them had failed. The Greek city-states, for example, where each man entered the assembly representing himself alone and, therefore, usually voted in his own interest alone, oscillated between tyranny and anarchy, never establishing an enduring balance of public and private interests. Nor were other democracies able long to escape either domestic autocracy or foreign domination.

But if the founding fathers lacked a reliable guide, they did have a stern warning. The centuries old, not then terminated, struggle for power between the king and parliament had taught them that in such a contest the rights of the people are pretty sure to be trampled by both contestants; and the logical means of protection against that was the system of checks and balances.

Some of them—Hamilton, for a conspicuous example—did understand that such a system, if brought to perfection, would result in impotence, a government hung on dead center, unable to move in any direction. They had an example in the Polish monarchy of the seventeenth century, so effectively checked and balanced by the requirement of a unanimous vote of the nobles that it was brought to ruin by sheer inertia. But the highly practical Americans were aware that their own system was by no means so delicately adjusted, since even the veto of the President could be overridden, and they assumed correctly that its very imperfections would prevent a complete deadlock.

What they did not take into account, or did not give sufficient weight in their accounting, was the possibility that in making absolute power unattainable, they had checked ambition, especially in the legislative branch, severely enough to discourage the development of effective leadership there. This was a contingency extremely remote in a government of undivided powers. Leadership originally vested in the monarch, could not be wrested from him except by leadership developed elsewhere—in a court favorite, perhaps, or in the legislative or even in the judiciary. The complete disappearance of the fourth power of government was one danger against which the Americans did not prepare, presumably because they did not envisage it.

It can be plausibly argued, nevertheless, that this country has suffered more, very much more, from excessively static than from excessively dynamic government. The example customarily cited is the inertia of James Buchanan as the danger of secession was visibly mounting; but the monumental uselessness of Buchanan was merely a continuation of a condition that had afflicted the Presidency ever since the administration of James K. Polk. The Pennsylvanian's misfortune was merely that he happened to be in office at the time when the lack of effective leadership produced its logical result. Buchanan is its spectacular example, but the condition has been characteristic of the Presidency more often than not.

Evidence to support this assertion is not far to seek. How many Americans can name offhand eighteen of the individuals who have held the office? Everyone remembers Washington, Jefferson, Jackson, Lincoln, Wilson and the second Roosevelt because great significance attaches to their names. Perhaps most of us recall also the first Roosevelt, John Adams, Monroe (on account of the Doctrine), possibly Cleveland; but beyond that the typical American grows vague. The reason is that none of the others exercised the power of the initiative in any memorable way. Hoover, Truman and Eisenhower are excluded from this account because all three are still living as these lines are written.

The half dozen first named, pretty generally regarded as the Big Six, are a remarkably varied assortment as regards their intellectual and cultural endowments, but they are alike in one respect—Washington established the Presidency and each of the other five added materially to its power. Each was, in Washington's words, "the chief of some prevailing faction," but that any turned the situation "to the purposes of his own elevation, on the ruins of Public Liberty," as the "Farewell Address" grimly predicted, will be asserted only of Franklin Roosevelt, and of him only by blind and bitter partisanship. To the vast majority of Americans they were great Presidents, the greatest in the list.

Here, then, is what at first glance seems to be a mystery, a cause not followed by its logical effect: the vast accretion of power that Washington apprehended has come to the Presidency, but the calamitous results that he feared have not followed. This odd circumstance can be explained only on the theory that the President has added to his power by occupation, but not by usurpation; that is to say, the addition to the Presidency has not been a subtraction from either of the other two branches. They retain unimpaired to this day all the powers delegated to them in 1789. If the Presidency has advanced relatively, it is by assuming the power of the initiative, never clearly envisaged by the Constitution makers, and, if it had been, probably incapable of legal definition.

Some years before he entered the White House Woodrow Wilson noted the fact. In *Constitutional Government,* published in 1908, he observed that "the President is at liberty, both in law and in conscience, to be as big a man as he can. His capacity will set the limit; and if Congress be overborne by him, it will be no fault of the makers of the Constitution—it will be from no lack of constitutional powers on its part, but only because the President has the nation behind him and Congress has not. He has no means of compelling Congress except through public opinion."

What a tremendous exception that is, probably Wilson did not fully realize in 1908, although he had the example of Theodore Roosevelt before his eyes. But Wilson himself demonstrated it during his first two years in the White House, and the overwhelming proof was furnished by the second Roosevelt in his first Hundred Days. A President who can seize the initiative at all is assured of some success; and one whose first few moves receive popular approbation is irresistible.

The recourse of Congress is to seize the initiative itself, and occasionally—as, for instance, in the case of Andrew Johnson—it has done so. Congress, too, is at liberty, both in law and in conscience, to be the biggest thing in the nation if it can. But the historical record of congressional efforts to assume leadership makes depressing reading. Certainly the most brilliant, and perhaps the most honorable, of those men who have seized leadership outside the White House were Alexander Hamilton and Henry Clay; but Hamilton succeeded only in hobbling—and infuriating—John Adams, while Clay was a millstone hung around the neck of every President of his own party. In later days the Reconstruction policy imposed upon the country by Thaddeus Stevens brought upon his memory an odium that still persists; and if the almost equally powerful legislative leaders, Thomas B. Reed and Joseph G. Cannon, are remembered more favorably it is because of their more amiable personalities rather than for their triumphs of statecraft.

The member of Congress, senator or representative, is not in a favorable position to exercise national leadership. One of its essentials, and one that is increasingly important as government becomes more complex, is the capacity for swift and decisive action. In this respect the President enjoys an inestimable advantage in that his close associates are his subordinates, whereas those of a member of Congress are his equals. The President can order, where the congressman can only argue. For this reason a weak President can contend on better than equal terms with a legislator immeasurably his intellectual superior—a John Tyler can frustrate a Henry Clay.

The first genius to appreciate this situation to the full and to exploit it was Andrew Jackson. The magnitude of his achievement is evidenced by the fact that the tradition still persists that Old Hickory was a simple soul, rough, but transparent. In fact, Jefferson himself was not more complex and devious.

Jackson was the first to understand the implications, for the President, of the fact that the votes are cast by individuals, although the country does not consist exclusively of individuals. The country includes territory, wealth, land and water, forest and field, mountain and plain, ecological variations that are wide and highly important. Individuals are, however, one constant in this giant aggregate of variables. Since the President is the sole elected official chosen by the whole country—for who ever voted for or against a Vice President?—he alone can afford to neglect the variables and devote his whole attention to the constant.

A senator from Texas, for example, must represent the Texans, of course, but he must represent oil also, as a senator from Montana must represent copper and one from Oregon, lumber. Not long ago the late Senator Neuberger acknowledged that publicly, and said that if any senator had failed to represent the dominant economic interest of his state, the fact had escaped Mr. Neuberger's notice.

Jackson's triumphant career was based on his success in convincing men and women that he represented people in a special way that no other official could. But he did more. He persuaded them that the President is, and of right ought to be, the people's man, speaking for them and for no local or nonhuman interest whatsoever. Jackson, more than any other President, established the claim of the Presidency to the power of the initiative. Incidentally, he also furnished at least one glaring illustration of its dangers. "John Marshall has made his decision; now let him enforce it," may not have been his exact words, but they certainly portray his attitude in the Indian lands case. By withholding the comity due from one branch of the government to another he, in effect, vacated a ruling of the Supreme Court—as clear a usurpation of the power of the judiciary as can be imagined. But there can be no shadow of doubt that it asserted the leadership of the Presidency in the nation at large, not merely in the executive branch.

Nearly a hundred years passed, however, before the claim was formalized by Wilson in his public announcement that he proposed to be head of his party, as well as head of the state. Even then the opposition professed to regard Wilson's statement as scandalous, although every strong President since Jackson had held leadership of the party; and to this day there is some dispute as to where the power of the initiative should lie.

Curiously enough, opposition to Wilson's position has included some of the Presidents themselves. Harding is the obvious example, but it may be argued that he was incapable of leadership in any circumstances; McKinley and Benjamin Harrison are better illustrations. Their distaste for the Wilsonian doctrine is understandable, if not particularly creditable, for it imposes upon the President formidable responsibility. If he is to lead the country successfully he must be resourceful, energetic and resolute, all to a high degree. This is hard labor, not to be undertaken willingly by a man who approaches the office in the spirit of the remark attributed, doubtfully, to Giovanni de'Medici, "Since God has given us the Papacy, let us enjoy it."

But evidence is already abundant and increases daily that the Presidency is the right location for the power of initiative. Since 1914 the tempo of events has accelerated to such an extent that crises tread upon one another's heels, and capacity for rapid and decisive action may soon be, if it is not already, the price of national survival. The Korean affair is an instance still vividly in mind; President Truman's course may not have been the ideal one, but his action was swift; and in politics as in military operations it is better to do any intelligent thing than to lose time searching for the perfect move.

In a world as tense as that of the twentieth century, speed in seizing the initiative seems likely to increase, rather than to diminish in importance; which suggests that the dominance of the Presidency in that respect is more likely to be strengthened and extended than to be reduced. Hitler, being only human, could not always be wrong, and he hit upon a great truth in his assertion of "the leadership principle" as essential to successful government in the modern world. Certainly a huge democracy, such as the United States, stands in as grave danger from lack of leadership as from usurpation of power.

It is not that usurpation is inconceivable in this country. Jackson's case was not the only one. Lincoln in suspending the writ of habeas corpus where the courts were still open, unquestionably infringed the prerogative of the judiciary, and Theodore Roosevelt, in ordering the motto, "In God We Trust," left off the coins, invaded Congress' exclusive right to coin money. Jefferson was inclined to think that he usurped powers of both legislative and judiciary in making the Louisiana Purchase. But the usurpations thus far have been either pardonable, as conducing to the general welfare, or unsuccessful, or so trifling as to come under the rule *de minimis*. . . .

This is, however, no guarantee that they will retain that character; and a generation that has been appalled by such apparitions as Mussolini, Hitler and Stalin knows only too well what horrors may rise from a perversion of leadership. The Twenty-second Amendment, forbidding any man to hold the Presidency more than ten years, is evidence of our extreme sensitiveness to the remotest possibility of the rise of dictatorship here. Our immediate peril, in fact, is probably much less the risk of submitting to tyranny than the risk of hobbling necessary leadership by hysterical efforts to ward off tyranny.

At the same time every thoughtful American must regard the development of the Presidency with something less than ebullient enthusiasm. It is clearly necessary to lodge the power of the initiative somewhere, and the hands of the President seem to be its logical repository, because he alone can exercise it effectively. It is clearly necessary, also, to insist that he shall exercise it, and to avoid electing any man incapable of doing so. In prudence as well as in equity it is clearly necessary to support the President strongly in the legitimate exercise of this power.

But it is not to be denied that this course, however necessary, involves a calculated risk, and it is always possible to miscalculate. This possibility must be taken into account in any extrapolation of the historical development of the Presidency. The tricky factor is the enormous potential of the force that we call public opinion. Against it, neither legislative, executive, judiciary, nor even the Constitution itself can stand. It has hitherto been the constructive power in erecting the political fabric of the republic; but a power capable of so gigantic a feat obviously could be terrifically destructive were it channeled in that direction.

To put this power absolutely in the hands of one man would be suicidal. We have had a grisly demonstration of that in the case of the German people, when the potent majority of them committed their minds and consciences to Hitler and blindly followed him to destruction.

That the American people will go to any such extreme seems highly improbable. Our historical experience, our educational methods, even to some extent our prejudices and superstitions militate against it. Artemus Ward's complacent proclamation, "I am not a politician, and my other habits are good," was something more than a jape. It reflects a skepticism of Whitman's "elected persons" that is deeply embedded in the American character —a prejudice perhaps touched with superstition, but one that operates against any attempt at the deification of Caesar.

It would be unrealistic, however, to deny that there are forces in the modern world that operate in the other direction; nor are they confined to the ideologies of Marx, Lenin or Mao. We seem, indeed, relatively immune to ideologies. In no large country has the Communist Party had less success in recruiting the masses, and even the Socialists have never polled as many as 1,000,000 votes. But there are conditions, not theories, that are subjecting the traditional American system to a considerable strain.

Some of these conditions are technological, others political. Communication, for instance, has been perfected to the point at which one man may speak to the entire nation; and with the aid of television he may bring to bear upon an audience of many millions all the resources of dramaturgy— not rhetoric and euphony only, but gesture also, as well as "wanton Wiles, Nods and Becks and wreathed Smiles," and if you think these are ineffective, remember that David Garrick, the actor, once said that he would give 100 guineas to be able to say "ah" as the Rev. George Whitefield, the evangelist, could say it.

The assistance of technology is available equally to statesmen and to demagogues. The statesman may employ it to inspire the nation to great deeds; but the demagogue may use it to foment all the evils inherent in hard psychology. Since demagogues as a rule outnumber statesmen, it is evident that the mass media of communication, especially the newer ones, radio and television, must subject the common sense of the American electorate to a severe test.

The political organization of the modern world also is a condition and not a theory. American military and economic power is now the chief defense of political liberty abroad as well as at home. When the Constitution assigned to the President the conduct of foreign relations, the work consisted almost exclusively of safeguarding American interest; its expansion to cover the whole free world obviously has put the President in a different position. His power has been greatly increased, but so has his vulnerability; the President in self-defense is being forced more and more to act as his own Secretary of State. Even Mr. Eisenhower, who disliked and distrusted this development, was finally forced to accept it.

A President of a different temperament, however, might find it very much to his taste. Think what Theodore Roosevelt, for example, might have done with the leadership of the free nations! That idea is in a sense a test of the division in American political philosophy—one school holding that so dynamic a character given Eisenhower's opportunity would have ruined us, the other holding that lack of dynamism in the Presidency is the cause of at least half our present difficulties.

The mocking devil of it is that both schools seem to be right. A generation that has witnessed the passing of Mussolini, Hitler and Stalin must shudder at the idea of leadership concentrated in an individual; at the same time, a generation numbed by fifteen years of cold war must be appalled by the possibility of a total paralysis of leadership.

The rather dismal conclusion of the whole matter would seem to be that the American who seeks to peer into the future, no matter what his philosophy, has reason to shudder.

But was it ever otherwise? Our Constitution, said Justice Holmes, is an experiment, but only, he added, as all life is an experiment. It is unrealistic to ignore the fact that it is dangerous to be free, but it is equally unrealistic to ignore the fact that this nation has lived dangerously yet has survived for nearly 200 years. In that period the Presidency has gradually acquired powers that would have staggered the writers of the Constitution, and the prospect, at least for the years immediately ahead, is that the welfare of the nation and the world will necessitate entrusting greater, not diminished, authority to the office.

This may be the road to dictatorship, but it is the road we have been following because we could find no other. And there are optimists who do not believe that it leads inevitably to tyranny. Unreasonably, perhaps, they see the history of the United States as the aged Jefferson described it in that famous letter to the still-older Adams: "Laboring always at the same oar, with some wave ever ahead threatening to overwhelm us and yet passing harmless under our bank, we knew not how, we rode through the storm with heart and hand, and made a happy port . . . and so we have gone on, and so we shall go on, puzzled and prospering beyond example in the history of man."

THE JOHNSON WAY WITH CONGRESS
Tom Wicker

Tom Wicker of the *New York Times* Washington bureau regularly reports White House news.

"For 32 years," said Lyndon B. Johnson in his first Presidential address to Congress, "Capitol Hill has been my home. I have shared many moments of pride with you—pride in the ability of the Congress of the United States to act, to meet any crisis, to distill from our differences strong programs of national action . . . I firmly believe in the independence and integrity of the legislative branch. And I promise you that I shall always respect this. It is deep in the marrow of my bones."

Probably no part of Mr. Johnson's speech was more heartfelt. The ninth President of the United States to have served in both Houses of Congress, the fourth Senator to have reached the White House in this century, one of the most effective floor leaders ever to serve in the Senate, Mr. Johnson has made it plain since November 22 that he is one of the most thoroughgoing Congressional men ever to become Chief Executive.

That can be said of him not just because he has applied himself with skill and assiduity to the problems of achieving legislation that had seemed lost or stalled; Mr. Johnson also has brought the legislative branch—or at least its leadership—closer than it has been in years to the arena of action, to that area of ultimate power where, decisions are taken, policies made, directions set. The latter case, if sustained, may yet prove the most important result of the President's ardent wooing of Capitol Hill.

It has been no pallid hothouse courtship but a many-splendored thing. Senator Harry F. Byrd of Virginia, for instance, is empowered to tell the press that the President will show him the Federal Government's budget before submitting it to Congress or to anyone else. Senator Richard Russell of Georgia and others are asked to vote informally on an important policy decision concerning Panama. Well-known members of Congress are whisked off from parties to the White House, there to swap ideas until midnight or beyond with a President who seems genuinely interested in what they think.

When Robert Kennedy returns from his mission to Indonesia and Malaysia, he is dismayed to find himself in the White House delivering not a privileged communication to the Chief Executive but a general report to Mr. Johnson and a flanking group of members of the legislative branch—including J. W. Fulbright of Arkansas and Hubert Humphrey of Minnesota.

Members of Congress get treatment at the White House of a cordiality unmatched in their memories: their wives danced with by the President and taken on a tour of the residential quarters by the First Lady, themselves briefed on world affairs by Secretary of Defense McNamara and Secretary of State Rusk. When Mr. Johnson nominates Carl Rowan to head the U.S. Information Agency, he provides Mr. Rowan with precise and knowing advice about which Senators to call on and what to say to them in order to make his nomination more popular.

A Senator like Olin D. Johnston of South Carolina gets Presidential congratulations via the telephone for a document he has caused to be printed in the Congressional Record. An obscure House member finds himself in the White House spotlight, receiving a ceremonial handshake and fountain pen from the President in return for his minor part in getting a bill passed.

When the extended foreign-aid fight keeps Congressmen in town almost until Christmas Eve—and on the surface seems to threaten an all-out struggle between Congress and President—a White House holiday reception is hastily organized for friend and foe alike, Charlie Halleck as well as Carl Albert. And it is Lyndon Johnson who at the party's height pulls an elegant White House chair into the middle of the state dining room, climbs on its damask seat and pours the following oil:

"We're Americans first . . . we're proud of our ancestry and hopeful for our posterity . . ." The President goes on to say that he hopes he and the Congressmen can "disagree without being too disagreeable." He reminds them that "you only have one President, you only have one Congress, and you only have one judiciary and your country is no stronger than your Government."

That is just the kind of medicine members of Congress like—pain-killing and not too hard to swallow.

This extended form of the celebrated "Johnson Treatment" has a palpable effect on Congress. Republicans, of course, in an election year have been getting in their usual oratorical licks, but compared with the criticism John Kennedy used to get, that directed at Mr. Johnson has been no more forceful (to borrow a phrase from Everett Dirksen) "than a snowflake on the bosom of the Potomac." And the Republican-Democratic coalition that put over the civil rights bill for the White House stayed notably glued together under the greatest of strains.

Southern Democrats—those honey-voiced avengers of Appomattox and the Brown Decision, thorns in the flesh of every Democratic President since F.D.R.—have turned finger-lickin' good in the presence of a Chief Executive from south of Mason-Dixon. "Judge" Howard Smith of Virginia, to cite a striking example, concedes on national television that where Barry Goldwater might have carried the South against John Kennedy, he will run like a dry creek against Mr. Johnson. Southerners in the house conduct their none too fierce fight against the Kennedy-Johnson civil rights bill on the plane of a law school course in constitutional theory. It is obvious by now that the Southerners want Mr. Johnson to succeed. Whom else can they get who will be as sympathetic?

More important, Congress as a legislative body gives the impression that it is coming alive. Where it had seemed bogged down in ineptitude and sloth, defiant of Kennedy, disregardful of editorial contempt and ignorant of the national interest, it now seems to be responding with bill after bill to a President who knows how to arouse it, and what makes it tick.

It is a classically romantic drama—unsung new President makes good; rags to riches. Unfortunately, like most such dramas, it is a little larger than life. Mr. Johnson has not really passed a miracle on Capitol Hill. His achievement in Congress has been substantial, not magical.

For instance, skeptics find no trace of magic in Mr. Johnson's handling of the perennially defiant Representative Otto L. Passman of Louisiana. Mr. Passman, the scourge of foreign aid, once was summoned to the White House by John Kennedy for a showdown. When the smoke cleared, Kennedy told his aides with a shudder: "Don't ever bring that man here again."

When Mr. Johnson in his turn called Mr. Passman in for another showdown, there must have been the greatest display of jawbone since Samson slew that horde, for the Texan and the Louisianan rank as two of the most voluble politicians of our time. But in the end, what did Mr. Johnson get for his pains? "He got zero," an Administration official reports.

Nor has Mr. Johnson converted Representative Clarence Cannon of Missouri into a spender. In pursuit of his war against outgo, the wizened Chairman of the House Appropriations Committee has summarily abolished a subcommittee that used to deal with the annual supplementary appropriations requests. Now such requests must be broken down by departmental totals, each separate total to be handled by the departmental subcommittees, and considered together with the next year's regular budget. The net effect is to put off until May 15, for example, a full committee hearing on a supplemental space appropriations request that was submitted early this year. A President would need to be a real magician to do anything about it because in that kind of infighting Clarence Cannon has got the power.

A more important retort is often made, however, to those who claim that Lyndon Johnson singlehandedly got Congress moving again. It is that nothing much has been done on Capitol Hill since November 22 that would not have been done—perhaps a little more slowly—had Kennedy lived.

One fact not widely credited was that, at Kennedy's death, the record of the 88th Congress was by no means so horrendous as some editorial writers contended. The Senate had ratified the test-ban treaty; the House had passed the tax bill, and Congress had approved a precedent-breaking measure that helped head off a national railroad strike (ordinarily, any Congressman would rather break a metatarsal than a precedent). Moreover, two major education bills were on the verge of passage. Each was in a Senate-House conference, having been approved in both Houses.

When Mr. Johnson took over, the most important objectives were to move the civil rights bill through the House Rules Committee and the House itself; and to move the tax-reduction bill through the Senate Finance Committee and the Senate itself. Here is a brief accounting, as objective as possible, of Mr. Johnson's contribution to the achievement of both objectives.

Tax Reduction: The President's reduction of the budget below the level of that submitted by Mr. Kennedy last year undoubtedly pleased Senator Byrd and other fiscal conservatives and improved the climate for tax reduction. A number of informed sources, however, doubt that it produced the votes for passage. There never was much doubt, they say, that the bill would pass the Senate, or even the Finance Committee. The real question was when.

Lyndon Johnson disagrees emphatically. "That tax bill never would have been gotten out of the Finance Committee unless the budget had been cut below $100 billion," he declares.

Those who disagree say the Johnson budget-cutting and the President's considerable rapport with Senator Byrd certainly helped speed the bill through the Finance Committee, but not by any great number of days. They concede that these factors probably kept the Senator from trying to hamstring the bill with amendments and limitations—although they are not sure that he would have tried to do so in any case.

They also concede that Mr. Johnson talked Senator Dirksen of Illinois out of an attempt to put off final passage until March. But they contend that it was before Mr. Johnson came into office that the most crucial time was lost. As a result of exhaustive hearings in both the House Ways and Means Committee and the Senate Finance Committee, it became impossible to get passage before Christmas.

On one score, however, no one questions Mr. Johnson's effectiveness. It is agreed that he contributed directly to the fight to preserve excise-tax revenues in the bill. With personal telephone calls, he laid the groundwork (and Presidential assistant Lawrence F. O'Brien followed through in person) for switching two votes and producing a 9–8 victory on this issue in the Finance Committee.

And when the committee finally had approved the bill, Mr. Johnson was on the phone almost immediately—not to a Senator but to Elizabeth Springer, its staff director.

"This is the President," he said (according to one version). "How soon can you have the tax bill report going to the printer?"

"Four P.M.," Mrs. Springer replied.

"Well, let's push it up all we can," Mr. Johnson said.

Then he called James Harrison, the head of the Government Printing

Office. "I want you to have that report out in the morning," he told Mr. Harrison. (This was characteristic. As a young legislative assistant 30 years ago, Lyndon Johnson was known for his ability to figure out what low-level official actually was responsible for a given piece of work, and to deal effectively with that official.)

Civil Rights: Here again, Mr. Johnson's contributions were valuable but not necessarily in the sense of producing needed votes that might not otherwise have been had. Sources in a position to know report that the existence of a petition that would have taken the bill out of the hands of the House Rules Committee was the major factor in forcing Chairman Smith of Virginia to permit the measure to go to the House by the end of January.

There never were enough signatures on the petition actually to make it effective. But there were enough to threaten Judge Smith's position and there were enough to force a number of members of the House into an uncomfortable position. They had refused to sign the discharge petition on the ostensible grounds that they believed the Rules Committee would act on its own sooner or later. The favorable response to the petition forced them to bring pressure on the chairman to make good their own promises that he would act.

President Johnson has confided to acquaintances, however, that the discharge petition was a stratagem he disliked, no doubt "in the marrow of the bones." No Congressional man is sanguine about such an undermining of the power of the Establishment.

Nevertheless, the President swallowed his objections and used his influence to get 10 Texas Representatives to sign the petition—no mean achievement, since only four of these same Texans actually voted for the civil-rights bill when it came to a final vote.

The bipartisan coalition that passed the bill had been put together by John Kennedy and Republican leader Charles Halleck of Indiana—but it had to be held together under the tense conditions of House debate. The bill's supporters in both parties give Mr. Johnson ample credit for maintaining a strict and necessary bipartisanship during those crucial days in February. They also credit him with an effective job, in the weeks before the debate, of keeping public pressure on Congress. The fact that he was a Southerner, they think, accounts in part for the lack of bitterness in the Southern opposition. But Mr. Johnson took no part at all—having no need to—in the tactical battle of the House floor.

But the President's decisions, phone calls and pressures form only half the story. Perhaps more significant than any of these positive actions is the fact that, coming in such tragic circumstances into his heavy responsibilities, Mr. Johnson avoided the numerous pitfalls into which a less surefooted leader might have stumbled.

No one will argue that tax reduction went through the Senate and the civil rights bill through the house *more slowly* because John Kennedy was dead. Yet, it could easily have happened that way. One or both bills could have been lost and Congress could have overrun a hesitant leader—just as it tried unsuccessfully to do when House Republicans sought to put restrictions on the executive branch's ability to work out a sale of wheat to the Soviet Union.

Now the greatest of Mr. Johnson's challenges is before him—the filibuster in the Senate against the most significant civil rights bill in history. He is doubtful the Senate will vote to end the filibuster, owing to the historic reluctance of small-state Senators to strike down unlimited debate—their last weapon, as many of them see it, against the big urban centers.

To illustrate the difficulty of cutting off a civil rights filibuster, one Administration strategist estimates that in order to attract the necessary Republican support, the move would have to be supported by three key Senators—Dirksen of Illinois, Bourke B. Hickenlooper of Iowa and George Aiken of Vermont. Those three represent almost all shades of Republican opinion, all sizes of Republican states, and both East and West.

Nor does Mr. Johnson have much room for maneuver and compromise—the weapons by which, as Majority Leader, he wriggled the 1957 and 1960 civil rights bills through the Senate. The Southerners' main target is the public accommodations section, but it is precisely this section that Mr. Johnson believes he must keep in the bill at all costs. It is a political necessity for him to do so because the section has become symbolic of the Negro's whole effort to win his rights legally and politically. If it fails, or is compromised into banality, the Negro may turn to more direct methods.

To bring such men as Aiken, Dirksen and Hickenlooper into some sort of unity with the disparate individuals of his own party, to find some politically feasible compromise formula—these are legislative problems that will challenge to the utmost a leadership that, on the record of Mr. Johnson's years in the Senate and his months in the White House, seems to rest, first, on an ability to find common ground on which men can stand; second, on a sort of relentless persuasiveness, and third, on decisiveness—approaching ruthlessness—in pursuing a course once determined upon.

Ever since the rights bill passed the House, there has been talk in Washington that Mr. Johnson was seeking a compromise formula to present to the filibustering Southern Senators. If so, it would be in his established *modus operandi.* An Administration official, wise in the ways of Congress, offers this assessment of one part of that method: "Kennedy came too late to many of his problems in Congress. He would hold back, let things develop, come in at the top of the crisis. Johnson likes to stay ahead and anticipate what will happen and how to meet it."

But beyond the fates of even such major legislation as tax reduction and civil rights, Mr. Johnson's affinity for Congress—the feeling "in the marrow of his bones"—offers him at once a greater opportunity and a greater peril.

The danger arises from the fact that a President cannot always act as his own Majority Leader and Congress cannot always be his main reliance in matters large and small. If Mr. Johnson involves himself too readily in the minutiae of Congressional procedure and politics, if he expends his prestige and power too rapidly on matters of secondary importance, the whole scope and course of his magistracy will be affected and not for the better.

And while no President can proceed far at home or abroad without substantial backing from Congress, there comes the inevitable time when he must push ahead either without it or without as much of it has he would like. Moreover, Congressional leaders—products of a system based on local districts and states and their interests—are not always the most far-seeing and disinterested advisers.

Mr. Johnson is reported to have been disillusioned by the vote he once called for when he had gathered Congressional and Administration leaders together to discuss Panama. He wound up with no majority for anything and had to make his own decision anyway. When later crises arose in Cyprus and over the Guantanamo water supply, the Congressional leaders were much less in evidence at the White House.

Mr. Johnson's opportunity, if realized, could be of importance beyond any conceivable single bill. It is somehow to achieve, not just on one measure or in one session, but in the broadest sense, a new atmosphere of mutual respect and mutual confidence in which Congress and President can work together effectively—coequal branches in fact as well as in theory.

One speaks for the national interest; the other for the vast diversity of local interests. Seldom in American history have they functioned in real harmony. Lyndon Johnson and the 88th Congress seem more willing than most to work together, and that fact may yet prove the first step toward a real "miracle" on Capitol Hill.

THE PRESIDENCY AND THE PEACE

McGeorge Bundy

McGeorge Bundy was Special Assistant for National Security Affairs to President Kennedy and holds the same position under President Johnson. A graduate of Yale University (1940), Bundy was a Lecturer and Associate Professor of Government at Harvard University before becoming Dean of Harvard's Faculty of Arts and Sciences in 1953, the job he relinquished to join the White House staff.

It is with some sense of temerity that a member of the White House staff undertakes to comment on the large topic of the Presidency and the Peace.

Loyalty and affection are so normal in such service that detachment is difficult.

Nevertheless, the importance of the topic and the enforced familiarity of close experience with the presidential task may justify a set of comments whose underlying motive is to express a conviction that is as obvious as the daylight, in general, and as fresh as every sunrise, in particular: a conviction that the American Presidency, for better, not for worse, has now become the world's best hope of preventing the unexampled catastrophe of general nuclear war.

Moreover, both charity and sorrow can be good lenses for perception, and it may therefore be possible to consider the subject without impropriety by focusing upon the years of John F. Kennedy.

The tragedy which has moved his Administration from politics to history may allow to his critics and excuse in his friends some generosity in the assessment of his three years. His death revealed his greatness, and the grief of the world was less for his tragedy than for its own—in that he had shown his spreading grasp of his duty to mankind as Chief Executive for Peace.

THE PURPOSE IS PEACE

To focus on the Kennedy years is not to forget those before, and still less the firm continuation after November 22. The Presidents of the nuclear age before Mr. Kennedy also made the service of peace the first of their purposes, and the determined commitment of President Johnson to this same end, matured in decades of direct knowledge of our nuclear world, has been made plain in his own words and actions already. Indeed one purpose of a retrospective assessment is to clarify purposes which are as important to the President today as to the President last year.

A President in search of peace has many powers, but none is more relevant or more effective than his power as Commander-in-Chief. The President is keeping the peace as long as he keeps his own nuclear power in check, and with it the nuclear power of others. The most obvious of his powers, apparently so simple and so negative, can be used for peace in a number of ways.

POWER PREREQUISITE

The prerequisite, of course, is that this power should exist, and that there should be confidence in its future as well as its present effectiveness. Nothing is more dangerous to the peace than weakness in the ultimate deterrent strength of the United States. In the quarter century that man has known the atom could be split, each American decision to enlarge its powers has been the President's alone. More subtly, but with just as great importance, the choices of methods of delivery and their rate of development have also been presidential.

As important as having strength is being known to have it; and here, if anything, the presidential authority and responsibility are still more clear. This is the lesson of Sputnik, and of the "missile gap" which was forecast and feared by responsible and well-informed men both in and out of government between 1957 and 1961.

There was ground for doubt and need for rapid action; the ground and the need were recognized, and important steps were taken, but an appearance of complacency led to an appearance of weakness, with considerable costs abroad. These costs would surely have been greater had it not been for the remarkable personal standing of President Eisenhower.

HONEST SURPRISE

At the beginning of the Kennedy Administration there was need both for further action and for a re-establishment of confidence. The new President himself had feared the missile gap and had pressed his concern in the campaign.

It was with honest surprise and relief that in 1961 he found the situation much less dangerous than the best evidence available to the Senate had indicated the year before. His Administration moved at once to correct the public impression, and thereafter, throughout his term, he encouraged and supported policies of action and of exposition which aimed to insure not merely that American strategic power was sufficient but that its sufficiency was recognized.

The adequacy of American strategic strength is a matter of such transcendent importance that it must always be a legitimate topic of political debate.

"How much is enough?" is a question on which honest men will differ, and interested parties will find room and reason for their claims. Thus, it is natural that in the present political year we have ranging shots already from the fringes, some saying that our strength is too little and others that it is too great.

Just as it is the responsibility of the Commander-in-Chief to insure the adequacy of our strength, so it is his task, either directly or through his principal defense officers, to meet and overcome such criticism.

The present Administration will not be lax in the exposition of the real situation, and no one who has closely examined the present and prospective balance of strategic strength can doubt that this year any assertion that we are weak will be found wanting to the point of irresponsibility.

EQUAL OBLIGATION

There is an equal obligation to meet the arguments of those who think we are too strong. When these arguments grow out of fundamentally different views on the purpose and meaning of effective strategic strength, it may be necessary to agree to disagree.

"Unilateral disarmament" is a tainted term, but it does embody something of what is desired by most of those who criticize our present strength as gravely excessive.

The Presidents of the nuclear age have recognized that the law of diminishing returns applies to strategic missiles as to all other commodities; they have also agreed with President Johnson's comment that our nuclear defense expenditures can never be justified as WPA for selected towns or states.

But they have all rejected the gamble of limiting our strategic strength in terms of any absolute concept of what is enough.

They have measured our strength against that of the Soviet Union and have aimed at strategic superiority; that superiority has had different meanings at different stages, but seen from the White House its value for peace has never been small.

Yet even in this rejection of the underlying arguments which move so many of those who find our strength excessive, a President who cares for peace will respect their general concern. It is entirely true that nuclear strength can be provocative, that it is full of the hazard of accident or misuse and that it imposes upon its commander, in his own interest as in that of mankind, a passion for prudence.

All the Presidents of the nuclear age have understood this responsibility and have sought to meet it by insisting on disciplined and responsible control of this power.

In the case of President Kennedy, the pressing need was that as the number and variety of weapons systems increase, there should be ever more searching attention to effective command and control. To him, this was a better answer to the dangers of accident than some arbitrary limitation of numbers; a thousand well-controlled and safely designed missiles could be less dangerous than a hundred of lower quality, as well as more effective in deterrence.

POWERFUL AVERSION

A related point was the President's powerful aversion to those nuclear weapons which could be used effectively only in a first strike. In 1961 and 1962 he faced a series of judgments on major systems; he always preferred the system which could survive an attack as against the system which might provoke one.

In the same way and for related reasons, he preferred the system which was on the high seas or at home to that which required a base abroad and evoked a real or pretended charge of encirclement from Moscow.

The Commander-in-Chief must be strong, then, but also restrained. And as his strength must be recognized, so must his restraint. The doctrine of "massive retaliation" was never as absolute as Secretary Dulles at first made it seem, and its real weakness lay not in the undoubted fact that against certain kinds of aggression a nuclear response would be necessary, but in the appearance of a bomb-rattling menace which it created.

The Presidency does well to avoid this appearance; in the Kennedy Administration the rule was that statements of strength and will should be made as calmly as possible. The President himself watched constantly to prevent the appearance of belligerence, and when the White House watch nodded—as in one magazine account in which a single phrase out of context was seized upon by Soviet propaganda—he made his dissatisfaction plain.

A similar discipline was enforced throughout the Administration upon both civil and military officials. Those who have read speech drafts for clearance know how seldom there is need for major change and how often divergence between presidential purposes and a speaker's draft can be corrected by revision which reconciles the real purposes of both.

And again it is not only the act of coordination but the appearance of it which is helpful. The nuclear age multiplies the mistrust that peaceable men must feel toward military men who appear not to be under effective control, and nothing adds more to a President's reputation abroad than recognition that he is Commander-in-Chief in fact as well as in name.

PRESIDENTIAL CONTROL

Yet the Kennedy years show again, as the terms of strong Presidents have shown before, that harmony, not conflict, is the normal relation between the armed services and the Presidency.

The maintenance of clear presidential control over military policy and over public statements gave rise to some criticism, and intermittently there were assertions that this or that military need was being overridden, this or that viewpoint silenced.

Energy and strength in the office of the Secretary of Defense produced similar worries, and challenges to cherished privileges were not unresisted.

But the center of emphasis belongs on the fact that the Presidency has these powers in this country; a President who uses them firmly, with a defensible concept of the national security, can count on the support of the officers and men of the armed forces. The American tradition of civilian control is strong and the tradition of loyalty among professional officers high; the services are eager for a strong and active Commander-in-Chief. The armed strength of the United States, if handled with firmness and prudence, is a great force for peace.

ROOSEVELT'S WEAKNESS

The President who seeks peace must have a clear view of the Soviet Union. The one great weakness of Franklin Roosevelt was that he did not; he had not the advantage of living, as all his successors have, through the realities of the years after 1945. Nothing is gained for peace by forgetting Czechoslovakia or Hungary or the recurrent menace to Berlin, or Korea or Southeast Asia or any of the dozens of times and places where Communists with help from Moscow have sought to put an end to liberty.

Mr. Kennedy had this clear view. He had it before he became President; he confirmed it in his first state papers; he understood not only the unrelenting ambition and the ruthlessness of communism, but also the weakness and disarray of much of the non-Communist world. And for almost two of his three years—from the very beginning until the offensive weapons were gone from Cuba—he had an exposure to Communist pressure in Berlin, in Laos and in the Caribbean which could only confirm the somber estimate with which he entered office.

Against these pressures he was firm, and to meet them more effectively he greatly strengthened the defenses of the United States—not merely in strategic weapons for basic deterrence but also in forces designed more precisely to meet the hazards of each point of pressure.

The reserves who were called up for Berlin never fired a shot in anger, but military service by Americans has seldom made a more effective contribution to the defense of freedom and the keeping of peace.

The new kinds of strength deployed to South Viet-Nam have not finished that hard job, but they have prevented an otherwise certain defeat and kept the door open for a victory which in the end can be won only by the Vietnamese themselves.

And never in any country did President Kennedy leave it in doubt that Communist subversion is always the enemy of freedom, and of freedom's friends, the Americans.

Yet always—and again from the beginning—he put equal emphasis on the readiness of the United States to reach honorable settlement of all differences, the respect of the United States for the reality of Soviet strength and the insistence of the United States that both sides accept and meet their joint responsibility for peace.

He rejected the stale rhetoric of the cold war; he insisted not on the innate wickedness of communism but on its evil effects. The Communist world was seldom if ever "the enemy." Characteristically, as in his Inaugural Address, the President used a circumlocution whose unaccustomed clumsiness was proof that it was carefully chosen: "those nations who would make themselves our adversary." Characteristically, too, what he there offered them was a request "to begin anew the quest for peace."

And he pressed in this same direction himself. In Laos, in Berlin, and most persistently of all in the search for a test ban, the President's powers, from beginning to end, were used toward the goal of agreement. Agreement must never be surrender; that would be no service to peace. The firmness of the United States under pressure was made plain both in Berlin and in Southeast Asia. But firmness was a means to honorable settlement, not an end in itself.

Harboring no illusion about the difficulty of success, the President nevertheless persevered. He was convinced that at the least it was essential to leave no doubt, in all these issues, of the good will and peaceful purpose of the United States.

If there were to be a continued arms race, or a test of strength it must be plain where the responsibility lay. But the larger truth, as he saw it, was that in these areas of difference there was real advantage to both sides in reliable agreement—if only the other side could be brought to see its own real interests, free of ambition that would be resisted and of fear that was unjustified.

THIN RESPONSE

In 1961 and 1962 the invitation to seek peace together met a thin response. True, the threat to Berlin, so noisy in 1961 and so sharpened by the confession of Communist bankruptcy which was the Wall, seemed slightly milder in 1962. And an agreement was reached on Laos, imperfect in its terms and in its execution but much better than no agreement at all. It was in Laos above all that one could see the advantage to both sides of even the most incomplete disengagement as against a tightening and sharpening of confrontation.

But no agreement at all had come in the field nearest the President's heart—that of limiting the nuclear danger. On the contrary, Soviet tests had led inexorably to American tests. It was somehow a measure of the Kennedy temper and purpose that of all the Soviet provocations of these two years it was the resumption of testing that disappointed him most.

The Cuban missile crisis was the most important single event of the Kennedy Presidency. As the President himself pointed out afterward, it was the first direct test between the Soviet Union and the United States in which nuclear weapons were the issue.

Although vast amounts have been written about the crisis, we still have no solid account of one half of it—the Soviet side. What is not known of one side limits our ability to assess action on the other, and this limitation should warn us against judgments that this act more than that, or one advantage more than another, was decisive. It does not prevent a more general judgment of the main elements contributing to success.

What is at once astonishing and wholly natural is the degree to which the clear components of this success are precisely those to which the Presidency had been bent and not only in the Kennedy Administration; strength, restraint and respect for the opinions of mankind.

That strength counted we cannot doubt—though it is typical of the uncertainties of assessment that the partisans of specific kinds of strength remained persuaded, afterward as before, of the peculiar value of their preferred weapons.

Believers in nuclear dissuasion as an all-purpose strategy asserted the predominant role of strategic superiority; believers in the need for conventional strength, while not usually denying the role of SAC in the success, were convinced that what mattered most was usable non-nuclear strength at the point of contest.

Interesting as this argument may be, it can have no certain conclusion. Prudence argues for a judgment that all kinds of military strength were relevant. The existence of adequate and rapidly deployable strength, at all levels, was the direct result of the reinforcement of balanced defenses begun in 1961.

A further element of strength in this crisis was the firmness and clarity of the presidential decision to insist on the withdrawal of the missiles. This was not merely a matter of one speech or even of one decision from a week of heavy argument. It was a position clearly stated, and internationally understood, well before the crisis broke. It was reinforced in its power, and the Communist position correspondingly weakened, by the repeated Soviet assertions that no such weapons were or would be placed in Cuba.

The strength of this position, like the strength of the available military force, was reinforced by its disciplined relation to a policy of restraint. That nuclear weapons should not be strewn around as counters in a contest for face was a proposition commanding wide support. Any impulse to discount or disregard the direct threat to the United States, as a problem for the Americans to solve, was deeply undercut by awareness of the difference between American and Soviet standards of nuclear responsibility as revealed in this moment of danger.

More broadly, the strength and restraint of the American position in October stood in striking contrast to the position in which others found themselves.

As a first consequence, and to a degree that exceeded predictions, the allies of the United States both in this hemisphere and in Europe were clear in their support, though in public comment, especially in the United Kingdom, there was evidence of the difficulties we should have faced if we had been less clearly strong, restrained, and right.

It can be argued, of course, that in this crisis the opinions even of close allies were not crucial, and it does seem probable that such critical decisions as the turnaround of armsbearing ships and the announcement that the missiles would be removed were not determined by OAS votes or by world opinion. This particular crisis might have been successfully resolved even in the face of doubt and division among allies whose immediate power at the point of contest was negligible.

But so narrow a judgment neglects two great hazards. Immediately, a serious division among the allies might have provoked action elsewhere, most dangerously at Berlin (and indeed in all the postwar annals of the bravery of West Berlin there is no moment in which the courage and strength of the Berliners—and indeed of all free Germans—have been more important in discouraging adventure).

And even if no such adventure had been attempted, the position after the crisis would not have been one in which "the quest for peace" could easily be led from Washington. It was and is the central meaning of this affair that a major threat to peace and freedom was removed by means which strengthened the prospects of both.

The October crisis came out better than President Kennedy or any of his associates had expected. The analysis suggested above would not have been compelling in the discussions of the week of October 15, and the predominant reaction in Washington on October 28 was one of simple and enormous relief.

In the weeks after the crisis, attention was diverted, first by backstairs gossip over who gave what advice and then by a renewal of political debate over Cuba, a problem of another order of meaning than the missile crisis and one which had rightly been left essentially as it was while the major threat was removed.

And finally, it was far from clear, in the immediate aftermath, that "those who had made themselves our adversary" in such a sudden and shocking way would now be ready for a different relation.

But what is important for our present purposes is that what shaped American action in this crisis—what set and sustained the tempered response, both to danger and to success, was the President. And while the man in the office was Kennedy, with a taste and style of his own, I think it is right to claim that the office as well as the man was embodied in the resolution, restraint and responsibility that governed in these weeks.

As the great disappointment of 1961 was the renewal of testing, so the great satisfaction of 1963 was the limited test-ban treaty.

The withdrawal of missiles from Cuba did more than end a specific crisis of great gravity. It also signaled an acceptance by the Soviet government, for the present at least, of the existing nuclear balance. In that balance there is American superiority, as we have seen, but it is a superiority that does not permit any lack of respect for the strength of the Soviet Union. No safer balance appears possible at present. No overwhelmingly one-sided margin is open to either side, and it was one lesson of the Cuban affair—as of many others since 1945—that it was well for peace that Communist strength should be matched with a margin.

But the purpose of this margin must still be peace, and the aim of policy must still be to get beyond conflicting interests to the great common need for safer prospect of survival. This is the meaning of the limited test-ban treaty.

If the missile crisis was the proof of American strength in conflict, the test-ban treaty was the proof of American readiness to work for this common purpose. And whatever the moving forces on the Soviet side, in the non-Communist world the Presidency was the necessary center of action.

A special and distinguished role was played by the British Prime Minister, but Macmillan would be the first to recognize that it was mainly through his close relation to two Presidents that he was able to make the British contribution effective.

POWER WITH ENERGY

It is only the American President who can carry the American Senate and the American people in any agreement on arms control, and it is only with American participation that any such agreement can have meaning for the Soviet government.

Unless a President uses these powers with energy, arms control agreements are improbable. The momentum of the arms race—the power at work to keep it going almost without conscious new decision—is enormous. Military men in all countries find it hard to approve any arms control proposal which is not either safely improbable or clearly unbalanced in their own favor.

In the United States, only a strong Commander-in-Chief with a strong Secretary of Defense is in a position to press steadily for recognition that the arms race itself is now a threat to national security.

Only the President can insure that good proposals are kept alive even after a first rejection, and that new possibilities are constantly considered—so that there may always be as many proposals as possible on the table waiting for the moment of Soviet readiness. The readiness to meet all threats must be matched by a demonstrated readiness to reach agreement.

In the case of the limited test-ban, it was President Kennedy himself who reached the conclusion in the spring of 1963 that the United States would not be the first to make further atmospheric tests. That quite personal decision, recognized at the time as fully within the presidential power and announced in an address on peace whose power and conviction were immediately recognized, was as likely an immediate cause as any for the announcement, less than a month later, that the Soviet government would now be willing to sign an agreement which had been open for two years.

There followed a period of negotiation and then a debate on ratification, and in these again the Presidency was central. The test-ban treaty, as we have all told each other a hundred times, is only one step, and President Johnson has made clear his determination to seek further steps with all the energy and imagination the Government can command.

Meanwhile, the lesson of the test-ban is that no step at all can be taken in this field unless the President himself works for it. A President indifferent to arms control, or easily discouraged by Soviet intransigence or irresponsibility or inclined to a narrow military view of the arms race, would be a guarantee against agreed limitation of armaments.

Conversely, where there is zeal in the search for agreement, refusal to accept initial disappointment as final, a cool and balanced assessment of the risks of agreement against the risks of unlimited competition and a firm use of the powers of the office, the Presidency can become—as in this case—an instrument of hope for all men everywhere.

In concentrating attention upon the great requirements of strength and a love for peace, and in using as examples of such very large matters as the missile crisis and the test-ban treaty, I do not pretend to have exhausted the connections between the Presidency and the Peace, even as they showed themselves in the short Kennedy years.

There is more in the Presidency that the special powers of the Commander-in-Chief or the special responsibility for pressing the hard cause of disarmament. There is more, too, than a need for understanding of Soviet realities.

The Presidency is a powerful element in the strength or weakness of the United Nations, as every Secretary General has known. The Presidency remains the headquarters of the Great Alliance, as even the most separated of national leaders has recognized.

The Presidency is an indispensable stimulus to progress in the Americas. The Presidency must make the hard choices of commitment that have brought both honor and difficulty, as in Korea in 1950 or in South Viet-Nam in 1954.

The White House visit and the White House photograph are elements of democratic electioneering not just in the United States but wherever the name of the American President can bring a cheer.

The death of a President men loved has shown how wide this larger constituency is. Allies, neutrals and even adversaries attend to the Presidency.

When the American President shows that he can understand and respect the opinions and hopes of distant nations, when he proves able to present the interests of his own people without neglecting the interests of others, when in his own person he represents decency, hope, and freedom—then he is strengthened in his duty to be the leader of man's quest for peace and in the age of nuclear weapons. And this strength will be at least as important in meeting danger as in pursuing hope.

NEW PROBLEMS

The administration in Washington, led now by President Johnson, will face new problems and make new decisions, and as time passes the new imprint of a strong mind and heart will be felt increasingly—in the presidency, in the Government and in the world.

President Kennedy would have been the last to suppose that the purely personal characteristics of any President, however loved and mourned, could or should continue to determine the work of the Presidency after his death.

President Johnson will conduct the office in his own way. Yet the short space of three months is enough to show plainly that the pursuit of peace remains his central concern, while the effective transfer from one administration to the next has reflected the fact that loyalty to President Kennedy and loyalty to President Johnson are not merely naturally compatible but logically necessary as a part of a larger loyalty to their common purpose.

And as we remember John Kennedy, let us separate the essential from the complementary. The youth, the grace and the wit were wonderful, but they were not the center. There lay courage, vision, humanity and strength, tested on the path to the office and tempered by the office itself. It is these qualities, applied to the greatest issues, that belong not only to the man but to the job.

It is my own conviction that this kind of President and this kind of Presidency reflect the general will of Americans. Temperate use of strength, respect for honest difference, sympathy for those in need and a readiness to go our share of the distance—these qualities, which I have described in phrases borrowed from our new President, are qualities of the American people.

They have their opposites in our character, too, but these are what we honor; these we expect of our Presidents.

In the terrible shock of President Kennedy's death there were so many—perhaps too many—who saw the foul deeds of a few days in Dallas, and not the dead President himself, as the embodiment of the real America. They were wrong.

As a man, as a President, as a servant of the peace, he was what we are, and his achievement belongs to us all. Strengthened by his service, the Presidency continues, and so does the quest for peace.

8 THE PUBLIC EXECUTIVE

Many Americans—Republicans and Democrats alike—have displayed a long-standing, if less than reasoned, suspicion of "Big Government." They tend to view bureaucracy as a necessary evil at best and to regard civil servants as generally inadequate and inefficient. "Unbusinesslike" is the damning phrase frequently applied to the civil-service system and "bureaucrat" is the individual condemnation. Yet, despite the popular saying "Those who can, do; those who cannot, go into the public service," many Americans fear the public servant's power—his supposed ability to regulate lives, his alleged tendency to build empires. Even the sophisticated have fallen prey to certain questionable beliefs—for example, that policy and execution should be kept separate, and that the quick solution to administrative problems lies in a neat, symmetrical government structure outlined by simplified flow charts and hierarchical diagrams.

Before attempting an analysis of such stereotyped thinking, however, let us isolate some of the possible goals that may prove acceptable to Americans of all political persuasions. First, what do we expect of our public executives—our "bureaucrats"? In the broadest sense, we expect them to facilitate social achievements, whether in meeting the progressive challenges of "new frontiers" or in consolidating the rewards of an "enlightened conservatism." More than mere governmental efficiency is involved in this expectation, since we also expect our civil servants to assure governmental stability through periods of social development and change. It is their task to make things come out as planned, and to provide the greatest amount of government service for the least possible cost.

What kind of public servant, then, do we want, and what are the tasks we assign him? If he is to meet fully the demands we make upon him, he must combine the qualities of responsibility, leadership, and initiative. Furthermore, he must understand fully the nature of democracy, and possess a strong sense of public service—a sense of mission. Above all, he must possess that all-too-rare ability to distinguish goals from techniques; the tax collector, for instance, must never succumb to the delusion that revenue raising is one of the ends of government.

We must consider some of the problems faced by the public executive before we can understand his role. Perhaps his most important problem is the magnitude of his task—a magnitude completely unknown to his counterpart in even the largest corporate entity, such as General Motors or General Electric. Moreover, his is a complex of responsibilities that the business executive finds bewildering. He is not only held to account by the press, with its speedy public disclosures; by the Congress with its appropriation power; and by the courts, with their prerogative of review. He must answer, even as his business counterpart must answer, to his chief executive and to his immediate agency superiors. In all his dealings, he must be a paragon of propriety, keeping a wary eye out for ethical temptations unknown to the business world and maintaining a moral posture beyond reproach. "Conflict of interest" is his ever present shadow.

What are his rewards for such demanding service? In addition to the accidental public distortions of his labors, deliberate attempts to disparage and discredit him are often his lot—not only on the part of political attackers but on the part of well-equipped pressure groups and, sometimes, elements of the press itself. In the face of all this verbal abuse, the public executive must, nonetheless, not only continue to operate the vast machinery of administration but carry out the delicate process best described as "the engineering of consent." He finds, even on the highest levels, that his authority is diffuse and that decisions are made by groups rather than individuals even though departmental shortcomings are all too frequently attributed to individuals—especially to those presumably in charge. His primary role is often one of coordination—of compromise rather than command—as he is called up to persuade the unyielding, to cajole his organization, and to better his "public relations." A generalist, he supervises specialists who are technically far more knowledgeable than he, but who are often hesitant to act, because of the myopia of their own expertness. In short, the task of the American public executive, as Harlan Cleveland has put it so well, is to "make a mesh of things," though his efforts may bring accusations of responsibility for the "mess in Washington."

We shall now examine the role that public-executive leadership plays in our government in action.

THE POLICYMAKER AND THE INTELLECTUAL
Henry A. Kissinger

Henry A. Kissinger, who served as one of President Kennedy's top foreign-policy advisers, is Associate Director of the Harvard Center for International Affairs. An educator, lecturer, and government specialist, he is the author of *Nuclear Weapons and Foreign Policy, A World Restored: Castlereagh, Metternich and the Restoration of Peace, The Necessity for Choice: Prospects of American Foreign Policy,* and many other books.

Any observer of the American scene must be struck by the tentative quality of our policy both foreign and domestic. Major parts of the world are undergoing revolutionary upheaval; but we seem hardly aware that peoples abroad find increasingly little in America with which to identify themselves. Beyond any disagreement or dissatisfaction over specific policies there exists an evergrowing distrust or at least incomprehension of America's purposes.

It would be comforting to believe that this state of affairs is due to particular mistakes of policy that can be reversed more or less easily. Unfortunately the problem is more deep-seated. Our policymakers' lack of vigor is matched by that of many of their critics. It has been a long time since there has been a real debate on policy issues beyond a bland competition for slogans such as coexistence or flexibility.

The stagnation is often ascribed to the fact that our best people are not attracted into government service. But it may be pertinent to inquire how qualified our eminent men are for the task of policymaking in a revolutionary period. Others trace the cause of our difficulties to the lack of respect shown the intellectual by our society. However, a case could be made for the proposition that in some respects the intellectual has never been more in demand; that he makes such a relatively small contribution not because he is rejected but because his function is misunderstood. He is sought after enthusiastically but for the wrong reasons and in pursuit of the wrong purposes.

ADMINISTRATIVE STAGNATION

One of the paradoxes of an increasingly specialized, bureaucratized society is that the qualities rewarded in the rise to eminence are less and less the qualities required once eminence is reached. Specialization encourages administrative and technical skills, which are not necessarily related to the vision and creativity needed for leadership. The essence of good administration is co-ordination among the specialized functions of a bureaucracy. The task of the executive is to infuse and occasionally to transcend routine with purpose.

Yet while the head of an organization requires a different outlook from that of his administrative subordinates, he must generally be recruited from their ranks. Eminence thus is often reached for reasons and according to criteria which are irrelevant to the tasks which must be performed in the highest positions. Despite all personnel procedures and perhaps because of them, superior performance at the apex of an organization is frequently in the deepest sense accidental.

This problem, serious enough in the private sector, is even more complicated in government. In a society that has prided itself on its free-enterprise character, it is inevitable that the qualities which are most esteemed in civilian pursuits should also be generally rewarded by high public office. But very little in the experience that forms American leadership groups produces the combination of political acumen, conceptual skill, persuasive power, and administrative ability required for the highest positions of government.

Our executives are shaped by a style of life that inhibits reflectiveness. For one of the characteristics of a society based on specialization is the enormous work load of its top personnel. The smooth functioning of the administrative apparatus absorbs more energies than the definition of criteria on which decision is to be based. Issues are reduced to their simplest terms. Decision making is increasingly turned into a group effort. The executive's task is conceived as choosing among administrative proposals in the formulation of which he has no part and with the substance of which he is often unfamiliar. A premium is placed on "presentations" which take the least effort to grasp and which in practice usually mean oral "briefings." (This accounts for the emergence of the specialist in "briefings" who prepares charts, one-page summaries, etc.) In our society the policymaker is dependent to an increasing extent on his subordinates' conception of the essential elements of a problem.

The bureaucratization of our society reflects not only its inevitable specialization but also certain deepseated philosophical attitudes all the more persuasive for rarely being made explicit. Two generations of Americans have been shaped by the pragmatic conviction that inadequate performance is somehow the result of a failure to properly understand an "objective" environment and that group effort is valuable in itself. The interaction of several minds is supposed to broaden the range of "experience" believed to be the ultimate source of knowledge.

Pragmatism, at least in its generally accepted forms, produces a tendency to identify a policy issue with the search for empirical data. It sees in consensus a test of validity; it distrusts individual effort or at least individual certitude and it tends to suppress personal judgment as "subjective."

The low valuation of personal views produces a greater concern with the collection of facts than with an interpretation of their significance; therefore the myth in our government that intelligence does not advise, it only reports. It leads to a multiplication of advisory staffs and a great reliance on study groups of all types. Each difficulty calls into being new panels which frequently act as if nothing had ever been done before, partly, at least, because the very existence of a problem is taken as an indication of the inadequacy of the previous advice.

The situation is compounded by the personal humility that is one of the most attractive American traits. Most Americans are convinced that no one is ever entirely "right," or, as the saying goes, that if there is disagreement each party is probably a little in error. The fear of dogmatism pervades the American scene. But the corollary of the tentativeness of most views is an incurable inward insecurity. Even very eminent people are reluctant to stand alone, and they see in concurrence one of their chief tests of validity.

Philosophical conviction and psychological bias thus combine to produce in and out of government a penchant for policymaking by committee. The obvious insurance against the possibility of error is to obtain as many opinions as possible. And unanimity is important, in that its absence is a standing reminder of the tentativeness of the course adopted. The committee approach to decision making is often less an organizational device than a spiritual necessity.

In this manner, policy is fragmented into a series of *ad hoc* decisions which make it difficult to achieve a sense of direction or even to profit from experience. Substantive problems are transformed into administrative ones. Innovation is subjected to "objective" tests which deprive it of spontaneity. "Policy planning" becomes the projection of familiar problems into the future. Momentum is confused with purpose. There is greater concern with how things are than with which things matter. The illusion is created that we can avoid recourse to personal judgment and responsibility as the final determinant of policy.

The debilitating tendency of this approach is often obscured in the private sector of our society because the goals of our economic effort are relatively limited. They involve less the creation of a policy framework than successfully operating within one—itself a conciliatory procedure. But when the same method is applied to national policy, its limitations become dramatically apparent. Many of our policymakers begin their governmental careers with only superficial acquaintance with the problems of their office. This is partly because the rise to eminence has often absorbed most of their energies, partly because civic consciousness, where it exists, most often finds its outlet on the local level. Whatever the reason, few of our executives (or lawyers with business background) can benefit in government from the strong will which is often their outstanding trait and which gained them success. Consciously or not, our top policymakers often lack the assurance and the conceptual framework to impose a pattern on events or to impart a sense of direction to their administrative staffs. Their unfamiliarity with their subject matter reinforces their already strong tendency to identify a policy problem with an administrative breakdown and a policy solution with an aggregate of administrative proposals.

The impact on national policy is pernicious. Even our highest policy bodies such as the National Security Council, are less concerned with developing overall measures in terms of a well-understood national purpose than with adjusting the varying approaches of semi-autonomous departments. The elaborateness of the process is compounded by the tendency of advisers to advise; for silence may be taken to mean not that the idea under discussion is good but that the adviser is inadequate. The committee system is more concerned with co-ordination and adjustment than with purpose.

A policy dilemma is produced because the advantages and disadvantages of alternative measures appear fairly evenly balanced; otherwise there would be no need for discussion. (This leaves aside the question to what extent the committee procedure encourages a neutral personality to which the pros and cons of almost any course of action always seem fairly even and which therefore creates artificial dilemmas.) But in assessing these alternatives the risks always seem more certain than the opportunities. No one can ever prove that an opportunity existed, but failure to foresee a danger involves swift retribution. As a result, much of the committee procedure is designed to permit each participant or agency to register objections, and the system stresses avoidance of risk rather than boldness of conception.

Our method of arriving at decisions and the attitudes of our officials distort the essence of policy. Effective policy depends not only on the skill of individual moves but even more importantly on their relationship to each other. It requires a sense of proportion; a sense of style provides it with inner discipline. All these intangibles are negated where problems become isolated cases each of which is disposed of on its merits by experts in the special difficulties it involves. It is as if in commissioning a painting, a patron would ask one artist to draw the face, another the body, another the hands, and still another the feet, simply because each artist is particularly good in one category. Such a procedure in stressing the components would lose the meaning of the whole.

The result is a paradox: the more intense the search for certainty by means of administrative devices, the greater is the inward insecurity of the participants. The more they seek "objectivity," the more diffuse their efforts become. The insecurity of many of our policymakers sometimes leads to almost compulsive traits. Officials—and other executives as well—tend to work to the point of exhaustion as one indication that they have done all that could be asked. The insecurity of many of our policymakers sometimes is also shown by the fact that almost in direct proportion as advisory staffs multiply they are distrusted by those at the top. Officials increasingly feel the need for "outside"—and therefore unbiased—advice. Memoranda that are produced within the bureaucracy are taken less seriously than similar papers that are available to the general public. Crucial policy advice is increasingly requested from *ad hoc* committees of outside experts. (See, e.g., the Gaither Committee on national defense or the Draper Committee on economic assistance.)

These committees are often extraordinarily useful. They provide a fresh point of view. They can focus public discussion. They make possible the tapping of talent that would otherwise be unavailable, particularly in the scientific field. (A good case in point is James Killian's method of operation as science adviser to the President.) They may even galvanize the bureaucracy. Nevertheless they suffer from serious drawbacks. Whatever the previous experience of the members, they require extensive "briefing." This places an additional strain on the bureaucracy, while the members of the committee are frequently ready to make their best contribution at the point when the group is disbanded. Then again, the committee is inevitably drawn from the same segment of society as the top officials. Its members have therefore also been victims of the prevailing administrative pace. And the committee process, with its trend toward the fragmentation of policy and its bias toward simplified approaches, is almost as pervasive in *ad hoc* groups as in regular governmental committees.

In some respects *ad hoc* groups can even be said to represent an important diversion of talent. The number of outstanding individuals with experience in a given field is severely limited. As a result the same group is called again and again on related tasks. Its discussions soon become predictable and sometimes even stereotyped. The ideal situation would be a "leap-frogging" process in which the current high officials expend their intellectual capital while others, usually outside government, develop new concepts and approaches. But constant membership on committees causes many of their members to stagnate and freezes them at the level of the experience or effort that gained them their reputation.

Moreover, outside groups are handicapped by the fact that unless they constitute themselves into a pressure group seeking to mold public opinion—a function beyond their scope and usually contrary to their purpose—they can be effective only if they convince the bureaucracy. If they are too far in advance of existing thinking, they are ignored. If they only confirm what has already been considered within the government, they are unnecessary. *Ad hoc* committees generally can be effective only in a narrowly circumscribed area which may be somewhat ahead of official views but which rarely touches the essence of the problem: to challenge the existing assumptions or to define a new sense of direction.

The committee system not only has a tendency to ask the wrong questions, it also puts a premium on the wrong qualities. The committee process is geared to the pace of conversation. Even where the agenda is composed of memoranda, these are prepared primarily as a background for discussion, and they stand and fall on the skill with which they are presented. Hence quickness of comprehension is more important than reflectiveness, fluency more useful than creativeness. The ideal "committee man" does not make his associates uncomfortable; he does not operate with ideas too far outside of what is generally accepted. Thus the thrust of committees is toward a standard of average performance. Since a complicated idea cannot be easily absorbed by ear—particularly when it is new—committees lean toward what fits in with the most familiar experience of their members. They therefore produce great pressure in favor of the *status quo*. Committees are consumers and sometimes sterilizers of ideas, rarely creators of them.

For all their cumbersome procedure and their striving for "objectivity," there is something approaching frivolity about many committees. Ideas are accepted because no one can think of an objection fast enough; or they are rejected because they cannot readily be grasped. Unfortunately, not everything that sounds plausible is important and many important ideas do not seem plausible, at least at first glance, the only glance permitted by most committees. Rapidity of comprehension is not always equivalent to responsible assessment; it may even be contrary to it. The result is a vicious circle: in the absence of well-understood goals each problem becomes a special case. But the more fragmented our approach to policy, the more difficult it becomes to act consistently and purposefully. The typical pattern of our governmental process is therefore endless debate about whether a given set of circumstances is in fact a problem, until a crisis removes all doubts but also the possibility of effective action. The committee system, which is an attempt to reduce the inward insecurity of our top personnel, leads to the paradoxical consequence of institutionalizing it.

The result is that American policy displays a combination of abstractness and rigidity. Our method of arriving at decisions and the qualities it reflects and rewards place a greater premium on form than on substance. Thus on any given issue some paper will be produced for almost any eventuality. But because policy results from what are in effect adversary proceedings, proposals by the various departments or agencies are often overstated to permit compromise, or phrased vaguely to allow freedom of interpretation. In any case, what is considered policy is usually the embodiment of a consensus in a paper. The very qualities which make the consensus possible tend to inhibit sustained and subtle effort: for the statement is frequently so general that it must be renegotiated when the situation to which it applies arises.

The rigidity of American policy is therefore a sympton of the psychological burden placed on our policymakers. Policies developed with great inward doubt become almost sacrosanct as soon as they are finally officially adopted. The reason is psychological. The *status quo* has at least the advantage of familiarity. An attempt to change course involves the prospect that the whole searing process of arriving at a decision will have to be repeated. By the same token, most of our initiatives tend to occur during crisis periods. When frustration becomes too great or a crisis brooks no further evasion, there arises the demand for innovation almost for its own sake. Yet innovation cannot be achieved by fiat. Crisis conditions do not encourage calm consideration; they rarely permit anything except defense moves.

The combination of unreflectiveness produced by the style of life of our most eminent people in and out of government, faith in administrative processes, and the conversational approach to policy accounts for much of the uncertainty of our policy. It leads to an enormous waste of intellectual resources. The price we pay for the absence of a sense of direction is that we appear to the rest of the world as vacillating, confused, and, what is most worrisome, increasingly irrelevant.

THE DEMAND FOR INTELLECTUALS

In a revolutionary period, then, it is precisely the practical man who is most apt to become a prisoner of events. It is most frequently the administrator who is unable to transcend the requirements of the moment. Are there any groups in our society who can overcome this impasse? How about those who are not engaged in administrative tasks nor part of large organizations; the individuals who devote themselves to furthering or disseminating knowledge—the intellectuals?

Any survey of the contemporary American scene reveals, however, that the problem is more complicated than our refusal or inability to utilize this source of talent. Many organizations, governmental or private, rely on panels of experts. Political leaders have intellectuals as advisers. Throughout our society, policy-planning bodies proliferate. Research organizations multiply. The need for talent is a theme of countless reports. What then is the difficulty?

One problem is the demand for expertise itself. Every problem which our society becomes concerned about—leaving aside the question whether these are always the most significant—calls into being panels, committees, or study groups supported by either private or governmental funds. Many organizations constantly call on intellectuals. As a result, intellectuals with a reputation soon find themselves so burdened that their pace of life hardly differs from that of the executives whom they advise. They cannot supply perspective because they are as harassed as the policymakers. In his desire to be helpful, the intellectual is too frequently compelled to sacrifice what should be his greatest contribution to society: his creativity.

Moreover, the pressure is not only produced by the organizations that ask for advice: some of it is generated by the self-image of the intellectual. In a pragmatic society, it is almost inevitable not only that the pursuit of knowledge for its own sake should be lightly regarded by the community but also that it should engender feelings of insecurity or even guilt among some of those who have dedicated themselves to it. There are many who believe that their ultimate contribution as intellectuals depends on the degree of their participation in what is considered the active life. It is not a long step from the willingness to give advice to having one's self-esteem gratified by a consulting relationship with a large organization. And since individuals who challenge the presuppositions of the bureaucracy, governmental or private, rarely can keep their positions as advisers, great pressures are created to elaborate on familiar themes rather than risk new departures that may both fail and prove unacceptable.

The great valuation our society places on expertise may be even more inimical to innovation than indifference. Since the American intellectual is so strongly committed to the same pragmatic values as the rest of society, it produces a tremendous overspecialization. This in turn makes it difficult for the intellectual to introduce a general perspective even from the vantage point of his own calling. Panels of experts are deliberately assembled to contain representatives of particular approaches: a committee on military policy will have spokesmen for the "all-out war" as well as for the "limited war" concept. A committee on foreign policy will have proponents for the "uncommitted areas" as well as specialists for Europe. These are then expected to adjust their differences by analogy with the committee procedure of the bureaucracy. Not surprisingly, the result is more often a common denominator than a well-rounded point of view.

This tendency is compounded by the conception of the intellectual held by the officials or organizations that call on him. The specialization of functions of a bureaucratized society delimits tasks and establishes categories of expectations. A person is considered suitable for assignments within certain classifications. But the classification of the intellectual is determined by the premium our society places on administrative skill. The intellectual is rarely found at the level where decisions are made; his role is commonly advisory. He is called in as a "specialist" in ideas whose advice is compounded with that of others from different fields of endeavor on the assumption that the policymaker is able to choose the correct amalgam between "theoretical" and "practice" advice. And even in this capacity the intellectual is not a free agent. It is the executive who determines in the first place whether he needs advice. He and the bureaucracy frame the question to be answered. The policymaker determines the standard of relevance. He decides who is consulted and thereby the definition of "expertness."

The fact that the need for excellence is constantly invoked is no guarantee that its nature will be understood. Excellence is more often thought to consist in the ability to perform the familiar as well as possible than in pushing back the frontiers of knowledge or insight. The search for talent consists more frequently in seeking personnel for well-understood tasks than in an effort to bring about an environment that constantly produces new and not yet imagined types of performance. The "expert" not uncommonly is the person who elaborates the existing framework most ably, rather than the individual charting new paths.

The contribution of the intellectual to policy is therefore in terms of criteria that he has played a minor role in establishing. He is rarely given the opportunity to point out that a query delimits a range of possible solutions or that an issue is posed in irrelevant terms. He is asked to solve problems, not to contribute to the definition of goals. Where decisions are arrived at by negotiation, the intellectual—particularly if he is not himself part of the bureaucracy—is a useful weight in the scale. He can serve as a means to filter ideas to the top outside of organization channels or as a legitimizer for the viewpoint of contending factions within and among departments. This is why many organizations build up batteries of outside experts or create semi-independent research groups, and why articles or books become tools in the bureaucratic struggle. In short, all too often what the policymaker wants from the intellectual is not ideas but endorsement.

This is not to say that the motivation of the policymaker toward the intellectual is cynical. The policymaker sincerely wants help. His problem is that he does not know the nature of the help he requires. And he generally does not become aware of a need until the problem is already critical. He is subject to the misconception that he can make an effective choice among conflicting advisers on the basis of administrative rules of thumb and without being fully familiar with the subject matter. Of necessity the bureaucracy gears the intellectual effort to its own requirements and its own pace: the deadlines are inevitably those of the policymaker, and all too often they demand a premature disclosure of ideas which are then dissected before they are fully developed. The administrative approach to intellectual effort tends to destroy the environment from which innovation grows. Its insistence on "results" discourages the intellectual climate that might produce important ideas whether or not the bureaucracy feels it needs them.

For these reasons, research institutes set up by governmental agencies have sometimes reflected the views of their sponsor even when they were financially independent. As long as the sponsoring agency retains the right to define the tasks of its research agency—or even the majority of these tasks—it will also determine the point of view of the product. The uniformity of the administrative approach is after all primarily the result less of fiscal control than of all the intangibles of fellowship and concern produced by association with a particular group and constant concentration on the same range of issues. It is not overcome if the "outside" research institute has no greater possibility for applying a wider perspective than its sponsoring agency has.

Thus though the intellectual participates in policymaking to an almost unprecedented degree, the result has not necessarily been salutary for him or of full benefit for the organization using him. In fact, the two have sometimes compounded each other's weaknesses. Nor has the present manner of utilizing outside experts and research institutes done more than reduce somewhat the dilemmas of the policymakers. The production of so much research often simply adds another burden to already overworked officials. It tends to divert attention from the act of judgment on which policy ultimately depends to the assembly of facts—which is relatively the easiest step in policy formation. Few if any of the recent crises of U.S. policy have been caused by the unavailability of data. Our policymakers do not lack advice; they are in many respects overwhelmed by it. They do lack criteria on which to base judgments. In the absence of commonly understood and meaningful standards, all advice tends to become equivalent. In seeking to help the bureaucracy out of this maze, the intellectual too frequently becomes an extension of the administrative machine, accepting its criteria and elaborating its problems. While this too is a necessary task and sometimes even an important one, it does not touch the heart of the problem: that purpose must dominate the mechanism if we are to avoid disaster. The dilemma of our policy is not so much that it cannot act on what it has defined as useful—though this too happens occasionally—but that the standards of utility are in need of redefinition. Neither the intellectual nor the policymaker performs his full responsibility if he shies away from this essential task.

RECHARGING THE BATTERIES

This is not a call for the intellectual to remain aloof from policymaking. Nor have intellectuals who have chosen withdrawal necessarily helped the situation. There are intellectuals outside the bureaucracy who are not part of the maelstrom of committees and study groups but who have nevertheless contributed to the existing stagnation through a perfectionism that paralyzes action by posing unreal alternatives. (If we have the choice between rebuilding our cities or launching a satellite, we must choose the former.) There are intellectuals with the bureaucracy who have avoided the administrative approach but who must share the responsibility for the prevailing confusion because they refuse to recognize the inevitable element of conjecture in policymaking. (How can we be *sure* about Soviet motives? How can we be *certain* that in say thirty years the Soviet system will not be like ours?) The intellectuals of other countries in the free world where the influence of pragmatism is less pronounced and the demands of the bureaucracies less insatiable have not made a more significant contribution. The spiritual malaise described here may have other symptoms elsewhere. The fact remains that the entire free world suffers not only from administrative myopia but also from self-righteousness and the lack of a sense of direction.

One reason why intellectuals outside the administrative machines have not made a greater contribution is that for them protest has too often become an end in itself. Whether they have withdrawn by choice or because of the nature of their society, many intellectuals have confused the issues by simplifying them too greatly. They have refused to recognize that policymaking involves not only the clear conception of ideas but also the management of men. In the process analysis has been too often identified with policymaking.

But the equivalence is not absolute, particularly if analysis is conceived too rigidly. Effective policy fits its measures to circumstances. Analysis strives to eliminate the accidental; it seeks principles of general validity. The policymaker is faced with situations where at some point discussion will be overtaken by events, where to delay for the sake of refinement of thought may invite disaster. Analysis, by contrast, can and must always sacrifice time to clarity; it is not completed until all avenues of research have been explored. The difference between the mode of policy and the mode of analysis is therefore one of perspective. Policy looks toward the future; its pace is dictated by the need for decision in a finite time. Analysis assumes an accomplished act or a given set of factors; its pace is the pace of reflection.

The difficulty arises not from the analytic method but from the failure to relate it to the problems of the policymaker. The quest for certainty, essential for analysis, may be paralyzing when pushed to extremes with respect to policy. The search for universality, which has produced so much of the greatest intellectual effort, may lead to something close to dogmatism in national affairs. The result can be a tendency to recoil before the act of choosing among alternatives which is inseparable from policymaking, and to ignore the tragic aspect of policymaking which lies precisely in its unavoidable component of conjecture. There can come about a temptation to seek to combine the advantage of every course of action; to delay commitment until "all the facts are in," until, that is, the future has been reduced to an aspect of the past.

As a consequence, on many issues the short-run and manipulative approach of the bureaucracy and its adjuncts is opposed, if at all, by an abstract, dogmatic moralism that all too often cannot be related to the problem at hand. The technicians who act as if the cold war were its own purpose are confronted by others who sometimes talk as if the cold war could be ended by redefining the term. The Machiavellianism of short-term expedients much too frequently has as its sole antagonist a Utopianism that seems more concerned with registering a dissent than with contributing a sense of direction. The self-righteousness that sees in conscientious co-ordinating procedures a sufficient gauge of valid policy is little affected by a perfectionism that segments policy into cycles of domestic and foreign concerns (do we have the moral right to act abroad as long as there is a Little Rock?); or by a fastidiousness that spends more energy on establishing a moral equivalence between our attitudes and those of Communism than on defining the moral content of what we stand for. (Since we and the Communists distrust each other, an attempt on our part to claim superior morality is the most certain means to prevent a lasting peace.)

Thus if the intellectual is to deepen national policy he faces a delicate task. He must steer between the Scylla of letting the bureaucracy prescribe what is relevant or useful and the Charybdis of defining these criteria too abstractly. If he inclines too much toward the former, he will turn into a promoter of technical remedies; if he chooses the latter, he will run the risks of confusing dogmatism with morality and of courting martyrdom—of becoming, in short, as wrapped up in a cult of rejection as the activist is in a cult of success.

Where to draw the line between excessive commitment to the bureaucracy and paralyzing aloofness depends on so many intangibles of circumstance and personality that it is difficult to generalize. Perhaps the matter can be stated as follows: one of the challenges of the contemporary situation is to demonstrate the overwhelming importance of purpose over technique. The intellectual should therefore not refuse to participate in policymaking, for to do so would confirm the administrative stagnation. But in co-operating, the intellectual has two loyalties: to the organization that employs him as well as to values which transcend the bureaucratic framework and which provide his basic motivation. It is important for him to remember that one of his contributions to the administrative process is his independence, and that one of his tasks is to seek to prevent unthinking routine from becoming an end in itself.

The intellectual must therefore decide not only whether to participate in the administrative process but also in what capacity: whether as an intellectual or as an administrator. If he assumes the former role, it is essential for him to retain the freedom to deal with the policymaker from a position of independence, and to reserve the right to assess the policymaker's demands in terms of his own standards. Paradoxically, this may turn out to be also most helpful to the policymaker. For the greater the bureaucratization and the more eminent the policymaker, the more difficult it is to obtain advice in which substantive considerations are not submerged by or at least identified with organizational requirements.

Such an attitude requires an occasional separation from administration. In all humility, the intellectual must guard his distinctive and in this particular context most crucial qualities: the pursuit of knowledge rather than of administrative ends, the perspective supplied by a nontechnical vantage point. It is therefore essential for him to return from time to time to his library or his laboratory to "recharge his batteries." If he fails to do this he will turn into an administrator, distinguished from some of his colleagues only by having been recruited from the intellectual community. Such a relationship does not preclude a major contribution. But it will then have to be in terms of the organization's criteria, which can be changed from within only by those in the most pre-eminent positions.

THE HIGHEST OF STAKES

Ultimately the problem is not the intellectual's alone or even primarily. There is no substitute for greater insight on the part of our executives, in or out of government. Advice cannot replace knowledge. Neither Churchill nor Lincoln nor Roosevelt was the product of a staff. As long as our executives conceive their special skill to be a kind of intuitive ability to choose among conflicting advice and as long as they see this skill largely in administrative or psychological but not substantive terms, their relationship with the intellectual will produce frustration as often as mutual support. The executive, while making a ritual of consulting the intellectual, will consider him hopelessly abstract or judge him by his suitability in achieving short-term ends. And the intellectual, while participating in the policymaking process, will always have the feeling that he never had a chance to present the most important considerations. The executives' lack of understanding of the process of reflection and the fragmented nature of their approach to policy causes them to place a premium on qualities in intellectuals which they can most easily duplicate in their own organization. It leads them to apply administrative criteria to the problems of creativity, thereby making it difficult to transcend the standards of the moment. The intellectuals' unfamiliarity with the management of men makes them overlook the difficulty in the application of their maxims.

The solution is not to turn philosophers into kings or kings into philosophers. But it is essential that our leadership groups overcome the approach to national issues as an extracurricular activity that does not touch the core of their concerns. The future course of our society is not a matter to be charted administratively. The specialization of functions turns into a caricature when decision making and the pursuit of knowledge on which it is based are treated as completely separate activities, by either executives or intellectuals. Our society requires above all to overcome its current lassitude, to risk itself on new approaches in a situation different from our historical expectation. This sense of purpose cannot come from a bureaucracy, and it will not come from our present leadership groups if they continue to see the challenge primarily as a succession of technical problems.

It is true that many of the difficulties described here are due to qualities which also account for the strength and vitality of our society. Against the background of our sudden projection into world affairs we have undoubtedly performed creditably. Unfortunately, our period offers no prizes for having done reasonably well; it does not permit us to rest on historical comparison. Our sole measure is our ability to contribute a sense of direction in a world in turmoil.

The stakes could hardly be higher. The deepest cause of the inhumanity of our time is probably the pedantic application of administrative norms. Its symbol may well be the "commissar," the ideal type of bureaucrat, who condemns thousands without love and without hatred simply in pursuance of an abstract duty. But we would do ourselves an injustice if we ignored that the commissar is not just a Soviet but a universal phenomenon—the Soviet system has simply encouraged it in its most extreme form. He is the administrator whose world is defined by regulations in whose making he had no part, and whose substance does not concern him, to whom reality is exhausted by the organization in which he finds himself. Our challenge is to rescue the individual from this process; to escape from the pretentiousness and stultifying quality of an atmosphere in which all sense of reverence for the unique is lost in the quest for reducing everything to manipulable quantities. The way we face this challenge will be the ultimate test of our long-proclaimed belief in the dignity of the individual.

POWER AND ADMINISTRATION

Norton Long

Norton Long is a Professor of Political Science and Director of the Education and Transportation Center at Northwestern University.

There is no more forlorn spectacle in the administrative world than an agency and a program possessed of statutory life, armed with executive orders, sustained in the courts, yet stricken with paralysis and deprived of power. An object of contempt to its enemies and of despair to its friends.

Reprinted from the *Public Administration Review,* the journal of the American Society for Public Administration, Autumn 1949, by permission of the publisher.

The lifeblood of administration is power. Its attainment, maintenance, increase, dissipation, and loss are subjects the practitioner and student can ill afford to neglect. Loss of realism and failure are almost certain consequences. This is not to deny that important parts of public administration are so deeply entrenched in the habits of the community, so firmly supported by the public, or so clearly necessary as to be able to take their power base for granted and concentrate on the purely professional side of their problems. But even these islands of the blessed are not immune from the plague of politics, as witness the fate of the hapless Bureau of Labor Statistics and the perennial menace of the blind 5 per cent across-the-board budget cut. Perhaps Carlyle's aphorism holds here, "The healthy know not of their health but only the sick." To stay healthy one needs to recognize that health is a fruit, not a birthright. Power is not only of the considerations that must be weighed in administration, but of all it is the most overlooked in theory and the most dangerous to overlook in practice.

The power resources of an administrator or an agency are not disclosed by a legal search of titles and court decisions or by examining appropriations or budgetary allotments. Legal authority and a treasury balance are necessary but politically insufficient bases of administration. Administrative rationality requires a critical evaluation of the whole range of complex and shifting forces on whose support, acquiescence, or temporary impotence the power to act depends.

Analysis of the sources from which power is derived and the limitations they impose is as much a dictate of prudent administration as sound budgetary procedure. The bankruptcy that comes from an unbalanced power budget has consequences far more disastrous than the necessity of seeking a deficiency appropriation. The budgeting of power is a basic subject matter of a realistic science of administration.

It may be urged that for all but the top hierarchy of the administrative structure the question of power is irrelevant. Legislative authority and administrative orders suffice. Power adequate to the function to be performed flows down the chain of command. Neither statute nor executive order, however, confers more than legal authority to act. Whether Congress or President can impart the substance of power as well as the form depends upon the line-up of forces in the particular case. A price control law wrung from a reluctant Congress by an amorphous and unstable combination of consumer and labor groups is formally the same as a law enacting a support price program for agriculture backed by the disciplined organizations of farmers and their congressmen. The differences for the scope and effectiveness of administration are obvious. The Presidency, like Congress, responds to and translates the pressures that play upon it. The real mandate contained in an Executive order varies with the political strength of the group demand embodied in it, and in the context of other group demands.

Both Congress and President do focus the general political energies of the community and so are considerably more than mere means for transmitting organized pressures. Yet power is not concentrated by the structure of government or politics into the hands of a leadership with a capacity to budget it among a diverse set of administrative activities. A picture of the Presidency as a reservoir of authority from which the lower echelons of administration draw life and vigor is an idealized distortion of reality.

A similar criticism applies to any like claim for an agency head in his agency. Only in varying degrees can the powers of subordinate officials be explained as resulting from the chain of command. Rarely is such an explanation a satisfactory account of the sources of power.

To deny that power is derived exclusively from superiors in the hierarchy is to assert that subordinates stand in a feudal relation in which to a degree they fend for themselves and acquire support peculiarly their own. A structure of interests friendly or hostile, vague and general or compact and well-defined, encloses each significant center of administrative discretion. This structure is an important determinant of the scope of possible action. As a source of power and authority it is a competitor of the formal hierarchy.

Not only does political power flow in from the sides of an organization, as it were; it also flows up the organization to the center from the constituent parts. When the staff of the Office of War Mobilization and Reconversion advised a hard-pressed agency to go out and get itself some popular support so that the President could afford to support it, their action reflected the realities of power rather than political cynicism.

It is clear that the American system of politics does not generate enough power at any focal point of leadership to provide the conditions for an even partially successful divorce of politics from administration. Subordinates cannot depend on the formal chain of command to deliver enough political power to permit them to do their jobs. Accordingly they must supplement the resources available through the hierarchy with those they can muster on their own, or accept the consequences in frustration—a course itself not without danger. Administrative rationality demands that objectives be determined and sights set in conformity with a realistic appraisal of power position and potential.

The theory of administration has neglected the problem of the sources and adequacy of power, in all probability because of a distaste for the disorderliness of American political life and a belief that this disorderliness is transitory. An idealized picture of the British parliamentary system as a Platonic form to be realized or approximated has exerted a baneful fascination in the field. The majority party with a mandate at the polls and a firmly seated leadership in the cabinet seems to solve adequately the problem of the supply of power necessary to permit administration to concentrate on the fulfillment of accepted objectives. It is a commonplace that the American party system provides neither a mandate for a platform nor a mandate for a leadership.

Accordingly, the election over, its political meaning must be explored by the diverse leaders in the executive and legislative branches. Since the parties have failed to discuss issues, mobilize majorities in their terms, and create a working political consensus on measures to be carried out, the task is left for others—most prominently the agencies concerned. Legislation passed and powers granted are frequently politically premature. Thus the Council of Economic Advisers was given legislative birth before political acceptance of its functions existed. The agencies to which tasks are assigned must devote themselves to the creation of an adequate consensus to permit administration. The mandate that the parties do not supply must be attained through public relations and the mobilization of group support. Pendleton Herring and others have shown just how vital this support is for agency action.

The theory that agencies should confine themselves to communicating policy suggestions to executive and legislature, and refrain from appealing to their clientele and the public, neglects the failure of the parties to provide either a clear-cut decision as to what they should do or an adequately mobilized political support for a course of action. The bureaucracy under the American political system has a large share of responsibility for the public promotion of policy and even more in organizing the political basis for its survival and growth. It is generally recognized that the agencies have a special competence in the technical aspects of their fields which of necessity gives them a rightful policy initiative. In addition, they have or develop a shrewd understanding of the politically feasible in the group structure within which they work. Above all, in the eyes of their supporters and their enemies they represent the institutionalized embodiment of policy, an enduring organization actually or potentially capable of mobilizing power behind policy. The survival interests and creative drives of administrative organizations combine with clientele pressures to compel such mobilization. The party system provides no enduring institutional representation for group interest at all comparable to that of the bureaus of the Department of Agriculture. Even the subject matter committees of Congress function in the shadow of agency permanency.

The bureaucracy is recognized by all interested groups as a major channel of representation to such an extent that Congress rightly feels the competition of a rival. The weakness in party structure both permits and makes necessary the present dimensions of the political activities of the administrative branch—permits because it fails to protect administration from pressures and fails to provide adequate direction and support, makes necessary because it fails to develop a consensus on a leadership and a program that makes possible administration on the basis of accepted decisional premises.

Agencies and bureaus more or less perforce are in the business of building, maintaining, and increasing their political support. They lead and in large part are led by the diverse groups whose influence sustains them. Frequently they lead and are themselves led in conflicting directions. This is not due to a dull-witted incapacity to see the contradictions in their behavior but is an almost inevitable result of the contradictory nature of their support.

Herbert Simon has shown that administrative rationality depends on the establishment of uniform value premises in the decisional centers or organization. Unfortunately, the value premises of those forming vital elements of political support are often far from uniform. These elements are in Barnard's and Simon's sense "customers" of the organization and therefore parts of the organization whose wishes are clothed with a very real authority. A major and most time-consuming aspect of administration consists of the wide range of activities designed to secure enough "customer" acceptance to survive and, if fortunate, develop a consensus adequate to program formulation and execution.

To varying degrees, dependent on the breadth of acceptance of their programs, officials at every level of significant discretion must make their estimates of the situation, take stock of their resources, and plan accordingly. A keen appreciation of the real components of their organization is the beginning of wisdom. These components will be found to stretch far beyond the government payroll. Within the government they will encompass Congress, congressmen, committees, courts, other agencies, presidential advisers, and the President. The Aristotelian analysis of constitutions is equally applicable and equally necessary to an understanding of administrative organization.

The broad alliance of conflicting groups that makes up presidential majorities scarcely coheres about any definite pattern of objectives, nor has it by the alchemy of the party system had its collective power concentrated in an accepted leadership with a personal mandate. The conciliation and maintenance of this support is a necessary condition of the attainment and retention of office involving, as Madison so well saw, "the spirit of party and faction in the necessary and ordinary operations of government." The President must in large part be, if not all things to all men, at least many things to many men. As a consequence, the contradictions in his power base invade administration. The often criticized apparent cross-purposes of the Roosevelt regime cannot be put down to inept administration until the political facts are weighed. Were these apparently self-defeating measures reasonably related to the general maintenance of the composite majority of the Administration? The first objective—ultimate patriotism apart—of the administrator is the attainment and retention of the power on which his tenure of office depends. This is the necessary pre-condition for the accomplishment of all other objectives.

The same ambiguities that arouse the scorn of the naive in the electoral campaigns of the parties are equally inevitable in administration and for the same reasons. Victory at the polls does not yield either a clear-cut grant of power or a unified majority support for a coherent program. The task of the Presidency lies in feeling out the alternatives of policy which are consistent with the retention and increase of the group support on which the Administration rests. The lack of a budgetary theory (so frequently deplored) is not due to any incapacity to apply rational analysis to the comparative contribution of the various activities of government to a determinate hierarchy of purposes. It more probably stems from a fastidious distaste for the frank recognition of the budget as a politically expedient allocation of resources. Appraisal in terms of their political contribution to the Administration provides almost a sole common denominator between the Forest Service and the Bureau of Engraving.

Integration of the administrative structure through an over-all purpose in terms of which tasks and priorities can be established is an emergency phenomenon. Its realization, only partial at best, has been limited to war and the extremity of depression. Even in wartime the Farm Bureau Federation, the American Federation of Labor, the Congress of Industrial Organizations, the National Association of Manufacturers, the Chamber of Commerce, and a host of lesser interests resisted coordination of themselves and the agencies concerned with their interests. A Presidency temporarily empowered by intense mass popular support acting in behalf of a generally accepted and simplified purpose can, with great difficulty, bribe, cajole, and coerce a real measure of joint action. The long-drawn-out battle for conversion and the debacle of orderly reconversion underline the difficulty of attaining, and the transitory nature of, popularly based emergency power. Only in crises are the powers of the Executive nearly adequate to impose a common plan of action on the executive branch, let alone the economy.

In ordinary times the manifold pressures of our pluralistic society work themselves out in accordance with the balance of force prevailing in Congress and the agencies. Only to a limited degree is the process subject to responsible direction or review by President or party leadership.

The program of the President cannot be a Gosplan for the government precisely because the nature of his institutional and group support gives him insufficient power. The personal unity of the Presidency cannot perform the function of Hobbes' sovereign since his office lacks the authority of Hobbes' contract. Single headedness in the executive gives no assurance of singleness of purpose. It only insures that the significant pressures in a society will be brought to bear on one office. Monarchy solves the problem of giving one plan to a multitude only when the plenitude of its authority approaches dictatorship. Impatient social theorists in all ages have turned to the philosopher king as a substitute for consensus. Whatever else he may become, it is difficult to conceive of the American president ruling as a philosopher king, even with the advice of the Executive Office. The monarchical solution to the administrative problems posed by the lack of a disciplined party system capable of giving firm leadership and a program to the legislature is a modern variant of the dreams of the eighteenth century savants and well nigh equally divorced from a realistic appraisal of social realities.

Much of the administrative thought, when it does not assume the value of coordination for coordination's sake, operates on the assumption that there must be something akin to Rousseau's *volonte generale* in administration to which the errant *volonte de tous* of the bureaus can and should be made to conform. This will-o'-the-wisp was made the object of an illuminating search by Pendleton Herring in his *Public Administration and the Public Interest.* The answer for Rousseau was enlightened dictatorship or counting the votes. The administrative equivalent to the latter is the resultant of the relevant pressures, as Herring shows. The first alternative seems to require at least the potency of the British Labour party and elsewhere has needed the disciplined organization of a fascist, nazi, or communist party to provide the power and consensus necessary to coordinate the manifold activities of government to a common plan.

Dictatorship, as Sigmund Neumann has observed, is a substitute for institutions which is required to fill the vacuum when traditional institutions break down. Force supplies the compulsion and guide to action in place of the normal routines of unconscious habit. Administrative organizations, however much they may appear the creations of art, are institutions produced in history and woven in the web of social relationships that gives them life and being. They present the same refractory material to the hand of the political artist as the rest of society of which they form a part.

Just as the economists have attempted to escape the complexities of institutional reality by taking refuge in the frictionless realm of theory, so some students of administration, following their lead, have seen in the application of the doctrine of opportunity costs a clue to a science of administration. Valuable as this may be in a restricted way, Marx has more light to throw on the study of institutions. It is in the dynamics and interrelations of institutions that we have most hope of describing and therefore learning to control administrative behavior.

The difficulty of coordinating government agencies lies not only in the fact that bureaucratic organizations are institutions having survival interests which may conflict with their rational adaptation to over-all purpose, but even more in their having roots in society. Coordination of the varied activities of a modern government almost of necessity involves a substantial degree of coordination of the economy. Coordination of government agencies involves far more than changing the behavior and offices of officials in Washington and the field. It involves the publics that are implicated in their normal functioning. To coordinate fiscal policy, agricultural policy, labor policy, foreign policy, and military policy, to name a few major areas, moves beyond the range of government charts and the habitat of the bureaucrats to the market place and to where the people live and work. This suggests that the reason why government reorganization is so difficult is that far more than government in the formal sense is involved in reorganization. One could overlook this in the limited government of the nineteenth century but the multi-billion dollar government of the mid-twentieth permits no facile dichotomy between government and economy. Economy and efficiency are the two objectives a laissez faire society can prescribe in peacetime as over-all government objectives. Their inadequacy either as motivation or standards has long been obvious. A planned economy clearly requires a planned government. But, if one can afford an unplanned economy, apart from gross extravagance, there seems no compelling and therefore, perhaps, no sufficiently powerful reason for a planned government.

Basic to the problem of administrative rationality is that of organizational identification and point of view. To whom is one loyal—unit, section, branch, division, bureau, department, administration, government, country, people, world history, or what? Administrative analysis frequently assumes that organizational identification should occur in such a way as to merge primary organization loyalty in a larger synthesis. The good of the part is to give way to the reasoned good of the whole. This is most frequently illustrated in the rationalizations used to counter self-centered demands of primary groups for funds and personnel. Actually the competition between governmental power centers, rather than the rationalizations, is the effective instrument of coordination.

Where there is a clear common product on whose successful production the sub-groups depend for the attainment of their own satisfaction, it is possible to demonstrate to almost all participants the desirability of cooperation. The shoe factory produces shoes, or else, for all concerned. But the government as a whole and many of its component parts have no such identifiable common product on which all depend. Like the proverbial Heinz, there are fifty-seven or more varieties unified, if at all, by a common political profit and loss account.

Administration is faced by somewhat the same dilemma as economics. There are propositions about the behavior patterns conducive to full employment—welfare economics. On the other hand, there are propositions about the economics of the individual firm—the counsel of the business schools. It is possible to show with considerable persuasiveness that sound considerations for the individual firm may lead to a depression if generally adopted, a result desired by none of the participants. However, no single firm can afford by itself to adopt the source of collective wisdom; in the absence of a common power capable of enforcing decisions premised on the supremacy of the collective interest, *sauve qui peut* is common sense.

The position of administrative organizations is not unlike the position of particular firms. Just as the decisions of the firms could be coordinated by the imposition of a planned economy so could those of the component parts of the government. But just as it is possible to operate a formally unplanned economy by the loose coordination of the market, in the same fashion it is possible to operate a government by the loose coordination of the play of political forces through its institutions.

The unseen hand of Adam Smith may be little in evidence in either case. One need not believe in a doctrine of social or administrative harmony to believe that formal centralized planning—while perhaps desirable and in some cases necessary—is not a must. The complicated logistics of supplying the city of New York runs smoothly down the grooves of millions of well adapted habits projected from a distant past. It seems naive on the one hand to believe in the possibility of a vast, intricate, and delicate economy operating with a minimum of formal over-all direction, and on the other to doubt that a relatively simple mechanism such as the government can be controlled largely by the same play of forces.

Doubtless the real reasons for seeking coordination in the government are the same that prompt a desire for economic planning. In fact, apart from waging war with its demand for rapid change, economic planning would seem to be the only objective sufficiently compelling and extensive to require a drastic change in our system of political laissez faire. Harold Smith, testifying before the Senate Banking and Currency Committee on the Employment Act of 1946, showed how extensive a range of hitherto unrelated activities could be brought to bear on a common purpose—the maintenance of maximum employment and purchasing power. In the flush of the war experience and with prophecies of reconversion unemployment, a reluctant Congress passed a pious declaration of policy. Senator Flanders has recorded the meager showing to date.

Nevertheless, war and depression apart, the Employment Act of 1946 for the first time provides at least a partial basis for the rational budgeting of government activities. The older concept of economy and efficiency as autonomous standards still lingers in Congress, but elsewhere their validity as ends in themselves is treated with skepticism.

If the advent of Keynesian economics and the erosion of laissez faire have created the intellectual conditions requisite for the formulation of over-all government policy, they do not by any means guarantee the political conditions necessary for its implementation. We can see quite clearly that the development of an integrated administration requires an integrating purpose. The ideals of Locke, Smith, Spencer, and their American disciples deny the need for such a purpose save for economy and efficiency's sake. Marx, Keynes, and their followers by denying the validity of the self-regulating economy have endowed the state with an over-arching responsibility in terms of which broad coordination, however, has run well ahead of the public's perception of it and of the development of a political channeling of power adequate to its administrative implementation.

Most students of administration are planners of some sort. Most congressmen would fly the label like the plague. Most bureaucrats, whatever their private faith, live under two jealous gods, their particular clientele and the loyalty check. Such a condition might, if it exists as described, cast doubt on whether even the intellectual conditions for rational administrative coordination exist. Be that as it may, the transition from a government organized in clientele departments and bureaus, each responding to the massive feudal power of organized business, organized agriculture, and organized labor, to a government integrated about a paramount national purpose will require a political power at least as great as that which tamed the earlier feudalism.

It takes a sharp eye or a tinted glass to see such an organized power on the American scene. Without it, administrative organization for over-all coordination has the academic air of South American constitution making. One is reminded of the remark attributed to the Austrian economist Mises; on being told that the facts did not agree with his theory, he replied *"desto schlechter fur die Tatsache."*

It is highly appropriate to consider how administrators should behave to meet the test of efficiency in a planned polity; but in the absence of such a polity and while, if we like, struggling to get it, a realistic science of administration will teach administrative behavior appropriate to the existing political system.

A close examination of the presidential system may well bring one to conclude that administrative rationality in it is a different matter from that applicable to the British ideal. The American Presidency is an office that has significant monarchical characteristics despite its limited term and elective nature. The literature on court and palace has many an insight applicable to the White House. Access to the President, reigning favorites, even the court jester, are topics that show the continuity of institutions. The maxims of LaRochefoucauld and the memoirs of the Duc de Saint Simon have a refreshing realism for the operator on the Potomac.

The problem of rival factions in the President's family is as old as the famous struggle between Jefferson and Hamilton, as fresh and modern as the latest cabal against John Snyder. Experience seems to show that this personal and factional struggle for the President's favor is a vital part of the process of representation. The vanity, personal ambition, or patriotism of the contestants soon clothes itself in the generalities of principle and the clique aligns itself with groups beyond the capital. Subordinate rivalry is tolerated if not encouraged by so many able executives that it can scarcely be attributed to administrative ineptitude. The wrangling tests opinion, uncovers information that would otherwise never rise to the top, and provides effective opportunity for decision rather than mere ratification of pre-arranged plans. Like most judges, the Executive needs to hear argument for his own instruction. The alternatives presented by subordinates in large part determine the freedom and the creative opportunity of their superiors. The danger of becoming a Merovingian is a powerful incentive to the maintenance of fluidity in the structure of power.

The fixed character of presidential tenure makes it necessary that subordinates be politically expendable. The President's men must be willing to accept the blame for failures not their own. Machiavelli's teaching on how princes must keep the faith bears re-reading. Collective responsibility is incompatible with a fixed term of office. As it tests the currents of public opinion, the situation on the Hill, and the varying strength of the organized pressures, the White House alters and adapts the complexion of the Administration. Loyalties to programs or to groups and personal pride and interest frequently conflict with whole-souled devotion to the Presidency. In fact, since such devotion is not made mandatory by custom, institutions, or the facts of power, the problem is perpetually perplexing to those who must choose.

The balance of power between executive and legislature is constantly subject to the shifts of public and group support. The latent tendency of the American Congress is to follow the age-old parliamentary precedents and to try to reduce the President to the role of constitutional monarch. Against this threat and to secure his own initiative, the President's resources are primarily demagogic, with the weaknesses and strengths that dependence on mass popular appeal implies. The unanswered question of American government—"who is boss?"—constantly plagues administration. The disruption of unity of command is not just the problem of Taylor's functional foreman, but goes to the stability and uniformity of basic decisional premises essential to consequent administration.

It is interesting to speculate on the consequences for administration of the full development of congressional or presidential government. A leadership in Congress that could control the timetable of the House and Senate would scarcely content itself short of reducing the President's Cabinet to what in all probability it was first intended to be, a modified version of the present Swiss executive. Such leadership could scarcely arise without centrally organized, disciplined, national parties far different from our present shambling alliances of state and local machines.

A Presidency backed by a disciplined party controlling a majority in Congress would probably assimilate itself to a premiership by association of legislative leadership in the formulation of policy and administration. In either line of development the crucial matter is party organization. For the spirit of the party system determines the character of the government.

That the American party system will develop toward the British ideal is by no means a foregone conclusion. The present oscillation between a strong demagogic Presidency and a defensively powerful congressional oligarchy may well prove a continuing pattern of American politics, as it was of Roman. In the absence of a party system providing an institutionalized centripetal force in our affairs, it is natural to look to the Presidency as Goldsmith's weary traveler looked to the throne.

The Presidency of the United States, however, is no such throne as the pre-World War I *Kaiserreich* that provided the moral and political basis for the Prussian bureaucracy. Lacking neutrality and mystique, it does not even perform the function of the British monarchy in providing a psychological foundation for the permanent civil service. A leaderless and irresponsible Congress frequently makes it appear the strong point of the republic. The Bonapartist experience in France, the Weimar Republic, and South American examples nearer home, despite important social differences, are relevant to any thoughtful consideration of building a solution to legislative anarchy on the unity of the executive.

The present course of American party development gives little ground for optimism that a responsible two party system capable of uniting Congress and Executive in a coherent program will emerge. The increasingly critical importance of the federal budget for the national economy and the inevitable impact of world power status on the conduct of foreign affairs make inescapable the problem of stable leadership in the American system. Unfortunately they by no means insure a happy or indeed any solution.

Attempts to solve administrative problems in isolation from the structure of power and purpose in the polity are bound to prove illusory. The reorganization of Congress to create responsibility in advance of the development of party responsibility was an act of piety to principle, of educational value; but as a practical matter it raised a structure without foundation. In the same way, reorganization of the executive branch to centralize administrative power in the Presidency while political power remains dispersed and divided may effect improvement, but in a larger sense it must fail. The basic prerequisite to the administration of the textbooks is a responsible two party system. The means to its attainment are a number one problem for students of administration. What Schattschneider calls the struggle for party government may sometime yield us the responsible parliamentary two party system needed to underpin our present administrative theory. Until that happy time, exploration of the needs and necessities of our present system is a high priority task of responsible scholarship.

THE EXECUTIVE AND THE PUBLIC INTEREST
Harlan Cleveland

Assistant Secretary of State for International Organization Affairs under Presidents Kennedy and Johnson, Harlan Cleveland served as Dean of the Maxwell Graduate School of Citizenship and Public Affairs at Syracuse University. He is a former editor of *The Reporter* magazine.

About eleven years ago, I was sitting against the wall of a Senate committee room, watching two political executives sell a lend-lease appropriation to the greatest, or at least the most deliberative, body in the world. My capacity on this occasion was as a briefcase carrier—one of those anonymous civil servants who sit behind government witnesses at these affairs, handing them scribbled calculations and bits of advice on bits of paper. The witnesses were Leo Crowley, the Wisconsin politician who headed the Foreign Economic Administration, and his deputy Oscar Cox, who as one of the New Deal's brightest lawyers had drafted that extraordinary piece of legislation, the Lend-Lease Act.

From *The Annals of the American Academy of Political and Social Science,* September 1956. Reprinted by permission.

The scene was a study in contrast. Crowley seemed more senatorial than the Senators, a languid, paunchy man with a mane of white hair, a florid complexion, and a deceptively benign expression. Cox was thin and efficient, his jerky gestures matching his crisp and factual eloquence. He was easy to carry a briefcase for: he already knew its contents by heart.

Most of the questions were taken by Cox. Before a Senator had finished asking his question, Cox was way ahead of him, guessing what was on his mind and starting to reply in impressive, uncompromising detail. Crowley leaned back, utterly relaxed, sometimes putting in a comment or telling a joke to keep things moving. Finally a Senator asked Crowley a question about one of the most intricate features of the lend-lease program, and I learned an important lesson.

"Well, I'll tell you, Senator," Crowley said in his Middle-Western accent, "I've always wondered how that works too. Let's see if Oscar can explain it to us."

Soon the hearing was over, the lesson complete. Two or three of the Senators were clapping Crowley on the back, saying what a fine presentation he had made. Cox, who had made it, was alone at the other end of the room, stuffing his papers back into his efficient-looking briefcase.

ADMINISTRATION AND POLITICS

A discussion of that political animal, the government executive, should start with some picture of the jungle in which he lives and works and, if he is fit enough, survives. From the requirements of survival in this jungle, the talents needed by the top political executives can readily be deduced. Beyond this we need to consider the civil servant as a political executive.

Let us start with the proposition that government is a mixture of politics and administration, accommodation and logic, consent and decisions—a blend, in short, of Crowley and Cox.

We instinctively demand that our Presidents be "double firsts"—that they be great politicians and great administrators too. Of course they usually do not succeed on both counts. Franklin Roosevelt, who is possibly unsurpassed in this century as a builder of consent in war and peace, was as casual an administrator as ever hit Washington. Harry Truman, whose reputation and training were in politics, proved himself an able and orderly administrator, but when it came to building consent for a government program he can hardly be rated better than fair. President Eisenhower, whose forte was military administration, has combined a remarkable talent for evoking consent with an equally remarkable tendency to appoint as administrators of his policies men who disagree with them.

Yet if we seldom or never get quite the perfect Presidential blend, we continue to pine for that rare amalgam—the man who can run the executive branch and still get along with most of the other Americans, in and out of Congress, who think they are anointed to run the government too.

What is not so clear in much of the literature of public administration is the fact that every official of the executive branch must in some measure combine the two qualities we look for in a President, the ability to manage and the talent to build political support for what is managed. In my own limited experience and observation, I have yet to encounter a government official with any responsibility at all who did not have this dual function. Mark this proposition well: it is bedrock to everything I have to say on this subject. Government is a mixture of administration and politics all the way up and down the line, not merely at something called the political level where people called political executives get jobs by a process called political appointment. As Peter Odegard puts it, "Policy and administration are the Siamese twins of politics and are associated at virtually all levels of the administrative structure." Or, as Paul Appleby wrote back in 1945, "So long as the people vote and have unrestrained the right to complain, the whole process of administration is in a sense political on every level."

Does this seem obvious? Does it go without saying that, in a free society, government is politics? I shall be glad if you agree so quickly. But I should give fair warning: if you take seriously what I have just said, you will, I think, have to disagree with much of what the second Hoover Commission on Organization of the Executive Branch of the Government has said in its 1955 Report on Personnel and Civil Service.

THE DIFFUSION OF POWERS

What is it about our government that makes it so political a jungle? The standard explanation is the constitutional separation of powers, the built-in checks and balances, the fact that everybody is in every act but nobody seems to be in charge of the performance.

Woodrow Wilson called this "administration by semi-independent executive agents who obey the dictation of a legislature to which they are not responsible." He was sure that Congress ran the show, described legislation as "the originating force," and complained that the "blind processes" resulting from the division of power made that power irresponsible. But Wilson was too pessimistic about the ability of the government to function in spite of this division of power and purposes—or better, perhaps, because of it.

He was certainly overimpressed with the power of the legislature in his academic days, though as President he later underestimated its veto power when it came to getting the League of Nations ratified. The legislature is powerful and can do a massive wrecking job, as we know from our own recent history. But the men who wrote our Constitution were clear about the "dangers from legislative usurpations." "One hundred and seventy-three despots would surely be as oppressive as one," Madison said in one of the Federalist papers; ". . . an elective despotism was not the government we fought for."

Despite the periodic flurries of legislative usurpation, we do not have an elective despotism. But we do have a Congress that participates with appalling vigor in the task of running the executive branch of the government. We have, indeed, a system that not only separates the general constitutional powers but diffuses the power of decision on quite specific matters. One of the very first things I ever had to do in Washington, as an "intern" in the office of Senator "Young Bob" LaFollette, was to stand in for the Senator at a hearing in the Veterans Administration on a compensation case. I recall being struck at the time by the distortion of functions thus dramatized: here I was, a legislative bureaucrat horning in on the efforts of executive bureaucrats to perform a judicial function.

Each official in each branch of the government has a chance to exercise two (and occasionally even three) of the constitutional powers at once; and by the same token, each of the three branches sooner or later gets a crack at nearly every major public issue.

The result of this diffusion of power is not merely, as Peter Odegard says, that "Congress has . . . found ways and means for interposing itself between the President and his executive subordinates and thus confusing the clear line of bureaucratic responsibility." Each executive official, whether politically appointed or not, has to spend an unconscionable amount of his time and energy telling Congress what he is doing, and why. In my last year with the Mutual Security Agency, I spent the equivalent of six months out of the twelve preparing and presenting on Capitol Hill the detailed exposition of the program I was supposed to be helping "administer."

CONGRESSIONAL COALITIONS

Nor is it enough for an administrator to defend a program from political attack. He finds himself actively promoting a political coalition in its support. For our Congress, which I have heard described to a group of visiting Frenchmen as a model of party discipline, is of course as choice an example of coalition government as the notorious French Assembly.

If there is any doubt that Congress is managed by complex, *ad hoc* coalitions which shift with every issue, look for a moment at the record of the Eighty-third Congress. In this supposedly Republican Congress, the fluctuating balance of power swung against the administration on foreign aid and public housing, but supported the President on farm price supports and (by one vote) the Bricker Amendment. A coalition majority could be put together for confirming the New Deal, reducing taxes, hitting slightly the funds for defense, continuing the 1950 version of United States foreign policy, and allowing some of its committees to trample on Executive toes. On hardly any of these issues could one party get its way solely with the votes it could deliver from its own side of the aisle.

We see the same pattern operating in the Eighty-fourth Congress, which is theoretically led by the Democrats. There was an excellent example in the Senate last spring, when thirty-one Republicans and twenty-two Democrats beat twenty-four Democrats and fourteen Republicans and sent the natural gas bill to Thomasville, Georgia, to be vetoed by a Republican President.

Because Congress is the way it is, every executive must help splice together the particular coalition that will pass his appropriation and protect his program and his reputation from damage. (His coalition may be very different from another one being fashioned for a different purpose by a colleague in the next office.) If every executive has congressional relations as an important segment of his duties—even though he may not himself carry a bulging briefcase up Pennsylvania Avenue to the "Hill"—every executive has to have some of the instincts of a politician. In this sense, the "political executives" in the government are not just the holders of those seven to eight hundred "noncareer executive" posts to which the Hoover Commission Report refers. The number of officials who are involved in this kind of politics is actually well up in the thousands. Under our constitutional diffusion of powers, the federal government would hardly operate at all if they were fewer.

THE INSIDE TRACK

Many distinguished writers have pondered whether the American Congress adequately represents the American people, but this is an academic question about which I have never been able to get excited. For the American people do not limit their representation in Washington to electing half a thousand Congressmen. The people are directly represented in the executive branch, too.

When I say "the people," I mean what David Riesman intends by the phrase "veto groups." In *The Lonely Crowd,* Riesman observed that political leadership has passed from businessmen as a class to . . . a series of groups, each of which has struggled for and finally attained a power to stop things conceivably inimical to its interests and, within far narrower limits, to start things. . . . Among the veto groups competition is monopolistic; rules of fairness and fellowship dictate how far one can go.

The tidelands group refrained from going too far; the natural-gas lobby, consisting of some of the same people, so outraged the public conscience that a President thought to be favorable to its objectives had to turn against the natural-gas bill. The farm group's effective power is enormous; the smaller effectiveness of the labor group may be traced, at least in part, to the fact that it overplayed its hand during the New Deal.

What Riesman did not mention is the fact that the power of these new-style lobbies can be roughly measured by the strength of their surrogates within the executive branch of the government. The Department of Agriculture has long been regarded, by both the farm organizations and the rest of the government, as a farmers' defense league inside the federal bureaucracy. Organized labor, particularly the Congress of Industrial Organizations, substantially controlled the National Labor Relations Board during the period (in the 1930's) when the Board was clearing the way for the rapid expansion of the CIO. The housing program, created by the New Deal for the purpose of getting houses built, placed itself in the hands of the speculative builders and the savings and loan associations to such an extent that moral corruption shaded over into pecuniary corruption. The organized veterans have their own preserve in the Veterans Administration. The Commerce Department has for some years had a Business Advisory Council whose function, in effect, is to bring to bear on internal government decisions an organized business opinion. Defense contracts are habitually given out by men recruited from the businesses that are getting the business, and regulations are drafted by surrogates of the industries to which they apply. The National Recovery Act was declared unconstitutional early in the New Deal, but "self-government of industry" is an established practice with a venerable tradition behind it.

During the Korean War, John Corson has said, ". . . the Office of Price Stabilization official in charge of price regulations for the apparel industry (in 1951) was borrowed from a leading firm in this industry. His aide, who specializes in women's woven underwear, is "on loan" from Barbizon, one of the principal competing manufacturers in this field. A succession of five or more chiefs of the Iron and Steel Division in the National Production Authority have been loaned by their companies, the major companies in the steel industry. The acting director of the Equipment and Materials Division of the Defense Transport Administration for most of 1951 was on loan from the American Car and Foundry Company. He actively promoted, for the Defense Transport Administrator, a plea that the NPA make available sufficient steel to build ten thousand freight cars a quarter; his firm meanwhile is engaged in the production of freight cars.

From time to time this sort of thing gets out of bounds, as in the recent cases of Air Force Secretary Talbott and Chairman Hugh Cross of the Interstate Commerce Commission, both of whom admitted error in using their official positions to advance their private interests. Much more often, there is no formal "conflict of interest." It is considered normal and natural for a steel man to lubricate with government contracts the growth of steel production; for a housing man to get more housing built by having the government absorb a good part of the risk; for a farmers' representative to promote aid for farmers from inside the Department of Agriculture; for a labor organizer temporarily in the government to promote the right of labor to organize. We have institutionalized the inside track.

OUTSIDE INTERESTS AND THE PUBLIC INTEREST

The political executive consequently has to do more than run his shop and deal with Congress. He has to maintain a complex network of horizontal relations with the veto groups whose interests his actions may affect, with others who think their interests might be affected, and with the surrogates of these groups in both the executive and legislative branches of the government.

I am trying hard not to pass any moral judgment on this system, but merely to describe how it seems to work. Given the nature of our society, it is almost bound to work this way. The government is, after all, the least bureaucratic of the major interest groups with which it has to deal. Turnover of government personnel is high, especially at the top. Even if this were not true for other reasons, we make sure of it by having reasonably frequent elections. The same is not true of the major aggregations of veto power outside: in business, labor, agriculture, and a good many other categories, elections are merely a facade for maintaining the same leadership from year to year and even from decade to decade. If you do not like the President of the United States, you can vote against him every four years. If you do not like the President of General Motors or the head of a labor union, you can only wait for him to die.

The difference in tenure between government and outside interest groups is critical. If the outside leaders know more about the subject than their opposite numbers inside the government, if they are providing key experts, advisers, and sometimes even the political executives themselves, the views of the regulated are likely to be pretty influential with the regulators. In the United States, the road to the riskless society that Europeans call socialism is paved with the incestuous intention of nearly every major economic interest to bring the government into its affairs as the risk-taking partner.

Where, in this picture, does the "public interest" appear? Not, certainly, through the organized political parties, which inflate like balloons at election time and are of small consequence in governmental decision making the rest of the time. No, the defense of the public interest rests in the hands of the people as a whole, who cannot do anything much about it, and of the President they elect, who can.

THE BUCK PASSES UP

Whether, under our system, the government ultimately serves the public interest or merely obliges the private and sectional Trojan horses encamped inside the walls of the federal bureaucracy, depends on the President to an extraordinary and alarming degree. He is the chief mediator among the veto groups, the one political executive whose whole job is to consider the situation as a whole. He is the one remaining safety man available to stop a specialized interest which breaks through the normal line of checks and balances and threatens to gain too much yardage at the expense of other groups.

In a revealing passage of his autobiography, Mr. Truman regarded it as quite natural that nobody should consider the public interest but the President:

> I was always aware of the fact that not all my advisers looked at the problem in the same manner I did. This was nothing unusual, of course. It is

> the job of the military planners to consider all matters first and always in the light of military considerations. The diplomat's approach is—or in any case should be—determined by considerations of our relations to other nations. The Secretary of the Treasury thinks in terms of budget and taxes. Except for the members of his personal staff, each Presidential adviser has and should have a departmental outlook.

Though we sometimes make gods or supermen of our Presidents, they have not generally been more moral than most of us. The difference is that in the White House they are compelled to stand a little higher on the mountain than anybody else, and they consequently see farther at the horizon. It is this unique and lonely vantage point that lends grandeur to the American Presidency.

Not More Decisions

Yet the President's high rank does not necessarily mean that he makes more "decisions" than other political executives below. Indeed it is arguable that in our government the higher one's rank the fewer decisions one makes. The man who buys paper clips makes a number of unreviewed decisions without consultation—what size and shape of paper clip, from whom to buy, at what price. As you go up the ladder of authority each official is beset with more committees, more horizontal clearances, more veto groups and political personalities whose views must be reconciled or discounted before the "final decision" is reached.

I once tried to get this important idea across to a very bright businessman who had just been appointed a division director and had promptly started to operate as if he were solely responsible for the program co-ordinated by that division. One day, months after he had taken office, I knew he would survive the transition to becoming a public servant, for he came to me and said: "I'm director of this program, but that doesn't mean I direct anybody, does it? I mean I don't make any decisions. I'm really a sort of broker, I guess."

The President's role as chief broker makes possible a certain order in the bureaucratic jungle. It is no accident that matters which frequently get to the White House are so often better handled than matters that do not. The Housing Agency worked off in a corner by itself for years, dealing direct with the housing industry and hardly ever creating a crisis requiring Presidential attention. As a result corrupt practices like "mortgaging out" under Section 608 came to be regarded by some as the natural order of things until Congress finally made a political scandal of it. The foreign aid program, on the other hand, has spent more than fifty billion dollars since World War II, with hardly a trace of scandal. Why? Could it be because so many departments and agencies were always fighting for the right to manage foreign aid that the program was a matter of monthly, even weekly, concern to the President himself?

The saving grace of our executive bureaucracy, then, is that nearly everybody in it works for the President. To be sure, each political executive is also responsible horizontally to four or five congressional committees; he has to deal with several outside interest groups whose leaders feel the executive is answerable to them; and within the executive branch he is constantly evading his own responsibility by burying it in collective decisions by interdepartmental committees. But when the chips are down on any one issue, all political executives are accountable to the President—which is another way of saying that if they get into a tight spot, they can generally pass the buck to him.

The King Can Do No Wrong

The buck passes up: many of the most serious crises in our government's operations come from temporary lapses in following the first law of the jungle. Many elements of the present federal security system—a major subject in itself when it comes to considering why it is so hard to get and keep good political executives—are a travesty of this principle. For the system legitimizes the downward passing of the buck, and even prepares ahead of time an endless file of scapegoats for administrative error and sacrificial lambs for periodic congressional slaughter. It encourages a reversion to the old English principle that the King can do no wrong: if the government errs, it must be some spy in the ointment. One lesson of our recent madness is clear—legislative usurpation generally takes the form of trying to find the disloyal official down the line on whom the blame for bad policy can be laid. The depth of the Army-McCarthy crisis was revealed when it became clear that Secretary Stevens, Counsel John Adams, and General Zwicker were to be left standing out in the rain without the umbrella of Presidential backing. The natural-law reply to that insistent question, "Who promoted Peress?" was always plain: "The President did. Want to make something of it?"

Perhaps the Hoover Commission Task Force had this in mind when it declared: "Public servants who are unfairly attacked deserve to be defended, and the public interest also requires it. . . . Defense is the corollary of discipline. Both are essential." Government is politics, but the executive branch has to be run by executives. And in government as in other hierarchies, the buck can travel in one direction only—up.

QUALITIES OF LEADERSHIP

The habitat of both political executive and civil servant is thus a political government. To be successful every government official needs to be aware of outside considerations, available to the concerned committees of the Congress, willing to work in a goldfish bowl, earnest in cultivating his public relations—because his personal public relations are the relations between the people and their government. He must be adept—increasingly so as he rises in rank and responsibility—in helping to build the coalition of outside forces which will provide a "political base" for the program in his charge. He must therefore not be afraid to advocate new policies if he thinks the old ones are worn out, nor can he flinch from becoming identified with the administration of which he is a part and defending his program in public. Since every government executive is something of a political executive, these are to some extent the conditions of work for bureaucrats at every level. They are the main conditions of work for an executive near the top of the heap, whether he is appointed from the outside or lifted out of the civil service from within.

In this jungle of close decisions, openly arrived at, the political executive must have certain natural talents and certain acquired tastes. Everybody who has given any thought to public administration has his pet list of these qualities. Here is mine.

Imbued with the Public Interest

First, he must be imbued with the public interest.

When I was a child, I was told to ask myself three questions before opening my mouth to say anything: "Is it kind? Is it true? Is it necessary?" If I had remembered this advice very often, silence would nearly always have overtaken speech.

Whenever a political executive says, does, or decides anything, he also needs to ask himself a question: Where does the public interest lie? The public interest cannot of course be defined in general. But in our society we have a pretty fair index ready at hand, if we approach each action or decision with the following query, in mind: Would this decision—and the procedure by which it was made—stand the test of detailed public scrutiny?

Asking this question must be second nature, automatic, instinctive. It was not all, in many a famous political scandal. In our own time General Vaughan did not have it on his mind during the deep-freeze affair. The men who tried to slip Dixon-Yates in through the back door (when they could have carried out the Eisenhower power policy by less circuitous and more durable means) must surely have forgotten to ask themselves what would happen if somebody wanted to know what was going on.

There are, of course, a few public officials who never do get the word, even when forcibly reminded. Several days after resigning as Secretary of the Air Force under a conflict-of-interest cloud, Harold Talbott turned up at a Southampton, Long Island, hotel in an Air Force vehicle and was helped in with his baggage by two or three Air Force officers. The action raised the question whether Mr. Talbott had any idea at all what had hit him in Washington.

General Matthew B. Ridgway, in a recent article in the *Saturday Evening Post,* revealed a different kind of fuzziness.

> As Chief of Staff (he wrote) I quickly learned that though my own recommendations were made on a purely military basis, the decision of the Defense Department were based on considerations other than clear-cut military needs. They were based on budgetary considerations, political considerations, on the advantage to be gained in the field of domestic politics by a drastic reduction in military expenditures . . .

How does one get to be a four-star general without learning that at the government level there is no such thing as a decision which is "purely military" or purely anything else, whether the public official making the decision is in or out of uniform?

The retort of President Eisenhower, who had one more star and a little civilian experience to guide him, was right to the point:

> His responsibility for national defense is, you might say, a special one, or, in a sense, parochial. He does not have the over-all responsibility that is borne by the Commander in Chief, and by him alone, when it comes down to making the recommendations to the Congress.

Leader of Men

Second, the political executive must be a leader of men, with a "sense of action." The very size of the government, and the complexity of the horizontal clearances, required to make anything happen, create the temptation to assume that somebody else has the initiative, that it is the other fellow's move. For the effective bureaucrat, it is always his own move.

Chester Barnard has written that a leader needs five qualities: vitality and endurance, decisiveness, persuasiveness, a sense of responsibility, and intellectual capacity—in that order of importance. He points out that only the last, intellectual capacity, can be increased by training. For the rest, . . . there is no substitute for the experience of recognizing and seizing opportunities, or for making one's own place unaided and against interference and obstacles; for these kinds of ability are precisely those that followers expect in leaders.

I suspect that Mr. Barnard would agree that for the political executive intellectual capacity should rank higher on his list than last place. A political executive, unlike a business executive, cannot possibly delegate his thinking to a vice-president for ideas. It is a condition of survival in the jungle that he do his own homework and be in intellectual command of the subject matter of the program for which he is responsible. When a congressional committee or an important "veto group" wants to know the story and asks embarrassing questions, no understudy with a mimeographed statement will fill the bill.

His Own Public Relations Man

Third, it is obvious from our earlier survey of the jungle that the political executive must be his own public relations man. One reason businessmen get into trouble in government is that many of them are accustomed to delegating to others the task of dealing with the public. In January 1953, toward the end of two long days of senatorial hearings on his General Motors stock holdings, Charles E. Wilson revealed how much he had learned about public relations at the age of sixty-two.

> The thing that perhaps I overlooked myself (he mused) was that not only did I have to operate honestly and fairly without prejudice, but all the people should also think that that was the way I was operating, and that part of it I did not quite appraise.

Where had he been? Presumably producing cars and trucks while somebody else worried about what the public would think.

The contrasting case is of course that of Paul Hoffman. By handling his own public relations from the start, he sold the Marshall Plan and himself in the same package: to millions of people in the early days of that singular project, he was the Marshall Plan. And his ideas about public relations permeated the organization he built to administer the European recovery program. I remember his telling us once in a staff meeting that we should answer every letter the day it came in, even if all we could say was that we would reply in detail later on. "When I ran a filling station," he went on, "I found that a man wouldn't wait for gas more than two or three minutes if nobody paid any attention to him. But if you gave him a big hello and explained that there were several cars ahead of him, he would sit there quite happily for a quarter of an hour!"

A Mixed Career

Fourth, the political executive should, preferably, have a mixed career. It has often been a mistake to bring into the government, especially in very high posts, men who have never before worked with or in a public bureaucracy, who have never had to live with the "public interest" from day to day. But it is also true that a lifetime public servant lacks something if he never leaves the bureaucracy; he loses track of the concerns which most of the people think about most of the time. Indeed, the very experience of dealing, year in and year out, with matters of great scale and moment can be a narrowing one; I am sure I am not the only ex-government person to whom the thousands looked like millions for a few months after leaving Washington.

It is beyond my scope in this paper—and probably beyond my powers anyway—to set forth a neat procedure to make sure that prospective political executives in the civil service get some private experience and budding

Assistant Secretaries now in private business or universities or foundations try the bureaucracy for a while. But I would be willing to bet that an objective study of political executives over the last generation would reveal that men with mixed careers behind them had been more effective and lasted longer in their jobs than those less favored by variety in their lives.

A Rare Combination

That is the list. Our political executive must be imbued with the public interest; he must be a leader of men; he must do his own thinking and be his own public relations man; and he should preferably have had some public and some private experience. As the Hoover Commission's Task Force noted:

> The combination of abilities is relatively rare. . . . His foresight must equal the hindsight of a host of critics, both amateur and professional, who are free to be as narrow in their point of view and time perspective as they care to be. The rules of the game of national politics allow no margin for error . . . To lead the life of a political executive of high rank amidst the asperities of American politics is a test of toughness, of intelligence, and of devotion to the public interest.

"Such talents," the Task Force concluded with classic understatement, "are valuable to the Nation but hard to find."

"DRAWING A LINE"

How far down from the President should political appointment and political expendability be the rule? On this, the perennial question in discussions of civil service reform, the Hoover Commission and its Task Force were very clear: A sharp line must be drawn between political and administrative functions. And when they draw it, what a curious boundary it turns out to be.

The second Hoover Commission must be seen as a recession in the seventy-year drive to have civil servants take over the government. From Wilson's professorial days until a few years ago, the general idea has been to reduce to a minimum the number of jobs with a tinge of politics. Wilson himself was not sure, when he published *Congressional Government* in 1885, whether the Secretaries in the Cabinet should be regarded as political or nonpolitical officers. The idea of a strong civil service has been so powerful in this country—even if the prestige of the actual civil service has not—that as late as December 1952 a National Planning Association report seriously suggested that most or all of the President's own staff should be drawn from the career service.

But the reformers overshot their mark. More and more people, especially those who had to run the executive branch of the government, became concerned about the short supply of political executives good enough and knowledgeable enough to manage the government of our big democracy. The second Hoover Commission therefore kept its enthusiasm for civil service reform within bounds, and sought to enlarge the number of political executives, now about seven or eight hundred by Hoover Commission count —though it prudently did not say how many more political executives there should be. Then it added a proposal for a senior civil service of 1,500 to 3,000 individuals, a special tribe of career men and women who have demonstrated their ability to survive and advance in the bureaucracy and are rewarded with personal rank and the permission to serve in any agency that will hire them.

Task Force Definitions

The Task Force wisely abandoned the traditional idea that you can distinguish between two kinds of people, those who determine policies and those who carry them out. But firm in their resolve to separate the political transients from the permanent boarders, the experts laid out a more complicated boundary line, more appropriate to the uneven terrain. Political executives should, they said, be appointed to:

> a) All positions filled by Presidential appointment, with or without confirmation by the Senate;
>
> b) All positions having vested in them statutory authority or executive delegations of authority requiring the incumbents to make final decisions in the establishment of governing policies, programs, objectives, and in the enunciation of principles which will control the action of subordinates in the implementation of the foregoing;
>
> c) All positions, the duties of which require the incumbents to act publicly in advocating new policies and in justifying or defending the governing policies or the basic principles or philosophy which controls their department or agency policies. Such duties would include direct participation with, or representation of noncareer executives in public debate, evaluate discussions, and justifications of departmental policies, programs, or activities.
>
> d) Most positions of a personal and confidential nature, such as personal aides, confidential secretaries, and personal chauffeurs. . . .

Article of Faith

I confess that all this enthusiasm for drawing a sharp line between politicos and careerists leaves me very cold. It is, I know, an article of passionate faith that pervades the literature on this subject. Hardly a month goes by without a scholarly admonition about the "rigid protection of bureau chiefs from political connections and duties"; or a civil service advocate making the misleading analogy between a lawyer's advice to his client and a civil servant's advice to his politically appointed boss; or an expert viewing with alarm the fact that government, the product of politics, is political. In a recent book, Dr. Leonard D. White argues the point so vigorously that in one passage about the making of decisions he draws a rather unattractive picture of a civil servant:

> At the highest levels, only the confidence that comes from an inner conviction of the "rightness" of a course of action and the moral support that comes from the representative capacity of the man who must act can sustain the strength to decide. The career service does not normally breed this type. Its decisions are based primarily on the logic of efficiency rather than on the calculated risks of an uncertain future.

How Government Works

Of course a line does have to be drawn, in the sense that you have to distinguish which jobs are going to be filled by political appointment and vacated by political action, and which jobs are going to be filled by civil servants and vacated under Civil Service safeguards. For this purpose the Hoover boundary is as good as any. What I object to is the Commission's quite unrealistic picture of what will be going on below that line: the image of an executive branch with a few political chiefs making policy and publicly defending it, while the drones below are carefully screened off from the ugly realities of the world of politics. But is this truly the way the government works, or the way a government under our Constitution can possibly work?

The Hoover group draws its line between "departmental management" and "bureau management." Thus in the New Deal Department of Agriculture, the heads of the Agricultural Adjustment Administration, the Farm Security Administration, and the policy-making Bureau of Agricultural Economics, all of whom ran highly controversial programs, would have been career men. Could Congress be kept from summoning such men as witnesses to explain their actions? Should such men as these be protected from the effort to explain to farm groups and business groups and labor groups and the press why they think their innovations are in the public interest? If a ranking bureaucrat cannot help build public support for the segment of the government's work for which he is responsible, is he even the right man for the job? Is there really this clear distinction between "factual material" and the policies which rest on them, between diagnosis and prescription, between "government" and "politics"?

SOURCES OF CONFUSION

The Commission's vision of how the government should work "below the line" strikes me as so exotic that I have tried very hard to think how this dreamworld came into being. There are, I think, three sources of confusion. One may be a misreading of British experience. Another source of confusion is the idea that the erection of defenses against the spoils system is still the cardinal item on the good-government agenda. And a third derangement stems from a concept of "political neutrality" which confuses party politics with the politics of national policy. We might look briefly at each of these confusions in turn.

The False British Analogy

It is easy for a student of American government to be dazzled by the eminence and prestige of British civil servants compared to the low opinion generally expressed about our own bureaucrats in Washington. It is, none the less, faintly ridiculous to make the British model our own. In Britain the Civil Service has an aristocratic tradition; it was the preserve of an upper class. Moreover, the political character of Cabinet Ministers and their immediate staffs was clearer from the outset; since they had to be politicians to get into the House of Commons to begin with, no British scholar is recorded as having asked, as Wilson did about American Cabinet officers, "Are the Secretaries political or non-political officers?"

Apart from their class origin, from what comes the prestige of a British permanent under secretary? Surely not from any system that divorces him from formulating policy or becoming identified with a policy in the public mind. The reverse is true. Indeed, I would suggest that nowadays British civil servants derive much of their prestige from the general knowledge that the civil servants run the government and the political Ministers are left with little room for political deviation from the "nonpolitical" advice they get from their permanent staffs. In many Ministries an independent study would I think reveal that almost the only function performed by the political Minister is the rather specialized task of explaining to his fellow parliamentarians what the civil servants are doing in his Ministry, and why they say they are doing it.

When Hugh Gaitskell gave way to R. A. Butler as Chancellor of the Exchequer several years ago, I was privileged to watch the civil servants in the Treasury put on a routine demonstration of their power. Shortly after the Conservatives took over, Mr. Butler went to a North Atlantic Treaty Organization Council meeting and publicly agreed with the American Secretary of the Treasury, John Snyder, about the need for early convertibility of sterling—a policy which his predecessor Mr. Gaitskell had been resisting with the enthusiastic backing of the Treasury staff. I was in London not long afterwards, and I vividly remember the quiet strength with which the Treasury civil servants assured me, "Don't worry about it, the Minister will be taking a different line in a few months, after he learns the facts." And indeed, after he learned the facts which the civil servants gave him to learn, nothing more was heard from the Chancellor's office about making sterling convertible with the dollar as soon as possible.

It is, in fact, not convertible yet. Either the facts or the civil servants—or possibly both—have produced an impressive continuity of policy.

The British model is not for us. Our Constitution does not exactly encourage the legislature to lie down and be walked on by an executive of its choice, an oversimplified but not too inaccurate description of British politics. Congress does not choose our President, and it therefore is not beholden to him and cannot be bullied by him. The separation of powers forces us to have the open government which is natural for our open society. With us, civil servants have to be not only responsible to the public interest but responsive to Congress, a myriad of popular organizations, and the press. In our political government there is no room for a bureaucratic manager who is "above politics."

Civil Service: Stifled by Reformers?

Because every program has a political origin, and every public manager must also be something of a politician, the spoils system seemed the natural way to run our national government a hundred years ago. A yard fight has long since reversed Senator William L. Marcy's famous dictum, "To the victors belong the spoils of the enemy." Yet the descendants of the original civil service reformers are still fighting the battle to protect and enlarge the place of the civil service in the scheme of things. In the process they may stifle the growth of the service itself.

Why do I say this? Because I think back to the days when I first joined the government, fresh out of school. In those days there were a good many examples of "government people" reaching high positions in the government. Daniel Bell, a civil servant who became Under Secretary of the Treasury, was held up to us as a model. Joseph Grew, a senior Ambassador and an Under Secretary of State, similarly has served as a symbol of the summit for young Foreign Service Officers. Now, sixteen years later, I find the Hoover Commission telling me that civil servants should not aspire to any post in which they make final decisions, enunciate principles, publicly advocate new policics, justify or defend existing policies, basic principles, or philosophy, or participate in something called "evaluative discussions." That sounds to me like retrogression in the kind of top position a junior civil servant can aspire to.

For purposes of comparison, consider the State Department. Of its ten statutory Assistant Secretaries today, seven are for practical purposes career men who also served under Democrats. There are 75 Chiefs of Mission (72 Ambassadors, 3 Ministers); of these posts 43 are held by career and 32 by non-career people. Of the most important ambassadorial posts, four—Moscow, Tokyo, Buenos Aires, and Rio de Janeiro—are held by career Ministers. A Foreign Service Officer or departmental official can, therefore, get to be an Assistant Secretary and an Ambassador—perhaps a Chief of Mission in several different countries in turn—before he completes a distinguished career.

The best civil servants should be able to look forward to comparable rewards of rank and prestige. They cannot do so today, by and large, and they will never be able to aspire beyond the Bureau level if the Hoover Commission prevails.

But, it will be said, let them become political executives and you make them expendable. This may not necessarily be so; it does not always work that way even in the State Department, which is surely as politically sensitive an agency as we are ever likely to have in the United States government. But even if it be true that the road to glory is strewn with turnover statistics, all is not lost. At this level a senior government official can often find an equally useful job outside the government; it is my impression that the political executives had nothing like the difficulty getting relocated that civil servants had in the 1953 exodus from Washington.

To get the best young people into the civil service, civil servants need to be encouraged to cap their career by becoming political executives, with the glory as well as the risks that choice entails. I see no other course that will enable the government to compete successfully for the very best talent coming out of college.

Party Politics and Policy Politics

The Hoover Commission's passion to separate politics from administration takes its most extraordinary form when the Commission gets to talking about "political neutrality." When I first read the Commission's report I could not believe that a body predominantly composed of practicing politicians could possibly have meant what the Report said. For the Commission has built into its remarks on this subject an appalling confusion between party politics and policy politics.

Most of the policy questions which come up in the executive branch of the government, of course, have little to do with party politics. They are nevertheless highly political. As we have seen, each high administrator uses up a good part of his time and energy building and maintaining a political base to support the program for which he is responsible. In the early days of the Marshall Plan, Paul Hoffman spent nearly all of his time successfully promoting the plan, in the United States and in Europe as well. Douglas McKay, until recently Secretary of the Interior, spent a good part of his time defending the Eisenhower administration's electric power and conservation policies, and the defense of his farm views seems to be almost a full-time job for Secretary of Agriculture Ezra Taft Benson. The higher one goes in the executive hierarchy, the less time there is for outside groups (including other agencies of the government) to support the segment of the government for which one is responsible.

Policy politics of this kind is not at all the same thing as party politics, though there is of course some overlap. The party in office has to run generally on the issue of what it thinks and what it is doing. But the campaign oratory generally has to do with what may be done rather than what is being done. And sometimes, as in the case of Secretary Benson at this moment, the demands of policy politics may run counter to the shortrun interests of party politics. Chairman Leonard Hall of the Republican National Committee would probably settle for a little less rigorous honesty in looking at the farmer's plight; certainly the Democrats, veterans of their own many confusions between party and policy, are making the most of this one.

A "Neutralist" Service?

Bearing in mind this distinction between the two meanings of the word "political," I invite your attention to the Hoover Commission's description of the neutrality required of senior civil servants:

> They should keep clear of all political activity, preserve their neutrality in matters of politics . . . This means that they must avoid such emotional attachment to the policies of any administration that they cannot accept change and work in harmony with new leaders. Senior civil servants would necessarily refrain from all political activities that would affect adversely their ability to perform their official duties fairly, or that would tend to identify them personally with a political party or its policies. . . .
>
> The senior civil servant should make no public or private statements to the press except of a purely factual nature. He should make no public speeches of a political or controversial character. . . .

The civil servants described in these quotations unquestionably exist. But few of them reach, and none of them should reach, the seniority and rank which would otherwise qualify them for membership in the Hoover Commission's senior civil service.

How can a senior government official, whose touchstone is the public interest, be expected to be "neutral" in dealing with a Senator who is plugging for some private interest that happens to be important in his state? Reading the Hoover Commission Report, I tried to picture myself, during the time when I was presenting the Mutual Security program to the Congress, being "neutral" about the reactions of Congressman John Taber, or about whether the bipartisan coalition which always wanted to cut foreign aid would have its way that year. Far from being "neutral" and avoiding emotional attachment, a bureaucrat in that position has the responsibility—not just the obligation to his administrative superiors but the duty to his own concept of the public interest—to be very active in the effort to build a congressional coalition in support of his program.

Avoid Emotional Attachment?

And how on earth can a senior government official "avoid emotional attachment to the policies of any administration"? To begin with he has to help make them. Correction: he "provides facts and background data." But by a curious coincidence he usually provides just those facts and background data that support the adoption of what becomes the administration's policy.

Even if he had nothing to do with establishing the policy, the Hoover Commission wants him to be "neutral" and to "avoid emotional attachment" on such questions as these:

Whether the federal government or the Idaho Power Company should pre-empt the Hell's Canyon power site.

Whether the federal government should aid schools in states that have not complied with the Supreme Court's desegregation decision.

Whether the federal government has any responsibility to assure a supply of polio vaccine for every child.

Whether the farmers need more subsidies or more competition.

Whether accused subordinates should be allowed to face their accusers and know the charges against them.

Whether we should or should not aid the Nationalist Chinese on Formosa.

Whether we need to be ahead of the Russians in the production of guided missiles.

Whether, in a particular situation, we should or should not go to war.

In the case of each of these issues, and dozens more, there are political executives and senior civil servants working side by side to develop the policy and sell it to the Congress and the public at large. For grown men working on matters like these, the avoidance of emotional attachment is nonsense.

Certainly a man who is protected in his job should avoid party work. There are plenty of examples even of top political executives who have operated on that basis. Republicans Robert A. Lovett and William C. Foster ran the Defense Department without getting into politics in the party sense of the word, and General George Marshall, who stayed clear of party politics in spite of extreme provocation, furnishes another notable example. But the Hoover Commission's ban on controversy and emotion goes far beyond party politics into the politics of national policy.

A senior civil service that took literally what the Hoover Commission has said about "political neutrality" would be a pool of eunuchs, a special breed of Americans who stay out of trouble by staying out of sight. No political executive in his right mind would want one of them assigned to his office. A government staffed with people who "avoided emotional attachment" would be like a hospital full of doctors and nurses who did not care whether their patients lived or died, just so the proper professional procedures were followed.

As anyone knows who has worked in Washington, it is not "neutrality" but vigorous advocacy that overcomes inertia in our big bureaucracy. Too much emphasis on neutrality would shift the whole government into neutral.

9 EQUAL JUSTICE UNDER LAW

No branch of American government has come under more violent attack in recent years than the judiciary. Justices of the Supreme Court have been vitriolically assailed and, in some cases, even their impeachment has been urged.

Since the 1930s, the Court has been embroiled in emotionally charged issues of great historical import—first in the economic realm, more recently in the many areas of personal freedom. Criticism of the Court in these decades has come from many ideological quadrants. In the early 1930s, liberals sharply criticized the "nine old men" for repudiating much of the New Deal. In recent years, white-supremacists in the South have defied the Court's long-overdue rejection of the "separate-but-equal" doctrine, while religious zealots in the North have sought to circumvent judicial reaffirmation of the traditional separation of church and state. Meanwhile, defenders of states' rights, allying themselves with archconservatives of all regions, have assailed the Court's involvement in the "political" arena of state legislative malapportionment.

This motley array of complaints has shared but one common view—the belief that the Court has been guilty of usurping legislative and even administrative prerogatives. In the words of one recent right-wing commentator, the court has been "power hungry and tyrannical."

In order to make a reasoned judgment, it seems desirable to suggest some criteria by which a judiciary may appropriately be judged in a democracy. High on the list must come the question of whether the system serves to protect the individual—if necessary, against public officials and government itself. A corollary question is whether impartiality exists—equality of treatment and of access for all, regardless of wealth, power, privilege, and prestige. In the engraved words above the marble columns of the Supreme Court itself, is there "Equal Justice Under Law"? Second, are the courts independent—are they truly free to arrive at judgments that, no matter how controversial, reflect the studied opinions of mature, competent, and diligent men of good will? Or do the courts yield to the pressures all around them, reflecting now the "vested interests"—be they racial, religious, or economic—and now the majoritarian hysteria of the moment, directed against a currently detested minority? This latter point suggests perhaps the most important question of all—Is justice the concern of the entire community? For without ultimate public support or acceptance of its views, no judicial system, no matter how strong, can long continue as the protector of a waning set of freedoms.

Traditionally the courts have occupied a powerful, if not always hallowed, place in the American system of government. Judicial review, that power of the Supreme Court to pass final judgment upon the constitutionality of state and federal legislation, as well as upon the decisions of the lower courts, has been a keystone of that system. Indeed, judicial review has been accurately described as one of the few uniquely American contributions to the science and art of democratic government. Popular acceptance of this "check and balance" in our system has guaranteed the judiciary an equal role among the three branches of government. It also means that judges and courts must inevitably be involved in functions that are, at least in part, legislative or even administrative. Thus, if the judiciary is to remain independent, the people, and the other branches of government, must accept possible (and even likely) court vetoes over statutes (progressive and otherwise), judicial "legislation" that interprets and sometimes modifies the "will of Congress," and judicial "administration" that sets the pace for desegregation and shapes the boundaries of legislative districts.

In a democracy, the public must ultimately support and obey all decisions of the court—not only those of which it approves but those that it thoroughly deplores. For only if there is public willingness to be guided by a rule of law can the judiciary continue to play its important independent-balance-wheel function in our complex government in action.

THE ROLE OF THE COURTS: CONSCIENCE OF A SOVEREIGN PEOPLE

J. Skelly Wright

Born and raised in Louisiana, Federal Judge J. Skelly Wright now sits on the United States Court of Appeals in Washington, D.C., where his voice continues to strike a "note of conscience in the breast of America."

There is abroad in this country a major debate concerning the role of the courts in expanding individual freedom and in increasing respect for human rights.

One school of thought, known as the advocates of judicial restraint, has advised the judges to move cautiously. Judges cannot give the people more freedom than the people themselves want or deserve, they tell us. And whatever freedom the people want or deserve cannot be kept from them by the judges. So from this point of view, it is useless for the judges to concern themselves with expanding the sphere of human freedom. It may be worse than useless, for judicial protection of individual rights may well encroach on the powers and prerogatives of other branches of our government, thereby upsetting our Constitutional system of checks and balances. Thus, it is said, it is to state legislatures and to Congress, rather than to the courts, that the people must look for the protection of their rights. Moreover, if the judges take the burden of defending and expanding freedom upon their own shoulders, then the people may grow lazy and less vigilant, and neglect their own duties in protecting freedom. It is the efforts of the people themselves, expressed through the election of their chosen representatives, which underlie whatever freedom exists in our nation. Or so the advocates of judicial restraint would have it.

But the rival school of thought, derisively called the judicial activists, has taken quite a different view. For them, it is the duty of the courts to do all in their power to protect those freedoms which our Constitution grants. The courts will not be able to do all that is necessary by themselves. The courts have no army like the President, nor can the judiciary declare war as Congress can. But the courts can act as the collective conscience of a sovereign people—just as once nations had chancellors to act as conscience to the king. With courts performing their duty of proclaiming the eternal rights and liberties of the people, the people will not be slow to defend the banners raised by the courts. And the President and Congress will fall in line. This judges must do, according to the judicial activist, in deciding the cases and controversies involving the rights of human beings.

Moreover, freedom under our Constitution is not subject to any elections, state or Federal. The fundamental freedoms announced in the Bill of Rights are inalienable, and the protection of those rights, by the Constitution itself, is consigned to the courts. With the late Justice Robert H. Jackson the activists say:

> The very purpose of a Bill of Rights was to withdraw certain subjects from the vicissitudes of political controversy, to place them beyond the reach of majorities and officials and to establish them as legal principles to be applied by the courts. One's right to life, liberty, and property, to free speech, a free press, freedom of worship and assembly, and other fundamental rights may not be submitted to vote; they depend on the outcome of no elections.

WITNESSES AND THE FLAG

Perhaps the most dramatic demonstration of the difference between these two schools of thought occurred during the Second World War, when the Jehovah's Witnesses experienced a wave of persecution in our country because of their unusual religious beliefs and practices. Matters reached a climax when a number of local school boards required that schoolchildren—including Jehovah's Witnesses—give a daily pledge of allegiance to the flag. The Jehovah's Witnesses refused to do this, for they felt that such an act was contrary to the Bible's command "Thou shalt have no other gods before me." As a consequence of this refusal, Jehovah's Witnesses across the country faced the prospect of having their children expelled from school, arrested as truants, taken from their parents, and sent to reform schools.

Eventually this problem arrived at our highest tribunal; the Supreme Court announced that it would not interfere with the requirement of the pledge of allegiance. It recognized a major conflict between the freedom of belief of the individual child and his parents versus the power of the state to command allegiance. But, said the court, the reconciliation of that conflict must be left to the people and their elected representatives—this could not be done for them by judges. If the responsibility for protecting the freedom of the individual were left to the people, said the court, the people would rise to that responsibility.

But without guidance from the Supreme Court, the people misread their responsibilities. From the standpoint of religious freedom and respect for human rights, the effect of that Supreme Court decision in the first flag-salute case was disastrous. School board after school board adopted new requirements commanding the flag salute, on pain of expulsion or other penalties. And often the school boards would quote the very words of the Supreme Court opinion in justification of their action. In many cases the salute to the flag was used simply as a device to expel the unpopular Jehovah's Witnesses. The words of the Supreme Court, that the protection of freedom could best be left the responsibility of local authorities, were perverted and used as an excuse for what was in effect religious persecution by the local school boards.

At the same time, and worse than the official action against the Jehovah's Witnesses, was the nation-wide wave of mob violence, attempts at lynching, and physical brutality against the Witnesses—all in the name of patriotism and support for the Supreme Court's opinion. Conditions were such that within three years after the first flag-salute case was decided, a second one reached the Supreme Court. In a dramatic reversal, the court ruled that no authority, state or Federal, could dictate the religious beliefs of any citizen. Schoolchildren could not be coerced into reciting pledges of allegiance when to do so would violate their freedom of religion. Specifically, the children of Jehovah's Witnesses could not be expelled from school because their religious beliefs prevented them from giving the flag salute.

The Supreme Court decision was honored by the local boards. Much of the official persecution of the Jehovah's Witnesses diminished. The new Civil Rights Section of the Department of Justice—founded by the former Attorney General, later Mr. Justice Frank Murphy—helped communicate the Supreme Court ruling to local authorities, and to the people, explaining that the freedom of belief of the Witnesses was protected by law. The rest is history. The Jehovah's Witnesses have been let alone. At least they have been allowed to practice their religion.

Thus, in the very midst of the Second World War, a court defended—

indeed expanded upon—Constitutional freedoms. It did so despite the opposition of political authorities. It did so in behalf of one of the most unpopular of freedoms—especially in wartime—the freedom *not* to salute the flag.

The Supreme Court's defense of freedom of religion did not cease with the war. The school-prayer cases of the very recent past demonstrate once again that the court is alert to even minor abridgments of fundamental freedoms. Once again the apostles of judicial restraint have been critical. But religious freedom in this country is safer today because the Supreme Court has shown the people why even a minor inroad on religious freedom cannot be tolerated.

PROTECTION FOR THE POOR

The courts have also been expanding the sphere of human freedom in the field of criminal law. It has often been said that "History will judge the quality of a civilization by the manner in which it enforces its criminal laws." The Supreme Court has taken the lead in ensuring that our enforcement of criminal law receives the approbation of history. In decision after decision it has sought to upgrade and civilize the manner in which our criminal laws, state and Federal, have been enforced.

The court has demonstrated a determination to diminish the part that poverty plays in the administration of criminal justice—the type of trial a man gets must not depend on whether he is rich or poor. Following this thesis, the court has recognized the right to counsel in both Federal and state criminal trials and has required the state and the national governments to supply a lawyer for the indigent person. More than this, the Supreme Court has required the state and Federal governments to provide a proper appeal for indigents by paying the costs thereof, including a transcript of the testimony taken at the trial. Thus the court has sought to remove the handicap of poverty so that the indigent, too, may receive a fair trial under our law.

Coerced confessions have also received the condemnation of the current court. Under the Anglo-Saxon system of criminal justice, as distinguished from the Continental system, a defendant has a right to remain silent, not only at the time of trial but, most importantly, after his arrest before trial. The Supreme Court has been at pains to condemn, as uncivilized and as a reproach to our system of criminal justice, not only physical pressure, but psychological pressure as well, designed to force an accused to confess.

Perhaps the keynote case on the subject of coerced confessions and third degree is Chambers v. Florida. There a young Negro was accused of committing a heinous crime that had excited a large number of the white citizens of Florida. Without access to a lawyer or even to members of his family, young Chambers was questioned by the police for days on end while a mob bent on his destruction roamed outside the jail. Under these circumstances, it was said that he confessed to the crime. After his conviction in the state courts of Florida, the Supreme Court heard the case. In reversing that conviction and in denouncing the conditions under which a confession was extracted from Chambers, Mr. Justice Hugo L. Black sounded what has come to be the new creed for the court:

> Under our constitutional system, courts stand against any winds that blow as havens of refuge for those who might otherwise suffer because they are helpless, weak, outnumbered, or because they are non-conforming victims of prejudice and public excitement. . . . No higher duty, no more solemn responsibility, rests upon this Court, than that of translating into living law and maintaining this constitutional shield deliberately planned and inscribed for the benefit of every human being subject to our Constitution—of whatever race, creed or persuasion.

The Supreme Court has not satisfied itself with merely outlawing confessions that are demonstrably involuntary. Taking cognizance of the fact that most confessions are obtained while the accused is alone in police custody immediately after arrest and before being transferred to judicial custody by a committing magistrate, the court has held that where there is unnecessary delay in bringing the accused before the committing magistrate, any confession made during this period of unnecessary delay shall not be received in evidence. Thus the court has sought to outlaw not only coerced confessions but also confessions obtained under circumstances presumptively coercive.

In the protection of rights under the Fourth Amendment against unreasonable searches and seizures, the Supreme Court has also been active. The midnight knock on the door, the hallmark of the totalitarian police, does not pass muster in this country. The court not only has outlawed evidence obtained from unreasonable searches and illegal arrests. By an application of the so-called fruit-of-the-poisoned-tree doctrine, it has ordered excluded from trial of a criminal case all evidence derived from the evidence illegally obtained. "Knowledge gained by the government's own wrong cannot be used by it," says the court.

Through its decisions in criminal law, the court has given rich meaning to our ideal of equal justice under law. Persons accused of crime, as a class, have little claim to sympathy with the public or to influence with political authorities. It would be easy, even popular, to constrict the rights of those who stand at the bar of justice. But the courts have reminded us that the rights of all citizens are safe only to the extent that the rights of each accused person are protected. The phrase "It's his Constitutional right" has entered the common language as a link between the ideals of our civilization and the recognition of the rights of the lowliest offender.

Of course, these civilizing advances in the manner of enforcing criminal justice have also been the subject of criticism. The court itself has been condemned for recognizing the rights of "criminals." What the detractors fail to recognize, of course, is that the Bill of Rights outlined in the first eight Amendments to the United States Constitution are the rights of all citizens of the United States, and until an accused is proved guilty beyond a reasonable doubt after a fair trial, he also, as a citizen, is entitled to those rights.

EQUAL VOTES

The reapportionment cases mark another important area in which the Supreme Court has affected our freedom. When we say "This is a free country," one of the things we mean is that we are a free people who govern ourselves. In order for us to govern ourselves, we require fair apportionment. If, for practical purposes, it were primarily the farmers and small-town residents who voted, and the votes of city people hardly counted at all, then to that extent we would be less a free country.

Reapportionment cases highlight the debate on the role of judges in preserving freedom. And these cases point out the importance of general acceptance, of popular support, of aid from executive and legislature, and of reaffirmation by the national conscience. For many years, judges would not decide reapportionment cases—no matter how unfair the reapportionment, no matter what laws or Constitutional provisions were violated, no matter how many people were denied an effective right to vote. Judges would not decide such cases because, as some of them saw it, a court decision about legislative apportionment could have no effect unless the legislature and the people accepted the decision. And no one could count on, or predict, whether there would be legislative or popular support. And so, though as a matter of law the courts had the power to decide apportionment cases, as a matter of judicial wisdom they generally abstained from these issues. Reapportionment was held to be a political issue that addressed itself to the people.

But the Supreme Court has now declared that such cases are proper for judicial decision. The court has now found that in many areas the political system restrained the people from acting, that there was developing in this country a condition in some respects similar to the rotten-borough system that disgraced England two centuries ago. So the court, in effect, authorized the courts in each state to hear apportionment cases as they came up and to apply to voting the principle of equal protection our Constitution ordains. Some people would resist to the end the court's efforts in this field, and that the nation's refusal to accept the challenge and rise to the responsibility given them by the courts would become a national disgrace. But the results have been quite different, and the response to the judicial spark has been broader and stronger than anyone could have predicted. In state after state, citizens' groups have stepped forward, swiftly and effectively, to demand enforcement of the Constitutional principles of equality of which the Supreme Court had reminded them. Soon local courts took up the matter of reapportionment. And in some states, even before the question came before the local courts, legislators and governors have supported reapportionment proposals of their own. Now, by and large, citizens generally—from the man in the street to newspapers and preachers—have said "at long last" to the principle that a state's apportionment must conform to the standards of equality required by our Constitution.

MAKING A TRUISM TRUE

Of the areas in which courts, particularly the Supreme Court, have been active in promoting the freedom of us all, the one of first concern to us today is racial justice. The Supreme Court decisions in the field of racial equality have attempted to secure an actual freedom for the Negro from the bonds of discrimination and bigotry—and a freedom for the white from having to live in a society where such injustices occur. That these freedoms belong to the white and to the Negro is solid Constitutional law—nothing could be more clear than that the Thirteenth, Fourteenth, and Fifteenth Amendments to the Constitution were adopted exactly for the purpose of raising the former slave to the level of first-class citizen. The court decisions of our day are but long-delayed steps forward in giving actual effect to that Constitutional law.

The question remains, Will these decisions receive the support of the people, or will they remain only words in the mouths of the judges? Will the other branches of the Federal government, the Executive and Congress—and the state and local governments—respond to the challenge of these Supreme Court decisions and make a reality today the promise of a hundred years ago?

In pleading for passage of the Civil Rights Act of 1963, the Attorney General of the United States began his remarks to the Congress with this statement:

"For generations, Americans have prided themselves on being a people with democratic ideals—a people who pay no attention to a man's race, creed, or color. This very phrase has become a truism. But it is a truism with a fundamental defect: it has not been true." Is there an honest person in this country today who will deny this statement? Are there enough people in this country today so depraved that the Supreme Court's efforts in behalf of racial justice shall be in vain?

In answering these questions, we should first take notice that the landmark 1954 school-desegregation case has received both more support and more opposition than any other case in our century. The support it has received is tremendous. Organizations sprang up to implement its philosophy, people who had been apathetic to all things public suddenly took a new interest in the commonwealth, a wave of idealism swept the country—especially among college youth—to see the old Constitutional principle of equal justice given effect in the problems of the day. Even foreign nations looked at us with new respect as we began to practice what for so long we had merely preached.

But the civil-rights cases also provoked opposition. Men whose positions had been entrenched upon the foundation of old injustices resisted the righting of wrongs. Unthinking men, men used to old customs and old thoughts, refused to alter their ways. And many others were fearful; being unused to change, they were not ready to accept what was for them a revolution in their lives.

And so these court decisions that have inspired such enthusiasm from many of our citizens stand in need of even further support. The voices of the judges have struck a note of conscience in the breast of America, and America has been stirred to new efforts in behalf of an old idealism. But so entrenched an evil is not so easily overcome. The rock of selfishness, the hard core of racial injustice, is not so easily dissolved. Idealism alone is not enough. There must be a recognition by all our people that we have been wrong, morally wrong, in our treatment of the Negro. There must be a day of repentance. There must be a determination to redress the injustice of the past and a firm resolve by all branches of the government, and by the people, that the long suffering of the Negro shall not have been in vain.

Thus we see that in the areas of religious freedom, criminal law, reapportionment, and racial justice the courts have indeed played a leading role in expanding human freedom in our time. And for this they, particularly the Supreme Court, have been subjected to a barrage of calumny and vilification in some parts of our country. Even some thinking men, men of good will whose roots in the fight for human freedom go very deep, deplore the leadership the current Supreme Court has given in the fight for social and political justice. They say they fear the rule of judges. I say their fears are foolish fancies. In expanding human freedom, the judges have nothing to enforce their rule but the conscience of America. And as long as we are ruled by the informed and challenged conscience of America, we have nothing to fear.

INSIDE VIEW OF THE HIGH COURT

William J. Brennan, Jr.

William J. Brennan, Jr., has served as Associate Justice on the Supreme Court since 1956. This article was adapted from an address he gave at Maxwell Air Force Base in Alabama in 1963.

Throughout its history the Supreme Court has been called upon to face many of the dominant social, political, economic and even philosophical issues that confront the nation. But Solicitor General Cox only recently reminded us that this does not mean that the Court is charged with making social, political, economic or philosophical decisions. Quite the contrary. The Court is not a council of Platonic guardians for deciding our most difficult, and emotional questions according to the Justices' own notions of what is just or wise or politic. To the extent that this is a governmental function at all, it is the function of the people's elected representatives.

The Justices are charged with deciding according to law. Because the issues arise in the framework of concrete litigation they must be decided on facts embalmed in a record made by some lower court or administrative agency. And while the Justices may and do consult history and the other disciplines as aids to constitutional decision, the text of the Constitution and relevant precedents dealing with that text are their primary tools.

It is indeed true, as Judge Learned Hand once said, that the judge's authority "depends upon the assumption that he speaks with the mouth of others: the momentum of his utterances must be greater than any which his personal reputation and character can command; if it is to do the work assigned to it—if it is to stand against the passionate resentments arising out of the interests he must frustrate—he must preserve his authority by cloaking himself in the majesty of an overshadowing past, but he must discover some composition with the dominant trends of his times."

However, we must keep in mind that, while the words of the Constitution are binding, their application to specific problems is not often easy. The Founding Fathers knew better than to pin down their descendants too closely. Enduring principles rather than petty details were what they sought. Thus the Constitution does not take the form of a litany of specifics. There are, therefore, very few cases where the constitutional answers are clear, all one way or all the other, and this is also true of the current cases raising conflicts between the individual and governmental power—an area increasingly requiring the Court's attention.

Ultimately of course, the Court must resolve the conflicts of competing interests in these cases, but all Americans should keep in mind how intense and troubling these conflicts can be. Where one man claims a right to speak and the other man claims the right to be protected from abusive or dangerously provocative remarks the conflict is inescapable. Where the police have ample external evidence of a man's guilt, but to be sure of their case put into evidence a confession obtained through coercion, the conflict arises between his right to a fair prosecution and society's rights to protection against his depravity. Where the orthodox Jew wishes to open his shop and do business on the day which non-Jews have chosen, and the Legislature has sanctioned, as a day of rest, the Court cannot escape a difficult problem of reconciling opposed interests. Finally, the claims of the Negro citizen, to borrow Solicitor General Cox's words, present a "conflict between the ideal of liberty and equality expressed in the Declaration of Independence, on the one hand, and, on the other hand, a way of life rooted in the customs of many of our people."

If all segments of our society can be made to appreciate that there are such conflicts, and that cases which involve constitutional rights often require difficult choices, if this alone is accomplished, we will have immeasurably enriched our common understanding of the meaning and significance of our freedoms. And we will have a better appreciation of the Court's function and its difficulties.

How conflicts such as these ought to be resolved constantly troubles our whole society. There should be no surprise, then, that how properly to resolve them often produces sharp division within the Court itself. When problems are so fundamental, the claims of the competing interests are often nicely balanced, and close divisions are almost inevitable.

Supreme Court cases are usually one of three kinds: the "original" action brought directly in the Court by one state against another state or states, or between a state or states and the Federal Government. Only a handful of such cases arise each year, but they are an important handful. A recent example was the contest between Arizona and California over the waters of the lower basin of the Colorado River. Another was the contest between the Federal Government and the newest state of Hawaii over the ownership of lands in Hawaii.

The second kind of case seeks review of the decisions of a Federal Court of Appeals—there are 11 such courts—or of a decision of a Federal District Court—there is a Federal District Court in each of the 50 states.

The third kind of case comes from a state court—the Court may review a state court judgment by the highest court of any of the 50 states, if the judgment rests on the decision of a Federal question.

When I came to the Court seven years ago the aggregate of the cases in the three classes was 1,600. In the term just completed there were 2,800, an increase of 75 per cent in seven years. Obviously, the volume will have doubled before I complete 10 years of service. How is it possible to manage such a huge volume of cases? The answer is that we have the authority to screen them and select for argument and decision only those which, in our judgment, guided by pertinent criteria, raise the most important and far-reaching questions. By that device we select annually around 6 per cent—between 150 and 170 cases—for decision. That screening process works like this: When nine Justices sit, it takes five to decide a case on the merits. But it takes only the votes of four of the nine to put a case on the argument calendar for argument and decision. Those four votes are hard to come by—only an exceptional case raising a significant Federal question commands them.

Each application for a review is usually in the form of a short petition, attached to which are any opinions of the lower courts in the case. The adversary may file a response—also, in practice, usually short. Both the petition and response identify the Federal questions allegedly involved, argue their substantiality, and whether they were properly raised in the lower courts. Each Justice receives copies of the petition and response and such parts of the record as the parties may submit. Each Justice then, without any consultation at this stage with the others, reaches his own tentative conclusion whether the application should be granted or denied.

The first consultation about the case comes at the Court conference at which the case is listed on the agenda for discussion. We sit in conference almost every Friday during the term. Conferences begin at 10 in the morning and often continue until 6, except for a half-hour recess for lunch. Only the Justices are present. There are no law clerks, no stenographers, no secretaries, no pages—just the nine of us. The junior Justice acts as guardian of the door, receiving and delivering any messages that come in or go from the conference.

The conference room is a beautifully oak-paneled chamber with one side lined with books from floor to ceiling. Over the mantel of the exquisite marble fireplace at one end hangs the only adornment in the chamber—a portrait of Chief Justice John Marshall. In the middle of the room stands a rectangular table, not too large but large enough for the nine of us comfortably to gather around it. The Chief Justice sits at the south end and Mr. Justice Black, the senior Associate Justice, at the north end. Along the side to the left of the Chief Justice sit Justices Stewart, Goldberg, White and Harlan. On the right side sit Justice Clark, myself and Justice Douglas in that order.

We are summoned to conference by a buzzer which rings in our several chambers five minutes before the hour. Upon entering the conference room each of us shakes hands with his colleagues. The handshake tradition originated when Chief Justice Fuller presided many decades ago. It is a symbol that harmony of aims if not of views is the Court's guiding principle.

Each of us has his copy of the agenda of the day's cases before him. The agenda lists the cases applying for review. Each of us before coming to the conference has noted on his copy his tentative view whether or not review should be granted in each case.

The Chief Justice begins the discussion of each case. He then yields to the senior Associate Justice and discussion proceeds down the line in order of seniority until each Justice has spoken. Voting goes the other way. The junior Justice votes first and voting then proceeds up the line to the Chief Justice who votes last. Each of us has a docket containing a sheet for each case with appropriate places for recording the votes. When any case receives four votes for review, that case is transferred to the oral argument list. Applications in which none of us sees merit may be passed over without discussion.

Now how do we process the decisions we agree to review? There are rare occasions when the question is so clearly controlled by an earlier decision of the Court that a reversal of the lower court judgment is inevitable. In these rare instances we may summarily reverse without oral argument. The case must very clearly justify summary disposition, however, because our ordinary practice is not to reverse a decision without oral argument. Indeed, oral argument of cases taken for review, whether from the state or Federal courts, is the usual practice. We rarely accept submissions of cases on briefs.

Oral argument ordinarily occurs about four months after the application for review is granted. Each party is usually allowed one hour, but in recent years we have limited oral argument to a half-hour in cases thought to involve issues not requiring longer argument. Counsel submit their briefs and record in sufficient time for the distribution of one set to each Justice two or three weeks before the oral argument. Most of the members of the present Court follow the practice of reading the briefs before the argument. Some of us often have a bench memorandum prepared before the argument. This memorandum digests the facts and the arguments of both sides, highlighting the matters about which we may want to question counsel at the argument. Often I have independent research done in advance of argument and incorporate the results in the bench memorandum.

We follow a schedule of two weeks of argument from Monday through Thursday, followed by two weeks of recess for opinion writing and the study of petitions for review. The argued cases are listed on the conference agenda on the Friday following argument. Conference discussion follows the same procedure I have described for the discussion of certiorari petitions. Of course, it is much more extended. Not infrequently discussion of particular cases may be spread over two or more conferences.

Not until the discussion is completed and a vote taken is the opinion assigned. The assignment is not made at the conference but formally in writing some few days after the conference. The Chief Justice assigns the opinions in those cases in which he has voted with the majority. The senior Associate Justice voting with the majority assigns the opinions in the other cases. The dissenters agree among themselves who shall write the dissenting opinion. Of course, each Justice is free to write his own opinion, concurring or dissenting.

The writing of an opinion always takes weeks and sometimes months. The most painstaking research and care are involved. Research, of course, concentrates on relevant legal materials—precedents particularly. But Supreme Court cases often require some familiarity with history, economics, the social and other sciences, and authorities in these areas, too, are consulted when necessary.

When the author of an opinion feels he has an unanswerable document he sends it to a print shop, which we maintain in our building. The printed draft may be revised several times before his proposed opinion is circulated among the other Justices. Copies are sent to each member of the Court, those in the dissent as well as those in the majority.

Now the author often discovers that his work has only begun. He receives a return, ordinarily in writing, from each Justice who voted with him and sometimes also from the Justices who voted the other way. He learns who will write the dissent if one is to be written. But his particular concern is whether those who voted with him are still of his view and what they have to say about his proposed opinion. Often some who voted with him at conference will advise that they reserve final judgment pending the circulation of the dissent. It is a common experience that dissents change votes, even enough votes to become the majority. I have had to convert more than one of my proposed majority opinions into a dissent before the final decision was announced. I have also, however, had the more satisfying experience of rewriting a dissent as a majority opinion for the Court.

Before everyone has finally made up his mind a constant interchange by memoranda, by telephone, at the lunch table, continues while we hammer out the final form of the opinion. I had one case during the past term in which I circulated 10 printed drafts before one was approved as the Court opinion.

The point of this procedure is that each Justice, unless he disqualifies himself in a particular case, passes on every piece of business coming to the Court. The Court does not function by means of committees or panels. Each Justice passes on each petition, each item, no matter how drawn, in longhand, by typewriter, or on a press. Our Constitution vests the judicial power in only one Supreme Court. This does not permit Supreme Court action by committees, panels, or sections.

The method that the Justices use in meeting an enormous caseload varies. There is one uniform rule: Judging is not delegated. Each Justice studies each case in sufficient detail to resolve the question for himself. In a very real sense, each decision is an individual decision of every Justice. The process can be a lonely, troubling experience for fallible human beings conscious that their best may not be adequate to the challenge. "We are not unaware," the late Justice Jackson said, "that we are not final because we are infallible; we know that we are infallible only because we are final." One does not forget how much may depend on his decision. He knows that usually more than the litigants may be affected, that the course of vital social, economic and political currents may be directed.

This then is the decisional process in the Supreme Court. It is not without its tensions, of course—indeed, quite agonizing tensions at times. I would particularly emphasize that, unlike the case of a Congressional or White House decision, Americans demand of their Supreme Court judges that they produce a written opinion, the collective expression of the judges subscribing to it, setting forth the reasons which led them to the decision. These opinions are the exposition, not just to lawyers, legal scholars and other judges, but to our whole society, of the bases upon which a particular result rests—why a problem, looked at as disinterestedly and dispassionately as nine human beings trained in a tradition of the disinterested and dispassionate approach can look at it, is answered as it is.

It is inevitable, however, that Supreme Court decisions—and the Justices themselves—should be caught up in public debate and be the subjects of bitter controversy. An editorial in *The Washington Post* did not miss the mark by much in saying that this was so because "one of the primary functions of the Supreme Court is to keep the people of the country from doing what they would like to do—at times when what they would like to do runs counter to the Constitution. . . . The function of the Supreme Court is not to count constituents; it is to interpret a fundamental charter which imposes restraints on constituents. Independence and integrity, not popularity, must be its standards."

Certainly controversy over its work has attended the Court throughout its history. As Professor Paul A. Freund of Harvard remarked, this has been true almost since the Court's first decision:

> When the Court held, in 1793, that the State of Georgia could be sued on a contract in the Federal courts, the outraged Assembly of that state passed a bill declaring that any Federal marshal who should try to collect the judgment would be guilty of a felony and would suffer death, without benefit of clergy, by being hanged. When the Court decided that state criminal convictions could be reviewed in the Supreme Court, Chief Justice Roane of Virginia exploded, calling it a "most monstrous and unexampled decision. It can only be accounted for by that love of power which history informs us infects and corrupts all who possess it, and from which even the eminent and upright judges are not exempt."

But public understanding has not always been lacking in the past. Perhaps it exists today. But surely a more informed knowledge of the decisional process should aid a better understanding.

It is not agreement with the Court's decisions that I urge. Our law is the richer and the wiser because academic and informed lay criticism is part of the stream of development. It is only a greater awareness of the nature and limits of the Supreme Court's function that I seek. I agree fully with the Solicitor General: It is essential, just because the public questions which the Court faces are pressing and divisive, that they be thoroughly canvassed in public, each step at a time, while the Court is evolving new principles. The ultimate resolution of questions fundamental to the whole community must be based on a common consensus of understanding of the unique responsibility assigned to the Supreme Court in our society.

The lack of that understanding led Mr. Justice Holmes to say 50 years ago:

> We are very quiet there, but it is the quiet of a storm center, as we all know. Science has taught the world skepticism and has made it legitimate to put everything to the test of proof. Many beautiful and noble reverences are impaired, but in these days no one can complain if any institution, system, or belief is called on to justify its continuance in life. Of course we are not excepted and have not escaped. Doubts are expressed that go to our very being. Not only are we told that when Marshall pronounced an Act of Congress unconstitutional he usurped a power that the Constitution did not give, but we are told that we are the representatives of a class—a tool of the money power. I get letters, not always anonymous, intimating that we are corrupt. Well, gentlemen, I admit that it makes my heart ache. It is very painful, when one spends all the energies of one's soul in trying to do good work, with no thought but that of solving a problem according to the rules by which one is bound, to know that

many see sinister motives and would be glad of evidence that one was consciously bad. But we must take such things philosophically and try to see what we can learn from hatred and distrust and whether behind them there may not be a germ of inarticulate truth.

The attacks upon the Court are merely an expression of the unrest that seems to wonder vaguely whether law and order pay. When the ignorant are taught to doubt they do not know what they safely may believe. And it seems to me that at this time we need education in the obvious more than investigation of the obscure.

ALSO ON THE BENCH: "DOMINANT OPINION"
Alan F. Westin

Alan F. Westin is Associate Professor of Law and Government at Columbia University, and is the author of *The Supreme Court: Views from Inside.*

During the past six months, hardly a day has gone by without some influential figure in American public life denouncing the United States Supreme Court. Twenty-five United States Senators and 75 Representatives in this period have delivered speeches in Congress attacking the Court's constitutional outlook. Hostile editorials have appeared in over 150 newspapers. Arthur Krock of *The New York Times* has complained that the Court's "big brother" attitude constitutes a clear case of "judicial usurpation." Police officials and state judges have attacked the justices for "handcuffing" law enforcement.

The American Bar Association has heard its outgoing president lash the Court for gravely undermining "property rights," "internal security," "good citizenship," and other key values of our system. Many Catholic and Protestant church leaders have criticized the justices for rulings allegedly "secularizing" national life and "protecting immorality" from prosecution, and a shudder of apprehension greeted the Court's recent announcement that it would review two cases involving Bible reading and Lord's Prayer recitation in public schools. When asked recently what businessmen thought of the Court, the general counsel of one major corporation replied: "Well, it pays to be a Negro or a Communist if you want justice from the Warren Court. Business doesn't get it."

Is this criticism only a continuation of the protests that Southerners, conservatives and fundamentalist religious leaders have been aiming at the

Court since the middle nineteen-fifties? Does the recent increase in their volume point to another Court-curbing debate in 1963, comparable to the fight over the Jenner-Butler Bills in 1958? Most important of all, how is the public responding to the Court's disputed rulings of the nineteen-sixties, and does the Court respond in turn to the public?

Any discussion of Supreme Court criticism must start with the recognition that the justices are subject to many direct and indirect controls under our constitutional system. Constitutional amendments and Congressional legislation can reverse unpopular rulings. The Constitution specifically gives Congress control over the Court's appellate jurisdiction and this can be used to cut off the Court's review of specific areas of controversy. Presidents are usually able to appoint new justices and can deliberately seek to change the voting balances within the Court through these appointments. State and Federal officials can mount embarrassingly effective resistance to the Court's orders, ranging from subtle inaction to open defiance, since the justices must usually look to elected officials to enforce their orders. The bar and bench can raise influential protests against the Court's legal arguments and its professional competence. And every Supreme Court, finally, is acutely sensitive to any continuous, widespread mistrust of its decisions by the general public.

Reflecting these realities, no Supreme Court in American history has ever defied for long the sustained will of "dominant opinion" in the nation. When the Court has met the determined will of these dominant forces—as it faced the Radical Republicans in 1866–68 or the New Deal in 1936–37—the existing Court majority has always modified its disputed doctrines to uphold the measure insisted upon by dominant opinion. As Reed Powell said, the Court knows how to execute the "switch in time that saves nine."

The troublesome question in these political-judicial crises, of course, is how to define and measure "dominant opinion." Clearly, the justices do not have to consult public opinion polls about their decisions, or party platforms or even the results of specific elections in which the voters hear debate over issues being considered by the Court. By "dominant opinion," we mean the active consensus of an era as represented in the "passionate truths" held by the majority of elected state and Federal officials; the leaders of the most influential economic, civic and religious groups, and those mass media trusted by the politically active public.

When wholesale criticism of its doctrines begins to dominate these key sectors, the Court must reconsider its checks on dominant opinion or else risk reprisals on charges of being "arrogant, unrepresentative and willful."

But the justices must also decide whether any given flood of attacks really represents dominant opinion or something less than that. If opinion in the nation is broadly divided over the Court's disputed doctrines, or if the Court is really the target of critics who are in dissent from the dominant opinion of their era, then the Court is not in ultimate crisis and the justices can pursue their views of the Constitution in the normal traditions of judicial independence and defense of "unpopular" constitutional rights.

Finally, it must also be realized that the storms that rage over the Court involve only a few of its rulings. Of the 250–275 cases it decides on their merits each year, fewer than a dozen normally make up the "constitutionally sensitive" cases that stir fundamental debate. Yet all the skill and wisdom displayed in the vast majority of its rulings will not alter the fact that it is by these sensitive cases that the Supreme Court will be judged, in its day and by history.

With these factors in mind, the constitutionally sensitive decisions of the present Court which have aroused so much criticism in the nineteen-sixties can be considered under four major headings: the continued application of earlier, disputed constitutional rulings; the Court's extension of existing doctrines beyond their previous boundaries; the entry of the Court into new fields of controversy, and its performance in the wide range of cases involving issues of internal security.

The first set of decisions under debate involves constitutional positions laid down by Court majorities before 1960. The present Court has simply been applying these. In segregation cases during 1960–62, for example, the Court struck down state racial discrimination practices at about the same pace as between 1954–59—drawing a similar volume of protest from Southern segregationists and their "hard conservative" allies like William Buckley Jr., who jointly deplore judicial interference with Southern "gradualism" in race relations. New issues, such as the sit-in demonstrations, have not yet been reached.

In cases involving Federal powers of taxation, spending and regulation of industry, the Court has continued to uphold Congressional measures despite the protests of corporate spokesmen that many of these activities are constitutionally forbidden to the national government. In the area of labor-management relations, the Court has continued to uphold Federal and state power over collective bargaining relationships—Federal pre-eminence—again despite complaints from business and conservatives that these are either private or local matters.

On each of these issues, it seems clear that the present Court is moving in lockstep with the active consensus of this era. Public opinion and national political majorities support judicial activism in behalf of Negro civil rights and judicial self-restraint in matters of industrial relations and welfare programs. On these questions, the South, business and "hard conservatives" are the voice of pre-1929 and pre-World War II America. History has simply outrun their constitutional positions.

The second group of rulings under attack is made up of decisions in which the present Court has been extending significantly constitutional positions first adopted by earlier Court majorities. In the field of church-state relations, for example, the Court's ruling in 1961 that an oath of belief in God could not be required for holding state office, and the 1962 decision striking down a nondenominational prayer composed by the Regents in New York for the public schools, carried judicial review of public religious practices on to new ground.

The same is true with respect to state police methods and trial rules.

While the Court has grappled with the meaning of "due process" for decades, a major step was taken in 1961 with its ruling that all evidence obtained illegally by police must be excluded from state criminal trials. Again, in dealing with government censorship of books and films, the Court of the nineteen-sixties has broadened considerably the area of constitutionally-protected expression.

These increased "interferences" with the action of elected officials account for much of the recent rise in Court criticism. The school prayer case set off more denunciation of the justices than any ruling since the segregation cases rallied Southern officialdom against the Court. When Congressman Glenn Cunningham of Nebraska commented this year that the Court's motto seemed to be "Obscenity, yes; prayer, no," he expressed the level of bitterness that many critics feel.

In matters of religion, censorship and law enforcement, national opinion and civic groups are deeply divided. This means that the Court has not received anything like the mandate from dominant opinion that it had had in the field of segregation or Federal regulation of industry. If anything, I think the balance of opinion probably tips to the side of the critics. It may be in instinctive recognition of this, therefore, that the Court has actually adopted quite guarded and flexible positions in these areas and has consciously refused to accept the absolute doctrines urged by Justices Black, Douglas, Brennan and Warren.

Thus the Court majority has *not* held that movies must be free from all censorship, or that every religious expression in public schools violates the Constitution, or that state criminal procedure must conform exactly to Federal practice. The majority has chosen to advance more slowly, probing to see how fast and how far civil libertarian positions, previously rejected by local political majorities, can now be installed and obeyed because the Supreme Court says they should be.

The third main area in dispute involves the Court's wholly new departure in the state legislative apportionment case of 1962. Over the sharp protests of Justices Frankfurter and Harlan that the Court had deliberately avoided this "political thicket" for many years and should keep out of it still, six members of the Court voted that the citizen denied equal protection of the laws by discriminatory districting was entitled to judicial relief.

With the prospect that Federal judges will now oversee the constitutional fairness of apportionment in 50 states, critics have charged that this is an unprecedented invasion of States Rights and an improper intrusion by judges into the elective politics of the nation. Since the ruling threatens the present rural-conservative advantages in districting and promises to strengthen the representation of urban-suburban areas, the first public response divided largely along that line. Yet the significant thing is how much public support at the grassroots level the Court's ruling seems to be gathering day by day.

Before the decision, only liberal stalwarts were seriously pressing for judicial intervention in this area. Many students of American politics had seemed resigned to gross gerrymandering as a permanent blemish on our democracy. But once the Court stepped in and unclogged the political process, a heavy flow of editorial and public support has developed for making districts fair—preferably by the states themselves but under minimum standards set by the courts. The alarmed cries of conservative critics seem to be falling on unappreciative ears.

The fourth and final group of decisions under attack is in the charged area of internal security, where critics contend that the justices have been steadily "hamstringing" the nation's fight against subversion. Last May, for example, the Chairman of the Senate Judiciary Committee, Senator James Eastland of Mississippi, stated that between 1953 and 1962, the Court had "sustained the position advocated by the Communists" in 46 out of 70 cases involving "Communist or subversive activities." By such decisions, the Senator said, the justices are "lending aid and comfort to the conspiracy" seeking to destroy this nation. Similar charges are heard often from some bar associations, civic groups, and law-enforcement officers, and, of course, as the constant theme of the Radical Right.

Apart from their outrageous premise that judicial protection of constitutional rights is adopting a "Communist position," these attacks have a distinctly ironic character. During the Court-curb debates of 1958, internal-security stalwarts roundly denounced the Court for a dozen or more rapid-fire rulings in 1956-57 that upset Government anti-subversive prosecutions. The Court had questioned the scope of investigations by the House Committee on Un-American Activities, state investigations of "subversion" unconnected with state employees, state loyalty criteria for admission to the practice of law, Federal authority to withhold statements made to the Government by witnesses now testifying in Federal trials, the scope of Federal prosecutions of Communists under the Smith Act and dismissals of state employes for claiming the Fifth Amendment.

Civil libertarians greeted these decisions with cheers and many read them as high constitutional roadblocks against official "McCarthyism." But a storm of protest arose from conservatives. Congress swiftly passed a statute limiting the breadth of the ruling giving defendants access to witness's statements in Government files. Hostile Congressional investigations were held on several other rulings and a sharp Court-curb bill was defeated in the Senate by a 41–40 vote. As late as 1962, Congressional forces were still working to "undo" the Court's "mischief" of 1957; this spring saw the passage of an act reversing the Court's 1957 definition of a key Smith Act term.

By 1962, the Court majority had reacted by distinguishing or diluting virtually all of the bold and assertive rhetoric of the 1957 rulings. While the Court majority did not overrule earlier decisions, it permitted the House Un-American Activities Committee, Federal Smith Act prosecutors, state legislative investigators, state employment officials and state bar admission committees to do almost exactly what the 1957 rulings had seemed to forbid.

The Court's shift came not through the appointment of new justices but through a change in emphasis by Justices Frankfurter and Harlan. In 1956–

57, they had voted with Chief Justice Warren and Justices Black, Douglas and Brennan to provide a majority for striking down extreme Government internal security measures. After 1957, however, Justices Frankfurter and Harlan voted with Justices Clark, Whittaker and Stewart to form a majority that upheld Government power in cases paralleling those of 1956–57.

What prompted this shift? The 1956–57 cases had reviewed internal security actions taken during the hysterical peak of the early nineteen-fifties. In 1957, anti-McCarthy sentiment was strong in the nation and the moment seemed ripe for judicial intervention against anti-Communist measures that were "popular" but, in the mind of the Court's majority, cut dangerously and unnecessarily into American civil liberties. So the Court freed some convicted people, wrote stirring opinions reaffirming our libertarian heritage, and warned Government to take more care in the future.

But when many officials of the states and nation responded by deliberately repeating their anti-Communist programs, when the public did not make such conduct politically unprofitable and when Court curb measures gained ominous momentum, the showdown was at hand. Should the Court transform the warnings of 1956–57 into flat commands outlawing those Government measures? And could the Court make such rulings stick?

To many Americans, and to Warren, Black, Douglas and Brennan, the answer was clear—of course, the Court should strike down "unconstitutional action," or else what are courts and the Constitution for? But for some of the justices, this answer was not enough. The insulation and isolation of the judiciary from elective responsibility, the need to encourage respect for the Constitution within the political process itself and the presence of sustained support for measures the justices might think desperately unwise but Constitutionally on the border lines—these considerations are often paramount in moments of political-judicial crisis. Such factors were probably in the minds of Frankfurter and Harlan, leading them to follow the course of judicial self-restraint and to limit rather than extend the scope of the 1956–57 doctrines.

Could the Supreme Court have held fast to the larger implications of its 1956–57 rulings? The Court *did* remain firm on some sharply criticized rulings, such as those involving passport procedures, Federal loyalty-security programs and state sedition laws. Could it have maintained more? Given the ambiguous, if not hostile, position of the Eisenhower Administration toward the libertarian rulings of 1957 and given the strength of the Court's critics in Congress, an assertion of the full Warren-Black-Douglas-Brennan position would probably have produced swift reversals and even broad Court-curbs. Yet, though post-war generalship is easy, it is hard to believe that as complete a retreat as the Court carried out after 1957 was inescapable.

The Court could have asserted itself more, and even if some of its libertarian rulings had been reversed by Congress or by amendment, the debates stirred by this action would have turned the attention of the public to civil liberties in the cold war in a more systematic and educative way than has been achieved by the mere re-assertion of anti-Communist crusades by some elected officials.

Looking over the present Court's performance in these four major areas under dispute, many people may deny that any justices have been affected by dominant opinion in this way—for if they had, it would have to be considered either as timidity on their part or as a betrayal of the independent status given to the Court by the Founding Fathers for the protection of the Constitution. These people would explain that constitutional cases must be decided as a matter of right and wrong, with the law-trained Justices "finding" the meaning of the Constitution through use of constitutional records, prior decisions and basic canons of construction. These "findings" should be announced in utter disregard of dominant opinion.

Such an approach confuses the usual function of the justices as the nation's highest law court with its more complicated, more vital but less regular role as keeper of our constitutional checks and balances. In this latter capacity, the justices must function as constitutional statesmen, applying the brilliant but ambiguous phrases of 1789 or 1868 to economic, military, political, social and inter-group conditions then undreamed of. The Court must also try to apply to modern circumstances those continuing conflicts that the framers of the Constitution knowingly locked into our political system—conflicts between majority rule and minority rights, Federal authority and local control, the private domain and the public sector. In these areas, it should be remembered, the terms of the Constitution involve such highly elastic concepts as "due process of law" and "establishment of religion."

As constitutional statesmen, the justices must arrive at some ultimate accommodation with dominant opinion. The imperatives of democracy and the need for broad confidence in the Court require this. But the justices must seek to influence dominant opinion as well. The creative challenge is to find exactly the right combination of judicial command, creative suggestion and respectful non-interference that will lead those entrusted with political power in the states and nation to live by the expanding ideals of the American Constitution.

When the Supreme Court opened its 1962–63 term, Justice Frankfurter was already in retirement. Justices Byron White and Arthur Goldberg took their seats at the two opposite ends of the bench, symbolizing by their physical location that the Court's doctrinal boundaries, for the moment, are as undetermined as the constitutional philosophies of the new Kennedy appointees. These two men now hold the Court's balance of power, and with their votes could come important changes in the direction or emphasis of the Court's rulings on sensitive issues.

In this situation, both supporters and critics of the Court can be sure that their efforts to mold dominant opinion in the nation on the great constitutional questions will have a profound impact on the Court of the nineteen-sixties. The justices are listening, and is this not as it should be in a constitutional democracy?

10 THE BILL OF RIGHTS AND INDIVIDUAL FREEDOM

Recent years have witnessed a new and dangerous interpretation, on the part of many Americans, of the rights so bloodily attained by their revolutionary forebears. Despite its national heritage, a substantial segment of the public has been all too willing to accept the un-American doctrines embodied in the phrases "Fifth-Amendment Communist," "Where there's smoke there must be fire" (a saying that ignores the fact that the vilifier himself may have lit the smudge pot), and "There is no right to government employment." In the midst of all these slogans lies the suspicion that the Supreme Court has been "too soft"—too soft in permitting, even perhaps abetting, the escape of Communists and criminals from the clutches of the law.

Such widespread attitudes as these create a doubt whether the Bill of Rights, if introduced today, could be adopted. But what are the rights involved? Where did they originate? Where are they set forth? Whom do they protect against whom?

The "civil rights" stemming from our historical heritage are far broader than the highly publicized racial protections. They include such Anglo-Saxon common-law doctrines as the presumption of the innocence of the accused, the individuality of guilt, the right to confront one's accusers, and the right to know the nature of the charges on which one is held in custody. In addition to these guarantees, common to all our states but one (Louisiana, where Roman code law served as historical foundation), there are the protections afforded in the body of the Constitution itself—prohibitions against the enactment, by Congress or state legislatures, of bills of attainder or *ex post facto* laws, and a strict and limiting definition of treason.

More important than such prohibitions, however, are the many protections incorporated within the Bill of Rights—the first ten amendments. These protections are more specifically found in the substantive guarantees of the First Amendment, and in the procedural guarantees of the Fourth, Fifth, and Sixth. The First Amendment incorporates the five great freedoms—freedom of speech, of the press, of assembly, of religion, and of the vital right to petition. (In some recent decisions, the Supreme Court seems to have been tending toward the protection of such unwritten supplements as a right to travel and a right to read.) Since such abstract substantive rights are of little worth without their implementation, the Fourth, Fifth, and Sixth Amendments provide certain procedural safeguards, including those against self-incrimination, double jeopardy, cruel and unusual punishments, and excessive bail. In addition, these amendments guarantee the accused a speedy and public trial, trial by jury, indictment by grand jury in the event of a major crime, and adequate representation by counsel.

The Bill of Rights was originally drawn up to protect the individual against the central government alone. Today its guarantees have come, by that court doctrine known technically as "substantive due process," to be applied largely (but not yet in their entirety) against the states. Nonetheless, the Constitution applies these many protections only against government in all its forms; it has afforded few protections for the individual against the encroachments of his fellow citizens. The notable exception to this rule has stemmed from the judicial finding that the Thirteenth Amendment, prohibiting slavery, makes illegal the enforcement of contractual obligations that create virtual conditions of peonage or serfdom. The Constitution is a dynamic document, however, and the Fourteenth Amendment in particular contains clauses, including the guarantee of "equal protection of the laws," that may in the future be interpreted to expand this area of individual freedom.

As a further protection against government—against the possible abuses and excesses of bureaucratic procedures and decisions—another major doctrine has been developed. It is the doctrine of "administrative due process." In a series of decisions, judges have ruled, among other things, that hearings before administrative tribunals must be fair and impartial, and that the accused, individuals and corporations alike, must be afforded advance notice and a full opportunity to present evidence in their behalf. In addition, there are rules of federal-court procedure, built up through "case law" and based on a high regard for the due-process clause of the Constitution. According to these strictures, wiretap evidence has been ruled inadmissible in federal courts, and federal enforcement officers have been held to high standards of procedural conduct.

Although these constitutional guarantees have effectively armored the individual against possible persecution by the federal government, a similar degree of protection for the accused has not yet been fully applied against the states. In the American federal system, the police power—that most dangerous of all government weapons—has been reserved to the states. And it is in the state exercise of this power that observers have noted the most significant current infringements of individual liberty.

These are the fundamentals of the American protective system; but, as the late Chief Justice Charles Evans Hughes so pungently put it, "The Constitution is the Supreme Law of the Land, but the Constitution is what the judges say it is." If we are to understand the rights of the individual in our society, we must examine in some detail the processes of the judiciary and of law enforcement, with their all-too-frequent local encroachments on protected rights as well as their abridgment through social pressure and economic sanction. Since human freedom is indivisible, all are equally important in the task of "securing these rights" in a government in action.

THE BLACK SILENCE OF FEAR
William O. Douglas

William O. Douglas, Associate Justice of the United States Supreme Court, has consistently supported the cause of individual freedom from his place on the bench. An avid hiker and explorer, he is the author of *Strange Lands, Friendly People, Of Men and Mountains,* and many other books.

There is an ominous trend in this nation. We are developing tolerance only for the orthodox point of view on world affairs, intolerance for new or different approaches. Orthodoxy normally has stood in the path of change. Orthodoxy was always the stronghold of the status quo, the enemy of new ideas—at least new ideas that were disturbing. He who was wedded to the orthodox view was isolated from the challenge of new facts.

The democratic way of life rejects standardized thought. It rejects orthodoxy. It wants the fullest and freest discussion, within peaceful limits, of all public issues. It encourages constant search for truth at the periphery of knowledge.

We as a people have probably never lived up to that standard in any of our communities. But it has been an ideal toward which most of our communities have strived. We have over the years swung from tolerance to intolerance and back again. There have been areas of intolerance when the views of minorities have been suppressed. But there probably has not been a period of greater intolerance than we witness today.

To understand this, I think one has to leave the country, go into the back regions of the world, lose himself there, and become absorbed in the problems of the peoples of different civilizations. When he returns to America after a few months he probably will be shocked. He will be shocked not at the intentions or purposes or ideals of the American people. He will be shocked at the arrogance and intolerance of great segments of the American press, at the arrogance and intolerance of many leaders in public office, at the arrogance and intolerance reflected in many of our attitudes toward Asia. He will find that thought is being standardized, that the permissible area for calm discussion is being narrowed, that the range of ideas is being limited, that many minds are closed to the receipt of any ideas from Asia.

This is alarming to one who loves his country. It means that the philosophy of strength through free speech is being forsaken for the philosophy of fear through repression.

That choice in Russia is conscious. Under Lenin the ministers and officials were encouraged to debate, to advance new ideas and criticisms. Once the debate was over, however, no dissension or disagreement was permitted. But even that small degree of tolerance for free discussion that Lenin permitted disappeared under Stalin. Stalin maintains a tight system of control, permitting no free speech, no real clash in ideas, even in the inner circle. We are, of course, not emulating either Lenin or Stalin. But we are drifting in the direction of repression, drifting dangerously fast.

What is the cause of this drift? What are the forces behind it? It is only a drift, for certainly everything in our tradition would make the great majority of us reject that course as a conscious choice.

The drift goes back, I think, to the fact that we carried over to days of peace the military approach to world affairs. Diplomacy, certainly in our relations with Asia, took a back seat. The military approach conditioned our thinking and our planning. The military, in fact, determined our approach to the Asians and their problems. That has been a great tragedy in Asia. And the tragedy to us at home has been about as great.

Military thinking continued to play a dominant role in our domestic affairs. The conspiratorial role of Soviet communism in the world scene was apparent to all who could read. This conspiratorial role of Soviet communism was, of course, backed by Russia's military strength. We, therefore, had to be strong in a military sense to hold off Russia. But we soon accepted the military role as the dominant one. We thought of Asia in terms of military bases, not in terms of peoples and their aspirations. We wanted the starving people of Asia to choose sides, to make up their minds whether they were for us or against us, to cast their lot with us and against Russia.

We did not realize that to millions of these people the difference between Soviet dictatorship and the dictatorship under which they presently live is not very great. We did not realize that in some regions of Asia it is the Communist party that has identified itself with the so-called reform program, the other parties being mere instruments for keeping a ruling class in power. We did not realize that the choice between democracy and communism is not, in the eyes of millions of illiterates, the critical choice it is for us.

We forgot that democracy in many lands is an empty word: that the appeal is hollow when made to illiterate people living at the subsistence level. We asked them to furnish staging grounds for a military operation whose outcome, in their eyes, had no perceptible relation to their own welfare. Those who rejected our overtures must be Communists, we said. Those who did not fall in with our military plans must be secretly aligning with Russia, we thought. This was the result of our military thinking, of our absorption in military affairs. In Asia it has brought us the lowest prestige in our existence.

The military effort has been involving more and more of our sons, more and more of our budget, more and more of our thinking. The military policy has so completely absorbed our thoughts that we have mostly forgotten that our greatest strength, our enduring power is not in guns, but in ideas. Today in Asia we are identified not with ideas of freedom, but with guns. Today at home we are thinking less and less in terms of defeating communism with ideas, more and more in terms of defeating communism with military might. The concentration on military means has helped to breed fear. It has bred fear and insecurity partly because of the horror of atomic war. But the real reason strikes deeper. In spite of our enormous expenditures, we see that Soviet imperialism continues to expand and that the expansion proceeds without the Soviets firing a shot. The free world continues to contract without a battle for its survival having been fought. It becomes apparent, as country after country falls to Soviet imperialistic ambitions, that military policy alone is a weak one; that military policy alone will end in political bankruptcy and futility. Thus fear mounts.

Fear has many manifestations. The Communist threat inside the country has been magnified and exalted far beyond its realities. Irresponsible talk by irresponsible people has fanned the flames of fear. Accusations have been loosely made. Character assassinations have become common. Suspicion has taken the place of good-will. Once we could debate with impunity along a wide range of inquiry. Once we could safely explore to the edges of a problem, challenge orthodoxy without qualms, and run the gamut of ideas in search of solutions to perplexing problems. Once we had confidence in each other. Now there is suspicion. Innocent acts become tell-tale marks of disloyalty. The coincidence that an idea parallels Soviet Russia's policy for a moment of time settles an aura of suspicion around a person.

Suspicion grows until only the orthodox idea is the safe one. Suspicion grows until only the person who loudly proclaims that orthodox view, or who, once having been a Communist, has been converted, is trustworthy. Competition for embracing the new orthodoxy increases. Those who are unorthodox are suspect. Everyone who does not follow the military policy-makers is suspect. Everyone who voices opposition to the trend away from diplomacy and away from political tactics takes a chance. Some who are opposed are indeed "subversive." Therefore, the thundering edict commands that all who are opposed are "subversive." Fear is fanned to a fury. Good and honest men are pilloried. Character is assassinated. Fear runs rampant.

Fear even strikes at lawyers and the bar. Those accused of illegal Communist activity—all presumed innocent, of course, until found guilty—have difficulty getting reputable lawyers to defend them. Lawyers have talked with me about it. Many are worried. Some could not volunteer their services, for if they did they would lose clients and their firms would suffer. Others could not volunteer because if they did they would be dubbed "subversive" by their community and put in the same category as those they would defend. This is a dark tragedy.

Fear has driven more and more men and women in all walks of life either to silence or to the folds of the orthodox. Fear has mounted—fear of losing one's job, fear of being investigated, fear of being pilloried. This fear has stereotyped our thinking, narrowed the range of free public discussion, and driven many thoughtful people to despair. This fear has even entered universities, great citadels of our spiritual strength, and corrupted them. We have the spectacle of university officials lending themselves to one of the worst witch hunts we have seen since early days.

This fear has affected the youngsters. Youth has played a very important role in our national affairs. It has usually been the oncoming generation—full of enthusiasm, full of idealism, full of energy—that has challenged its elders and the status quo. It is from this young group that the country has received much of its moral power. They have always been prone to question the stewardship of their fathers, to doubt the wisdom of traditional practices, to explode cliches, to quarrel with the management of public affairs.

Youth—like the opposition party in a parliamentary system—has served a powerful role. It has cast doubts on our policies, challenged our inarticulate major premises, put the light on our prejudices, and exposed our inconsistencies. Youth has made each generation indulge in self-examination.

But a great change has taken place. Youth is still rebellious; but it is largely holding its tongue. There is the fear of being labeled a "subversive" if one departs from the orthodox party line. That charge—if leveled against a young man or young woman—may have profound effects. It may ruin a youngster's business or professional career. No one wants a Communist in his organization nor anyone who is suspect.

And so the lips of the younger generation have become more and more sealed. Repression of ideas has taken the place of debate. There may not be a swelling crowd of converts to the orthodox, military view. But the voice of the opposition is more and more stilled; and youth, the mainstay in early days of the revolt against orthodoxy, is largely immobilized.

This pattern of orthodoxy that is shaping our thinking has dangerous implications. No one man, no one group can have the answer to the many perplexing problems that today confront the management of world affairs. The scene is a troubled and complicated one. The problems require the pooling of many ideas, the exposure of different points of view, the hammering out in public discussions of the pros and cons of this policy or of that.

There are few who know first hand the conditions in the villages of Asia, the South Pacific, South America, and Africa. There are few who really know the powerful forces operating from the grass roots in those areas—forces that are reflected in the attitudes of the men who head up the Governments in those countries. But unless we know those attitudes, we cannot manage intelligently. Unless we know, we will waste our energies and our resources. Unless we know, we are not in position to win even political alliances of an enduring nature. Unless we are eager to know, unless we invite a flood of information on these problems, unless we encourage every avenue of approach to them, we will live and act in ignorance. There are those who think that our present policy toward Asia will lead to disaster—for us. There are those who believe that in Asia we are fast becoming the symbol of what the people of Asia fear and hate. There are those who believe that the most effective bases we can get in Asia are bases in the hearts of

Asia's millions, not bases on their lands. There are those who believe that we must substitute a political for a military strategy in Asia; that when there is a cease-fire in Korea, we must make a political settlement with Red China; that if we apply to China the attitude we are now brilliantly exploiting in Yugoslavia, we can manage to make Soviet imperialism crumble.

There are those who are deeply opposed, many of whom put the issue beyond the pale of discussion. There are even some who make the crucial test of one's loyalty or sanity his acceptance or rejection of our present policy toward Asia.

The question of our Asian policy illustrates the need for a wide range of free public discussion. Asia poses probably the most critical issues of the day. Certain it is that if Asia, like China, is swept into the political orbit of Soviet Russia, the Soviets will then command or be able to mobilize (a) the bulk of the people of the world, (b) the bulk of the wealth of the world. If that happens, it is doubtful if we, with all our atomic bombs, could even win a war.

The great danger of this period is not inflation, nor the national debt, nor atomic warfare. The great, the critical danger is that we will so limit or narrow the range of permissible discussion and permissible thought that we will become victims of the orthodox school. If we do, we will lose flexibility. We will lose the capacity for expert management. We will then become wedded to a few techniques, to a few devices. They will define our policy and at the same time limit our ability to alter or modify it. Once we narrow the range of thought and discussion, we will surrender a great deal of our power. We will become like the man on the toboggan who can ride it but who can neither steer it nor stop it.

The mind of man must always be free. The strong society is one that sanctions and encourages freedom of thought and expression. When there is that freedom, a nation has resiliency and adaptability. When freedom of expression is supreme, a nation will keep its balance and stability.

Our real power is our spiritual strength, and that spiritual strength stems from our civil liberties. If we are true to our traditions, if we are tolerant of a whole market place of ideas, we will always be strong. Our weakness grows when we become intolerant of opposing ideas, depart from our standards of civil liberties, and borrow the policeman's philosophy from the enemy we detest.

This has been the direction of our drift. It is dangerous to the morale of our people; it is destructive to the influence and prestige of our country that is losing its human resiliency, and much of our inventive genius. The demands of orthodoxy already have begun to sap our strength—and to deprive us of power. One sees it from far-off Asia. From Asia one sees an America that is losing its humanity, its idealism, and its Christian character. From Asia one sees an America that is strong and rich and powerful, and yet crippled and ineffective because of its limited vision.

When we view this problem full face we are following the American tradition. The times demand a renaissance in freedom of thought and freedom of expression, a renaissance that will end the orthodoxy that threatens to devitalize us.

THE FIFTH AMENDMENT
Erwin N. Griswold

Erwin N. Griswold is Dean of the Harvard Law School. An educator who has held many public posts, he is the author of *Spend-Thrift Trusts, Cases on Federal Taxation,* and other books.

Old friends are good friends. Yet even with the best of friends problems sometimes arise. I have the feeling that this is in a sense the situation we find ourselves in with respect to the Fifth Amendment. It has been with us a long time. It is rather comforting to have around. Yet in the past few years it has come to our consciousness as it rarely has before, and it has been troublesome to many members of the public. It has seemed to me worth while, therefore, to undertake a review of the Fifth Amendment with the thought that ordinarily the better we understand something in human experience, the less fearsome it becomes.

Before going further it may be well to introduce our old friend itself. The Fifth Amendment contains a number of provisions which are commonplace. It is the source of our constitutional rule that serious criminal charges must be made by indictment of a grand jury. It provides against double jeopardy, against the taking of property without due process of law and against the taking of private property for public use without just compensation.

Along with these other provisions is the phrase which has currently come to the fore: "No person . . . shall be compelled in any criminal case to be a witness against himself." In this connection, it is well to mention the fact that the Massachusetts Constitution has a corresponding provision, which antedates that in the Federal Constitution. Article XII of the Bill of Rights in the Massachusetts Constitution, adopted in 1780, provides that "No subject shall . . . be compelled to accuse, or furnish evidence against himself." We are not dealing with either an alien or a novel doctrine. . . .

DESIGNED TO PROTECT THE INNOCENT

I am going to offer my own attempt to express the reason for the Fifth

From *The Christian Science Monitor,* February 15, 1954; also in the book *The Fifth Amendment Today* (Cambridge, Mass.: Harvard University Press, 1955), by Erwin N. Griswold. Reprinted by permission of the author.

Amendment, and why I think it is a sound provision of our basic laws, both federal and state.

I would like to venture the suggestion that the privilege against self-incrimination is one of the great landmarks in man's struggle to make himself civilized. As I have already pointed out, the establishment of the privilege is closely linked historically with the abolition of torture. Now we look upon torture with abhorrence. But torture was once used by honest and conscientious public servants as a means of obtaining information about crimes which could not otherwise be disclosed. We want none of that today, I am sure. For a very similar reason, we do not make even the most hardened criminal sign his own death warrant, or dig his own grave, or pull the lever that springs the trap on which he stands. We have through the course of history developed a considerable feeling of the dignity and intrinsic importance of the individual man. Even the evil man is a human being.

If a man has done wrong, he should be punished. But the evidence against him should be produced and evaluated by a proper court in a fair trial. Neither torture nor an oath nor the threat of punishment such as imprisonment for contempt should be used to compel him to provide the evidence to accuse or to convict himself. If his crime is a serious one careful and often laborious police work may be required to prove it by other evidence. Sometimes no other evidence can be found. But for about three centuries in the Anglo-American legal system, we have accepted the standard that even then we do not compel the accused to provide that evidence. I believe that is a good standard and that it is an expression of one of the fundamental decencies in the relation we have developed between government and man.

As said by that old tartar, Mr. Justice Stephen J. Field, who was reared in western Massachusetts, "The essential and inherent cruelty of compelling a man to expose his own guilt is obvious to everyone, and needs no illustration." And in words which he approved, it is the "result of the long struggle between the opposing forces of the spirit of individual liberty on the one hand and the collective power of the state on the other." *Brown* v. *Walker,* 161 U.S. 591, 637 (1896).

Where matters of a man's belief or opinions or political views are essential elements in the charge, it may be most difficult to get evidence from sources other than the suspected or accused person himself. Hence, the significance of the privilege over the years has perhaps been greatest in connection with resistance to prosecution for such offenses as heresy or political crimes. In these areas the privilege against self-incrimination has been a protection for freedom of thought, and a hindrance to any government which might wish to prosecute for thoughts and opinions alone.

But the privilege is broader than that. It is applicable to any sort of crime, even the most sordid. Don't we go too far in giving this protection to criminals? Isn't the claim of the privilege the clearest sort of proof that the person who claims it is guilty of a crime? This has been asserted by high authority, but I do not believe it is true.

Apart from its expression of our view of civilized governmental conduct, another purpose of the Fifth Amendment is to protect the innocent. But how can a man claim the privilege if he is innocent? How can a man fear he will incriminate himself if he knows he has committed no crime? Judge Magruder of our own First Circuit Court of Appeals has recently given some illustrations of this in his illuminating opinion in the Maffia case, decided last month.

There is, for example, the case of the man who has killed another in self-defense, or by accident, without design or fault. He has committed no crime, yet his answer to the question whether he killed the man may well incriminate him. At the very least it will in effect shift the burden of proof to him so that he will have to prove his own innocence. Indeed, the privilege against self-incrimination may well be thought of as a companion of our established rule that a man is innocent until he has been proved guilty.

In this connection let me quote from a Supreme Court decision written long before our present troubles. In *Burdick* v. *United States,* 236 U.S. 79 (1915), Mr. Justice McKenna wrote, "If it be objected that (Burdick's) refusal to answer was an implication of crime, we answer, not necessarily in fact, not at all in theory of law."

TWO HYPOTHETICAL CASES

Now let us turn to an area which is closer to that which has recently been of concern. I am going to ask you to assume two sets of facts. You may think that both of the sets of facts are unlikely, and that they do not correspond with any case you have ever heard of. All I ask is that you assume the facts. I am simply putting a hypothetical case; and the facts are not the facts of any specific case.

Here is Case 1. A man is a college teacher. He is an idealist and perhaps slow to recognize realities as idealists sometimes are. He has a great urge for what he regards as social reform. He is native born, went to American schools, and loves his country despite what he regards as its imperfections. You may not agree with his ideas but you would respect his honesty and sincerity. He believes himself thoroughly attached to the country and the Constitution, and he abhors anything involving force and violence. He is a good teacher and works hard on his subjects. He has always believed that as a good citizen he should be interested in politics. Neither of the established political parties provided what he wanted.

In the relatively calm period of the past middle 1930's, on the solicitation of a friend, he went to a Communist meeting and soon joined the Communist Party. At that time the Communist Party was perfectly legal, and regularly appeared on our ballot. He thought he was simply joining a political party. One of the reasons that led him to join was because he regarded fascism as highly immoral and a great danger to the world, and he felt that the Communists were fighting fascism in Spain at this time. His interest was not merely in protecting Spain, but because he thought that fighting fascism there was an important means of guarding against such a danger here.

Now you may say that this is all very unlikely. To this I reply that I am, for the moment, only assuming a hypothetical case I want. So these are the facts I put before you. You may feel that such a man must have been very naive or lacking in intelligence. To that I would make two replies: First, to say that involves the use of a large amount of hindsight. A man's actions at any time should be evaluated on the basis of the facts then available to him, and the state of his own mind on the basis of what he actually knew, and not by facts we learn later that were not known to him. And my second reply would be that the man may have been naive or obtuse. I would say that he was at least misguided and unwise. But I would point out that being obtuse or naive is a very different thing from being a traitor or a spy.

Let me add a few more facts, assumed by me as before. Our teacher was in a Communist cell, with other teachers. The Communists had great plans for this group. They wanted to use it to infiltrate American education. However, the Communist command was canny. They knew that many or all of the members of this cell of teachers were politically innocent, and that they would recoil quickly from any proposals for sabotage or the use of force and violence. So they treated this group with great care. The group was never subjected to the rigors of Communist discipline. It was a study group, and its discussions were kept on a high intellectual plane. The more sordid features of the Marxist doctrine were kept thoroughly in the background. Our teacher never engaged in espionage or sabotage or anything like that, and never saw or heard of any such activities by any member of his group. He would have been horrified by any such actions.

WHAT HAPPENS TO INDIVIDUALS?

Nevertheless, there were things from time to time which he did not like. He rationalized them in various ways—nothing can be perfect; the thing to do is to stay inside and work against excesses; and so on. Besides he was a stubborn fellow. Once having started out on something he thought was good, he did not give it up lightly. But he became troubled; and after the war he slowly drifted away from the group. He never formally resigned. He just turned away. By the time of the Korean invasion in 1950, he was thoroughly disgusted and saw that he had been used as a dupe. But he was also convinced in his own heart of the rectitude of his actions, if not of their wisdom; and he did not doubt that many of the people who had been associated with him in the venture were just as innocent of wrong-doing as he was sure he was.

Remember I am doing the assuming. You may feel that these facts do not fit an actual case. But I am not trying to state an actual case. I am just assuming a hypothetical case, which is one of the ancient rights of any law teacher.

Now let me turn to Case 2. This man is also a college teacher. He never joined the Communist Party. He never thought of joining the Communist Party. He knew a good deal about the realities of communism, and he was thoroughly opposed to it. He was, however, a man who was interested in causes. His father had been a minister who had dedicated his life to helping people. He himself had a great urge to participate in activities which he felt would help to alleviate suffering or contribute to social progress. In fact he was a sucker for almost any kind of an appeal. He contributed modest amounts to China Relief. He had always had a warm feeling for the Chinese. Sometimes he found himself on some of the letterheads of some of these organizations as a sponsor. He was not sure that he remembered giving permission to use his name this way; but the cause, as indicated by the attractive name of the organization, was one that appealed to him, and he did not bother himself much about it.

After a while he heard some rumblings that there might be some Communist influence in these organizations, but he was slow to believe that that could be true. In some of the organizations, he had been on committees with thoroughly respectable fellow citizens. He did not want to pull out, because he felt that this would let his friends down. Eventually, he heard that some of these organizations had been ruled to be subversive by the attorney general. But, he too, was a stubborn fellow. He believed in the stated objectives of these organizations. He was also a freeborn American, proud of his country's great traditions, and he allowed his name to be used by some of these organizations, as had been said in a recent article, "as a gesture of opposition to the procedure of prescribing organizations without giving them the right to be heard."

Well, that is the end of my assuming. Let us see what happens to these two individuals. Remember that both of these individuals feel that they are innocent of any wrongdoing. Each one is pure in heart, and perhaps a little too certain of his own rectitude. Each one may now regret some of the things he did, but he does not think that they were wrong. Each one is certain that he is morally innocent of any crime.

We will consider Case 1 first. He is the man who was a member of the Communist Party. He is summoned to appear before a congressional committee, and is asked whether he is a Communist. He answers truthfully: "no." Then he is asked whether he ever was a Communist. He is now surely subjected to a substantial risk, even though he honestly believes that he has committed no crime. He knows that a number of Communists have been convicted under the Smith Act of 1940, and more have been indicted. Our teacher perhaps magnifies his own predicament. He sees the jail doors opening up if he gives himself the evidence that he was once a Communist.

Interestingly enough, Section 4 (f) of the Internal Security Act of 1950 (commonly known as the McCarran Act) provides specifically that "Neither the holding of office nor membership in any Communist organization by any person shall constitute per se a violation of . . . this section or of any other criminal statute." But this was enacted after his period of party membership. It has been declared to be a crime to be a Communist in Massachusetts since 1951, but there may be some possible room to question the effectiveness of this statute in view of the provision of the federal act. That the federal statutes may displace state action is indicated by a decision of the Supreme Court of Pennsylvania just last week.

EXAMINER CHANGES TACK

After much internal torment, the witness finally decides to claim the privilege of the Fifth Amendment with respect to the question of his past membership in the Communist Party. Putting aside the question of his wisdom in doing this, can there be any doubt that the claim is legally proper? Past membership in the Communist Party is not a crime in itself; but admitting such membership may well be a link in a chain of proof of a criminal charge against him. Persons have been prosecuted under the Smith Act for membership in the Communist Party plus something else; if he supplies the proof of his own membership in the party, he does not know what other evidence may then be brought against him to show that he has committed a crime. Thus, an answer to the question will definitely incriminate him, that is, provide evidence which could be used in a prosecution against him. Yet, remember that he thoroughly believes that he is not guilty of any crime; and on the facts I have given he is not guilty of a crime.

There are other factors that influence his conclusion. His own experience is an ordeal. He does not want his friends to be subjected to it. He believes in their innocence of any crime. If he thought that they had committed crimes, he would promptly tell the proper officers of the government. By claiming the privilege against self-incrimination, he can refrain from naming any of his associates. He feels a strong sense of loyalty to them. He feels a strong sense of loyalty to his country, too; but since he is convinced that neither he nor his associates have in fact done anything wrong, his desire to protect them from having to experience his own predicament seems to him to have prevailing weight in the actual circumstances.

He claims the privilege. He cannot be prosecuted on the basis of any evidence he has provided. There can be no doubt, I believe, that his claim of privilege is legally justified. Yet, note that on the facts I have assumed he is not guilty of any crime. Of course his claim of privilege as to his membership in the Communist Party means that he must also claim the privilege as to all other questions which relate in any way to what he did, or to his associates in the activity. For if he answers any of those questions, it will clearly connote his own Communist activity. . . .

Let us turn to Case 2, which we can dispose of briefly; you will remember that that was the man who had lent his name to causes, and had contributed money; and the causes have now turned out to be Communist fronts, although they were attractively named, and many good Americans were, at one time or another, associated with them. But he was never a member of the Communist Party.

This man likewise is summoned before a congressional investigating committee. The mere fact that he is summoned shows that he is suspected of something rather serious, and he is badly worried. He is asked whether he is now a member of the Communist Party; and he answers "No." Then he is asked whether he ever was in the past. The answer is in fact "no," as we have seen. But he is now in great fear. If he says "No," then he may be subjecting himself to a real risk of prosecution for perjury. He may rightly fear that proof of the fact of his joining and contributing to so many agencies which have turned out to be front organizations might lead a jury to believe that he actually was a Communist.

Now it is probably true that fear of a prosecution for perjury for an answer given to a question is not a proper basis for a claim of the privilege. If it was, almost any witness could claim the privilege as to any question. But our man is in a somewhat different situation. If he says "no," to the question of the Communist membership, then in his own interest he may have to undertake to state and explain his membership and activities in the various front organizations. The net result may be that he will have to give much evidence which could be used against him in an attempt to prove that he was a member of the Communist conspiracy. It would appear, therefore, that he can properly claim the privilege even though his answer to the question as to Communist Party membership at any time would honestly and rightly be "No."

In both of the cases I have put, the privilege may be claimed although the individual was guilty of no crime. In the second case it may be claimed although the person was never a member of the Communist Party. In each case, the inference which would be taken from the claim of the privilege would in fact be unwarranted. The claim of the privilege is surely a serious business, but it is equally surely not the equivalent of an admission of criminal conduct . . .

OTHER REASONS WEIGHED

A witness lost in fear and confusion might turn to the privilege as a means of sanctuary from a situation which he feels himself incompetent to handle. Consider also how much the chance of a witness losing his calm and collected demeanor is enhanced by such things as television, radio microphones, movie cameras, flashing flash bulbs, and procedures which may not seem to him to be based upon the finest spirit of fairness. In connection with this I might mention the recent decision of the United States Court of Appeals for the Sixth Circuit in *Aiuppa* v. *United States,* 201 F.2d 287, 300 (1952), where we find the following language in the opinion:

> But, in concluding, we think it may not be amiss to say that, notwithstanding the pronouncements of the committee chairman as to intended fairness, the courts of the United States could not emulate the committee's example and maintain even a semblance of fair and dispassionate conduct of trials in criminal cases.
>
> Despite the enjoyment by millions of spectators and auditors of the

> exhibition by television of the confusion and writhings of widely known malefactors and criminals, when sharply questioned as to their nefarious activities, we are unable to give judicial sanction, in the teeth of the Fifth Amendment, to the employment of a committee of the United States Senate of methods of examination of witnesses constituting a triple threat; answer truly and you have given evidence leading to your conviction for a violation of federal law; answer falsely and you will be convicted of perjury; refuse to answer and you will be found guilty of criminal contempt and punished by fine and imprisonment. In our humble judgment, to place a person not even on trial for a specified crime in such predicament is not only not a manifestation of fair play, but is in direct violation of the Fifth Amendment to our national Constitution.

Ordinarily when the privilege of the Fifth Amendment is exercised, it is in a criminal trial. There a specific charge has been made and the prosecution has by evidence established a prima facie case of guilt of the particular crime charged in the complaint or indictment. Under such circumstances there is much more than the mere claim of the privilege on which to rest an inference of guilt.

In investigations, however, there are no carefully formulated charges. Evidence to support such charges has not been introduced and made known to the witness before he is called upon to answer. He has no opportunity for cross-examination of other witnesses, and often little or no opportunity to make explanations which might have a material bearing on the whole situation. In the setting of an investigation, therefore, the basis for the inference from a claim of privilege against self-incrimination is much less than it is when the privilege is exercised in an ordinary criminal trial.

There are two more matters to which I should like to make brief reference. The first of these is the rather technical legal doctrine known as waiver of the privilege. A clear instance of waiver occurs when a defendant in a criminal case voluntarily takes the stand. He then becomes subject to cross-examination, and must answer relevant questions. So far as witnesses at investigations are concerned, our current learning on this is based largely on the Supreme Court's decision in *Rogers* v. *United States,* 340 U.S. 367 (1951)....

This doctrine of waiver is, I believe, the true explanation of the refusal of some witnesses to answer such questions as "Have you ever taught Communist doctrine in your classroom?" or "Have you ever solicited students to join the Communist Party?" These refusals have been deeply disturbing to the public. Yet, answers to these questions may be "No"; but the witness nevertheless fears that he cannot give that answer without its being said that he has waived the privilege as to questions about the other sorts of Communist activity. Here again we have a situation where the obvious inference from the refusal to answer the question may be completely unwarranted.

Finally, I would like to make reference to one more problem which is collateral to that of the Fifth Amendment. Suppose a witness is summoned before an investigating committee. He does not claim a privilege against self-incrimination, and talks freely about himself, answering all questions about his own activity. He takes the position, however, that he will not answer questions about others. Or suppose a person first refuses to answer virtually all questions, claiming the Fifth Amendment privilege, but he later decides to waive the privilege as to himself. However, he refuses as a matter which he regards as one of principle to identify other people. What should be the situation with respect to such a person?

There have been a number of people who have been summoned before investigating committees and taken this position from the outset. They have answered all questions about themselves, and have refused to identify others. As far as I know, no academic person who has done this has been cited for contempt; nor has any such person lost his job. Should it be any different where the witness has first relied on the Fifth Amendment, but has later changed his position, waiving the privilege as to himself, but still refusing to answer as to others?

The problem is undeniably a difficult one. So long as the witness was claiming the privilege, it could be argued that he had done no wrong. If he had committed any crime, the evidence should be brought forth in the proper way and tried out in court. His refusal to answer was not evidence of any crime. This argument, however, is not available where he waives the privilege by refusing to answer questions relating to other persons. Then his Fifth Amendment privilege is wholly gone, and his situation presents new and rather different problems.

Whether he has committed a crime by his refusal to testify may be extremely difficult to tell. Even if he is cited by the legislative body, it will still be for the grand jury to decide whether to indict; it will remain to the courts to decide such questions as whether the committee was properly constituted, and whether the question asked was relevant to the inquiry. We should not forget that a prosecution for contempt was set aside within the past year by the Supreme Court on the ground that the questions asked the witness—as to the identity of his contributors—were not relevant to the particular inquiry. *United States* v. *Rumeley,* 345 U.S. 41 (1953).

However such questions go, though, would it not seem that such a person is at least in no worse a position morally than he was when he stood on the Fifth Amendment? He should not be worse off for being willing to speak fully and frankly about himself than he was when he would not talk at all. His refusal to tell on his friends may be both contrary to valid law and unwise. Nevertheless, it may be based on strong grounds of conscience.

UNIVERSITIES DEFENDED

Let me do a little more assuming; let us assume that the witness feels positive in his own mind that the persons with whom he was associated did no wrong to their country. They did not engage in espionage or sabotage or anything like that. They were merely hopeful but misguided people, as he was. Let us assume, too, that this is all far in the past. The persons in question are in other work. They have families to support. If their names are disclosed, they will surely lose their jobs. He must then resolve for himself the question whether he will give their names and subject them to the same sort of ordeal he has been through in order to save himself from further difficulty and possible prosecution. He may be wrong if he decides that he would not protect himself by sacrificing them. I recognize the legal obligation to testify as to others, and the general importance of this both in trials and in investigations. But can it be said clearly that his action is always immoral?

Of course he may be wrong in his judgment of these other people. They may be worse than he thinks they are. But we all have to use judgment on such things. A man may honestly feel that he cannot bring suffering to others in order to save himself. To a considerable extent such questions can only be resolved in a man's own conscience. We are a society which has long depended on and applauded the virtues of the rugged individualist.

I do not justify the past or present conduct of anyone. I seek only to explain. Because of claims of privilege under the Fifth Amendment, and refusal to answer questions, many members of the general public have come to have fear of our educational institutions, and general mistrust of academic people. I firmly believe that these fears are unwarranted. I have tried tonight to show how some of the things that have happened could have happened without there being anything rotten in the universities. It may be a serious error of judgment for an academic person to claim the privilege of the Fifth Amendment, or to refuse to answer questions; but the conduct, regrettable as it is, does not show the existence of treason, espionage, sabotage, or any other serious crime.

The great misfortune from all this, I believe, is that charges are made against our universities and other educational institutions, and more or less believed by some segments of our people. I think that it is easy to overestimate the extent of that belief, but it cannot be denied that there is disagreement, uneasiness, and even fear in some quarters. As I have said, I think these fears are not soundly based.

This is my 20th year as a faculty member at Harvard University, and I am thoroughly convinced that the university has acquitted itself well, and that it has been of great value to the country during that time. It is an injustice not only to the faculty members but to the country to allow any conclusion to stand that they are not good Americans or that they do not serve their country well. I think that the Harvard Law School with which I am intimately connected, is a great asset to the country and to the commonwealth and, in essence, one of the great conservative influences in our land. If there are any who think otherwise, let them examine the facts, carefully and thoughtfully.

And so I come back where I started. The privilege against self-incrimination embodied in the Fifth Amendment and in the commonwealth's Bill of

Rights has been a long time with us. It is, I believe, a good friend as well as an old friend. It embodies a sound value which we should preserve. As we increase our understanding of it, and the part it has long played in protecting the individual against the collective power of the state, we will have better appreciation of some of the basic problems of our time.

THE CURBING OF THE MILITANT MAJORITY
John P. Roche

John P. Roche is Morris Hilquit Professor of Labor and Social Thought and Chairman of the Department of Politics at Brandeis University. He has written a number of studies of the history of civil liberty in the United States, including *The Quest for the Dream.* Long active in the American Civil Liberties Union, he has also served as national chairman of Americans for Democratic Action.

For some curious reason, historians and political scientists have largely by-passed the history of civil liberties in the United States before the First World War. The consequence of this neglect has been the prevalence of an amazing set of clichés about the character of contemporary American society and the historic position of civil liberty in the American political tradition.

Once upon a time, so the story runs, the United States was a land of militant, inner-directed non-conformists, men who were as sensitive to the rights of others as they were fierce in the defense of their own autonomy. Then slowly over this green and pleasant land crept the miasma of orthodoxy, an enervating spirit of conformity which left in its wake an atomized population of other-directed status seekers gibbering the slogans of the moment, terrified of the FBI, and finding ultimate consolation only in the narcosis of mass culture. A nation of Thoreaus has in some subtle fashion been transformed into an atomic mass of dying salesmen.

Underlying all this nonsense, of course, is the myth of bucolic virtue which Richard Hofstadter so sensitively limned in *The Age of Reform:* the notion, profoundly Jeffersonian, that the rural yeoman is the paradigmatic Democratic Citizen and that cities are a source of civic degeneracy, a malignant cancer on the body politic. With this agrarian nostalgia is combined a heavy dose of sociological paranoia: a self-anointed intellectual elite has simply lost patience with a mass society that persists in spending its new-found leisure bowling or watching TV rather than reading Kafka, a society where the masses refuse to genuflect to their Cultural Betters. So the critics talk morosely of "the eclipse of community" and "the lonely crowd," conveniently forgetting that a mere half century ago it was precisely the firmly integrated rural community and the accompanying "idiocy of rural life" that set off the mad rush to urban anonymity.

Few historians, political scientists, or sociologists seem to love cities; the medieval German aphorism *"Stadt Luft macht frei"*—city air nourishes freedom—has seldom been echoed by American students of the process of urbanization. Suffice it here to note my conviction that it has been a major factor in the growth of liberty in the United States by bringing about the collapse of that "natural community" which brings nostalgic tears to the eyes of sociological critics of contemporary American culture. Within the cities the breakdown of ethnic ghettos—"natural communities" *par excellence*—has paralleled the demise of a rurally based, authoritarian social structure.

There is a singular durability in the myth that at some undesignated time in the past there was in the United States a golden age of individual freedom. Vernon L. Parrington (*Main Currents in American Thought*) and his followers probably established this tradition so far as modern American historians are concerned, although it should be added that the filio-patristic nationalistic writers, for their own reasons, assigned extraordinary virtue to the founders of the Republic. Parrington was quite explicit: American liberty hit its apogee with the Declaration of Independence and has been on the decline ever since. Jefferson is the folk hero of this tradition, and the basic analytic proposition on which the whole Parringtonian superstructure rests is that the centralized state is the enemy of freedom. The Hamiltonians thus become the sappers under the fortress of liberty, and it follows (quite properly in logical terms) that the increase in the power of the state has automatically led to a decline in the rights of the individual. The better to preserve the pristine ideal, Parringtonians regularly overlook the inconvenient facts that Jefferson opposed both John Adams's Sedition Law and Hamilton's mercantilism on *states'-rights* grounds. Here, for example, is Jefferson's Second Inaugural Address on the subject of religious freedom:

"In matters of religion I have considered that its free exercise is placed by the Constitution independent of the powers of the General Government. I have therefore undertaken on no occasion to prescribe the religious exercises suited to it, but have left them, as the Constitution found them, under the direction and discipline of the church *or state* authorities acknowledged by the several religious societies." (Italics added.) A few paragraphs later, he made the same differentiation between state and national *vires* in connection with the handling of seditious libels.

How can we account for this curious refusal to confront historical reality on its own terms? A generation that ruthlessly suppressed Tory speech and Tory press (not merely "overt" Tory acts), confiscated Tory property with a zeal and efficiency a Bolshevik could admire, and populated the wilds of Canada with its opposition, has somehow been acclaimed as "conservative."

A generation that employed loyalty oaths and disclaimer affidavits in a fashion that would bring joy to the heart of a Joseph R. McCarthy has similarly been credited with establishing civil liberties in the United States. The forty-second and latest *Annual Report* of the American Civil Liberties Union, for example, gives a stirring quotation from Jefferson and bemoans "our twentieth century resurrection of official orthodoxy," with the clear implication that "official orthodoxy" was a foreign product that Jefferson and his fellow libertarians barred from these shores.

STILL FIGHTING THE KING

If there was one thing on which John Adams and Thomas Jefferson always agreed, it was with respect to what has been called the doctrine of "American exceptionalism," the view that the truths of the Old world were not necessarily applicable to the realities of the New. It seems to me that, oddly enough, the source of historical confusion about civil rights has largely arisen from a refusal to recognize the validity of this insight. To put the point precisely, a set of analytic categories devised in Europe to cope with European development has been unthinkingly applied to the American scene. Thus because the political leaders of the American Revolution were not "Jacobins," they must have been "conservatives." Similarly the often terrifying realities of a savage, brawling frontier society and the brutal confrontations in the great Civil War and the lesser civil wars (between labor and management, white and Negro, Mormon and "gentile," Irish and nativist) have been converted into exercises in consensual group therapy because they refuse to fit the standards of European social theory.

What this means in concrete terms is that the European liberal doctrine that the centralized state is the natural enemy of freedom was simply transplanted to the American scene—where, I submit, it was essentially irrelevant. The centralized state, that "Mortal God" which in Europe emerged triumphant over the centrifugal tendencies of feudalism and the religious wars and in the process destroyed the "liberties" of the subject, of the town, and of the province or shire alike, never developed on this side of the water. To the European liberals, Thomas Hobbes was the enemy incarnate, and bravely they fought to put chains on Leviathan, to curb the power of a centralized bureaucracy, to mobilize the power of the community against the artificial "engines of tyranny" created at Paris or Westminster. But the "engines of oppression" were not successfully exported to the American colonies; British efforts to establish centralized colonial administration foundered—as young John Adams pointed out to a Boston discussion group almost two centuries ago—on the stubborn realities of local sovereignty. (And, it should be added, on British inefficiency.)

The American Revolution was—as Adams also pointed out—fought to retain *de facto* local sovereignty against British efforts to establish Leviathan on an international basis. It was fought to maintain the civil liberties of

Americans, i.e., the right of Americans to define their rights for themselves. No one ever suggested that a Tory could assert his rights against his patriot neighbors, and there was certainly no operating concept of "vested individual rights" against the community. John Locke was interpreted, as indeed he had been in his own day, as the theoretician of majority rule, as the tribune of the community, in its resistance to arbitrary, capricious, and above all unrepresentative governmental institutions. There was no appeal to "natural law" against the responsible decision of the society: for Locke and the Americans who set to work building their own governments, it was simply taken for granted that civil law defined natural law in any truly representative system. Bills of rights were thus designed to protect the citizen from the possible usurpations of the government, not from the decisions of his neighbors.

The Federal Bill of Rights, from this viewpoint, was not designed to preserve the liberty of the individual but to guarantee that *local* definitions of liberty would prevail. If one reads carefully the Amendments dealing with criminal procedure (IV through VII), he will appreciate the institutional sagacity of their sponsors: literally enforced, they would make impossible the development in the United States of a Tudor judiciary, that marvelous mechanism of centralization where the royal judge became in effect a local viceroy. (Those who noted the failure of the Federal government to indict former Major General Edwin Walker for incitement to riot against national authority in the wake of the Mississippi crisis last year will admire the effectiveness of the authors of the Fifth Amendment: a Mississippi grand jury refused to turn in a true bill and the United States government was helpless).

The community, then, is charged with protecting civil liberties from any perversion by the state. But, returning to the concept of American exceptionalism, has this curbing of the Federal government ever really been the problem in the United States? It is my contention that since the seventeenth century the basic civil-liberties problem has been not the arbitrary exercise of centralized power but the despotism of the militant majority. Thus while the growth of bureaucracy, particularly of the national government, and the expansion of national law proves to the Parringtonians that liberty is in decline, I look upon the same set of historical developments and find a growing tradition of impersonal bureaucratized justice and a withering away of decentralized authoritarianism. Moreover, I am prepared to argue that something "impossible" has happened, impossible that is in terms of the premises of European liberalism: the national government has become an instrument for protecting individual freedom.

AN INVISIBLE TERROR

Since this involves some drastic shifts in definition, let me set forth in more detail what I mean by the despotism of the militant majority. Until roughly the First World War, excluding the Sedition Act of 1798, it is impossible to find any national laws penalizing dissenting *opinion.* And until the great epidemic of criminal anarchy laws touched off by the assassination of President McKinley, the states had little legislation on the subject. It would, however, be a drastic error to draw from this absence of legislation the conclusion that freedom of opinion was universally respected. Or, if one wishes to quibble with this generalization, we can concede that freedom of opinion was everywhere respected—with the right to define *opinion* reserved to local juries. There was nothing "individualistic" about the common law, and in most states the old common-law remedies for non-conformity were adequate to the needs of the time. Thus a citizen who advocated birth control would find himself in court charged with "lewd behavior" and "breach of the peace" and, unless he could convince stalwart jurymen of the virtue of his cause, would wind up in the workhouse for six months. His opinions were not at issue; it was his "lewd behavior" that got him into trouble—and no one, anywhere, has a constitutional right to behave lewdly. If his opinions were the source of his behavior, that was his problem; his objective actions alone were involved in the trial. He might think whatever he wanted, but he might not behave lewdly.

Let us take another area—freedom of conscience, which most bills of rights guaranteed absolutely. Here we have a classic example of the legal assault on the Church of Jesus Christ, Latter Day Saints, by which the Mormons were savagely persecuted in Missouri and Illinois and eventually besieged and beaten in their Utah fortress. The Mormons, claiming divine inspiration, incorporated as part of their creed the doctrine of "celestial marriage," i.e., polygamy. Their neighbors, suffering perhaps from prurient envy, denounced them as bigamists and the majesty of the law was invoked. To their claim of freedom of religion, the judges and juries uniformly replied that bigamy was a crime, not an exercise of freedom of conscience. Freedom of religion stopped at the outer limits of the criminal code. (In Utah and Idaho, however, the jury system failed in its obligations: Mormon jurors acquitted Mormons. The consequence was that Congress, which had refused to act in defense of Southern Negroes who had been returned to virtual slavery by a militant majority, their white neighbors, passed a bill barring "bigamists," "polygamists," and "any person cohabiting with more than one woman" from voting or serving on juries and thus got the local majority back in sound hands!) A Mormon in jail for bigamy could hardly claim that his religious freedom had been violated; by definition (of twelve good men, well-chosen and true), religious freedom had been held not to include the right to be a bigamist.

To abbreviate a long story, I have been searching for some years for an early (say pre-1900) case in which a state court overruled a decision of a lower court on civil-rights grounds, that is, invoked a provision of a state bill of rights as a bar to prosecution. There are cases that conform to the Parringtonian ideal—where state courts have thrown out *statutes* as violative of a state bill of rights—but I have yet to find an instance in which an appellate state tribunal threw out the decision of a local jury on libertarian grounds. There must be some cases in this category somewhere, but they are fairly well concealed. Perhaps elected judges took a dim view of reversing and remanding the decisions of their constituents.

One of the marvels of the common law in this contest was (and is) its invisibility. No centralized state apparatus had been mobilized; the sheriff or chief of police handled the burden of prosecution; no statute was normally invoked; and the defendant was never put away for sedition but simply for "unlawful assembly" or "breach of the peace"—legal rubrics that are still, as recent Freedom Rider and sit-in litigation demonstrates, extremely difficult to handle at the appellate level. For technical reasons that need not concern us here, appellate courts have always been limited in their ability to go "behind" the record—to investigate *de novo* the facts in a case—so that to this day it is extraordinary to find an instance where sufficient legal sophistication is employed at the trial level to make possible an appellate reversal of a conviction for "breach of the peace." (The NAACP has been infuriating Southern prosecutors by providing precisely this expertise, carefully introducing into the trial record material that opens up the possibility of broad appeal.)

Although one can condemn the consequences of this system as "undemocratic," the system itself seems to have reflected the "will of the people." This pluralism of decentralized authoritarianism made it possible, of course, for a wide range of views to exist, each in its own haven of orthodoxy. "Law and order" in this milieu clearly meant what the local majority defined as such. A sheriff elected on a clean-up program in Nevada gave this position its finest expression: anyone who rejected the principles of "law and order," he proclaimed, would be "summarily hanged."

Now all of this—like the local campaign of extermination in the ante-bellum South against the Abolitionists—took place below the threshold of classic liberal sensitivity. Civil rights in the United States were secure, an Albert Jay Nock or William Graham Sumner would argue, adducing the absence of centralized, bureaucratized despotism. Also below their threshold were the exercises of sovereign power by economic feudalities, the great private governments of the last quarter of the nineteenth century and the first three decades of the twentieth. While the New York Central Railroad or the United States Steel Corporation, *inter alia,* fulfilled every definition of sovereignty except issuing postage stamps, the restrictions they imposed on their subjects were not violations of individual liberty. On the contrary, from this vantage point they were merely contractual obligations freely accepted as a precondition for making a living. A man might receive the economic equivalent of the death sentence—dismissal and blacklisting—for joining a union, and a union organizer might be forbidden even to discuss the merits of organization with workers who had signed "yellow dog" contracts (a limitation on freedom of speech which the Supreme Court accepted on the grounds that such a speech constituted incitement to breach of contract!), but none of the classic civil-rights issues were involved.

Indeed, civil-rights issues did not arise in this area unless the state attempted to intervene on behalf of the workers—by, say, banning the yellow dog contract, or requiring payment in coin of the realm rather than scrip, or limiting the work-week. The minute the state was sighted on the horizon, classical civil libertarians marshaled their forces for Armageddon.

MOB RULE AND THE LAW

To summarize an elaborate argument, if we examine the "state of civil liberties" in 1900 from the classical liberal viewpoint, we find that the United States was clearly the freest nation in the world (the otherwise sound British had a bad habit of passing Factory Acts and other invasions of Freedom of Contract). There was no centralized bureaucracy, no national police, no income tax, no national control of state and local government—the nation was a libertarian paradise. Yet, if one analyzed the same data from another angle, he might contend that the United States was a nation where the workers were at the mercy of their employers, Negroes were living in serfdom, religious and ethnic minorities were subjected to blatant discrimination, and the "rights of the individual" were those specified by a militant majority of his neighbors.

Patently it is a question of what "model" one employs. In the United States there existed both a weak and decentralized governmental apparatus *and* a fundamental absence of individual freedom for those to whom it was important: those who differed on basic issues with the rural, white, predominantly Anglo-Saxon Protestant majority. The majority was free—it held views approved by the majority, or by those local majorities which characterized a country still strongly regional in emphasis. Community authoritarianism also permeated those subcultures that were under attack by the great society: Brooklyn Jews who sponsored a Yom Kippur ball to demonstrate their liberation from the "superstitions" of the Orthodox were mobbed by their neighbors in the ghetto, and a hard-rock miner in Colorado who refused to respond to the bugle of the Western Federation of Miners could expect little sympathy on his painful ride out of town.

One final example may illuminate the shadowy place in my argument. On April 26, 1913, a tragic sequence of events began in Atlanta, Georgia, when Mary Phagan was found raped and murdered in the basement of Moses Frank's pencil factory, managed by his nephew Leo. Leo Frank was accused of the crime, indicted, tried, and convicted of murder. The evidence was flimsy and wholly circumstantial; the prosecution's key witness, Jim Conley, was certainly himself the murderer. But in no real sense was Frank on trial: the Jews were in the cage. "Our little girl—*ours* by the eternal God!" bellowed Tom Watson, the agrarian demagogue who was to be elected to the Senate in 1920 on a program that mixed equal parts of anti-war Populism, anti-Semitism, and anti-Catholicism, "has been pursued to a hideous death and bloody grave by *this filthy perverted Jew of New York.*"

Frank's lawyer was told bluntly, "If they don't hang that Jew, we'll hang you." In this atmosphere Frank was sentenced to hang (Watson editorially licked his chops at the prospect of vengeance on this "lascivious Jew"); eventually after successive appeals the United States Supreme Court rejected Frank's contention that the state of Georgia had denied him due process of law. Oliver Wendell Holmes, Jr., joined by Charles Evans Hughes, dissented brutally from the seven-justice majority which implicitly ruled (technically they declined jurisdiction) that Frank had been granted his full legal remedies under the Constitution. "Mob rule," said Holmes, expounding a position taken for granted by today's court, "does not become due process of law by securing the assent of a terrorized jury . . . it is our duty [to declare] lynch law as little valid when practiced by a regularly drawn jury as when administered. . . . by a mob intent on death."

It appears that by this time the Georgia judges were well aware of Frank's innocence. Conley had confessed to his lawyer, who, bound by the lawyer-client relationship, could not reveal the information. Finally, incapable of standing silent while Frank was railroaded to the gallows, the counsel confided the matter to Judge Arthur Powell, who was his intimate friend. The latter apparently passed the information on to Governor John Slaton, though still under the seal of secrecy. But with Watson on the war path, no one wished to assume responsibility for letting "the Jew" go free, or even for ordering a new trial. Finally with Frank about to hang, Governor Slaton risked his own neck and commuted the sentence to life imprisonment. Frank, secretly removed from Atlanta to Milledgeville Prison Farm, was immediately knifed by a fellow convict and was soon seized by a mob and lynched. "We regard the hanging of Leo Frank as an act of law-abiding citizens," observed the Marietta *Journal,* and Tom Watson chortled, "Jew libertines take notice!"

Back at the statehouse in Atlanta, only the intervention of armed troops prevented a frenzied mob from hanging Governor Slaton and dynamiting his home. When Slaton left office, and Georgia, three days after commuting Frank's sentence, his once promising political career was over. And when Tom Watson died in 1922, Eugene V. Debs sent his widow a letter praising this "heroic soul who fought the power of evil his whole life long." More appropriately the Ku Klux Klan sent a huge floral cross.

THE SOURCES OF FREEDOM

This was the militant majority in action, and one can find other episodes that equally demonstrate the unfettered passion of mob rule operating under the procedural formulas of "due process of law"—the extirpation of opposition during the First World War presents the interested student with an endless accumulation of relevant data. But the classical liberal would theoretically remain unmoved: the centralized state, that evil abstraction, played a minor role or none. (A. Mitchell Palmer's brutal raids in the immediate postwar period were the first nationally directed sedition hunt on a large scale since 1798, but Harding's victory put an end to any national concern with ideas—"good" or "bad.") The absence of a star chamber has been taken as proof of the existence of freedom of opinion, the lack of an FBI or a "security program" as evidence of unfettered individual freedom.

Actually, in the transformation of American life from the condign direct democracy of the "old order" to the regularized tradition of due process of law, enforced by national courts, a major share of the credit for converting civil liberties from privileges a community granted to its members to rights which can be defended against a militant local majority must be accorded to the intervention of the centralized state. The passage of the Wagner Act, for example, was one of the greatest acts of liberation in American history; decisions of the Supreme Court in school segregation, reapportionment, search and seizure, right to counsel, and other cases have played a notable part in the expansion of individual freedom; and one should not overlook in this context the work of the national Executive, such as President Truman's desegregation orders for the Federal administration and the armed forces and President Kennedy's housing order. The same pattern of governmental action has been instituted in many states.

And yet this state action for *individual* freedom—not group freedom, not majority freedom—still arouses the wrath of classical liberals; and contemporary liberals, who hold no general brief against the state, often seem hypnotized by the litany. Last December, for instance, the Center for the Study of Democratic Institutions held a potlatch in New York where speaker after speaker, mostly from civil-liberties circles, echoed the mordant warning that American liberty was in unprecedented jeopardy. No sane man will deny that the *potential* threats to American freedom from possible state action are far greater in 1963 than they were in 1833 or 1913. The great apparatus of Federal power *could* be employed for evil ends as well as good ones, and the real possibility of resistance to centralized power has vanished. But what indications are there that our modern Leviathan is driven by totalitarian compulsions? One hundred and nine once jailed Communists, many now busy lecturing to liberal-arts colleges? Without suggesting that one can adopt a quantitative scale in matters of this sort, I would submit that any sober evaluation of the contribution of the national government to the improvement or the decline of civil liberty must conclude on the basis of the evidence to date with a decision in favor of Federal intervention.

Anyone who cherishes the ideals of individual freedom and justice can never relax his efforts to push forward the frontiers of liberty. But the historian of civil liberty in the United States (though himself a civil libertarian who realizes that history can grant no absolution) has the obligation to assert the relative proposition that the contemporary American, despite the existence of a huge centralized state, is today free to enjoy a range of personal liberty unknown to his ancestors.

11 AMERICAN FOREIGN POLICY

American attitudes with respect to the conduct of foreign affairs have been reflected in two somewhat contradictory beliefs—both questionable. The first is embodied in the fundamental public acceptance of the idealistic Wilsonian doctrine of "open covenants openly arrived at." The second, best represented by the saying "Never lost a war, never won a peace," has reflected a widespread American fear of negotiations.

This fear, unsubstantiated though it may be, stems—at least in part—from the doubt of many Americans about the personnel conducting their negotiations. The political appointment of ambassadors has been widely criticized, and the caricature in "Call Me Madam" commonly accepted as more truth than fiction. Even the career diplomat, it is commonly supposed, is chosen more for his social graces and Ivy League background than for his intellectual capacity and general ability. The appellation "striped-pants cookie pusher" has been widely applied to foreign-service officers, and *The Ugly American,* highly critical of our diplomats, became a best seller. Furthermore, the excesses of the McCarthy period have left an indelible mark on foreign policy in the form of an ongoing scapegoatism. Having been persuaded that Owen Lattimore, General George C. Marshall, and/or the State Department "lost China," the public logically enough then sought to discover who had "lost Cuba."

This oversimplification of the conduct of policy has carried over into policy itself. First, Americans have unrealistically assumed that neat, permanent "settlements" can be achieved in an ever changing, problem-beset world. Second, our foreign policy has long reflected an outdated combination of isolationism and xenophobia. Although Washington's admonition against entangling alliances has been remembered, his reasoning that neutralism was the only prudent course for a weak, young nation has been forgotten. Further neglecting their history, Americans have displayed a twentieth-century abhorrence of revolution as a means to freedom from colonial domination. Coupled with this has been their dogmatic view of communism's immutability—their stereotype of a Kremlin-dominated monolith of Marxist granite. Consequently, American policy for more than a decade was most applauded when it was most oriented to the "containment" of communism, whereas the more inspired, positive strokes, such as the Marshall Plan and the Point Four Program, bore the brunt of the critics' attack.

Although the danger that war might result from such oversimplifications is obvious, a contrary American bent has provided a stabilizing factor in a precarious world. This factor is the widespread American abhorrence of war, coupled historically with an ultimate willingness to resort to force if necessary in defense of an ideal. (Some Americans, however, carry this willingness too far, so that we often hear the screams of the modern American "war hawks" that armed hostilities provide solutions and should not be avoided in the effort to "settle things.")

With these conflicting attitudes in evidence, it is not surprising that Americans have entertained immediate foreign-policy goals that have contradicted more rational long-term principles.

Can it be seriously argued in the 1960s that "lining up people on our side," "eliminating communism," or "preserving American sovereignty" should be our principal objectives? Fortunately, the impact of such slogans abroad appears to have been lessened by an obvious reluctance to undertake a forced Americanization of the world.

What better goals may be suggested? Many Americans would start with two of FDR's "Four Freedoms"—freedom from want and freedom from fear—and place a peaceful, prosperous world first in their list of objectives. Second, they would assist the other people of the world to achieve *their* goals, by supporting democratic elements in all nations—politically, economically, and socially—while avoiding any show of support or sympathy for totalitarians, even those "on our side." Americans of this persuasion would place their chief reliance upon aid, education, and friendship rather than upon military or economic coercion.

The ultimate goal acceptable to most Americans is the establishment of an enduring world peace enforced through law. Keeping in mind the achievements of the eighteenth century, some look to a world federalism, capable of representing the individual directly and of operating upon him directly rather than through his national government. Though some would label this goal "utopian," still the dream persists.

The task of formulating and effectuating an American foreign policy to attain these goals is tremendous. It is complicated by the constitutional problems that stem from the separate influences of fifty state governments in a system where, theoretically, responsibility for the conduct of foreign affairs lies only with the central government. It is further complicated by the separation of powers within the national government, which requires that the president consult a Congress that is only indirectly charged with foreign-policy determination. There is a growing need for coordination—internally among departments (such as State, Defense, Treasury, Agriculture, and Commerce), and externally with international organizations (not only with the United Nations and its many specialized agencies but also with the sometimes neglected Organization of American States). Compounding these broader problems are some of the more specific difficulties—the bureaucratic inertia that lends to existing policy the force of momentum, the need for a president who can win the support of his own State Department, and the need for secrecy of negotiations in spite of repeated press sniping and the destructive demagogic criticism that has been all too much a part of the postwar world.

The need seems clear—the need for a more realistic, a more objective, critical appraisal of American foreign policy. And yet the well-intentioned efforts to "take politics out of foreign policy"—to achieve a bipartisan policy—have sometimes seemed to thwart the realization of these goals just as much as has destructive partisanship. Thus the determination and conduct of foreign policy continue to play a perplexing, preeminent role in our government in action.

WHAT MAKES U.S. FOREIGN POLICY?
J. William Fulbright

J. William Fulbright, U.S. Senator from Arkansas, is Chairman of the powerful Senate Committee on Foreign Relations. A career educator, he also served as a university president before entering the Senate.

My remarks will surely disappoint those who want me to invent for this occasion new solutions to troubles in Berlin, Tibet, the Middle East, Africa, Southeast Asia, Latin America, the Formosa Strait or, to bring the matter very close to home, Little Rock, Arkansas. I feel that we have had quite enough of speechmaking by public men who invent policies on the spur of the moment from a misplaced sense of duty—the sense that they owe it to the press, or perhaps to themselves, to be the source of new sensations.

Instead, I would like to explore for a bit the question of what makes U.S. foreign policy—a subject, I hope, of some interest to ourselves and our allies.

Now I confess that when I put this question to myself, that when I thought about it a bit, the answer I came up with appeared in Book Eleven of St. Augustine's *Confessions*. There the author raised the question of what God was doing before He created the Heaven and the Earth. A possible answer, St. Augustine said, was this: "He was creating a Hell for people who pry too deep."

Still, despite the measure of truth in this reply, it is worth while to pry into my question, and for two reasons. First, the answer may shed some light on why we do or don't do some things in this or that particular sector of a troubled world. Second, the challenge inherent in my question is not confined exclusively to America. It was raised for all democracies as far back as 1835 by Alexis de Tocqueville when he wrote:

"Foreign politics demand scarcely any of those qualities which are peculiar to a democracy; they require, on the contrary, the perfect use of almost all those in which it is deficient . . . Democracy can only with great difficulty regulate the details of an important undertaking, persevere in a fixed design, and work out its execution in spite of serious obstacles. It cannot combine its measures with secrecy or await their consequences with patience." These are qualities, he concluded, that more especially belong to a form of social organization where the government is ruled by one man or a handful of men.

How true is this?

The paradoxical, indeed the frightening fact is that de Tocqueville's comment is a great deal more applicable today than it was when he made it.

Consider what happened between 1783, when we won our independence, and 1853, when the Gadsden Purchase rounded out our present continental limits. All of this territory was acquired by power and diplomacy, by a skillful maneuvering through the maze of European politics. And at the same time, we managed—with the help of the British fleet—to protect a whole series of nationalistic revolutions to the south from the unholy intentions of the Holy Alliance.

Moreover, throughout the whole of this process, while much was done by the action of individual Presidents, a great deal was done as a direct result of Congressional action or by the direct play of public pressures, rising from a people whose life was being progressively democratized.

FOUR NEW CHALLENGES

The key point is that the conduct of foreign affairs did not appear to be an elite function, limited to specialists in and around the Executive. Neither the electorate nor the Congress was ever overawed by the Executive claim to exclusive knowledge, or its claim that it would be against the national interest to disclose the facts relevant to a foreign-policy decision. Foreign policy was debated in remote frontier outposts as well as in seaboard cities, with a shrewdness and a knowledge of great power rivalries that astonish any modern reader who browses through the records of these debates preserved in our national archives.

The stakes of foreign policy in those days were both visible and finite. They meant the difference between having a hostile power on our frontier or not having one. The contrast with our present circumstances is obvious. The stakes of our foreign policy today are real enough but infinitely more complex. Whereas once upon a time our real national interests were clear and immediate and generally agreed upon, they are so no longer.

They put four hard challenges to the basic workings of our democratic system.

For one thing, if ever the line between domestic and foreign affairs could be drawn, it is now wholly erased. Whether we realize it or not, we can no longer assure ourselves that what we do in one place is unrelated to what we do in a second place; that if we slip domestically, the effect will not be felt abroad—or the other way around. The strength of the American economy, for example, enters directly as a factor in our power to build a versatile military establishment, or to export capital in ways that will contribute to the orderly growth of newly independent peoples. In a reverse view, if those people and their resources along with those of our European allies should ever be drawn into the Communist orbit, it is difficult to see how we could for long maintain our present economy or, indeed, anything resembling our present way of life.

Secondly, because America's paramount strength has vested in us the role of leadership for a coalition diplomacy, our Executive and Legislative organs of government must bear two constituencies in mind. One is the voting constituency from which the chief officers of American government draw their title of office. The second constituency begins at the three-mile limit. It is formed by many hundreds of millions of people around the globe who, though they don't cast a single vote in any American election, are vitally affected by the decisions of American lawmakers.

Out of this there arises a recurrent dilemma. In the event of a conflict of interest between the two constituencies, which one should have a prior claim on the support of the American lawmaker? If the prior claim is that of his nonvoting constituency, then he risks a repudiation by American voters. If the prior claim is that of his voting constituency, then he risks the loss of trust by the nonvoting constituency—whose support he must have if he is to attain what both constituencies want above all other things, namely, the conditions for a just peace.

Thirdly, the very process of coalition diplomacy tends to exercise a gravitational pull that centers the business in the hands of the Executive, and downgrades the role of the Congress and the electorate as direct parties to the affair. For the Congress is simply not structurally equipped to deal simultaneously with all the day-to-day problems of coalition diplomacy. And the people, for their part, are even less well equipped to follow the intricate twists and turns of any contemporary diplomatic transaction.

The fourth difference between the past and present represents so great an intensification of the old problem of amateur-expert relations in government as to constitute an almost new problem. What I have in mind here is the fact that many of our leading questions of foreign affairs nowadays are entwined with infinitely complicated scientific and technological questions. For example, should we or should we not stop the testing of the hydrogen bomb? Should we put more or less effort into missile-launching submarines or into the support of foreign allied armies? You can search all the great treatises on the American polity from the *Federalist* papers on forward and they will not give you a single clue to the right answer. Even that second great source of popular doctrine, *Poor Richard's Almanac,* which is so much evoked today, also fails in this respect.

Public ignorance of these newstyle political-scientific-military questions is widespread, to put it mildly, and reaches into high places, including the United States Senate. It is matched by the respect and awe we hold for the expert practitioners of these new arts—a respect which we do not accord experts in other fields. The economists of this country rarely, if ever, agree on precisely the monetary policy to be followed by the Federal Reserve Board. But this does not in the least inhibit people who don't know the difference between Adam Smith and John Maynard Keynes from expressing the most profound judgments on the matter. Yet these same people are quite willing to leave vastly more important questions to a handful of scientists and military strategists who sharply disagree among themselves.

One reason for this paradox, I suggest, is that whereas the economists carry on their disputes in public, what the military scientists have to say is funneled almost exclusively to the Executive, where the cutoff stamp of Top Secret comes into play. But what is cut off simultaneously is any real power by the people or the Congress to judge whether the agents of the Executive acted wisely or not on the basis of the word they alone were privileged to hear.

BIPARTISAN OR UNPARTISAN?

All of these new challenges work in their own way to give a new sense of awesome relevance to what de Tocqueville had to say about the inherent difficulties a democracy faces in the conduct of contemporary foreign politics.

There is one more difficulty that deserves mention, for it arises, paradoxically, from the effort of a democracy to respond to the new challenge. It has to do with the very nature of bipartisanship—in theory an instrument of national unity but more often in recent practice a gag on legitimate discussion. Time and again we have lately found ourselves in situations where the Executive, consulting itself, has announced a policy, whereupon the cry goes out that it cannot be debated, since this would show the world that we are divided. What we must do, instead, is to swallow our doubts about the wisdom of the policy. We must rally to the Executive in a great show of national unity. Nor does the matter end there. Later on, when the doubtful wisdom of the policy becomes apparent in the formidable world of actual practice, the members of the opposition party are again silenced. For if they raise their voice, they invite the rebuke: "You voted for that policy when it was sent down here to the Congress. Why are you squawking about it now?"

I am not implying that anything and everything ought to be fair game for partisan politics. Far from it. Foreign policy ought in fact to be nonpartisan or unpartisan—words which the late Senator Vandenberg preferred to bipartisan. Nonpartisanship means that policies are criticized and debated on their merits, not in a partisan electioneering context.

I would add but one more footnote to this. From what I have been able to judge of America's European allies, the thing they fear most is not a healthy debate conducted by Americans on foreign-affairs issues. Their greater fears arise over precipitate announcements of foreign policy which neither Congress nor the country has properly considered.

If the difficulties I have been considering seem more acute in their American context, it is only because the blinding light of attention is focused on America in its role as the mainstay of the western coalition. But if we shift the spotlight to any of the other leading democracies in this coalition, we get the impression of a single image repeating itself in various degrees, like an object seen in a hall of mirrors.

Today, for example, Europe is caught in the crisis for which the word "Berlin" stands as the graphic symbol. Each nation there looks at its neighbor and all look at the United States with a sense of wonder whether all will stand together or fall separately in the event the Soviets mean to breach the peace. Yet on the occasion of the tenth anniversary of NATO recently observed in Washington, I asked myself why it was so necessary for one member after another to assure all the rest that he could be trusted to carry out the purpose of NATO.

I asked myself why the speech given by (the then) Acting Secretary of State Christian Herter—the speech in which he merely repeated America's ten-year-old commitment to honor its NATO obligations—should have been considered the highlight of the anniversary. And I also wondered why the crisis over Berlin should have so menacing a face and should have led to an uneasy feeling, which has even been voiced in some quarters, that we have already been defeated on the ground by the Soviets.

By any arithmetic test of potential strength, it is *we* who should be giving the Soviets sleepless nights and not the other way around. For if the population and the industrial resources of Europe and the United States were really mobilized to act in concert, and if that strength were translated into a military dimension, the aggregate would exceed by far anything the Soviets could muster in the foreseeable future. Think of it. The United States and its NATO allies constitute 460 million people organized in a highly industrialized power complex. The Soviet Union, with its problematic allies in eastern Europe, can muster only 300 million. Yet here we are, frightened by the present preponderance of the Soviet strength in conventional arms, and frightened also by the all too exact knowledge that a resort to nuclear arms under conditions of nuclear parity might result in a dead Europe instead of the live one we all want to preserve.

How have we arrived at this incongruous position? Sometimes I wonder if we have correctly assessed the changed situation that now confronts us. It is true that at the end of the Second World War there may have been opportunity for choice in the methods of our foreign policy. By cold logic we could have taken the imperialist course. We had a monopoly of nuclear weapons. Indeed, we had shown that we were prepared to use them. It is conceivable that we could have pressed this temporary advantage to impose a dictated peace upon the Soviets, forcing their withdrawal within the Soviet perimeter. Instead we chose not to use the nuclear weapon as an instrument of policy but to work in concert with our allies to build what we hoped would be a more durable peace.

TENTATIVE BEFORE THE INEVITABLE

Whatever the choices of the past, today we no longer have any choice. Today the nuclear weapon has no utility as an instrument of foreign policy. It cannot attain the objectives which lie beyond war. It can only ring down the last-act curtain for us and our enemies alike.

Then why are we so tentatively committed to the only course that lies open to us? Why do we hesitate before the commitments of manpower and resources that can preserve the balance for the West? Why do we appear listless before a challenge that is so obviously demanding of our greatest energies?

Take the area of military strategy alone. Even before the Soviets attained their present nuclear position, it was perfectly apparent that our own atomic superiority was not a substitute for conventional forces. It was wholly clear that placing our entire reliance on these weapons would one day confront us with the choice of blowing up the world simply to contain the sort of probing operation the Russians use to test our will.

The founders of NATO realized this. Their first plans called for ninety-plus divisions. And yet, as the countries of NATO have steadily prospered, their concept of what they can afford to do has steadily narrowed.

What has been missing is not the material capacity to support adequate conventional forces but the will to do so. Our spirit, on both sides of the Atlantic, has gone soft.

Is it not ironical that the blaze of selfless idealism burned brightest in Europe and in America when the havoc of World War II still met the eye at every turn? In that hour, as I recall it, the cry went out from the best spirits among the victors and the vanquished alike for a new sense of fraternity and for an end to the national divisions that twice led the flower of European youth to the slaughterhouse. The best spirits of Europe, as I recall, wanted to stand as one family, respecting the cultural diversity of their individual members but united in the pursuit of a political destiny sought in common by all members.

And is it not ironical that as the rubble was swept from the streets of Europe, and as the signs of a progressively expanding prosperity rose where rubble once had been, the visions of a Europe twice united—within itself, and with its North American offshoot—grew progressively more cloudy? Here was a cause that should have enlisted the concentrated and sustained energies of the leaders and the led on both sides of the Atlantic. Instead, European leaders fully as much as American leaders began to think in terms of their voting constituencies at the expense of their nonvoting constituencies. I deeply regret the recent recriminations between two of our chief NATO allies—recriminations that have been echoed out of all proportion in the popular press. Their differences, I suspect, arise not so much over substantive issues as over a sense of frustration at the lack of an energizing force that will give life to our alliances.

Now it is not my purpose, as the saying goes, to be a prophet of doom and gloom. I am merely saying that the choice facing European democracies was and is just this: Federate or perish. And the task facing America is to so conduct itself that it will help nurture those tentative roots toward federation like Euratom and the Common Market that have managed to take hold—to nurture them with the object of creating a real European Union. Beyond that, our purpose must be to bring into being that system of interlocking commonwealths—to use Max Ascoli's apt phrase—that can bolster our security.

I know all about the vetoes practical men stand ready to catalogue. I heard them in 1945 and the list has not changed one bit today. The only thing that has changed is the urgency of ignoring what practical men have to say. The march of history is fast outstripping us. Europe and America have enormous resources for survival, indeed for the mastery of any challenge hurled our way by the Soviets. But those resources will not be mobilized, they will remain in their present state of disarray, until public men and the publics on both sides of the Atlantic fit those resources into a grand design for closer union. In striving to bring this design to pass in our own time, we may make mistakes; but in striving, we may find our salvation. If we do not strive for it at all, our epitaph will read: They chose to stand still, and so were lost forever.

FOREIGN POLICY ON CAPITOL HILL

Thomas L. Hughes

Thomas L. Hughes is a well-known Washington lawyer who was legislative counsel for Senator Hubert Humphrey from 1955 to 1958 and an administrative assistant to Representative Chester Bowles from 1959 to 1960.

Last June during hearings conducted by the Foreign Relations Committee of which he was to become chairman eight months later, Senator J. William Fulbright volunteered some illuminating if pessimistic comments on the role of Congress in foreign policy. "I admire your persistence and optimism," he told a prominent witness who had been criticizing American policies in many parts of the world. "I must congratulate you on it . . . In a way I am flattered that you think the Senate can do something about this, and in another way I am a little disappointed that you have such illusions about your own government. You should understand it better than that."

After Mr. Fulbright had spent about ten minutes elaborating on this theme, the witness desperately countered: "Senator, surely you are not saying that the government of the United States, in which I include the three branches, is incapable of making good sense."

To which the senator replied: "I am asking you if you really think it is."

It goes without saying that the Constitutional status accorded the Executive and Congress is a standing invitation to struggle for control over foreign relations. Almost every candidate for national office, and a mounting percentage of national aspirants temporarily running for state and local office, have left little doubt that this foreign-policy struggle is bound to occur anyway—that it is simply enhanced by the explicit sanction given to it in the Constitution.

In this struggle the Executive branch enjoys certain advantages. In addition to the specific Constitutional power, party control, and the President's clearly defined responsibility to a national constituency, these advantages include a number of technical assets in the field of foreign relations: superior information, expert analysis, centralized planning, co-ordinated policy formulation, and speed and flexibility in execution.

But what happens when the Executive branch abandons its prerogatives and defaults on its obligations? It is now a common complaint, by no means restricted to Democrats, that the administration lacks those very attributes which have usually distinguished Executive pre-eminence in the foreign-policy field.

WHO'S IN CHARGE?

One of the principal difficulties is that it is impossible to fix with any certainty the responsibility for the formulation of foreign policy in the present administration. Bearing upon it from different directions are decisions that are made, modified, or postponed in the State Department, the Pentagon, the Atomic Energy Commission, the National Security Council, the Central Intelligence Agency, and—far from least—the Treasury and the Bureau of the Budget. Many of the relationships within the Executive branch are as tense, and some of the animosities as entrenched, as are those between the Executive and Congress. Disarmament policy in the past three years has been one obvious and critical example.

Strong Presidential leadership is essential if Executive policy is not to be splintered among these competing centers of power. Instead, the top-level leaderlessness to which we have become accustomed simply serves to invite Congressional interest and participation, thus further dispersing the decision-making power. For the centers of power are even more widely scattered in Congress than in the Executive, and this is especially true in the area of foreign policy.

Indeed, any assumptions about the role of Congress in foreign policy and any assumptions about an alleged Congressional reaction to a foreign-policy issue are always open to doubt. There is hardly any such thing as a "Congressional reaction" except as a tough-and-ready projection of past committee decisions and of the present temperament of the Senate and the House leadership.

Of course it is in the temporary interest of the Executive to complain about a "Congressional view" and of some in Congress to complain about an "Executive view." The temptation to seek scapegoats is always present and often seized. Members of the Executive and Congress, each group feeling uneasy about the other, at times happily exploit the situation in covering their own inadequacies when addressing the outside world. The expectation of trouble from Congress has often been useful to the Executive branch as a protective device in negotiating with foreign governments. For a State Department whose natural inclination may be to drift anyway, it is the easiest thing in the world to rationalize inaction on grounds of prospective trouble with Congress, or to suggest that what might otherwise be an imaginative foreign policy is being frustrated by Congressional attack. In much the same way, popular fancies concerning the motivations and capabilities of State Department personnel have been deliberately given the false credence by political speeches from irresponsible congressmen.

OVERLAPPING POWERS

But it is not the formal struggle between Congress and the Executive that causes the most trouble. The routine ebb and flow of Executive-Congressional business, the multiple and circuitous processes that defy, overrun, and undercut jurisdictional lines and even the Constitutional doctrines of the separation of powers—these actually constitute the chief reason why, as Senator Fulbright has suggested, no one is really "in control."

The committee system is a case in point. It is not very systematic as systems go. One reason here too is the hobbling effect of jurisdictional overlap. The committees in Congress that have recognizable jurisdiction over some area or other of foreign policy include at least the following: Foreign Relations, Aeronautical and Space Sciences, and Finance in the Senate; Foreign Affairs, Ways and Means, and Science and Astronautics in the House; and one in each body of these—Appropriations, Agriculture, Armed Services, Government Operations, Commerce, Judiciary, Banking and Currency, Interior and Insular Affairs, plus the Joint Committee on Atomic Energy.

The Appropriations Committees have in large measure become third Houses of Congress. Their eroding impact on the two foreign-affairs committees has been increasingly in direct proportion to the growth and importance of funds to foreign policy. The end is not in sight, as the opening skirmishes in this year's foreign-aid battle have clearly indicated.

Since 1946, when committee jurisdictions were refined in the Legislative Reorganization Act, a process of cellular division into subcommittees has prompted even more jurisdictional controversy. It scarcely matters that some of the subcommittees never meet; their chairmanships are considered worth a major amount of civil strife. Indeed, the competition within committees and among subcommittees surpasses in exasperation and dissonance anything that troubles the manager of the Metropolitan Opera.

A CONGRESSMAN'S DAY

Needless to say, this tangled web of personal ambition, parochial interest, and partisan maneuver makes countless demands on a congressman's time. The picture is well known of the busy legislator arriving breathless and late at a committee meeting, leaving it early only to be late at the next. Each new Congress seems destined to face tasks more complicated than its predecessor. Even the most intelligent and dedicated congressman can devote only spasmodic and fragmentary attention to foreign affairs.

Under the circumstances, it is the most natural thing in the world for the average congressman to continue to simplify the external world out of all semblance to reality. He cannot escape the complexity of the domestic problems that stream across his desk. He is sorely tempted, therefore, to shift his favorite stereotypes and oratorical flourishes to the area of foreign affairs. It is a form of relaxation. It offers a change of pace.

Out on the stump a congressman is impelled more and more to venture into foreign policy simply as a device for blunting the attack of his opponents on domestic policy. Foreign policy, the last great redoubt for Congressional oratory, lends itself to grandiose expressions of sentiment that are helpful to the campaigning congressman's momentary reputation and are not easily susceptible to convincing counterargument or meaningful repudiation.

The temptation to tell minority nationality groups what they wish to hear, with ornate orchestrations on the emotions of war and peace, is a traditional and invaluable opportunity in many political campaigns. Moreover, many congressmen have found from experience that foreign affairs is a sufficiently important topic so that everybody is interested, and a sufficiently elusive one so that the non-differentiating audience can be charmed equally by Senator Goldwater one week and Senator Kennedy the next. However nightmarish it may seem to sober political scientists, every campaigning congressman is willing to consider himself an authority on foreign affairs should the occasion arise, and there are few standards of expert judgment that mean much to a congressman's audience.

Once in office, the congressman comes up against the barriers to effective action that have already been mentioned. When an individual member of Congress tries to hurdle these barriers, he does so episodically, usually by means of a foreign-policy speech, an "investigation," or a hasty visit abroad. No matter how hard-working and dedicated, he will on such occasions be accused of a variety of misdemeanors, including junketing, publicity seeking, and harboring Presidential ambitions. He may even be conspicuously and contemptuously silenced by an outbreak of Philistinism on the part of his own party leadership. Counterinducements from many sources, less publicly expressed, are the more usual inhibitors against a sustained display of intelligence and initiative by an individual congressman in the course of official duties.

Meanwhile, the congressman is under constant pressure from his constituents to play a disruptive role. Every special interest routed through a congressman's office for action by an Executive agency upsets the smooth functioning of Executive operations, disturbs established procedures, may trespass on accepted standards—and is designed to do so. More and more, these interruptions are connected with foreign policy in the fields of contracts and personnel. Indeed, a particular congressman's interest and attention have often been first directed to a particular agency's operation by means of such a service case. The result is that an individual congressman, perhaps from purely personal or political motives, mounts a sortie into what is theoretically supposed to be an administrative function. All over Washington in a score or more of agencies, this is the most important kind of Congressional penetration of Executive responsibility. It is not the "broad policy lines" that Congress is examining or proposing. From time to time in a halfhearted way Congressional committees do try to undertake general appraisals of foreign policy. But the day-to-day preoccupation is with individual questions of immediate and limited relevance, and perhaps of rather more selfish concern to a congressman.

DOES ANYBODY VETO?

The textbooks once said that Congress made the laws and Presidents enforced them. In reality the Executive now initiates much, if not most, important legislation and Congress modifies it. The President proposes and Congress disposes. The veto power, once supposed to be in the hands of the President, is no longer in his hands alone. Indeed, as issues become more complex, the experts are telling us that all Congress can really do is exercise an enlightened veto on Executive proposals. The same experts are likely to tell us that all the American voter can do is exercise a public veto on policies selected for him by competing elites.

A crucial question then emerges: What if there is not much policy competition, and what if there are hardly any elites to choose among? What if the Executive, now having the power of legislative initiative, doesn't actually initiate much, and what if the Congress, now having the power of veto, doesn't exercise it? What if there is little proposing and less disposing?

The Senate Foreign Relations Committee itself, for instance, has been under the control of the opposition party for the last four years. Individual members of that committee—especially Fulbright, Humphrey, Mansfield,

Kennedy, and Morse—have provided helpful and constructive criticisms of our current role in world affairs. Indeed, the committee has long regarded itself as a special and independent guardian of American foreign policy. Yet it is astonishing that with all its tradition the committee has not exerted itself more. It has done little to demonstrate its independence. Over the last few years, the committee has been applauded chiefly for its acquiescence in administration policy. Explanations for this semi-paralysis may be found in various places. One place to look is the Senate Democratic cloakroom, where the "principles of accommodation" have been elevated to the status of a new and demonstrably effective art form under the Texas leadership.

In the current Washington atmosphere there is a clear and present danger of too many accommodators being overly accommodating. Some men may be born accommodators, but in this respect our age has been unusually blessed. As a result, there are not enough polar positions left to require accommodation. As soon as everybody blandly starts to assume the role of Henry Clay, there is less and less left to compromise toward or away from. At the moment an objective observer might feel that we could stand a few more Calhouns and Websters expounding enough firmly held convictions to make the leadership's manipulations worth while.

"TALKING POLITICAL"

Another factor in the situation is a difficult one for the public and many of the participants to accept. There has been increasingly widespread acknowledgment inside Congress of the value of reducing cloakroom talk to the lowest common denominator when politicians get together. Senators and representatives find that life is much easier if they explain themselves to one another in terms of political opportunism. In this way a number of otherwise distasteful feelings about one another become palatable. Principles no longer get in the way of working relationships. Even friendships can result. "Talking political" takes everybody off the hook—at least in personal terms.

Naturally a concerted depreciation of issues as issues is inevitable in this situation. If the Southern hierarchy cannot abide a Humphrey and a Douglas because they appear to believe what they say on a thorny subject like civil rights, a mediator will intervene to explain that, after all, the Northern senators have to say it. And vice versa. The political explanation, even when it does violence to the character and personalities of the men involved, is acceptable and understandable, while an image of sincerity would be intolerable. There is general agreement that if everyone were sincere, and if sincerity were translated into real stubbornness, Congress simply could not operate. Nor could the principles of accommodation.

Clearly, senators and representatives resent being made out to be more opportunistic than they are. But most of them enjoy heightening their reputations among their fellows. Often these reputations suffer from taking strong lone-wolf positions on foreign policy.

It is true that the principles of accommodation are more frequently applied to domestic than to foreign-policy matters. But the appeal is often irresistible in the foreign field as well. It is applied whenever the President puts Congress on the spot, as with the Formosa Resolution and the Eisenhower Doctrine, by forcing a choice between sound foreign-policy inclinations and a publicly embarrassing repudiation of the President. It is also applied in the *quid pro quos* that tacitly link agriculture votes to mutual security, patronage to Un-American Activities appropriations, and Supreme Court legislation to immigration bills. Foreign policy in Congress is caught up in the political life of the institution, and that is not entirely auspicious for a fresh approach to foreign affairs.

THE CONFIDENCE GAME

Curiously enough, another part of the explanation for Congress's semi-paralysis in foreign affairs is the role of so-called confidential information. Members of the Foreign Affairs and Foreign Relations Committees often insist *pro forma* on obtaining classified information from the Executive. A good case can be made that they should have it, but it is even more fascinating to wonder why the Executive branch does not give it to them more readily. Congressmen both want and enjoy the feeling of consultation, and the psychological benefits likely to be derived are all to the State Department's advantage. Moreover, if the information bears out the State Department's policy position, the congressman who receives it is rendered relatively more helpless as an adverse critic.

Everyone accepts the fact that the reasoning behind certain policies cannot be grasped without the special information available to the Executive. This fact, however, is often useful to an administration even when it doesn't have a very thoughtful or imaginative policy to sell. Discussion on a highly confidential basis with individual senators or representatives or with committees frequently serves a dual purpose. First, the congressmen are flattered; they like the confidential aspect of being let in on something, and they like to hint to others that they know something in confidence that they only wish they were at liberty to disclose. Second, the introduction of a confidential element throws the average congressman's own analysis off balance; he respects those who know more secrets than he does, and his own confidence is jolted by this confidential disclosure.

If, as part of this process, a certain amount of credit can be bestowed upon the congressman by the Executive, consultation can really become the "oil of government," criticism of Executive policy can be blunted, and persuasion through participation can reach new heights of effectiveness. After all, persuasion is a continuing process, and it can be helped along in a variety of ways. As Congressional committees and the Legislative Reference Service both draw increasing numbers of personnel from Executive agencies for their own staffs, there is no reason why the liaison cannot blossom at all levels.

No reason except prudence. For this sort of liaison is not desirable per se, any more than contention between the branches is desirable per se. The vital questions are not of institutional means but of substance. A tremendous amount of time can be spent by Congress in working out its relationships with the Executive, and by the Executive in smoothing its relationships with Congress. But the concentration on reconciling these essentially operational problems of government constantly deflects attention from policy.

To the degree that the chief problem for either branch becomes the other, attention is distracted from the world scene, which is providing more than enough challenges for both. If our sights are trained and our time is consumed trying to promote mutual respect and deference between the Executive and Congress, we can easily be caught in a descending spiral of ineffectiveness in meeting mounting world problems. It is possible to check and balance a government—especially ours—into a kind of irrelevant equilibrium.

Now, it is one thing for a dynamic, forceful, imaginative administration to concern itself with buttressing its Congressional support, promoting an atmosphere of mutual concession, winning the personal friendship of opposition leaders to run administration errands, and seeking advance public-relations support by Constitutionally unnecessary policy resolutions. But it is, to say the least, a good deal less significant for a timid, retrenchment-minded administration to go to this effort. If the main objective is merely to perpetuate past policies and hold onto the *status quo*—and if compromise is required even to achieve this limited aim—then the topic we are discussing comes down to one of distinctly third-rate importance: the promotion of relations for the sake of relations.

The gentle picture, so often drawn for us by sophisticated columnists a few years ago, of Secretary Dulles and the late Senator George "co-ordinating" foreign policy over coffee at a Mayflower Hotel breakfast table had even then a slightly passe aroma. Historians may regard it as one of the major curiosities of our time that when the international situation required a major effort at critical thinking and new approaches, a weak and declining administration was piously embraced by a strong and "responsible" opposition party in Congress.

WHITHER BIPARTISANSHIP?

The evocation of bipartisanship continues to be a significant factor in Washington. Since 1955, with different parties in control at either end of Pennsylvania Avenue, the blanket of bipartisanship has become especially useful in covering up legitimate struggles in the name of a nondescript "unity." The appeal for bipartisanship has conspired with an overconcentration on Executive-Congressional relations to produce an end result of sham battles, undisguised credit and publicity seeking, and little forward thrust toward new world policies. Bipartisanship as a living endorsement of mutually understood means and ends in foreign policy is one thing; bipartisanship as a mere cliche is another. Indeed, a threadbare bipartisanship can undermine the whole democratic process.

Surely in these days of dynamic conservatism and prudent progressivism, one of our major problems is to retain enough difference between the two parties to provide at least some vestige of meaning in the voters' choice. Yet the morning after the 1958 elections, following the most dramatic overturn of Congressional seats in twenty years, the Republican Secretary of State and the Senate Majority Leader hastened to say that there were no foreign-policy implications in the elections because foreign policy was, of course, a bipartisan affair. The implications could not be more subversive of democracy, in theory or practice. In effect, this means that as far as the life-or-death questions of foreign policy are concerned, you may vote either way. In any event, your vote will not disturb the continuing political moratorium on foreign-policy change.

Bipartisanship on the military and economic defense of western Europe ten years ago was vigorous, substantive, and meaningful. To a large extent it still is, as the party alignments on the Berlin crisis prove. But what about the vast areas of new non-European problems, from Africa to China, from missiles to space? What about new developments in Europe itself? Can we really afford to depoliticize the crucial work of policy-making in these broad areas where a consensus has not begun to form?

A HOPEFUL FERMENT

These are the real issues of the moment, and the calamity is that we must face them without sustained Executive leadership for at least another twenty-one months. Uncertainties over State Department leadership complicate the situation even further. "I do not think there is the remotest chance for Congressional control of foreign policy," Fulbright has said. And he is certainly right. Congress cannot hope to take over large-scale Executive tasks. The odds against far-reaching changes are probably insurmountable.

But even minor changes can become cumulatively significant. Congress, after all, has some tasks of its own that must not be shirked. The same Constitution that calls upon the Executive branch to "make" foreign policy demands the "advice" of the Senate, and in practical terms this injunction now applies to the House also.

At the moment the situation on Capitol Hill is in ferment. The Senate and the House are full of new blood. Many of the new members departed from tradition and campaigned constructively on foreign-policy issues. Moreover, the two main foreign-policy committees are in a period of transition. In addition to its new chairman, the Senate Foreign Relations Committee has four new members; aside from *its* new chairman, Dr. Thomas E. Morgan, the House Foreign Affairs Committee has eight new members. Some of the new committee members on both sides of the Hill are men of special competence—like Albert Gore, Frank Church, and Chester Bowles.

For the first time in years these two committees can become focal points for such realignments as are possible on Capitol Hill. They are capable of conducting frank and thoughtful public discussions of world affairs that could release new energies and attract new allegiances. They can bring conscientious criticism to bear on policies that are increasingly losing their way. And they can join with their enlightened colleagues, however few, against the odds, however great, to help move the foreign policy of their government off dead center, out of the rut of full-time adjustment to the principles of accommodation into the enormous new realities of world affairs.

FOREIGN AID HAS SUCCEEDED
Barbara Ward

Barbara Ward, a British economist, is the author of many books, including *India and the West* and *The Rich Nations and the Poor Nations.*

Against all the Cassandra warnings of hatchet work to come, the Foreign Aid Bill has gone through the House in a uniquely untruncated state. Yet one can still say no more than that the tendency to reduce aid, which has been gathering momentum in Congress for several years, has been halted, at least for the time being. A trend has been checked, time gained for reappraisal. But not even the most potent political magic can be expected, year in, year out, to force through programs from which public opinion is thoroughly alienated.

Is this the case with foreign aid? Have the American people, after a 17-year experiment, decided against it? Has Congress in recent years accurately reflected a growing popular disillusion? If so, is it one that can no longer be reversed? There is time, this year, to ask these questions. And on the answers depends any possibility of renewing and sustaining economic assistance for the longer run.

The first difficulty lies in establishing the facts. Whenever public opinion polls test the popular reaction to foreign aid in general terms, the answer is invariably that a sizable majority believe that aid should continue. It cannot be said that the American people have gone on record against economic assistance. Yet every Congressman who opposes aid tends to include among his reasons the argument that it is highly unpopular in his own constituency.

A lot, of course, depends upon the way in which the question is put. "Would you use some of America's abundant wealth to fight hunger, misery and ignorance abroad?" invites the generous answer: "Yes." The question: "Would you continue to shore up corrupt and lascivious generals with your aid money?" invites an equally emphatic negative.

Foreign aid can cover either or both propositions, and since many Congressmen display a built-in tendency to distrust Federal spending and an equal tendency to confine it, if possible, to expenditures which have immediate impact on American voters—especially, their own—it is quite conceivable that the supposed unpopular reactions from the grass roots are in response to heavily loaded questions: "Would you rather see this fertilizer plant set up in Adel County or Bombay?" "Would you rather have flood control on the Upper Missouri or the Lower Nile?" The sampling is very far from clinically pure and the evidence must therefore be held to be somewhat inconclusive.

These loaded questions point to an even greater difficulty in the way of judging either the effectiveness of foreign aid or the real nature of popular reactions to it. Any judgment implies some standard of comparison. A teacher in a slum area contriving to pass on some instruction and a little sense of purpose to a class of potential juvenile delinquents may, in fact, be doing a far more testing and brilliant job than a university instructor successfully coaching a group of straight-A students. Most judgments, therefore, imply expectations—of what it is reasonable to achieve in given circumstances and hence of what the circumstances actually are.

At this point, one encounters the most formidable of all obstacles to the forming of any clear and convincing judgments about the success of foreign aid. Such judgments depend directly upon people's expectations—and there are some good reasons for supposing that, over the past 17 years, the link between American expectations and world facts has not always been very close.

Can one, without caricature, give some sort of profile of America's worldwide hopes and interests in the postwar years? Certainly a central strand is the concern for freedom—freedom from colonial rule by Western powers, freedom from post-colonial domination by Communists. But this is an aspiration at a very high level of generality. When Americans have thought in concrete terms about the policies needed to create or preserve freedom, it is arguable that their minds have been strongly colored by two great historical experiences—one old, one new, but both felt to be relevant.

The old experience is America's own anticolonial revolution. The archetype for the world is a band of vigorous men acting together to throw off colonial rule, setting up the institutions of free government, keeping foreign tyranny at bay and setting to work, by their own free efforts and enterprise, to develop a whole underdeveloped continent. When a Sukarno comes to Washington and speaks of the leadership Jefferson and Lincoln have offered an aspiring world, the American subconscious stirs with sympathetic images of freedom won and tyrants overthrown.

The new experience is the triumphant success of the Marshall Plan. After 1947, a group of free nations, shattered by war, endangered by Communist pressure, prostrate in the wake of an appalling winter, were enabled, by American aid, to rebuild the foundations of their shaken continent. In four years, they achieved new standards of wealth and unity and decisively defeated the risk of Communist expansion. American assistance, though vast—some $13 billion in free grants—was only the spark to ignite a whole conflagration of local investment which, in its turn, launched the European community into a new orbit of growth in which it has happily circled ever since. With this triumph behind them, Americans have understandably been inclined to believe that capital assistance, judiciously injected at strategic points in stagnant economics, can provide the extra element of elan needed to insure take-off into sustained growth.

Out of these two experiences it has been all too easy to construct an ideal pattern of aspiration for the world at large—that of responsible local leaders throwing off colonialism in the name of free government and then, supported by appropriate American aid, building up independent economies, closed to Communism and open to productive private investment. Aid, in such a context, is largely what the distinguished Clay Committee thought it should be—an instrument of American foreign policy designed to frustrate the spread of Communism and to foster not only the public but also the private development and management of free economies—certainly not an ignoble aim but, in the event, wildly out of line with the realities of the post-colonial world.

For what in fact is the record in recent years? There have been one or two resounding examples of success within the framework of America's expectations. Greece, Israel, Taiwan—all have been massively aided. All have used the aid to strengthen and diversify their mixed economies. All are now more or less in orbit, economically. None has succumbed to left-wing extremism.

But one cannot call the achievement typical. Whether the arena is Asia or Africa or the less developed parts of Latin America, the normal pattern is a shaky economy still far from "self-sustaining growth"; a government of dubious stability and authoritarian leanings, announcing a wide variety of "Socialistic patterns" for its economy: an international stance which, far from upholding anti-Communism, refused to take sides, proffering an equal variety of variants on the theme of nonalignment—and all this in spite of a continuing undercover threat of Communist subversion.

There are exceptions to this discouraging picture. India has maintained the rule of law and a functioning democracy among a population that makes up nearly half the "third world." Egypt and Guinea have accepted Communist aid and locked up local Communists. Venezuela has survived a violent Castroite onslaught with democratic procedures and rates of growth intact. But these can be dismissed as exceptions. The norm remains. And if Americans are gloomy about the apparent results of a decade of assistance to the developing nations, it would be less than candid to maintain that they have not a good deal to be gloomy about.

But how much of the disillusion is due to fact, to reality, how much to disappointed expectations? The world seen from Westchester County (or Sunningdale or Passy, for that matter) may look a little less than reassuring. But this is not the only view. How, for instance, may it have looked from Peking in the early nineteen-fifties? The view from there would certainly not have raised the same expectations. Indeed, it would not have overlapped at all in any but the crudest geographical sense. Yet it would have seemed real enough to the Chinese and remarkably close to *their* historical experience.

All around the world they would have seen poor, colored nations on the point of getting rid of Western tutelage, or, in more flamboyant language, "throwing off the imperialist yoke." The economies of these countries in some ways repeated China's own early obstacles to growth—stagnant, often bankrupt agriculture; modernization chiefly confined to the import-export sectors and concentrated in large, foreign-dominated coastal cities; industry in an embryonic state and largely in foreign hands. In politics a small, wealthy local group would be likely to be in close and even compromising touch with foreign interests; foreign businessmen, administrators, technicians and visitors would hold aloof on the other side of a color bar. Local education, though it would be large enough to spark hope, would be neither technical nor widespread enough to underpin a vigorous, modernizing economy (one thinks of the Congo, with only 12 college graduates at the time of its independence). In short, the typical post-colonial pattern could be held to be one of societies aware of new opportunities, open to the "revolution of rising expectations," but frustrated by internal unbalance and caught between an old world that would not die and a new order still unborn.

Only violence, it was easy to feel, would break the impasse. Like Russia in 1917—a comparable case of deadlock—China in 1949 embarked on the Leninist short cut to modernization—Lenin himself had thought that the conquest of the world might lie through Peking and Delhi. In China, in the early fifties, the worldwide triumph of Communism, as the "contradictions" of the ex-colonial world turned into revolution, must have seemed a foregone conclusion. Aid in the shape of loans and guerrilla instruction would simply hasten a historic inevitability.

Two views, two sets of expectations, one world, presumably one reality—but who has proved to be nearer the facts? So far, at least, one has surely to admit the curious paradox that while the Communists' picture of the developing world is on the whole more accurate, their expectations have proved to be far wider of the mark.

The developing world of the sixties *is* definitely more like China of the late forties than Europe at the same time or America in the days of the Founding Fathers. Economics *are* unbalanced as aresult of the old Western dominance which stimulated exports and little else. Trade patterns *do* induce one-crop dependence and unsatisfactory primary prices. Western investment plans and tariff structures *do* tend to favor growth where it is already profitable—in the developed world—while poor countries grow poorer still. All this experience of disequilibrium and dependence *does* create its resentments—racial resentment, economic resentment, growing realization of the gap between rich nations and poor.

Meanwhile, new governments, composed all too often of no more than a fringe of fully literate and experienced men, could hardly be more unlike the Madisons and Jeffersons of America's own revolution. Nor can one compare the reactions of the sturdy yeoman electorate of the United States in the late 18th century with the inchoate ambitions and measureless miseries of the poor majority in today's new states. A double revolution of equality sweeps the world—against the elite at the national level, against the wealthy West at the world level.

It is a crisis apparently tailormade for Communism. Yet, by and large, Communist pressure is no more effective today than it was 10 years ago. In fact, it can be argued that in some areas it is receding, as Africa develops strange new varieties of home-grown Socialism, as Latin America learns the lean look of the Castro experiment, as Eastern Europe wriggles out of Soviet tutelage and as the Communist bloc tears itself apart in a new ideological struggle in which one element is, precisely, China's denunciation of Russia as a "bourgeois" state.

Why have Communist expectations for the developing world been even more brutally disappointed than Western hopes? Certainly, no one will assign all the credit to foreign aid. Communist policies have often contributed to their own discrediting. Their aid—as in Africa—has often been expensive and unfit for tropical conditions. On occasion, their technicians have been shown to be without the needed skills or languages. They have been caught out in subversion. They have even been found guilty of such "capitalist tricks" as unloading unwanted goods, or reselling tropical produce at less than world market prices.

Again, many new governments have proved fully as anxious as any American could wish to avoid substituting Eastern ideological control for Western colonialism. President Nyerere's present maneuvers to regain control over Zanzibar have precisely this aim in view. Nasser, Toure, Nkrumah —to name some of America's possibly less favorite leaders—do not wear "positive neutrality" as a cloak. It means what it implies—independence from either great world bloc. For, as President Nkrumah once put it: "When the bull elephants fight, the grass is trampled down."

Such detachment may rile Western enthusiasts, but at least they can console themselves with a reminder that they are supposed to believe in variety. It is infinitely more galling for the Communists, for whom world uniformity is the aim.

Yet while allowing for Communist mistakes and for the developing nations' own sturdy sense of independence, one must also give Western policies—above all, the policies of economic assistance—some credit for the continuance of a largely open world. Western aid to the development plans of India and Pakistan in the shape of crucial foreign exchange and surplus food supplies has permitted the huge subcontinent to secure industrial growth of the order of 8 per cent a year and to keep just ahead in the task of producing more food for its bursting population. America's assistance to Latin America has offset the decades-long fall in primary prices and at least permitted trade to continue at the old levels. Western aid of all kinds to Africa has brought about an educational revolution in a continent in which a shortage of skills of all kinds is the greatest obstacle to growth. A dozen universities, primary schools for half the population, places for perhaps 4 per cent of the children in secondary education—these are targets either achieved or within reach as a result of Western activity.

It can therefore be argued that foreign aid has succeeded in the profoundest sense—at the level of human imagination and understanding. It has begun to change the whole context within which the developing nations, the vast majority of mankind, look at the West and assess Western policies and intentions. This does not mean that aid cannot be better administered and better used. A very valuable tightening up of the administrative machinery is now taking place in America's agency for aid. The international agencies have also acquired a great deal of valuble experience about the best methods, the best channels, and the right kind of supervision to be applied in aid programs.

Nor, in the longer run, is even the check to potential Communist expansion the most important feature of the aid effort. Its *positive* possibilities in building up the institutions and solidarity of a brotherly world order are ultimately of far greater significance and, for Western nations—wealthy beyond the dreams of avarice—of much greater moral validity as well.

But, given the present questioning mood of America, the first point to be made, when the effectiveness or continuance of aid is discussed, is that even within the single context of checking Communism the program cannot be said to have failed. On the contrary, the failure—the setback, the surprised disappointment—is largely on the Communist side. For this reason, if for no other, any decision to support foreign aid is profoundly in America's interest.

12 GOVERNMENT AND THE ECONOMY

The economic beliefs of many Americans clearly reflect the impact of nineteenth-century *laissez-faire* thinking. First, many believe in "More business in government, less government in business"—a slogan posited on the assumption that business, because of its profit motive, is always efficient and that government, lacking this spur, is basically inefficient. Closely related to this assumption is the view that private spending is desirable but that public spending should be feared and avoided. This view is often tied to a belief in a "balanced budget"—a belief that runs counter to current business practices, where borrowing is judged on its merits. Underlying this belief is the feeling that public debt is always dangerous, but private debt is normal. The conclusion frequently drawn is that government should always be run on a "pay-as-you-go" basis—even though this generally means, in the words of an experienced city manager, that "You pay but you don't go!" Finally, there is the view that *planning* is a nasty word—one with socialistic or communistic overtones—and something to be avoided by government, even though planning has, for many years, been the mark of enlightened businesses.

Before attempting to make a full evaluation of some of these American myths, it is necessary to establish clearly in our minds the goals generally entertained for the American political economy. Several suggestions may be advanced. The first is equality of opportunity—within the limits of the individual's ability. Second is freedom of choice—though not for the benefit of one at the expense of others; freedom is not license. Third is the goal of raising the standard of living for all, by establishing certain minimum levels of shelter, nutrition, and clothing—levels that may be exceeded but that should never be denied. Fourth is the achievement of a seemingly contradictory "dynamic stability"—so that there may be a regular and continuous growth of the economy, along with a levelling of cyclical fluctuations. Finally, there is the desirability of business and government each occupying its appropriate sphere of action. Here Americans have, in the long run, tended to follow a pragmatic rather than doctrinaire viewpoint, adhering to Lincoln's dictum that government must do for the people those things which they cannot do at all for themselves or cannot do so well.

Before proceeding to the specific problems it may be desirable to review briefly the historical pattern of governmental intervention in the economy. Far from being the product of any one political party, of any given political leader, or even of any "outside influence," the American government's programs clearly have stemmed from historical necessity—particularly from crises such as wars and depressions. In area after area, an observable pattern has emerged. First there has been a felt *need*—such as the need, in the case of the railroads, for linking our East and West Coasts. Following recognition of the needs have come grants of public *privilege*. Again in the case of the railroads, tremendous amounts of land as well as construction subsidies were provided by the government. Almost invariably, such privileges have been followed by *abuse*—in the instance of the railroads, flagrant abuse, such as legislative bribery, illegal rebates, and charging more for short hauls than for long. Inevitably, abuses have been followed by increasing public demands that "something be done about it"—that is, that government provide *regulation*. Such pressures led first to state and local regulatory attempts, then, as these fell short of the mark, to demands that the federal government intervene, in the form of the Interstate Commerce Commission. In the case of the railroads, during World War I, a fifth step followed—governmental *ownership* and operation.

With this background in mind, what are some of the major problems facing us today as we debate the government's role in an expanding economy? One problem is the battle over the allocation of resources—the public sector versus the private sector—in which most observers agree that a balance is needed. Another is the question of the administered economy. Twentieth-century economies do not operate in accordance with Adam Smith's "unseen hand"; they are directed by powerful human fingers. The question is, in whose interest and by whom are they guided? Are they guided by government, in the form of indirect or direct controls, or by industry, in the guise of market restrictions and cartel agreements? The third major problem is that of spending for defense. What is the impact of annually committing some 10 per cent of our gross national product to the military? What economic alternatives do we have in the unlikely event that a general disarmament agreement were negotiated? Finally, what about the climate of opinion in which government must operate to promote economic growth? How is the public to achieve a clear view through the repeated propaganda smoke screens belched forth by special interests all the way from labor through agriculture to industry?

These are some of the problems that must be assessed in attempting to understand the economic concerns of our government in action, its purpose in promoting and in regulating business, and its programs in the field of monetary and fiscal policy.

HOW PLANNED IS OUR ECONOMY?

James Tobin

James Tobin is Sterling Professor of Economics at Yale University and a former member of the Council of Economic Advisers.

For Americans of sufficient age and memory, much current political debate about government and business must sound comfortably familiar. Like the New Deal and Fair Deal before it, the New Frontier has provoked shrill warnings that an "anti-business" Administration seeks to supplant the "free-enterprise system" with a "planned economy." Some public defenders of free enterprise, their natural hostility to government muted during eight years of Republican rule, have scarcely concealed their enthusiasm at finding Washington once again occupied by the enemy.

The Kennedy Administration has been puzzled and hurt to find itself cast in this role. Unlike its Democratic predecessors, the New Frontier leaned over backward to avoid earning an "anti-business" label and to forestall suspicions that it contemplated radical changes in U.S. economic institutions. Evidently there is still considerable misunderstanding—between the Administration and its critics, and in the public at large—about the role of government policies and plans in a private enterprise economy such as ours.

To what extent can and does the Federal Government plan and control the American economy? Do the economic measures of the Kennedy Administration, including the pending tax bill, involve any increase in Federal planning and control?

To answer these questions, it is essential to begin with a simple distinction, all too rarely respected in public discussion. The distinction is between *plans* and *controls*. In the context of everyday life, planning simply means "thinking ahead," basing current actions and decisions on rational calculation of their future consequences. In discussions of government and the economy, however, *planning* connotes to many people an elaborate regime of coercive *controls* over the daily economic behavior of business managers, workers, and consumers. There is no necessary connection between the two. Clearly there is a great difference between planning one's own actions and coercing the actions of others, between using forethought and using force.

DIRECT CONTROLS

Government controls over the activities of specific business firms and individuals—specifying the quantities of materials they can buy and stock, the kinds and quantities of goods they can or must sell to different customers, the prices they may or must charge—are familiar to the American people from the Second World War. No one in his right mind wishes to revive the battery of war-time controls unless another full-scale military mobilization is forced upon us.

A few controls, some Federal, others state and local, are permanently scattered over the peacetime economic landscape. These are quite a mixed bag. Some, like the strengthened drug legislation adopted in the wake of the thalidomide scare, are meant simply to safeguard public health or safety. The rates and services of public utilities are regulated, on the grounds that customers of natural or government-franchised monopolies lack the automatic protection of competition. Elsewhere, some direct government interventions, like those under the anti-trust laws, are intended to preserve or restore competition. Other interventions are designed to shelter producers from competition among themselves and with others; examples are agricultural price and production controls, minimum wages, "fair trade" laws, oil production and import quotas.

In short, the direct economic controls we have in peacetime serve a variety of very special purposes, or cross-purposes, and interests. They are administered by special Federal and state agencies, many of which enjoy considerable autonomy. These controls are certainly not available to any Federal Administration as instruments of an overall economic strategy or "plan."

The Kennedy Administration's approach to special-purpose direct controls has varied pragmatically with the subject matter. If the President has favored tighter production controls over farmers in order to save Federal money, he has also proposed to dismantle many government regulations restricting competition in the transportation industries.

INDIRECT CONTROLS—THE BUDGET

To carry out a general policy to promote economic stability and growth, the Government must rely on quite different instruments, mainly on fiscal and monetary measures. These are general, impersonal and diffuse in their effects upon economic activity. Unlike the detailed controls of war-time, these measures do not supplant markets or prevent the forces of supply and demand from determining the prices and quantities of goods and services bought and sold. They do not work through orders to particular firms or individuals to take, or to refrain from taking, specific actions. But they do affect the general market environment in which businessmen and consumers freely make choices and decisions. For these reasons, they are sometimes called "indirect controls."

The major indirect controls are Federal expenditures and receipts. The Federal Government now spends over $65 billion per year to buy goods and services (11 per cent of the gross national product), and distributes in addition more than $45 billion in veterans' pensions, social security and welfare benefits, grants-in-aid to state and local governments, and other "transfer payments" for which no current productive services are rendered.

Government expenditures affect, first of all, the economic fortunes of the individuals and businesses who actually receive the Government checks. But as the initial recipients respend the money, Government outlays are quickly and widely diffused over the whole country. Consequently an increase in Federal expenditures, whatever its initial purpose and distribution, is an injection of general purchasing power into the economy. Just like injections of purchasing power from private sources, a rise in Federal spending tends to increase sales, jobs, incomes, profits, and sometimes prices, throughout the economy.

On the other side of the budget ledger, taxes drain purchasing power from the economy. Higher taxes affect first of all the tax payers on whom they are levied. But the reduction in their ability to spend spreads to the whole economy, generally reducing sales, jobs, incomes, profits and sometimes prices.

The converse is also true. The major economic proposal of the Kennedy Administration has been the $11 billion income-tax cut now before the Congress. The Administration became convinced in 1962 that full employment could not be restored or maintained without a new and substantial stimulus to consumer and business spending.

The budget, therefore, packs tremendous power for inflation or deflation, for growth or stagnation, for unemployment or full employment. This power neither vanishes if ignored nor increases if acknowledged. To plan the budget with a view to over-all economic balance does not add to the Government's power over the economy. It is only an attempt to exercise this power rationally rather than blindly.

In almost all advanced countries, the economic power of the budget has long since been explicitly acknowledged. In France, Germany, the United Kingdom, the Netherlands, Sweden—to name a few countries which in other respects differ widely both economically and politically—the Government budget is regarded as a major instrument of general economic planning, not simply as an accounting device to facilitate internal governmental housekeeping.

In those countries the Government attempts through each year's budget to achieve a balance between aggregate purchasing power and the capacity of the country to produce. The budget is consciously made tighter—with higher taxes relative to expenditures—if excessive purchasing power threatens inflation or balance-of-payments difficulties. It is consciously made easier—through lower taxes or higher expenditures—if deficiencies of total demand threaten to produce unemployment and excess capacity.

In our own country, unfortunately, the economic use of the Government budget is only now emerging from the area of ideological controversy. Indeed it is probably anxiety over the budget—rather than any proliferation of direct controls—which is at the bottom of many current complaints about "economic planning."

Some business leaders, particularly in the Committee for Economic Development, have long since joined the great majority of economists in advocating flexible budget policy. But a large segment of business opinion, and of general public opinion, regards it as heresy to frame the Federal budget with any end in view except strict balance of administrative expenditures and receipts. The evils of deficit financing are a favorite theme of political orators. We are hearing a great deal about them during the debate on the proposed tax cut. We will hear even more in 1964.

INDIRECT CONTROLS—MONEY

The other main "indirect control" is monetary policy. Under the Constitution the Federal Government has the inescapable power and responsibility of a central government "to coin money, regulate the value thereof."

As the economy has developed, bank checks have supplanted coins and paper currency as the usual means of payment. The Government therefore has acquired, mainly through the Federal Reserve Act of 1913, significant control of the aggregate volume of bank deposits and bank credit. Banks are required to hold a certain percentage of their deposits as reserves, either in vault cash or on deposit with Federal Reserve Banks. The percentage required can be within limits varied by Federal Reserve authorities. More important, the "Fed" controls, principally by open market transactions in government securities, the aggregate dollar volume of reserve assets available to the banks to satisfy the requirements.

These are indirect and impersonal controls. Although they decisively affect general monetary and credit conditions throughout the economy, they do not interfere with the free choices of individual banks, depositors and borrowers, or with competition among banks for deposits and loans.

Not even the most doctrinaire advocate of laissez-faire favors free enterprise in the minting of coins or the printing of paper currency; and few would argue that the quantity of bank-created money can safely be left to unfettered competition among private banks. There is no escape from the fact that the Government possess and must exercise monetary powers over the economy. Tight money restricts, and easy money encourages, private borrowing and spending. The only issue is whether these powers are to be exercised for narrowly defined monetary objectives or, in planned concert with the Government's fiscal powers, for the broad objectives of economic stability and growth.

PLANS AND THE LAW

Critics who detect tendencies toward economic planning in Washington should recall the Employment Act of 1946. This act, passed by heavy bipartisan majorities, charges the Federal Government to concert the various measures at its command in the interest of achieving "maximum employment, production, and purchasing power." The President and his Council of Economic Advisers are directed to keep track of trends in employment, production and purchasing power, to compare levels actually obtaining with the "maximum" levels desired, to consider how Federal policies might improve the performance of the economy, and to report to the Congress on these matters at least once a year.

With this act as a solemn expression of national policy, no Administration, Democratic or Republican, can avoid a modest amount of economic planning. At all times—and especially when the yearly budget and legislative program are being prepared—the President, his Cabinet officers and advisers, and the Federal Reserve authorities must be asking themselves: Is total demand in the economy likely to be deficient or adequate or excessive? Should the Government give demand a boost, by spending more or taxing less or by an easier monetary policy? Or should demand be checked either by a tighter budget or more restrictive credit policies?

Of course, economic diagnosis and therapy are far from being exact sciences. There is always plenty of room for disagreement about appropriate policy. That is precisely why the Employment Act provides, in the Joint Economic Committee of the Congress, machinery for a critical appraisal of the President's diagnosis and recommendations.

In addition to its pending tax bill, the Kennedy Administration has also proposed to sharpen the tools of fiscal and monetary management. In January, 1962, the President proposed three measures to reinforce the Federal Government's arsenal of anti-recession weapons: (1) A procedure by which the President could make temporary uniform reductions not exceeding five percentage points in personal income tax rates, (2) a standby program of public capital expenditures, to be triggered by increases in unemployment, and (3) permanent improvement of unemployment insurance, including automatic lengthening of benefit periods during times of high unemployment.

None of these proposals involves new Government controls over individuals or businesses; none of them thrusts the Government into new areas of activity. But they would greatly strengthen the Government's hand in carrying out the purposes of the Employment Act. Unfortunately the Congress has not acted on any of these proposals.

Along with the central objective of the Employment Act, high employment, the Administration has emphasized two other economic objectives. One is the long-run growth of the economy, and the other is restoration of balance between the nation's international payments and receipts.

HOW MUCH GROWTH?

Unlike its predecessor, which was sometimes contemptuous of "growthmanship," the present Administration explicitly aims at a higher growth rate—specifically to reach 4½ per cent per year in the sixties, compared to the 2½ per cent realized in the years 1953–60. As one means toward this end, the Administration has sought to encourage business investment—by maintaining as easy credit conditions as international monetary conditions permit, by reforming the tax treatment of depreciation, and by offering a 7 per cent credit against taxes for expenditures for new equipment.

Some purists, both liberal and conservative, have objected to using the tax system to stimulate investment. But their purism seems misplaced, if it means that a tax structure shot through with loopholes which serve narrow private ends should not be adapted to serve a ranking national objective. At any rate, these measures can scarcely be described as "antibusiness."

The Administration's interest in growth does not mean new controls over business or individuals. No one is to be ordered to grow! All that the growth orientation implies is a somewhat different emphasis in the use of traditional instruments of policy—the budget, the tax structure and monetary control.

At the same time, more explicit long-range economic planning, both public and private, may help to promote economic growth. France has found it useful for the Government to cooperate with business and labor in projecting the French economy ahead for four or five years. The French plan indicates a feasible rate of growth for the economy as a whole (5½ per cent per year under the current plan, for 1961–65), together with corresponding estimates of the growth of major sectors, public and private.

These estimates are in no sense compulsory. But they give French businessmen valuable guidance and mutual confidence. Each industry can make the investments which growth requires with some assurance that similar investments by others will expand its markets.

A somewhat similar exercise by the Committee for Economic Development in 1943, "Markets After the War," helped to raise the sights of American businessmen to the unprecedented levels of peacetime demand of which a prosperous American economy was capable. The Conservative Government in Britain, in the hope of raising Britain's sluggish growth rate, is importing French planning procedures. Development of cooperation and trust between Government, business and labor in the United States may some day permit similar procedures—which involves no Government controls—to be used in promoting steadier and faster economic expansion in this country.

WAGES AND PRICES

But does not the dramatic steel-price episode of April, 1962, prove that the Administration seeks to substitute government controls for private decisions? It proves, if anything, the opposite, for the Administration's actions were part of a determined effort to defend the dollar *without* new controls.

Ever since the war, pressures for wage and price increases, arising from concentrations of wage and price-making power in unions and corporations, have been a major problem in all democratic industrial countries. Indirect controls—that is, restrictive monetary and fiscal measures—can eliminate these pressures, if at all, only at heavy costs in unemployment and underproduction. In some countries, notably the Netherlands, the answer to this cruel dilemma has been government control of wages and prices.

This is certainly an unacceptable solution for the United States. But in the face of serious balance-of-payments difficulties, the U.S. cannot afford new twists of the wage-price spiral. Whatever their disagreements on other matters, the Councils of Economic Advisers of both Presidents Eisenhower and Kennedy have agreed on the principles of non-inflationary wage and price behavior. Both Presidents have tried to throw the moral weight of the Presidency and of public opinion on the side of restraint in wage negotiations and price decisions. Nevertheless, as many recent events demonstrate, these decisions remain in private hands.

The Government has been involved, one way or another, in every labor-management dispute and settlement in steel since the war. No Administration can regard a stoppage in so basic an industry as a purely private concern to which the Government is indifferent. Vice President Nixon and other officers of the Eisenhower Administration arranged the settlement which ended the 116-day steel strike of 1959. The settlement reached in early 1960 involved a 3.7 per cent per year increase in hourly employment costs but was accompanied by no price increase.

In 1962, the Kennedy Administration sought to encourage the parties to reach a new steel labor contract without a strike well before the June 30 deadline. But, as the President had made clear to everyone as early as the previous September, the Administration did not seek peace at any price level. The President and Secretary Goldberg sought a non-inflationary settlement, holding the wage increase within the range of productivity gains in order to permit stability in steel prices.

It was a fair assumption that the 1962 settlement met this test—the increase in hourly employment costs, 2½ per cent per year, was the most moderate since the war. The ink was scarcely dry on the new contracts when U.S. Steel precipitated the famous events of April 10–13. After using his moral influence to obtain moderation from the union, the President could scarcely have failed to speak out against the announced price increase. . . .

The economic record of the New Frontier does not justify the dark suspicions and heated attacks of which it has been the target. Probably there is today a greater and more stable social consensus on the frontiers between government activity and private enterprise than at any time in this century.

No influential opinion—least of all in a Democratic Administration which entrusts communication satellites to a private corporation—supports nationalization of any private industry. (And only the lunatic fringe on the right wants to denationalize the post office or abolish the public schools.) No one—least of all a Democratic Administration which reforms the tax system to encourage business investment and proposes to lower top-bracket income tax rates—is seriously proposing massive government efforts to redistribute income and wealth. No one—except perhaps some business groups—seeks to use government power to shift the present balance of power between organized labor and management. No one seriously advocates any general extension of the list of direct government controls over the economic activities of individuals and business firms. These may have been the great issues that aroused the ideological battalions in the past, but they are not very relevant today.

Plenty of issues remain. But they are not for the most part questions of widening or narrowing the sphere of government activity. Rather they are differences of view about national priorities among various government activities—defense, space, education, etc.—and between public and private uses of economic resources. Or they concern the best use of existing government powers to achieve full employment, stability and economic progress.

It is not surprising that many observers differ with the Kennedy Administration's policies and proposals. What is surprising, in the 1960's is that some critics have regarded the Administration's economic program—and sometimes the very fact that it has a program—as an occasion for summoning the troops to a new anti-government crusade.

For surely it is a proper concern of the Government whether the economy is in recession or prosperity, whether unemployment is 7 per cent or 4 per cent of the labor force, whether prices are rising or reasonably stable, whether the dollar is weak or strong abroad, whether the gross national produce is $500 or $570 or $600 billion, and whether the G.N.P. is, on average, growing at 2½ or 4½ per cent per year. If conscious and coherent policy to discharge these responsibilities is "planning," then the Administration is guilty.

THE NATIONAL DEBT AND THE PERIL POINT

J. David Stern

Born in Philadelphia and a graduate of the University of Pennsylvania, J. David Stern began his career in journalism in 1908. Four years later, he bought the *New Brunswick Times,* the first of a string of papers across the country whose fortunes he directed in a liberal tradition. As publisher of the *Philadelphia Record* and the *New York Post,* he became a power in eastern politics and a close friend and adviser of F.D.R.

If a man had twenty pounds a year and spent nineteen pounds, nineteen shillings, and sixpence, he would be happy, but if he spent twenty pounds sixpence, he would be miserable.

Thus Mr. Micawber expounded his theory of economics to David Copperfield. In modern terms: Balance the budget and all is well: unbalance it on the minus side and you are on the road to hell.

My generation (I am seventy-seven years old) was brought up on this theory, buttressed by eighteenth-century maxims in *Poor Richard's Almanack,* such as: "The first [vice] is running in debt." "Beware of little expenses; A small leak will sink a great ship," and many others of the same ilk. (Nor are these eighteenth-century proverbs entirely forgotten. Printing Industries of New York recently sent Dr. Walter W. Heller, chairman of the Council of Economic Advisers, a specially printed, deluxe book of Ben Franklin's warnings against debt.)

Bankers swelled the chorus. They extolled thrift and savings accounts, discouraged debt. In those days banks did not have small-loan departments.

From *Atlantic Monthly,* January 1964. Reprinted by permission.

Small loans were left to "loan sharks," who charged exorbitant interest and were less respectable than pawnbrokers. Only the improvident patronized stores which gave long-term credit.

Conditioned by such propaganda, I was scared when I borrowed $10,000 to buy my first newspaper in 1912. It did not lead to disaster. Having made this first plunge, I kept on going deeper and deeper into debt during my thirty-five years of publishing seven newspapers. When I retired in 1947 my newspapers, radio station, and paper mill owed $5,500,000. My debt had increased 550-fold, but the value of my properties had grown almost a thousand-fold, from $12,500 to $12 million. So there was a margin left for old age.

My experience was not unusual. Most businesses borrow to expand. Credit has been as essential to industrial growth as were steam and electric power. Look over the balance sheets of giant corporations, the "blue chips," in Wall Street parlance. They are all in debt.

Our point of view has changed. Debt has become respectable, not only for the businessman but for the householder. Installment buying is a major force in our economy. The government encourages newlyweds to start their married life in a home bought for next to nothing down and with a forty-year mortgage. Through its Small Business Administration it helps small enterprises to grow by going into debt. And the banks have changed their tune. Now they advertise and promote small loans more than savings accounts. Debt is no longer regarded as evil in itself. It is what you do with the money after you borrow it that really matters; how well you invest and not the fact of borrowing is the true yardstick.

In our expanding economy Micawber seems forgotten—except in one most important instance. When the federal government debt is at issue, Micawber's ghost walks again and resurrects the ancient shibboleths. A protean ghost, it usually assumes the form of an elder statesman to croak, "Debt will ruin the nation." It has been repeating that refrain as far back as I can remember. Sixty years ago it was predicting that a $500 million appropriation for the Panama Canal would bankrupt the country. Thirty years ago, taking the form of General Robert E. Wood, president of Sears Roebuck, it went about the nation alerting the populace to the danger of President Roosevelt's profligacy. In the guise of General Wood, Micawber's ghost ended every speech with a warning that when the federal debt reached $25 billion, the dollar would be worthless. While performing his Paul Revere stunt the ghost pointed with pride to President Hoover, who balanced the budget, achieved a billion-dollar surplus, and reduced the national debt during the first three years of his Administration. Readers over fifty remember what happened in 1932. At the same time, General Wood, in the flesh, was borrowing money in order to expand his company into the largest retail organization in the world.

Micawber's ghost warns us that the spendthrift Democratic Administration is leading the government into bankruptcy. And our newspapers and magazines, largely controlled by ultraconservative wealth, give the front page to this foreboding.

Typical of this concerted effort to scare the living daylights out of the average citizen was the lead article in the *Reader's Digest* for May, 1963, entitled "The Real Truth About the Federal Budget." "Incredible. Inviting disaster. Staggering," shouts the ghost from the floor of Congress, this time in the guise of Congressman Clarence Cannon, chairman of the House Appropriations Committee, a fitting embodiment of Micawber's shade since Cannon is almost as old as Micawber and a character straight out of Dickens.

By the end of the *Reader's Digest* article the ghost has assumed an even more appropriate corporeal form, that of Senator Harry F. Byrd, chairman of the Senate Finance Committee, boss of Virginia, and president of the Micawber Chowder and Marching Club, which proudly flaunts its slogan, "Debt is a dirty word." So faithful is Byrd to Micawber's theory of economics that he has forbidden the state of Virginia to contract any more debt. As a result, Virginia's cities and counties must finance essential public works, schools, water, sewers, and so forth, at much higher rates of interest than the state could command. So Byrd's loyalty to Micawber is costing his fellow citizens many millions of dollars a year. Virginia lags behind other states in urgently needed improvements, and some of the leaders in Byrd's own organization are in open revolt. What does the ghost, posing, as Byrd, have to say at the close of the article?—"This loose spending must stop." No matter how many shapes the ghost takes, it is consistent.

Another typical Micawber article was the lead in the *Saturday Evening Post* of May 18, 1963. The title "Spending into Trouble" is followed by a subhead "We are stealing from our grandchildren in order to satisfy our desires of today." This time the ghost speaks through President Eisenhower. Like the *Reader's Digest* tirade, it is packed with half truths and forebodings of doom from debt. Neither these two pieces nor any of the warnings which clutter our press have comparative statistics on which an intelligent appraisal of the national debt can be based. Nor do they measure the national debt against growth in business, wealth, and population.

Without some frame of reference, discussion of the debt is meaningless. Such attacks on the Kennedy Administration's fiscal policy are tedious repetitions of Micawber's theory: balance the budget or ruin.

What are the facts?

The nation is growing faster than its debt.

Its debt is shrinking in proportion to its wealth and ability to pay.

As a result of World War II, our national debt in 1947 was $257 billion. That was 10 percent more than the gross national product, or total business done in that year. In 1962 the national debt was 55 percent of the gross national product, proportionately half as much as it had been fifteen years before.

The GNP is a useful yardstick for economists. But let us use a more familiar tape measure: take-home pay, or personal income after taxes, or "personal disposable income," as the President's Council of Economic Advisers calls it.

In 1947 the national debt was 151 percent of net personal disposable income; in 1962, 80 percent. Here are the figures of the Administrations from Truman through Eisenhower to Kennedy:

	National Debt (billions)	*Net Disposable Personal Income (billions)*	*Percentage of National Debt to Personal Income*
1947	$257	$170.1	151%
1952	267.4	258.7	112%
1957	275	308.8	90%
1962	304	382.7	80%

Not only is the national debt decreasing in relation to personal income and volume of business; it is also decreasing in proportion to population. Since 1947 the population has increased 29 percent, the national debt 18 percent. The above figures can be restated on a per capita basis as follows:

	Population	*Per Capita Personal Income*	*Per Capita National Debt*	*Percentage of Per Capita Debt to Per Capita Income*
1947	144,126,000	$1180	$1783	151%
1952	156,947,000	1521	1700	112%
1957	171,278,000	1803	1600	81%
1962	186,591,000	2051	1600	78%

We can translate this table into the budget problems of a family of five. Mr. and Mrs. John Doe and their three children consider the household budget. "In fifteen years our debts are down," says Mr. Doe. "From $8900 to $8000," complains Mrs. Doe. "I don't call that much." "But at the same time my take-home pay has nearly doubled," replies Mr. Doe. "So we are really much better off. By budgeting ten percent of the family income we could pay off all our debts in eight years. It would have taken twice as long at the rate we were going fifteen years ago. That's progress."

As far as the national debt is concerned, we are certainly making progress. But during the past fifteen years corporate debt has increased 204 percent; personal debt, including home mortgages, 389 percent; state and local government debt 400 percent. These facts are never mentioned when Micawber's ghost damns the national debt. We will now all rise while the ghost leads us in singing the patriotic song "Debt's OK, in every way, for everyone, but not for Uncle Sam."

Without considering the income and resources of a debtor it is impossible to calculate whether his debt is too great. I am reminded of a profound question, worthy of an elder statesman, propounded by my granddaughter, aged six.

"How much is too much?" she asked.

" 'Too' and 'much' are connecting words," I explained. "meaningless unless hooked to things or ideas. A pile of hay might be too much for a horse, too little for an elephant. Five pieces of candy are too many for you, too few for your birthday party."

This is childish talk, but no more childish than debates in Congress on setting a fixed-dollar limit to the national debt, rather than a limit based on a percentage of GNP, national income, or some other composite frame of reference.

Why is the public kept in ignorance of the comparative statistics which would enable it to judge for itself the financial state of the nation? I have already mentioned one reason. Our communications are controlled by wealthy ultraconservatives who are congenitally allergic to government spending. Another reason is that our articulators, the columnists who write so entertainingly, the commentators who talk so glibly, are, generally speaking, weak on figures. They avoid statistics and percentages. Their excuse is that the public would not understand or be interested. I have long felt that they do not give their audience credit for the intelligence with which it is endowed.

But the chief fault lies with the present Administration, which has done little to counteract conservative propaganda. In one address, President Kennedy did compare the national debt to the gross national product, but he neglected to explain GNP, a technical term familiar to less than a tenth of his audience. Nor, as far as I have been able to discover, has any other spokesman for the Administration discussed the relative size of the national debt against any frame of reference.

Under these circumstances it is easy for Micawber's ghost to rouse the rabble by denouncing federal spending and debt, which imply more taxes. Even though the present proposal is to borrow to lower taxes, conservatives growl their disapproval just as Pavlov's dogs responded with conditioned reflexes. And why does this difficult ghost haunt the United States instead of his native land where the debt burden is proportionately double the amount in this country and yet is not a political issue?

The ghost is also helped by the awesome words "billion dollars," a frightening sum of money to the individual. For Uncle Sam, $1 billion is the equivalent of $100 for a family with an income of $8550—slightly more than one percent of the income. To counteract the billion-dollar scare propaganda, the Administration must drive home lessons in proportion and take the bigness out of "billion" by homely contrast of government finance with everyday transactions. To give an example: a country dentist, with an income of $10,000, asks his bank for a $1000 loan.

"What for?" asks the village banker, not like big-city bankers, who nowadays lend without asking. Besides, he is suffering from a toothache, which makes him momentarily disinclined to grant a loan, even to a Rockefeller.

"To modernize my office," the dentist replies.

"Why go heavier into debt?" the banker snarls. "You still owe on your home and car."

"With better equipment I could increase my practice," the dentist explains.

"I could treat patients more quickly and with less pain." The phrase "with less pain" gets the banker where it hurts, and the loan is granted.

The proposal to borrow $11 billion to stimulate business by lowering taxes is in about the same proportion to government income as the dentist's loan to his income. And the Administration's plan is designed to alleviate some of the pains with which the body politic is presently afflicted—unemployment, depressed areas, racial tensions. Only in a period of full employment can we hope to make any real progress in upgrading the employment of minority groups, which is one of the essentials in solving the racial problem.

Even a banker, grouchy with a toothache, would not denounce the dentist's loan as spending "into decadence and peril." But those are the words Micawber's ghost, speaking through Eisenhower, used to describe President Kennedy's plan. And nowhere in the many attacks do I find mention, let alone consideration, of the ills and injustices which the plan is designed to cure.

Most men of wealth, particularly those who started poor and acquired affluence late in life, are emotional about money. It is hard for them to think objectively about the magic force which changed their lives. This King Midas syndrome explains their aversion to John Maynard Keynes, greatest economist of the twentieth century. Keynes defined money as a no-par share in the purchasing power of a nation, an abstraction, an entry on a bank ledger. Such a concept is anathema to Midas, who harbors the subconscious desire to possess money he can bite. Keynes held that a nation in depression should borrow and spend more than its income. President Franklin D. Roosevelt took his advice. He incurred deficits for unemployment relief and public works, which were factors in curing the Depression.

Many a business has gone into debt to rescue itself from decline. In 1933, at the height of the Depression, my competitors stopped all circulation promotion. I borrowed $250,000 to put a couple of hundred unemployed to work soliciting subscriptions for the *Philadelphia Record*. To borrow wisely, at the right time, is the key to many a business success. Commodore Vanderbilt said, "A millionaire isn't the man who has a million but the man who can borrow a million."

President Eisenhower writes, "I know that the economic theorists (have) convinced themselves that what . . . counts is the relationship between the debt and the gross national product. . . . As long as the debt doesn't grow out of proportion to the gross national product, they believe, the country will remain in sound financial condition. But what they don't point out is that nobody really knows where this theoretical peril point might be."

There is a peril point in nearly everything we do, but if that were to keep us from doing, we would be a backward nation. There is a peril point in pioneering, and some of our Founding Fathers got mighty close to it. There is a peril point in drinking, so we were persuaded to try prohibition. There is a peril point in swimming out into the ocean. If you haven't strength to return, you drown.

Because we sent General Eisenhower what he needed to win the war, the national debt rose to 110 percent of GNP. Perhaps we were approaching the "peril point." But no one suggested cutting down our shipments of ammunition.

Now the national debt is 55 percent of GNP, so we are far from the peril point. The real peril is that federal, state, and local taxes take too large a percentage of national income and thus retard economic growth. The President's Council of Economic Advisers figures that we are approaching that peril point. It wants to avoid it by lowering taxes. If this tactic stimulates the economy, reduces unemployment, absorbs the teenagers entering the labor field in greater numbers each year, the GNP will soar well over $600 billion, and the government's income will exceed its budget. That should make everybody happy, including Micawber's ghost.

The debate as to which comes first, balancing the budget according to Micawber or balancing the economy according to Keynes, is not an abstract controversy. It is fundamental to the immediate problems which vex the nation today. If President Eisenhower is looking for peril points, he can find them in a growing population with a static economy.

If your only excuse for shouting "fire" in a theater is that you do not like the actors, you are going to spend a long time in jail. Shout "ruin and disaster" about the state of the nation and the First Amendment will protect you, even if you have as little reason to cry your alarm as when you cried "fire" because you disapproved of the actors.

The peril point is not in the budget but in the minds of reactionaries. As Senator Joseph S. Clark of Pennsylvania has said, "Perhaps no topic (national debt) in our time has been the victim of so much nonsense."

Our nation is growing faster than its debt. Those words are the magic formula to lay Micawber's ghost.

CAN OUR ECONOMY STAND DISARMAMENT?

Gerard Piel

Gerard Piel, who served as Science Editor of *Life* magazine from 1938 to 1944, is the publisher of *Scientific American,* a periodical that, during the past fifteen years, has become one of the most influential expositors of the atomic age.

There is a tempo in the common experience of our species that is racing ahead of the biological clock. Events all out of scale with the rate and dimen-

From *Atlantic Monthly,* September 1962. Reprinted by permission.

sions of life processes have transpired and impend. If mankind had time, I would have no doubt about the outcome. Human heredity, however, is accumulative and selective and is transmitted by teaching and learning. Man, in consequence, has evolved more rapidly than all of the inventions of nature. As the beneficiaries of this late, new phase of evolution, we cannot fail to call it by the name of progress. But, all too suddenly and unprepared, we have come to a fork in the road. The progress of which I speak has disclosed the noblest and most generous ends to human life and has placed in our hands the means to accomplish them here on this earth. In the command of those same means, progress has given the power of irrevocable decision to our historic capacity for cruelty and folly.

The promise of tomorrow is no less convincing than the threat that there may be no tomorrow, and I do not despair. My hope comes from what I know is in the hearts of the best men among us, and my confidence from what I know is in their heads. By one reckoning, we have two years. There were twenty-five years, time for one generation to grow up, between 1914 and 1939. June, 1962, is not quite twenty-three years since August, 1939.

Instability is inherent in the most sensible and humane argument for stability in the present impasse in world politics. Our national security is defended, we are told, by our power to retaliate. The Soviets do not dare to try to overwhelm us with their nuclear striking power, because they know that we could overwhelm them in return. This is the balance of terror. It is said to be secure against rational strategies, at least, on either side. That is, no statesman presently in power is likely to find a reason for attempting the first nuclear strike, which would expose his own constituency to annihilation by the other side.

In recent months, however, even this insecure notion of security has been undergoing serious stress and revision. Unofficial leaks and official disclosures from the highest quarters in our government tell us that there is a considerable imbalance in the balance of terror. From the President himself, from the Secretary of Defense and his undersecretary, from senators and congressmen, and from the back door of the Pentagon, we have learned that our country is equipped with a ready nuclear strike force that dwarfs the Soviet ready strike force in destructive power. In other words, there is no missile gap, nor any bomber gap, and there never was. Throughout the eight years of their stewardship, the Republicans stoutly denied, against the claims of the Democrats, that there was such a gap. Now the Democrats are in office, and they are denying it in turn. In fact, they have released sufficient information to permit estimates that our ready strike force outnumbers and outweighs that of the Soviet Union by at least five times.

To appreciate the significance of this situation requires some consideration of the technical details. The destructive power of nuclear weapons is commonly expressed on a somewhat misleading scale of tons of chemical high explosives. Thus, a one-megaton nuclear weapon is, by definition, equivalent to a million tons of TNT. Hans Bethe has calculated that this is just a little less than the combined explosive power of all the old-fashioned bombs dropped on Germany in the course of World War II. To a certain extent, the comparison must be discounted. A ten-megaton bomb is not ten million times more destructive than a one-ton high-explosive blockbuster, because a nuclear weapon discharges all of its devastating energy at one point in space. The radius of destruction by blast increases only as the cube root of increase in explosive power. The destruction at that point is the more complete, however, because the weapon discharges its energy at a single instant in time.

But blast is only part of the story. The exploding nuclear bomb evolves into a gigantic fireball—three and a half miles in diameter in the case of a ten-megaton bomb. The incendiary effect of the thermal radiation from the fireball increases as the square root of the increase in explosive power. In other words, the bigger bombs yield more destruction by fire than by blast.

Thus, the blast from a ten-megaton bomb will obliterate an area five miles in radius, but the heat from the fireball will incinerate an area within a radius of twelve miles. If you draw these circles around the Statehouse in Boston, for example, you will see the central city destroyed by blast and the entire metropolitan region enveloped in fire. With the handy circular slide rule furnished by the government along with the new weapons-effects handbook, you can calculate that an attack with a total weight of about 1000 megatons directed against the 111 largest metropolitan regions in the country could yield up to 100 million casualties. The effects of fallout may be neglected in these calculations, because the airbursts that would maximize the effects of blast and fire produce no local fallout.

My object in presenting these figures is to show that the civilian population is highly vulnerable to nuclear attack. This means, in turn, that a purely deterrent strike force need be of no more than modest size. Fewer than 1000 megatons—a few hundred megatons—emplaced in secure or hardened bases have enough retaliatory killing power to keep the enemy from striking your population first. If both sides would commit themselves to a second-strike strategy, the arms race could terminate in a draw with relatively small deterrent forces on each side.

Most citizens, I suppose, have been under the impression that we have no more than a deterrent force, one that just about offsets its Soviet counterpart. It comes as a surprise to realize that we are armed on a different scale entirely. Our nuclear force is of a size, in fact, that brings into the realm of feasibility another kind of strategy. The objective of this strategy is to knock out the enemy's deterrent. To appreciate what this implies, we must return to the technical details.

Against a hardened target, such as an underground missile-launching silo, the blast and fire of an airburst are of little avail. The attacker must groundburst his weapon in the hope of engulfing the target directly in the crater or of bringing it at least within the so-called "plastic zone" of disrupted terrain surrounding the crater. When a ten-megaton bomb is employed for such a purpose, its effective radius shrinks to less than a mile. To be confident of success, an attacker must be prepared to dispatch two or more big weapons to every hardened target. The destruction of the 1000 hardened Minuteman missile installations contemplated in the Administration's present military program, for example, would require an attack with the astronomical dimension of 20,000 megatons. A hit at each target calls for pinpoint location of the target, a continent away, and fantastically accurate guidance of the missiles. The preparation of such a counterforce attack, therefore, implies resolute intelligence work and endless research and testing, as well as a huge preponderance of striking power.

Now, there is a school of military strategists and publicists who argue for a counterforce strategy in justification of our overwhelming nuclear superiority. As a matter simply of engineering, they say that it is possible for us to strike first and disarm our antagonist. We could then hold his civil population hostage under the threat of a second strike, to be aimed at his cities. On moral grounds, they claim, we are entitled to such a pre-emptive strike because our antagonist would do it to us if he could.

But the pre-emptive strike, also known as "retaliation in advance," is still not a rational strategy. Its proponents concede that we would have to be ready to absorb some "acceptable" number of casualties—up to one third of our population, say—because we cannot be sure of knocking out all the Soviet nuclear striking power. That is why the pre-emptive strategists are numbered among the most ardent advocates of civil defense. On the other hand, the popular apathy toward civil defense would indicate that ordinary citizens have not yet adopted this approach to the solution of world problems.

I do not believe that the advocates of the pre-emptive strike have had any significant influence on U.S. military planning. Certainly no responsible civilian or uniformed official of our government has ever voiced such a proposal.

The official justification for our present military posture takes a different line. Thanks to our superiority in nuclear striking power, it is said, the second-strike capability that would remain to us after a first strike by the enemy would be vastly greater than his first strike. The built-in contradiction that makes nonsense of this statement scarcely calls for explicit exposure: an enemy so heavily outgunned could not conceivably be contemplating a first strike.

So long as the game of nuclear war is played on paper, however, there is never a last word. It can still be argued that our overwhelming nuclear power promotes our security because it interdicts a first strike from the other side. A corollary to this argument is that the other side should also feel more secure in our possession of a potential first-strike capability. They have been given to understand, in fact, that we would never strike first, except on some intolerable provocation.

Yet, somehow, our nuclear armament has failed to promote stability in world politics. The Soviet Union called off the moratorium on nuclear testing last year and reversed the hopeful downward trend in its military expenditures. When disarmament talks resumed this year in Geneva, the Russians proved to be more than ever obsessively concerned with their geographical security and resistant to early inspection.

Our enormous armament also complicates our own approach to disarmament. We would have to do so much more disarming than anyone else that ratification by the U.S. Senate would constitute a bigger miracle than an agreement at Geneva.

Meanwhile, the prolongation of the arms race darkens the prospects of the world. If the present conference at Geneva should break down, it cannot be reconvened without the presence of China, which is on the verge of becoming a nuclear power. By that time, there will be other new nuclear powers demanding or resisting invitations to the conference. France is the first second-class power to realize that the nuclear weapon is the ultimate equalizer and to adopt this dangerous route back to the summit. As the number of players in the game approaches the nth number, the hazard from irrational strategies, or from mere accident, must increase. In the words of C. P. Snow, "We know, with the certainty of statistical truth, that if enough of these weapons are made—by enough different states—some of them are going to blow up!"

As citizens responsible for our self-government, we are confronted by grave questions concerning our responsibility in the creation of this dangerous situation. How did we come into the possession of such overwhelming capacity for violence? Since there is no rational military or political justification for it, we must look elsewhere for the answer.

I think the answer is not difficult to find. Beyond any doubt, the history of the last decade of our domestic life shows that the ruling compulsions were economic. Any student of the stock market can tell you what happens on the rumor that peace is breaking out. The oscillations of the business cycle since the Korean War can be traced, every one of them, to variation in the rate of government expenditure for arms. Military expenditure has taken up more than half of the federal budget and fully a quarter of our manufacturing output throughout this period. In the fiscal management of our economy, in other words, armament has played the same role as public works in the first two Administrations of Franklin D. Roosevelt. After ten years of this kind of pump priming, is it any wonder that our magnificent industrial establishment should have burdened us with such an enormous surplus of weapons?

Now we have to ask ourselves another question. How did our economic housekeeping fall into such disarray as to create this threat to our continued existence? To approach the answer this time, we must turn from economics to technology.

During the past twenty-five years our technology entered upon the era of automatic production. The real work of extracting nature's bounty from soil and rock and transforming it into goods is no longer done by human muscles, and less and less by human nervous systems. It is done by mechanical energy, by machines under the control of artificial nervous systems, by chemicals, and by such subtle arts as applied genetics. While the impact of these developments upon industry has attracted most of the attention, their impact upon agriculture has amounted to a revolution. Since 1939, employment on the farm has dropped from one fifth of the labor force to less than one tenth, from one worker out of five to one out of eleven. A mere six million farm workers, working fewer acres, are bursting our granaries, year after year, with unconsumed abundance. Adding up all the farmers and miners and all of the construction and factory workers, we find that not much more than one third of the labor force is engaged in producing all of the abundance that chokes the channels of distribution. Most of the rest is employed in the task of distributing the abundance, keeping books on it, and repairing and servicing its component parts. To complete our census of the labor force, we must face the most portentous of all the consequences of automatic production: more than 25 percent of the labor force today finds employment outside the normal domestic, private sector of our economy. These people are employed in the arms industries or on the public payrolls, in uniform or in civilian clothes—or they find no employment at all.

Mention of unemployment brings us back to economics. The most critical problem confronting our economic system is the insidious growth of unemployment. With each ripple in the business cycle, the number of workers left high and dry on the beach has increased. Yet, for everyone else, this has been a period of ascending prosperity. It is apparent that the disemployment of workers, both blue-collar and white-collar, has overtaken the growth of the economy and the now "classical" techniques for administering the cycle of recession and recovery from Washington.

Since no one can tell us how to get these surplus workers back to work, perhaps the time has come to ask why we must find jobs for them. Surely the aim is not to increase production. On the contrary, a little reflection shows that the objective is to increase consumption. Economists agree that the maintenance of a high level of consumption is the key to the health of the economic order. Jobs must be found for the jobless, therefore, in order to qualify them as consumers of abundance.

Our economic system and our economics are confounded by abundance because they have their roots in the history of scarcity that lies back in time beyond the industrial revolution. That revolution has come suddenly to fulfillment in our lifetime. We find it difficult to achieve equitable distribution of abundance precisely because our economic institutions are designed to secure inequitable distribution of scarcity. In the more distant past, such inequity sustained the glory of civilization. Under the management of capitalism, it financed the industrial revolution.

John Maynards Keynes told the story in his famous parable of the cake that was never to be consumed. Writing forty-two years ago, at the end of

World War I, Keynes observed that "the immense accumulations of fixed capital, built up during the half century before the war, could never have come about in a society where wealth was divided equitably." This "remarkable system," he said, "depended for its growth upon a double bluff or deception. On the one hand the laboring classes . . . were compelled, persuaded or cajoled . . . into accepting a situation in which they could call their own very little of the cake that they and nature and the capitalists were cooperating to produce. And on the other hand the capitalist classes were allowed to call the best part of the cake theirs . . . on the tacit understanding they consumed very little of it in practice."

In drawing the lesson from his parable, Keynes indulged himself in a heretical forecast of the day when the cake might be cut: "when there would at least be enough to go around. . . . In that day overwork, overcrowding and underfeeding would have come to an end, and men, secure in the comforts and necessities of the body, could proceed to the nobler exercise of their faculties."

For most other economists and for the owners and operators of the system, the perpetual growth of the cake remained "the object of true religion." It remains so today, sustained by the almost unanimous conviction of the community that high wages are bad (because they increase current consumption) and big profits are good (because they go to increase productive capacity.)

The first portent that the system had fulfilled its purpose came in the 1930s. The economics of scarcity was then confronted by the paradox of poverty in the midst of plenty. Strangely enough, as Clarence E. Ayres has pointed out, it was Keynes who saved the true religion with his "investment subterfuge." The Keynesian technique for administering the business cycle calls for increase in the current rate of investment on the downturn of the cycle, with the government supplying the funds, by deficit financing if necessary. Investment creates consumers but no addition to the consumable surplus, and so it delivers a powerful stimulus to the entire economy. The priming of the investment pump by the government was a scandalous notion when first put into practice by the New Deal, but now it is a constitutional function of our federal government.

More investment could not long serve, however, as the remedy for too much investment. Our economic system has found another way to certify citizens as consumers. The production of armaments, it turns out, can serve something like the same economic function as investment: it certifies additional workers with paychecks to consume the surplus, and yet it certainly makes no addition to the consumable surplus. By this device, by dumping a quarter of our industrial output into the sink of armament, we have achieved affluence if not abundance. For a few years, we even attained full employment. But now, in 1962, despite a 25 percent increase in military expenditure, the number of unemployed again exceeds the number of unemployed at the last recovery peak.

There are other signs that the time has come to cut the cake. The progress of technology has stirred a new ingredient into the recipe. It is the sorcerer's ingredient that so astonished the apprentice. The cake now grows out of its own substance at no cost to the abundance of its consumable output. Despite the huge appetite of the military establishment, no certified consumer goes without any good that he hankers for. Admittedly, some 50 million of us continue to be ill-fed, ill-clad, and ill-housed, but idle plant and rotting surpluses testify that we have more than enough to go around.

There is no doubt that disarmament would compel the cutting of the cake. The first word that follows disarmament in any economic analysis of the prospect is "depression." But the authors of these studies hasten to dispel, as they say, "any misconceived or exaggerated apprehensions" about the "potential economic impact of an agreement." As you read on, you are enthralled to learn what promise the future holds, when we are at last disarmed and freed to cultivate the arts of peace. In the first place, both Republicans and Democrats agree that disarmament would bring no corresponding cut in the expenditures of the federal government. The major portion of the funds released by disarmament is to be invested in the enrichment of our land and our people.

In a memorandum on the economic and social consequences of disarmament addressed to the Secretary-General of the United Nations, the Kennedy Administration declares that this country has "a backlog of demand for public services comparable in many ways to the backlog of demands for consumer durable goods and housing and producers plant and equipment at the end of World War II." By way of illustration, the memorandum shows there is demand for an additional $10 to $15 billion in our annual expenditures for education, an additional $4 billion for control of environmental pollution, and $12 billion more each year for conservation and development of natural resources. A parallel study by the National Planning Association sees need for a total annual investment of $66 billion in the realms of education, mass transportation, urban renewal, natural resources, and scientific research; this compares to a current annual investment of $30 billion in the public domain.

To the Eisenhower Administration, we are indebted for a glimpse of what the federal budget might look like after a first substantial step toward disarmament. Such figures as $7.5 billion for education, $3.7 billion for public health, $3.2 billion for urban renewal, $4 billion for resource development, and $3 billion for space research and a total increase in the federal civilian budget of about $30 billion show that Republicans can be as imaginative spenders as Democrats are reputed to be.

The Kennedy Administration has yet to make such a full-dress forecast. But a report issued by the Disarmament Agency finds it possible to pick up some of the slack from disarmament by putting $9 billion into space research. With the Galaxy out there beyond the solar system, we have no cause to worry about depression!

The consensus is clear: we can offset the reduction in the arms budget by worthwhile and overdue investment in the upgrading of our human and material resources and the enhancement of our domestic existence. The possibilities inherent in the expenditure of Pentagon-size sums of these objectives stagger the imagination.

The prospect of disarmament confronts us, therefore, with a lesson, a vision, and a question. The lesson is that the public sector—comprising the federal, state, and local governments—must continue directly and indirectly to certify a major and a growing percentage of our consumers with purchasing power. From 25 percent today, the figure is bound to go up, not down, on the day after disarmament. There is no return to normalcy in sight. On the other hand, the continued expansion in the scope and power of the government lays serious hazards to self-government. The exercise of citizenship should commend itself in leisure time.

The vision is the vision of the Founding Fathers—the realization of the values, as Ayres has catalogued them, of freedom, equality, security, abundance, and excellence in the life of the people.

The question is, What are we waiting for? If education should indeed command twice the present annual expenditure at some future date, then the children now in school are being cheated. If our cities cry out for $100 billion worth of reconstruction in the course of a half decade, some years hence, we are losing time and corrupting precious human resources in the slums and ghettos of the present. The same reasoning applies to the topsoil now going down the drain and the forests going up in smoke.

A hint of the answer to this question of why we are losing time is contained in the recent economic report of the Disarmament Agency. At one point, the report declares: "the chief obstacles . . . would be political resistance rather than deficiencies in our economic knowledge." It is difficult for anyone, including even the Secretary of Defense, to resist the demands on the public treasury laid by the armed forces. Those demands are now backed by the substantial economic interest of a giant industry exclusively devoted to armament. No such absolute moral sanction supports the claims of education, for example, and no comparable vested interest stands to gain from them. In many fields, as in natural resources and urban redevelopment, the expansion of governmental activity is bound to bring public and private interests into sharp collision. There are good grounds for the view that it will take disarmament and the threat of a great depression to overcome political resistance to our passage into the age of abundance.

But the politics of the situation can also be stated the other way. We are unlikely to get disarmament unless we are ready to embrace and vigorously advance the economic alternatives to armament. The large round numbers I have quoted from the reports and studies made thus far must be translated into programs and engineering drawings. Local and individual initiative has an important role to play in this effort, especially in those regions and industries in which armament expenditures are now concentrated. While the federal government need not and cannot assume the entire burden, a real commitment to disarmament on the part of the Administration would begin to bring the New Frontier into view on this side of the far horizon.

The choice one way or the other cannot be postponed much longer. The arms budget is losing its potency as an economic anodyne. It is concealing less and less successfully the underlying transformation of our economic system. Progress in the technology of war, as in all other branches of technology, is inexorably cutting back the payroll. With the miniaturization of violence in the step from A-bombs to H-bombs, from manned aircraft to missiles, expenditure on armaments has begun to yield a diminishing economic stimulus. Armament in any case holds out no endless frontier. By some estimates, we are already armed with the equivalent of ten tons of TNT for every man, woman, and child on earth. We acquired this monstrous capacity for destruction by a subterfuge. There is surely little to be gained, economically or militarily, by raising that figure to twenty tons. Even in the postponement of disarmament, the economic and social consequences of abundance must be recognized and accommodated in our politics. If we had acquired the kind of armament most of us thought we had, scaled to the "rational" strategy of deterrence, we would be in the midst of abundance today.

In all that I have said, I have dealt with the state of our nation in isolation from the world-wide political crisis that so heavily conditions our domestic situation. I have done so deliberately, in the conviction that our country's domestic situation plays no inconsiderable role in shaping the nature of the world crisis. It goes without saying that we do not command all the variables in current history. But we can and must put our own house in order, or we will surely lose what command we now claim. We have come to the fork in the road.

13 THE WAR ON POVERTY

The peculiarly American paradox of poverty in the midst of natural abundance was spotlighted during the great depression of 1929–1939. Farmers, unable to buy coal, burned wheat to keep warm, while coal miners, unable to buy bread, went hungry because of mine layoffs and shutdowns.

The overwhelming nature of the depression, an across-the-board economic collapse that left bank presidents and corporate managers among the unemployed, commanded full public attention and brought ultimate public action, once we had been persuaded, in the magic words of FDR, that "the thing we had most to fear was fear itself." Today's problem, however, poverty in the midst of unprecedented prosperity, is much more invidious and much more difficult to cope with, because it has left so many untouched. "Pockets of unemployment," as the economist phrases it, do not affect those who dwell outside the "pockets."

From the European point of view, it is astounding that the wealthiest nation the world has ever known, in Gunnar Myrdal's incisive wording, has "the highest rate of unemployment, . . . the worst and biggest slums, and . . . is least generous in giving economic security to its old people, its children, its sick people and its invalids." From the viewpoint of the underdeveloped world, whose nations lack the resources (both human and natural), the education, the institutions, and the capital for development, it seems incredible that a nation possessing a wealth of these resources permits so many of its own areas to remain underdeveloped.

To the American, however, things appear in a different light. So often warned against "loss of freedom" and "weakening of initiative," he seems to have an obsessive fear of "big government," even though it be his very own government—a government viewed by the rest of the world as a model of democratic responsibility and responsiveness. He fails to see any possible analogy to the wealthy miser who ultimately dies of malnutrition midst his hoards of coins and dollar bills, stock certificates and bank books.

Historically, the American people have rallied to all-out wars against foreign enemies and aggressors. The dominant question in the latter half of the twentieth century may well involve their response to an equally urgent war against poverty. But, before that war can be declared, a better understanding of it is required—we must identify the enemy and lay out the prospective lines of attack. For the mechanistic, physically oriented assaults of the past have all too often been unsuccessful, as in the public housing and slum clearance programs. Only recently have we begun to question the conclusion that slums create slum dwellers, rather than vice versa. Only recently have we begun to understand that improved formal education, urgently needed though it may be, reaches the ranks too late—that the future drop-out, the prospective juvenile delinquent, and the slum maker of tomorrow is already a year or two retarded before he steps inside the kindergarten door.

The problem of poverty in today's America is as much a familial and societal one as it is an economic one. At what stage do the seemingly normal aspirations that motivate the average family become so blunted and battered that striving for improvement slows or is cast aside as impractical? If this apathy becomes endemic, or contagious, how can society best combat it? What hope, what renewed effort can defeat it? Removing discriminatory barriers to jobs, opening channels of communication, and providing greater physical mobility through job training are feasible as well as necessary. But, since the problem involves so fundamentally the hopes and aspirations of people, it is not a failing effort but a failure to make the effort that may prove the most difficult handicap.

Thirty years ago it was fear that was most to be feared. Today it may be ignorance and apathy—lack of awareness of the problem, lack of concern over its solution—that are most to be feared. Will the American people respond wholeheartedly to this different call to arms? Or will they, through ideological fears or misguided partisanship, through a lack of understanding or a lessened sympathy, reject a government in action in the war against human misery and degradation, in the war against poverty?

THE WAR ON POVERTY
Gunnar Myrdal

Ever since he published *An American Dilemma* more than twenty years ago, the Swedish economist Gunnar Myrdal has been accepted as a sort of wise and benevolent uncle by Americans. It is said of Mr. Myrdal that Americans will willingly listen to harsh things from him that would anger them coming from almost anyone else.

Having to live with large pockets of poverty-stricken people in their midst is not a new experience in the American nation. Right from slavery the masses of Negroes formed such pockets, both in the rural South and in the cities South and North. Such pockets were also formed by other colored people who immigrated to work as laborers from Asia, Mexico and Puerto Rico. Most American Indians in their reservations were also poor and isolated as they are today. There were also, as there are still, pockets of "poor whites," ordinarily of old American stock, who lived by themselves in abject poverty and cultural isolation.

I believe it is important to have in our minds this broad picture of the historical reality of American poverty as a background to the discussion of the problems facing us today. The regular, prosperous Americans have be-

From *The New Republic,* February 8, 1964. Reprinted by permission.

come accustomed to living with unassimilated groups of people in their midst, about whom they know in a distant and general way that they are very poor. The fact that in earlier times they themselves lived under the risk of being thrown out of work and losing their livelihood, if only temporarily, made it easier for them to feel unconcerned about the people who more permanently were enclosed in the pockets of poverty. Otherwise, the existence of all this poverty in the midst of progressive America stood out in blunt contradiction to the inherited and cherished American ideals of liberty and equal opportunity, as these ideals increasingly had been interpreted, particularly since Franklin D. Roosevelt and the New Deal.

Automation and other changes are all the time decreasing the demand for unskilled and uneducated labor. Standards are rising fast even in household and other menial work. Something like a caste line is drawn between the people in the urban and rural slums, and the majority of Americans who live in a virtual full-employment economy, even while the unemployment rate is rising and the growth rate of the economy is low. Except for a lower fringe, they experience a hitherto unknown security, for it is a tacit understanding in America, as in the rest of the Western world, that a recession will never again be permitted to develop into anything like the Great Depression. But there in an underclass of people in the poverty pockets who live an ever more precarious life and are increasingly excluded from any jobs worth having, or who do not find any jobs at all.

I want to stress one important political fact. This underclass has been, and is largely still, what I have been accustomed to call the world's least revolutionary proletariat. They do not organize themselves to press for their interests. The trade union movement comprises only about one-fourth of the workers, mostly in upper strata who in the main belong to the prosperous majority. To a relatively higher extent than normally they do not register and vote at elections—even apart from the large masses of Negroes in the South who are prevented from doing so.

In very recent times we have seen one important break of this empirical rule of the political apathy of the poor in America. I am, of course, referring to the rebellion of the Negroes in Southern and Northern cities. Without any doubt, this is a true mass movement—so much so that the Negro leaders in the upper and middle class have had to run very fast to remain in the lead, as have, on the other side of the fence, the Administration and other whites responsible for American policy.

I am not at this time going into the question of how this movement, so exceptional to what has been the pattern of passivity on the part of the poor in America, has come about. But I should mention two things about which I am pretty sure. One is my belief that the outbreak of this rebellion just now is not unconnected with the high and, as a trend, rising rate of unemployment, which as always runs much higher—about double—for Negro workers than for whites. Another thing of which I am convinced is that this movement wil not abate unless very substantial reforms are rapidly undertaken to improve the status in American society of its Negro citizens. I am optimistic enough to forecast that in the next 10 years the Negroes will get legal rights equal to the white majority, and that these will be enforced. What will still be needed are, in particular, social sanctions to defend the Negroes' equal opportunities to employment, against the resistance of trade unions more than employers and the business world, particularly big business. And even when all this is accomplished, the Negro masses will nevertheless continue to suffer all the lasting effects of the disabilities and disadvantages of their poverty, their slum existence and their previous exclusion from easy access to education and training for good jobs.

Indeed, it is easy to understand why some of the Negro leaders, and some white liberals, are now raising the demand for a new Marshall Plan to make good the effects of the maltreatment in America of the Negroes from slavery and up till this day. Nevertheless, I am convinced that this demand for a discrimination in reverse, i.e., to the advantage of the Negroes, is misdirected. Nothing would with more certainty create hatred for Negroes among other poor groups in America, who have mostly been their bitterest enemies as they have been the only ones who have felt them as competitors. Moreover, special welfare policies for Negroes are not very practical. Negro housing cannot very well be improved except as part of a plan to improve the housing situation for poor people in general. The same is true of education. Special welfare policies in favor of the Negroes would strengthen their exclusion from the main stream of American life, while what the Negroes want is to have equal opportunities.

What America needs is a Marshall Plan to eradicate poverty in the nation. This is a moral imperative. The unemployed, the underemployed and the now unemployables are also America's biggest wastage of economic resources. The poor represent a suppressed demand which needs to be released to support a steady rapid growth of American production. The goals of social justice and economic progress thus are compatible. A rapid steady economic growth is impossible without mobilizing the productive power of the poor and clothing their unfilled needs with effective demand. The existence of mass poverty in the midst of plenty is a heavy drag on the entire economy.

The statistics on unemployment in America do not tell the whole story. Besides the four million unemployed there are the workers who are only part-time employed, those who have given up seeking work, and all the underemployed. It is an ominous fact that even the prolonged upturn in production from 1961 and onward has not implied a substantial decrease in the rate of unemployment. Nobody seems to expect that the continuation of the present boom will bring down unemployment to a level that could be considered even to approach full employment. And nobody assumes that there will not be a new recession, if not this year then the next. It is reasonable to expect that the unemployment rate will then reach a new high point. There are definite signs that the trend is rising.

For this there are explanations. I believe it is important to stress that none of the specific explanations put forward makes a rising trend of unemployment inevitable, or could by itself prevent the attainment of full employment. Only in conjunction with each other do these influences have the present disastrous result. If in the Sixties exceptionally many young workers enter the labor market, this should not necessarily mean more unemployment. Production could expand rapidly enough to absorb them, and all the new workers could have been properly educated and trained so that they fitted the demand for labor as it has been changing. Long ago, Professor Alvin Hansen and other economists, including myself, used to think that in rich countries, where capital is plentiful, a rapid population increase would rather act as a spur to expansion. It would stimulate the demand for new housing and all the goods and services accessory to housing, and for new schools, teachers, and productive capacity.

Likewise, automation should not by itself lead to unemployment if output expanded enough and the labor force were adjusted to fit the change in demand, caused by automation itself among other things. There are countries with full employment that have an equally rapid pace of automation. There, automation is viewed as driven forward by the scarcity of labor, higher earnings and a rising consumers' demand for products and services: in America, as a cause of unemployment.

OUR CHANGING SOCIETY

What type of society are we moving toward in the modern rich countries? A continually smaller part of our total labor force will be needed in agriculture, manufacturing industry, heavy transport, distribution of commodities, banking and insurance. If we could countervail Parkinson's law, which for various reasons is working with particular force in America, even many sectors of public service would demand less labor.

It is the serious lag in adjusting the education and training of our labor force to the needs of this new society which is the general cause of the situation where we have serious overemployment in some sectors of our economy, at the same time as there is an uncomfortably large and growing residue of structural unemployment and underemployment that cannot be eradicated by an expansion of our production that is feasible.

Against this background it is easy to establish the broad lines of the policies that we will have to apply in order to cure our economic ailments. Huge efforts will have to go into education and vocational training, not only on the higher levels but on the level of grade schools and high schools. Particularly will we have to lift the level of elementary education for the poor people in the urban and rural slums, who are not now getting an education that fits them to the labor market. We must at the same time undertake the retraining of the older workers who are continuously thrown out of jobs without having the abilities to find new ones in our changing society.

I see it as almost a fortunate thing that America has such vast slums in the big cities and smaller ones in the small cities; so many dwellings for poor people that are substandard; so many streets that need to be kept cleaner; such crying needs for improved transport. To train unskilled workers to do such jobs should be easier than to make them teachers or nurses.

INCREASED PUBLIC SPENDING

It should be stressed, however, that a primary condition for success is rapid and steady economic expansion of the national income. Without an increased demand for labor, no efforts for training and retraining workers on a mass scale can succeed. This is the important argument for the view that expanding the economy is the essential thing. Expansion is, in a sense, the necessary condition for any effort to readjust the supply of different types of labor to demand.

A common characteristic of all the reforms directed at raising the quality of the labor force and eradicating poverty in the midst of plenty is that the increased expenditure will be public expenditure. Even when poverty is gone, when there is little or no unemployment or underemployment, a relatively much larger part of the nation's needs will have to be met by collective means. In the future society toward which we are moving, where our productive efforts will increasingly have to be devoted to the care of human beings, health, education, research and culture, and to making our local communities more effective instruments for living and working, public spending will be an ever larger part of total spending. This is because it is not very practical and economical, and in most cases not even possible, to rely on private enterprise for filling these types of demands.

This brings up the problem of balancing or not balancing the federal budget. Large sections of the public and Congress hold, on this question, an opinion that has no support in economic theory and is not commonly held in other advanced countries: that, in principle, expenditures of the federal budget should be balanced by taxation.

A recent experience from my own country Sweden must seem curiously up-side-down to Americans. In a situation of threatening overfull employment and inflationary pressure, the Swedish social democratic government, which has been in power almost a third of a century, felt that it needed to put on brakes, and decided to raise taxation to a level where, for a while, we actually had a balanced budget in the American sense. The political parties to the *right* of the party in power criticized the government fiercely for overtaxing the citizens, and insinuated that this was a design to move our economy in a socialistic direction, by robbing the citizens and private business of the funds they needed. So differently can the problem of balancing the budget appear in two otherwise very similar countries. In fact, you have examples nearer at hand. When the railroads were built in America, the federal government favored the railroad companies in various ways, which occasionally broke the rule of balancing the budget.

The analogy that a nation must handle its purse strings with the same prudence as an individual is false. An individual is not in the position to borrow from himself. Moreover, if the implication is that the government should not borrow even for productive purposes, it is a rule which no private householder follows, or should follow, if he is wise and prudent. And we know that there has been a huge increase, both absolutely and relatively, of private borrowing by business as well as by consumers.

This does not mean that Congress should not carefully weigh each dollar that is spent and each dollar that is taken in by taxation or other means. But the weighing should be in terms of progress and welfare for the nation. I can see no virtue in America having decreased its national debt in postwar years to half its size compared with the national income, while abstaining from undertaking a great number of public expenditures that would have been highly productive from a national point of view. America has been satisfied for a whole decade with a rate of growth of only a little more than one percent per head, and with unemployment rising to the present high level. In the interest of public enlightenment I would wish my American colleagues to spend a little more of their time disseminating some simple truths about budget balancing and related issues. America cannot afford to remain the rich country that has the highest rate of unemployment and the worst and biggest slums, and which is least generous in giving economic security to its old people, its children, its sick people and its invalids.

THE PERMANENT POOR

Harry M. Caudill

Harry M. Caudill, an attorney in Whitesburg, Kentucky, is the author of the best-selling *Night Comes to the Cumberlands,* a perceptive appraisal of the problems of Appalachia.

The Cumberland Plateau of Kentucky is one of the great natural resource regions of the American continent. Industrialists bought up its great wealth three quarters of a century ago and soon after 1900 commenced the large-scale extraction of its timber and minerals. When the development of the eastern Kentucky coalfields began, mining was largely a manual pursuit. Mining machines were replacing mules and ponies, and electricity was making it possible to do an increasing number of tasks with electric power rather than muscle power. Nevertheless, some of the undercutting of coal, much of the drilling, and practically all of the loading into cars were done by armies of grit-blackened miners. Industrial wages enticed thousands of

From *Atlantic Monthly,* June 1964. Reprinted by permission.

mountaineers to turn from the plow and hoe to the pick and shovel. Hordes of Negroes were induced away from the cotton rows of Georgia, the Carolinas, Tennessee, Mississippi, and Alabama and forsook plantation life for the mines. Shiploads of Europeans were brought to the southern coalfield. The extraction of the region's mineral wealth was undertaken in the atmosphere of a tremendous industrial boom.

The Depression destroyed the coalfield's prosperity, but the Second World War revived it, and for a few years the boom returned and the miner was again a useful and honored citizen. The coal industry depended upon his skill and courage, and steel production, electric-power generation, and other basic industries were dependent upon coal. The collapse of the war and of the post-war boom is now history, and we have an opportunity to reflect upon the social, political, and economic consequences that result when a modernized industry is able to cast aside three quarters of its workmen within the span of a decade.

In the post-war years technologists were able to design and manufacture machines of remarkable power and efficiency. Their genius was nowhere better demonstrated than in the coal industry. Devices were developed for boring directly back into the face of the coal seam, and chewing out immense quantities of the mineral, thus eliminating the need to undercut or blast the seam. Simultaneously, the conveyor belt displaced the tracks, mining locomotives, and strings of cars in many mines. Roof bolting made its appearance. This method of supporting the roof eliminated the need for wooden props and proved most effective. A single mechanical loading machine could load more coal than two dozen hardworking shovelers.

Machines were costly, but investment capital was plentiful. The mine operators borrowed from the banks and mechanized and automated the mines and tipples to a remarkable degree. Big, amply financed operations bought up their small competitors. Many inefficient and nearly worked out pits suspended operations altogether. Thus in a few years the fragmented and archaic coal industry became surprisingly modern and technologically advanced. The operators were delighted. Corporations that were bankrupt only a few years before now basked in a sustained new prosperity. For example, Consolidation Coal Company, which had been in receivership, paid off all its obligations and acquired a controlling interest in Chrysler Corporation.

While a new optimism pervaded the offices of the automated and mechanized companies, disaster befell thousands of the men who had depended for so long upon the old industry. By the thousands they found the scrip offices and payroll windows closed in their faces. Mining companies for which they and their fathers had worked, in some instances for two generations, simply vanished altogether. Some three fourths of eastern Kentucky's miners found themselves without work. They had become the victims of a materialistic social order which venerates efficiency and wealth above all other things and largely disregards social and human consequences. When they were no longer needed, their employers dropped them as a coal miner might have thrown away the scrip coins of a bankrupt company.

The legions of industrial outcasts were left with three choices. They could leave the area and find work elsewhere if employment of any kind could be found. Many thousands followed this course, and the population of the mining counties subsided dramatically. A third of the people fled from the shadow of starvation.

They could remain within the region and attempt to live by mining coal from the thin seams not monopolized by the big and highly efficient operations. These men could operate small "doghole" mines with little equipment and trifling capital, pitting their arms and backs against the tireless machines of their big competitors. They were goaded to desperation by the fact that in a camp house or a creek shanty a wife and five to ten children depended upon them for clothes and bread. They had been educated for the mines at a time when little formal education was required for that calling. Thus, in the contest with the big coal corporations they could contribute little except their muscles and their will. Thousands entered these small mines, often "gang-working" as partners and sharing the meager profits at paydays.

In the third situation was the miner who for one reason or another could not or would not leave the area, and found that however hard he toiled in the small mines his income was too meager to provide for the needs of his household. He and his family became charges of the government. Federal and state agencies came to his relief with a wide variety of cash and commodity doles. He was confined to a kind of dull, bleak reservation-existence reminiscent of that imposed by military fiat on the reservation Indians of the Western plains.

Living by welfare, without work and without purpose save existence, these numerous mountaineers settled down to while away the years and await developments.

The men who left the region for the great cities of the North and Middle West did not always find smooth sailing. The rapid process of industrial modernization which had first, and so dramatically, waved its wand across the eastern Kentucky coalfield had penetrated into the immense industrial complexes of the nation's cities. Assembly lines which had traditionally required hundreds of swarming workmen were reorganized, and wonderfully efficient machines were introduced into the automobile and other great manufacturing industries. In many instances, these machines were guided by sensitive electronic masters which, with belts of punched plastic and electric current, could impose unerring and immediate obedience.

In some respects, to be sure, eastern Kentucky is unique. Its people were dependent for fifty years on but a single industry, and, remarkably, they were an industrial people living in a rural rather than an urban setting. The coal industry, like extractive industries generally, invested little of its profits back in the region and allowed its communities to maintain schools of only the most rudimentary sort. It created an environment which left its workmen almost totally dependent upon their employers for bread and leadership, then provided only a small measure of the former and practically none of the latter. Nevertheless, the collapse of coal as a mass hirer of men left in the Kentucky mountains a splendid case study of the social and political implications arising from the displacement of men by machines.

Government at all levels was wholly unprepared for the dramatic developments that ensued. To be sure, these developments were a logical outgrowth of the continuing industrial revolution, which, once set in motion, appears to be destined to carry us inevitably toward a day when a few people and many machines will do the work for a leisurely population of consumers. But between the first spinning jenny and the distant utopia lie many pitfalls, some of which yawn before us today.

In short, government in our democratic society proved practically bankrupt of ideas when confronted with this new challenge. Hoping against hope that expansion in other industries would eventually absorb the displaced miners, government agencies waited. When the stranded miner had exhausted his unemployment insurance benefits and his savings, when he had come to the ragged edge of starvation and was cloaked in bewilderment and frustration, government came to his rescue with the dole. It arranged to give him a bag of cheese, rice, cornmeal, beef, butter, and dried milk solids at intervals, and in most instances to send him a small check. Having thus contrived to keep the miner and his family alive, the government lost interest in him. Appropriations were made from time to time for his sustenance, but little thought was given to his spirit, his character, his manhood. He was left to dry-rot in the vast paleface reservation created for his perpetuation in his native hills.

And, inevitably, he fell prey to the politicians who dispense the bread and money by which he lives. Coal mining and thirty years of subservience to the scrip window had already done much to impair the mountaineer's ability to adapt well to rapidly changing circumstances. He had dwelt too long as a kind of industrial serf in company-owned houses, on company-owned streets, in company-owned towns. For too long the company had buffered him from the swift-flowing social and economic tides swirling in the world outside his narrow valleys. When his employers cast him aside, he still possessed only a single valuable remnant of his birthright—the ballot. He was essential to the politicians because he could vote, so he was placed in a sort of suspended animation in which he came fully to life only at election time. He became increasingly dependent upon the political machines that ran his counties. He accepted the food doles and the welfare checks and ratified the arrangement by voting for the men and women who thus sustained him. The politicians expanded their operations into other fields where public funds could make the difference between life and death. In all too many counties they captured the school systems, thereby acquiring large new sums to be dispensed as patronage. The positions of school-teacher, bus driver, lunchroom director, truant officer, and a multitude of others were treated as so many plums to be dispensed to the acquiescent, the obedient, and the meek. The union of school politics and welfare politics resulted in a formidable prodigy indeed. Its power was quickly recognized at Frankfort and Washington. New political pacts were made, and a wide range of state jobs were placed at the disposal of the local overlords. Thus their power became virtually complete.

Today in many Kentucky counties political machines of remarkable efficiency are to be found. Their effectiveness surpasses Tammany Hall at its best. In a typical county the school board and state agencies control the biggest payrolls. The politicians who run them can also reach and influence the many small merchants, automobile dealers, and service station operators with whom they do business. Thus they are masters of the majority of those who still work for a living.

The state and federal governments act as tax-collecting enterprises, which funnel vast sums into the hands of merciless and amoral local political dynasties. The county machines dispense the funds so as to perpetuate themselves and their allies at Frankfort and Washington. Increasingly, these omniscient organizations manage to gather into their hands funds and gifts from private charities, including even the American Red Cross. Taxpayers in fifty states, oblivious to what their dollars buy, pay little heed to this ominous course of events.

These developments raise a disquieting question which Americans have never confronted before:

How fares the American concept of government of the people, by the people, and for the people when a clear majority become permanently dependent upon and subservient to their elected leaders?

Indeed, can democratic government survive at all in such a setting?

The situation in eastern Kentucky is new to the American scene, but much of the pattern is as old as Rome.

In ancient Italy the social order was remarkably healthy so long as the populace consisted, in the main, of freeholding farmers and self-employed artisans and artificers. The scene darkened when Roman armies conquered distant territories and sent home multitudes of captives. The rich bought up the small plots of farmers and cultivated the resultant plantations with the labor of slaves. Other slaves were set to work in mass manufactories. Because of their great numbers, their carefully planned organization, and their specialization, they were able to produce far more cheaply than their self-employed, free competitors. The corporations that ran these huge enterprises provided grain, leather goods, cloth, and weapons for the empire. The free men and women flocked to the towns and cities to cluster in slums. To keep them orderly the government fed them, clothed them, and entertained them with games. An astoundingly complex system of doles and subsidies was perfected to sustain the idled millions of Roman citizens. In idleness the Roman decayed. He became bitter, vengeful, irresponsible, and bloodthirsty. The mutterings of Roman mobs came to speak more loudly than the voice of Caesar. Rome withered within, long before alien armies crashed through her walls.

These ancient events cast shadows of portent for us today. The machine is a far more profitable servant than any slave. It is untiring, wears out slowly, and requires no food or medication. Technological progress is inexorable and moves toward perfection. What will be the final consequences of it all for the American ideals of equality, liberty, and justice?

We are in the throes of a rapidly quickening new technological revolution. Fifty years ago 700,000 American coal miners were able to mine less coal than 140,000 dig today. Experts tell us that coal production may double by 1980 without any increase in the number of miners. Automobile production increases year by year, but the number of workmen declines. In every field of manufacturing, sensitive, accurate, unfailing steel monsters crowd men and women from workbench and turning lathe, from well and mine. On the land the number of farmers decreases as farms are consolidated into giant tracts. Tractors and mechanical cotton pickers and threshers have rendered the farm laborer as obsolete as the coal miner of 1945.

New turns of the technological wheel are in sight. In twenty years nuclear power may render all fossil fuels obsolete, valued only for their chemical derivatives. If this occurs, new legions of workmen will follow the coal miner into abrupt obsolescence.

On the material side, this revolution undoubtedly represents only progress. It brings us more and more goods for less and less work, thus bringing to fruition one of mankind's ancient dreams.

But what of man's social, spiritual, and political aspects? Is it possible we are moving rapidly forward on the one hand and going backward to barbarism on the other?

What is to become of the jobless miner who takes his family to a Chicago housing development, there to press in upon a onetime automobile assembler from Detroit and a discarded tool and die maker from Pittsburgh? What results when these men and their wives and children are joined by a Negro from Mississippi whose job as a cotton picker was taken over by a machine, or by a white hill-farmer from Tennessee whose ninety acres could not produce corn in competition with the splendidly mechanized farms of Iowa? Are the mushrooming housing developments of the great cities to become the habitations of millions of permanently idled people, supported by a welfare program as ruinous as the one devised by the Caesars? Are whole segments of American citizenry to be consigned to lifetimes of vexatious idleness, resentment, and bitterness? Are these centers to become vast raw slums out of which will issue the ominous rumblings of titanic new mobs?

And what torrents of new bitterness will be added to the nation's bloodstream when computers send multitudes of white-collar workers into abrupt idleness in the mortgaged houses of suburbia?

In my opinion these questions pose the foremost issue of our time.

It strikes me that our scientists may develop the explosive power to send a few Americans to Mars while, simultaneously, our society prepares a vastly greater explosive power among disillusioned millions of Americans who remain behind on our own battered planet.

The industrialists who run the eastern Kentucky coalfield laid careful plans for the creation and use of mining machines but cast aside their mining men as one might discard a banana peel. Most of the victims of this callous treatment accepted their fate resignedly. Some did not, however, and in the winter of 1962–63 the hills in four eastern Kentucky counties resounded with gunfire and nocturnal explosions. For several months a situation bordering on anarchy prevailed across a wide region. Tipples and mines were blasted. Automobiles, power lines, and mining machines were destroyed. Such acts were committed by desperate men seeking to strike at a social and economic order which had rejected them.

Today the challenge of eastern Kentucky is a great national challenge. If we can triumph over it, the solutions we find will offer hope to the entire nation. Increasingly, the agony of eastern Kentucky is but a part of the misery that afflicts great cities, mill towns, and mining regions everywhere. The pain grows out of the evil paradox of mass idleness in the midst of booming production.

Liberty, like a chain, is no stronger than its weakest part. If the freedom and well-being of a part of the people are lost, the freedom and well-being of all are mortally imperiled. If the nation writes off our southern highlands as unworthy of rescue and rehabilitation, then the nation as a whole is unworthy of survival. As an optimist and a liberal I believe that the nation will rise to the challenge of the depressed and backward Appalachian region, and that in so doing, it will find many of the answers that democracy requires for survival throughout the nation.

A population equivalent to the present population of New York State is being added to the nation every four or five years. Technology eliminates some 40,000 jobs each week. These facts tell us that we must successfully master new frontiers of social justice, and do so in a hurry, or become another nation of regimented serfs.

A social and political crisis of the first magnitude will confront America before the end of another decade. Substitutes for such presently accepted goals as full employment will have to be found. Fresh definitions of the concepts of work, leisure, abundance, and scarcity are imperatively needed. Economic theories adequate to an infant industrial revolution are wholly unsatisfactory when applied to a full-fledged scientific revolution such as that which now engulfs us. The complexity and interdependence of the scientific-industrial nation call for national planning and action. Government must and will intervene more and more in the nation's industrial life. The destiny toward which we move is a national economy under the law. A radical change in public attitude toward law and government is necessary if the general welfare is to be achieved without the total sacrifice of individual liberty. Having bargained for the benefits of technology on all fronts, law is our only means of assuring that it serves the common good.

In 1963 the American economy brought unprecedented prosperity to some 80 percent of the people. Simultaneously, a segment of the population as numerous as the inhabitants of Poland consisted of paupers, and 5.5 percent of the nation's breadwinners were without jobs. Clearly a new tack must be taken soon unless America the Beautiful is to become a crazy quilt of bustle and sloth, brilliance and ignorance, magnificence and squalor.

For more than a dozen years the prevailing political ideology has implemented a *de facto* return to the Articles of Confederation. This doctrine holds that action at the state or local level is admirable while any direct effort by Washington to deal with social or economic malaise is un-American and dangerous. The result is a growing paralysis of the national government as an instrumentality of the public will. This reasoning has brought tremendous outpourings of federal grants-in-aid to states and communities, under circumstances which entail much waste and, often, minimal benefits.

In eastern Kentucky, and in many other depressed areas, the state government will not act effectively to combat poverty and economic decline because it is allied to or controlled by the interests that produced the problems. Thus, state officials talk piously about reform but strenuously oppose any real effort to attack the status quo. They respond to the political machines nurtured by welfare grants and founded on impoverished and dependent citizens. It is not too much to expect that, as matters now stand, federal funds trickling through state treasuries will finance the rebuilding of new political machines in practically every state—machines more odious than those once bossed by Crump, Pendergast, and Hague.

Common sense and past experience argue strongly for a system of federally administered public works. Only in America are able-bodied men permitted to loaf in idleness amid a profusion of unperformed tasks. Should not the thousands of jobless Kentucky coal miners be set to work reforesting the wasted hills, building decent consolidated schoolhouses and roads, and providing decent housing in lieu of the dreadful shacks that now dot every creek and hollow? And why not a modernized version of TVA—a Southern Mountain Authority—to develop the immense hydro- and thermal-power potential of the Appalachian South for the benefit of the entire nation, and to stop the hideous waste of the land now being wrought by the strip-and-auger-mining industries? What of the possibility of an educational Peace Corps to break the old cycle of poor schools, poor job preparation, poor pay, and poor people?

Unless the nation can profit from the terrible lesson eastern Kentucky so poignantly teaches, new multitudes of once prosperous Americans may find themselves slipping inexorably into an economic mire that breeds poverty, despair, dependency, and, eventually, revolution.

THE POLITICS OF POVERTY
Douglass Cater

Douglass Cater, former Washington editor of *The Reporter* magazine, joined the White House staff in 1964 as a special assistant to President Lyndon B. Johnson. He is the author of *Power in Washington.*

At least one public-spirited lobbyist in Washington who had been working long and hard to stir up a fight against poverty in the United States was caught by surprise to learn that President Johnson was declaring "unconditional war" on this ancient enemy. There had not been the usual bureaucratic rumblings to indicate such a major governmental initiative in the making. Nor did it seem a particularly auspicious time, Congress being already bogged down on two issues marginally related to this one: civil rights and tax reduction. Two key Kennedy programs directly aimed at poverty—the Area Redevelopment Administration and the Appalachian project—were in serious difficulties. The request of ARA for more funds had been rebuffed by the House of Representatives last summer; and the Appalachian project, though zealously promoted by Under Secretary of Commerce Franklin D. Roosevelt, Jr., was having trouble getting past the preliminary stage of Budget Bureau clearance.

Amid such disarray, how did the ambitious scheme for a frontal war on poverty come into being? The origins of an idea in the nation's capital are always difficult to trace, especially after a President sponsors it and thereby puts a premium on plagiarism.

This one seems to have had at least partial beginnings in the Council of Economic Advisers, where it was stimulated not so much by any sudden sympathy for the poor but by tough problems of fiscal policy. Last year's Council Report, concentrating on the need for a tax cut, failed even to mention hard-core poverty. But as Council Chairman Walter Heller began to look beyond the tax cut and ponder the inevitable downturn in the government's rate of spending for defense, space, and related activities, he recognized the combined advantages of a broad attack on the deep-seated economic distress that economists describe as "structural" (as distinguished from "cyclical") and that publicists have labeled "pockets of poverty." On June 3, Heller directed a memorandum to his staff soliciting their views on the subject. "Specifically, what lines of action might make up a practical Kennedy anti-poverty program in 1964?" he inquired. He also commenced quiet agitation within the Executive branch and even test-marketed the idea during a speech at the Communications Workers convention. He failed to get much response from either his audience or the press.

Heller was more successful with the President, who, of course, had long been sensitive to the economic decline in Massachusetts caused by industrial migration to the South. Thanks to the Presidential primary system, Kennedy had been fully exposed in West Virginia to poverty of a scale and severity that he had never before seen. As he later sought to repay his political debt to that state, he faced the fact that even more desperate conditions existed in the mountainous country of eastern Kentucky and that poverty was endemic to the whole Appalachian region stretching from Pennsylvania to the foothills of north Alabama.

The late President was displaying increasing concern over the problem during the final months of his life. Last fall, moved by Homer Bigart's eloquent account in the *New York Times* of conditions in the Cumberland Plateau as winter approached, he hurriedly directed Under Secretary Roosevelt to mobilize all the emergency funds available to relieve the families of unemployed miners. On the evening before he left on the fateful trip that terminated in Dallas, Kennedy gave tentative assent to Heller's request to proceed with a poverty program. If he had lived, some advisers believe Kennedy would have surely worked hard to change the trend that, over the past decade, had allocated a fairly puny portion of the budget to Federal welfare services. But considering the stalemate on the legislative front, they doubt that a full-scale war on poverty would have started with such a bang.

The fact that Johnson moved so swiftly on Heller's proposition even as he was determinedly slashing away at the budget has aroused a certain amount of skepticism in Washington. It offered obvious tactical advantages by opening inviting prospects to liberals in Congress while dealing out hard and immediate realities to conservatives like Senate Finance Committee Chairman Harry Byrd. The cost of the new program will not become clear right away. The coming year's budget, according to its drafters, earmarks five hundred million dollars in new obligational authority for a special poverty package along with at least another six hundred million for beefing up existing programs or starting new ones. But actual expenditures in fiscal 1965 could amount to only half of this—not a very substantial outlay compared to the size of the task. Though nobody seems to have a precise notion about what an unconditional war on poverty should cost, everybody agrees that it won't be cheap.

Johnson supporters profess not to be worried that their man will shy away from the budget realities. They point out that while he may not have any theoretical commitment to Keynesian economics, the new President does have an abiding concern for human beings. As a youth he had more than a speaking acquaintance with poverty, and later, working for the New

Deal's National Youth Administration, he served a valuable apprenticeship trying to eradicate its corrosive effects.

WHO ARE THE POOR?

Amid the newly aroused public interest, there has been not a little back-biting over why the policymakers have dallied so long. One complaint is that the publicists have failed to make this a particularly burning issue. At a recent "Pockets of Poverty" conference in Washington, economist John Kenneth Galbraith felt obliged to defend himself against accusations that he had misled everybody by his writings about *The Affluent Society*. Galbraith argued that "One of my principal purposes was to urge that growing wealth will not, of itself, solve the problem of poverty." But he ruefully admitted that more people had read the title than the book.

Much of the recent literature directly addressed to poverty has been couched in a jargon that politicians cannot comprehend, much less find compellingly translated; it has revealed the distressing fact that at least one-fifth of our population still lives in rather abject conditions. While this would seem to represent some improvement over the "one-third of a nation" that concerned FDR, statisticians estimate that those in the bottom fifth have been getting a stationary share of the nation's goods and services during the past three decades even as the gross national product has grown vastly. They seem to be caught in a rut of privation that deepens as the economy moves ahead. They are not simply confined to big geographic pockets such as Appalachia, but include millions living in city, town, and country from coast to coast.

In the attempt to search out the poor and identify them, sociologists have developed categories of families having "poverty-linked" characteristics—nonwhites, families whose heads are females, males aged fourteen to twenty-five or over sixty-five, individuals with less than eight years of schooling, inhabitants of some farm areas, and families in which there are more than six children under eighteen. These are the ones who are most apt to fall into the rut and, once in, have the most difficulty climbing out. A recent study made by the National Policy Committee on Pockets of Poverty reached the alarming conclusion that these poverty risks have been on the increase and that "Unless remedial steps are undertaken, there will be considerably more poor even with a more affluent America." Of those who fall into these categories, the committee's study concludes: "Their poverty is the result of special circumstances, rather than of . . . the rate of economic activity. Their lot cannot be said to be the direct result of inadequate growth rate as they are not part of the economic structure. . . . It will not do to argue—as most policymakers and economists do—that poverty will be done away with by policies aimed at bringing about full employment."

This year's Report of the Council of Economic Advisers presents statistics that in general show a declining incidence of poverty in these risk groups.

But it, too, soberly concludes with the prediction that ". . . in the future economic growth alone will provide relatively fewer escapes from poverty. Policy will have to be more sharply focused on the handicaps that deny the poor fair access to the expanding incomes of a growing economy."

But there has been more dramatic testimony of what the policymakers are up against. *Night Comes to the Cumberlands,* written two years ago by Harry Caudill, a lawyer and a former state legislator from Whitesburg, Kentucky, describes eloquently the misery of his region, which nature has endowed so abundantly with beauty and mineral resources. Caudill points out that the causes of its present predicament are ancient and deeply rooted. A way of life based primarily on coal mining led inevitably to company-style paternalism and left employees helpless as markets declined and automation moved in. Caudill makes a scathing indictment of the politics that failed and still fails to protect the interests of this region and its people. There was first of all the failure of local and county politics to impose an adequate tax base during boom times, thereby permitting the gradual decay in schooling and other local social services. State politics not only failed to plan wisely for the region's future but even today permits the scandalous exploitation by strip and auger mining in which newfangled mechanical monsters lay waste the mountainsides as a cheap way of getting at the coal veins. A farm owner whose ancestors bargained away his mineral rights for as little as fifty cents an acre may find his land ruined and his streams clogged without possibility of redress. Soon, Caudill warns, the Cumberlands may be unfit even for the tourist trade that has been its brightest prospect.

Finally, Caudill indicts national politics for ignoring the plight of this region even while dealing so generously with the nearby Tennessee Valley. Emergency Federal programs for Appalachia have mainly had the result of accustoming these despirited people to life on the dole. Federal welfare, he also points out, has been dispensed in a way that reinforced the rule of the county courthouse satrapies, stubbornly resistant to progress.

Another eloquent book, Michael Harrington's *The Other America,* also published in 1962, describes less remote parts but people just as isolated from the main life in this country. The poor, Harrington argues, have become invisible. Even those who huddle in the cities have not been able to identify themselves or their problems so that others will pay attention. Unlike earlier generations who could aspire to break out, today's poor often inherit a legacy handed down from generation to generation.

Harrington, too, indicts a political system that launches massive programs in agriculture, housing, Social Security, and the rest while almost entirely neglecting the genuine poor. Social Security does not cover them. Minimum-wage laws specifically exempt them. Even slum clearance, wryly labeled "Negro removal," usually only complicates their existence. He points out that government welfare unwittingly contributes to broken homes and illegitimacy by denying help to the family whose father is hopelessly unemployable even if able-bodied. School-lunch programs have not nourished the communities that could not afford to transport the surplus foods or the children who could not make even the token payments.

Both Caudill and Harrington have written angry books, reminiscent of an earlier literature in America. They depict poverty that feeds on itself and politics that has advanced little in its mentality from the day of the soup kitchens. But though the situation they describe is deeply disturbing, the nature of the remedy is by no means clear-cut. The politics of poverty today poses problems no less baffling than the economics of poverty.

WHAT CAN BE DONE?

Caudill and others have suggested that the best way to rehabilitate Appalachia would be to create a Federal authority closely patterned along the lines of the Tennessee Valley Authority. TVA's success story after three decades has aroused a great deal of envy among nearby valley folk who watched its planners and technicians—calling on the blessed trinity of water, electric power, and fertilizer—perform their economic miracle in this once benighted valley. But in hindsight, the political success story is no less miraculous. First promoted by Nebraska's Republican Senator George Norris, who lacked a self-serving constituent interest in the region, TVA was able to build a political base that withstood the assaults of the private-power lobby and survived eight years under a President who called it "creeping socialism." It did not merely survive, it converted the subalterns whom Eisenhower sent down to be directors and continued to expand its resources to meet the region's needs.

Some skeptics in Washington argue that TVA's experience is so freakish as to have no relevance for Appalachia. In the first place, they claim, the technical feat of developing a river basin that was confluent by nature is scarcely applicable to a mountain chain where even near neighbors share little sense of identity in their misfortunes.

Is it possible to devise a program that spans rural eastern Kentucky and industrial western Pennsylvania? Recent experience indicates that the problems are not merely technical. There were great hopes that a bold start was being made with the Area Redevelopment Administration, the first program enacted under Kennedy after being twice vetoed by Eisenhower. Its chief purpose was to supply long-term, low-interest loans to induce private industry to locate in depressed areas and thereby create jobs. When, after only two years' experience, the House voted down new authorizations for ARA, it was quite evident that this new venture had aroused little enthusiasm. Some of the opposition came from such men as Representative W. Pat Jennings, Democrat of Virginia, whose district was one of those most in need of assistance.

Their miscellaneous complaints indicate the nature of ARA's political predicament: the loans were too few and too tardy in being granted; assistance was not reaching the most depressed communities; industries were being enticed from higher-cost areas; and, finally, ARA was promoting such frivolous projects as ski lifts and motels.

Quite possibly, Administrator William L. Batt, Jr., has been over-optimistic in claiming that a hundred thousand permanent jobs will result from the $192.6 million ARA has invested to date. But clearly, not all his troubles were of his own making. Jockeying in Congress set the terms that permitted more than a thousand separate areas to qualify for ARA's limited largesse. As a concession to the Federal bureaucracy—a formidable political power—ARA has been required to work mainly through existing Federal agencies, slowing things considerably. Though the desire for haste may have led to a few dubious projects, Batt and his associates argue vehemently that motels and ski lifts, as in the experience of Vermont, can bring great prosperity to rural regions. And it is sad but true, they admit, that some of the areas in most desperate need have the hardest time meeting criteria imposed by the statutes.

The rise and decline of ARA suggests that the politicians lack the patience to allow time for a long-range developmental program to prove itself. Even among the Kennedy aides, there were signs of diminished enthusiasm after the debacle in the House. Officials of ARA were unexpectedly heartened when Johnson, in his State of the Union message, called for expansion of their "small but successful" program.

Both congressmen and local politicians have shown greater partiality for an alternative method of aid inaugurated during the Kennedy administration—the Accelerated Public Works Program. Through stepped-up Federal help in building various community facilities, with the ironic exception of schools, APWP has managed to pump more than $850 million into depressed areas. It can move swiftly and its benefits are highly visible. Batt, who also administers this program, estimates that more than 220,000 jobs have been created, but he points out that they average only one year's duration. Improving public facilities may improve a community's capacity to attract industry, he argues, but it is hardly a substitute for programs like ARA that are designed to have a more lasting impact.

The priorities of politics have also left their mark on the Commerce Department's effort to put together a program specifically designed for Appalachia. As a concession to the eight participating governors of that region, the notion of a TVA-type regional authority was rejected in favor of a Federal corporation that would share its powers with the state governments. Voting was to be equally divided between Federal and state authority, thus in effect requiring unanimity for all major decisions. Such an arrangement aroused a great deal of enthusiasm in the state capitals, but at last report it was running into serious opposition among Budget Bureau experts who are doubtful not only about its constitutionality but also whether it represents sound policy for the Federal government.

Other doubts have been voiced about the governors' dominant interest in launching a massive and politically lucrative road-building program.

"Every citizen of Appalachia to live within twenty-five miles of a sixty-mile-an-hour highway," the slogan goes. This traditional method of public works, generously subsidized by the Federal government, has its benefits both direct and as a pump primer for depressed areas.

FIGHTING INERTIA

But $4.50-an-hour road-engineering crews hardly fall into the impoverished class. Those who are most intimately involved with the problems of the poor are concerned that such a program should not be regarded as the sole thrust of an unconditional war.

Just a quick visit to the battlefronts can provide convincing evidence of how intractable poverty's problems really are. In the hill country of western Tennessee last summer, I toured an area that has remained largely untouched by TVA's regenerative force. Even in communities not distant from the billion-dollar industrial development along the stretch of the Tennessee River, I came upon squalor reminiscent of the poverty-ridden South of the depression period. Poverty's habits are persistent, as TVA's planners readily concede. There are those inhabitants of the region classified as "innovators" who have acted quickly to adopt new ideas and techniques. Others, the "responders," have waited to be shown, while still others, even after decades of demonstrated experience, cling resolutely to the outmoded. Changing human custom, say the planners, is the most unpredictable activity in which they engage, whether it consists of persuading a community to undertake needed reforms or a farmer to try new and better fertilizer practices. It is also a slow business.

Poverty's habits in the metropolitan centers of the nation are every bit as intractable. A decade ago, New Haven, Connecticut, began a vigorous effort to resist the awful urban blight that was spreading rapidly. Today, New Haven stands as a pioneer in urban renewal. But Mayor Richard Lee, who has led the renewal forces, denies vigorously that rebuilding the city physically was the most important problem. As the slums were cleared, Lee ran into indescribable conditions among what the sociologist euphemistically calls "multi-problem" families. They could not be helped merely by moving them away from their former misery. Many had been on the welfare rolls since the early 1930's. Second and third generations were growing up helpless to take their places in normal society.

New Haven's Community Progress, Inc., a combined public and private enterprise, found itself pulled into a widening range of rehabilitation. A "homemaking" program helps these social delinquents learn the elementals of family living so that they will not perpetuate slum conditions in new surroundings. Community schools accept a fuller educational role than one designed for children only, and adult literacy programs are facing up to the fact that it is not only immigrants who cannot read or write. Neighborhood employment centers bring job counseling to those who lack the imagination to venture afar. A massive campaign has been launched to reclaim high-school dropouts—a group, constituting forty-eight per cent of the young people from low-income neighborhoods, who have started on the vicious cycle of underprivilege.

What comes clear in New Haven's experience is that living has grown too complicated for a sizable number of those who dwell in the cities. The poverty risks, once they meet any kind of chance misfortune, lack the resources to recover from it. To get at their problems requires a variety of undertakings going far beyond a stepped-up program of public works or fight for full employment. Mayor Lee, a dynamic salesman of his city's effort, argues emphatically: "You can't win the war against poverty with stirring slogans. You have got to have earthy people willing to take on the dirty work." A cheering part of the New Haven story has been its recruitment of outstanding civil servants who prefer this task to the lure of Washington.

IT WILL BE A LONG WAR

The concerted effort at Federal, state, and local levels for which President Johnson is calling could inject government into social planning on a scale never before attempted. Inevitably, there will be outcries against such encroachment. But there is already encroachment of a different sort when individuals and whole communities can be buffeted with sudden fury by forces outside their control. There is the recent example of the shock with which South Side Chicago has endured in five years' time the loss of industries that employed fifty thousand workers and indirectly brought a livelihood to an estimated half a million. No city by itself can plan against such hazards, and it is regrettable that state government has been callous to metropolitan needs. As automation begins to have its mounting impact, the plight of those who were already technologically obsolete can only grow worse. There is every reason why government cannot ignore the people who, in Johnson's phrase, are living on "the outskirts of hope."

Not all the resistance can be expected from the Goldwater philosophers who still tend to equate poverty with God's judgment against the undeserving. The more subtle opposition will come from those coalitions—among bureaucrats, congressmen, and pressure groups—who would assert different priorities and who have the power and expertise to make themselves felt. Poverty has so far lacked a power base in Washington capable of sustaining its claims. As with foreign aid, there will be constant temptation to shift this program off target in order to win more immediate or more obvious political benefits. Dealing with underdeveloped people can be as baffling at home as abroad.

Will Johnson show the perseverance to keep his program on target? Though his activities to date are still largely at the propaganda stage, there are some promising signs. Despite his budget economies, he approved a more than twofold increase in funds for the Labor Department's Manpower

Retraining Program, which is now getting into high gear. He has enthusiastically accepted the proposal to assist draft rejectees, who are a prime source of the nation's social and economic misfits. He is disposed to concentrate on youth while there is still time to eradicate poverty's awful heritage. He is reported determined to find new ways to break the impasse that has blocked Federal aid to education at the lower school levels.

According to those who have worked with him, the new President is anything but dogmatic about the way this war should be waged. He favors a variety of pilot projects, collaborating with governors like Terry Sanford of North Carolina and mayors like Richard Lee who show a willingness to take new initiatives. So far, there is a heated rivalry among Washington officials over how to set up the GHQ to direct his operation.

The war on poverty is going to demand experiment, not only in the programs themselves but in building political institutions capable of surviving the long haul. In Washington, it means forming a political coalition that will not be inclined to follow the line of least resistance. Outside Washington, it means finding the politicians and the public servants who are willing to take on what Mayor Lee calls the dirty work.

In the year's report to the President, the Council of Economic Advisors suggested facetiously that $11 billion in direct handouts annually could raise the nation's poor to a minimum standard of living. Johnson's dilemma is whether his war can be waged with better economics and better politics.

14 BIG BUSINESS IN POLITICS

The belief system of the American public with respect to big business has undergone a series of ups and downs in the nineteenth and twentieth centuries. Whereas business dominated the post-Civil War period, with the finest talents devoted to rapid industrialization, the turn of the century brought marked changes, thanks in no small part to the revelations by the "Muckrakers" of business malpractices. Demands from aggrieved farmers, laborers, and consumers that government "do something" about the abuse of power by the Trusts, the Railroads, the Meat Packers, and Wall Street (all capitalized in the reformers' lexicon) led to repeated regulatory attempts, first on the state level, and then, after the states were constitutionally foreclosed from action by a conservative Supreme Court, on the federal level.

Spurred first by the ebullient Teddy Roosevelt, then by the more studious and even more effective Woodrow Wilson, Congress attempted to plug the regulatory loopholes of the 19th-century Sherman Antitrust and Interstate Commerce Acts. Under this vigorous leadership, the federal government broadened the field of government regulation with the Pure Food and Drug Law, the Clayton and Federal Trade Commission Acts, and the Federal Reserve Act. A climate favorable to such intervention was fostered by the public stereotype of the "robber baron," reinforced by the *caveat emptor* ("let the buyer beware") attitude of many a business tycoon.

With the subsequent wartime suspension of regulatory activities and the postwar retreat into "normalcy" under Harding and Coolidge, business came to regain its place in the public favor. Aided by the burgeoning arts of the public relations man, even the detested name of Rockefeller took on a new image—that of a kindly old gentleman handing out shiny new dimes to eager youngsters. "The business of America is business" became the watchword of the early 1920s. Even the gross corruption revealed in the Teapot Dome scandal could not shake the new-found faith of the ordinary American that "every day, in every way, things were getting better and better"—under business auspices, of course.

The Great Depression, and the failure of prosperity to reemerge from around an interminable series of promised "corners," brought ultimate political and economic upheaval. Business became the target for renewed regulatory activity, once Franklin D. Roosevelt—aided, perhaps unwittingly, by the Supreme Court—had written off his New Deal's misguided attempt, in the form of the NRA, to hand over government's regulatory powers to the very ranks of big business itself. Reviving his namesake's earlier cries against the "malefactors of great wealth," FDR gained from a compliant Congress an unprecedented series of economic reforms; and in so doing, he added a new list of alphabetical agencies to the Washington scene—the SEC, the FPC, the NLRB, and so on.

Once again, business had to begin the slow climb back into public esteem. The generally distinguished performance of American industry during World War II and the postwar reconversion period (despite the occasional wrongdoing revealed by the investigations of a Truman or a Kefauver committee) brought a steady resurgence, once again aided by a postwar reaction against governmental controls.

This time, however, business was no longer content to await passively the shaping of its image by others. It embarked upon a vigorous positive campaign to create a favorable climate of opinion. Sustained by the new tools of market research, "community relations" took its place alongside the ever increasing hard sell of "new and better products." Looking still further ahead, some industrialists perceived the need for greater direct political involvement on the part of its managers and its white-collar workers, to counter the reputed success of organized labor in "getting out the vote." With a mixture of motives, some highly laudable, others less commendable, more and more businessmen joined in. Thus emerged upon the American scene the Practical Politics Seminar. Originating in Syracuse, New York, during 1958, under the auspices of the General Electric Company and the Syracuse Manufacturers' Association, this program of learning through observation and participation was later adopted, modified, and "nationalized" by the U. S. Chamber of Commerce. Big business had again emerged, through an ingenious and highly valuable method of education (some might say indoctrination), to take its place alongside the more traditional lobbying, institutional advertising, and "community-of-interest" endeavors.

But before passing judgment on either the wisdom or the virtue of business' new involvement in politics, it seems desirable to suggest some appropriate goals for business in a democratic capitalistic society. The first might be the social desirability—indeed the necessity—of the profit motive, since only through this motive does human incentive seem likely to be adequately spurred. Second is the goal of free competition—competition not only in advertising and in services, in gimmicks, gadgets, and brand names, but in price as well—save in those areas where natural circumstances compel the grant of a monopoly or near monopoly, as in the public utility industry. Third is the goal of freedom—so long as it is consistent with the public interest: freedom to enter or leave a business, to produce new goods or to cease the production of outmoded; freedom of access—to raw materials, to labor and to markets; and the freedom to inform the public about the merits of one's products. In short, a favorable climate for business seems a justifiable goal, so long as business plays its part in making that climate favorable for others as well. Indeed, it seems obvious that our government in action, motivated by a concern for the interests of all, is not likely to prove hostile to those enlightened businessmen who have identified their own best long-run interests with those of the people as a whole.

THE TROUBLED CONSCIENCE OF AMERICAN BUSINESS

Bernard D. Nossiter

Bernard D. Nossiter, who was recently a Nieman Fellow at Harvard, has reported on economic affairs for the *Washington Post* since 1955. He adapted this article from his book, *Myths and Mythmakers in the Modern Economy.*

What is fast becoming a traditional American rite—the periodic hassle over steel prices—has again brought into the open some of the most troubling questions that American businessmen have to face. How can an executive—with the best will in the world—be sure that he is acting in the public interest? How can he tell what it is? And what should he do if his duty to the public conflicts with his idea of his duty to his stockholders?

Practically everybody now believes that the price of steel, and the wages which help to determine it, are matters of vital public interest. Several studies have fixed on increases in steel prices as the chief cause of inflation during the Eisenhower era. But there is nothing in logic or fact that makes the price of steel any more or less important than the price of oil, autos, cement, electrical machinery, or other major commodities. There is also a growing recognition that in many of these industries a comparative handful of executives make the crucial decisions.

However, some business theoreticians have invented a new doctrine, the concept of the Corporate Conscience, to assure us that all is well. This idea would, of course, have dismayed Adam Smith. In his simpler age, the restraints of conscience had no place in business behavior. For the classical economists insisted that each man's hand could, and should, be turned against every other's. Out of this conflict, in which each pursues his own self-interest, the maximum well-being of all would automatically result.

But this doctrine rested on a crucial assumption—the existence of perfect competition. In a world where no single entrepreneur was big enough to affect the price and supply of his industry's output, the consumer was king. Guided by supply and demand, then resources would flow to their most efficient use and would be priced according to their contribution to the satisfaction of impersonally determined wants. So long as every businessman aimed single-mindedly at making the biggest possible profit he would inevitably serve the public interest.

If theory and practice didn't quite jibe—if women and children toiled in mines and poverty was the lot of most—this was no indictment of the theory.

From *Harper's Magazine,* September 1963. Reprinted by permission.

Human imperfections, the stickiness of wages, or the fecundity of the poor were interfering with an elegant model.

Today, of course, the gap between the reality of concentrated economic power and the fiction of perfect competition is too wide to be ignored. While most economists are reluctant to surrender the attractive classical model entirely, the fact of concentration is taken for granted by laymen and necessarily (if tacitly) recognized by public-policy makers. Typically, modern industries are dominated by a handful of producers. In steel, autos, aluminum, electrical machinery, cigarettes, chemicals, and many more, the major firms must take account of each other's moves and generally follow the policies of a recognized leader.

Unlike the little businessman of the classical competitive world who received his signals from impersonal markets, the executives of a General Motors, a General Dynamics, or a General Electric can exercise considerable discretion over their price, employment, output, and investment decisions. In such an economy, narrow self-interest no longer insures a state of bliss for the whole society; decisions lack the automatic sanction of Adam Smith's invisible hand. What, then, does justify the businessman's behavior? What is there to guarantee that his use of economic power will serve the public interest?

Thoughtful commentators and businessmen have fully understood this theoretical vacuum. To fill the gap, they have proclaimed a new breed of managers whose decisions are guided by a profound sense of social responsibility.

In its simplest form, the new doctrine of legitimacy runs along these lines: ownership in the large, modern corporation is so widely diffused among tens of thousands of stockholders that none is powerful enough to exercise control. Therefore control is vested in a largely self-perpetuating group of officer-managers. These managers are in an almost impregnable position. They operate the machinery through which their nominal superiors, the corporate directors, are elected. And the cost of rounding up enough shares to oust the directors in a proxy fight is extremely high. But this is a good thing. It largely frees the manager from the selfish interest of shareholders in stock prices and dividends; it enables him to balance carefully the conflicting claims of all groups in society.

The conventional wisdom on this subject was well expressed last year by executives from corporate, theological, and educational institutions who sat on the Business Ethics Advisory Council of the Secretary of Commerce. They said:

> Every business enterprise has manifold responsibilities to the society of which it is a part. The prime legal and social obligation of the managers of a business is to operate it for the long-term profit of its owners. Concurrent social responsibilities pertain to a company's treatment of its past, present, and prospective employees and to its various relationships

with customers, suppliers, government, the community, and the public at large.

SCRIPTURE ACCORDING TO JOHN (HARVARD)

The prophets of corporate responsibility are not always clear whether modern executives have attained the new state of grace or whether they merely aspire to it. However, there is general agreement that schools of business administration play a strategic role in the scheme. They are the spawning grounds of the enlightened organization man, imparting the values and techniques that train commonplace undergraduates for a life of responsible service in the corporate temple.

Adolf A. Berle, a leading apostle of the new creed, observes in *The 20th Century Capitalist Revolution:* "At least two great business schools—Harvard and Columbia—have offered programs of background information and thinking in the larger ranges of social organization to selected business executives." These programs are helping to create, he says, "a body of sophisticated thinking, whose aim, properly analyzed, is a conception of community making for the good life." Corporations are leading the way to a modern "City of God" because their managers are tending to respond to the promptings of conscience or some inchoate higher law.

Because of its crucial seminarian role, let us examine the scripture according to the most prominent business school, the one at Harvard. A cursory examination of the 1962–63 catalogue confirms the Business School's concern with the moral revolution. Its 116 pages contain at least eight separate references to right conduct.

A Harvard Business School student, we are told, "develops a concept of ethical values and of social responsibility in the making of concrete business decisions." Elsewhere, the catalogue is sprinkled with phrases like "the responsibility that business leaders have to society" and "the responsibilities of business to the American society as a whole."

Harvard's Divinity School, older and perhaps less optimistic, does not claim as much.

The Business School offers a half-year course exclusively devoted to the precepts of corporate responsibility. It is labeled "Business, Society, and the Individual" and is known as BSI in the acronymic world of the embryo corporate executives. "The primary concern of this course," that catalogue tells us, "is realistic managerial decision-making in business situations in a private-enterprise economy which requires profit, and which is complicated by the presence of issues of public responsibility, fairness, integrity, right and wrong, personal conscience."

BSI, like "Creative Marketing Strategy" or "Factory Management," is an optional course offered to second-year students. Unfortunately it was not given this past year because its professor George Albert Smith, Jr., was on leave in Switzerland. However, he left behind his own text, 762 pages of documents and cases.

The heart of the Business School's method is the case system, the study of situations drawn from the actual world of business. Professor Smith's cases range over a bigger territory than Salesman Willy Loman dreamed of. Can a study of these cases teach us how the sentiments of the catalogue are translated into practice by decision-makers in executive suites? Do they develop a technique to replace competitive markets and strike a balance between the competing claims cited by the Business Ethics Advisory Council?

Some of the BSI cases pose rather simple, Sunday school issues of honesty. Should a dealer in motor scooters who divides promotion expenses with his distributor, permit his advertising agency to pad the bills in order to shrink his share of the costs? Should a business-school student, offered an expense-paid trip for a job interview by two different firms in the same city, collect his expenses twice? Some of the cases raise broader questions of responsibility. How should the steel executives respond to President Kennedy's request for price restraint? Should a candy manufacturer with a plant in the Philippines introduce machinery that would lay off half his work force?

There are, of course, no textbook solutions to these questions. George Smith does not profess to be a Solomon. Nor does he claim to be a new Adam Smtih, developing a theory that provides ready answers for decision-makers. Near the end of his text, George Smith quotes another business-school scholar, Richard Eells of Columbia:

> The well-tempered corporation is a system of private government with self-generated principles of constitutionalism that match corporate authority to corporate responsibilities and impose restraints upon corporate officialdom for the protection of the rights of persons and property against abuse of corporate power.

Thus, Eells, who has also been in charge of something called "Public policy research" at General Electric, lets the cat out of the bag. For he suggests that the principles of responsible corporate behavior cannot be blueprinted. They are "self-generating" or, in effect, somehow divined. Both Smith of Harvard and Eells of Columbia, it is safe to say, would be dismayed at the suggestion that these principles can be discovered by studying the entrails of chickens. There is no reason to believe, however, that this respected method of ancient Rome is much less fruitful than the doctrines of BSI.

Indeed, Smith's cases suggest that the main use of his course lies in introducing students to the variety of pressures that will affect their power when they reach the executive suite. BSI may teach less about beneficent decision-making than about the way to handle possible adversaries, such as government, labor, consumers, and suppliers.

This is no warrant for cynicism, however. If the New Creed and the Business School can't supply simple guides to decision-making, this does not mean that corporative executives are not genuinely concerned about the gulf between their power and its sanction, between their performance and their aspirations.

Some evidence on this score was turned up by the Reverend Raymond C. Baumhart, a Jesuit priest and former student at the Business School. He sent readers of the *Harvard Business Review* a provocative questionnaire that drew 1,700 replies, mostly from men who said they were either "top management" or "middle management" in the corporate world. Nearly half of them agreed with a statement that American businessmen tend to ignore ethical laws and are preoccupied chiefly with gain. Four of seven thought that businessmen would breach a code of ethics if they thought they could get away with it. Four of five said there are practices generally accepted in their own industry which they personally regarded as unethical. Among these generally accepted "unethical" practices, they cited lavish entertaining to seek favors; kickbacks to customers' purchasing agents; price fixing; and misleading advertising.

These replies do not add up to a world of amoral executives, accepting the corporate life for what it is. Instead, they indicate that these businessmen are uneasy about their own role and that of their fellows. Their distress is understandable. Nothing in the logic or practice of concentrated corporate industries now compels socially responsible decisions or even defines what they are. No formula explains how competing claims are to be gratified. No theory fixes responsibility on specific actors in the corporate drama.

HOW TO DELEGATE BLAME

In the style of the Business School, let us look at a few cases to illustrate the difficulties of socially responsible decision-making.

In any roster of leading concerns, the General Electric Company—the fourth-ranking industrial corporation in sales in 1960—would clearly shine. As Berle himself said in his celebration of the new creed, "The General Electric Company is, justly, one of the most respected of American corporations. Its management has been able and of unquestioned integrity."

GE, of course, was also the kingpin of the greatest criminal price conspiracy in the history of the antitrust laws. Indeed, GE has been running afoul of the antitrust laws for half a century. Between 1911 and 1952, the company had been ordered to abandon some illicit practice, or been convicted, or pleaded unwilling to contest, in thirteen other alleged breaches of the monopoly laws. So the remarkable cases to which GE pleaded guilty in 1960 were hardly isolated incidents. Even more interesting, however, is the way the corporation and its chief officers regarded their responsibility.

The company's latest brush with the antitrust laws involved ranking corporation officials. During the 1950's, the government charged, they had met secretly with other producers of electrical machinery to agree on and sometimes raise prices and to allocate shares of markets. The conspiracies—and there were many separate ones—ranged from giant turbine-generators to watt-hour meters. They embraced billions of dollars in sales.

GE's highest management repeatedly asserted that blame could attach only to those who participated directly in the price-rigging and market-sharing rings. How could this be? Simply because the corporation had issued a directive instructing its executives to obey antitrust laws and not to engage in agreements or discussions with competitors over prices and other competitive matters. Three GE officials were jailed, eight others given suspended sentences, and five more were fined. All of them came from just three of GE's divisions. But the man directly in charge of these three divisions, Arthur F. Vinson, was sure no serious fault lay with him.

Vinson, a Group Executive and Vice President, was questioned by the Senate Antitrust and Monopoly Subcommittee about his relation to the conspirators. "It was my duty," he said, "to have trustworthy, capable management in place and I delegated that authority and depended on them to do this job."

At another point, Vinson pictured himself as a sort of philosopher, aloof from the hurly-burly of prices and sales. He said, ". . . it is my job to coach, guide, and help and be knowledgeable to the extent that you can." At most, he would acknowledge some flaw in his Socratic dialogue. Vinson concluded his testimony by saying, "I think we could do a better teaching job" on antitrust matters. "Perhaps we didn't do enough talking about it."

On the next rung of the corporate ladder stood President Robert Paxton. In his view, "a handful of people" had "departed from proper conduct." He, himself, could be blamed only for "an unsuccessful supervision." The guilty handful, he said, "were supposed to be mature businessmen. They are supposed to be people who conduct themselves properly."

Before he moved up to the presidency, Paxton had preceded Vinson directly in charge of the tainted divisions. But Paxton insisted that GE's troubles flowed from some black lambs who had strayed from the fold because of their earlier, pre-GE rearing; neither the shepherds nor the sheep pen were faulty. He told the Senators, "Too much of the morality of the business life has to be taught by the employer. It should have been taught by a church; it should have been taught by a school; and above all things, it should have been taught at home, but it isn't."

The highest executive at GE, Chairman Ralph J. Cordiner, at first adopted a somewhat ambiguous stance before the Subcommittee. In his formal statement he said, "As chief executive officer, I accept my share of responsibility for what happened, even though I did not know of these secret violations of the law or condone such acts." But under questioning, it became clearer that Cordiner regarded his "share of responsibility" as minute, and he returned to the Vinson-Paxton thesis of a corrupt few. "Finally," he said, "this comes down to the individual attitude of an individual person and how responsive they are to the teaching and the belief and the conviction."

Speaking as a corporate entity, GE was as emphatic as Cordiner that guilt lay elsewhere. The 1960 annual report declared:

> The Company pleaded *nolo contendere* to thirteen of these indictments, while pleading guilty to six others upon being advised by counsel that the Company may be held *technically responsible* (my emphasis) for the acts of its employees even when they have violated a clear, long-standing Company Directive Policy setting up standards of conduct more stringent than requirements of the antitrust laws.

Responsibility, in this view, is individual and personal. Federal Judge J. Cullen Ganey, who received the indictments, examined much of the evidence, and sentenced the defendants, was not persuaded. Among other things, he declared:

> I am not at all unmindful that the real blame is to be laid at the doorstep of the corporate defendants and those who guide and direct their policy. While the Department of Justice has acknowledged that they are unable to uncover probative evidence which could secure a conviction beyond a reasonable doubt of those in the highest echelons of the corporations here involved, in a broader sense they bear a grave responsibility for the present situation. . . .

But at least in public, business leaders rallied behind GE and Cordiner. John W. McGovern, then President of the National Association of Manufacturers, told an inquiring newspaper, "In a large organization, you can't know every detail. Things like that could happen but people at the top would not be aware of it."

And the President of the Chamber of Commerce, Arthur H. Motley, observed: "As business gets bigger and more decentralized, a code is written and top management expects everybody to operate with it. But it must be followed through personally. It's possible to establish a policy that's not followed."

This confronts the creed with a peculiar dilemma. Are corporate leaders responsible when things go well, but not accountable when they don't, because the large corporation is too complex?

WHERE THE FORD GOLD WENT

This dilemma apparently troubled Henry Ford II, chairman of the Ford Motor Company and a GE director. Shortly after GE and the other electrical companies were sentenced, Ford declared that "it is the job of our corporate executives to keep their own houses in order."

In an address entitled "Business Ethics in 1961," Ford said: "I'm afraid it is little use to drag out the old bad-apple alibi to explain away things—the idea that there are always a few bad ones in every barrel. There is really only one thing for top executives to do at such a time as this. That is to forget the alibis and the explanations and have the fortitude—the plain guts—to stand up and say: 'This is our failure. We are chagrined and sorry. It will not happen again.' "

Ford's attempt to resurrect the doctrine of responsibility was confounded one week later. He and the other GE directors—drawn from the cream of American finance and industry and including a former Harvard Business School dean—publicly endorsed GE's management. They continued Cordiner in his newly enlarged role of both Chairman and President.

If the price conspiracy illustrates the difficulty of fixing responsibility, Ford's own company offers a prime example of the problem of determining just what is responsible corporate conduct.

In his speech on ethics, Ford confidently asserted: "Business today understands well how its actions may impinge not only on the lives of individuals but also upon the goals and policies of our nation both home and abroad." Former members of the Eisenhower Administration, not known for their antipathy to the corporate view, might well have done a double take at this. For Ford played a curious part in one of the Administration's climactic dramas. In October 1960, international speculators suddenly began betting feverishly against the dollar, pushing up the price of gold. Behind this outburst lay the deficit in the United States' international accounts. The speculators were betting that the deficit and the resultant loss of gold would force the United States to devalue, paying more dollars for an ounce of gold. The President and his treasury Secretary, Robert B. Anderson, took to national television to tell the nation that the situation was perilous. "All Americans ought to be profoundly concerned," Anderson said.

After the election, Mr. Eisenhower, now a lame duck, moved decisively to curb the outflow of dollars and gold. Among other measures, he ordered the Department of Defense to reduce by 15,000 a month the number of dollar-spending servicemen's wives and children overseas. He even hinted that the United States might have to trim its military expenditures on the North Atlantic Treaty Organization, and sent Anderson on a humiliating and largely unsuccessful mission to drum up help from the West Germans.

In the midst of these alarums and excursions, the Ford company announced it was about to add about 360 million of its own dollars to the unfavorable balance of payments. The sum was greater than all of the estimated savings in the first year of the Eisenhower orders. Ford was to spend the money to buy up the remaining 45 per cent of the shares in its British manufacturing subsidiary. The Detroit parent already owned 55 per cent, more than enough for absolute control. But the chairman declared that the remaining 45 per cent was needed for "greater operational flexibility and to coordinate better."

Simple observers were puzzled at how flexibility and coordination could be improved by enlarging a 55 per cent share to 100 per cent. But students of Ford's finances thought they had a clue. The company's cash and marketable securities had climbed by more than $200 million in 1959 to $666.3 million. In other words, excess cash was burning holes in Ford's pockets. At the same time, the British plant was earning nearly 40 per cent more on its assets than the corporation as a whole; sales of autos and trucks by the English firm had expanded during the 1950s about fifteen times as fast as those of the American company. Ford appeared to be acting like a classical entrepreneur, putting its idle cash into the more profitable overseas venture.

Anderson personally telephoned Ford asking him to soften the blow. But Ford, like the West Germans, was not about to do favors for lame ducks. In the week that Ford sent its check to London for the shares, the United States' stock of gold dropped another $204 million.

The point of this essay is not to argue that businessmen are greedy, hypocritical, or irresponsible. Rather it is to suggest that corporate executives, by training and outlook, are ill-equipped to make difficult judgments in the swampy area of social responsibility. This is a burden that cannot and should not be placed upon them. As Theodore Levitt, a business consultant, has said, the theory of the socially responsible executive conjures up "a frightening spectacle of a powerful economic functional group whose future and perception are shaped in a tight materialistic context of money and things, but which imposes its narrow ideas about a broad spectrum of unrelated non-economic subjects on the mass of man and society."

TOO SIMPLE AN ANSWER

Berle, eloquent champion of the conscience-ridden executive, saw through to some other major difficulties of his thesis. "If corporations are to make industrial plans," he asked, "what are the criteria of these plans?" In a world of perfect competition, this question is irrelevant; the consumer is king and his choices, through the market, guide business decisions. But in a world of corporations emancipated in some measure from the market, no such criteria exist.

Moreover, Berle observed, modern corporate managements have "substantially absolute power." Even if agreement could be reached on what is and is not responsible behavior, there is no mechanism to make the corporate hierarchs accountable. Society generally has no process it can use to recall erring executives or hold a referendum on crucial corporate decisions. If GE's chief officials disclaim responsibility, society is powerless to contradict them effectively.

If the corporate conscience is an uncertain instrument, what can take its place? How can legitimacy and sanction be restored to economic decision-making? For many economists, the answer is simple—too simple, in fact, for life outside the academy. They say: Let's restore competition. Their favorite method is a more vigorous antitrust policy. The more sophisticated economists, however, know that with the best will in the world, the Justice Department won't (and shouldn't) be able to recreate a world of atomistic competitors, no one of them big enough significantly to affect an industry's price or output. These neo-trustbusters argue for a more limited goal. With considerable persuasiveness, they urge that greater competition and more reliance on impersonal forces would have considerable value in some industries.

This does not mean, for example, fracturing the steel industry into hundreds of small corporations. Efficient production in steel requires large aggregations of capital. But it is doubtful that these need to be as large as the three firms which now control more than half of the industry's output. The American producers' belated introduction of new steel-making techniques pioneered in Europe testifies that the biggest are not necessarily the liveliest.

The neo-trust-busters recognize that if anti-monopoly regulation is to become more than a shield for business as usual, the laws will have to be amended drastically. Courts are reluctant to break up corporations—at most, they will adopt such heroic expedients only to cope with obvious misconduct. Under present laws, they won't do it simply to reduce market power.

An amendment to the Sherman Act proposed by Professors Carl Kaysen and Donald Turner of Harvard could be helpful. They would split up into viable units any corporation exercising "unreasonable" market power. "Unreasonable" power would be assumed wherever, for example, one firm accounted for half an industry's sales or four firms accounted for 80 per cent. The giants could escape division only by showing that their preeminence arose as the result of gains in efficiency or if the cost of a breakup would be too great.

Even with such an amendment—and apart from a few economists, the pressure for it would not lift a small balloon—great sectors of private economic power would remain. This stubborn fact has led others to suggest that we should keep the existing structure, but harness it by new devices to responsible ends. In effect, this idea revives the concept of responsible decision-making—but declares that its definition is too elusive to be left exclusively to the business schools or the corporate managers.

FOR THE WORLD AS IT IS

Other groups, consumers, the government, labor might be enlisted to help shape crucial economic decisions through a variety of devices. One approach was embodied in a bill proposed by Senator Joseph Clark and Representative Henry Reuss a few years ago. Their measure would require dominant corporations (and unions in important industries) to spell out their price and wage plans before some public panel. The panel might then mobilize public opinion behind a set of recommendations.

Another approach—indicative of noncoercive planning—has been tried with some success in Scandinavia, France, Holland, and Japan and is now being introduced into Britain. This technique brings together representatives of labor, management, other interest groups, and government. They try to agree on a specific set of attainable economic objectives and then voluntarily translate them into policies for individual industries and plants. President Kennedy's Council of Economic Advisers quietly tried a dry run at this more than a year ago. But corporation economists, horrified at the implications of even noncoercive planning, were hostile. The President has also created a Labor-Management Advisory Committee with government and public representatives; despite its difficulties in agreeing on even platitudinous statements, it is another stab in the same direction. So too are the government's suggested wage and price guideposts which have caused the steel industry and the White House so much anguish.

All of these hesitant stirrings in Washington reflect a slow-growing recognition that we no longer live in the world of Adam Smith—and we have not yet reached a world of corporate philosopher-kings, whose intuitive consciences will guide them to make their decisions in the public interest. Indeed, we are never likely to reach it; and it is unfair to our corporate executives to pretend that we will.

Today, much private economic power exists in a political void. But this might be filled by broadening the narrow apex of private decision-making, by ensuring that other groups besides corporate managers shall bring their influence to bear on the crucial choices in the great corporations. A society that regards itself as pragmatic need not be bound by any particular solution to this problem, but could fruitfully experiment with several. A domestic brand of noncoercive planning may prove most useful for the economy as a whole. It might well be supplemented by price-wage hearing panels in a few industries along the lines of the Clark-Reuss bill.

None of these devices could or should be extended to every nook and cranny of the economy. They should focus instead on the significant sectors, on those industries whose economic size and concentration arm their managers with a strategic grasp on the material well-being of the whole country. Some new arrangements like these will have to be devised if the legitimacy that perfect competition once provided for economic decisions is to be restored to those areas of concentrated power that cannot and should not be broken up.

SHOULD BUSINESS GO IN FOR POLITICS?

Charles P. Taft

Charles P. Taft, a leader in civic reform, has held many public and government posts. Mayor of Cincinnati from 1955–1957, he is also the author of *City Management, The Cincinnati Experiment, You and I and Roosevelt, Democracy in Politics and Economics,* and other books.

Americans read almost daily now that businessmen should go into politics. This has been said before, but not so often or so broadly. A few years ago business leaders were being urged to work at the local political level. Now, every salaried employee in some companies is being called upon to select the party that best represents his point of view and work for that party in his neighborhood.

This sounds good, especially to one who has watched local groups seek businessmen candidates for, say the City Council in such a well-governed and progressive city as Cincinnati. The task of finding candidates is harder every year, it seems. Perhaps, one thinks, this movement can help. But how "civic" is it?

Business has been in politics a long time. I have been told that at the end of the seventeenth century the sons of Robert Taft, a wheelwright, of Mendon, Mass., became select men of the town and worked hard to get a bridge built to the west over the Blackstone River—where coincidentally no doubt, they owned some land.

Certainly the "robber barons" were in politics up to their ears, from Jim Fisk and Commodore Vanderbilt to the copper miners of Montana. Railroaders, liquor dealers, insurance men, shipping magnates, fair-traders and price discounters are only a few of the businessmen who have found it necessary to go to State Legislatures and Congress. Makers of fire-department equipment, concrete and blacktop purveyors, claypipe manufacturers, road and building contractors all are concerned with who is Mayor, City Manager, Councilman or Governor.

Companies of any size have a trouble shooter, part or full time, who knows his way around in politics. He may also be the one who decides what campaign contribution is made to what politician by what officer—from his personal salary, of course.

Government regulation in the state or national capital makes a common front essential to an industry. Government contracts may be the lifeblood of the business, as with most airframe companies. So trade associations grow and prosper, and larger companies have branch offices in Washington.

Then what is new about the business-into-politics movement? One thing is its scale. One nationally known corporation has trained a battalion of 500 executives to spread the gospel of company views on public issues. Another new element is that the present movement, upon examination, begins to assume some of the aspects of a public-relations operation. There is even a New York advertising firm organized last year specifically to advise companies in this limited field.

Is all this good or bad? How far will it get?

There is a lot of sound thinking behind a program for a "better business climate." A big local plant is usually a sitting duck for a rabble rouser on a City Council. It shouldn't be; its intelligent leaders—and its employees on lower levels—ought to fight back.

But there is something wrong with the broad drive to get employees into politics. Even the political P. R. firm warns business men to look out. Democratic National Chairman Paul Butler, in a joint interview last May with Thruston B. Morton, his Republican counterpart, said: "With . . . narrow purposes in mind they are going to end up alienating the general public, creating suspicion of the business community and doing a clumsy job of obtaining even their narrow objectives." And Mr. Morton warned: "If business men are to achieve a maximum effectiveness in politics, they must work toward this goal as citizens rather than as spokesmen for, or representatives of, just one segment of our total economy."

Henry Kaiser and George Romney, both pretty good judges of sound business public relations, have stood against the whole idea of business telling its employees to go into politics—apparently for just the reasons Butler and Morton gave.

That warning is sound. What is really self-interest, however justifiable, ought to be advanced with some degree of attractive modesty and humility. What is good for General Motors is not necessarily good for the country—or the city.

A second thing wrong with the campaign is that it is, in fact, aimed at labor. This central motivation—to rival big labor and beat down labor organizations—is openly stated in many cases. An executive of a large corporation, in a speech to the Business Advisory Council last October, urged more vigorous political action by business men because of his "personal" appraisal of the A.F.L. C.I.O. as the "most aggressive and successful force in politics." This power, he said, is "principally in the hands of other (than racketeer) union officials, who nevertheless put forth ideologies and proposals which result in inflation, concentration of power in central government, damage to progress and withering of freedom." I cannot remember any endorsement of political participation by business not closely related to emotion about the labor problem.

You may ask why this campaign should not be aimed at labor. There are two good reasons.

One is that labor is not as effective at the polls or in Congress or the State Legislatures as is assumed in this emotional reaction. The Taft-Hartley Act was passed by more than a two-thirds margin over President Truman's veto and the labor reform bill that recently passed the House was certainly not the one labor wanted. At the local level labor seldom really works *for* a candidate—only once since 1925 in Cincinnati, for example.

Labor can vote *against,* when the issue is something like the "right to work," and when people in general feel it is simply punitive, not constructive. And if labor comes out to vote on such an issue, it may knock off a candidate incidentally, as it did Senator John Bricker in Ohio last November. But although workers may get herded out to register, they do not vote as "labor." In fact, they do not vote at all. Their local leaders have their hands too full with union politics to spend much time on local, state or national party politics.

The other reason against just "opposing labor" is that a wholly negative campaign, for all that it may be temporarily effective, does not work in the long pull. As Arthur Motley, the publisher of *Parade Magazine* and a leader in the successful fight to elect Representative John V. Lindsay against the opposition of the Republican organization in New York's Seventeenth District last November, has put it: "I can see no future for business and our kind of economy if we're merely going to have 'big business' opposing 'big labor' in the political arena."

This leads us to my third general objection to the "business into Politics" campaign—the fact that it looks, and sometimes acts, as if it were against all progress. For example, an official of one of our largest corporations, active in the movement, has talked about "successful Republican candidates who were pulled far to the left in their campaign obligations and promises." The head of another company, located in New Jersey, which conducts one of these programs, has been reported organizing to prevent the renomination of Clifford Case as Senator from that state because his record is "indistinguishable from the Americans for Democratic Action." Yet Case in four years is recorded as supporting President Eisenhower 85 per cent of the time, compared with 83 per cent for former Senator H. Alexander Smith.

There is an interesting schizophrenia here. The National Association of Manufacturers and the United States Chamber of Commerce are officially opposed to any program like public housing, and want urban renewal stopped or reduced rapidly. Yet many of their distinguished members belong to organizations in Pittsburgh, Cleveland, Cincinnati, Boston or San Francisco which are the civic spark plugs for urban renewal as the only cure for the blight at the heart of practically every large city in America. In that connection they support public housing. They go to state capitals and to Washington and say so, while the N.A.M. and Chamber of Commerce present resolutions to the contrary in the same places.

It may be argued that if business men want to go into politics to oppose labor, urban renewal or Senator Case, that is their privilege. To this I answer that we are talking about politics, and that politics, as the art of the possible, is no place for anti-intellectual absolutism about economics and social sciences, or about individuals, either. I do not advocate compromise with principles but I do mean that in these areas nobody knows all, that humility learns more than arrogance, and that an intelligent and honest opponent may have a little—just a little—in which he may be right.

My final objection to the "go into politics" movement is that it generally neglects local government where public servants provide us with streets, sewers, hospitals, police protection, water and garbage disposal. Rather, the movement's sponsors back the local "organization" for supposedly doing the job for the Republican candidates for President, Senator, Congressman or Governor. (Let us face it: these sponsors work with Democrats because they have to in most large cities, but they are all Republicans.)

The truth is that a local Republican organization does very little for the four named officials on the Republican ticket, especially if there is a real fight on. It is much more interested in the Probate Judge (Surrogate in New York), the Auditor (tax assessor), the Sheriff and the County Commissioners.

My late brother, Senator Robert A. Taft, now highly revered by the organization in Cincinnati, always ran well *behind* those local officials, and it was not the Cincinnati or any other local organization that pulled him through for re-election in 1944 by just 17,000 out of well over 2,000,000 votes in the state of Ohio.

Local government—good, efficient local government—is where any political movement ought to begin, especially when, as today, most national domestic issues, including labor corruption, have their roots there. And from local government, too, come those good candidates for national office whom this movement is looking for.

But few spokesmen for the moment even think of local government when they make their speeches. I heard a top corporation man describe the whole program to a president's round table of the American Management Association. When he had finished I asked if what he said applied (1) to local government, and (2) to a city with an independent local movement like our Cincinnati Charter Committee and (3) to places like Detroit or Dayton where the national parties take no part in local elections. (A poll taken last April showed that 60 per cent of American cities with more than 50,000 population have no Republican or Democratic activities.) The answer was that, of course, the program applied there, too. I can only say there is very, very little in his company's literature to show it.

Yet there is much that business men could do in politics. They are urgently needed. Clearly, since I have been so critical, it is up to me to lay out some guide lines.

(1) One thing that business men are doing, and that they should do more of is exemplified by the Cleveland Foundation, the Citizens Development Committee in Cincinnati and the Allegheny County Group in Pittsburgh. These organizations back master plans for their areas, and help and encourage local officials of either party to carry these plans through. Their business-men members go to state capitals and Washington to help cut through red tape or get new legislation.

(2) Business men should take adult courses in economics, as members of the Committee for Economic Development do. Too many of the vocal ones rely on self-constituted research organizations that tell them what they want to hear instead of on professionally recognized groups like the National Bureau for Economic Research, the Brookings Institution or the National Industrial Conference Board.

(3) Business men ought to write their own speeches and do a lot of their own homework. They should practice persuasive speaking, seek critical comments on their technical proficiency. Few business men can stand up to comparable labor leaders, mostly for want of practice and training in both sound economics and public speaking.

(4) Business men who go into politics should learn first that the "pros"

have no interest in their participation except as moneybags or fat cats, and perhaps as rubber stamps for the ticket.

To put it affirmatively, the place to begin is usually with a fight—*against* the organization—to get good candidates nominated and elected in both the party primary and the election. Talking about starting in the precincts of your own party organization is eyewash, because intelligent young business men are the last thing the local machine wants. It wants order-takers who will produce votes for the slate at the primary. After that, of course, the voters probably have little choice.

This is not a sorehead's gripe. I can get myself elected in my home town against the organization. I have done it in eleven primary or general elections, and I have lost in only three.

But my point is shown by the White Plains Republican primary fight of a couple of years ago, in which a group of insurgent beginners lost by only 1,000 votes in 20,000, and by last fall's victory for an anti-organization Republican Congressional candidate in New York's Seventeenth District. A group of young Republican business men has even analyzed the marginal districts around the country and set out to show, with some success, what a good plan can do, with good local leadership.

Every good American ought to be in politics, because through politics his government is run in a way that provides justice for his rights, and the services that make it possible to live as pleasantly as few in history have lived before. Business men can help make the word "politician" an honorable tag, even an intellectual tag, and have all kinds of fascinating fun doing it. But no one should fall for the canned slogan: "Join the party of your choice and start working in it at the precinct level (and, boy, let's sock these damned unions)."

HOW BUSINESSMEN CAN FIGHT "BIG GOVERNMENT"—AND WIN

David G. Wood

David G. Wood has been in public relations for the steel industry many years, in Seattle first and later in San Francisco. A graduate of the University of Washington school of journalism, he has worked for the Seattle *Times* and the Associated Press.

I am weary of hearing fellow businessmen attack Big Government. I'm even more bored with platitudes about defending the Free Enterprise System. And the charge that Nobody Understands the Role of Profits is just as tiresome.

From *Harper's Magazine,* November 1963. Reprinted by permission.

The latter was the theme of yet another speech I sat through at a major college campus last June. It was the annual awards banquet of the School of Business Administration. The speaker was the Director of Corporate and Public Affairs, whatever that means, of a major home-appliance manufacturer in the Midwest. He was out to convince his listeners that profits are the cornerstone of our society. Why senior students and faculty members in business administration, and businessmen from the surrounding communities, should need convincing is a point that escaped me. I guess he was really trying to tell the graduating students to go forth and save our system. The "how" was totally missing, an all too common aspect of these polished, inspirational Free Enterprise speeches.

I happen to believe so strongly in our Free Enterprise System and in the importance of profits to that system that I'm convinced they don't need defending. To do so is to state the obvious. That's why the speeches and the advertisements and the commercials and the house-organ articles are so boring.

Our economic system is, after all, a human institution. And no human institution I know of has ever achieved perfection. Improvement should be a goal of all businessmen truly intent on preserving the Free Enterprise System. But we never seem to talk about improvement when we make speeches. This would involve "how?" It would force us to consider methods and programs and objectives. It would be controversial, and businessmen try never to be controversial. Hence, we are boring.

The Director of Corporate and Public Affairs, in his speech at the banquet, cited a typical statistic from *Opinion Research, Inc.* Sixty-two per cent, or something like that, of all Americans think profits are too high. Does this mean profits *are* too high? Emphatically no, said our speaker, profits are dwindling every year. I work for the steel industry and I wholeheartedly endorse that part of his talk. Does it mean that the American people are being misled by educators and journalists into the belief that profits are too high? Despite the fact he was speaking before a considerable number of educators, our speaker implied that this was the case. He managed by a "we know you're with us" gesture to exclude the Business Administration professors from the leftist teachers who some businessmen are convinced dominate our campuses today.

At any rate, we were told, we businessmen must somehow overcome the power of the press and the schools and tell the people the Truth—that profits are not too high. They are too low. I don't believe the Director of Corporate and Public Affairs actually expects us to succeed. Who would invest their money in our corporations if the people did become convinced that profits are too low?

MARXISM, HIGH-SCHOOL STYLE

But let's use a little common horse sense. It is ridiculous that any businessman should become concerned for our Free Enterprise System just because most Americans think profits are too high. Nearly all Americans are consumers first and investors second, if at all. There would be something wrong with human nature if we didn't believe that anyone trying to sell us something is making too much money.

Businessmen also get excited around graduation time every spring because public-opinion surveyors measure the attitudes of high-school kids and decide that they don't know much about economics, and what they do know is all wrong. How many times have you heard in a speech or read in some company magazine that high-school students somewhere have communist tendencies? A majority had approved of "*from* each according to his ability, *to* each according to his needs." Shocking? Well, the speaker or house-organ editor obviously intends it to be, but I somehow never get very disturbed.

When you stop to think of it, that's a rather practical philosophy for a high-school student. After all, his earning ability is very small and—from what parents of teen-agers tell me—his needs are very great. If he's smart he's been trying to sell his father on the equity of this doctrine for years. Just before the son of our ex-next-door neighbors in Seattle was graduated from Shoreline High School there, we got a letter from his mother. She reported that he and his Senior Prom date were "planning a big time with dinner at Canlis if you please." She added, significantly, "We haven't even been there." Seattleites regard Canlis as their most elegant and expensive restaurant, catering chiefly to the expense-account crowd and, apparently, to high-school boys wishing to impress their girls. Here is a high-school senior willing to spend his father's money in a restaurant his father has always regarded as too expensive to take his mother to. Why should he question a neat idea like "from each according to his ability, to each according to his needs"?

One might argue it is the job of the schools to teach our children that this is a Marxist doctrine and therefore bad. I would answer that we can't teach them to think for themselves by hanging labels on ideas. It's better to let them figure out for themselves that this idea simply won't work in a free society. If a majority of them haven't figured it out by the time they are high-school seniors, it is perhaps because teenagers are what they are—a confusing mixture of selfishness and idealism. I think I like them that way.

Permit me to proceed, then, on the assumption that businessmen are wasting their time and energies, to say nothing of their money, on defending Profits and the Free Enterprise System. This is really not such an original idea. On the same subject more than a dozen years ago, *Fortune* magazine asked "Is Anybody Listening?" and concluded that no one was. *Fortune* went a step further by suggesting that businessmen were making people wonder what was wrong with the system that it constantly required so much defending.

Improvement, as I have already suggested, is the best defense. Instead of talking so much, businessmen ought to do more. If they did enough, they could quit worrying about Big Government. For the past thirty years most of the improvements—if you choose to call them that—in our Free Enterprise system have been made by the federal government. During most of that period government has drawn its leadership from areas other than the business community. Our governmental leaders have been pragmatists. If a problem existed in our society, they wanted to find a way to solve it without regard for labels or doctrines.

What I'm urging upon my fellow businessmen is to out-govern government. Let's identify problems and bring about solutions before government is forced to act. Every citizen of a free society possesses this privilege and responsibility. The leaders of a community are especially obligated to act. And businessmen are leaders—or should be. Lincoln was right. Government should do only what citizens cannot do for themselves.

One reason government has been doing so much is that businessmen have been doing so little. Perhaps we forgot how, during the tremendous scare of the Great Depression. But that has been over for a long time, and the Roosevelt reforms have not so changed our society that we are incapable of effective action.

What action? That question ought to be answered with a review of all the problems facing our country today and a discussion of what businessmen can do about them. That obviously is impossible here because: (a) I lack the space and (b) I lack the knowledge. I'll just have to satisfy myself that any suggestions made here will be more than the Director of Corporate and Public Affairs gave us in his speech.

WHO OUGHT TO PROVIDE JOBS?

One obvious criterion of a successful economic system is its ability to provide enough jobs. Ours is not doing as well as it should. Let's look at my young ex-next-door neighbor once again, the one whose tastes already run to Seattle's most expensive restaurant. As a high-school graduate this year he is joining a growing army of young men who are finding it increasingly hard to get work. California's youth-employment supervisor, Robert Hill, called jobless young people "social dynamite." He said in this decade twenty-six million youths will seek jobs, twice as many as in the 1950s.

Businessmen are going to have to assume more responsibility in getting these young people started on useful careers, especially with on-the-job training. We are demanding too high a skill from beginning workers. The kids complain that no one will hire them because they have no experience and then ask, the undeniable logic: How are we supposed to get experience?

Mr. Hill suggested that some companies might do better to hire fewer engineers, who are in short supply anyway and sometimes become bored with jobs that don't really require their full professional skills. Engineers' aides, who could be trained on the job, might make more sense.

The Peace Corps is a marvelous idea, perhaps the best of the Kennedy Administration so far, but the young people we send overseas must have skills if they are to be of any service. We businessmen ought to promote and favor any programs which will enhance human skills, even government programs. Our businesses will benefit eventually, just as they benefit from public education. Providing all the employment and on-the-job training we possibly can, consistent with efficient operating practices, should be the Number One goal of our private economy. Then if we still are unable to absorb the twenty-six million young people in this decade that Mr. Hill talks about, we must stop opposing federal and state programs. Serving in a government-sponsored civilian service corps, foreign or domestic, is infinitely preferable to joblessness. Business opposition to a domestic Peace Corps is the type of irresponsible negativism that causes our fellow citizens to dislike us, ignore us, or both.

Employment opportunities are not the only kind denied many Americans. Negroes lack so many opportunities that theirs has been a second-class citizenship in a society based on equal citizenship for all. This is wrong, and at long last two branches of the federal government—the judicial and executive—are taking meaningful action to assure equal rights for everyone.

There appear to be considerable number of business executives willing to condemn such use of federal power. Many others (or perhaps they are the same ones) join and finance anti-communist crusades. Using comparable energy and most likely less money, these same businessmen—through the power they possess in the American economy—could render government action unnecessary and deliver worldwide communism a staggering blow. Equal status for the American Negro would undermine communist strategy and propaganda everywhere. This one improvement in our own society could well be enough to turn the tide overwhelmingly in our favor throughout the world. I often wonder why the anti-communist crusaders won't change into pro-Negro crusaders. They would achieve their goal far sooner than with their present methods.

I would expect the truly responsible leaders of business and industry, however, to work toward equality for Negroes simply because it is right. I wish there were more evidence that they are so working. Undoubtedly, more is being done than the public generally realizes. Because the problems involved are potentially explosive, and because they are not concerned with winning votes, businessmen generally shun publicity in endeavors of this kind. All but one of the white business leaders of Birmingham who served on the biracial committee seeking a solution to the city's conflict, before the bombings this fall, refused even to be identified. They feared economic reprisals, a universal concern of businessmen. "What will my customers think?" is a question usually considered carefully prior to political or social activity. It's a shame Mr. Welch didn't ponder it more seriously before he founded the John Birch Society. If he had run true to business form, he might have decided to refrain for fear of offending all the country's communist candy consumers!

INVITATIONS TO GOVERNMENT MEDDLING

Even if we were free to publicize our bosses' actions to our hearts' content, it would be most difficult for industrial publicists like myself to convince anyone that everything possible is being done. The results just aren't there. I would welcome, for example, a steel industry report on what it has done to prepare Birmingham for its inevitable compliance with court rulings granting its Negro citizens equal status. After years of enlightened industrial influence, we might logically expect Birmingham to be more advanced in its social attitudes than it apparently is. It simply *has* to be more enlightened than the surrounding rural areas of Alabama. Yet its recent tragic history (not to mention its international press notices) raises serious doubts.

U.S. Steel is Birmingham's largest employer and therefore a powerful economic force there. It is faint praise to point out that under U.S. Steel's quiet leadership and influence Birmingham is a better city than it would otherwise be. A question that repeatedly has been asked, usually by indignant liberals, is, "Why hasn't John F. Kennedy done more about Birmingham?" Conservatives who truly believe what they preach ought to respond with "Why hasn't Roger Blough done more about Birmingham?"

Industrial leaders may have an excuse in the Deep South, where long-established customs, to say nothing of statutes, have precluded any dramatic moves by them toward equality for all. But neither law nor custom exists to discourage action in such enlightened cities as San Francisco.

Sunday, May 26, 1963, was proclaimed Human Rights Day by Mayor Christopher of San Francisco. Some 12,000 citizens paraded up Market Street and held a rally at the Civic Center to protest racial oppression and demand universal equality. The newspapers described it as "San Francisco's ringing answer to Birmingham." Significantly enough for the point I have been trying to make, the march was organized by the San Francisco Church-Labor Conference. Advance stories promoting the observance of Human Rights Day quoted ministers and labor leaders. Business leaders remained silent. Sponsorship did not include the Chamber of Commerce, or any other business organization.

The parade itself was a responsible, dignified demonstration. The chief of police called it "a heartwarming spectacle." In the words of the San Francisco *Chronicle,* "They were of all races, but the major races were white and Negro, about 50-50. They were of all faiths—rabbis, Protestant ministers of the Council of Churches, Maryknoll nuns, Christian Brothers, a Jesuit priest. They were of all classes, but predominantly labor."

Are we businessmen too stuffy and self-satisfied to associate ourselves with a gesture of this kind? If we fail to be counted as *for* anything as basic as equal citizenship for fellow Americans, how can we expect anyone to become excited about government's intrusion in business affairs? The freedom to raise steel prices would seem of small consequence compared with the freedom to vote, to work, to live (or even dine) anywhere the price is right, to assemble peaceably, or to enroll in the state university.

Instead of seizing the initiative—which is after all one prerequisite of leadership—businessmen permit the government to lead the way. I work in a major San Francisco office building where the tenant on one floor is a federal agency. The only Negro white-collar workers in the building—stenographers, clerks, and supervisors—are employed on that floor. The few non-government Negroes in the building are janitors, cafeteria busboys, and messengers. If government agencies can find qualified Negro workers, so can we. And we can easily get them because we pay more. But we are not doing so, and we are thereby inviting government interference into the conduct of our business in a situation where it is right and we are wrong. This is the worst possible position in which to be to carry on a fight against government regulation, the Welfare State, or Creeping Socialism. Scare phrases help but little if our policies are wrong to begin with.

WHY HIDE THE COST OF CREDIT?

Also as a mattter of right, credit buyers are entitled to fair and honest treatment. Public reports as well as personal experience lead me to the conclusion that they are not getting it. For several years, Senator Paul Douglas of Illinois has been trying, in vain, to obtain passage of a truth-in-lending bill. A similar bill at the state level died in committee at Sacramento recently. According to reporter Jack Miller of the San Francisco *News Call Bulletin,* "the cost-of-credit measure, opposed by a powerful alliance of business interests, was shunted to the oblivion of the Assembly Rules Committee."

What honest reason could there possibly be for not informing buyers exactly, in a percentage figure and in dollars and cents, what buying on time is going to cost them? Maybe the passage of another law *is* undesirable—but retailers themselves have shown no inclination to police the situation. Their attitude appears to be, as usual, to get whatever the traffic will bear, which is a remarkable amount if the facts can be disguised well enough.

To purchase a few dresses for our daughters at Christmas time, 1961, my wife opened an account at a Seattle store of a well-known national chain. The unitemized statement we received about the first of February was larger than my wife could remember having charged. Investigation showed that $6.09 had been added to purchases totaling $31.64—on an account, mind you, to be paid within ninety days. I wrote a stinging letter to the credit manager in Seattle, which was answered within a week by the Credit Controller at the firm's executive offices in New York. In it I said the additional charge amounted to 77 per cent annual interest, although I'll admit I was a little unsure of my ability to compute it accurately. But the Credit Controller didn't question that at all. He objected only to my use of the word "interest." He called it a "service charge to *partially* compensate us for the expense of having a credit office in the store." The emphasis is his, not mine. He would have us believe that his firm is losing money on its credit operation. A "service charge" of 77 per cent is merely partial compensation! He added that he disliked having a dissatisfied customer so would settle for our payment minus the $6.09 "service charge." In the future, he trusted, we would not want to use his credit facilities. What an understatement!

Legitimate businesses, more interested in selling products than credit, ought to oppose this kind of retailing with all the vigor they can muster. Newspapers and radio stations ought to refuse the sleazy advertising that sustains it. The Better Business Bureau—which incidentally received a copy of my letter and made no response at all—ought to disown firms guilty of outrageous and hidden credit charges. If they cannot solve the situation themselves, honest businessmen should support rather than oppose Senator Douglas' bill. Neither the Senator nor anyone else can prevent gullible persons from squandering money, but they can be given all the facts on which to base their decisions. The cost of credit is a fact that should be made crystal clear.

By and large, government has stayed out of those areas where private citizens, businessmen mostly, have done the job. Cultural activities of all kinds are generously supported by the business community. Federal aid for the arts has been suggested occasionally, but not taken too seriously. Most people probably regard it as unnecessary if not unwise. Higher education—especially the private colleges and universities—has received massive financial support from industry. I suppose educators will never regard it as sufficient, but the corporation (or its executives) is rare that doesn't maintain a generous program of support for higher education. United Funds—conceived, promoted, and conducted by businessmen throughout the country—have provided the money to keep much welfare and social work in private hands. No tax money is used and contributions remain voluntary, more or less. It seems unlikely that government financing of election campaigns will ever be adopted in this country. Businessmen and others, notably labor unions, have been willing enough to contribute the money for this activity so essential to a democracy. Medical insurance for employees has become a widespread fringe benefit provided by corporations. The only serious talk of government-sponsored medical care is for retired persons. Which brings up Medicare, an extension of Social Security to include a most obvious need of old age. When industry furthers a lie of the American Medical Association by calling Medicare "Socialism," it offers no solution. Let's find a better one than Medicare if we can.

Undoubtedly many business leaders will object to what I have said. Full employment, job training, fair employment practices, equal rights for all our citizens, consumer protection, medical care for retired men and women. I can hear the response of businessmen I know: "None of these things is our concern. Our job is to make a respectable profit for our shareholders."

To them I say, "Then stop raving about Big Government!" If private citizens with power and influence refuse to concern themselves with improving our society beyond offering new and better products, they have only themselves to blame if their power atrophies. Negativism is not leadership. And that is what the business community all too often exerts.

Until we businessmen demonstrate some positive leadership in the solution of social and economic problems, I'm afraid the country is better off in the hands of politicians and their allies, and labor leaders and the intellectuals.

15 BIG LABOR U.S.A.

What are the beliefs of the public about labor's rights and responsibilities on the American scene? Several notions seem to have gained credence in recent years. Perhaps the most prevalent is that labor in the 1930s not only redressed the historical imbalance of economic power against it but went on to gain an undue weight of its own in relation to business. Therefore, according to this view, the major task since World War II has been to redress the new inequality. Second is the opinion that organized labor, through such devices as the Political Action Committee (PAC) and the Committee on Political Education (COPE), has created a well-oiled, smooth-running political machine that would put Tammany Hall to shame. Finally, there is a widespread belief that workers, if free to follow their own wills, would seldom join a union, and that union members, if protected against "coercion," would abandon their leaders. This last conclusion has lent support, particularly in the southern states to a series of so-called "right-to-work" laws—more accurately labeled union shop-prevention laws—as well as to a whole rash of dubious preachments about the right of the individual to choose freely whether to join a union or not.

Such beliefs reflect a generally negative "public image" of labor. Union leaders are viewed as undemocratic—if not crooked—"bosses" who dominate their followers by force or violence. They are often held to be of low intellectual as well as ethical levels. Above all, they are felt to have created an un-American monopolistic restraint of trade through their "dictatorial control."

In order to form a more accurate picture than that displayed in these stereotypes, it is necessary to assess some of the fundamental weaknesses of the American labor movement. In the first place, the relative degree of organization should be kept in mind. Of the entire labor force, only one worker in four belongs to a union. If the field is limited to those in manufacturing, industry, and commerce, thus excluding agriculture, the figure is still only one in three. Moreover, any personal involvement with labor's political movements leads to the firm conclusion that their success has been far less than that of management's Practical Politics Seminar in marshaling either interest or participation on the part of the rank and file. Finally, labor has had its share of unenlightened leadership and undemocratic practices—although the percentage is perhaps no greater than in business, government, or the professions.

Despite conflicting views as to the proper role of labor in the American economy, government intervention in labor affairs has followed a pattern. As early as the nineteenth century, the federal government responded to the *needs* of labor by attempting to redress the basic business-labor imbalance with such statutes as the Sherman Act and the Clayton and Norris-LaGuardia Acts. In the New Deal period, it granted *privilege*, as in Section

7 (a) of the National Industrial Recovery Act (N.I.R.A.), in the Wagner National Labor Relations Act, and in the Fair Labor Standards Act. Finally, it moved to meet *abuses* in the postwar period, with the Taft-Hartley, Kennedy-Ives, and Landrum-Griffin measures all providing *regulation.*

But what are the appropriate goals for a labor policy that reflects the public interest rather than the interest of either conflicting party? Agreement may be found on several significant points, including first, the need to harmonize labor-management interests with those of the public, so that there will be neither damaging stalemate nor erosive collusion on the part of the well-organized at the expense of the unorganized. Second, such goals as equality of opportunity, minimal living standards for all, and the provision of education and training would seem basic to a generally acceptable policy. The prevention of exploitation, to protect the weaker economic element against the stronger (whether labor or management, depending upon the industry), and the prevention of discrimination against women, children, and minority groups are also necessary. Finally, there is the need for "Full Employment in a Free Society"—the need for a maximum utilization of resources as well as a maximum freedom of choice.

With some of these concepts in view, it may be possible to make a more accurate appraisal of government's interests in various areas of labor-management relations and of the vital part labor plays in our government in action.

THE MOHAWK VALLEY FORMULA
National Labor Relations Board

As recently as 1937, many sections of the country, where labor today is well organized, were racked by industrial strife and violence. One such area was the Mohawk Valley of New York State. The files of the National Labor Relations Board bear objective testimony to the successful efforts of one employer—Remington Rand of Ilion—to prevent union organization of its plants.

The systematic program advanced by that employer, and later exported for use elsewhere—by other employers as well as Remington Rand—has come to be known as "The Mohawk Valley Formula." The NLRB has summarized its details in the following steps.

First: When a strike is threatened, label the union leaders as "agitators" to discredit them with the public and their own followers. In the plant, con-

From the official reports of the National Labor Relations Board, 2 NLRB 664–666.

duct a forced balloting under the direction of foremen in an attempt to ascertain the strength of the union and to make possible misrepresentation of the strikers as a small minority imposing their will upon the majority. At the same time, disseminate propaganda, by means of press releases, advertisements, and the activities of "missionaries," such propaganda falsely stating the issues and the real issues, such as the employer's refusal to bargain collectively, are obscured. Concurrently with these moves, by exerting economic pressure through threats to move the plant, align the influential members of the community into a cohesive group opposed to the strike. Include in this group, usually designated a "Citizens Committee," representatives of the bankers, real estate owners, and business men, i.e., those most sensitive to any threat of removal of the plant because of its effect upon property values and purchasing power flowing from payrolls.

Second: When the strike is called raise high the banner of "law and order," thereby causing the community to mass legal and police weapons against a wholly imagined violence and to forget that those of its members who are employees have equal rights with the other members of the community.

Third: Call a "mass meeting" of the citizens to coordinate public sentiment against the strike and to strengthen the power of the Citizens Committee, which organization, thus supported, will both aid the employer in exerting pressure upon the local authorities and itself sponsor vigilante activities.

Fourth: Bring about the formation of a large armed police force to intimidate the strikers and to exert a psychological effect upon the citizens. This force is built up by utilizing local police, State Police if the Governor cooperates, vigilantes, and special deputies, the deputies being chosen if possible from other neighborhoods, so that there will be no personal relationships to induce sympathy for the strikers. Coach the deputies and vigilantes on the law of unlawful assembly, inciting to riot, disorderly conduct, etc., so that, unhampered by any thought that the strikers may also possess some rights, they will be ready and anxious to use their newly acquired authority to the limit.

Fifth: And perhaps most important, heighten the demoralizing effect of the above measures—all designed to convince the strikers that their cause is hopeless—by a "back to work" movement, operated by a puppet association of so-called "loyal employees" secretly organized by the employer. Have this association wage a publicity campaign in its own name and coordinate such campaign with the work of the "Missionaries" circulating among the strikers and visiting their homes. This "back to work" movement has these results: It causes the public to believe that the strikers are in the minority and that most of the employees desire to return to work, thereby winning sympathy for the employer and an endorsement of his activities to such an extent that the public is willing to pay the huge costs, direct and indirect, resulting from the heavy forces of police. This "back to work" movement also enables the employer, when the plant is later opened, to operate it with strikebreakers if necessary and to continue to refuse to bargain collectively with the strikers. In addition, the "back to work" movement permits the employer to keep a constant check on the strength of the union through the number of applications received from employees ready to break ranks and return to work, such number being kept secret from the public and the other employees, so that the doubts and fears created by such secrecy will in turn induce still others to make applications.

Sixth: When a sufficient number of applications are on hand, fix a date for an opening of the plant through the devices of having such opening requested by the "back to work" association. Together with the Citizens Committee, prepare for such opening by making provision for a peak army of police by roping off the areas surrounding the plant, by securing arms and ammunition, etc. The purpose of the "opening" of the plant is threefold: To see if enough employees are ready to return to work; to induce still others to return as a result of the demoralizing effect produced by the opening of the plant and the return of some of their number; and lastly, even if the maneuver fails to induce a sufficient number of persons to return, to persuade the public through pictures and news releases that the opening was nevertheless successful.

Seventh: Stage the "opening," theatrically throwing open the gates at the propitious moment and having the employees march into the plant grounds in a massed group protected by squads of armed police, so as to give to the opening a dramatic and exaggerated quality and thus heighten its demoralizing effect. Along with the "opening" provide a spectacle—speeches, flag raising, and praises for the employees, citizens, and local authorities, so that, their vanity touched, they will feel responsible for the continued success of the scheme and will increase their efforts to induce additional employees to return to work.

Eighth: Capitalize on the demoralization of the strikers by continuing the show of police force and the pressure of the Citizens Committee, both to insure that those employees who have returned will continue at work and to force the remaining strikers to capitulate. If necessary, turn the locality into a warlike camp through the declaration of a state of emergency tantamount to martial law and barricade it from the outside world so that nothing may interfere with the successful conclusion of the "Formula," thereby driving home to the union leaders the futility of further efforts to hold their ranks intact.

Ninth: Close the publicity barrage, which day by day during the entire period had increased the demoralization worked by all these measures, on the theme that the plant is in full operation and that the strikers were merely a minority attempting to interfere with the "right to work," thus inducing the public to place a moral stamp of approval upon the above measures. With this, the campaign is over—the employer has broke the strike.

LABOR'S LONG TRIAL IN HENDERSON, N.C.
Douglass Cater

Douglass Cater, special assistant to President Lyndon B. Johnson, was formerly Washington editor of *The Reporter* magazine. He is the author of *The Fourth Branch of Government* and *Power in Washington.*

Last month, the state prison in Raleigh, North Carolina, released a convict on parole who has been on the mind and conscience of a great many North Carolinians. He is Boyd Payton, long a regional director for the Carolinas of the Textile Workers Union of America. As director, Payton had a large role to play in the strike the Textile Workers called in late 1958 against the yarn and thread mills of John D. Cooper, Jr., located in Henderson. It lasted two and a half years and was formally terminated by the TWUA only on June 1 of this year. Meanwhile, Payton, along with seven other union members, had been sent to prison for conspiring to damage Cooper's property.

The question of Payton's guilt—indeed, the broader question of guilt and innocence in this prolonged and violent labor-management conflict—has caused grave disagreement within a state that is one of the South's leaders in industrial progress. Several prominent citizens, including Jonathan Daniels and Harry Golden, have questioned whether Payton received justice. Others, among them the textile manufacturer Spencer Love, whose own mills are non-union, have not questioned the verdict but suggested that justice be tempered with mercy.

The trial involved at least two men now prominent in the Kennedy administration: Secretary of Labor Arthur Goldberg, as chief counsel for the AFL-CIO, carried the appeal to the Supreme Court, and Secretary of Commerce Luther Hodges, who was governor at the time of the trial, declined to grant a pardon or commutation of sentence. When the present governor, Terry Sanford, reduced the sentences of Payton and the others, making them eligible for parole, he denied that he was disparaging earlier judgments but added: "The Executive is charged with the exercise in the name of the people of an . . . important attitude of a healthy society—that of mercy beyond the strict framework of the law."

The facts of the Henderson case are still in dispute. According to the prosecution's version, in late May, 1959, Harold Aaron, an unemployed textile worker living in a different part of the state, was contacted by a TWUA representative and invited to go to Henderson for the purpose of bombing the plant's boiler room. After some hesitation, Aaron notified an

Reprinted from *The Reporter,* September 14, 1961.

agent of the State Bureau of Investigation, then proceeded on his mission. He met with three or four local union members in a motel room that had been duly "bugged" by the SBI and discussed plans. There was evidently talk of using dynamite and Molotov cocktails. On the night of June 13, three of the union men met at an agreed rendezvous with Aaron and were picked up by SBI agents. Subsequently, Payton and four others were also arrested and charged with being party to the conspiracy.

AN OPEN-AND-SHUT CASE

Against the background of violence accompanying the strike, the outcome of the case was predictable. A special judge appointed by North Carolina's chief justice ran the trial with an iron hand. (At one point, according to the defense appeal submitted to the Supreme Court, he called in the defense attorneys and said, "If you want to be sons of bitches then I can be a bigger son of a bitch than all of you put together.") Jurors impaneled from a neighboring county had a vivid impression of what had been happening in Henderson, and some had relatives who had taken over the jobs of the strikers in the mills. All eight defendants were found guilty as charged. The judge handed down stiff sentences, with Payton's six to ten years among the stiffest. The Supreme Court of North Carolina upheld the verdict (with one judge dissenting in the case of Payton) and the U.S. Supreme Court declined jurisdiction.

From the defense point of view, the case had several legal loopholes. First, it had been a conspiracy in which no dynamite or other instruments of destruction were found on the men at the time of arrest. Privately, the defense admitted that the men had talked a good game but had never really intended to go through with it. Publicly, the defense attorneys dismissed the tape recordings, which were not admissible in court, as simply the evidence of drunken conversation among embittered men.

More fundamentally, the defense attorneys argued that conspiring with a state agent to do something that he had no intention of doing did not constitute a crime. Aaron's record included jail sentences for offenses ranging from drunken driving to assault with a deadly weapon. (Just recently he was convicted in Virginia for assault and battery in a scrap with another man over a girl.) Only one of the defendants had a police record. (He had been arrested a short time earlier for picketing.) Aaron was paid by the SBI —$1,100 it later turned out—and during the motel-room conference furnished liquor to a group of men who were out of work, frustrated, and susceptible to temptation. There was only Aaron's word as to who initiated the idea of wrongdoing.

Finally, there was no evidence that Payton himself knew what was being cooked up. He had not attended any of the meetings with Aaron. His total involvement, according to the courtroom testimony, was to accept a telephone call from Aaron intended for someone else. Aaron said he identified himself as "the boy from Leaksville," and Payton warned him that the call was passing through a hotel switchboard. That was all. It hardly contradicted Payton's claim that he believed Aaron was simply being hired as a union spy to infiltrate and report on the situation inside the struck mills.

The courtroom drama, with both sides resorting rather doggedly to legalisms, did not tell the real story of what went on in Henderson. The clash of forces that had occurred in this small city near the state's northern border was reminiscent of the industrial strife of an earlier era. More than one man was caught in a situation beyond his control.

Boyd Payton came to Henderson with a good reputation. A Presbyterian elder, Sunday-school teacher, and family man, he was well liked in his home town of Charlotte. He was an international vice-president of the TWUA and had considerable experience in union work. He had once served on an advisory committee appointed by Governor Hodges.

But Payton's experience did not equip him for dealing with John D. Cooper, Jr., who had run the mills in Henderson for the better part of this century. The union representatives who had organized the mills fifteen years earlier always found Cooper a stern negotiator but an honorable one. The union was unprepared for the dogmatic stand he took when the contract came up for renewal in 1958. They had offered to extend it *in toto,* with no boosts in wage or other benefits, but Cooper demanded renegotiation of practically every clause.

In the subsequent recriminations, Cooper claimed that he was prepared to accept the union so long as it accepted the fact that he was boss. He complained about the two locals' eagerness to take disputes to the independent board of arbitrators provided for in the contract and to indulge in technical fine points in winning these appeals. In reply, TWUA representatives argued that arbitrations had averaged less than two yearly, with Cooper winning about as many as he lost. They insinuated that the old man was not really acting as his own boss but was engaged in union busting for a combine of industrialists.

The negotiations, hopeless from the start, bogged down over Cooper's demand for a right to veto arbitration. Reluctantly, the union called the workers out in November, 1958—an ideal time, they pointed out, to help Cooper meet the seasonal slump in the textile market.

It was a quiet battle during the winter months until Cooper announced plans to resume production. On February 16, state highway patrolmen stood guard while fifty six of the approximately one thousand strikers and an undisclosed number of new comers answered the plant whistles. Next day, the violence began.

MAYHEM AND MEDIATION

During the months that followed, the violence at Henderson attracted nation-wide attention. It was an ugly business, turning neighbor against neighbor and dividing the town into suspicious factions. At one point, Cooper tallied fifty-six acts of violence against his property and employees. Nonstrikers' cars were battered by rocks and brickbats. Acid was thrown on carding machines in the mills. Gunfire shattered plant windows. Most frightening of all, dynamite was exploded and Molotov cocktails set off. Henderson became accustomed to terror.

From the union's point of view, the violence was seen as a series of unreasoned and uncontrollable acts by men and women, most of them with only grade-school educations, who had been turned out of their jobs after years and sometimes decades in Cooper's mills. They felt panic when they saw outsiders from as far as sixty and seventy miles away come in by car each day to earn $40 to $60 a week—good wages in a low-income agricultural area.

The objective of the violence according to the union's view, was to create fear but not actual hurt. Much of the dynamiting went off in open spaces without damage. Considering all the commotion, it was remarkable that so few were injured and no one was killed.

The union men argued that not all the violence was on one side. It was curious, they said, that only the mills' older carding machines had been damaged by acid. Cooper had more to gain than they did by creating conditions that would draw state police to guard his mills. The TWUA posted reward notices alongside management's in the effort to find the culprits.

One set of accusations and counteraccusations took a bizarre turn. Late in February, 1959, Payton was hospitalized with a mild concussion; he claimed that he had been assaulted outside his motel room by someone wielding an empty softdrink bottle. A month later, Payton reported that his car had been forced off the road, and that he had been injured by rocks thrown through the windshield. A wound over his eye required two stitches.

But the same afternoon, North Carolina's Attorney General Malcolm Seawell told the press that Payton had not been attacked at all. He charged that SBI evidence, including the glass from the broken windshield, proved it was a "hoax" perpetrated by the union official himself. SBI director Walter Anderson, a subordinate of Seawell, later voiced the conviction that Payton's earlier beating had also been self-inflicted as a means of attracting sympathy for the strikers.

Payton, offering $10,000 to anyone who could prove a hoax, promptly demanded a retraction from Seawell. When this was unsuccessful, he took legal steps preparatory to filing suit against the state attorney general for slander and defamation of character. Before he could get anywhere, however, the roles were reversed. Payton was under indictment for the conspiracy to dynamite the mill, with Seawell serving as his chief prosecutor and the SBI furnishing the evidence. What it really meant, in the view of the union, was that state officialdom had entered into its own conspiracy with management to break the strike.

In their angry recriminations, not even Governor Hodges was free from censure. According to the union, Hodges had acted promptly to protect the mills and scabs, diverting so many patrolmen from their customary duties that highway deaths increased notably. He took his time, however, about responding to the union's appeal that he serve as arbitrator for renewed negotiations.

When Hodges did act, the results were scarcely satisfactory. On April 18, 1959, after he had held a series of personal consultations, local newspapers carried a photograph of the smiling, snowy-haired governor, carnation in lapel, holding aloft the hands of Cooper and Payton. Headlines announced, "Pact Ends Bitter Henderson Strike." By the terms, the union agreed to a compromise of the arbitration clause. As a further bitter pill, the newcomers employed by Cooper who had been working the single shift in the struck mills were guaranteed continued job status. Nonetheless, there was jubilation in Henderson next day as union members voted to accept the pact.

Jubilation turned to shocked outrage and renewed violence a day later when Cooper calmly announced that he had already hired a full complement of workers to man his second shift. Openings for the strikers would be limited to the third shift. This meant jobs for barely a fourth of the more than one thousand men and women who had gone out five months earlier.

After a futile attempt to intercede, Hodges complained that Cooper had misled him "intentionally or otherwise" about the second shift. But he also rebuked the union because of the renewed violence and refused to arbitrate further. Shortly afterward, the governor ordered in several hundred National Guardsmen on whom the state legislature had bestowed civil arrest powers. Within a few days, Cooper reopened his third shift and announced that only thirty-three jobs remained unfilled.

The strike dragged on for two more years while the national headquarters of the Textile Workers poured $1,220,000 into Henderson and other contributions for relief benefits ran an additional $233,000. But the strike had been broken. In a recent interview, Cooper claimed that he had no difficulty in quickly reaching and surpassing his previous production. A small and chipper old man, he declared that not long ago he turned down a woman striker who had wanted to come back to the job she held since the First World War. He was full up.

Cooper denied that he bore any grudges about the past. He was more deeply vexed these days about the way our government was letting foreign textiles cut into the U.S. market. Was he aware of the State Department's current efforts to negotiate a voluntary reduction of Hong Kong products? Cooper said that he was. Fingering his lapel, he remarked that the silk suit he was wearing had been made in Hong Kong.

"PART OF A PATTERN"

Labor representatives insist that the Henderson strike has a bigger meaning than Cooper's successful defiance of a remarkably cohesive group of strikers. A recent TWUA report notes, "Cooper's . . . foibles didn't cause the strike. Henderson is not an isolated instance nor are the issues at stake peculiar to Henderson alone. Henderson is part of a pattern . . ." Tracing the pattern in the South, where more than eighty per cent of the cotton textile industry is now located, it concludes, "In recent years TWUA has spent several million dollars on organization work in the South. The union frankly admits that the few thousands of workers it enrolled were totally disproportionate to the time and effort and money spent."

The catalogue of hardships recited by the union is a long one.

a) In Cordova, North Carolina, constant surveillance of organizers and union adherents frustrated four years' effort to form a union at Frank Ix & Sons, Inc.

b) In Cordova, North Carolina, propaganda attacking the unions for "compulsory mongrelization" was distributed in the plant of Burlington Industries, Inc., the country's largest textile chain.

c) In Elkin, North Carolina, the organizers at the Chatham Manufacturing Company, not allowed to rent a meeting place in an empty theater, the YMCA, courthouse, or the school auditorium, finally called the workers together in an open field.

d) In Wilson, North Carolina, the Chamber of Commerce announced publicly that it would "actively fight any attempt by union organizers to bring a union into the local industries."

e) In Alexander City, Alabama, the TWUA organizer was ordered out of town by the chief of police, beaten by thugs, and kept under the constant scrutiny of a local officer who was fond of saying to the workers, "My gun will belch fire and smoke if I catch anyone joining."

But the most crushing failure reported by the union occurred five years ago in Darlington, South Carolina, when employees of Deering, Milliken & Co. finally voted to have TWUA become their bargaining agent. Stockholders were summoned, and company head Roger Milliken abruptly announced the closing down and dismantlement of a cotton mill that provided the community's largest source of purchasing power. The experience at Darlington, even more than at Henderson, has hung like a pall over the union's organizing campaign in the South.

The failure is by no means limited to the Textile Workers. Though the AFL-CIO declines to give out statistics, officials admit privately that recurrent efforts to launch an Operation Dixie have been pretty disastrous. In North Carolina, according to the state director, only nine per cent of industrial workers are organized. This is no better than ten years ago, and probably less than at the end of the Second World War. One company after another, unionized in the North, has successfully resisted union efforts to accompany its southward expansion.

The more realistic union officials admit that formidable obstacles lie in the way of any breakthrough. First of all, there is the smoldering racial situation, which, though singularly absent from the Henderson strike, serves to divide and disrupt labor's efforts throughout the South. Despite the urgent efforts of the national unions, most locals practice discrimination. Quite apart from bargaining relations, labor leaders cannot hope to help themselves in Southern politics when large numbers of their rank and file are voting unquestioningly for the white supremacists.

More immediate obstacles, they claim, are the laws, Federal and state, that have put labor relations in the newly industrialized South on a completely different footing from the rest of the nation. Taft-Hartley, buttressed by the right-to-work laws adopted by most of the Southern states, has proved an effective instrument for the employer who desires to keep out the union by fair means or foul. As evidence of this, the TWUA reports that during the five years before the passage of the act, it won fifty-eight per cent of its representation elections and later successfully organized over three-quarters of the plants. In the first five years after the passage, the Textile Workers won only thirty-seven per cent of the elections and then were able to organize less than half of the plants.

The evil, the TWUA asserts, is not all in the law. In addressing itself to labor's complaints of unfair practices, the National Labor Relations Board has become so bogged down in procedures and niggling precedents that it has become almost useless. A worker unfairly fired for union activities and obliged to wait years to be reinstated teaches his co-workers a grim object lesson.

In their case against the last-ditch defiance of trade unionism going on in the South, AFL-CIO spokesmen issue a solemn warning. They argue that it is absurd to expect that the region can continue unorganized indefinitely. If democratic and uncorrupted unions like the Textile Workers are beaten back, the vacuum will surely be filled by those like Jimmy Hoffa's Teamsters which will be cynical and ruthless in grabbing power. The rumor of prospective moves by the Teamsters is already circulating around North Carolina's capital at Raleigh.

But the North Carolina state AFL-CIO is also making a more positive plea for public support. A recent report of its Committee on Economic Affairs, entitled "How Much Does Opposition to Unionism Cost North Carolina?," contains some startling claims.

It accepts the boasts of North Carolina's rapid industrial growth (new plant investment has been running ahead of every other Southern state). Yet during the past decade, the gap between the average hourly earnings of industrial workers in North Carolina and in the nation as a whole has grown rather than decreased. On the average, the North Carolina industrial worker is paid seventy-five cents an hour less, although his products are apt to sell at national market prices.

Undoubtedly there are many reasons for this disparity. But the AFL-CIO report claims it is also significant that North Carolina's percentage of union membership is the lowest in the South. As the state and the region try to move ahead, the report warns, "There are no democracies which have achieved an industrial society without making room for the labor movement and its contribution. . . ."

A PRISONER IS RELEASED

Reporters are not permitted to interview prisoners in North Carolina, but a short time before his release, Boyd Payton was allowed to answer questions put to him through an intermediary. He stated that he has not been at all embittered by his prison experience. He had passed his time teaching the illiterates among his fellow convicts how to read, an occupation he found highly gratifying. His class was meeting overtime as his release date drew near.

Payton said that he had thought about the union's problems while in prison and had become more deeply convinced than ever that both labor and management need to achieve a new attitude in tackling their problems. There is still a tendency on both sides to approach one another as in the 1930s with a conviction of inevitable clash. But times have changed. The labor union needs to convince management of its willingness to work for their mutual good. In the textile industry particularly, with its problems of competition and contraction, Payton feels the union, too, had not always shown enough of this cooperative spirit.

Since his release Payton has been working to prepare new evidence in hopes of obtaining a full pardon from the governor. Among other things, the TWUA can offer sworn affidavits from its representatives that subsequent to Payton's conviction, Aaron offered in exchange for pay to forget other incriminating evidence he claimed to have against the union. Coupled with Aaron's Virginia conviction, they argue, this thoroughly destroys the credibility of the state's sole witness.

A perennial optimist, Payton refuses to be downcast about his union's future in the South. In a telephone conversation, he pointed out that only recently the Textile Workers had won an election—the Cone Mills in Salisbury, North Carolina—the first in years. Maybe, he felt, the lesson of Henderson had not been all loss.

WHAT'S WRONG IN THE HOUSE OF LABOR?

Robert Bendiner

Robert Bendiner is a well-known free lance writer who contributes to the *New York Times Magazine, The Reporter,* and other periodicals. He is the author of *The Riddle of the State Department.*

Of the more imposing piles of marble, tile, and cool green glass erected in the city of Washington since the Second World War, at least a dozen are the luxurious headquarters of trade unions, each the capitol of a labor satrapy that is proud to spend millions of dollars in membership dues on such visible proofs of wealth and status. Sharing a Sixteenth Street block with the elegant Carlton Hotel and its ground floor with a large firm of stockbrokers, for example, is the Hod Carriers Union. Out of consideration for the Carlton's management it tactfully agrees to call the structure the Moreschi Building, after its president, but the fact remains that the Hod Carriers have arrived. From the most important of these seats of government, George Meany, erstwhile plumber and now president of the AFL-CIO, daily walks just the distance required to enter his large limousine, which, complete with uniformed chauffeur, is provided by the merged federation. To a colleague who once proposed walking to a hotel three minutes away, President Meany replied with the simplicity that is his hallmark, "What the hell do you think I have a Cadillac for?"

Yet at this moment, when at least the business agents of the meek seem to have inherited the earth, the American trade-union movement is on the downgrade, its spirits low, its operations static, its horizons narrow, its public image dismal, and its forces engaged in precisely the kind of family feuding that preceded the splitting of the old AFL in the days of William Green. The difference is that where the stodginess of the AFL was challenged in 1935 by the drive and vision of industrial unions in the making, the dispirited federation today is challenged only by Jimmy Hoffa's Teamsters, an organization that has plenty of drive but no more vision than it takes to provide a home away from jail for such laboring men as Johnny Dio and Tony "Ducks" Corallo.

Is there a connection between surplus fat in high places and the lethargy that has come over the federated house of labor? Walter Reuther, whose moral fervor has not faded since he ran up a seven-year record of perfect Sunday-school attendance in his youth, suggests outright cause and effect. "The AFL-CIO code of ethics was adopted in the roulette room of the Monte Carlo Hotel in Miami Beach," he says with evangelical scorn, "and in February, at the height of the season, at that. That's what's wrong with labor."

Much more is wrong, of course, as Reuther, for one, can explain colorfully and at length—just as Hoffa's future status in the labor movement is far more complicated a question than whether sin will win over outraged virtue.

To understand Hoffa's growing power, to appreciate the excellent chance he has of forcing his way back into the federation that expelled his union for corruption in 1957, requires only a glimpse inside the fortress he expects to storm. The scene suggests nothing so much as an assembly of old-time Chinese war lords sucked into an alliance that was painfully inevitable at the time and has been inevitably painful ever since. That confirmed old maverick John L. Lewis called the turn six years ago, when the AFL and the CIO merged their fortunes. They were united, he said, by "a rope of sand."

Even if the alliance were not torn by jurisdictional feuding—and it is torn almost to the point of paralysis—it would be creaking under the strain of holding together those labor leaders who believe in more bread and butter plus a few social platitudes and those who want labor to be the vanguard of enlightenment and reform from here to Tibet.

On the surface the latter group, mostly from the old CIO, has about given up. The merged federation's political, social, and economic policies are geared to the lowest common denominator, and there is no question that the body as a whole is much more conservative than the hosts that followed Lewis in the 1930's, Philip Murray in the 1940's and Reuther in the 1950's. Resolutions still pour forth at conventions, but they are perfunctory compromises, watered down in advance to avoid debate and to arouse no alarm in the most Republican member of the Building Trades. Pro-labor congressmen complain that except when strictly trade-union matters are at issue, they have to call up union headquarters and urge them to send their lobbyists around to support bills in the general interest.

But this surrender of spirit has left a backwash of resentment that is surprisingly bitter and articulate. Making the rounds of union headquarters, I repeatedly heard comments like this one from the political representative of a large union: "Something's missing in the labor movement now. Everyone seems tired out except Hoffa. There's mediocrity or weariness everywhere you turn." An old-time organizer, at least twenty-five years in the business, shook his head sadly. "This is the most frustrating period of my life in trade unions—there's no lift." A veteran educational director of a big union observed that "the spirit of crusading" had gone out, leaving him with "a feeling of discontent and disenchantment." Almost as an afterthought he remarked, "I think the merger is coming apart at the seams."

AN INVENTORY OF GLOOM

It is easy for the outsider, especially if his memories go back to the turbulence of the 1930's, to make invidious comparisons between Lewis and Meany, but the fact is that most of organized labor's problems are by no means self-made. They are forced by external events, and they go far to explain the low spirits that now prevail, especially in former CIO circles. The chief of these developments, with a few facts about them, follow:

1. Automation and other technological advances have had a stunning effect on the industrial unions that were the heart of the old CIO—autos, steel, electric, and textiles. All told, the industrial unions are reliably estimated to have lost 800,000 members in the past five years. At the same time, most of the nonmanufacturing unions—especially the Teamsters, Hotel and Restaurant Workers, Railway Clerks, Meat Cutters, Retail Clerks, and Carpenters—are doing well and going up in the table of relative union strength.

2. Figures put out by the AFL-CIO to show the "changes that unions

have helped bring about in American life" unintentionally indicate why some of the fight may have gone out of the federation. A typical union member today is between thirty-five and forty-four, married ten years, and as likely to own a home and mortgage in the suburbs as to rent a flat in the city. The chances are that there is another wage earner in the family, probably part-time, raising the household income to the middle brackets. A car, a checking account, and a small savings account fill out the picture. What the survey does not say but what union leaders freely admit is that strikes are an unwelcome interruption for these credit-burdened middle-class workers. Moreover, taxes and socially oriented politics are no more popular among them than in the local Chamber of Commerce. And neither union nor government gets credit from them for the various forms of social security they enjoy and take for granted. Members under forty tend to believe that people have always had vacations with pay and that collective bargaining and social security came in with Jefferson and are part of the Constitution.

3. As the number of production and maintenance workers decreases, the number of clerical, technical, and service workers has gone up, until there are now as many white-collar workers as there are blue. But the white-collar worker is, for psychological and social reasons, by far the hardest for the unions to recruit. Forty per cent of nonfarm workers are now in this category, but they represent less than fifteen per cent of the unions' membership. Fortifying the nonmanual worker's reluctance to sign up, many employers are by now shrewd enough to match the best that unionized employers in the field have to offer in the way of wages, hours, benefits, and job security. The employee saves in dues, assessments, and social prestige, and the employer saves in time and aggravation. What would happen if there were no union yardstick in the field is a question that both parties are too satisfied to raise.

4. Congressional action has hurt the unions and slowed down their drive. The Landrum-Griffin Act, inspired by the McClellan Committee's revelations of knavery in the Teamsters, did no visible harm to Mr. Hoffa's union, which has in fact supplanted the Auto Workers as the largest in the country. It *has* hurt smaller unions that relied on the Teamsters to win their strikes by imposing secondary boycotts, now forbidden, and refusing to handle "hot cargo."

5. The race issue has hamstrung union organizers in one of the greatest areas of opportunity still open, the South. Sharing enthusiastically in the mores of their region, Southern unionists often turn out to be members of the White Citizens' Councils or at the very least advocates of Jim Crow locals. Spending an international's funds on this sort of organizing inevitably stirs up resentment among anti-segregationists, North and South, while any show of integrationist tendencies is cheerfully used by Southern employers to turn racial passions against the union. Failure of the various Operations Dixie can be attributed to several factors, but not least to this one. It accounts, too, for the hollowness of labor-convention resolutions on segregation and

the eloquent scorn with which they are regularly denounced by President A. Philip Randolph of the Brotherhood of Sleeping Car Porters.

6. So much have certain industries been affected by the current flood of foreign goods, made at low wages, that at least a dozen unions in the federation have been driven to urge some form of protectionism. The Amalgamated Clothing Workers, which has been the most vocal on the subject, does not concede that it has abandoned labor's traditional free-trade policy, but last May, after failing to get a quota imposed on the import of Japanese shirts and suits, the union declined to do any further work on Japanese fabrics. Similarly, the largest local of the Brotherhood of Electrical Workers voted a boycott on electronic parts from Japan, and a large Machinists local protested the use of Japanese tools and dies by a California aircraft company as long as local craftsmen were being laid off. Officially, on the other hand, the federation is for free trade as much as ever. Through the International Labor Organization and the International Confederation of Free Trade Unions, it has been working since the war to foster anti-Communist unions abroad and raise foreign labor standards. Meany and Reuther do not want to see that work undone, but neither can they afford to be unsympathetic to member unions that have been feeling the weight of competitive cheap labor. According to Jacob S. Potofsky, president of the Amalgamated, rising imports have cost his union twenty-five thousand jobs in the past three years.

"ORGANIZING COSTS TOO MUCH"

Problems of this magnitude would tax the greatest of labor statesmen, and few union leaders place George Meany in that category. His talents lie rather in deferring showdowns, postponing action almost as a matter of principle, and riding out all storms that arise. To his admirers, especially in the Building Trades, he is, if not a statesman, at least a skilled tactician. No one else, they feel, could hold the federation together a month. But to the crusaders of the old CIO he seems to be given chiefly to marking time and avoiding decisions, finding satisfaction merely in holding on and even more satisfaction in gin rummy.

If the federation itself were holding its own, if temporizing were the price of unity, the guarantor of peace, and the promise of future advance, Meany's approach might well suffice. But neither the federation nor organized labor as a whole *is* holding its own, absolutely or relatively. At the time of the merger the AFL-CIO claimed fifteen million members. Expulsion of the Teamsters and a few smaller, similarly tainted unions cost the federation about 1.5 million members, and since then it has dropped another million by Mr. Meany's own reckoning. At the same time new jobholders have been coming into the labor market at the rate of 850,000 a year, or nearly 3.5 million since 1957. Meany concedes that the federation would have to be signing up nearly half of these merely to hold onto its roughly twenty-five per cent of the total nonfarm work force, that is, to stand still. But with an absolute loss of a million instead, it is clear that the AFL-CIO is slipping at an accelerated rate.

Little of the loss is due to unemployment, since most unions carry jobless members on their active rolls even if they are not paying dues. The loss is simply a failure to organize—in part because of the difficulties already suggested, in part out of weariness and sheer inertia, and in part because the AFL, with its tradition of decentralization, has never gone in for national organizing drives from the top. It has chosen to concentrate on the well-being of those already in rather than on proselytizing the unblessed. The CIO came into the merger, I was told, prepared to put four million dollars into a fund for organizing, expecting the larger AFL to contribute six million. The plan evoked rousing indifference and has long since been put to rest.

Apart from the fiasco in the South, the most conspicuous failure to break fresh ground has been in the factory farms of California. As recently as February of this year the AFL-CIO Council renewed a pledge to support its Agricultural Workers Organizing Committee, engaged in trying to break employer resistance in the Salinas and Imperial Valleys. But by June the council suddenly concluded that the drive was costing too much. The AWOC had never had more than 3,500 workers signed up at one time, Meany said, and it had cost something like half a million dollars. David Dubinsky of the International Ladies Garment Workers, siding with his old friend and gin-rummy partner, is reported to have murmured that he could buy union members cheaper than that. No one seemed to recall what it had cost to organize steel in the high old days of the 1930's. No one seemed to care that earlier in the year Jimmy Hoffa's men had with suspicious ease obtained a contract from the biggest lettuce grower in the state—perhaps, it was hinted, because Hoffa had given assurances of favored treatment and perhaps because he offered, in fact, no objection to the hiring of cheap Mexican labor if local workers should prove hard to get.

In any case, Norman Smith, who directed the federation's organizing committee, noted with some bitterness the vacuum that had been left for Hoffa to fill. The committee had already forced up the wages of California farm workers by twenty million dollars a year and compelled employers to cut down on the use of the exploited Mexican *braceros*. But it would be the Teamsters who would reap the benefit. If Meany had been working for Hoffa, he said, "he could not have picked a more opportune time . . . to announce the suspension of our operations."

THE RAIDING GAME

With jobs being lost to automation and organizing in the doldrums, the old American trade-union game of raiding has once more become the rage. When the two great labor bodies merged, there was no immediate intention to unite the parallel unions that had grown up—in electrical work, textiles, chemicals, meat packing, and other fields. Such a course would have required many high offices, not to mention the high salaries that went with them. As Meany put it at the time, "We can go after unity the long way or the short way. The short way is to merge into one trade-union center which will protect the integrity of all affiliates. The long way is to solve all of our problems before merging. Which will it be?" It was the short way, of course, and the best that was hoped for was that the unions would respect each other's borders and live in peaceful coexistence until such time as they might choose to merge.

Obviously, nothing of the sort has happened. The Metal Trades unions have fought the Auto Workers, the National Maritime Union is at daggers drawn with the Seafarers International, the Amalgamated Clothing Workers raids the domain of the Retail Clerks, the Airline Pilots Association makes war on the Flight Engineers, and the Sheet Metal Workers carries on a prolonged and deadly feud with the Steelworkers, even at plants where a strike is in progress. The Building Trades have fought both the Auto Workers and the Machinists at government missile bases, to the grave detriment of labor as a whole; and according to Meany, at least six vice-presidents of the federation, all chiefs in their own unions, have at one time or another repudiated the AFL-CIO no-raiding agreement. Beyond mere raiding, fraternal unions within the federation have dragged each other into court and before the National Labor Relations Board and have boycotted each other's products. Building Trades unions have even been known to call wildcat strikes rather than yield to their brothers in Reuther's Industrial Union Department.

Efforts have been made, of course, to damp down the fires and establish effective arbitration machinery, but neither the general climate in the federation nor Meany's determination has been up to making it a reality. Two years ago he appointed a committee on jurisdictional problems, which brought in a report favoring binding arbitration, and the federation's 1959 convention gave its approval. But when the Executive Council proceeded to set up the machinery, the craft unions, which are Meany's chief source of support, recoiled at the thought of being bound by an arbitrator's findings. After months of battling, reminiscent of the pre-CIO days of the mid-1930's, industrial-union chiefs met unofficially in a New York hotel last April and drew up a rebellious demand for a swift end to the fratricide. A letter signed by Reuther was sent off to Meany recording the "deep feeling of shame and sadness" with which the group had reviewed conditions prevailing under the "law of the jungle." Once more the demand was made for effective machinery, and ten days later the thirty protesting leaders called on Meany to deliver much the same message orally, using words like "sabotage" and "favoritism" for good measure. They were told that all their complaints would be investigated in due course, and they went away unimpressed.

The next day Meany publicly characterized Reuther's implied charge of bias as "an absolute lie." A delegation of craft unionists then called on him, in turn charging Reuther & Co. with bad faith. They had gone "95 per cent of the way" with him, they said, and went on to suggest that he was taking the "anti-building trades line" of Senator McClellan, who had in fact made unkind references to their behavior at the missile bases. Complaining wearily that the industrial-union men were trying to blame him for all the federation's troubles, Meany shortly afterward called on A. J. Hayes, president of the Machinists, to head a special panel charged with presenting a peace plan to the June 26 meeting of the Executive Council. But the plan was not ready in time, and peace was put off once more. If Hayes, an AFL man himself and chairman of the Ethical Practices Committee, is genuinely hopeful, then he has drastically changed his mind since last December. He observed then that "the AFL-CIO is in danger of a break-up because of interunion disputes. It now appears very doubtful that any sensible solution will be found to these major problems which are festering and gnawing at the federation's very foundations."

CAN THE TEAMSTERS RETURN?

With slight variations the same sentiment is to be heard from other union chiefs. Reuther, with more circumspection, says he is "deeply concerned about the ability of the federation to continue unless it begins to deal with some of its basic problems." Jimmy Hoffa, with no circumspection at all, publicly gives the organization only eighteen months more to hold together unless it sees the light and readmits his Teamsters. Otherwise internal discord and inaction will finish it off, he predicts. "People are discouraged and won't put up with this nonsense much longer." Not a minute longer, in fact, than Hoffa can help. He fully understands the differences, personal and otherwise, that are tearing the federation apart, he is in a position to exploit them, and the divide-and-conquer strategy has already proceeded farther and faster than the casual observer imagines.

In spite of the federation's solemn injunction against fraternizing with expelled unions within its ranks, Hoffa has avowed allies, undercover allies, and potential allies, waiting only for Meany to relax his fierce opposition before they declare themselves. Probably the most outspoken and influential of the Hoffa champions is Joseph Curran, the tough and salty president of the National Maritime Union, whose arguments and rationalizations for taking back the Teamsters pour out in a flood. "Anyone who would stand up and say that he didn't want the Teamsters back is not a trade unionist," he starts off, adding, "That applies to *anyone*." This would seem to dispose of most of the federation's Executive Council, but Curran makes a pass at taking them off the hook. "Mind you," he says, "I'm talking about the Teamsters, not Hoffa." For himself, however, even that distinction is out. "Hoffa's been cleared by the courts, hasn't he? Who am I to say he's guilty—or you? Of course some people aren't satisfied with the courts, or with democracy either."

This is the commonest argument to be heard in Hoffa's favor. In view of the succession of sullen goons who appeared before the McClellan Committee and the volumes of uncontroverted evidence that the union is crawling with extortionists, racketeers, and sweetheart contractors, the argument does not seem quite fitting for a member of the Ethical Practices Committee. Neither does the point that none of the Teamsters' ex-convict officials has been in jail within the past five years, the technical limitation laid down in the Landrum-Griffin Act. But Curran has other arguments, and he brings them up at every meeting of the Executive Council: expulsion is not the way to handle a union's offenses; it has played into the hands of labor's enemies, who are using Hoffa to get at all of organized labor; disciplinary measures short of expulsion would have been more effective, since making Hoffa an outcast has only encouraged "under the table" dealings with him—unlike Curran's, which are all open and aboveboard. Finally, Curran asks, "Why demand reform concessions from Hoffa, who is legally in the clear, and not from Maurice Hutcheson," the Carpenters' president, who was actually convicted?

The Teamsters are important to Curran's Maritime Union, which needs their support on the New York waterfront, especially since it is presently engaged in a savage feud with the Seafarers International Union. Indeed, the Teamsters can have a decided impact on the well-being of almost any union, since the refusal of its truck drivers to pick up or deliver goods can often make the difference between a quick and successful strike and a long-drawn-out failure. This is the chief source of Hoffa's hold on other unions and the reason that three AFL-CIO union heads—George Baldanzi of the Textile Workers, T. J. Lloyd of the Meat Cutters, and Sal B. Hoffman of the Upholsterers—defied the ban on fraternization to attend the Teamsters' last convention. Baldanzi made precisely this point, and Harry Bridges, likewise on hand for the proceedings, was reported to have credited the Teamsters with a greater contribution to the national good than any program of President Kennedy's. It may be worth noting, in passing, that Hoffa's understandable dislike for the Kennedy brothers (as counsel to the McClellan Committee, Robert took him over the bumps, and as Presidential candidate, Jack publicly decried his being out of jail) gives him more in common politically with both Republicans and leftists than with a pro-administration man like Reuther. Bridges had been to many another convention at which the name of Roosevelt brought on a standing ovation, but at Hoffa's convention the honor was not for Franklin or even Theodore. It was for John, who serves the Forgotten Man as the Teamsters' investment counselor.

Although the Building Trades unions grudgingly went along with Meany in voting for the Teamsters' expulsion, Hoffa has had little reason to believe that their heart was in it or to doubt that they constitute his greatest bloc of potential support in the federation. At meetings of the council, Curran says, Building Trades people invariably come up to him after his customary pitch for the Teamsters, clap him on the back, and say, "Joe, we think you're right, but if George says no, it's no." So much do they count on Meany's support in the endless jurisdictional wrangling, one industrial-union leader explains, that they are willing to put up with his whim regarding Hoffa.

"Whim" may be an unfair word to use in this connection, but to many responsible people in the federation—AFL and CIO alike—no other word will describe Meany's position. "Principle" won't do because there is Hutcheson, convicted of a land swindle, still sitting beside him on the council and yet to hear an unkind word from the president's lips. Some of Meany's supporters explain that he can put up with a bit of skulduggery as charitably as the next fellow as long as it is in the family, but that he draws the line at having crooks brought in from the outside, especially thugs from the underworld of organized crime. Privately he is said to have made the point, too, that Hutcheson's offense, unlike Hoffa's, was a personal act, having nothing to do with union corruption.

But none of this stands too close an inspection. Meany was just as adamant about expelling James Cross and his Bakery Union as he was about the Teamsters, though the Bakery corruption was without benefit of the underworld. To make matters more confusing, he once visited Sing Sing to pay a friendly call on Joey Fay, one of the worst of the labor racketeers. An explanation more frequently heard is simply that Hutcheson is an old friend of Meany's and Hoffa is not. It's a personal obsession, one union chief says, "Meany's hatred for Hoffa is deeper than any personal hatred I've ever seen."

Scattered through the federation are pools of troubled water in which Hoffa can fish profitably, as he is believed to be doing right now, in time to produce the maximum disruption at the federation's December convention. In James Carey's International Union of Electrical Workers, weakened by last year's nearly disastrous strike against General Electric, an anti-Carey faction is thought to lean toward Hoffa. The Amalgamated Clothing Workers is definitely divided on the question and would gladly vote for the Teamsters' readmission if only Meany would give the word. A. Philip Randolph, incensed at the federation's slowness to shake off all traces of segregation, reports that the Teamsters are generally good on racial matters, that Negro members of the union regard Hoffa as fairminded. He would like to see a "united labor movement, including the Teamsters if they were able to comply with the code," Randolph told me, winding up with something stronger: "I haven't seen any success in the court cases against Hoffa. I would not vote against the re-entry of the Teamsters, even with him." For further indication of how the land lies, Hoffa men point out that several unions, like the Typographers and the Hotel and Restaurant Workers, voted against expulsion in the first place; that, like the NMU, Captain William V. Bradley's Longshoremen are a close ally; and that even the board of the Machinists, whose president headed the Ethical Practices Committee, was originally two to one against the suspension.

WHO ARE JIMMY'S ALLIES?

But the biggest question mark in the future of Jimmy Hoffa is the attitude of Walter Reuther. That there should be any doubt on this score may seem at first incongruous. Reuther's concern for "trade-union morality" is almost Calvinist in its intensity, while Hoffa's is hardly noticeable. Reuther's questioning mind accepts no boundaries—political, technical, national, or international—while Hoffa, aside from opposing restrictive labor bills, limits his lobbyists to such objectives as thc discouragement of piggyback traffic on the railroads; internationally, his advice to his labor colleagues is "Stop trying to save the world—get down to saving the United States." Yet the air is crackling with rumors and suspicions that Reuther is not nearly so adamant as Meany against the re-entry of the Teamsters, that an accommodation of some sort is in the wind, and that when it comes it will drastically rearrange the power alignment within the federation.

To stir up speculation of this sort is naturally in Hoffa's interest. One can pick up reports at Teamsters headquarters that Richard Gosser, an official of the UAW, has been sounding out Hoffa lieutenants on a *rapprochement,* possibly an eventual understanding whereby the Auto Workers will support the return of the Teamsters and in time the Teamsters will support Reuther for the presidency of the federation. Hoffa uses markedly different language in discussing the two top powers of the federation, both of whom pressed for his expulsion. Meany is "that dopey, thick-headed Irishman," but Reuther "is not stupid like Meany" and "he's enough of a politician to know that to get anywhere, organized labor has to function as a group."

What greatly stimulated the rumor market and shocked some of Reuther's admirers was the mildness of his reaction to flat statements that he wanted the Teamsters readmitted: "Obviously I would like to see a unified labor movement, but it would have to be on the basis of all organizations which belong being willing to accept the standards of trade-union morality required. Under no circumstances would I take the Teamsters back carte blanche."

Discussing these rumors in the handsome Detroit office that graces what was once Edsel Ford's estate, Reuther flatly denied having had any contact with Hoffa, directly or through intermediaries, since the expulsion. When I asked whether he might nevertheless favor readmission, he chose at first to stand by the statement he had made on television a few days before—that any union seeking affiliation with the AFL-CIO would have to meet "certain basic minimum standards of trade union morality" and that the Teamsters "certainly do not" do so. But he took pains to add that if the Teamsters Union *could* be taken back without compromising those standards, "their return would be an asset to the whole labor movement."

After an hour's talk with the man whose mind is still the freshest and most invigorating in trade-union officialdom, I came away with the impression that while he is no more indulgent of Teamster corruption than he has ever been, he is far from happy with the all-out or all-in positions taken by Meany on the one hand and, say, Curran on the other. The double standard applied to Hoffa and Hutcheson bothers him, and I gathered, too, that he feels there would be more chance of reforming the Teamsters if they were brought within the federation than left for good to go in their wild and maverick way. In a showdown, I believe, he would still vote against outright readmission—his public image would be badly tarnished if he did not—but it does not follow that he would actively fight it. In fact there are signs that he would not. It would not surprise me if, instead, he were to press for the setting up of some sort of machinery whereby an offending union could be straightened out without having to be banished.

Why all this concern for a single union, especially one as gamey as the Teamsters? The concern, I think, is not for the union as such, much less for its presiding genius. It is for the AFL-CIO itself, which has been so weakened by feuding and inertia that it could be seriously endangered by the rival attraction of a runaway Teamsters Union, ready and willing to organize all comers and raise a bit of hell in the process. It might be safer, the theory seems to be, to bring the swashbucklers back into the house of labor than to let them constitute an attractive nuisance in the back yard.

LABOR UNIONS ARE WORTH THE PRICE

Max Ways

Max Ways, an assistant managing editor of *Fortune* magazine, has devoted a lifetime to journalism, including reportorial work on the *Baltimore Sun* and *Philadelphia Record* and an editorial stint for *Time* magazine. He is the author of *Beyond Survival.*

From their seasonal habit of flocking to resort hotels, George Meany and his fellow members of the AFL-CIO executive council are misleadingly called the Old Men of the Seashore. An old slander that soft resort living makes soft labor leaders has been revived in recent years and was often repeated by an unfriendly press during last winter's meeting of the council at Bal Harbour, a ganglion of Miami Beach. By 1963 it ought to be plain to all that the leaders of American labor are hard-fibered men, dedicated in some cases to their cause, in other cases to their own power, and in most cases to both. Whether they happen to be at resorts or back in their (by no means Spartan) offices, their waking hours are obsessed by the increasingly complex business of steering their unions through an era of rapid change. Many of these leaders rose to power—and keep themselves there—by such labyrinthine intrigue as would bewilder a Renaissance duke and make a Wall Street lawyer blanch. Such men are not likely to be corrupted by the less than Lucullan pleasures of Bal Harbour's expensive hostelries.

Right now and in the years ahead they are sure to need all their resilience and their inventive resource. For a mighty wave of denunciation is rolling in upon the unions. Indignation over strikes rose in vehemence through 1962 and especially in early 1963, when a long-shoremen's strike posed a major economic threat, and a strike and lockout of New York newspapers exasperated nerve centers of U.S. opinion.

After these disputes were settled, few people noticed that an extraordinary degree of labor peace prevailed, however insecurely, throughout the nation. Instead, there was an acute awareness of other strike dangers ahead, including that of a nationwide railroad strike. Americans seemed convinced that the burden of strikes was increasing, although the standard statistical indicators suggested the contrary. In 1962 time lost in strikes was only one-sixth of 1 percent of time worked, doubtless less than the cost of the common cold or the common hangover. But merely correcting the statistical picture was not going to assuage the indignation; the public (or significant parts of it) had lowered its boiling point on strikes. Therein lay grave danger to the unions—and to others.

The widespread demand that strikes be replaced, at least in essential industries, by "some better way" shies away from the question: *what* better way? Representatives of management and labor avoid strikes in hundreds of contracts signed every month, but unless the strike remains as a possibility no genuine collective bargaining can occur. When George Meany says, "Strikes are part of the American way of life," he is not exulting in labor's power to disrupt, but rather expressing awareness that there are no known alternatives to collective bargaining that would not do far more damage to the American system. All the foreseeable substitutes involve, directly or indirectly, massive extension of government power to fix wages and other conditions of labor. Although collective bargaining as it is now practiced in the U.S. does involve many serious departures from an ideal market system, it is a lot closer and more responsive to markets than any system of government intervention could be.

Labor and management, intent upon their continuing contest, may be underestimating the threat to collective bargaining. Unions often lean to Washington for support in obtaining settlements; every such incident increases the belief that only government can bring labor accord. For its part, management tends to welcome the present wave of anti-union feeling without examining its sources and direction. Clearer understanding might convince management that it has deeper interests parallel to the deeper interests of Meany & Co.

THE THUNDER IS ON THE LEFT

The present anti-unionism needs to be sharply distinguished from two preceding waves—that which produced the Taft-Hartley Act, withdrawing some union privileges granted by the Wagner Act, and that which produced the Landrum-Griffin Act, aimed at the corruption that had been disclosed in some unions. Both of these statutes, especially the former, had the backing of the business community and of groups concerned over union infringement of individual rights. Some of these groups continue to seek additional legislation to outlaw the union shop, subject unions to various forms of antitrust discipline, and ban industry-wide strikes. These proposals do not seem to have picked up much, if any, momentum from the present wave of anti-strike and anti-union indignation.

The wind, indeed, is now blowing from exactly the opposite direction—from the left, if "left" is accepted as meaning the tendency to expand central government power at the expense of the market economy. Three related elements are responsible for the recent change in public opinion toward strikes and unions: the cold war, the intense "activism" of the Kennedy Administration, and the rift, widening for years, between the unions and their erstwhile admirers, "the liberal intellectuals."

As the cold war continues year after year, there is an increased tendency to consider it a total struggle, with a score to be kept in such indexes as the growth rates of national economies. A production loss is treated as a loss of ground on a military front, and national harmony in the face of the enemy takes on a heavy emphasis. In such a context, strikes offend. (And not strikes alone. Wide swings in stock-market prices, bankers' caution in refusing loans, managers' hesitation over plant expansion, consumers' insistence on buying what they want instead of what some learned governess of the public weal thinks they ought to have—all these have been denounced for debilitating the national muscle.) The cold war should indeed be an inhibiting factor against major strikes; but if the public, exaggerating strike damage, pushes this feeling to extremes it may impair the spring that makes the U.S. economy tick. The real issue of the cold war—freedom—may be compromised.

From the first, the Kennedy Administration, by advertising its activism in settling labor disputes, made strikes more conspicuous and therefore more repugnant. Arthur Goldberg, as Secretary of Labor, rushed about the country, busy as a small-town cop on Halloween. He even re-established the national harmony by getting the Metropolitan Opera back in production. This triumph was no trivial mistake. It became a kind of bench mark, and comparison set in. If an opera strike merited federal intervention, where was the strike so local, so humble, so remote from the essential national interest that it should not be dignified—and headlined—by federal attention? Every time a strike gets national publicity, the public, ever conscious of the cold war, falls more and more into the belief that strikes are seriously, perhaps fatally, sapping the national strength.

Having stirred up the public by its own intense activity, the Kennedy Administration now begins to discover that, *because the public is so stirred up over strikes,* a much greater degree of federal intervention in labor disputes may be necessary. In February of this year Goldberg's successor, Willard Wirtz, made a most remarkable speech to the National Academy of Arbitrators. He said clearly, cogently, emphatically, that the public was exaggerating the damage done by strikes. But "neither the traditional collective-bargaining procedures nor the present labor-dispute laws are working to the public's satisfaction, at least as far as major labor controversies are concerned. It doesn't matter any more, really, how much the hurt has been real, or that if collective bargaining can't produce peaceable settlements of these controversies, the public will." And Wirtz added: "I agree with that decision."

The public, he thought, was giving labor and management a "last clear chance" to develop bargaining techniques that would avoid "crippling shutdowns," or else there might be established a court of labor-management relations to do the job. Wirtz dutifully pronounced the ritual anathema upon such a court and upon compulsory arbitration in general. But in his speech he transformed a wave of diffuse public indignation into a public "decision" to see that strikes in major industries do not occur. Who is going to carry out that "decision"? Three guesses.

Antistrike impatience is further magnified as events pass to the people through those who report, interpret, analyze, and comment upon public affairs, and who exercise a considerable long-range influence on popular judgment. In default of a more apt name, this group of scholars, journalists, and speechmakers is referred to as "the intellectuals," for a generation their preponderant political cast has been even less aptly known as "liberal." The liberal intellectuals have wished to alter the course of U.S. society by stressing the role of the national government as a symbol of the direct and total "public interest" and downgrading the interplay of private interests. Although strikes are rather naked displays of private interest, the liberal intellectuals formerly defended strikes because they were conducted by unions, and unions were deemed hostile to the market economy.

Some years ago the liberal intellectuals began to weaken in their defense of strikes because such ideas as "the national strength" and "the national growth rate" had come to have an overpowering grip on the liberal imagination. Later came a deeper shift: the liberal intellectuals increasingly realized that American unions were inextricably merged with the market system. This disillusionment has now given birth to an inaccurate and unfair picture of the character and condition of American unionism. The same group that ten years ago gave labor leaders too much credit for the improved lot of the American worker now heaps on labor leaders too much blame for the discords of American life. Unions are said to belong to the past while government is seen as the main hope of the future in labor situations, as in so many other fields.

Among the charges now leveled from the left at the unions are these: they have deserted "social unionism" for "market unionism," thus losing the enthusiasm, prominent in the Thirties, for reshaping society; their growth has stopped because they lack the energy to organize the unorganized, either the unskilled (particularly Negroes) or the white-collar workers; labor's leaders are old, old with "tired blood" and "hardened arteries"; strikes today are not a sign of restless militancy but of senile frustration and obstinacy; such outworn men and such institutions are obviously unable to cope with the rapid changes of American industrial life.

This picture of the unions is—to give it an old, outworn name—malarkey.

CUSHIONING PAINFUL CHANGE

At a resort-hotel poolside, it's true that nobody (well, hardly anybody) on the AFL-CIO executive council is likely to start singing, "I dreamed I saw Joe Hill last night," or otherwise to indicate a burning desire to free the workingman, overturn the oppressors, or remake the world. But complacent they are not; insensitive to the problems and opportunities of the American future they are not; stupid they are not; exhausted they are not.

These are, however, haunted men; what haunts them is not some ghost from the past but the uncertainties of the U.S. industrial prospect. "Automation" is the center of their daily practical problems. Their attitudes toward the present period of rapid technological and organizational change are formed within a profound ambivalence they share with the men and women they represent and with Americans generally. All demand the fruits of progress and at the same time resist such painful changes as the breaking up of work patterns, the discarding of skills, the shifting of relative wage rates, and the loss, however temporary, of jobs.

The top leaders of American unions are too smart to oversimplify the problem as one lesser labor leader does: "Look. You can't stop progress in this country. I tell the bosses that and I tell the men that. You can't stop progress. *You can only slow it down.*" The vast majority of American labor leaders say—and honestly believe—that technical advance should move faster. Few of them think they know "the" answer to the problem of how to speed progress and at the same time cushion the painful impact of change. Just now, their public answer is a shorter work week to reduce unemployment, but this is less a practical goal than a symbolic way of calling attention to the insecurity that dogs the men they represent. The unions' more practical and less visible answer is an infinitely complex edifice of arrangements, worked out industry by industry, company by company, and craft by craft, by which they seek—sometimes clumsily and outrageously but sometimes with brilliant ingenuity—to adjust the economic facts of a progressive technology to the social and psychological fact of man's profound resistance to being changed by forces outside himself, or pushed around, or treated as a thing.

TEEMING WITH INNOVATION

The effort toward giving union members a sense of participation in the control of their working life is and always has been at the heart of American unionism. Accelerated technological change increases the pressure from below on the leaders to provide the protection workers want; at the same time it increases the danger that the steps the unions take to fulfill their function will exact too great a price from the U.S. economy.

This dilemma—and not the cost of strikes—is today's and tomorrow's real "labor problem," and much union energy in recent years has been directed toward dealing with the difficulties posed by the pressures of rapid industrial change. To handle this task unions themselves have had to change, to improvise new devices in dealing with employers, with one another, and with their own members. Although accused of stagnation, the unions are, in fact, teeming with innovation and efforts toward internal improvement.

The Steelworkers, for example, is not a model union; some of its old friends complain that the fire and enthusiasm of its early years have been frozen into a bureaucracy. But bureaucracy can be another name for competent, functionalized administration, and this union has constructed working channels of two-way communication running from the plant floor to the top of a vast (900,000-member) structure. It does much of its bargaining on a national basis, yet it is able to handle effectively the host of individual grievances that arise in the plants. This is no small achievement. Many British unions that bargain nationally have lost touch with the shop stewards, who often disrupt production by acting independently of the national body; on the Continent national unions have, in general, even less top-to-bottom structure than in Britain. In consequence, workers' specific grievances, instead of being resolved within a contractual framework, melt into an ugly lump of politicized class grievance against the bosses and the system.

The Steelworkers and management are now trying to remove a wide range of issues from the pressures of deadline negotiations. The Human Relations Committee is a year-round joint study group investigating such questions as seniority and work rules. These matters can be of immense importance to individual workers, but, unless the rules are knowledgeably and carefully written, they can impose inefficiencies that cost much more than the benefits are worth. It's too early to say whether steel's Human Relations Committee will do any real good, but at least a sane and novel approach has been made. More interesting is the recent agreement worked out between the Steelworkers and Kaiser Steel Corp. Groups of Kaiser workers now receiving incentive pay may vote to give this up (each getting a substantial lump-sum payment for a transitional period); these workers and all others will receive a third of cost savings Kaiser makes by automation or in any other way; to minimize the displacement of workers that may result from cost cutting, workers will be protected by new job-security provisions and strengthened seniority rules. None of the authors of this plan hails it as "the" answer for industry in general or even for the whole steel industry. It is to be a four-year experiment in one company where management and workers, apparently, are acutely aware of the need for cutting costs in the face of competition, while giving the workers as much protection as possible.

Walter Reuther's United Automobile Workers is another union that can hardly be accused of stagnation either in collective bargaining or in efforts to improve the quality of its internal organization. For years the UAW has vainly proposed to the automobile companies that joint study groups be set up in advance of negotiations. This year for the first time the automobile companies seem interested in exploring the plan. Meanwhile, in the way it runs its own affairs the UAW has made a novel approach to the protection of individual members aggrieved by union decisions. Such cases are bound to occur where unions are large, their contracts and procedures complex, their staffs expert, and their officers possessed of the self-confidence that comes with experience in which the rank and file cannot share. Reuther, than whom there is no more self-confident man, is proud these days of having established in the UAW a "supreme court" of seven eminent men, not members of the union, who can decide appeals by aggrieved members against UAW organs or officers, including Reuther. This "court" has heard 122 cases, and its existence is said to have had a substantial effect in making UAW leaders at all levels more careful of the rights of dissidents.

WHEN THE PLUMBERS GO STARRY-EYED

The four biggest unions in the U.S.—the outcast Teamsters, the Steelworkers, the UAW, and the Machinists—account for a highly significant quarter of all organized workers, and these four are all exceedingly lively unions. But the vigor and change reach further down. Even the unions of the building trades, usually the prime example of reactionary, restrictive "business unionism," show signs of effort toward internal improvement. In recent years they have reduced the damage done by interunion conflict over job jurisdiction.

The plumbers' union, not in the past a progress-minded group, has responded to the challenge of changing technology by operating one of the best training programs of any union. Purdue University helped to train instructors. Scores of locals have set up their own classrooms. Journeymen as well as apprentices are the students. Not long ago the union's president, Peter T. Schoemann, presented diplomas to a group of trainees whose average age was sixty. "What are you old birds going to school for?" asked Schoemann, who is sixty-nine. He was told, "We got tired of holding the pipe while the young men made the weld. Now we've learned to make the weld and they can hold the pipe." Strictly "selfish," of course—but the kind of motivation that built a great nation.

Heart of the training program is lavishly illustrated textbooks that cost several hundred thousand dollars to develop. Union leaders hold out the pipe fitters' manual, inviting the awe and admiration usually reserved for the *Book of Kells*. When the plumbers go all starry-eyed about a training book, it is certain that not all sense of progress has disappeared from the American labor movement.

WHY UNIONS AREN'T GROWING

Management will be deluded if it accepts the widespread opinion that the unions' failure to increase their proportion of the total work force is a sign of weakness. Membership figures must be read against the background of union history and in the framework of present U.S. employment trends.

In the first place, the labor movement—unlike the telephone business and the diaper-wash industry—is not comfortably pinned to the population curve. Membership in American unions has always advanced in sprints and these sprints are connected more with broad changes in U.S. life than with the quality or energy of labor leadership. The biggest numerical gains, in fact, have been associated with wartime or postwar labor shortages. In terms of percentage of the labor force, the unions have done better at holding their World War II gains than they did in the years after 1920. American unionism since 1945 has passed through searing vicissitudes—struggles in some unions over Communism, the effects of the Taft-Hartley law, the McClellan investigation—without any substantial exodus of members. (By contrast, the postwar struggles over Communist leadership in some French unions lost millions of members who have never reappeared in French unions.)

Moreover, U.S. unions have been working against a tide: production workers, among whom unionism has always been strongest, have been declining in proportion to the total work force. Some liberal intellectuals, in their present antiunion mood, will not accept this excuse for union "stagnation"; they demand that unions make more strenuous efforts to break out of their old strongholds and organize the unskilled (especially Negroes) and the growing number of white-collar workers. But in both categories the obstacles to union progress are too deep-seated to be overcome by mere improvement of union leadership or a surge of union organizing "energy."

Before the mid-Thirties unskilled industrial workers were mainly white—and unions made little headway in organizing them. Many unskilled production workers—along with skilled and semiskilled—were enrolled during the rapid progress of industrial unionism from 1936 to 1945. But this still left outside of unions many unskilled workers in the service trades, which are now expanding, and in numerous pockets of employment not accessible to industrial unionism. These unskilled workers today have a high proportion of Negroes, Puerto Ricans, and Mexicans, but race is not among the main reasons why more are not organized. Unskilled workers are so easy to replace that they have little inherent bargaining power—the stuff unionism can mobilize and make more effective, but which it cannot create. Moreover, service workers, rarely concentrated in large groups, tend to be harder to organize than factory workers.

In some quarters the idea seems to be that the 1,750,000 Negroes now in unions could be multiplied if labor leaders took a much stronger stand in championing Negro rights and aspirations. In fact, union leadership has a good recent record of anti-discrimination—a record that has undeniably hurt union organizing drives among southern white workers. Whatever may be the ethical merits of the case for even stronger union policies favoring under-privileged groups, there is little chance that adoption of such policies would result in a big net gain in union membership. Those at the bottom of the social escalator may "need" unionism most, but unionism has been most effective within a middle band of workers who have substantial pre-union bargaining power.

WHY THE WHITE-COLLARS ARE UNORGANIZED

Above the middle band lies the unions' other area of frustration, the white-collar workers, of whom less than 15 percent are unionized. Market demand for white-collar workers has been stronger than for production workers. Just before, during, and just after World War II, however, production workers apparently were closing the pay-and-working-condition gap between themselves and the white-collars. This overtaking movement has ceased, and the white-collars may be drawing away again.

Many of the fringe benefits (e.g. sick pay, vacations) on which blue-collar unions are now concentrating have for years been standard in much white-collar employment. The main white-collar advantage—and the one that makes this group hard to unionize—is continuity of job, "the annual wage." Hourly paid production workers, subject to layoff at management discretion, are less reluctant than white-collar workers to interrupt their pay by striking. Where a very high proportion of a white-collar group has been organized (e.g., actors) there is often a background of discontinuous employment. The upper levels of white-collar workers have one other pertinent advantage over production workers: a measure of built-in control over the pace and pattern of their own work. Managers usually don't need a union to tell them that "overbossing" of technicians results in lost efficiency.

The majority of white-collar workers are not likely to be organized unless there are major shifts in the terms of their employment. Such shifts may appear. Years ago, when white-collars were a small minority in most businesses, it was easy to provide them with continuous employment; today the growing proportion of white-collar workers represents in many companies a cost rigidity that is hard to take when business is slack. If management tries to meet this difficulty with white-collar layoffs, or if office automation is too rapid, or if white-collar jobs become overbossed, there may be huge union gains among this group. But in the absence of such changes it is hard to believe that a mere stepping up of union "energy" is going to organize millions of workers who have, without unions, an increasing market power already superior to that of unionized production workers.

WHAT DOES UNIONISM COST?

The present wave of anti-union feeling raises again the question of what effect unions have on the economy. In such an appraisal there are some bear traps for the unwary. The two groups that sound off most loudly about the effect of unions are labor leaders and labor baiters; they tend to agree with each other in rating the impact of unionism very high. The labor leader gives unions credit for a generation of rapid gains by workers, and the labor baiter says almost the same thing when he fixes upon unions the chief blame for rising costs and prices. The truth seems to be that the economic impact of unions is not so great as either group asserts.

In a remarkably clear, concise, and balanced new book, *The Economics of Trade Unions,* Albert Rees of the University of Chicago, working from a number of detailed studies, has arrived at some sophisticated opinions about the cost of unions. One way of getting at the wage effect is to compare the wage rates of union members with those of unorganized employees doing comparable tasks. Rees's educated guess is that the over-all difference at any point in time amounts to between 10 and 15 percent. In some industries that are almost completely organized, unions reach periods when they are unable to raise the relative wages of workers at all. An example is the Amalgamated Clothing Workers, once one of the most effective unions. Since the war it has been stymied, and the usual cries have been raised of tired, old leadership. But the Amalgamated had excellent leadership in depth, and it is hardly plausible that the sudden lowering in the union's effectiveness is traceable mainly to leadership. The explanation, according to Rees, is that the market factors heavily condition union effectiveness. In the men's clothing field, the postwar market has been soft and many employers are in trouble. In such a situation, even the strongest union must choose between scaling down its wage demands or accepting greater unemployment among its members.

Following the late Henry C. Simons and others, Rees believes that union action in raising wages tends to decrease employment opportunities. (Even where the number of jobs increases, the expansion of employment is slower than it would have been if wage rates had not been pressed upward by union action.) Usually, unemployment in an industry acts as a brake on wage demands. The great exception to this for years has been the United Mine Workers, which forced up wage rates while making no effort to slow the mechanization that was spurred by rising labor costs. The number of coal miners declined from about 450,000 in 1947 to 119,000, while hourly earnings almost doubled.

Rees says that it cannot be proved that unions measurably increase "the workers' share" of total income at the expense of the owners of capital. Union gains are probably paid for by other workers or consumers. On the other hand, Rees defends unions against the charge that they are solely or mainly responsible for "cost-push inflation." Unions can aggravate inflationary dangers arising from monetary or other causes, but their "push" on costs becomes inflationary only when wrong policies are pursued elsewhere in the economy.

The chief cost of unions is not strike losses or cost-push, but the distortions and rigidities that unionism introduces into the market system. Rees says: "If the union is viewed solely in terms of its effect on the economy, it must in my opinion be considered an obstacle to the optimum performance of our economic system."

He has, however, more to say. Although he is an economist, Rees knows that life is not an exercise in economics. American unions rose not in response to an economic theory, but as a complex institutional form of expressing the complex reactions of workers to the pressures of industrial society. "By giving workers protection against arbitrary treatment by employers, by acting as their representative in politics, and by reinforcing their hope of continuous future gain, unions have helped to assure that the basic values of our society are widely diffused and that our disagreements on political and economic issues take place within a broad framework of agreement." He notes that American manual workers are committed to the preservation of a political democracy and a free-enterprise economy and that they are not, "as in many other democracies, constantly . . . attempting to replace it with something radically different." Rees concludes: "The economic losses imposed by unions are not too high a price to pay" for the psychological, social, and political benefits.

WHAT ABOUT "THE RIGHT TO MANAGE"?

Even if this judgment is true about the past and present, what are the prospects? Are the future costs imposed by unions on the economy likely to become "too high"?

In recent years direct union pressure on wage rates has slowed down a bit. But a great deal of present labor activity and conflict is on fronts other than wages; most of these issues are connected with adjustments to technological change; many of them involve the possibility of high economic loss by union infringement on management's "right to manage."

While this danger is real, the actual picture is more complex and more balanced than is generally supposed. In the first place, unions in many industries have had the effect of speeding up the pace of technological improvements. One railroad executive put it this way: "If it wasn't for those damn unions, we'd be using as many man-hours to do every job as we did twenty years ago. Every time they get an increase, we have to get off our duffs and find a cheaper way to do things."

This quote represents an important hidden truth about "the right to manage." If it is assumed that complete managerial control exists prior to any union infringement on management power, then every concession to unions in the form of work rules and other limitations represents a diminution of management power. Examination of the masses of these limitations that have been written in the last fifty years—and are still being written—might lead to the conclusion that management is gradually being pushed into a corner where it has less and less control than it had fifty years ago, and its control decreases year by year.

The explanation lies in the falsity of the original assumption that "complete management" preceded union interference. Complete management, the total subjection of action to rational control, never exists. Whether confusion be attributed to original sin or to the undomesticated Freudian id, the truth is that in human affairs, individual or group, the segment of unmanaged activity exceeds the segment of managed activity. (Saints and the Bell Telephone System may be exceptions to this rule.) Masters never exercise complete rational control over slaves, nor parents over children, nor any man over himself, nor managers over a work process.

For example, the imposition by unions of seniority rules in layoffs seems to be an encroachment on the right to manage. But before the unions interfered, the selection of the particular individuals to lay off was often not really a management decision (i.e., it was not worked out rationally in terms of the interest of the enterprise). Foremen and supervisors, unguided by policy from above, selected by favoritism or at random the workers to be retained or laid off. Nobody in his right mind would argue that seniority was the most efficient or economically rational way of selecting workers for continuous employment or for promotion. But in many cases what seniority rules replaced was not rational management but merely power exercised in a way that seemed unfair and arbitrary to workers. It seemed so because that's what it was.

The struggle over the control of labor is not simply management vs. unions. The older struggle is that of management vs. chaos, or unmanagement. Unions make it a three-cornered fight. Nobody can promise that union encroachments upon "the right to manage" will not advance faster than management's ability to win from chaos new frontiers of rational control. In industries where that has happened the costs of unionism may be disastrous. But the general record of a hundred years of unionism indicates that—so far—union power and management effectiveness have *both* advanced together.

FEATHERBEDS FOR SALE

When they encroach upon the right to manage, American unions are not trying to take over enterprises; they are trying to restrict or cushion change or to give the workers a sense that some power over the job is in their hands. Since American unions are themselves immersed in market psychology, every union encroachment has a price at which it may be traded for some other potential union advantage.

A most remarkable example of this occurred on the West Coast in 1961. For thirty years Harry Bridges had built up a fantastically restrictive set of work rules. Unneeded men were required for all sorts of specific jobs around the docks. When Bridges was asked what these supernumeraries should be called, his cynical humor answered: "Witnesses." The burden was becoming so intolerable to employers that they "bought" all the restrictive work rules in a single package in return for large employer payments into a special fund that will make possible earlier retirement and larger pensions for longshoremen. The agreement endangered some hundreds of dockworker jobs, but these were held by "B-men" without voting rights in Bridges' union. The employers have obtained, at a price, a free hand to improve productivity on the West Coast wharves.

What Bridges did in a wholesale deal, other unions do all the time on a retail basis. Much has been heard lately about the printers' insistence on "setting bogus" or "dead horse." But it is less widely known that "dead horse" is often stored up, unset, on the spike and then traded off at the end of a contract term for small additions to wage or other concessions. After the east-coast longshoremen's strike was settled in February, there was a sudden flare-up on a Manhattan pier, where an employer had introduced an unusual distribution of the work gang between the pier, the deck, and the hold. The workers considered this a violation of an agreement to maintain local work patterns unchanged; apparently they had it in mind that the right to change the pattern could be "sold" in some future negotiation. Union officials had to tell them that on this particular pier the right had already been conceded to the shipowner.

The proliferation of specific work rules in American union contracts is not paralleled in other industrial countries—but the actual situation in other countries is not necessarily better from management's point of view. British managers are conscious of worker resistance to automation and change even though that resistance has not been embodied in specific contractual provisions. One result is that the hidden worker resistance in Britain is used by managers to reinforce their own inertia, with the consequence that the pace of industrial change in Britain is slower than in the U.S. One rogue whale of a shipowner in New York holds that the slowness of technological change on the waterfront there is attributable mainly to the inertia of shipowners, who for decades were dealing with a weak and racket-ridden union. Now that the east-coast longshoremen are somewhat stronger they may make wage and other bargaining gains; squeezed, the shipowners may be forced into cost-cutting improvements.

The U.S. practice of writing specific rules into contracts at least exposes the featherbedding to view where it can be argued about, bargained about, and sometimes traded off. It is somewhat more difficult for management to deal with the deep-seated worker resistance, which surfaces only in unofficial slowdowns and general foot-dragging.

EXEGESIS ON THE FAMOUS WORD "MORE"

The extreme untidiness, the messiness, of collective bargaining in the U.S. is apparent on all sides. One union is deciding to stress wages while another decides to de-emphasize wages and stress security; or the same union reverses its emphasis from one year to another. But these shifting decisions do not express mere whim; they are responses to changing conditions in various industries, and changing fears and desires of particular groups of workers. So untidy, so shifting, so relative is the American labor scene that it *must* be deeply involved in that most untidy, shifting, and relative of all human institutions, the market.

This involvement is no accident but the development of the character that Samuel Gompers imprinted on American unions as boldly as his signature, which adorns the charters that hang in Washington union offices. For Gompers' great invention was the word "more" as a description of what the unions wanted. Usually this word is recalled as an example of the unions' unappeasable voracity; but in its original context and its long-range effect its significance is different. On New York's East Side when Gompers was young, a hundred ideologies of labor competed with one another. His predecessor as head of the Cigar Makers, Adolph Strasser, rebelled against the belief that unions should be considered instruments for gaining utopian goals. In 1873, testifying before a U. S. Senate committee, Strasser was asked, "What are your ultimate ends?" And he answered: "We have no ultimate ends. We are going on from day to day. We are fighting only for immediate objects—objects that can be realized in a few years." Gompers, accepting the thought, boiled it down to "more, now."

Thereby the U.S. labor movement committed itself to the U.S. market system. Again and again ideologues, many of them Marxists, have tried vainly to turn American unions from their "purposeless" pursuit, their concentration on responding to immediate pressures and on improvement within a short perspective of a few years. Gompers' "more" was a non-utopian acceptance of limits rather than an arrogant demand. He didn't want to get to an ideal society; where he wanted the workers to go was merely ahead.

In its refusal to define an ultimate goal of its activity, the labor movement Gompers shaped is not so different from business. Because of the limited ends they have in common, because of their involvement in the messy quicksands of the market, both the businessman and the labor leader have drawn upon themselves the antagonism of modern intellectuals. Unions, whenever they can be hopefully interpreted as instruments toward ideological goals, attract the affection and support of intellectuals; but when they descend into the obscure specifics of practical bargaining, their highbrow friends—and not the Marxists alone—desert them.

This is understandable if not excusable. After all, one of the highest functions of an intellectual is to imprison the buzzing fly of life in the clear amber of definition. The service is indispensable if society is to understand itself, even a little. But the service is difficult to perform, and many modern intellectuals slothfully insist that the fly crawl into the amber of its own accord. This demand is the featherbedding of the intellectuals.

Anybody who wants to understand the labor movement had better start with the object itself in all its historical complexity and the multiple contradictions and defects of its present position. He had better not start with a preconceived notion of what a labor movement, considered as an instrument for attaining the ideal society, ought to be. An example of the latter approach is the complaint of a liberal intellectual, disillusioned with unions, who declared that government intervention must increase because "collective bargaining has failed to solve the labor problem." Indeed, it has failed—and in a free society there can never be any "solution" to the labor problem, the price problem, the investment problem, or the woman problem.

WHY GOVERNMENT SHOULD STAY OUT

Accepting unions and collective bargaining with their inherent and ineradicable defects does not imply accepting all present union practices or pressures. Such acceptance does not preclude further legislation cutting back the degree to which government influence is thrown on the side of unions. To say that unions in general "are worth the price" is not to say that the union shop is inviolable or that the restrictive practices of the stagehands' union are worth what they cost. The future of collective bargaining, moreover, depends as much upon employer resistance to excessive union demands as it depends upon employer concessions to reasonable demands. What is "excessive" and what is "reasonable" can be determined only company by company, and year by year. The terms on which labor is performed—in their impermanence, complexity, particularity, and susceptibility to market pressures—are *prices*. Terms of this sort are not appropriate subjects for government action, because the basic mode of government action is law, which is supposed to be stable, uniform, and general.

When raw wage rates were the main subject of collective bargaining, it was hard enough to imagine how a government in peacetime might set wages. But it is infinitely harder now that the emphasis in bargaining has shifted to the more complex and particular field of arrangements for cushioning the social impact of rapid technological change. If a government imposed, say, the Kaiser plan on one company, it might be tempted to impose it on others where specific conditions were different. Or else government would abandon its appropriate mode of action—legality—and would decide each labor case on its particular circumstances; that way lies the corruption of constitutional government, a more serious matter than the inefficiencies of collective bargaining. Even assuming—and this is quite a large assumption—that any given Administration would be evenhanded in its treatment of management and labor, the more fundamental objection to government intervention remains: the difficulty of determining labor prices by legal machinery. As the recent strike of French coal miners indicates, an essential industry will not necessarily be protected against work stoppage merely by making a strike "illegal."

THE DEVIL WE KNOW

The Kennedy Administration certainly does not *want* to take over the role now performed by collective bargaining. But an impatient public opinion, goaded by the Administration's own activism, could come to consider as "inevitable" massive government intervention in labor disputes. In fact, such a trend is probable unless the President resolves to hold intervention to an absolute minimum. Reflecting on his own experience and not speaking in criticism of his successors, former Secretary of Labor James Mitchell has said that it is always easier for a government official to intervene than not to intervene in major labor disputes. When those telegrams from governors begin to arrive in Washington, when the congressional delegations troop to the Labor Department and the White House, when the editorials scream that the government must "do something" to end a strike—it's hard not to say, "We'll look into it and see what we can do." Looking leads to judgment, and judgment to government pressure for specific terms of settlement. Soon no real bargaining occurs anywhere because one side or the other thinks it will get a better break in Washington than in a test of bargaining strength.

The American labor movement today is certainly no worse than it ever was, and a strong case can be made that it is getting better. Unions and techniques of collective bargaining may not improve fast enough to meet the challenge of the years ahead. The same doubt can be cast on management—and on government. Unions are not only the devil we know, but they are also institutions that fit this society far better than would government regulation of the terms of labor.

16 BIG AGRICULTURE AND THE FARM PROBLEM

The public knowledge of American agriculture sometimes seems limited to an awareness of problems arising from the shopper's daily contacts. The man in the street knows that he must pay an increasingly high price for food at the same time that he spends a sizable portion of his tax dollar for support of programs that keep those prices up. But he is little acquainted with the increasing spread between the higher prices the consumer must pay and the lower payments the farmer must accept. He possesses a fundamental belief, sometimes more fancied than real, in the family farm as a part of the "American way of life." But he seldom realizes the inroads on small farming made by corporate agricultural enterprise, nor does he apprehend the magnitude of capital investment required to operate even a relatively modest one-man farm. He views the farmer as essentially a conservative isolationist, interested primarily in preventing governmental intervention in domestic agricultural matters and in foreign affairs.

Notwithstanding this lack of public perceptiveness, certain agricultural goals have emerged as generally acceptable to the nation at large. First, there is agreement on the necessity of adequate production of a wide variety of foodstuffs. In recent years, increasing numbers have come to support American participation in attempts to solve world food problems, reflecting an instinctive sympathy toward the goal of a well-fed One World. Second, Americans have had a long interest, sometimes emotional, in the conservation of natural resources. Even when unwilling to support minimum income standards for the farm population, Americans have been willing to pay farmers to adopt sound conservation practices. In some instances, the basic contradictions have produced a mixed reaction; prosperity for the farmer and the lowest possible food prices for the consumer have proved difficult to achieve simultaneously. On the other hand, elimination of rural poverty has been a widely acceptable goal.

But what, basically, is the "farm problem"? In the background, there was the overexpansion of agricultural production during two World Wars followed by postwar aftermaths of resumed foreign competition and the resultant declines in American incomes. In the 1920s, the end result was catastrophe for the individual farmer—thousands of mortgage foreclosures, which, combined with unfavorable weather in some areas and drought in others, drove many families out of agriculture and into the cities—often at untold costs in human suffering and misery.

Nonetheless, the farmer's long-run problem has primarily been his own amazing efficiency. Gains in American industrial productivity are well known, but agricultural advances have been even more spectacular. Improved crops, improved methods, and new implements have contributed to a technological breakthrough that allows an ever decreasing farm population not only to feed increasing urban numbers but to produce a vast surplus of food each year. However, the reward for these achievements has been a precipitous drop in farm income. Relatively, the demand for farm products in a prosperous economy has been a declining one—reflected in the lesser percentages of national income earned each year by agriculture.

In the market place, the farmer is caught in a triple squeeze. First, he is competing with thousands of his fellows to sell identical crops which can command no premium and where his individual output has no influence on the available supply. Second, he is dealing with a diminishing number of buyers, who are not always averse to secret price agreements among themselves—as revealed in the Ohio tomato market a few years back. Third, he must purchase his implements and supplies in a market that has become increasingly monopolistic and price-administered. Hence a "farm gap" continues to grow—while the farmer's prices are dropping, his costs are rising.

The farmer's basic problem is further complicated by America's foreign relations—difficulties with tariff agreements, the problem of nontransferable currencies, and the task of feeding the underdeveloped nations. All these have hindered an orderly expansion of potential export markets in a hungry world.

As if these problems were not enough, the farmer must also contend with cyclical ups and downs ranging from recession and depression to periodic credit shortages, weather uncertainty, and recurrent drought and dust-bowl conditions.

Small wonder that the farmer for nearly a hundred years has sought a strengthened role through organized pressure groups such as the Grange and the more recent Farm Bureau Federation and National Farmers' Union. In these groups, he has found strength beyond his numbers in certain governmental phenomena—including the marked overrepresentation of rural areas in state legislatures, the availability of two United States Senators for even the smallest farm state, and finally the balance-of-power position the farm vote has occupied in presidential elections.

Consequently, the primary question for analysis is not whether or not there will be a farm program. Rather it concerns the nature of that program in our government in action.

WHAT MAKES THE FARM PROBLEM

Murray R. Benedict

Murray R. Benedict, Professor of Agricultural Economics at the University of California since 1931, has served as a consultant on farm

From *The New Republic,* July 27, 1959. Reprinted by permission.

problems to public and private organizations. He is the author of many pamphlets, articles, and books, including *Farm Policies of the U.S. 1870–1950* and *Can We Solve the Farm Problem?*

It is hard for our highly urbanized society to understand the underlying causes of the "farm problem" or why, after nearly four decades of argument and expenditure of many billions of dollars, it has not been solved. In the first place, this is not primarily a party issue; party differences here tend to be matters of degree or direction rather than of basic concept. Even in the 1920's, the Congressional approaches to the farm problem were surprisingly nonpartisan. In the very first years of the decade, the farm bloc was causing political headaches for a Republican Administration backed on most issues by a predominantly Republican Congress. Much later, in the 80th Congress, the bills put forward by the House and Senate committees, both headed by Republicans, differed more than did the positions traditionally taken by spokesmen for the two major parties.

The depression of the 1930's brought fairly general agreement that something drastic had to be done to help the farmer. Generally speaking, farm-state Congressmen and farm leaders of both parties worked together to devise workable programs. And what they did, in the main, was to give the Administration almost a free hand to try any or all of the plans that had been seriously proposed. In its basic elements the current program is still essentially the one that took shape in that period. However, the setting has changed and the program has been subjected to severe distortions that grew out of wartime needs and legislation.

In the 1930's, the major cause of farm distress was a drastic decline in demand. Farm production was not badly out of line with the needs of the people of this and other countries. But with millions of workers unemployed and other millions on low or uncertain incomes, a normal flow of farm products could not be sold at prices that seemed fair either to farmers or to those responsible for making legislative and administrative policy. The impact of depression was not the same in the farm and nonfarm sectors of the economy. Nonfarm workers and businesses had to take their punishment in the form of unemployment and sharply reduced average incomes. Industrial production was cut back quickly and drastically. Agriculture, an atomistic and highly competitive industry, tended to maintain output and to take its losses in the form of sharply reduced prices.

It would have seemed logical to encourage agriculture to continue to produce the food and fibre needed and to restore quickly the purchasing power of consumers so that these needed supplies could move at prices the farmers could live on. But restoring demand after a severe depression, like the recovery of strength after a severe illness, is a slow process.

Meanwhile, farm prices were virtually at all-time lows and the overriding demand, both in business and agriculture, was for action on the price front. In agriculture, this took the form of efforts to cut back production in a variety of ways ranging from the plowing up of cotton and the slaughter of little pigs to the imposition of acreage controls and the subsidized destruction of fruits. But controlling production in highly competitive agriculture is by no means easy. This was not a situation in which boards of directors could decide how much to produce and could allocate resources accordingly. Neither was it one in which strongly organized unions could induce, or coerce, workers to refrain from working at less than standard rates. Instead, it was one in which there were at that time more than five million independent entrepreneurs, each making his own decisions as to how much to produce and most of them with strong incentives to produce as much as possible.

Production controls were thus only moderately successful, perhaps fortunately, so far as the economy as a whole was concerned. For if agricultural production could actually have been reduced enough to restore farm prices to the levels considered appropriate, it would have meant throttling down all of the economy to the low tempo then prevailing in the nonfarm parts of the economy. Consumers would have had less to eat and the cost of living would have been significantly higher. Farm prices did improve some though they were still low as late as 1940. Meanwhile, there was an abundance of food for those who had even a modest amount of buying power.

Up to that time there was no clear indication of the great technological revolution that was to come later. Yields of most of the major crops hadn't changed much in the 75 years for which records were available. Hence the effort to cut down production by reducing acres planted seemed logical. But the great agricultural machine had within it as yet unsuspected potentials for rapid expansion of production. The incentives for full use of these potentials were lacking, and parts of agriculture were being deliberately held down to keep output from expanding.

That situation was suddenly changed by the outbreak of World War II. Demand strengthened; prices began to improve; and unemployed labor was rapidly drawn out of agriculture. The coming need for more and more food, which a fully employed labor force would be abundantly able to buy, soon became apparent. Government policy shifted from an attempt to keep the lid on production to a positive effort to lift it. Outlets were assured; price incentives were provided; and production goals replaced quotas. Farmers had almost every incentive to put the industry into high gear and to produce as much as they could. Furthermore, there was a substantial reservoir of new machines, new techniques and new knowledge that had not been drawn on in the two preceding decades of low prices and capital starvation.

The results exceeded the most optimistic expectations. In spite of a growing scarcity of labor, agricultural production increased by more than 20 percent between 1939 and 1944, though it was already high in terms of past performance. Even under war conditions, and with heavy demands from abroad, US per-capita food consumption increased by more than 6 percent in the same period. Vast quantities of food were supplied to the armed forces and to our allies. Thanks in part to the effective response of agriculture and in part to favorable weather, consumers were spared the tight rationing and austere diets that most European countries had to contend with during the war years. The surplus problem was temporarily a thing of the past, and it was not to reappear until the end of the decade.

But in the effort to encourage all-out production and partly in response to the strong political power of agriculture, high levels of price support for farm products were written into the laws during the war years, including promises that these levels of price support would be continued for at least two years after the war. Later they were extended throughout the 1940's and into the 1950's. Agricultural production continued to increase and, at least until the end of the decade, this increase was needed.

As well as supplying the strong domestic demand, it enabled the United States to come to the rescue of a battered Western Europe on a scale never previously approached even in wartime. Much of Europe was stripped of livestock and short of machinery, fertilizers and manpower. Its processing and transportation facilities had been destroyed or damaged and, to add to the difficulties, it encountered a 1946–47 winter of almost unprecedented severity and an extremely severe and widespread drought in the summer of 1947.

Our response was effective and generous. It was made possible by two things, continuing high production in US agriculture and the special financing provided by the Marshall plan. Even during what some Europeans refer to as "The Hungry Period" minimum requirements for survival were provided. In 1948 alone we exported more than half a billion bushels of wheat, almost all of it to Western Europe. At the same time our own people were eating more and better food than ever before.

This abnormal need had slackened by 1950. Troublesome surpluses were in fact beginning to appear in some lines as early as 1949. The demand for farm products was revived temporarily, and largely speculatively, by the outbreak of war in Korea but soon slacked off and the era of evermounting stocks of storable agricultural commodities was upon us.

As a result of 10 years or more of strong incentives for all-out agricultural production, forces had been set in motion that were to plague us from 1953 on. Agriculture was geared for high production. Immense amounts of capital, in the form of machinery, organization, soil fertility and know-how had become available. As yet, there was little incentive for farmers to slow down production. Farm prices, on what was virtually a free market basis, had been well above "parity" in the late 1940's and early 1950's. Parity itself is a generous yardstick, one that for two decades was looked upon as something to be hoped for but probably not to be achieved. In the speculative boom of 1951, farm prices rose to alltime highs, thus giving further impetus to the technological revolution that had already gained a good deal of momentum. The new Administration coming in in 1953 and faced by rapidly mounting surpluses urged some easing down of the wartime price incentives then in effect, but there was not only strong political opposition to such a course but very real doubt that lower prices would actually bring about the desired easing off of production. Once production capacity has been built up in agriculture it takes a very drastic decline in prices to cause it not to be used.

Labor was being withdrawn from farms and acreages were being held down, but the technological revolution could not be stopped. For American agriculture it was perhaps as fundamental and difficult to deal with as the industrial revolution that had unsettled Western Europe so profoundly in the period around 1800. No longer are American farmers accepting new ideas reluctantly and slowly. They are welcoming them eagerly and reaching out for more, that is, for new forms of organization, improved strains of crops and animals and new production techniques. Once such a process is underway, improvements that may at first be undertaken as a means of improving profits must be adopted as a way of reducing losses. Consequently, they tend to spread throughout the industry very quickly. The farmer who does not "go modern" soon drops hopelessly out of the running. Greater productivity would seem not to be something to be deplored, but so far as food is concerned, once a nation is as well fed as ours now is demand can grow only about as fast as population grows. If production increases faster, prices fall to unacceptably low levels or unused stocks pile up. Since our policy has been to support prices, the imbalance shows up in the form of burdensome and costly stocks held by the government. This relates mainly to a fairly small number of products but they are important ones; for example, wheat, the feed grains, cotton, tobacco and, potentially, hogs. The products directly supported probably do not account for more than 35 to 40 percent of the total output of agriculture, but if these are cut back the problem spills over into other lines that are now managing fairly well without government price support. The prices of beef cattle, fruits and vegetables, poultry products and, as of now, hogs are not supported by the government.

But if we have more production capacity than we need, it is reasonable to ask why we don't simply withdraw enough of it to bring the situation into balance. That process *has* been going on for quite some time, but the upsurge in productivity has been at an even faster pace. (Farm output in 1956 was more than 40 percent above that of 1939). The average number of persons employed in agriculture *has* declined markedly, from 12.7 million in 1935 to 7.9 million in 1956, and it is still going down. In 1910 the number so employed was 13.6 million though the total population of the United States was then only 91.9 million, scarcely more than half what it is now. In most countries, well over half the population is engaged in agriculture. Here, about 12 to 13 percent of the employed labor force produces agricultural products so abundantly that we are concerned as to how to make effective use of them.

But, even so, this does not explain why we should not reduce the number of farm workers still further if we still have too many. Part of the difficulty arises from the distribution of skills and resources within agriculture. The most efficient half of the agricultural labor force produces about 90 percent of the agricultural products that go to market. This leaves another 1.5 to 2 million farmers who not only do not fare well but cannot easily shift from agriculture to something else. Many are past middle age and have no other skills. Family and community ties hold them where they are. Pulling up stakes and relocating takes money and some little courage, especially if one has a family. Many of the younger farm people are, however, shifting to other occupations as is abundantly evident from the figures given above. But to make fully and quickly the adjustment that appears to be needed would involve more hardship and more drastic measures than society appears to be willing to countenance. Hence the process of human readjustment seems almost certain to be a slow and difficult one. A similar problem on a smaller scale has long been evident in the soft coal industry.

Much more significant is the fact that migration away from agriculture of small-scale, low-production farmers will not solve the problem. They will not take their farms with them, and the most likely outcome is that such lands will be merged into the larger, more efficient farms and will then produce more than they do now! However, the spread of industry and other lines of business to the rural areas has enabled hundreds of thousands of these small-scale farmers to supplement the returns from their farms with other income, and their average financial situation has, in fact, improved materially in recent years despite the fact that their income from agriculture has remained almost constant since 1945.

Though the over-all results do not reflect it, the adjustments made in US agriculture have actually been far more impressive than most people realize. Last year's record-breaking wheat crop was grown on an acreage that was nearly a fifth smaller than the 1947-1956 average. It was 30 percent under the peak acreage of 1949. The cotton acreage harvested in 1958 was less than 12 million. In the 1925-1930 period we were growing almost four times as many acres of cotton. The story is similar for many of the other crops. In 1958 we grew 3.8 billion bushels of corn on 73.5 million acres whereas in the early 1930's we were growing around 2.5 billion bushels on more than 100 million acres. The appallingly wasteful potato crops of the period around 1950 were actually grown on an acreage that was less than half what was considered normal and necessary in the early and middle 1930's.

I cite these figures not as either a defense or condemnation of current or past programs but merely to explain why adjustment has proved so difficult. The factors that go into agricultural production are land, labor, capital, organization and technology. Of these, only the land factor can be brought under effective control, and even that is far from easy. Land taken out of one crop tends to be shifted to some other crop. Under American conditions, improved technology, once it is developed, tends to be adopted quickly and widely. Also it tends to feed on itself and to continue to grow. Capital investments are extremely difficult if not impossible to control. Labor will shift only as it has inducements and opportunities that make such shifting attractive. This leaves the burden mainly on the land factor. Hence the acreage control schemes and soil conservation programs of the 1930's and the soil bank plan of the present period. But land can't be taken out fast enough to offset wheat yields that have moved up from around 14 bushels in the pre-World War II period to 27.3 bushels in 1958, or a cotton output that averaged less than 200 pounds per acre prior to the middle 1930's and is now well over 400 pounds. Similar but less easily measured improvements have been occurring in the livestock industries.

Clearly we do not want to go on producing and storing things for which we have no use. But as in most other major economic adjustments, peoples' lives, homes, investments and skills are involved. If we are to avoid very great hardships to very large numbers of people, changes are bound to be somewhat slow and halting. The stocks we have built up do not consist of the kinds of things most needed either in our own economy or in the world at large, but we need to find ways to make more effective use of them and, as soon as possible, to stop building them up unless we do have use for them either here or abroad. There are political obstacles to be overcome as well as economic ones, and the problem may become more troublesome before it gets better. But we are at least coming to have a better understanding of the nature of it, which is an essential step toward solution. In the meantime, we can console ourselves to some extent by keeping in mind that an economy of overabundance is far easier to live with than one of extreme scarcity.

HOW THE FARMERS GET WHAT THEY WANT

Theodore Lowi

Theodore Lowi is Assistant Professor of Government at Cornell University and specializes in the field of political theory.

In his Farm Message of January 31, President Johnson proposed that Congress establish a bipartisan commission to investigate the concentration of power in the food industry. In the same message the President called for new legislation to strengthen farmer co-operatives, to encourage their expansion through merger and acquisition, and to provide them with further exemptions from the anti-trust laws.

This was the beginning of the "Johnson round" in agriculture. It is part of a familiar pattern. An attack on the food industry's market power, coupled with proposals for expanded and stronger farm co-operatives, is obviously not an attack on concentration itself. Rather it is an attack on the intervention of nonagricultural groups into strictly agricultural affairs.

That agricultural affairs should be handled strictly within the agricultural community is a basic political principle established before the turn of the century and maintained since then without serious re-examination. As a result, agriculture has become neither public nor private enterprise. It is a system of self-government through a delegation of national sovereignty. Agriculture has emerged as a largely self-governing federal estate within the Federal structure of the United States.

President Johnson recognized these facts within three weeks of his accession when he summoned a conference of agricultural leaders to formulate a program by which agriculture should be served and regulated. The most recent concession to agriculture's self-government was the wheat-cotton bill. Because cotton supports were too high, the cotton interests wrote a bill providing for a subsidy of six to eight cents a pound to mills in order to keep them competitive with foreign cotton and domestic rayon without touching the price supports. On the other hand, wheat supports were too low because wheat farmers last year in referendum overwhelmingly rejected President Kennedy's plan to provide some Federal regulation along with supports. The wheat section of the new act calls for a program whereby wheat farmers may voluntarily comply with acreage reduction for subsidies of up to seventy cents a bushel but without the Federal supply regulations. The press called this a major legislative victory for Mr. Johnson, but the credit is not his. That the press could see this as a victory for anyone but organized cotton and wheat is a testimonial to the total acceptance by President, press, and public of the principle that private agricultural interests alone govern agriculture and should do so.

The reasons for agriculture's self-government are deep-rooted, and the lessons to be drawn are important to the future of American politics. For a century agriculture has been out of step with American economic development. Occasional fat years have only created unreal expectations, to be undercut by the more typical lean years.

Quite early, farmers discovered the value of politics as a counterweight to industry's growth and concentration. Land-grant and home-steading acts were followed by governmental services in research and education. Continuing distress led to bolder demands. First there were efforts to effect a redistribution of wealth in favor of agriculture. As a debtor class, farmers saw inflation as the solution, and Bryan was their spokesman for cheaper money and cheaper credit. The monopolies, the railroads, the grain merchants and other processors, the banks, and the brokers were to be deprived of power over the market by dissolution or by severe restraints. Next, farmers sought solutions by emulating the business system: the co-operative to restrain domestic trade and international dumping over high tariff walls to restrain international trade. Yet all these mechanisms either were not enacted or did not live up to expectations.

With the coming of the New Deal and with its help, organized agriculture turned to self-regulation. The system created during the 1930's has endured to this day, and with only a few marginal additions and alterations is accepted almost unanimously by farm leaders. Self-regulation might have taken several forms, the most likely one being a national system of farm-leader representation within a farmers' NRA. Instead, a more complicated system of highly decentralized and highly autonomous subgovernments developed, largely for Constitutional reasons. Agriculture was the most "local" of the manufacturing groups the Federal government was trying to reach. The appearance if not the reality of decentralizing Federal programs through farmer-elected local committees helped avoid strains on the interstate commerce clause of the Constitution. But this avoidance of Constitutional troubles created very special political difficulties.

THE LOCAL COMMITTEES

The Federal Extension Service shows how the system works. It is "co-operative" in that it shares the job of farm improvement with the states, the land-grant colleges, the county governments, and the local associations of farmers. The county agent is actually employed by the local associations. In the formative years, the aid of local chambers of commerce was enlisted, the local association being the "farm bureau" of the chamber. In order to co-ordinate local activities and to make more effective claims for additional outside assistance, these farm bureaus were organized into state farm bureau federations. The American Farm Bureau Federation, formed at the Agriculture College of Cornell University in 1919, was used as a further step toward amalgamation. To this day there is a close relationship between the farm bureaus, the land-grant colleges, and the Extension Service. This transformation of an administrative arrangement into a political system has been repeated in nearly all the agricultural programs during recent decades. The Extension Service exercises few controls from the top. There are cries of "Federal encroachment" at the mere suggestion in Washington that the Department of Agriculture should increase its supervision of the extension programs or coordinate them with other Federal activities.

As the financial stakes have grown larger, the pattern of local self-government remains the same. Price support—the "parity program"—is run by the thousands of farmer-elected county committees that function alongside but quite independently of the other local committees. Acreage allotments to bring supply down and prices up are apportioned among the states by the Agricultural Stabilization and Conservation Service. State committees of farmers apportion the allotment among the counties. The farmer-elected county Stabilization and Conservation Committees receive the county allotment.

These committees made the original acreage allotments among individual farmers back in the 1930's; today, they make new allotments, work out adjustments and review complaints regarding allotments, determine whether quotas have been complied with, inspect and approve storage facilities, and perform as the court of original jurisdiction on violations of price-support rules and on eligibility for parity payments. The committees are also vitally important in the campaigns for the two-thirds vote required to fix high price supports. Congress determines the general level of supports, and the Secretary of Agriculture proclaims the national acreage quotas for adjusting the supply to the guaranteed price. But the locally elected committees stand between the farmer and Washington.

Most other agricultural programs have evolved similarly. Each is independent of the others, and any conflicts or overlapping mandates have been treated as nonexistent or beyond the jurisdiction of any one agency. The Soil Conservation Service operates through its independent soil-conservation districts, of which there were 2,936 in 1963, involving ninety-six per cent of the nation's farms. Each district's farmer-elected committee is considered a unit of local government. The Farmer Cooperative Service operates through the member-elected boards of directors of the farm co-ops. In agricultural credit, local self-government is found in even greater complexity. The Farm Credit Administration exists outside the Department of Agriculture and is made up of not one but three separate bodies politic, a triangular system mostly farmer-owned and totally farmer-controlled.

TEN SYSTEMS AND POLITICS

The ten principal self-governing systems in agriculture, in fiscal 1962, disposed of $5.6 billion of the total of $6.7 billion in expenditures passing through the Department of Agriculture. During the calendar year 1962, $5.8 billion in loans was handled similarly. This combined amount represents a large portion of the total of Federal activity outside national defense.

Each of the ten systems has become a powerful political instrumentality. The self-governing local units become one important force in a system that administers a program and maintains the autonomy of that program against political forces emanating from other agricultural programs, from antagonistic farm and non-farm interests, from Congress, from the Secretary of Agriculture, and from the President. To many a farmer, the local outpost of one or another of these systems *is* the government.

The politics within each system is built upon a triangular trading pattern involving the central agency, a Congressional committee or subcommittee, and the local district farmer committees (usually federated in some national or regional organization). Each side of the triangle complements and supports the other two.

The Extension Service, for example, is one side of the triangle completed by the long-tenure "farm bureau" members of the Agriculture Committees in Congress and, at the local level, the American Farm Bureau Federation with its local committees. Further group support is provided by two intimately related groups, the Association of Land Grant Colleges and Universities and the National Association of County Agricultural Agents.

Another such triangle unites the Soil Conservation Service, the Agriculture subcommittee of the House Appropriations Committee, and the local districts organized in the energetic National Association of Soil Conservation Districts. Further support comes from the Soil Conservation Society of America (mainly professionals) and the former Friends of the Land, now the Izaak Walton League of America.

Probably the most complex of the systems embraces the parity program. It connects the Agricultural Stabilization and Conservation Service with the eight (formerly ten) commodity subcommittees of the House Agriculture Committee and the dozens of separately organized groups representing the various commodities. (Examples: National Cotton Council, American Wool Growers Association, American Cranberry Growers Association.) These groups and congressmen draw support from the local price-support committees wherever a particular commodity is grown.

THE FARMER HAD HIS WAY

These systems have a vigorous capacity to maintain themselves and to resist encroachment. They have such institutional legitimacy that they have become practically insulated from the three central sources of democratic political responsibility. Thus, within the Executive branch, they are autonomous. Secretaries of Agriculture have tried and failed to consolidate or even to co-ordinate related programs. Within Congress, they are sufficiently powerful to be able to exercise an effective veto or create a stalemate. And they are almost totally removed from the view, not to mention the control, of the general public. (Throughout the 1950's, Victor Anfuso of Brooklyn was the only member of the House Agriculture Committee from a non-farm constituency.)

Important cases illustrate their power:

1. In 1947, Secretary of Agriculture Clinton P. Anderson proposed a consolidation of all soil-conservation, price-support, and FHA programs into one committee system with a direct line from the committees to the Secretary. Bills were prepared providing for consolidation within the price-support committees. Contrary bills provided for consolidation under soil conservation districts. The result: stalemate. In 1948, a leading farm senator proposed consolidation of the programs under the local associations of the Extension Service. Immediately a House farm leader introduced a contrary bill. The result: continuing stalemate.

2. In Waco, Texas, on October 14, 1952, Presidential candidate Eisenhower said: "I would like to see in every county all Federal farm agencies under the same roof." Pursuant to this promise, Secretary Ezra Taft Benson issued a series of orders during early 1953 attempting to bring about consoli-

dation of local units as well as unification at the top. Finally, amid cries of "sneak attack" and "agricrat," Benson proclaimed that "any work on the further consolidation of county and state offices . . . shall be suspended."

3. From the very beginning, Secretary Benson sought to abandon rigid price supports and bring actual supports closer to market prices. In 1954, as he was beginning to succeed, Congress enacted a "commodity set-aside" by which $2.5 billion of surplus commodities already held by the government were declared to be "frozen reserve" for national defense. Since the Secretary's power to cut price supports depends heavily upon the amount of government-owned surplus carried over from previous years, the commodity set-aside was a way of freezing parity as well as reserves. Benson eventually succeeded in reducing supports on the few commodities over which he had authority. But thanks to the set-aside, Congress, between fiscal 1952 and 1957, helped increase the value of commodities held by the government from $1.1 billion to $5.3 billion. What appeared, therefore, to be a real Republican policy shift amounted to no more than giving back with one hand what had been taken away by the other.

4. President Eisenhower's first budget sought to abolish farm home-building and improvement loans by eliminating the budgetary request and by further requesting that the 1949 authorization law be allowed to expire. Congress overrode his request in 1953 and each succeeding year, and the President answered Congress with a year-by-year refusal to implement the farm housing program. In 1956, when the President asked again explicitly for elimination of the program, he was rebuffed. The Housing subcommittee of the House Banking and Currency Committee added to the President's omnibus housing bill a renewal of the farm housing program, plus an authorization for $500 million in loans over a five-year period, and the bill passed with a Congressional mandate to use the funds. They were used thereafter at a rate of about $75 million a year.

5. On March 16, 1961, President Kennedy produced a "radically different" farm program in a special message to Congress. For the first time in the history of price supports, the bill called for surplus control through quotas placed on bushels, tons, or other units, rather than on acreage. An acreage allotment allows the farmer to produce as much as he can on the reduced acreage in cultivation. For example, in the first ten years or so of acreage control, acreage under cultivation dropped by about four per cent, while actual production rose by fifteen per cent. The Kennedy proposal called for national committees of farmers to be elected to work out the actual program. This more stringent type of control was eliminated from the omnibus bill in the Agriculture Committees of both chambers and there were no attempts to restore them during floor debate. Last-minute efforts by Secretary Orville L. Freeman to up the ante, offering to raise wheat supports from $1.79 to $2.00 were useless. Persistence by the administration led eventually to rejection by wheat farmers in 1963 of all high price supports and acreage controls.

The politics of this rejected referendum is of general significance. Despite all the blandishments and inducements of the administration, the farmer had his way. The local price-support committees usually campaign in these referendums for the Department of Agriculture, but this time they did not. And thousands of small farmers, eligible to vote for the first time, joined with the local leadership to help defeat the referendum. It is not so odd that wheat farmers would reject a proposal that aims to regulate them more strictly than before. What is odd is that only wheat farmers are allowed to decide the matter. It seems that in agriculture, as in many other fields, the regulators are powerless without the consent of the regulated.

Agriculture is the field where the distinction between public and private has been almost completely eliminated, not by public expropriation of private domain but by private expropriation of public domain. For more than a generation, Americans have succeeded in expanding the public sphere without giving thought to the essential democratic question of how each expansion is to be effected. The creation of private governments has profoundly limited the capacity of the public government to govern responsibly and flexibly.

LOOK—NO PRICE SUPPORTS

Gilbert Burck

Gilbert Burck is a member of the Board of Editors of *Fortune* magazine.

One of the major delusions of our time, propagated by farm-state politicians, is that U.S. farming is incurably sick and needs constant government aid and attention. Actually, the ailing and subsidized sector of U.S. farming is smaller than you may think. The federal government supports the price mainly of wheat, cotton, tobacco, corn and other feed grains, dairy products, and oilseeds. Subsidized commodities account for around 45 per cent of the farmer's cash marketing income (which came to $34 billion in 1958), and probably a smaller percentage of farm effort. The other 55 per cent of the farmer's income is mainly from livestock, vegetables, fruits and nuts, poultry and eggs. For these products farmers receive virtually no subsidy, usually want none, and certainly need none.

It is true that what might be called free farming is not rolling in clover. Nearly all its practitioners are caught in a price-cost squeeze, and egg producers are undergoing a readjustment that is permanently changing the business. Nevertheless, most "free" farmers are opposed to subsidies for the very simple reason that they encourage too many potential competitors. The farmers' self-interest, furthermore, here coincides with the national interest. Because the U.S. is already a very well-fed nation its demand for farm products is increasing only a little faster than population—say, at around 2 per cent a year. But farm productivity (output per man-hour) has been increasing more than three times as fast, at better than 6 per cent a year. That is why 7,500,000 farm workers today produce 75 per cent more than 12,700,000 workers produced twenty-five years ago, why the U.S. is in the enviable position of being able to devote not merely a steadily smaller *share* but a steadily smaller *amount* of its total resources to winning its daily bread, and why it will need even fewer farms and farmers in the future.

Subsidized agriculture wastes human and material resources on surpluses, inflates the price of land under quota, dries up markets by artificially raising prices, and fools people into staying on high-cost or redundant farms. Meanwhile, unsubsidized agriculture, governed in the main by market forces, generally adjusts itself to the consequences of rising productivity without mortgaging its future and without burdening the rest of the country.

The U.S. public hears plenty, pro and con, about the part of agriculture that is subsidized. *Fortune* decided to look around at the other part. In these times of stress, how are farmers, particularly the efficient farmers, doing in the $1.6-billion vegetable-growing business, the comparably large fruit-and-nut sector, the $3.3-billion poultry-and-egg business, and the $11-billion livestock industry? It turns out that free farming has some lessons for subsidized agriculture—and for all of the U.S.

THE RISK SPREADERS

Let's look at vegetable raising, which is a highly risky business in the sense that prices for specific products often vary wildly from season to season. The vegetable grower must have both the patience and the resources to spread the risk over a long time or over a large area, to treat part of every profit as a reserve against losses. As an extreme example, snap beans rose from 7.5 cents a pound in December, 1958, to 15.8 cents a year later, and cucumbers from 4.6 to 14.4 cents. A California farmer gets anywhere from $1.53 to $4.46 a bushel for potatoes, so he "plays" potatoes as other Californians play the races and calls it fun if he wins once in three or four tries.

To come out ahead of the game, the vegetable farmer needs a generous endowment of the combination of intuition and knowledge known as good judgment. Herman Zeldenrust, for example, a cocky, stocky young agronomist, runs a seventy-two-acre truck farm near Lansing, Illinois, only twenty-five miles south of Chicago's Loop. Zeldenrust grosses some $65,000 a year and turns in an "agreeable" net by going in for such specialties as chicory, escarole, Bibb lettuce, romaine, mustard greens, and turnip tops—as well as conventional cabbage, lettuce, radishes, and beans. "If you want to get on top of the market," he says, "you have got to have different things. But you also got to time them right." Even Bibb lettuce, which fetches as high as 65 cents a pound, can be a losing item at the wrong time. Zeldenrust hires only workers who agree to work in the rain—well protected by stout rain-wear. Because the market is rarely glutted after bad weather, he remarks that he makes his best money in the rain. "Give me the open market any day," he says. "The buyers have no mercy on me when I've got what they got too much of. But the time always comes when I've got a lot of what they got too little of."

It will be five years before James Ernie Podesto, Route 3, Stockton, California, can be sure how good his judgment is. An outgoing, articulate man of thirty-nine, he and two in-laws bought 125 acres on the installment plan ten years ago, and leveled and irrigated them. On another 125 rented acres he grew kidney beans and other row crops. But he felt sure their price would decline as California's production increased, and looked around for something else. Fewer and fewer acres, he discovered, were then devoted to cherries. Cherries are hard to grow and take fifteen years to reach maturity, but such considerations, because they discourage others, made Podesto all the more eager to produce them. He puts his own 125 acres to cherries, interplanting them with cling peaches and beans while they were maturing. In five more years, if his judgment was right, they should pay off handsomely; and so far it looks as if his judgment was right. "I just have faith in cherries," says Podesto.

Era of the Agribusinessman

In addition to market judgment, a vegetable farmer must also be a big-time, heavily capitalized manager—an agribusinessman, as the new cliche goes. For competition has been bearing down on prices, while costs of labor, capital equipment, and "boughten inputs" like fertilizer, service, parts, fuel, and seed have been rising steeply. To maintain profit margins, as well as to take full advantage of mechanization, the vegetable farmer is being forced to expand, often by buying out his less affluent or less able or less fortunate neighbor. In the 1920's some twenty acres of good land sufficed a hard-working truck farmer near the big eastern and midwestern cities, and in the 1930's perhaps forty acres. Today, however, he may need something like eighty acres, worth, say, $40,000 to $60,000, and another $60,000 worth of machinery and equipment, including a half-dozen specialized tractors. Why so many tractors on so little land? Mainly because the time otherwise wasted in changing equipment and wheel gauge at the height of the season is worth more than the overhead on the tractors.

How a relatively large plant for vegetables can be combined with judgment and ability is illustrated by the four De Jong brothers of Cook County,

Illinois. The De Jongs devote some 300 acres to such crops as green onions, spinach, green beans, radishes, cabbage, and Bibb lettuce, and they work the land intensively. Most of it is fully irrigated and yields two or more crops a year. Not counting the land, more than half of which they rent, the De Jongs put the replacement value of their total investment at more than $200,000; it includes fifteen trucks, twelve tractors with a battalion of equipment, six irrigation pumps, four miles of pipe, and $75,000 worth of buildings including greenhouses and four large refrigerated structures for cooling their produce. At the peak of the season the De Jongs employ as many as 150 migrant Mexican workers, for whom they must provide housing.

Not only have their produce mix and timing been unusually good, but they make a point of keeping up with all the latest wrinkles in fertilizers and insecticides. Carl Mees, the Cook County farm adviser, says they often know about a new development as soon as he does. The De Jongs are smart marketers too; they spread the risk by selling about 40 per cent of their produce in the South Water Market in Chicago, 30 per cent to roadside stands and nearby supermarkets, and 30 per cent to peddlers. Their investment and acumen enable them to gross more than $500,000 a year, or an astonishing $1,700 an acre, and of their net they say only that their profit margins have been declining, but that they're doing better than if they invested the money at interest.

In Love with Dichondra

In California, where growers raise much of their vegetable crop for processing or for distant markets and have long operated on a relatively large scale, the push is toward even bigger and more diversified farms. Aggressive Adolf Merwin, who with a son and son-in-law grosses $250,000 on an 800-acre place near Clarksburg, California, in the flat river valley south of Sacramento, earns an average of "only" $60,000 net. He estimates their total investment at $500,000 to $700,000, and figures he could put the same money into other things more profitably. To better his margin, he is constantly experimenting with new crops to supplement his tomatoes, sugar beets, and onion bulbs. His latest love is seed of dichondra, a lawngrass, to which he devotes some seventy-five acres. He harvests about 1,000 pounds to the acre and gets $1 a pound for it, and he has cut production costs by inventing a machine to harvest the seed.

For some time now, only heavy capitalization and intense cultivation have enabled a truck farmer to survive near or in the eastern metropolitan areas. Take the Farino brothers (Thomas, Patsy, and Vincent), who work sixty acres near Jamesburg, New Jersey, less than fifty miles from New York City. They raise a wide variety of truck such as lettuce, spinach, cabbage, endive, and onions, and by irrigating every square foot of the place get three crops worth more than $50,000 a year. Their capital investment including land "could not begin to be replaced at $100,000," and includes three trucks, seven tractors, a full complement of implements, a greenhouse, and a cooling shed.

"Patsy specializes in selling, Vincent in growing, and I in harvesting," says Tom. "We plan our production carefully and don't grieve about our mistakes because they should cancel out. Whether we're good or not shows up in what we have left at the end of a season. When we have a good year, we put money aside in a kind of sinking fund to protect ourselves against the bad years, which have been frequent. Costs are up and prices are down a little, but we are still making out O.K."

Tom Farino is eloquent on the subject of price supports, whose defects he feels are illustrated by the potato business in New Jersey. Beginning in 1943, the government supported potato prices chiefly as a wartime measure, but it continued those supports until 1951, and on a scandalously high level. Not only did it spend nearly $480 million supporting potato prices; much worse, so far as many farmers were concerned, it encouraged "everybody and all his brothers" to get into potato production. "Price supports on vegetables," says Farino, "would only encourage farmers to raise things people don't need and don't want."

Collective Marketing

Now that much of their produce is being sold directly to chain stores and other purchasers with immense buying power, vegetable farmers everywhere are paying more attention to marketing, and showing more interest in consolidating their selling power. They have got into processing and into federal and state sponsored marketing agreements, and have formed large cooperatives and bargaining associations. The marketing programs aim to "stabilize" prices either by setting standards that automatically exclude some produce from the market or by controlling members' volume, or by increasing demand through promotion and research. Such quasi-cartel arrangements, of course, are not new; they have sprung up since the 1930's, when they were exempted from antitrust. They have been set up to market some fruits, nuts, dairy products, and a few vegetables, and they have been most successful on the Pacific Coast, where the growing of many crops is concentrated in a relatively small area and thus can be cooperatively controlled. Some sixteen federally sponsored agreements were in force in California last year, as well as thirty-two state-sponsored marketing "orders," or laws that govern all producers of a given crop.

Fortunately for the American consumer, volume controls are airtight only when organized growers have a near monopoly on the product, which they rarely have—at least on a national basis. When they do succeed in raising prices very high, they usually find the consumer turning to substitutes or the market undermined by newcomers wanting to get in on a good thing. For both the farmer and the rest of the country, the most beneficial price-raising schemes are obviously those that are fallible.

Nevertheless, farmers continue trying to improve their marketing power, particularly against the chain stores. They complain that the chains "cut the top off the market"—i.e., prevent them from getting high premium prices on new vegetables by bringing them in from elsewhere till prices fall. Growers around Chicago used to haul their produce to the South Water Market, but by 1955 much of their output was going directly to the chains. "The chains argued that we should sell to them direct and save the commission merchant's cut," says Edward Koehler of Des Plaines, Illinois, "Trouble is now you never know what the price really should be—and how do you establish a price except in a market?" In 1956, Koehler and several dozen other farmers organized the Arlington Valley Growers' cooperative, and turned their marketing problems over to the produce-dealing firm of Robert L. Berner Co., which washes, cools, waxes, packages, stores, and markets their stuff. Berner spends upward of $10,000 a month calling distant markets, trying for a better price than local markets afford. Thus in 1958, when nearby growers were plowing cabbages under, A.V.G. members got $18 a ton for cabbage.

So goes the transformation of the vegetable-growing industry. Like any collection of small businesses caught between rising costs and prices determined by ferocious competition, it has been forced to consolidate, to employ more capital, to upgrade its management, and to market more cheaply and efficiently—in short, to offset narrowing margins by increased efficiency or greater volume or both.

Those Who Get Left

So far, we have been talking of the more prosperous, efficient vegetable farmers. What about the less efficient, the unlucky, and the capital-shy? The answer is that they are doing exactly what they should be doing for the good of themselves, the industry, and the U.S. economy—they are getting into other businesses or finding other jobs. Near Jamesburg, New Jersey, not far down the road from the Farinos, truck farmers are selling out to land developers, or getting jobs in other industries, or simply retiring. Out on Riverhead, Long Island, last February 21, occurred the first of a series of auctions of used tractors and implements whose owners reckoned the time had come to choose between becoming large-scale potato and cauliflower producers, and hardly making a living on their farms. In California's Sacramento Valley many "little" farmers with as many as 100 or more acres are getting out of the business, and recently there were three auctions a week.

Gloom in Plums

We are conditioned to shed a semi-automatic tear whenever a family leaves a farm; but is this, in an age of varied and expanding jobs elsewhere, such a tough prospect? Only if people move to new jobs can an economy grow faster than its population and so convert rising productivity into a higher living standard. This continuous redeployment, which benefits the country as a whole, is also good for the vegetable-growing business. The farmers who survive are the ones who will be able to judge their markets more accurately. As marginal producers quit, vegetable growing will be burdened with less blind competition. Because an entrepreneur must have a lot of capital as well as talent and experience to make good in vegetables, there will be less incentive for ex-farmers to return to, or for new ones to enter, the business unless prices and profit margins rise considerably. Then, of course, they would be tempted to get in, and so would keep prices from rising too high. All in all, the vegetable-growing business may never be a Gibraltar of stability, but the man who is smart and foresighted enough to take one year with another, to forfend against bad times, should continue to do well.

So too in the $1.5-billion fruit-and-nut industry. These days most fruit and nut growers are also being strapped by narrowing profit margins, the result of productivity increases generated by machinery, sprays, insecticides, breeding innovations, and the like. Times are tough for many. Frank Aberle, who raises Tokay grapes and plums on eighty acres near Lodi, California, says he's "never been so disappointed." Last year he pulled up twenty of his forty acres of plums. One fruit grower in Monmouth County, New Jersey, has 215 acres of apples and peaches, on which he grosses some $175,000. But he doesn't make enough these days, he says, to bring a fair return on the $150,000 to $200,000 he has invested in his plant. However, he goes on, 1959 was an exceptionally bad year, and good times are bound to come again as the fruit business consolidates itself.

In some ways, indeed, fruit farmers are better off than vegetable farmers. Because fruit farms usually take several years to mature and so require relatively large capital investments, the fruit business has been less bothered by the forays of the in-and-outers. The fruit farmer, moreover, finds it easier to gauge the market and to form cooperatives and enter marketing agreements.

The trend in fruit as in vegetable farming is toward bigness, diversification, and cooperative marketing arrangements. An extreme example of the last is the California Canners and Growers, known locally as Cal-Can, which was launched in 1957 by four bargaining associations that got members to put up 15 per cent of the value of their crop to buy two canning companies. The canneries did very well in 1958, and 650 member-growers received going prices or a total of $12 million for their crops. Cal-Can also made $2,900,000; and someday, after the company is well established, the farmer-owners expect to receive dividends from the operation.

THE REVOLUTION IN EGGS

As anyone who has shopped in a grocery store is well aware, eggs have rarely been so cheap as they were last year. Few farm businesses since the great depression have gone through the travail that the $1.5-billion to $2-billion egg-farming industry endured in 1959. Depending on his location, a fairly efficient producer cannot make money if he gets much less than 32 to 35 cents a dozen. Yet by the end of 1958 the average price received by farmers was sliding down toward that level; in May and June, 1959, it was hovering around 25 cents; and not until last autumn did it rise above 32 cents for a short while.

The reasons are many and cumulative. Egg raising used to be an easy business to get into; everybody from retired bookkeepers to grain farmers wanting to diversify became small-time egg farmers. Few businesses have been so plagued with part-time or marginal producers, many of whom had no idea of what their real costs were. Furthermore, the government, to help feed the world during World War II, began to support egg prices. Since it takes only six months to convert a fertile egg into an egg-laying hen, production responded handsomely—from 40 billion eggs in 1940 to 59 billion in 1944. Although eggs were in surplus by then, the government continued to support prices through 1950. Thus overstimulated, egg production stayed high, and actually hit 62 billion last year.

Meantime, egg "technology" was advancing by leaps and bounds. Modern housing, mechanized feeding and watering systems, and especially disease prevention, enabled farmers to keep 75,000 or more layers on a few acres. Egg "integration" or contract farming began to flourish. That is to say, feed companies or specially organized companies simply pay a farmer to produce the eggs. His base pay is usually 4 or 5 cents a dozen, but incentive payments, linked to quality, yield per hen, and egg prices, can theoretically almost double the base pay. Almost overnight, under such a system, an ordinary farmer is converted into an efficient, well-managed, mass egg producer.

Some companies, such as General Mills and Tennessee Egg Co., own the chickens themselves; others, such as Ralston Purina, extend credit to dealers who put the local growers under contract. General Mills, which markets eggs labeled "Sure Fresh," is one of the largest operators in the game, and is processing its own eggs in a new plant in Jackson, Mississippi, where it expects to be handling the output of 500,000 hens by August. In California, poultry and egg producers are doing their own integrating by buying feed mills and doing some marketing cooperatively. Perhaps more than a fifth of all the country's eggs are produced by contract farmers or those with other market hookups, and the percentage is increasing.

While all this was happening, and in part because of it, hen productivity was steadily rising. Better breeding and feeding and medical care sent average output per hen from 156 eggs a year in 1946 to 192 in 1955, and to more than 200 last year. At the same time, the national appetite for eggs abated measurably. Egg consumption per person, 392 in 1951, fell to 371 in 1955, and to around 350 last year. The laying-hen population declined a little too, but not enough to stay the inevitable glut.

The Fewer the Higher

The solution? Herman Demme, sixty-six, of Sewell, New Jersey, who has been in the egg business longer than most other large producers in the state, has a sure-fire solution. Demme's 18,000 hens lay some 3,600,000 eggs a year worth about $120,000, and he also breeds pedigreed hens and prepares a locally popular layer-breeding ration. He sells to nearby stores, dairies, supermarkets, and through his own retail outlet, and does better than most nearby egg raisers, but says he has made no money worth talking about for the last few years. Although his operation is bigger and more efficient than most, it has a hard time competing with some of the new 50,000 or 100,000-hen establishments—especially those in the Deep South, where costs are lower. Herman Jr., who had been in the business with Demme seven years, recently got a job with Procter & Gamble; and Demme now intends to sell out and retire. His solution for the egg crisis; let more farmers follow his example. "Fewer farmers, fewer hens, fewer eggs."

Some of Demme's neighbors have other notions. Jerome Taub, a poultry farmer in Franklin Township, started to raise a beard three years ago and vowed to let it grow until egg prices went up. He still has his beard, and is also running for the U.S. House of Representatives on the Democratic ticket. More than 1,500 South Jersey and Pennsylvania egg producers have asked to join Jimmy Hoffa's Teamsters Union. Hoffa has attributed the poultrymen's problem to the buying practices of the chains, which he has described with unintentional humor as manipulating distribution. Elsewhere egg "technologists" are experimenting with frozen scrambled and "pre-fried" eggs. The federal government has come to the aid of egg producers in a small way by purchasing some dried eggs for school lunches, and Senator Hubert Humphrey has introduced a bill enabling turkey, chicken, and egg farmers to form nationwide, federally sponsored marketing agreements.

But of course, the only lasting solution, as Demme and every other responsible producer knows and freely admits, is fewer eggs. This, indeed, is precisely what now seems in the offing; egg farmers almost everywhere are deliberately reducing production. The number of laying hens in the U.S. was down to around 300 million last March 1, against 350 million on March 1, 1952. More important, the number of "egg-type chicks" (chicks bred for laying power) hatched last February was 38 per cent below the number hatched in February, 1959 (52 per cent below in New Jersey). So egg production should decline by autumn, and egg prices should rise. This prospect, it is true, may encourage growers to keep their old hens laying longer, or may prompt some optimistic entrepreneurs to raise more egg-type chicks.

Yet the worst is probably over. Gradually the egg "situation" is improving for the egg producer—but a very different kind of egg producer. Like vegetable farming, egg production now demands capital, volume, and special techniques. Even for the big and efficient operators, profit margins will doubtless remain thin; instead of 5 to 10 cents a dozen, they may not rise above 2 or 3 cents. Given such margins, the little farmer cannot make a go of the egg business, and presumably will stay out of it. Certainly fewer newcomers will want to get into it.

Some observers, it is true, point out that, according to the 1954 census of agriculture, more than half the country's eggs came from small flocks that were probably sidelines. They argue that many part-time egg farmers can and probably will go on raising eggs even if prices are so low that efficient, large-scale producers lose money. This, however, is a highly dubious inference. Almost everywhere farmers are giving up raising "a few" eggs on the side as not worth the trouble. Unless they can feed their hens entirely on home-produced grains or table scraps, they often find that prepared feed, when bought in small quantities costs more than the eggs are worth. And the newcomers are often contract farmers, such as the Southerners who have found their cotton and tobacco acreage cut down by quotas and are supplementing their basic-crop income by raising eggs on a larger scale for the feed companies. As the egg business recovers its stability, such farmers will probably make money. Consumers will find eggs reasonable, and unburdened with a penny of subsidy.

Productivity in Broilers

Most of these observations are relevant to the poultry-meat business, which brings the farmer nearly $1.4 billion a year. In 1959 broilers, which make up the bulk of all poultry, fetched as little as 15 cents a pound (live)—against a postwar high of 36 cents and a high of close to $1 a pound (dressed) about the time of World War I, before the use of vitamins A and D made it possible for farmers to raise broilers cheaply in winter. Yet so efficient has the broiler industry become, the big operators can actually make a thin profit with the price down around 16 or 17 cents. More than 90 per cent of the broiler business is now done by contract or otherwise "integrated" farmers, who get about a penny a pound for their trouble and overhead. Feed dealers or feed manufacturers supply capital, rations, medicine, and technical advice; banks also supply capital to dealers and manufacturers. How the resultant cost and price cutting has broadened the market is strikingly illustrated by the figures: broiler prices declined from 29.5 cents a pound in 1945 to 18.9 cents in 1957. But commercial production rose from 1.1 billion to nearly 4.7 billion pounds, and sales from $327 million to $887 million.

NATION OF BEEFEATERS

More than $11 billion, or a third of the farmer's cash marketing income, is accounted for by meat animals—$7.4 billion by beef and veal, $3.4 billion by hogs, and $360 million by sheep. Beef producers have resolutely and regularly turned down price supports in favor of the free market (although lately some have been muttering about "protection" against imported carcasses); and except during periods of low prices, hog producers too have shown little interest in supports.

The price of both hogs and beef moves in cycles: as production increases, prices fall, whereupon production slows down and prices rise again. Actually the hog and beef cycles are much more complex than this. They vary in pattern and length, are affected by each other, and are further complicated by the price of feed. High hog prices, for example, may not boost production very much if the price of corn is also high.

Taking everything together, the beef industry is in good shape and has relatively little to worry about. In the past decade U.S. per capita consumption of beef has risen 30 per cent—from sixty-four to eighty-four pounds a year, while cash receipts to farms have risen by more than 50 per cent, from less than $5 billion to more than $7 billion. In 1951 beef cattle prices reached a postwar high of around 30 cents a pound. Although they declined to as low as 13.5 cents in 1955, they began to swing up again in 1957 and reached a high of 24.3 cents in the spring of 1959. They started to break again in the summer of 1959, and will probably decline for some time.

The price swing is not the same for all beef—cheaper beef like cow meat fluctuates more than fed steers and heifers. Much depends on the producer's judgment in deciding when to market for slaughter. According to Dr. Herrell DeGraff of Cornell University, economist for the American National Cattlemen's Association, a producer with an assured feed supply might well retain his young stock longer than normal at the beginning of an upswing, and then, as prices level off, sell calves instead of yearlings, and sell at weaning age when prices turn down. Circumstances alter cases, and there are enough potential combinations to keep a computer busy. Whatever happens, the beef producer can look for the eventual upswing. Per capita consumption of beef, by 1965, is expected to increase to some ninety-five pounds a year, or by 13 per cent.

The hog farmer's life has not been so happy as the beef producer's. The price of hogs dropped from around 25 cents a pound early in 1954 to 11 cents a pound in the winter of 1955–56, and nearly all producers lost money. The National Farmers' Organization and others began to agitate for a government-supported price, but experienced farmers knew that prices would very likely rise soon, so nothing came of the movement. Sure enough, prices rose to as high as 21 cents in 1958.

Then the cycle began all over again. Prices declined to 11 cents last winter, but farmers farrowed fewer spring pigs, and prices are now on the way up. As Claude W. Gifford, economics editor of the *Farm Journal,* keeps insisting, the notion that farmers always produce more when prices decline is one of the major misconceptions about U.S. agriculture. The smart hog farmer takes the cycle into account when he plans production. Unless he is prepared to absorb the lows at the bottom while cutting back his production, he won't be there to share in the profits at the top. "The efficient corn-belt hog farmers do not want price supports," says Keith E. Myers of Grundy Center, Iowa, executive secretary of the National Swine Growers Council.

Neither does Santo Miserendino of Westville, New Jersey, who is in the business of raising and fattening hogs on "edible plate waste," the latest euphemism for high-class garbage. Miserendino, who turns out about 3,000 "fat hogs" a year, says he needs a little more than 15 cents a pound to break even. Last year, when he produced nearly a million pounds, he lost a good deal. But this doesn't bother him in the least. When he makes money, he simply puts an adequate amount away against the down phase of the cycle. "You know it's coming," says Miserendino, "and you get ready for it and play with it."

FREE MARKET FOR ALL?

The lesson in all this for subsidized farming? As agricultural economists point out, there are important differences between basic-crop farming and the activities we have examined. The demand for vegetables and fruit responds sharply to price changes and fluctuates widely over the short run. The demand for wheat and corn, by contrast, is very little affected by prices. As income rises, as a matter of fact, people eat more meat and fowl, but steadily less food made from grain—regardless of prices. To turn subsidized commodities loose in the market place, the argument goes, would bankrupt farmers who produce them. And certainly so long as the market is overshadowed by monumental surpluses—there is enough wheat in storage to supply the U.S. for nearly three years—a free market would ruin many if not all producers. But these surpluses are a result of policies born in depression and war; and it is the aim of the Eisenhower Administration, and ought to be the aim of any future administration, to try to bring production and demand into some kind of balance. Once they were in fair balance, commodities now subsidized could doubtless be exposed to market forces once again.

U.S. farming, as we have seen, has changed enormously since the days when prices were first supported. Like U.S. business before it, farming has become more mature as it has become better organized and more heavily capitalized. The old theory that unbridled competition is bound to result in a boom-bust cycle of relative scarcity and high prices followed by overproduction and ruinously low prices has little relevance today. Farmers, of course, cannot shut off production as a factory manager can, and cannot plan production with the relative accuracy of the industrial manager. But a kind of innate stability has superseded the wild instability of the old days. The lesson taught by free agriculture is simply that farmers, even in these trying times, can and do adjust their production to market demand, without cost to the rest of the country, and at a profit to themselves.

17 BIG GOVERNMENT: WHAT ROLE?

"That government governs best which governs least." Perhaps better than any other brief statement, this often quoted remark of Thomas Jefferson's reflects the basic belief of the American people about government's proper role. Yet big government has grown up all around us. Indeed, a careful examination of Jeffersonian philosophy in practice might suggest that Jefferson himself would be among the first to reject an agrarian-oriented government for one attuned to a modern industrial society. Certainly, his conduct of the presidency, as exemplified in the purchase of Louisiana, indicates the necessity of a qualifying phrase—"that government governs best which governs least, *so long as it provides the government requisite to the times.*"

Despite the cries of "unconstitutional usurpation of power," despite the protests against bureaucrats' allegedly "taking away our freedoms"—taking our governance away from those state and local branches reputedly "closest to the people"—despite all these, government has not only grown larger but relatively stronger, more centralized, and more federalized over the past 175 years. Indeed, the process seems unlikely to lessen, let alone halt, in the foreseeable future.

Before we assess the complex functions of government in a modern society, we should ask ourselves: What criteria may be advanced for judging the desirability of this trend to more government? What objectively phrased questions may help clarify the emotional atmosphere?

Perhaps the best standard is the century-old urging of Abraham Lincoln that government do for the people those things they cannot do at all for themselves, or do so well. This approach may be offered in response to the related question about which level of government should undertake what tasks—local, state, or federal. That is, a rejection of bald ideology—of socialistic and *laissez faire* dogma alike—would suggest that government services should be performed on the level that is most capable of undertaking them.

Much of the history of government's ever expanding role suggests that Americans have, by and large, followed this suggestion. The rise of big government can be traced to a series of responses to felt needs—needs arising out of crisis situations (wars and depressions in particular) for which traditional approaches proved inadequate. In area after area, regulatory action has countered the abuse of publicly granted privilege by groups that had successfully pleaded their identity with the national interest. More often than not, initial control attempts were pursued at the state or local levels, and it was only after these attempts failed that federal action was demanded.

From this pragmatic approach, government has emerged in the latter half of the twentieth century with three clearly defined functions—a positive, a negative, and a third, which may be termed *conciliatory-representative*. The negative functions of government—the traditional police restraints, preservation of law and order, protection against invasion—have been vastly expanded in recent years to include protection of the public health, defense against fraudulent business practices, as well as the suppression of public nuisance, occasionally arising from an overly free use of private property. The positive functions—long with us in the form of a postal service, a protective tariff, and in the very grant of corporate privilege—have similarly been amplified in the present century to include social security, unemployment insurance, workmen's compensation, school lunch programs, and even the beginnings of medical care for the aged—in short, the "welfare state."

The third function of government, a product, for the most part, of the twentieth century, has stemmed from the rise of those "great aggregates of socioeconomic power"—the pressure groups. Not only in their demands and counterdemands for service to themselves and regulation of others have these groups made their weight felt. When opposing forces clash head-on or, at other times, join in conspiratorial agreement, we find the need for government intervention to protect the public interest. Since the power of these groups is not always "countervailed," it becomes the task of government to speak for the unorganized, to represent the consumer or the nonunion worker.

Constitutionally, these developments should not be too surprising, particularly in the light of the Supreme Court's early interpretations under Chief Justice John Marshall. For it was Marshall who, in the precedental case of *Gibbons v. Ogden,* clearly set forth the dictum that "all intercourse" among the several states constitutes interstate commerce. Thus, the way was paved for the modern use of the commerce clause to justify the federal government's entrance into a field of activities ranging from the prevention of false and misleading advertising (that crosses state lines) to the guarantee of civil rights for Negroes using buses and trains, or even restaurants and hotels (engaged in or catering to interstate commerce).

Even though, for a few brief years during the 1890s, the Court majority rejected many of these earlier interpretations, its reactionary doctrines, such as the infamous "separate but equal," have proven the real aberrations from the mainstream of our constitutional development. As noted in an earlier chapter, the Constitution may be, in the short run at least, "what the judges say it is." But, in the long run, the ultimate shape of our constitutional system will be determined by the wishes of the people, if not by the positive actions of a majority, then by those views—even of a minority—they are willing to accept. Thus, our government in action has remained a dynamic one, its role throughout our history changing in response to democratic dictates rather than through ideological fiat. What democrat, what republican would have it otherwise?

IS THE WELFARE STATE OBSOLETE?
Irving Kristol

Irving Kristol, who was co-founder and co-editor (1953–1958) of *Encounter* in London, is Senior Editor and Vice-President of Basic Books in New York. He has contributed to many magazines and has been an editor of *The Reporter*.

Ever since John Kenneth Galbraith, in *The Affluent Society,* popularized the distinction between the private sector and the public sector of our economy, these two categories have been the shuttlecocks of ideological debate. On the one hand, the liberals think it a scandal that this nation should spend as much on cosmetics as on space exploration (including missile development) . . . that automobiles should flourish while civic transit decays . . . that private vanities predominate over the public welfare. On the other, there are the conservatives for whom the contrast between private and public sectors is between "productive" and "nonproductive" expenditures, between the "voluntary" and "coercive" areas of American life, between individual, rational self-interest and public folly.

I think this debate is anything but insignificant or sterile, but I also think the terms in which it is defined are profoundly misleading. I would even say they are deliberately intended to mislead. Beneath this rhetorical controversy is a rather crude struggle for political and social power. The liberal community—i.e., the teachers, the journalists, the civil servants, the trade unionists, the leaders of minority groups, etc.—envisages the welfare state as the one institution through which it can exercise a power and authority over the nation's affairs which it does not otherwise possess. The conservative community—i.e., businessmen and their associates—sees the welfare state as a *parvenu* authority that usurps its traditional power and prerogatives, obstructs its habitual freedom of action. Each party doubtless sincerely believes that its sovereignty is most conducive to the common good. Whom the gods would make power-hungry, they first make sincere.

In some significant respects, of course, this conflict has already been decided in favor of the liberals. The need for huge government defense expenditures, the sheer massive complexity of our industrial society and the consequent necessity for increased regulation, the simple fact that businessmen are an electoral minority—these have made it inevitable that a modern democratic state will be a strong state, not a weak one. There is not much point in lamenting this development; and, so far as I can see, no reason to do so.

But true strength knows its own limits; and there is a real question as to

From *Harper's Magazine,* June 1963. Reprinted by permission.

whether the welfare state, as it is taking shape in America today, is not exhibiting delusions of omnicompetence. What is one to make, for instance, of the following extract from an interview with Mortimer Caplin, the Commissioner of Internal Revenue?

> *Q.* Would you clarify the tax status of one kind of situation that occurs frequently among business people: the case of a man who takes his wife, and a client and his wife, out for drinks, to dinner and to the theatre?
>
> *A.* I think that we first have to establish whether or not the expense is at all deductible. This is the first important question.
>
> *Q.* But suppose that this is the kind of entertainment that is deductible?
>
> *A.* Well, we're right in the midst of trying to interpret exactly where the lines are properly to be drawn. Hence, it's difficult for me to give you a definitive answer now.
>
> *Q.* Could you give it in general terms?
>
> *A.* Generally speaking, the committee reports indicate that the customer's wife is placed in a unique position. There is some indication that, in certain circumstances, you could get a deduction for the customer you're entertaining and for his wife—but no other outsider.
>
> *Q.* What about your own wife?
>
> *A.* The question of you and your wife is a more difficult one. There is a certain fuzziness surrounding this deduction under present law, and we're trying to determine the limits of the present state of the law, trying to reconcile many decisions, and also trying to evaluate the impact of the new legislation on this issue.

No doubt Mr. Caplin and his men will approximate as best they can to a Solomonic wisdom when confronting this and similar problems. But how realistic is it to assume that every Caplin will be a Solomon? Why on earth should the United States government be involved in making such precise determinations of such petty matters? How could *any* government presume to do so?

It is quite true that some businessmen have invited such regulation by their abuse of expense accounts. But it is of the essence of good government, not only to know what ought to be done, but also to discover ways of doing it that are not self-defeating. This is a lesson the welfare state is only just beginning to learn.

WHO SPENDS THE MONEY?

The terms "public sector" and "private sector," as commonly used, are summary answers to the question: Who spends the nation's money? Not: For what purpose? Not: With what consequence? Merely: Who:—government, or private associations and individuals?

For those whose hands are now on the purse strings, or are itching to take possession of them, this is obviously the crucial question. But for those of us who neither control the nation's wealth nor have grand certainties about how brilliantly we could dispose of it, this is just as obviously a secondary consideration. Only a fanatic would assert that a corporation's expenditures can never serve the common good while a government's expenditures invariably do—or vice versa. Yet these fanatical theses—gross specimens of what philosophers call the generic fallacy—are, if not openly affirmed, at least insinuated by the partisans involved.

Until recently, the public-sector advocates were bound to have the better of the argument. For one thing, the optimistic and rationalist temper of American thought worked in their favor: it is hard for Americans to be convinced that any problem cannot be "solved" by vigorous and purposive collective effort. For another, they had all the advantages of those who argue the ideal over those who defend the actual. Since the private sector was larger and more prominent than the public, it offered the easier target. Corporate corruption, inefficiency, and shortsightedness were fair game. Against them could be posed the high-minded and farsighted quality of proposed government planning—in housing, in transport, in education, in agriculture, in resources development, etc. It takes a great deal of political experience to breed an instinctive and intelligent skepticism toward government planning; the *arriviste* elites of the new underdeveloped nations have no particle of it; and the *arriviste* elites of the New Deal and the New Frontier did not have it either. Where, after all, could they have got it?

Well, they have it now. The famous pragmatic approach to government regulation and intervention, it has been discovered, has one slight drawback: the agencies and institutions that are created soon achieve a life of their own, beyond all trial and error. Among New Frontiersmen in Washington today, the word "bureaucracy" is used with the same bitter despair that used to be the hallmark of a reactionary. The kind of criticism of foreign aid that was once reserved for use by Representative Passman has recently been echoed by Chester Bowles.

In private, nowadays, almost every head of every department will concede that "things are out of hand"—that between the original idea and the terminal reality there is a long and disillusioning gap. The new men in Washington have discovered that in only rare instances can a large-scale plan encompass all the factors on which its success or failure depends. More important, they have discovered for themselves the basic law of administration: the number of capable people available to execute any plan is always less than the number needed—and the larger the plan, the greater the discrepancy. This is why the most planned of all human enterprises—organized warfare—is such a chaos and confusion.

What one tends to forget, when speaking of bold new government programs, is that the people who, in the last analysis, are going to create these programs in their own image are not the planners or the experts but the agency's permanent personnel of all grades—protected from reprisal by civil-service tenure, themselves not particularly interested in the program as such, but themselves also masters of all its legal and technical detail in a way that disarms criticism from top officials and ordinary citizens alike. In a limited program of foreign aid, one might hope to find enough enthusiastic and skilled "ugly Americans" to make a go of it. As the program mushrooms, it becomes the creature of the job-hungry second-rate.

It is in public housing, as a result of the work of Jane Jacobs and others, that this state of affairs has most dramatically impinged upon the liberal consciousness. Why is low-cost housing so hideously dreary? Why should the continuing "administrative expense" (as distinct from operating expense) on each low-cost apartment in New York City amount to thirteen dollars a month? Why must low-cost housing be so huge and permanent, thus making adaptation to changed circumstance practically impossible? When I was in Washington a couple of months ago, I asked a friend, who has taken an important job in the area of federally subsidized housing, what official recognition would be given to this new liberal dissatisfaction with what had been one of the major liberal programs. He shrugged and said:

"Everyone knows things have gone wrong, but no one knows how to go about setting them right. Do you see that row of thick volumes on that shelf? They contain the laws and regulations that govern the federal housing program—the kinds of buildings that may go up, the way they may be financed, and so on. It will take the present Administration five years to master them. It will take at least another five years to amend and revise them. And then it will take five more years for the reforms to have any practical effect. It needed a generation to construct the present juggernaut and set it in motion. It will need another generation to stop it."

A WAY TO GO MAD

Once one becomes aware of a problem, one tends to confront it around every corner. I can hardly pick up a newspaper these days without my anti-bureaucratic nerve being given a shock. The Internal Revenue Service announces that it will not recognize the general validity of a tax court case decided against it. (This means that each individual taxpayer covered by this case will have to go to court on his own!) Newbold Morris, New York City's Park Commissioner, denounces the suggestion that salesmen be allowed to carry merchandise samples in their private cars while driving on city parkways. (His reason: people ought to use parkways because of their beauty, not because of their utility!) The Rural Electrification Administration (did you know it still exists?) announces that, with American farms electrified, its mission is now completed—and so it will henceforth be selling its electricity at a discount (courtesy of government subsidy) to suburbs, in highly unfair competition with private (i.e., publicly regulated) utilities. The National Labor Relations Board decides that, when a family has a controlling interest in several corporations, in utterly unrelated fields, all of these companies have unlimited liability with respect to an unfair labor practice by any one of them. . . .

Or take this fascinating report from the *New York Times:*

> The city dedicated four rehabilitation brownstones on west 94th Street yesterday for low-rent public housing.
>
> They were the first rehabilitated public housing to be included in an urban project in the United States. Mayor Wagner was the main speaker at the ceremony. . . .
>
> At a cost of approximately $600,000 the fronts of the structures were renovated and their interiors were gutted and rebuilt into forty apartment units.
>
> The forty units replaced more than one hundred single-room occupancy units in what were four rundown buildings.

A bit of arithmetic reveals that these forty new apartment units cost $15,000 each. These are not commodious apartments, mind you—anything but. For that kind of money, wouldn't it have been more sensible for the federal government (whose money it is) to give New York City the authority to purchase for each family a suburban home, with garden, garage, and all? Or, for that matter, wouldn't it have made more sense to divide the $600,000 among the hundred original tenants, giving them $6,000 each as compensation with which to relocate themselves as they pleased, and permitting the land to be used for non-subsidized (and therefore tax-paying) construction? But under present laws and regulations governing federal aid for urban redevelopment, such actions are strictly forbidden. If New York City was to spend the money at all, it had to do so in that absurd way, and in no other.

One can go mad thinking too much on such incidents—and, indeed, it is precisely such incidents that do drive people mad, so that they come to regard all government expenditure as inherently, and by definition, wasteful. A more relevant response would be to concede the desirability of the ends pursued while focusing attention on new methods of achieving them. We might then find that the idea of a welfare state does not necessarily imply that the state should itself always dispense all welfare. Perhaps it would suffice for the state to establish a legal framework for a society in which individual welfare is recognized as a *social* responsibility without at the same time necessarily being a direct responsibility of the *state*.

ILLUSIONS ABOUT MEDICARE

For instance, the President's Medicare Bill might possibly be the best way of dealing with the problem created by the dual fact of medical care costing so much more than it used to and people living longer than they used to. On the other hand, it might not be—we shall require a couple of decades to find out. Would it not, therefore, be prudent to establish that governmental medical insurance will not be the *only* way? Monopolies are sometimes necessary evils, but we ought not to concede the necessity prematurely. We already have a nongovernmental pattern of medical insurance—two-thirds of the American population is now covered by surgical and hospital insurance issued by non-profit organizations such as Blue Cross or Blue Shield or by private insurance companies. Why not encourage this natural growth, parallel to any state insurance scheme that is set up? Why not give individuals the option to choose among a plurality of insurers? It is one thing to make medical insurance compulsory; it is quite another to make only one *kind* of medical insurance compulsory.

Any medical insurance program is going to cost the taxpayer money. The mute appeal of a state-run monopoly is the illusion that over a period of time, and in some undefined way, people may get more than they put in, either because the federal government will magically "close the gap" or because "someone else" (the rich or the employers or whoever) will be called upon to make up the difference. This idea is appealing, but baseless. It is as appealing, and as baseless, as the notion that government money is something additional to the people's money, instead of being identical with it. It is as appealing and as baseless, as the belief that the steeply progressive income tax significantly reduces the tax burden of the average citizen. In a society and economy such as ours, where government expenditure is so infinitely greater than the ability of the rich to pay for it, such egalitarian fancies are mischievous and deceitful. Just because most people, most of the time, feel poorer than they think they ought to be, it does not follow that they are "underprivileged." Indeed, it is this very majority who will have to subsidize medical care for the truly poor—under whatever program is instituted.

The question of how much the American people wish to spend on medical care, as against other things (such as education, leisure, etc.) is something the American people are in the process of deciding. But if, as seems likely, they decide to compel themselves to spend more than they are now doing, it does not follow that only the federal government is competent to spend it for them—and certainly not for all of them.

What holds for Medicare may hold for other areas of the public sector as well. Public-welfare outlays by federal, state, and municipal governments have doubled since 1955, and now amount to more than $40 billion a year. (This excludes expenditures on education by states and municipalities.) This money has not been "wasted"—but can anyone claim that it has been spent as efficiently as it might have been? Or that we have nothing to learn from the experience of these years?

It is right for the government to see to it that public needs are adequately met. It is not always necessary for the government to do the job itself. Certainly the present system of rapid transit in our cities and suburbs needs improvement. But so long as this problem is the football of local politics—and that will probably be forever—relying exclusively on the distribution of federal funds to the cities may make it worse rather than better. There are some good municipally owned transit systems; and there are some awful ones. Why put all our eggs in one basket? Might it not also be advisable to give generous tax advantages to those firms which invest their retained profits in rapid-transit development? After years of experience with New York's subway system, I am not all averse to seeing it owned and operated by General Motors. Perhaps what is good for General Motors will be good for me. It couldn't be worse. And it would be a lot easier for the city to regulate GM than it is for me to regulate New York City.

Similarly, our foreign-aid program must be continued. To a greater extent than we like to admit, the distribution of this aid will be determined by political and military considerations, and we may as well resign ourselves to that fact. But need we also insist upon fanciful "development" schemes, laboriously contrived, solemnly approved, and blithely ignored thereafter? Why should not the United States, in collaboration with its wealthier allies, simply give to the country in question a sum totaling one-half (or some such fraction) of all private foreign investment there, so that the recipient could become an equal shareholder in all such enterprises? Whether the latter kept the shares, or sold them to its citizens and spent the cash in any way it saw fit, would be its own affair. This would help lay the ghost of imperialism; it would leave it to businessmen to determine jointly with the beneficiary nation what development scheme is most appropriate in each case; and it would allow the recipient government a latitude to accomplish those tasks that private business was loath to undertake. Would there be more waste and less progress than under present arrangements?

Once one gets into the swing of thinking along these lines, all sorts of intriguing possibilities emerge. Would it not be interesting to explore these possibilities instead of persisting in the sterile argument over the relative merits of the private and the public sectors? It is always the taxpayer's money that is going to be spent for purposes of improving his welfare. But it does not always follow that it is the tax collector who can spend it most wisely or efficiently.

The important thing is that welfare be improved and enlarged. The means by which we proceed to do this may be as various and as flexible as we wish them to be. And the more various and flexible—the more open to innovation, the more susceptible to reform and revision—the better. Waste and inefficiency there will always be, but the less monumentally it is institutionalized, the less incorrigible it is. Surely a good motto for an open society is: keep it open.

WILL GROWTH INCREASE FEDERAL CONTROL?

Edward T. Chase

A writer on public affairs and a consultant to private industry and to the government, Edward T. Chase has also served as organizer of

From *Atlantic Monthly*, August 1961. Reprinted by permission.

national conferences on urban planning, transportation, and medical economics.

It is clear that the highly charged debate over our economic growth rate and the integral question of private versus public spending will be the central domestic issue of the 1960s. The manner in which the Kennedy Administration attempts to resolve this problem will determine our governmental framework for a generation. In particular, it will establish the pattern of relationships between the federal government and our other great power system, free enterprise, or what economists call more precisely the price-market system.

It was Allen W. Dulles, director of the Central Intelligence Agency, who first predicted economic suicide if we did not change our ways. As the controversy evolves, there is an increasing realization that growth and private versus public spending—a polarity Americans had not thought about in twenty-five years—have to do with our very survival. Only recently, the chairman of the Council of Economic Advisers, Professor Walter W. Heller, suggested that government intervention in the economy may not need to be directing, but simply stimulating. "One of the chief arguments for a more positive program for economic growth," Dr. Heller stated, "is that it is far easier to achieve many of our common goals by enlarging the size of our economic pie than by transferring income and wealth from one group to another.

But Federal Reserve Board Chairman William M. Martin, Jr., differed with him over this point. He contended that, in the case of chronic unemployment, for example, general stimulation of the economy will not be enough. We have the modern paradox of employment and unemployment simultaneously at record peaks. Affirmative government intervention in specific programs of training and job placement is needed to overcome the kind of persistent structural unemployment now so common. In effect, Martin was saying that a stepped-up economic growth rate alone, while desirable and even essential, is an incomplete solution. This hard lesson will have to be learned again and again, because it applies not only to unemployment but to a whole series of economic problems.

The consequences of our failure to learn are serious in the extreme; we can lose in the competition with Communism for the allegiance of the world's newly emerging nations, because our own example will prove unpersuasive. We can lose something even more precious—our sense of confidence that our own social institutions are both effective and serve worthy ends. In this latter respect, the morale of the younger generation is at stake.

The urgency of the growth debate is comprehensible only in the light of two basic forces: 1) our demographic change, by which I mean population growth, a change in the age complexion of the American population, and the population's massive shift into our urban and suburban centers; 2) technological progress. Take a vivid example fraught with political tension, medical care for the aged. Many readers, like the author, have parents over sixty-five. According to official government reports, 55 per cent of all people sixty-five and over (including those still working) have less than $1,000 cash income per year. About a third have liquid assets up to $200, in case of an emergency. Only a tiny fraction have substantial assets readily convertible to cash. And illness strikes the aged two to three times more frequently than the rest of the population; their hospitalization is much longer—the costs run 120 per cent higher than those for the rest of us; and for drugs and medicines the disproportion is even greater. Meantime, medical costs, which have doubled since the war, continue to spiral, with hospital costs advancing relentlessly 5 to 6 per cent each year. Scientific progress has meant marvelous but very expensive new equipment, drugs, and procedures.

Technology has equipped medicine with the means to control the death rate and thus make those over sixty-five the nation's fastest growing population group, and at the same time it has made our industrial plant so productive as to eliminate the aged as an essential part of our work force. Thus, relatively few can earn even minimal annual incomes.

The elderly, increasing in number at the rate of one million every three years, while tolerably fed, housed, clothed, are largely unprotected by health insurance. Only about 40 per cent have even fragmentary health-insurance coverage, according to the Department of Health, Education, and Welfare. Even if the growth of health insurance continues at the booming rate of earlier years, still only about 56 per cent of the aged will be covered by 1965. Yet, after food, clothing, and shelter, medical care has come to be accepted as the fourth basic social right, a right regardless of income.

What bearing has this situation on the question of growth and private versus public spending? This much is clear: a rise in the economic growth rate by itself is beside the mark. Though economic growth is necessary for many reasons, we are learning that growth in a modern industrial society also can be dismayingly irrelevant. In the instance at hand, the bulk of the elderly lack the financial means to afford the health insurance they desperately require; whereas the insurance industry, operating in the market system, cannot hope to insure the aged at premium rates on which the companies can break even, let alone make a profit, for these rates are set by the costs of medical care in the first place.

What we witness, in short, is the spreading phenomenon that goes to the root of the growth debate: the incapability of the price-market system, for technical reasons beyond its purview, to supply an essential public need. The only recourse is government support or provision of the service. And, given the strapped financial situation of the states, the federal government usually must step in.

URBAN CONGESTION

Medical care for the elderly is by no means an isolated example of what the twin forces of technology and demographic change are doing to our society, and, more particularly, to our reliance upon the price-market system as the key determinant of how our wealth is allocated. Consider urban congestion and urban renewal. The problem of urban congestion has become a national nightmare, and its most critical aspect is the alarming decline in mass transportation facilities. As commuter railroad services are terminated, as whole lines fold, as transit companies founder under rising costs and declining patronage, automotive vehicles and the facilities encouraging them proliferate. America's fabulous technological achievement in mass-producing highways and private automobiles has made the giant, sprawling metropolitan complex possible. Here is the locus of the population explosion. At the same time, this accomplishment mortally threatens public transportation as a profit venture.

Can a "hands off, let private growth solve this" position succeed? Obviously not, because the market system simply cannot cope with such a mammoth deficit operation. Hence, substantial government subsidies, tax relief, and even outright takeover of mass transportation systems have become commonplace. And such measures alone do not remedy the situation. Substituting government financing for the market system is not a sufficient answer, since the proper planning of transportation facilities and of land use is the essence of the matter. Support without planning means wasting tax moneys on moribund or irrational organizations; for example, inefficient railroads, or authorities building highways which add to the traffic problems of cities. The congestion, air and land pollution, destruction of neighborhoods, the hideous disarray of our urban complexes are usually traceable to a lack of integrated planning from a central vantage point. The lesson has been made clear again and again that without government intervention either by an authority transcending petty political jurisdictions or by some federal entity, the imbalance will grow between private automotive transportation and public mass transportation. If we intend to rescue our cities before this situation becomes irretrievable, we must come to accept more rather than less government "interference" in realms where the invisible hand of the market has hitherto held sway.

The same holds true in the closely related case of urban slum clearance and rehabilitation. Of all the domestic tasks confronting mid-century America, none has a higher priority than the physical renewal of our cities, where two thirds of our entire population live. Will an increase in our economic growth rate, even up to 5 per cent annually, benefit matters here? Precious little. The evidence shows that mere demand does not register in the tremendously costly and complicated task of rebuilding cities. Only with the intervention of the federal government through the clever mechanism of the "Title 1" program, which makes a profit incentive possible, can the forces of the market be brought to bear on the slum-clearance problem. Only the most hidebound conservatives would contend in 1961 that we should leave the survival of our cities up to the vagaries of market values. The role of government is as inevitable here as it is in regulating the natural monopolies of water, gas, electricity, and telephone service.

The controversy grows hotter in areas where it is only beginning to be appreciated that the market system is failing to fulfill the need. For instance, it is uncertain whether Americans will yet tolerate the principal of large-scale government participation in acquiring and preserving open land. Open land is disappearing at a rate of a million acres a year, for superhighways, airports, and suburban sprawl. We prosecute for food pollution, and even for air and water pollution. Yet, apart from local anti-billboard regulations, we have not begun to invoke comparable powers to prevent land pollution. Is there any doubt but that controls must be forthcoming, and would be, if they were not stigmatized as antibusiness by vested business interests?

RESEARCH AND DEVELOPMENT

Now consider the specialized issue of air transportation. It typifies a whole category of vital technical problems and poses a fundamental question about the government's part in financing industrial research and development. The government has recently announced that supersonic commercial airliners are coming in the immediate future. Their production cost is well beyond the capacity of the private aviation companies. No conceivable acceleration in their growth will render these corporations able to meet the burden of producing the supersonic commercial airliner. Also, it is estimated that the world market will be able to sustain only one producer. Therefore, the first nation to create an effective supersonic airplane will achieve monopoly. It will achieve something more—the national prestige that goes with such an achievement. What is essential again is not growth alone, but bold governmental decision on a matter of resource allocation.

This example raises the point that government intervention may be essential to achieve economic growth itself, besides accomplishing a given project. How big should government's role be in subsidizing industrial invention and innovation? These activities are at the heart of economic growth. There is evidence that the price-market economy is by no means sufficiently effective in seeing to it that we are devoting enough resources to "R and D" (as the knowing call research and development), to invention, to innovation. The fantastic success of government research and development in military technology is prompting economists to examine their potential in industrial areas as well.

The terrible gap between our actual economic productivity and our potential productivity is another reason why Washington economists contemplate a revolutionary research and development role for government. The gap in 1960 between actual and potential output was $30 to $35 billion, or 6 to 7 per cent of our total output. This amounts to two thirds of what we spend on national defense, almost twice what we spend on public education, and about one and a half times what we spent in 1960 on new homes.

The gap in mid-1961 between what we are producing and what we can produce is approaching $50 billion. A basic reason for this higher figure is that recoveries from recent slumps have been incomplete, never quite regaining previous peaks in employment and productivity. Steel and oil have been operating at hardly better than 50 per cent of capacity for a long period. This holds for several other major sectors of the economy. Small wonder that the President's Council of Economic Advisers testified to Congress that "Even the world's most prosperous nation cannot afford to waste resources on this scale."

Our leading economists are, therefore, considering radically broader applications of research and development. Inventiveness, knowledge, and highly technical skills are the crucial contributors to growth. The newest stress is upon the primary value of investment in people versus machinery. Large-scale federal subsidy and direction will be necessary in re-educating, retraining, and relocating the victims of technological change, who range from unskilled farm laborers to skilled transport workers displaced by pipelines.

POLITICAL ACTION AND PUBLIC NEED

Paradoxically, at the height of its achievement in producing goods and services, the American price-market system is revealing alarming inadequacies, not only as a self-regenerating force for limited resources. Professional economists and political leaders and the educated public are becoming uncomfortably aware of this. The general public will remain ignorant and complacent for only a short time. In consequence, control of the economy is becoming a government concern, not because of subversion or ideological considerations but because the impersonal forces of technology and demography are requiring it.

The corporation, which is the work horse of the economy (four fifths of Americans work for corporations), increasingly will find its main endeavors directed by law instead of by the invisible hand of the competitive market. Now, so far as the corporation is concerned, intervention by law hitherto has been aimed strictly at keeping the market free, because the health of the free market has been judged primary to national well-being. Even today no one disputes the fact that the competitive price-market system founded on private property and the profit incentive remains our most effective instrument for distributing consumer goods and services.

But, because the market is failing to solve vital social needs, a completely new kind of intervention will occur. Corrective action will not mean simply a stepping up of the traditional kinds of government interference, such as trust busting, tariffs, and regulations. It will be something quite strange to Americans. There is one major precedent that illustrates this new kind of government role—the Full Employment Act of 1946. That act was the first instance where the national government stipulated by law that the goals of full employment and equitable income distribution were to be a federal legal concern and were not to be left up to the price-market system.

At that time, the end of World War II, all but a handful of economists predicted nationwide unemployment. This anticipated crisis stimulated passage of the law. But the crisis did not materialize, owing to the immense, underestimated backlog of demand created by the war. The thinking behind the act was not "radical" in the invidious sense of the term; namely, a socialistic demand that we scrap the American way and try something different. Rather, the philosophy was one of tacit acknowledgment of an essential role for the market system, supplementing it with political action in the interest of rational resource allocation and public need. The whole thrust of the growth debate is for extensive implementation of this principle.

A NATIONAL ECONOMIC BUDGET

The United States must develop a new kind of national economic budget, quite different from the federal budget as we have known it. The traditional budget has actually involved some limited planning and allocation of resources, but only on a short-term basis. In the future, the budget will have to embrace all our national resources viewed against national goals over a long term. Such a budget, goals oriented, would be more than a mere annual federal accounting. It would comprise an integrated, comprehensive, continuing plan for the entire nation. It would mean five-or-six-year projections of the use of our national resources and output in terms of employment, growth, foreign policy objectives, housing, roads, welfare, and other such goals.

One of the appeals of such a budget (apart from the inexorable logic of the forces making it a necessity) is that, enunciated by the President, it would act as a means for rallying public opinion, for articulating a meaningful program for the American economy beyond the sheer aggrandizement of material wealth. In its broadest aspects, it would amount to a working agreement on the priorities for the use of our total resources. In its narrowest aspects, it would amount to national programing of explicit policies.

RATIONING OUR RESOURCES

Such a budget is not going to be achieved overnight, but it will come within the decade. It must come, because long-range blueprints and decisions on use of resources are an essential ingredient of the future. Though perhaps not a matter for jubilation, it certainly should not be a matter for dismay. Walter Lippmann hinted at such a conception of the budget in his commentary on President Kennedy's first budget. His remarks also indicated why even a tentative move in the direction of a goals-oriented budget will not be accomplished immediately. "It is a complicated thing," he wrote, "to explain that the Federal budget is not only an accounting of revenues and expenditures. It is also a great fiscal engine which as a matter of national policy has to be managed in such a way as to promote a stabilized growth of the economy. It is a makeweight which has to be swung from deficit to surplus and from surplus to deficit to compensate for the ups and downs of the business cycle. There is nothing sinister or mysterious in this idea. But it is a *new* idea." Lippmann went on to write that the notion of a budget covering a number of years, instead of just one year, will require that the President himself educate the people. For, "most of what he has promised to do, most of what for the long pull urgently needs to be done, depends on explaining this theoretical issue to the people."

THE TEST OF OUR INVENTIVENESS

Resistance to the idea can be expected. It will be charged that bureaucratic planning and reduced profit incentive will stifle the market system; the public will be the victim of a noncompetitive, flaccid economy, with Communist-style suppression of cherished individual freedoms just around the corner. But this risk is justified by disagreeable facts: that we are operating drastically under our productive capabilities, slump or no slump, and have been for some time; that the imbalance between satisfying public needs and fulfilling private demands continues to worsen; and that the public already is victimized by noncompetitive, administered prices in industries making up a third to a half of our economy—basic industries like steel, electrical equipment, and autos—and by industry-wide union wages, combining to create a relentless wage-price rise that is the despair of economists.

There is an inherent possibility of a constitutional crisis. American political inventiveness, our justly famous instinct for freedom, is going to be put to the most difficult test it has had in a century. This is because any successful society must have a theory, a clear comprehension of principle, for what it is doing. Such an understanding is essential if a society intends to achieve great ends, and as the precondition for the kind of congressional action required. The Council of Economic Advisers serves as an example of the type of organization needed. This might well be made by law into a powerful agency for national planning.

The intense pressure for planning is building up from many directions. Presidential adviser Dean James Landis, for one, has suggested that the federal regulatory agencies, through better formulation and coordination of their policies, could be the key to revitalization of major sectors of the economy. But the most fundamental pressure of all is exerted by the fact that the United States now competes in a world of government-controlled economies. Meanwhile, our own economy remains substantially guided by disparate private corporate interests. The strategies of these corporations reflect their primary obligations to shareholders. No formal compunction exists to relate these obligations to the common interest. The American myth about the free, competitive system and its miraculously beneficent role runs counter to legal and political regulation of economic affairs.

Our hope must be that genuine public understanding of our true condition will do two things. It will act to eliminate the anxiety that comes from the unknown, and the resultant dangerous nonsense about subversion. It will thus release us to exercise to the full America's unmatched talent for combining individual freedom with optimum collective performance. In this light, President Kennedy's striking statement in his State of the Union Address, "Before my term has ended, we shall have to test anew whether a nation such as ours can endure. The outcome is by no means certain," can be appreciated as more than rhetoric. Survival is, indeed, the issue.

INSTRUMENT OF FREEDOM
Brooks Hays

Brooks Hays, a member of the Tennessee Valley Authority's board of directors, was a member of the U.S. House of Representatives from Arkansas for eight terms. In Congress, he served on the Banking and Currency and the Foreign Affairs Committees and was also a member of the President's Commission on Intergovernmental Relations.

There is no more puzzling and controversial section of our constitution than the clause in its preamble dealing with promoting "the general welfare." Even though it is puzzling and contentious, this provision has paradoxically been one of the most useful in enabling our governmental system to adapt to the changing needs of the times.

That which the federal government should do in the interests of "the general welfare"—the apportionment, that is, of powers and responsibilities between the state and local units and the federal government—is a decision which each generation of Americans has made for itself. Some decisions have been made out of necessity, some out of expediency. Some have been wise, others questionable. Some we would agree with today, others we would dispute. But the fact that these decisions were made, and had to be made, is evidence of the need to adapt to changing conditions.

What governments should or should not do for the general welfare cannot be decided once and set for all time. The guidance even of our constitutional forefathers is valid only for the times in which they lived. We can offer them our gratitude, however, for not placing us in a constitutional strait jacket; for giving us, in fact, the flexibility of government to enable us to adapt as the need requires. Much of this flexibility is in the general welfare clause.

Change is forced upon us not so much by the will of man as by the course of history. It is not the abstract thought of the political theoretician that persuades us to mold our institutions but the facts of our times, the problems we confront, and the need to meet them head on. When wise men saw that private toll roads and ferries were no longer adequate for the growing volume

From *National Civic Review,* January 1961. Reprinted by permission.

of our national commerce, they offered as a solution a national system of highways, bridges and canals. A great national debate arose over the constitutionality of these "internal improvements." Presidential candidates were elected and defeated on the issue. In the end, the right and duty of the federal government to enter this important field of national communications was sustained by the courts and by the electorate.

Scientific progress brings changes in our way of living which are reflected in our governmental processes. With the invention of steam locomotion came the railroads and the opportunity to unite our eastern and western states with rapid communication. Land grants from the federal domain helped make possible our transcontinental rail network. As railroading grew, competition between lines also grew. Freight rates became important economic factors in many sections of the country—too important, in fact, to leave entirely in private hands. Thus the Interstate Commerce Commission came into being to regulate both destructive competition and unwarranted freight charges.

With the coming of electricity another new industry was born toward which the people soon developed a great common concern. Inherently monopolistic in nature, this industry was left to the states to regulate in the federal interest. State regulation failed in the late 1920's and early 1930's and the federal government stepped in to promote the general welfare with the Public Utility Holding Company Act and other measures. The Tennessee Valley Authority was created to provide, among other things, a demonstration of how an electric power system can be operated efficiently and profitably in the public interest.

Resource development similarly became an important part of the general welfare. Great interstate rivers overflowed their banks creating flood disasters of national proportions and requiring national remedies. As electricity became more significant in the economy, great natural hydro-electric power sites remained undeveloped. Engineering science made available the multipurpose dam with which floods could be controlled, power generated, rivers made navigable and thousands of acres irrigated. The very size of the task of mastering these great streams made it obvious that the national government had to take a strong hand in development.

National and world events have forced changes in our concept of the role of government in relation to "the general welfare." The great depression convinced all America that the federal government can never again stand idly by while business cycles make people jobless and hungry. Federal action to counteract both inflation and deflation is now accepted national policy, regardless of party politics.

The current trend of world events offers prospects of federal action beyond our imagination: atomic research with its infinite potential; rockets and satellites bring us to the horizon of space travel and revolutionary new communications methods. The importance of these sciences to national defense is so critical and urgent, and their cost so titanic, that only the federal government can undertake them. So we have a whole new realm of federal responsibility destined to radiate into every corner of our lives and penetrate our society to an extent we cannot fortell.

The prospect leads to the question every one of us is asking: Is this trend to federal power inexorable? Are we facing the demise of strong state and local governments? Or is there a way we can adapt our institutions so that the strong federal power so necessary to our national existence can be employed to make stronger state and local governments? I am convinced there is such a way. My formula has two parts:

1. Federal programs of the present and of the future must be so organized and so established as to assure a large measure of local participation.

I base this tenet on the conviction that decisions affecting primarily local interests should be made primarily by local people through the governmental institutions responsible to them at the local level.

It is often said that the federal government should do only what the states cannot do. I think this is a tale which falls by its own oversimplicity. For example, the federal government has not only an interest but also a responsibility for getting done jobs that states can do but won't. The efforts made by the individual states are often uneven in matters such as housing for example, or highways or health or education. Some states make great efforts, others exert the bare minimum. Federal action becomes necessary because state and local governments either fail or refuse to act.

There are also instances in which state action is less preferable than federal action because it would be actually harmful to other states. This can be true in the regulation of the river. A single state may set out to develop the stream to its own advantage but in so doing it may deny to other states the water and water rights to which they are entitled and which they need. The kind of controversy and bitterness which can result from such situations is all too well known. Yet the federal government can develop an entire watershed to serve many needs in the total region.

2. The second half of my formula for preserving a balanced federal-state-local framework holds that state and local governments must be equipped, organized and staffed to take decisive action in solving the problems of their people. Another one of those rules which we too often accept without thinking is that "the least government is the best government." It is as simple as a fairy tale and has about as much validity. Failure to govern, or refusal to govern, is the closest thing to anarchy; and anarchy cannot be tolerated.

One of the facts we must face, though our wishes may be to the contrary, is that our society is a complex one and our interrelationships are extremely close. The interests of the farm are linked with those of the city, labor with business, national defense with civil rights, and resource development with housing and education, with wages and profits. Where the federal government refrains from action, state and local governments cannot refuse or neglect to assert their authority. They must be perceptive of the problems about them. They must be active and intelligent, fair and impartial, and above all imbued with a sense of the public interest. The initiative they show will have much to do with the ultimate answer to the question of the balanced growth of state and federal power.

I am confident this formula will work because I have seen it work in the Tennessee Valley. Let me quote from a speech by Barrett Shelton, editor of the *Decatur Daily* of Decatur, Alabama. Mr. Shelton has lived the life of the Tennessee Valley since before TVA. He saw the erosion of the soil and felt its consequences in his business and in the welfare of his community. He, with his neighbors, experienced the despair of what seemed to be a hopeless future; and the arrival of TVA seemed to them the coming of the alien force of federalism to reshape their lives whether they liked it or not. Said Mr. Shelton:

> Into this dismal, perplexed economic setting one late midwinter afternoon came David Lilienthal, then a member of the Board of Directors of the Tennessee Valley Authority. Four of our citizens, who had long been hopeful of improving conditions generally, met him in conference. We were almost frankly hostile for he represented to us another way of thought and another way of life. And our conversation might be summarized in this fashion, "All right, you're here. You were not invited, but you're here. You are in command, now what are you going to do?"
>
> Dave leaned his chair back against the wall and the twinkle of a smile came into his eyes, as he said gently and firmly, "I'm not going to do anything. You're going to do it."
>
> He went on to tell us something we never knew before. He went on to say that TVA would provide the tools of opportunity—flood control, malaria control, navigation on the river, low-cost power, test-demonstration farming to show how our soils could be returned to fertility, a fertility lost through land erosion, another wayward child of a one-crop system. He told us the river would no longer defeat man but would become the servant of man. "What you do with these tools," he said, "is up to you."
>
> Dave Lilienthal had passed the task right back to us, right back to local control. He let us know that simple economics could be applied in the Tennessee Valley and that the faith, determination and sweat of the people would bring about the result we had eagerly sought for so many years.

Mr. Shelton went on to relate that this counsel from an administrative head of this great new federal agency actually was the signal to the local people to roll up their sleeves and get to work. They undertook to create new farm processing plants. They persuaded the local ice company to put in a packing plant. They pooled local capital in order to establish a milk processing center. The object was to create a steady payroll for both the community and the farmers. Soon the Tennessee River became navigable to Decatur's doorstep and flour millers began importing midwest grain for distribution in the south. A cooperative established a fertilizer mixing plant. Soon this organization saw the possibility of selling seed commercially and put in a seed cleaning plant. An alfalfa drying plant was set up.

This was a small beginning for Decatur, Alabama, but it was like the beginning of a giant snowball. Decatur today is a prosperous, growing community. It is a service center for the surrounding agricultural area and its waterfront on the Tennessee River now includes industrial plants from among the "who's who" of American industry.

The story of Decatur is an example of the result of the operation of the TVA formula—resource development brought to successful fruition through local initiative.

In 1933 TVA was given the huge synthetic nitrate facilities built by the government at Muscle Shoals, Alabama, during the First World War. It was told by Congress to use these facilities in the interests of agriculture, principally for the production of chemical fertilizer. TVA might have set up an entirely federal organization to do this work. Instead, it enlisted the cooperation of the state agricultural colleges. Their experiment stations through the years have been the chief testing grounds for the new experimental fertilizers turned out by TVA scientists. The college extension services have been the principal media for adult education among the farmers in the modern use of improved fertilizers. Decisions as to the best cropping practices to be encouraged in the interests of the state economy thus are local decisions, not federal, made by state employees and state officials acting in the state interests.

This form of cooperation—TVA and the agricultural colleges—extends into two thirds of the states, and the methods and the results are similar. The colleges are stronger. They serve the people better.

The TVA power program also is a cooperative venture with local interests. TVA is the producer and wholesaler of electricity. Retail distribution is performed by local distribution systems owned by the cities in urban areas and by farmer cooperatives in the rural areas. These distribution systems are locally managed and financed independently of TVA. The tremendous growth in the use of electricity in the valley is due in large part to the vigorous initiative of these local institutions.

The private sector of the Valley's economy has been similarly strengthened by the investment of public funds in TVA facilities and without damage—indeed, with positive benefit—to other regions. Federal funds invested in New York harbor increase the business volume of that port but do not detract from the commerce of New Orleans or San Francisco. Federal funds invested in the Columbia River basin development provide greater opportunity for industry in the Pacific northwest but do not detract from the potential of California or Pennsylvania.

Just so, funds invested in the natural resources of the Tennessee Valley have provided new opportunities for commercial and industrial growth in the Tennessee Valley without taking away from any other section of the country. For example, over $800 million have been invested in new or expanded industrial plants along the Tennessee waterway since 1933. This is private enterprise using new "tools of opportunity"—flood-free sites, water transportation, precious water itself for processing, as well as low-cost electricity.

These are not acts of industry piracy of which TVA has been so often accused. Nor are they even a luring of industry. The industrial development of the Tennessee Valley has been the natural result of industries using resources to the best advantage for themselves, their consumers and the nation. The federal government provided the tools. State and local governments and private interests have made the basic decisions as to how the tools should be used.

The other half of this picture—this struggle to maintain state and local institutions in their rightful place in our governmental structure—is the necessity on the part of state and local governments to organize themselves and staff themselves so they can take over responsibilities that belong to them.

Now this is not an automatic process. It means attracting trained and perceptive people into state and municipal governments. To attract them, you will have to pay them well. You will have to give them assurance that politics and the spoils system will not endanger their working security and that of their staff; they will have to have some assurance that acts of political expediency will not undermine the results of their labors. You will have to support their decisions and recommendations against the frustrating attrition of special interests.

Vigorous state and local governments require the existence of an administrative organization within governments able to anticipate problems, analyze them and make the necessary decisions. Planning bodies, therefore, are an integral part of the decision-making process at both the state and local level.

The task of government today is not to oppose federalization. Nor is it its task to aggrandize state's rights. Neither is it to compromise principles of democratic government. This is no time for a doctrinaire approach by which we denominate all federal action as bad and all state and local action—or even inaction—as good.

We must face facts. We must look honestly at our problems. If we do, we will recognize the tremendous events taking place in the world which affect us personally and locally and yet demand our national attention. We will recognize that people can be inventive in their governmental operations. They can rise above special interest and adapt their governmental machinery to new conditions. State and local governments can be honorable and capable and responsible to the electorate and at the same time work closely and effectively with the federal government to accomplish their goals and solve their problems.

Democratic government is the instrument of freedom. Freedom encourages thought and invention and everlasting change in our society. Democratic government must keep pace with the change that democracy itself makes possible. Ingenuity is as important in government as in science or business or farming. We have seen a merging of federal and state efforts in the Tennessee Valley with results that have surpassed our hopes. I am convinced it is a pattern which can be adapted to other valleys, to other regions and to many current problems of government.